Learn Advanced JavaScript Programming

Yehuda Shiran and Tomer Shiran

Wordware Publishing, Inc.

Library of Congress Cataloging-in-Publication Data

Shiran, Yehuda.
Learn advanced JavaScript programming / Yehuda Shiran and Tomer Shiran.
p. cm.
Includes index.
ISBN 1-55622-552-0 (pb)
1. JavaScript (Computer program language) 2. Internet programming. I. Shiran, Tomer. II. Title.
QA76.73.J38S46 1997 97-26719
005.2'762--dc21 CIP

2320 Los Rios Boulevard
Plano, Texas 75074

Printed in the United States of America

ISBN 1-55622-552-0
10 9 8 7 6 5 4 3 2 1
9709

All inquiries for volume purchases of this book should be addressed to Wordware Publishing, Inc., at the above address. Telephone inquiries may be made by calling:

(972) 423-0090

Contents Summary

Table of Contents

Chapter 1

Introduction to JavaScript

The World Wide Web

You may recall that only a few years ago the Internet served mostly as a way to send and retrieve electronic mail to and from other users on the net. As the computer industry rapidly developed and advanced, hardware and software became more efficient and more powerful. The modem speed increased, and prices dropped. The time when only text ruled the Internet came to an end then. Several software companies released Web *browsers* which enabled data transfer over the Internet. The *World Wide Web*, a unique "branch" of the Internet, still serves as a means for exposing data to the net, so it can be accessed from anywhere in the world.

Almost every company provides information to the public via a Web site. Some even use the Web for promotion and online sales of their products and services. Many individuals create Web pages for fun, telling visitors about their hobbies, favorite music, and so on. Some companies, such as Geocities (http://www.geocities.com), have entered the business of providing free space and services for Web page authoring and maintenance, in return for posting commercial advertisements.

Competition on the Web

Site popularity is often measured by the number of *hits* the site receives. Many Web pages show off their hit count to impress surfers. Just to get a feel of the magnitude involved, Netscape claims that tens of millions of people visit its site daily. Although Microsoft does not believe this number, there is consensus among Internet users that the number of hits is a good measure for comparing two sites. A site posting 10,000 hits per week is obviously ten times more popular than a 1,000-hits-per-week site.

The competition for surfers' attention is tremendous. In order to start understanding how fierce the competition is, imagine you are broadcasting on one of 600,000 channels that can be seen on a TV set. Rather than simply channel surfing, the viewer must conduct a proactive search to find something interesting to browse. What is the chance of a casual surfer hitting your channel? Indeed, the chances are very slim and you have to understand this, because only then will you appreciate the role of an attractive site and other marketing techniques described in this chapter.

The World Wide Web (WWW) is constantly growing as new Web servers and pages are connected. It is estimated that over 15,000 domain names (such as netscent.com) are registered daily. Each domain name is eventually associated with a Web server or a virtual server. Your Web site is truly useless if people do not visit it. There are several ways to attract Web surfers to a site:

- Advertising. You can advertise your Web site on pages that belong to other companies or individuals by placing some text or images on their page. The user loads the page and sees a banner at the top of the page, so when he or she clicks the banner, the advertiser's site is loaded. Many large companies also tend to advertise via traditional methods such as newspapers, magazines, television, and radio. Although this method is somewhat less efficient, it works surprisingly well for well-established companies.
- Submission. Once you have a Web site, people should know that it exists. Most people and small businesses do not have enough resources to advertise via banners that can cost up to tens of thousands of dollars a month. The most common free promotion method is to submit the URL and description of a Web page to search engines and directories. Those services live by providing an easy way of retrieving desired Web pages. For example, a search engine returns URLs of pages that are related to a specific topic that the user searched for. AltaVista, Infoseek, Excite, and Lycos are just some examples of such search engines, because there are hundreds available on the Web. Directories such as Yahoo! gather Web pages by subject so the user can find pages related to a given subject.
- Attractive Site. The most important way to attract users to your site is by creating an engaging site. Most Web surfers tend to

stick to sites that they have visited before and where they have found interesting, new material every visit. The most "effective" way to deter people from revisiting your site is by allowing it to become stale.

Extending HTML

HTML is a very limited document-formatting language. It is based on *tags* which instruct the browser how to display a chunk of text or an image. As such, the HTML is limited to a static, one-way interaction with the user. The Web page can be as sophisticated and attractive to the surfer's eyes as it can possibly be, but the user cannot interact with the page. Interaction cannot be static—it requires constructs such as `if` statements and `for` loops, which are not part of the HTML syntax.

These missing constructs are found in JavaScript. This object-oriented language provides Web page authors with the power to reach a very high level of interaction between the user and the document. The power of the language is best witnessed from the pace of its evolution. Browser providers are coming out with new extensions and features every few months, leapfrogging each other in their constant quest for market dominance. The leading browser-provider companies are thus setting the standards in Web page authoring features, with JavaScript being of special importance.

CGI Programs

You are probably familiar with popular search engines such as Yahoo!, Infoseek, AltaVista, and Excite. Have you asked yourself how these engines work? They are based on CGI (Common Gateway Interface) scripts. CGI extends the interaction between the user and the document to a higher level where the document communicates with the Web server on which the Web pages reside. When you click the Submit button on Infoseek's form, your browser sends your entries from the HTML form to the server, where the CGI script processes the data and sends it to another program running on the server. The results are then transmitted to the user's browser.

CGI scripts can be written in any language, Perl and C being the most popular ones. Objectively, Perl and C are more complicated to program than JavaScript, and therefore CGI scripting is usually mastered only by experienced programmers.

You are now in a position to understand why search engines need such powerful machines to run their devices. A typical search engine receives several million requests per day. For example, suppose a provider needs to answer one million search requests per day. A simple calculation shows that that server must process approximately ten one-second-long requests per second. Each of these ten requests is a CGI script executing on the server.

Helpers, Plug-ins, Applets, and CGI

Web page authoring consists of several layers. The more powerful the layer is, the more complex it is to program. The fundamental layer is HTML. As we have explained earlier, JavaScript extends HTML to a dynamic user-page interaction. Helpers, plug-ins, and applets extend JavaScript's capabilities even more.

Helpers

Browsers are very powerful in converting HTML tags into attractive pages, as well as interpreting JavaScript scripts to animated commercials, but have some deficiencies in other areas such as understanding audio that comes in from a Web site. Your browser, though, is smart enough to use *helper* applications to do such jobs instead. The conversion of digitized sound to audio you can hear through your speakers is done by a program that resides on your hard disk and is launched by the browser.

Plug-ins

Another way to extend browser capabilities is by plugging an application into it. SmartSketchAnimator is an application from FutureWare Software, Inc. that displays a vector-based animation as efficiently as a .gif file. The disadvantage of the .gif file is that the user cannot interact with the detailed artwork. With FutureWare, the graphic object can be customized in such a way that a specific portion can appear highlighted when the user clicks on it. At this stage we will not discuss plug-ins, because a full chapter is dedicated to these mechanisms and their powerful connections with JavaScript.

Java Applets

OK, so you have tried HTML, JavaScript, helpers, and plug-ins (in this order) and you are still not satisfied with your Web page. There is still a rotating globe you want to place at the bottom left corner of your page. Sun Microsystems has answered this need by developing a language for the Web called Java. Talented programmers can use Java to build small applications (*applets*) that are downloaded to the browser upon hitting the appropriate page and then automatically discarded from memory when a new page is loaded. The applet concept is similar to the image file concept. As the .gif file is being loaded upon hitting the page which calls the appropriate image, so is the applet being loaded upon the browser's request. The applet, though, is more than a static combination of pixels; it is an independent program which executes when the page loads and is automatically terminated when the page unloads. The applet is a self-sustained, independent module, without any possibilities for user interaction during its execution.

The classic example for an applet is a scrolling LED banner, similar to the scrolling sign at Times Square. There is no better way to inform your visitors about changes you have made to your page. You can change your banner whenever you want to bring new items to the user's attention. This touch of animation can bring your page to life and create the perception of a dynamic, up-to-date one.

For a browser company to support Java applets, it needs to license the technology from Sun and build the proper hooks in the browser. The first one to do it was (you guessed right) Sun itself, with its HotJava browser. Netscape incorporated it later and so did Microsoft. Java applets are assets that people are accumulating, and every browser must support them to live up to the nonstop competition.

You have probably asked yourself about the origin of Java. The Java language is derived from C and C++ and is targeted for the more experienced programmers among us. Therefore, many Web page authors and casual programmers cannot adopt the language as easily as they have adopted HyperCard, ToolBook, or Visual Basic. JavaScript was created to answer this exact need.

CGI (Common Gateway Interface)

There are some tasks that cannot be accomplished by the browser on the client side. Building a common database for an engineering department must rely on a server accepting data and requests from all users and storing it for future access and processing. Such an application can be written in C, C++, Perl, or any other language. The communication protocol between the server application and the client browser is called CGI. You should buy a book on CGI if you intend to learn it, because it is far beyond the scope of this book and is very difficult to learn without detailed documentation.

What is JavaScript?

JavaScript is an easy-to-use object scripting language designed for creating live online applications that link together objects and resources on both clients and servers. While Java is used by programmers to create new objects and applets, JavaScript is designed for use by HTML page authors and enterprise application developers to dynamically script the behavior of objects running on either the client or the server. JavaScript's design and concepts represent the next generation of software for the Internet and is:

- designed for creating network-centric applications
- complementary to and integrated with Java
- complementary to and integrated with HTML
- open and cross-platform

With JavaScript, an HTML page might contain a form that processes data on the client side. A server-side JavaScript might pull data out of a relational database and format it in HTML on the fly. A page might contain JavaScript scripts that run on both the client and the server.

Who Can Benefit from JavaScript?

Generally speaking, Web surfers benefit most from JavaScript, because they have the opportunity to enjoy the language's capabilities in the form of games, animation, interaction, and so forth. But not only the common Web surfer can benefit from the language. Netscape Communications obviously benefits from JavaScript, because it gives them a competitive advantage over other Web browsers, especially Microsoft Internet Explorer, which is still in the process of catching up with Netscape Navigator's JavaScript implementation.

Many other companies believe that they will benefit from JavaScript and its descendants. The words of Rose Ann Giordano, vice president of the Internet Business Group at Digital Equipment Corp., demonstrate it:

> *"Tools like JavaScript will unleash a new wave of creativity and transform the Internet in ways no one can predict. JavaScript and other developments will demand increased system performance,* ***ideally met by Digital's Alpha systems architecture****."*

Jan Silverman at Hewlett-Packard also mentioned how JavaScript matches his company's plans in a press release:

> *"JavaScript is an exciting technology because it represents the next generation of software designed specifically for the Internet. Hewlett-Packard is committed to open standards and is a supporter of JavaScript because* ***it complements Hewlett-Packard's open systems architecture****."*

The History of JavaScript

JavaScript was originated by Netscape as LiveScript, developed in parallel with LiveWire server software. LiveScript was developed for several applications—we'll discuss two of them here. The first one is to enhance Web pages in a way that HTML cannot. The classic example is verifying a user's form entries. Instead of sending the data as is to the server and validating the data types there, the client handles all the validation and only then sends the data to the server for further processing. Another application for LiveScript (JavaScript) is the communication glue between HTML documents and Java applets. A scrolling banner, for example, can use information from the user's customized settings, sent to the applet by LiveScript. This data exchange is transparent to the server and, since there is no server-client communications, there is no response time penalty.

In December 1995, Sun Microsystems took over LiveScript development and changed its name to JavaScript. On the one hand, JavaScript is related to Java in its C++ object flavor. On the other hand, JavaScript's vernacular is much reduced compared to Java, in order to make it suitable for less experienced programmers and scripters. JavaScript's first and foremost advantage is in its ease of learning. Only then comes its features and capabilities which are important for Web page interactivity as well as for customizing solutions around prewritten applets.

In 1996 Microsoft introduced its first JavaScript-enabled browser, Internet Explorer 3.0. Netscape followed up a week later with another

JavaScript-enabled browser, Netscape Navigator. Internet Explorer was far from reaching Navigator 3.0's level in terms of JavaScript and lacked many important features and capabilities. In early 1997 the beta version of Netscape Navigator version 4.0 (Communicator) was released. Microsoft Internet Explorer was still far from reaching Navigator 3.0's level.

JavaScript in a Browser

Client-side JavaScript

Client-side JavaScript is the most common form of the language. The script should be included in or referenced by an HTML document for the code to be interpreted by the browser. Suppose you load a Web page with a JavaScript-generated banner. The browser begins interpreting the HTML code and then encounters a JavaScript script. If the script has no syntax errors, it is executed by the browser's built-in interpreter.

The JavaScript client-side mechanism features many advantages over traditional CGI server-side scripts. For example, you might use JavaScript to check if the user has entered a valid e-mail address in a form field. The JavaScript function is executed when the user submits the form, and only if the entry is a valid e-mail address (includes an @) is the form transmitted to the server for further processing, database storage, and so on. In this case, the user does not need to wait until the form is submitted over the network to the server and back to the client, only to be informed that a single character is missing.

Browser Objects

JavaScript is an object-based programming language. Its built-in object model is mostly based on the HTML content of the given Web page. The tight interaction between JavaScript and other browser objects (such as forms, browser windows, frames, and images) provides full control over various page elements and enables the programmer to create a link between "external" objects and "internal" ones. A classic example for such linking is a JavaScript script that invokes a Java applet from an HTML form.

JavaScript exposes objects and properties related to the browser's window, history list, status bar, frames, forms, links, and so forth. Furthermore, JavaScript can be used to trap user-initiated events such as button clicks, link navigation, and other actions that the user explicitly or implicitly initiates. You can create a distinct script for each event, enabling a smooth, logical interaction with the user.

What Can JavaScript Do?

In this section we take a look at a few interesting effects and programs created entirely with JavaScript. At this point, we will only focus on client-side JavaScript that is embedded in or referenced by an HTML document.

Games

You can create many interesting games with JavaScript. During our JavaScript-programming experience we have written tic-tac-toe games, a mastermind game, a Tetris game, and many others. There are basically two types of games which you can create via JavaScript:

- static games
- dynamic games

Static games are usually logical ones, and thus do not require much action or immediate responses. For example, you can play tic-tac-toe without any live action, because even reloading the entire page for each move does not interfere with the game itself (although it might be very boring). Static games do not require image replacements or animation. Dynamic games, on the other hand, require real-time action and animation. For example, a Tetris game requires that the blocks will fall down the screen smoothly, without having to wait each time for the screen to be refreshed. Dynamic games are often resource demanding and therefore must be programmed with efficiency in mind. It is almost impossible to create a dynamic game that works under Navigator 2.0x or MSIE 3.0x, because those browsers do not feature the `Image` object (explained in Chapter 25, Images and Graphics) that enables image swapping.

Small, simple games are usually embedded in existing Web pages, whereas large, complex games are most often placed on a separate page. Figure 1-1 shows a fairly complex game (an interesting implementation of Tetris, consisting of hundreds of lines of code) that makes up a Web page.

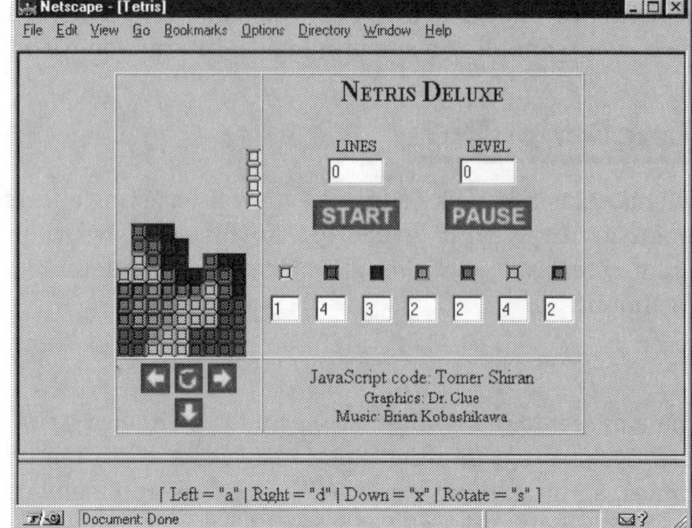

Figure 1-1. Some complex games require multiple frames, so it is preferable to put them on a separate page.

Banners

JavaScript is a full scripting language, so you can create an infinite number of distinct scripts. Nevertheless, some implementations became more popular than others due to the fact that they are easy to use and create interesting effects. Banners are a classic example of such scripts. A banner is a script that displays text in the browser's status bar or in a form's text field. The most common browsers are those that scroll and those that type in messages sequentially. The latter was first developed for this book and is known as a T-banner! Figure 1-2 shows how banners can significantly improve the overall look of a Web page.

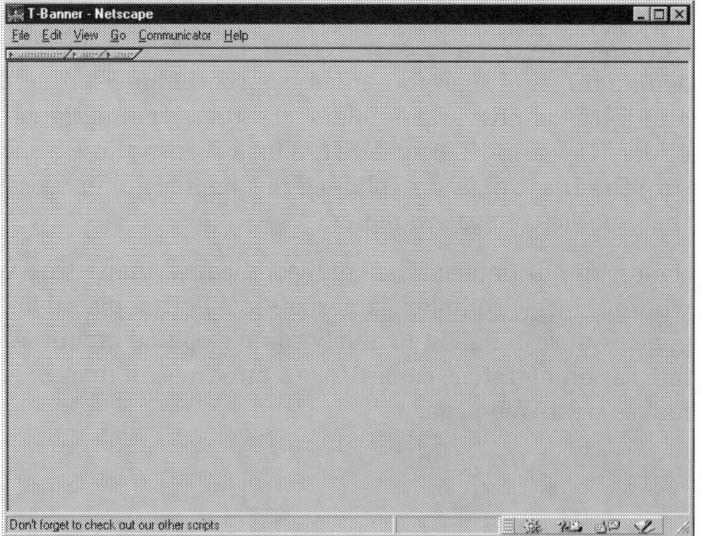

Figure 1-2. A status-bar banner adds interest to the page.

Form Validation

JavaScript is tightly connected to browser objects, including forms and their elements. Therefore, it provides a great amount of control over forms. A classic form-related script is one that validates a form's fields before it is submitted and cancels the submission to the server if an error is found in one of the fields. The advantage of using JavaScript in this particular example is that client-side validation is much faster than validation via transmission to the server and back to the client. For example, suppose you have a form that accepts data from the user, including his or her e-mail address. Let's assume that the e-mail address is essential, and that a string containing an "@" character is assumed a valid e-mail address. There are two options:

- You can choose not to validate the entries. In that case, when the user clicks the Submit button, the form is submitted to the server where a CGI script checks if the e-mail address field is valid and then processes the form. If the e-mail address does not contain an "@" character, the submission is denied and the appropriate message is returned to the user.
- You can choose to use client-side validation via JavaScript. In that case the validating script is loaded as a plain text (JavaScript code embedded in the HTML code). When the user clicks the Submit button, a JavaScript function is triggered to validate the form. If the e-mail address seems valid, the form is submitted to the server—otherwise an appropriate message is immediately displayed and the submission is canceled. Note that the user does not have to wait for the form to be submitted to the server and back to the client, only to receive a message informing him or her that the e-mail address field contains an invalid entry.

Figure 1-3 shows a simple form with a client-side JavaScript validation script that highlights an incorrect entry.

Figure 1-3. *A form with a validation script that selects an invalid entry (e-mail address without @ character).*

Miscellaneous

We have covered three important JavaScript implementations. However, like all other languages, it is obviously impossible to cover all or most of the possible scripts. You can use JavaScript to create almost anything you desire. For example, you can create an LED sign which once could be created only with Java. Figure 1-4 shows an LED sign created with nothing but JavaScript, so you don't have to program and compile any Java!

Figure 1-4. *A JavaScript-only LED sign (ticker).*

Bear in mind that client-side JavaScript is executed on the user's machine. That is, you do not have any direct access to the server's properties with client-side JavaScript. Although that may seem to be a disadvantage, it is sometimes very convenient to have access to client-side properties rather than server-side ones. For example, you can create a digital clock that shows the current time in the client's time zone, because JavaScript extracts the time from the client's operating system, be it Windows 95, Macintosh, Unix, or any other OS. Figure 1-5 demonstrates the digital clock.

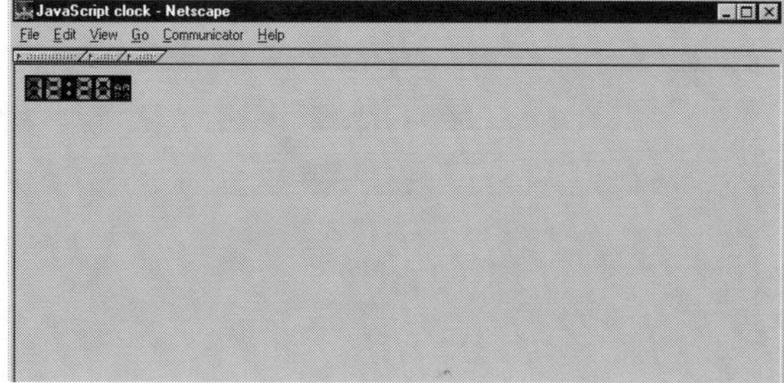

Figure 1-5. *A graphical clock representing the client's current time.*

The full control over browser objects is what makes client-side JavaScript so powerful. You can pop up windows and use them as remote controls linked to the original window. You can use one link to perform several operations or load various documents in separate frames simultaneously. You can also use JavaScript to create an online calculator or to draw graphs and curves. To attract visitors, you can enhance a Web page with JavaScript in many different ways.

We have introduced a few client-side JavaScript scripts in this section. Although client-side JavaScript is by far the most important and useful, there are many other implementations of the language. For example, you can use JavaScript for server-side applications using LiveWire compiler. Server-side JavaScript is actually an alternative to traditional CGI programming via Perl and C++. JavaScript is a very convenient language—therefore, it is being used alongside many other languages (such as VRML) and for various purposes. Another example of JavaScript use is for automatic proxy configuration. As you might already know, Netscape Navigator enables you to connect through a proxy server. You can configure the proxies manually by entering the correct values, or enter the URL of an automatic proxy configuration script, which is actually a JavaScript code. The JavaScript code is located in a text file on the server, but is not compiled like server-side JavaScript. You should know by now that there is plenty to do with JavaScript, and JavaScript is expected to be one of the most important programming languages, both for the Internet and for other general purposes. We will cover the most important implementations of the language in this book.

JavaScript and Java

JavaScript Resembles Java

JavaScript supports most of Java's expression syntax and basic control flow constructs. Take a look at the following **JavaScript** code segment:

```
for (var i = 0; i < 10; ++i) {
    /* statements come here */
}
```

Now take a look at the **Java** equivalent:

```
for (int i = 0; i < 10; ++i) {
    /* statements come here */
}
```

Notice the similarity. The only difference is the variable declaration (JavaScript is loosely typed).

JavaScript and Java are both based on objects, but their implementations differ. In both languages, many built-in functions are implemented as *properties* and *methods* of various objects.

JavaScript Differs from Java

JavaScript resembles Perl in that it is interpreted, not compiled. Java is referred to as a compiled language. Unlike most other programming languages, though, Java is not compiled to a native machine code, but rather to a Java byte code. Java byte code is an architecture-neutral byte-code compiled language. That is, an applet is compiled to Java byte code and then run by a machine-dependent runtime interpreter. Therefore, Java is much slower than general programming languages such as C++. Since Java is compiled, the common user cannot see the actual code behind the program. Nevertheless, when a user comes across a JavaScript script, he or she can generally see and even copy (legally or illegally) the code by simply using the browser to view the HTML source which contains the script (unless it is an external script). A compiled language has many other advantages. For example, a compiled program is much more efficient than one that is always interpreted directly from a text file, such as Perl and JavaScript. On the other hand, there are more than enough reasons to prefer an interpreted language over a compiled one. It is much easier and more convenient to debug and modify a program by simply modifying its text file rather than having to recompile it. Furthermore, most scripts and applets implemented in Java or JavaScript for Web usage do not require efficiency and are not resource demanding. Therefore, an interpreted language is somewhat more convenient.

Both Java and JavaScript are based on objects. However, their implementations of objects are different. JavaScript is an object-based language. It supports built-in, extensible objects, but no classes or inheritance. Its object hierarchy is not an inheritance one as in Java. JavaScript features two types of objects:

- Static objects—objects that combine general functions (methods) and data constructs (properties). The values of such objects' properties are usually read-only. A static object is a single object, and thus does not enable you to create instances of it. For example, the `Math` object in JavaScript is a static one, because you cannot create instances according to its template. Its methods are common mathematical functions, whereas its properties are mostly mathematical constants.

- Dynamic objects—objects by which instances are created. A dynamic object resembles a template. You do not touch or use the object directly. In order to take advantage of such an object, you must create an instance of it. For example, the `Date` object is a dynamic object in JavaScript. An instance of that object is associated with a given date. You can create as many instances of a dynamic object as needed.

Java, on the contrary, is fully extensible. A programmer can create numerous classes that group objects together. A *class* is a term used in object-oriented programming vernacular to refer to a set of related objects that share common characteristics. Java programmers create their own extensions to the base set of tools or classes. JavaScript's object model is somewhat simpler than Java's equivalent, so JavaScript's object implementation is much easier to accommodate than Java's model.

Another difference between Java and JavaScript is their time of *binding*. JavaScript features dynamic binding, so all object references are checked at run time. Java, on the other hand, is based on static binding, meaning that all object references must exist and be valid at compile time. However, an object-oriented language may require dynamic method bindings because polymorphism allows multiple definitions of methods sharing a common name, and calling such polymorphic methods often cannot be resolved until run time. The most obvious reason for this difference is that JavaScript is not compiled, so checking object references at compile time has no meaning. If you are not familiar with Java, you should pay no attention to these confusing terms—simply bear in mind that the object implementation in JavaScript widely varies from that in Java.

When you come to writing a script, you surely need to use variables. In order to use a variable you must declare it. Another difference between Java and JavaScript is that Java is *strongly typed*, as opposed to JavaScript which is *loosely typed*. That is, when you declare a variable in Java, you must specify its data type. For example, when you create a variable to contain integer values you must use the `int` keyword. In JavaScript, all variables are declared in the same way. Furthermore, a variable of one data type can contain a value of a different data type elsewhere in the script. This behavior resembles other popular languages such as Perl. This topic is discussed later in the book.

We have intentionally left the most critical difference to the end. You have noticed that all differences discussed thus far are related to the language itself. A very important difference between Java and JavaScript is that JavaScript is integrated with, and embedded in, HTML. Although Netscape Navigator 3.0 introduced an alternative in the form of external files, that is still the general situation. Java, on the contrary, is neither integrated with nor embedded in HTML. Applets (small Java programs) are always distinct from the HTML code and are only invoked by it. A space is reserved on the Web page for later execution if needed. If you have some experience creating HTML documents, JavaScript's implementations will be a piece of cake for you. When you create the HTML document for a Web page, you simply embed the JavaScript script according to its syntax and semantics.

Another significant difference between Java and JavaScript is the area in which they are executed. A Java applet resembles an image in that you give it a specified area on the page, and the applet executes independently in that area. Within the defined area, the applet can do virtually anything, including animation, games, and so forth. An applet does not have any effect outside its area. JavaScript, on the contrary, gives you access to the entire Web page. You can affect various elements in the page, provided that JavaScript is given permission to access them. For example, you can reference any form, link, image, and browser window via JavaScript. Netscape Navigator 3.0 introduced a new feature, *LiveConnect*, which enables Java to interact with JavaScript and vice versa. This tool makes it possible for a Java applet to interact with HTML elements through JavaScript, which is the connector in this case.

Java is not only a language for creating applets that run on Web pages, but rather a general purpose language that can create stand-alone applications. That is, you can create any application with Java, without any connection to the Internet or the World Wide Web. The classic example for a stand-alone application written entirely in Java is HotJava, the Web browser created by Sun Microsystems. On the other hand, JavaScript is not a stand-alone programming language. Like most scripting languages, JavaScript is interpreted and thus requires a specific application to run it. JavaScript currently works with Netscape Navigator, Microsoft Internet Explorer, the LiveWire server environment, and plug-ins. JavaScript applications will probably never function independently.

Java requires an appropriate multitasking operating system. Therefore, anyone running Unix platform, OS/2, Windows 95, Windows NT, or Macintosh should not have a problem viewing Java on the Web. Nonetheless, Windows 3.1 or Windows 3.11 users cannot benefit from Java because that operating system does not support multitasking. As opposed to Java, JavaScript's audience is not limited due to any operating system. Windows 3.1x users can enjoy JavaScript-enhanced pages exactly like other users. That is obviously a major benefit of JavaScript over Java. Not only Windows 3.1x users are missing Java—some users running multitasking operating systems cannot run Java applets from a Web page. This happens when a user is connected via a proxy server that disables Java due to possible security flaws.

JavaScript and Java are Complementary Languages

We have spoken with many people who believe that JavaScript is a scaled down version of Java. As you should already know, that is far from being correct. JavaScript cannot perform many tasks that Java can, whereas Java cannot do most things that JavaScript is capable of doing. As of Netscape Navigator 3.0x, JavaScript and Java can interact together using LiveConnect (see Chapter 31).

JavaScript's Current Status

JavaScript is currently under development, and will probably stay that way. The language specification is not complete yet. Each browser release introduces new features to the language. Therefore, you must take special precautions when creating scripts for the general public. First of all, you must follow the rules that enable you to hide the code from browsers that do not support JavaScript. Secondly, if the script works only on some JavaScript-enabled browsers, you must take that into consideration. You can use all versions of JavaScript to find out which browser the user is running, enabling you to provide a script compatible with the browser being used. If you implement this technique, you can avoid all errors by disabling the script if it is not compatible with the user's browser. In any case, you must assure that the user does not receive any annoying JavaScript errors that are an indication of a poorly designed Web site. The fact that JavaScript is under development has immense influence because the language is an interpreted language, not a compiled one. When using a compiled language, you must use an up-to-date compiler so it can compile your code. However, once the program is compiled, it will run on any machine with the designated operating system. Another related problem with JavaScript is that it is interpreted by a different interpreter every time. For example, it can be interpreted by Netscape Navigator 3.0 and Microsoft Internet Explorer 3.0. Therefore, your script must be suitable for all browsers, or at least the most popular ones. This problem is specific for JavaScript, not for all interpreted languages. For example, when you create a CGI script via Perl, you must only make sure that the Perl interpreter installed on the server meets the script's needs. If so, it will work for any browser that supports CGI (more than 99.99% of all browsers).

JavaScript is supported by many companies. At the same time Netscape Communications and Sun Microsystems announced JavaScript, more than 28 companies also announced that they would be endorsing JavaScript as the open scripting standard for the Internet, and many companies indicated that they were considering licensing the technology to include it in their own products.

The Future of JavaScript

JavaScript is perceived to advance in two vectors. The first one is in the direction of "serverless" CGI scripting. Small databases of information will be embedded in an HTML document and processed by JavaScript scripts. Cutting the server-client communication will sharply reduce the response time, which is still the number one problem in surfing the Internet. The second vector is pointing to Java applets. As applets become more and more powerful, more exciting opportunities will be available to use JavaScript to assemble existing building blocks.

As ActiveX and VRML become more powerful, JavaScript will work in concert with them, resulting in very powerful applications. JavaScript, a cross-platform language, is currently in use alongside many other languages. Among those languages are Java and some VRML. Furthermore, it has many other uses, such as automatic proxy setting scripts. In the future, other programs and languages will feature interaction with JavaScript. For example, Netscape is currently using JavaScript with LivePayment, a program that enables a Web site developer to receive *immediate* payments over the Web.

Motivation Summary

A Web page designer cannot afford to ignore JavaScript, because his competitors will not, beating him in Web design competition. Nevertheless, JavaScript has its limits and cannot perform every task. A few classic JavaScript-based solutions are as follows:

- User interaction with form elements (input fields, text areas, buttons, radio buttons, check boxes, and selection lists)
- Distributing small collections of database-like information with friendly interfaces to that data
- Processing the data on the client side before submission to the server
- Animation and live image swapping

This list is obviously an abbreviated one and does not include all possible uses of JavaScript.

Chapter 2

Reading This Book

How to Learn JavaScript

This chapter provides you with a detailed outline on how to make the most of this book. Whether you are composing your very first "Hello world" script or looking for an answer to a specific problem, this chapter will guide you through the shortest path to your goal.

Prerequisites

Most of the topics in this book require some knowledge of HTML. Since JavaScript is both based on and enhances HTML, there is no point in learning JavaScript before first creating your very own Web page. Although we explain the more difficult and advanced HTML tags, knowledge of advanced HTML is not a prerequisite.

A Programming Refresher

This book starts with a crash programming course using the JavaScript language. It may serve either as a refresher for experienced programmers or a basic course for nonprogrammers. Chapter 5 discusses data types, variables, identifiers, etc., while Chapter 7 describes JavaScript-supported operators and expressions. Conditional statements are covered in Chapter 8, functions and parameters in Chapter 9. Chapter 13 explains how to use arrays, and Chapter 15 shows JavaScript's portfolio of mathematical features.

How to Read This Book

This book includes material for advanced programmers as well. Even if you are a novice programmer, you should have no problem with the first ten chapters, including the comprehensive example in Chapter 10. The most effective way to learn a language is by examples, and you have plenty of those in this book. You should carefully read the example scripts and make sure you understand every line. Naturally, the examples at the end of the book are more complex than those at the beginning, so pace yourself accordingly.

If you are an experienced JavaScript scripter, it is suggested you skim through the beginning of the book until you encounter advanced material you are not fully comfortable with. Once you have digested the new material, skim to the next batch and so on. There are more than fifteen chapters of advanced material, so you'll find answers to most of your current problems.

The book can also be used as a reference resource. The index at the end of the book and the table of contents at the beginning are to help you find the material you are looking for.

The Structure of This Book

It's important to understand how the book is structured so you can plan your learning experience in the best possible way. The Table of Contents lists the chapters by name. This section provides you with a brief description of each.

- Chapter 3 covers Web page authoring tools. It outlines the main advantages and disadvantages of existing tools and provides you some guidelines on which tool to use for each specific task. This chapter also covers the basics on embedding JavaScript in an HTML document and hiding JavaScript code from old browsers that do not support JavaScript. The most exciting feature of this chapter is the famous "Hello World," or "Hello net," example script. As this chapter explains how to run a JavaScript script, understanding it is very important for new JavaScript scripters. You also learn in Chapter 3 why you might not be able to print JavaScript output generated with the `document.write()` method.
- Chapter 4 describes how an HTML file should be laid out and how JavaScript scripts should be included in it. The chapter talks

about the HEAD portion and the BODY portion of an HTML document and how scripts behave if posted in each of these sections. Chapter 4 stresses the difference between deferred scripts and immediate ones and when it is better to choose one over the other. While helping people all over the world debug their scripts, we found misplacement to be a frequent culprit. After reading through Chapter 4, you should know how to define functions and invoke them via a deferred script. If you have no programming background, reading this chapter is essential for understanding more advanced material later in the book.

- Chapter 5 is an introduction to programming with JavaScript. Since it covers the most important elements of the language, you should carefully read this chapter. It explains the differences between JavaScript and other languages resulting from the fact that JavaScript is loosely typed. The chapter discusses local and global variable declarations, data types, and literals. Each type of literal is explained separately and in depth. A list of escape sequences for special characters is also given. JavaScript entities, a relatively new JavaScript feature which enables the use of JavaScript values in HTML attributes, are introduced.
- Chapter 6 introduces the object-oriented programming concepts such as objects, properties, and methods. If you haven't been exposed to OOP, you'll find this chapter very helpful, as it overviews both general OO concepts as well as JavaScript's OO specific ones. This chapter also shows how to reference properties and methods using the "dot" syntax as well as the array convention. You may have heard about the OOP paradigm, but it is important for you to know exactly what objects are, how to access their elements, and so forth. Since the chapter explains the difference between OOP and OBP (object-based programming), some parts of this chapter are recommended even for the most advanced object-oriented programmers (C++, Objective C, Java, etc.). JavaScript is object based, as opposed to object oriented, so classes are not supported. Chapter 6 also covers the different types of objects supported by JavaScript.
- Chapter 7 is a complete reference of all operators featured by JavaScript. Most operators in this chapter are borrowed from C and Perl, but some are not. Since expressions are tightly related to operators, an in-depth discussion of expressions and evaluations in JavaScript is given. We have even uncovered an unpublicized evaluation tool, hidden in all versions of Navigator.

- Chapter 8 starts off by explaining dialog boxes, including `alert()`, `confirm()`, and `prompt()`. Although these methods are not related to the general topic of the chapter, they are required for demonstrations presented in the chapter. The chapter deals with control structures, from conditional statements to looping through properties. Because JavaScript does not support several known structures from other languages, we provide workarounds that use native JavaScript statements instead. For example, Chapter 8 shows how to use nested conditional statements in place of the missing `switch` statement, and how to use variables and conditional statements to escape complex situations, thus avoiding the `goto` statement which is not part of JavaScript's vocabulary.

- Chapter 9 presents a concept that may be unfamiliar to some of you—variable scoping. A thorough understanding of this topic is extremely important, because it is impossible to debug a script without knowing where each variable is valid. The chapter introduces some other difficult concepts, such as recursion and how to use variables in a recursive function. It shows the best way to organize your code with functions. You should not skip this chapter, because it is also an introduction to debugging. Chapter 9 formally discusses functions, including arguments, parameters, and returning values. If you are familiar with other languages such as C++, you should only need to skim through this chapter, familiarizing yourself with JavaScript-specific syntax.

- Chapter 10 is a good point for a break and assessment of what you have learned. In this chapter you learn to combine and implement what you have learned in the previous chapters. Study carefully the two comprehensive scripts, which are explained in great detail. The first example interacts with the user and asks him or her for his or her height, weight, and age. The script then returns the user's percentile in the population along with some other neat observations. The second script accepts a number in a given base and converts it to a different one. The script also creates a base-conversion table, demonstrating how to generate HTML output using JavaScript only.

- Chapter 11 presents events and event handlers. Handling events is the cornerstone of user interaction. JavaScript is mostly driven by events that occur on a Web page. An event is a specific action that the user performs, such as clicking a button, loading a page, and so on. All events are user initiated, so you can use event handlers to respond to various actions performed by the user. Chapter 11 covers events and event handlers in general, and several specific event handlers such as `onLoad`, `onUnload`, and `onError`.

- Chapter 12 discusses objects, properties, and methods. It explains how to create instances of a given object and how to use an instance. In this chapter you also learn how to create constructor functions, so you are not limited to JavaScript's object model. Chapter 12 is important because JavaScript programming is object based and thus requires a good understanding of objects. This chapter also shows how to debug an object by looping through its properties with a recursive algorithm. By nature, objects can be combined to create complex, nested structures, which are also explained in Chapter 12. This chapter also covers object prototypes by which you can add properties and methods to existing objects, even those that are built into the language.

- Chapter 13 comes back to the basic data structure of every language—arrays. The idea of arrays is simple and known to most of you, but pay attention to how we present two-dimensional arrays, which are not supported by JavaScript. Unlike other languages, arrays in JavaScript are objects, not explicit data types. Chapter 13 introduces array methods which enable advanced array manipulation. In addition, we developed several scripts that emulate all array function supported by Perl.

- Chapter 14 is mostly dedicated to the `Date` object. You can find detailed explanations on creating instances of this object and on using each of its methods and properties. Several examples are included to demonstrate how much more impressive scripts become when using the `Date` object. Chapter 14 deals with time-related methods of other objects.

- Chapter 15 brings you back to familiar turf, mathematics. If you have forgotten advanced math, then this chapter is a good refresher. The content, of course, is the mathematical functions that JavaScript provides you for accomplishing various tasks on your Web page. In this chapter we discuss the `Math` object, its methods (mathematical functions), and its properties (mathematical constants). A graph-plotting script is included as an example of using the `Math` object.

- Chapter 16 deals with strings, a very popular literal and data type in JavaScript. Web authoring involves a great amount of string manipulation of user input, document URLs, etc., so rarely will you encounter a script that does not handle strings. This chapter is probably one of the most important ones in the book, because several chapters and many scripts in the book are based on its contents. Even if you are an experienced Perl programmer, you will be surprised to find that JavaScript features more than enough string-related functions and methods.

- Chapter 17 discusses browser objects and the browser object hierarchy. Because there are many nested browser objects, this chapter focuses on the objects at the highest level. Chapter 17 is mostly theory, and thus does not deal much with JavaScript. It explains the relationship between a Web page's HTML content and the resulting browser objects.
- Chapter 18 talks about the thin bar at the bottom of the browser window—the status bar. It may not seem vital, but the status bar has several important uses worth devoting a chapter to. This chapter includes many examples, from scripts that display short messages associated with specific links to special banners. We have developed some unique banners explicitly for this book, including the famous T-banner and R-banner. It is not a surprise then, that a three-page article in *Boardwatch Magazine* was dedicated to these banners.
- Chapter 19 deals with the relationships between JavaScript programming and URLs. The chapter first explains the different portions of the URL specification, and then describes the common protocols of the Internet. The `location` object and its properties and methods are covered. The chapter answers almost every question related to URLs.
- Chapter 20 discusses JavaScript's `history` object. It explains how you can return the user to any entry in his or her history list. This short chapter also presents several security issues related to the history list and the `history` object in JavaScript. Among these topics you can find information on how to reload a page in two different ways, each with its own advantages and disadvantages.
- Chapter 21 explains the structure of the `document` object, which is a container for most JavaScript elements such as forms, images, links, etc. An advanced programmer should master this chapter, because it is a cornerstone of JavaScript programming. Chapter 21 deals with only a few aspects of the `document` object (colors and output streams); other aspects are covered in other chapters. Chapter 21 formally explains output streams and output methods and their relationship with immediate and deferred scripts.

Understanding output issues is very useful for advanced JavaScript programmers.

- Chapter 22 is dedicated to HTML forms and form elements. It naturally deals with the `forms` array and the `form` object. The chapter includes a lengthy explanation of form validation, which is one of the most powerful features of JavaScript. In Chapter 22 you learn how to use various form elements for both collecting input and providing immediate responses. This chapter includes many example scripts.
- Chapter 23 talks about links, anchors, and image maps. The hypertextual essence of a Web page is achieved by using these HTML constructs, which JavaScript can access and modify. Both novice and experienced programmers should be acquainted with this chapter. Links, anchors, and image maps are all related to linking two different documents or two points within a document, allowing fast and easy navigation between the two. You can use many different JavaScript methods to manipulate these native HTML elements.
- Chapter 24 covers a very interesting concept in Web programming—cookies. Cookies allow storage of information on the client side for a specified duration. Due to the nature of these data tidbits, the storage of cookies is not affected by any standard operation performed by the user. For example, cookies are not deleted when the user shuts down his or her computer. Cookies should be studied in conjunction with forms, because it is usually convenient to use cookies for storing form-entered data.
- Chapter 25 is intended for advanced programmers who are interested in using Netscape Navigator's most powerful features. In this chapter you learn about images and how to use them with JavaScript. Chapter 25 focuses on the `Image` object and the `document.images` array. It teaches you how to cache images before they are loaded or used in an animation. This chapter is a must if you are interested in creating live, dynamic effects.
- Chapter 26 describes `frames`. Frames let you divide your page into separate windows, each window being a target of a different document. You learn how to create frames with and without borders, how to use the event handlers for `onFocus` and `onBlur`, and how to emulate the `focus` and `blur` events. It also shows you how to target documents to the different frames. If you want to be consid-

ered an advanced page author, be prepared to learn frames and use them in your page.

- Chapter 27 elaborates on windows. It teaches you how to open and close browser windows from JavaScript. It shows you how to customize your windows, for example, by omitting the status bar and menus. Chapter 27 introduces the concept of remote windows which Yahoo! was the first to feature. The code extract that generates a remote window is provided in this chapter. The `onBlur` and `onFocus` event handlers are described as well. A JavaScript-based HTML editor is explained in detail to demonstrate the usage of the features discussed in this chapter. Chapters 26 and 27 teach you most of what you need to know about browser windows and frames and how to manipulate them.
- Chapter 28 deals with various number and string evaluation concepts in JavaScript. It also explains the differences between a function call and a function reference. It then shows how to take advantage of function references for compiling a function.
- Chapter 29 explains how to use the `navigator` object to determine the user's browser and platform. This information allows a Web page author to provide different content for each browser. Lastly, Chapter 29 elaborates on how to check if Java is currently enabled on the user's browser. This is very important when implementing LiveConnect applications.
- Chapter 30 shows how to embed a plug-in object in an HTML document (using the `<EMBED>` tag) and how to reference that plug-in from JavaScript. In this chapter, you learn how to determine which plug-ins are installed on the user's browser. Finally, Chapter 30 discusses the basics of LiveAudio and LiveVideo.
- Chapter 31 deals with LiveConnect, a feature of Netscape Navigator 3.0x and above. Using several examples, it shows how to use Java and JavaScript in concert. It also discusses the usage of LiveConnect to control LiveAudio and LiveVideo plug-ins from JavaScript.
- Chapter 32 is dedicated to layers, a feature introduced in Netscape Navigator 4.0 (Communicator). It explains how to create layers with HTML and how to control them with JavaScript.
- Chapter 33 describes JavaScript-accessible style sheets. This powerful capability, supported by Netscape Navigator 4.0 and above, lets you define the stylistic attributes of the page, including mar-

gins, padding, border width, and fonts. It explains how to create external style sheets, style sheets within the document, and style specification for specific elements. It also explains the mathematics of a text box, as far as its stylistic specifications are concerned.

- Chapter 34 discusses security issues. The concept of data tainting is dealt with in depth. It allows users to choose which information to expose and which information should be secured. It presents the concept and use of the window taint accumulator for URL to URL secured access.
- Chapter 35 focuses on a JavaScript authoring tool named Acadia Infuse. It shows ten top tips of Infuse, such as how to cleverly print your script, how to drag and drop new structures into your code, how to instantiate new objects, how to use special inline characters, visual trees, and tool bars, and how to reuse your own JavaScript codes.
- Chapter 36, last but not least, helps you in debugging your scripts. It shows common error messages and what is usually the cause for each. It then suggests several techniques to find and fix bugs, such as viewing intermediate HTML files, reopening the browser, commenting out suspicious lines, and watching and tracing variables. It also suggests some tips on avoiding bugs in the first place by, for example, building the script skeleton first, and only then completing the details.

Programming Style

As you read this book, you will see that we use a uniform coding scheme in all scripts. That is, we always use the same indentation practice and the same formation. For example, you will find that we always put the opening semicolon of a loop on the same line as the loop's keyword. Take a look at the following script segment:

```
for (var num = 0; num < 10; ++num) {
     [JavaScript statements]
}
```

Some JavaScript scripters prefer to use a different style:

```
for (var num = 0; num < 10; ++num)
{
     [JavaScript statements]
}
```

The same applies to comments. Consider the following comment:

```
/* Copyright (c) 1997. All rights reserved.
Permission given to use this script provided
that this notice is left as is. */
```

Instead we would normally use single-line comments, because we believe that they emphasize the comment:

```
// Copyright (c) 1997. All rights reserved.
// Permission given to use this script provided
// that this notice is left as is.
```

You should feel free to choose the style that you like most, because there is no such thing as an incorrect choice. However, if you have never programmed before, it is recommended that you use the same coding scheme we use. If you are an experienced programmer, you may prefer to stick with your habits. For example, most C and C++ programmers choose to place a semicolon at the end of each statement. Although not required, JavaScript works fine with semicolons, just as C++ does.

Reading Examples

A picture is worth a thousand words, and so is a good example. However, if you do not read an example properly, it isn't worth anything. When you encounter an example of a script segment, read through it and try to find what it does. Even if you cannot understand how everything is being accomplished, try to get the main idea. First, try to find where the execution starts. For example, if a JavaScript script includes a global function call, it is surely the first statement to be executed. Follow the natural flow dictated by the script. The most important part of a script is its comments, so you should read every one of them. It is probably more important that you read the comments first, rather than reading the statements without the comments.

The second stage in reading an example is reading the explanations that usually follow the script. Every script is provided with complete documentation, so you should understand every single statement. If you try hard and simply can't figure something out, don't hesitate to run the script under your browser. As a matter of fact, since it is difficult to learn computer programming without using a computer, it is recommended that you try executing all scripts.

Encouragement for Nonprogrammers

Learning JavaScript is much easier than mastering a full programming language such as C or Java. Using JavaScript, you can write small scripts which you can immediately execute and debug. The JavaScript interpreter gives you immediate feedback on your script correctness, and until you learn a compiled language, you'll never appreciate this powerful capability. Implementing a similar task in C or Java is probably more difficult.

The advantage of computers is that they do exactly what you tell them to do. The disadvantage of computers, on the other hand, is that they do exactly what you tell them to do. Think about this axiom and internalize it, because every programmer needs to come to terms with it before he or she can become successful. Programmers become frustrated usually because of two types of errors. The first type is syntax errors. The computer understands sentences that are written in the exact syntax as it is specified in this book (unless a mistake has been made). If you misspell a command or a function name, the computer won't understand it and will return an error message. The more difficult error to find is when the computer does not complain but does not do what you want it to do. This is one of the laws of programming—the computer does what you tell it to do, not what you want it to do. This kind of error, also called a semantical error, is usually found by careful debugging, which is explained later in the book. Another method to find semantical errors is letting someone else look over your shoulder and read your script. Another person will sometimes catch an error that is overlooked by the original author.

Experience also shows that a wrong assumption lies at the root of every difficulty in finding an error. Once an assumption is made, the programmer never tests its validity and, instead, is looking for the source of the problem elsewhere. It is a good idea to always repeat to yourself which assumptions you are relying on and validate each one of them. It is recommended you discuss the problem with a friend. A programmer may find an annoying bug just by explaining the program and its assumptions to someone else.

Warning for Programmers

Some people say programming experience in a procedural language such as C or Pascal may almost be a disadvantage to learning JavaScript. Although this judgment is controversial, there is indeed a big difference between them. JavaScript's object-oriented programming is very different from the procedural C language. The difference is classically demonstrated by mouse clicks. In a procedural language, the programmer is responsible for the screen appearance and everything that happens thereafter. Imagine a screen display of the classical Tetris game. The user has to program the blocks, the container, the score dial, etc. When the user clicks on a button (the Pause button for example), the program examines the coordinates of the click and compares those coordinates against all button coordinates on the screen (the programmer placed these buttons and therefore he or she stored the coordinates in the beginning of the program). Program execution then goes to the proper procedure and carries out the instructions associated with that button (pausing the Tetris game in our example).

Object-oriented programming is 180 degrees from the above. The Tetris Pause button is constructed as an object. An object is defined by its properties and by a set of operations defined to work with it. The Pause button's properties include its label, size, color, and icon. Operations defined for it may include the color change upon clicking and sending an instruction to another object to carry out the pause action. If a user clicks in a text entry field, the browser sends a message to the field to take care of the user actions as long as the insertion point is within the text field. An operation defined for a text field is written as a script segment. There is a script to handle typing in the field or clicking outside the field.

Don't be confused. JavaScript programming involves procedural construction as well. You will write a sequence of instructions in your script that will be in order. But when you work with JavaScript objects like form, radio button, text field, and image map, you will use their object properties and methods. Once you have defined the properties of the radio button, you won't have to worry about it any more. It will take care of itself and that's the beauty of object-oriented programming.

For those C programmers among you, you should feel very comfortable. Many language constructs were designed a la C style: Operator symbols, conditional structures, and repeat loops are almost identical.

Data typing is looser in JavaScript. Data is either a number (integer or floating), a string, a Boolean, an object, or `null`. Converting from one type to the other is straightforward. Since you are familiar with the language syntax, invest your time in the semantics, notably in object hierarchy which is not supported by C. Also, don't forget to master HTML.

Let the Show Begin

If you haven't got cold feet by now and are ready to jump in the water, then flip the page to the next chapter. Make sure you have Netscape version 3.0x and up or Microsoft Internet Explorer version 3.0 and up, as well as a text editor for the HTML documents. You are to embark on a new path that will take you to new adventures!

Chapter 3

Writing Your First Script

Essential Authoring Tools

In order to begin writing scripts, you need to know which text editor to use. HTML files are plain text (ASCII) files. Therefore, in order to add JavaScript to an existing HTML document, you need a text editor. You should not have any problem getting hold of a text editor for your computer.

Choosing a Text Editor

It is very important to choose the most suitable editor. The market is flooded with editors of various complexity and strength. Many text editors are also available as freeware and shareware. A simple text editor is probably the best for JavaScript programming. Most Web authors and designers use such editors because they allow plenty of freedom and enable the use of advanced features. Many different HTML editors and authoring tools are available, but you should avoid them. WYSIWYG (What You See Is What You Get) editors should not be used when adding or creating JavaScript. If you usually use a word processor that supports HTML extensions, feel free to use it. It comes in handy when you want to generate the simple HTML tags that apply to all documents. Even vi can do the job, if you know how to use it!

It is usually better to avoid powerful word processors such as Microsoft Word, because they do not deal with ASCII as a standard. However, if you do choose to use such an editor, always save your files as plain text. See Figure 3-1 for a demonstration.

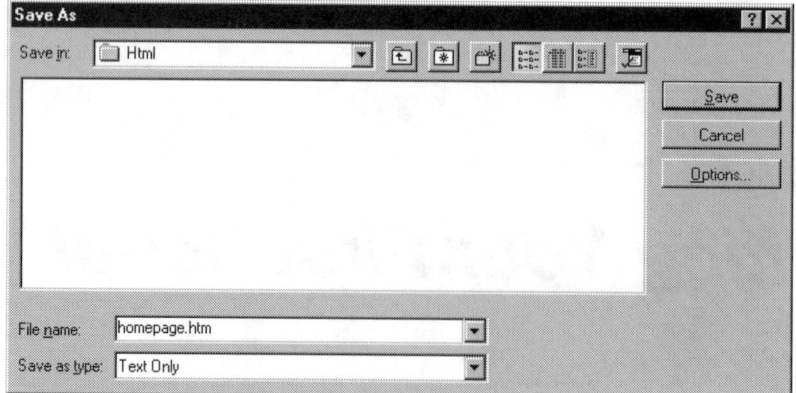

Figure 3-1. *Saving an HTML document in a word processor.*

Above all, it is important that you are comfortable with the text editor you choose and that it is easy to use.

The first JavaScript editing environment, Acadia Infuse, was introduced by Acadia Software. It offers an easy-to-use interface and enables fast and easy scripting. A trial version of this software is available on the CD-ROM. We discuss Acadia Infuse later in the book.

Choosing a Browser

Besides the basic programming tool, you need to be able to run your scripts and view their output. In order to run JavaScript, you need a compatible browser. Netscape Navigator 2.0x, 3.0x, and 4.0 currently support JavaScript. Microsoft Internet Explorer 3.0 and up also supports JavaScript (IE's implementation of JavaScript is called *JScript*).

It doesn't really matter which browser you choose, but using Netscape Navigator is probably the best. The Internet industry is quickly developing, so many new browsers will probably support JavaScript. When you load a local page that includes JavaScript, you do not have to be connected to the net—you can load it directly from your local disk. Overcoming JavaScript compatibility problems is often difficult, so we suggest that you have at least one version of Netscape Navigator and one version of Microsoft Internet Explorer.

Basic JavaScript Structure

In order to run client-side JavaScript, you must embed the code in the HTML document. Obviously, you cannot just place JavaScript statements in the source. There are several different ways to embed JavaScript scripts in HTML:

- As statements and functions using the <SCRIPT> tag.
- As event handlers using HTML tag attributes.
- As short statements resembling URLs.

The <SCRIPT> Tag

Internal Scripts

The <SCRIPT> tag is used to enclose JavaScript code in HTML documents. Here is the general syntax:

```
<SCRIPT LANGUAGE="JavaScript">

[JavaScript Statements...]

</SCRIPT>
```

The `<SCRIPT LANGUAGE="JavaScript">` tag acts like all other HTML tags. Notice that it must be followed by its closing counterpart, </SCRIPT>. Every statement you put between the two tags is interpreted as JavaScript code.

The LANGUAGE attribute is used to specify the scripting language. Although it is currently optional, you should always use it to accommodate future scripting languages. At present, the <SCRIPT> tag supports various languages including JavaScript and VBScript. JavaScript is the default scripting language, so the LANGUAGE definition is not required. When the browser comes across the precise name of the language, it loads the built-in JavaScript interpreter and then interprets the script.

JavaScript is case sensitive, but HTML is not. It does not matter whether you write <SCRIPT> or <script>, but try to be consistent. Be sure to write the name of the language properly, using capital letters where they are needed (although it does not matter to the browser).

External Scripts

Netscape Navigator 3.0 introduced a new SRC attribute for the <SCRIPT> tag, which enables the use of external scripts; that is, you can use a JavaScript script that is located in another file. This feature will eventually allow people to hide their scripts from the public, despite the fact that such action is not in keeping with the spirit of the Web. We will rarely use external scripts in the book, but remember that they exist, and you may find them helpful.

External scripts are useful when you need to integrate a long, sophisticated JavaScript script into an HTML file. This approach has several advantages:

- **Ease of maintenance.** The script is isolated from outside elements, such as nonrelated HTML code. The maintenance is much easier when the script stands alone.
- **Hiding from foreign browsers.** The code is automatically hidden from browsers that do not support JavaScript. The most basic rule of HTML interpretation, which enables the existence of various browsers, is that unrecognized tags are ignored (try typing `<Hello>` to your HTML document...). So if only the `<SCRIPT LANGUAGE="JavaScript">` and `</SCRIPT>` tags exist, an old browser will ignore all JavaScript-related elements.
- **Library support.** External scripts enable the use of JavaScript libraries, similar to the ones in C, C++, and other programming languages (e.g., `#include <string.h>`). You can reference general predefined functions in external scripts, thus avoiding duplication of functions or global declarations. Let's refer once again to C++. Think of `cout` as a simple function you have written. You must specify the source of the function in order to use it:

```
#include <iostream.h> // a directive to include the header file
void main()
{
   cout << "This is C++ programming"
}
```

  JavaScript has the same structure, except that only one external file is supported.

Here are some disadvantages of using an external file:

- **No back references.** As mentioned above, JavaScript scripts are mainly driven by user-initiated events. A click on a button calls a function, a selection of a form element executes another function, and so on. If you design your whole script in an external file, you will have difficulties in referring to the HTML definitions in the original file. For this reason, place only general functions in an external script.

- **Additional processing.** The JavaScript interpreter evaluates all functions found in your script header, including those defined in the external file, and stores them in memory. Thus, loading unneeded functions in an external file degrades the script performance.
- **Additional server access.** You know how irritating it is to wait until another page loads in the window, especially with slow modem connections. That is exactly the problem with the SRC attribute. When the browser comes across the tag which tells it to interpret JavaScript code in another file, it must first load that file. Such an action is time consuming. Most programmers say that efficiency is not as important as maintainability and clarity. However, loading a new page can cause more than the usual efficiency penalty. Always keep in mind that unnecessary HTTP hits to the server should be avoided.

Enough theory. Here is the syntax for defining an external script in the <SCRIPT> tag:

```
<SCRIPT LANGUAGE="JavaScript" SRC="yourFile.js">

[additional JavaScript statements...]

</SCRIPT>
```

Note that the extension of the external file must be ".js", just as the extension of an HTML file must be ".html" or ".htm". The name of the file does not have to include the full path—a relative (virtual) path is enough.

Suppose abc1.js contains the following code:

```
var counter = 100

function alertMe(message) {
    alert(message)
}

function writeMe(message) {
    document.write(message)
}
```

Do not pay any attention to the meaning of the statements. They are all explained in the following chapters. Here's the basic HTML file:

```
<HTML>
<HEAD>
<TITLE>Using external files</TITLE>
<SCRIPT LANGUAGE="JavaScript" SRC="abc1.js">
<!--

var digit = 8
alertMe("Hello!")
writeMe("Howdy!")

// -->
</SCRIPT>
</HEAD>
</HTML>
```

The preceding structure is equivalent to the following HTML document:

```
<HTML>
<HEAD>
<TITLE>Equivalent Script</TITLE>
<SCRIPT LANGUAGE="JavaScript">
<!--

 var counter = 100

 function alertMe(message) {
     alert(message)
 }

 function writeMe(message) {
     document.write(message)
 }

var digit = 8
alertMe("Hello!")
writeMe("Howdy!")

// -->
</SCRIPT>
</HEAD>
</HTML>
```

It is extremely important to understand the way external scripts are interpreted, because many different rules apply to JavaScript and HTML layout (this topic is discussed in the following chapter). Just keep in mind that an external script is actually interpreted as if it precedes the local script (enclosed by the `<SCRIPT>` and `</SCRIPT>` tags). The `<!--` and `// -->` tags are introduced in the next section.

JavaScript-only files should have the filename suffix ".js", and the server must map the ".js" suffix to the MIME type "application/x-javascript", which it sends back in the HTTP header. If the server does not map the .js filename extension to application/x-javascript, Navigator will not load properly the JavaScript file specified by the SRC attribute. In short, your server must be configured to reflect the proper MIME type—otherwise the browser does not respond properly with the data coming back in the HTTP response to the SRC-initiated request.

Hiding the Script

You have probably asked yourself what happens when someone loads your page with an old browser that does not support JavaScript. The solution to this problem is based on the commenting tags of both HTML and JavaScript.

Commenting tags in Netscape Navigator are <!-- and -->. The first one opens the comment block, and the second one closes it. A simple comment in a plain HTML document looks like this:

```
<!-- copyright 1997 -->
```

There are two types of comments in JavaScript:

- // to begin a short comment that does not exceed the length of one line
- /* and */ to enclose a comment of any length

The JavaScript interpreter ignores the opening HTML comment tag in JavaScript code. Take a look at the syntax you should use to hide the code from old browsers that do not support JavaScript:

```
<SCRIPT LANGUAGE="JavaScript">
<!-- hide code from old browsers

JavaScript statements...

// end code hiding -->
</SCRIPT>
```

In order to understand how this hiding works, picture the output of the preceding script in a browser that does not support JavaScript. Both the <SCRIPT> and the </SCRIPT> tags are ignored, like any other unrecognized tag. Everything between the HTML commenting tags is also ignored. This structure works fine with Navigator and IE, which understand the tags and interpret the script correctly.

Problems with Code Hiding

It is important to understand that Netscape Navigator does not use standard HTML. One difference is the commenting tag. While Netscape Navigator expects the sequence `<!-- comments -->`, standard HTML commenting syntax is `<! comments >`. Therefore, any *greater-than logical operator* in the JavaScript source indicates the end of a comment. The script statements beyond this character are interpreted as noncomment plain HTML code, causing the JavaScript statements to be printed to the page as plain text. The only workaround is to avoid using the > character in the script. For instance, you can replace `b > a` with `a < b`. In some situations, such as printing an HTML tag via JavaScript, it is more difficult to find a replacement for the greater-than character. Take a look at the following script:

```
<SCRIPT LANGUAGE="JavaScript">
<!--

document.write("<TABLE>")

// -->
</SCRIPT>
```

An old browser begins to interpret the code as a plain HTML comment when it encounters the <! sequence. It terminates the comment when it finds a > character which is present in the script itself. Therefore, an old browser will print the remaining portion of the script. Generally speaking, you must avoid providing a greater-than character literally in a script. The perfect workaround in this case is to assign the greater-than character to a variable without placing it literally in the script, and then evaluating the variable when needed. That would be as follows:

```
<SCRIPT LANGUAGE="JavaScript">
<!--

var gt = unescape("%3E")
document.write("<TABLE" + gt)

// -->
</SCRIPT>
```

Scan the script and notice that no greater-than characters are present. See Chapter 16, Handling Strings, for details on the `unescape()` function.

Alternate Content

A new HTML tag which enables you to provide alternate content for users who are using old browsers or who have disabled JavaScript is the <NOSCRIPT> tag. This tag and its closing counterpart </NOSCRIPT> are similar to the <NOFRAMES> tag which is used to provide alternate content to users who are not using a frame-enabled browser. The following example demonstrates how to add such content for users who don't run JavaScript:

```
<NOSCRIPT>

<B>This page uses JavaScript, so you need to get Netscape Navigator 2.0 or
later!</B><BR>

<A HREF="http://home.netscape.com/comprod/mirror/index.html">
<IMG SRC="NSNow.gif"></A><BR>

If you are using Navigator 2.0 or later, and you see this message, you
need to enable JavaScript by choosing Options | Network Preferences.

</NOSCRIPT>
```


You might be asking yourself how an old browser that does not even recognize scripts can interpret the <NOSCRIPT>…</NOSCRIPT> portion correctly. A JavaScript-enabled browser simply ignores that section when JavaScript is currently enabled. However, an old browser does not know this tag and ignores it. Therefore, it does not ignore the interior of a <NOSCRIPT>…</NOSCRIPT> portion, causing the HTML you put in between to be interpreted only by an old browser or one that has its JavaScript support disabled.

Placing JavaScript Code

When you want to place the script somewhere in the HTML document, you need to choose where to put it. Technically, you may place it anywhere between the <HTML> and </HTML> tags which enclose the whole document. Actually, the two possibilities are the <HEAD>…</HEAD> portion and the <BODY>…</BODY> portion. Because the <HEAD>…</HEAD> portion is evaluated first, it is generally a good practice to place the script there. You will find later another compelling reason to do so.

A single HTML document may contain any number of scripts. You can place some of the scripts in the <HEAD>…</HEAD> portion, and others in the <BODY>…</BODY> portion of the page. The following code demonstrates it:

```
<HTML>
<HEAD>
<TITLE>Multiple scripts</TITLE>
<SCRIPT LANGUAGE="JavaScript">

[JavaScript statements...]

</SCRIPT>
<SCRIPT LANGUAGE="JavaScript">

[JavaScript statements...]

</SCRIPT>
</HEAD>
<BODY>
<H1>This is a complex structure</H1>
<SCRIPT LANGUAGE="JavaScript">

[JavaScript statements...]

</SCRIPT>
</BODY>
</HTML>
```

Conventions

JavaScript syntax is very similar to C, C++, and Java. It includes functions, expressions, statements, operators, and more.

Using the Semicolon

The JavaScript interpreter does not pay any attention to carriage return characters in the source. It is possible to put numerous statements on the same line, but you must separate them with a semicolon (;). You can also add a semicolon at the end of a statement that occupies its own line, but it is not necessary. Take a look at the following statements:

```
document.write("Hello"); alert("Good bye")
```

```
document.write("Hello")
alert("Good bye")
```

```
document.write("Hello");
alert("Good bye");
```

All three sets are legal, and their results are identical.

JavaScript is Case Sensitive

You saw earlier that JavaScript is a case-sensitive language. It applies to all aspects of the language, including variable names (*identifiers*), functions, and methods (discussed later). The statement `document.write()`, for example, is legal, but `document.Write()` is not.

Comments

Comments are an important concept in all languages, especially in JavaScript. They help make programs simple and easy to understand. Comments are messages that can be put into programs at various points, without affecting the results. There are two different types of comments in JavaScript:

- **Single-line** comments are comments that do not exceed the length of a line. They must start and end on the same line of the source. These comments begin with a double-slash (//).
- **Multiple-line** comments are comments that may exceed the length of one line. Therefore, they require a sign that specifies the beginning of the comment, and another sign that specifies the end of the comment. The opening part is /* and the closing part is */.

Both types of comments are identical to the comments in C and C++. You should use comments to explain every part of your script.

```
// single-line comment
```

```
/* line 1 of the comment
   line 2 of the comment
   line 3 of the comment */
```

Using Quotes

In JavaScript, you often use quotes to, among other things, delimit strings. A common problem arises when using a pair of quotes inside another pair of quotes. Since the interpreter must recognize each set of quotes in order to pair them correctly, the creators of JavaScript made it possible to use two different types of quotes: double quotes (") and single quotes ('). If you need only one set of quotes, you can choose either of them as long as you terminate the quote with the same type of quote you used to open it. If you do not follow this rule, you will get a JavaScript error: "unterminated string literal." You must always alternate quotes properly:

```
document.write("<IMG SRC='cool.gif'>")
```

Your First Script

First of all, launch your text editor. Type Example 3-1 in the text editor and save it under a name of your choice. Make sure the name ends with either the .htm or .html extension. Next, launch the browser. Since the file is local, you do not need to be connected to the Internet to view the results. Now, load the file from the browser's menu. That's all there is to it. You can start enjoying JavaScript.

The following script is interpreted and executed immediately when you load the page containing it.

```
<HTML>
<HEAD>
<TITLE>Hello net.</TITLE>
</HEAD>
<BODY>
<SCRIPT LANGUAGE="JavaScript">
<!-- hide code from old browsers

document.write("<H1>Hello net.</H1>")

// end code hiding -->
</SCRIPT>
</BODY>
</HTML>
```

Example 3-1 (ex3-1.htm). *A simple "Hello net." script.*

This is a simple HTML document that includes a JavaScript script. Notice that its structure is the same as that of any other HTML document. The only new concept is the `<SCRIPT>` tag. We put the script in the `<BODY>...</BODY>` portion of the page, though you may put it anywhere between the `<HTML>` and `</HTML>` tags. For now, think of `document.write()` as a way to print expressions to the page. `write()` is actually a *method* of the document *object*. Objects, methods, and properties are introduced in Chapter 6, Object-Based Programming. The `write()` method supports any HTML syntax. Be aware, also, that all *strings* must be included in quotes.

Example 3-1's equivalent consists of two files, the HTML file and the external JavaScript file:

```
<HTML>
<HEAD>
<TITLE>Hello net.</TITLE>
</HEAD>
```

```
<BODY>
<SCRIPT LANGUAGE="JavaScript" SRC="sayHello.js">
</SCRIPT>
</BODY>
</HTML>
```

```
 // this file must be named sayHello.js
document.write("Hello net.")
```

Example 3-1 demonstrates the basic structure of a JavaScript program.

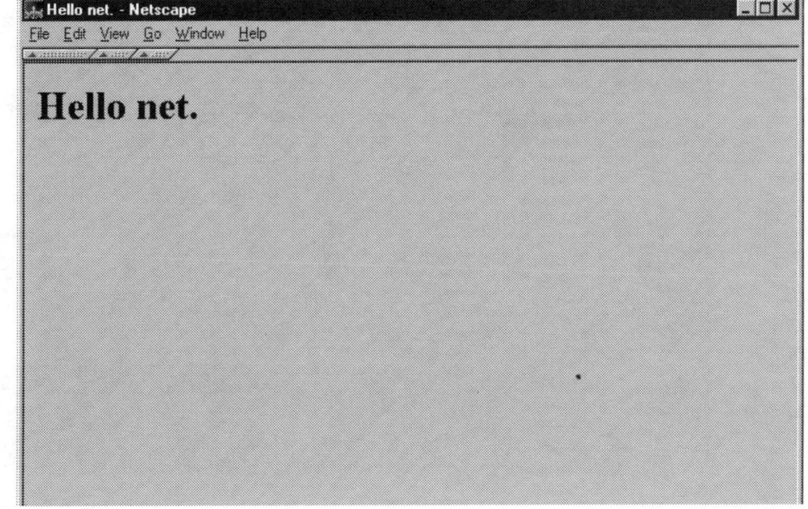

Figure 3-2. HTML content generated by the `document.write()` method.

Printing JavaScript Output

Netscape Navigator 3.0 and up enables you to print the JavaScript script output. Take a peek at the following example:

```
<HTML>
<HEAD>
<TITLE>Printing JavaScript</TITLE>
</HEAD>
<BODY>
<SCRIPT LANGUAGE="JavaScript">
<!--

document.write("This is JavaScript output.")

// -->
```

```
</SCRIPT>
<BR>
This is HTML output.
</BODY>
</HTML>
```

Example 3-2 (ex3-2.htm). *JavaScript and HTML output combined.*

In order to understand the printing concept, it is necessary to compare the screen output with the paper output.

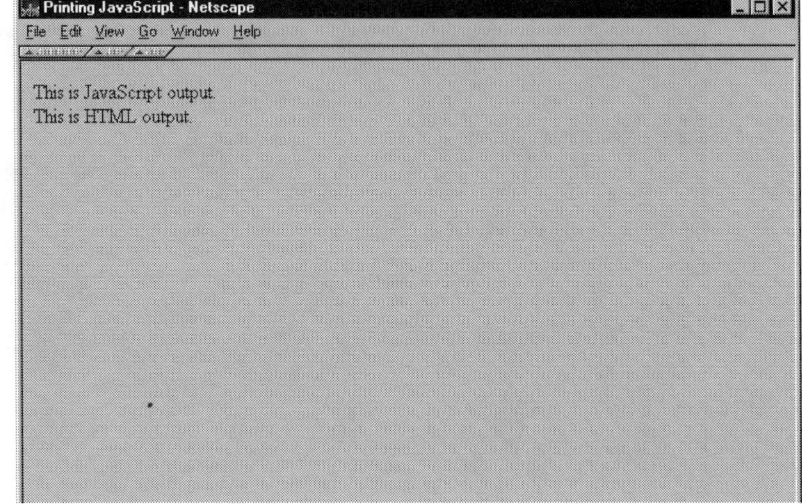

Figure 3-3. *One line of JavaScript-generated output and one of HTML output.*

If you try printing this page with Navigator 2.0x you will receive a page with a blank line followed by the second line—"This is HTML output." When printing it with Navigator 3.0 and up, or Internet Explorer, the printout is identical to the content of the browser window.

Updating a Page

Whenever you change the content of the page and you wish to see how it affects the final layout, you must reload the page using the Reload button. A JavaScript script is immediately interpreted upon initial loading of the page, and code that does not run immediately is stored in memory. Reloading the page refreshes the memory and generates a new version of the page layout (if you changed it, of course).

Summary

In this chapter you learned how to write scripts and add them to an HTML document. We covered the `<SCRIPT>` tag and other related topics. It is sometimes difficult to predict what other people see on your page, especially those who are using a browser that does not support JavaScript. Although you haven't seen any useful JavaScript script yet, we hope you understand that this is a powerful scripting language that can do much more than generate HTML content with `document.write()`. Once you get a grip on writing simple scripts, you will find it easy to move on to more complicated and interesting programs.

Chapter 4

JavaScript and HTML

Page Layout

Layout refers to transforming the plain text directives of HTML into graphical display on your computer. Generally speaking, layout is done sequentially. The browser starts from the top of the document and works its way down to the bottom. It transforms the plain HTML tags and text to a graphical interface. The browser recognizes many tags that instruct it how to perform the layout. There are tags that refer to images, tags that refer to forms, and many other tags. Obviously, the layout also occurs from left to right, so you may put an entire page on one line.

The browser deals with JavaScript code like it handles HTML code, scanning the source from left to right and from top to bottom. JavaScript has "tags" of its own by which it instructs the browser and determines the layout. However, JavaScript is not read exactly like HTML. In HTML, the browser acts immediately according to the elements it recognizes. Not all JavaScript code refers to actions that take place while the page is loading. Some parts are just kept in memory until they are called. For instance, if you write a function and do not call it, the browser does not do anything with it. This part of the script stays in memory, and can be invoked later.

Command Blocks

Command blocks are units of JavaScript commands. Although a command block acts exactly like a single one, it can actually perform many tasks. Commands are read and interpreted in the same way the browser interprets commands in the main scripting zone. Blocks are used in functions, loops, `if-else` statements, and many other

JavaScript statements. They allow you to reference more than one command in a single statement. A command block looks like this:

```
{
     first command
     second command
     third command
     .
     .
     .
}
```

All commands are enclosed in curly braces ({ and }). In order to remember the closing brace after the set, it is a good practice to type both braces first, and only then add the commands in between. Command blocks can also be interleaved (*nested*). Take a look at the following structure:

```
{
     first command of main block
     second command of main block
     third command of main block
     .
     .
     .
     {
          first command of nested block
          second command of nested block
          third command of nested block
          .
          .
          .
     }
     .
     .
     .
}
```

As shown in this example, it is a common practice to indent each nested block, according to its nesting level. The JavaScript interpreter is not influenced by these spaces (or tabs).

Functions

Functions allow you to group commonly used code into a compact unit that can be used repeatedly. Functions are a fundamental element in almost all programs. Each function consists of a set of JavaScript statements which are executed as if they were a separate program.

You define a function somewhere in the script, and call it later. Take a look at the syntax of a function:

```
function functionName([parameters]) {
    [statements]
}
```

The name of the function must be a set of letters, digits, and underscores (_), provided that the first character of the name is not a digit. In order to call the function (and execute the statements located in it), you need to specify its name. Example 4-1 shows how to define and invoke a function:

```
<HTML>
<HEAD>
<TITLE>Calling a function</TITLE>
<SCRIPT LANGUAGE="JavaScript">
<!--

printText()
function printText() {
    document.write("I am now inside the function.<BR>")
}

// -->
</SCRIPT>
</HEAD>
<BODY>
</BODY>
</HTML>
```

Example 4-1 (ex4-1.htm). *A simple function with one statement.*

The function `printText()` includes only one command (the `document.write()` method). When the function is called, all the command function blocks are interpreted. The output of this script is the same as the output of a script containing only the printing line inside the function; its output is shown in Figure 4-1.

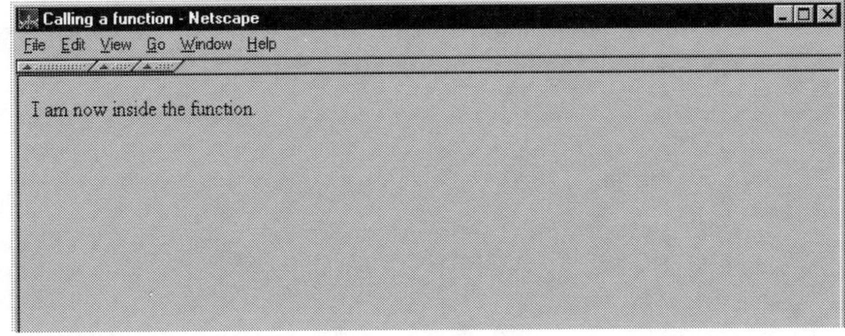

Figure 4-1. *HTML content generated by a function.*

Defining and Calling a Function

When the browser interprets scripts placed within <SCRIPT> tags, it stores functions in memory until they are called. You can call a function from within a script tag or from an *event handler*. Defining a function consists of first naming it and then assigning some commands to it, as shown in Example 4-1. It is important to understand the difference between defining a function and calling it, because it influences the way you build your document.

This often reminds me of the following situation. Mike tells Joe that he should take an umbrella with him and also provides him with instructions on how to use it. This is similar to the definition of a function. Now, Joe knows exactly how to use the umbrella, and he is prepared to do so. Two hours later, it begins to rain. The falling rain reminds Joe that he should use the umbrella, in the same manner as Mike taught him. The falling rain resembles the function call. Until now, the function was stored in memory, but it was not called, and therefore it was not executed. Just as certain events trigger a function call, rain calls for an umbrella. If someone instructed Joe to use the umbrella, as Mike taught him earlier of course, that would be like calling the function from within another script, rather than from an event handler.

Placing Scripts in Documents

You already know that not all JavaScript statements are executed immediately. Some need to be called in order to do something. In order to understand where to place a script in a document, you must know the difference between an *immediate script* and a *deferred script*.

Immediate scripts are ones that influence the layout of the page. For instance, a script that prints something to the Web page is usually an immediate script. Therefore, you must place immediate scripts exactly where you want their output to appear. The following example demonstrates how to place immediate scripts.

```
<HTML>
<HEAD>
<TITLE>Immediate script</TITLE>
</HEAD>
<BODY BGCOLOR="#ffffff">
<TABLE BORDER=5 CELLSPACING=5 CELLPADDING=25>
<TR>
```

```
<TD>
<SCRIPT LANGUAGE="JavaScript">
<!--

document.write("<IMG SRC='img4-2.gif' ALT='pencil icon' HEIGHT=71
WIDTH=53>")

// -->
</SCRIPT>
</TD></TR>
</TABLE>
</BODY>
</HTML>
```

Example 4-2 (ex4-2.htm). *A script in an HTML table cell, in the <BODY>…</BODY> portion.*

In Example 4-2, we included the script block in the <BODY>...</BODY> portion of the page. The only JavaScript statement included is the one that prints the image. In order to produce a frame around the image, we used an HTML table. Notice how we used plain HTML to create the <TABLE> tag and other table-related definitions and JavaScript-generated HTML to create images. Therefore, we had to position the script exactly where we wanted it to be—inside the table. Whenever possible, it is better to make the table a JavaScript output as well, because placing JavaScript scripts inside plain-HTML tables may expose a known bug in Navigator. The output of Example 4-2 is shown in Figure 4-2.

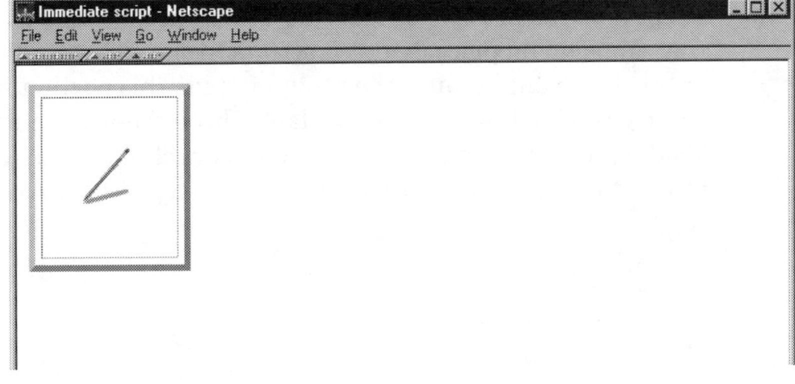

Figure 4-2. *JavaScript-generated output in an HTML table.*

Tip An important rule in HTML programming is to always specify the height and width of an image. You can specify them by adding `HEIGHT` and `WIDTH` attributes to the `<IMG>` tag. Both sizes are measured in pixels. For example, `img4-2.gif` in Example 4-2 has a height of 71 pixels and a width of 53 pixels. Do not forget to attach these attributes to all images in the following fashion:

```
<IMG SRC="imageURL" ALT="briefDescriptionOfImage"
HEIGHT=imageHeightInPixels WIDTH=imageWidthInPixels>
```

Many bugs in JavaScript can be avoided by specifying the height and width attributes of an image.

An immediate script does not necessarily generate any output. It can consist of virtually any valid JavaScript statement (such as variable declarations and loops). Statements in an immediate script are executed as they are being interpreted.

Deferred scripts are different from immediate scripts. They do not directly influence the final layout of the page. Deferred scripts just pass a set of instructions to the browser, which keeps them in its memory. These scripts usually include function definitions. A deferred script tells the browser what to do when another script tells it to do that. You should place deferred scripts in the `<HEAD>…</HEAD>` portion of the document because the browser loads this portion first, and therefore all definitions are available throughout the entire program. That is, the browser already has the instructions when another script tells it to execute them. Example 4-3 uses a deferred script.

```
<HTML>
<HEAD>
<TITLE>Deferred script</TITLE>
<SCRIPT LANGUAGE="JavaScript">
<!--

function makeDialogBox() {
     alert("Wonderful!")
}

// -->
```

```
</SCRIPT>
</HEAD>
<BODY>
</BODY>
</HTML>
```

Example 4-3 (ex4-3.htm). *A deferred script that displays a dialog box when invoked.*

This script does not influence the graphical layout of the page. The browser evaluates the script but does nothing except for storing the script in memory. This characteristic applies to all deferred scripts. Deferred scripts usually react to events that the user triggers after the page has been loaded.

Another advantage in putting deferred scripts in the `<HEAD>...</HEAD>` portion has to do with programming style and convenience. Placing all scripts in the `<HEAD>...</HEAD>` section enable easy maintenance and modification because you naturally know where to look for errors.

So far you know two types of scripts: immediate scripts and deferred scripts. Both types often need to be used in the same document. This is very simple—you just need to write the scripts and put each one of them in its appropriate place, as if it is alone.

4 Chapter

Tip Most of your scripts will be in the <HEAD>...</HEAD> portion of the HTML document. Always place the <TITLE>*title of the page*</TITLE> definition before the script, so the title appears in the title bar during the script's execution. If the script is deferred, you do not have to worry about this because evaluating a script does not take much time, and people will not notice the difference. It is generally a good idea to place immediate scripts in the <BODY>...</BODY> portion so that the viewable attributes of the page, such as the background, are evaluated before the script is executed. On the other hand, it is a good practice to place deferred scripts in the <HEAD>...</HEAD> portion.

Executing Deferred Scripts

Deferred scripts do not do anything immediately, but they are certainly not a decoration. In order to use deferred commands, you must call them from outside the deferred script. There are three ways to call deferred scripts:

- From immediate scripts, using the function mechanism
- By user-initiated events, using event handlers
- By clicking on links or image-map zones that are associated with the script

Calling Deferred Code from a Script

A function is a deferred script because it does not do anything until an event, a function, a JavaScript link, or an immediate script calls it. You've probably noticed that you can call a function from within a script. Sometimes you are interested in calling a function from the same script, and in other cases you might want to call it from another script. Both methods are possible.

Calling a function from the same script is very simple. You just need to specify the name of the function, as demonstrated in Example 4-4.

```
<HTML>
<HEAD>
<TITLE>Calling deferred code from its own script</TITLE>
<SCRIPT LANGUAGE="JavaScript">
<!--

makeLine(30)
function makeLine(lineWidth) {
    document.write("<HR SIZE=" + lineWidth + ">")
}
makeLine(10)

// -->
</SCRIPT>
</HEAD>
<BODY>
</BODY>
</HTML>
```

Example 4-4 (ex4-4.htm). *Function definitions and calls in the same script.*

Example 4-4 shows that a function can accept an argument. Also notice the "+" operator that combines *strings*. These topics will be discussed in later chapters. Let's follow the entire process for the makeLine(10) command. This command invokes the makeLine function and assigns the value 10 to a *parameter* named lineWidth. Then, the browser prints the string <HR SIZE=10> in the client window.

Since both the calling statement and the function definition are located in the same script, you can call the function before the function definition as well as after it.

The <HEAD>...</HEAD> portion in HTML is interpreted immediately when the page loads. Therefore, the script in Example 4-4 outputs two horizontal lines at the top of the page, as illustrated in Figure 4-3.

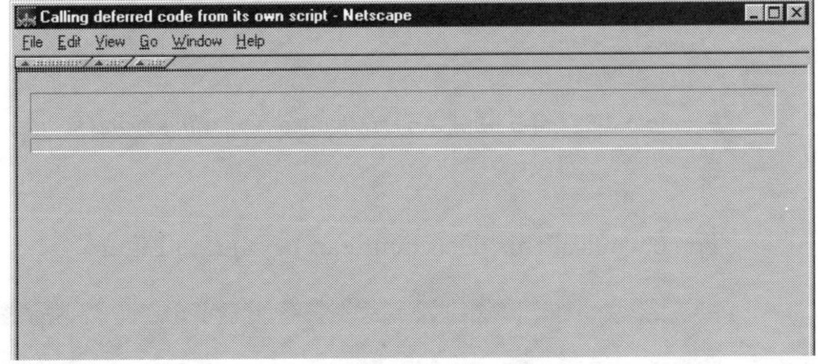

Figure 4-3. *Two horizontal rules of different sizes.*

But, what if you want more horizontal lines in the middle of the page? Example 4-5 does just that via function calls.

```
<HTML>
<HEAD>
<TITLE>Calling deferred code from another script</TITLE>
<SCRIPT LANGUAGE="JavaScript">
<!--

function makeLine(lineWidth) {
     document.write("<HR SIZE=" + lineWidth + ">")
}

// -->
</SCRIPT>
</HEAD>
<BODY>
<H1>JavaScript coming in handy.</H1>
<SCRIPT LANGUAGE="JavaScript">
<!--

makeLine(10)
```

```
// -->
</SCRIPT>
<BR>
This is a good example of how you can use JavaScript to
repeat certain procedures many times, without having to
write the same line over and over again. Whenever you
need a horizontal rule of any size, you call the function
makeLine() with the appropriate argument instead of writing
it again.
<SCRIPT LANGUAGE="JavaScript">
<!--

makeLine(4)

// -->
</SCRIPT>
</BODY>
</HTML>
```

Example 4-5 (ex4-5.htm). *An HTML document with several scripts, each consisting of a function call.*

The output of this document can be seen in Figure 4-4.

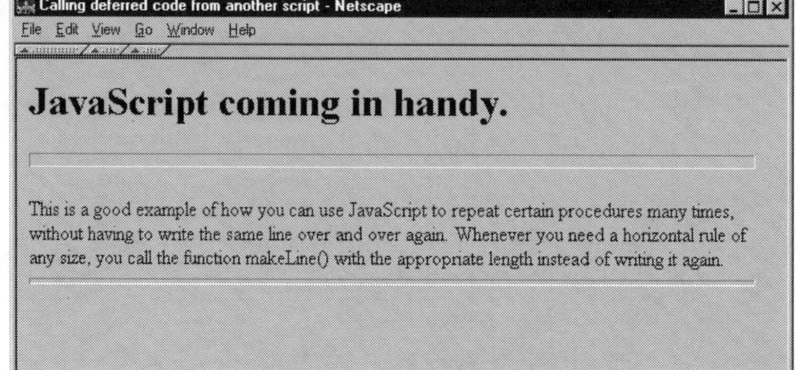

Figure 4-4. *Two horizontal rules created by the same function.*

Generally speaking, you can call a function from anywhere in the script, or, if the function is already evaluated, from any external script that the browser interprets. An error message will pop up if you don't obey this rule. For example, if an external script calls the function `makeLine()` before its definition, you will get an error message: "makeLine is not defined." You will probably see this message often while working on your first scripts.

Calling Deferred Code from Event Handlers

JavaScript applications are mostly driven by events that occur in the page. You may not have noticed, but when you load a page in the client window, many different events take place. Some of the events occur automatically when you load a page, while others, such as button clicks, form selections, and link navigation, are user triggered. As opposed to scripts that you embed in a document with a <SCRIPT> tag, you can add JavaScript statements to some known HTML tags. Event handlers, for example, are embedded in documents as attributes of HTML tags to which you assign JavaScript code. The general syntax is as follows:

```
<TAG eventHandler="JavaScript code">
```

Browsers that do not support JavaScript will pay no attention to the event handler attribute, but they will still evaluate the tag. One of the most simple event handlers is onMouseOver. This event handler is associated with the link or anchor tag. Its syntax is:

```
<A HREF="..." onMouseOver="JavaScript code">
```

This event handler is triggered when the user moves the mouse pointer over a link or an anchor. Take a look at the following example.

```
<HTML>
<HEAD>
<TITLE>Calling deferred code from event handlers</TITLE>
<SCRIPT LANGUAGE="JavaScript">
<!--

function thankYou() {
    alert("Thank you for pointing at me!")
}

// -->
</SCRIPT>
</HEAD>
<BODY>
<A HREF="http://www.netscape.com/" onMouseOver="thankYou()">Point at
                                   me.</A>
<BR>
<A HREF="http://www.intel.com/" onMouseOver="alert('Thank you for pointing
                                   at me!')">Point at me.</A>
</BODY>
</HTML>
```

Example 4-6 (ex4-6.htm). *Two links with event handlers, each invoking a different function.*

The new term in this script is the `alert("expression")` method. This is a built-in method of the window object. It shows the given `expression` (usually a message) in a pop-up dialog box. The syntax of this method is similar to that of `document.write()`. Objects and methods are introduced in Chapter 6, Object-Based Programming.

Example 4-6 demonstrates how to use event handlers. The page contains two links. The first link (to Netscape's site) uses the `onMouseOver` event handler. When you put the mouse pointer over the link, the function `thankYou()` is invoked and executed. This function, like any other function, is a deferred code. An event handler is similar to a `<SCRIPT>` tag in that both formats allow you to freely include JavaScript code. The second link in Example 4-6 uses the same event handler, but it does not call the `thankYou()` function.

Normally, you should avoid adding a lot of JavaScript code to an event handler script. Instead, you should use functions, as shown in the first link of Example 4-6. When your document becomes long and complicated and consists of many functions (ten functions in the same page, for example) it is better to place all functions in the `<HEAD>...</HEAD>` portion of the page, and invoke them from elsewhere in the document.

Event handler definition usually calls for alternating quotes. You often need one pair of quotes for the argument of a function and a second pair for the event handler attribute.

Calling Deferred Script from Links and Image Maps

The rest of this chapter is based on three concepts we have not defined yet: WWW, hypertext, and URL. *WWW* is a hypertext document system, linking related data from different documents. *Hypertext* is a technology used to thread information. The *Universal Resource Locator*, or *URL*, is the standard naming convention of documents on the Web.

The basic structure of a reference anchor (link) is:

```
<A HREF="documentURL">any text or images</A>
```

Instead of the *documentURL* in this example, JavaScript uses the `<A>` tag's `HREF` attribute to create a "link" to a script (function) that has already been evaluated. The placement of this tag is governed by the same rules affecting that of event handlers. For example, you can call a function from this tag only if the function was previously defined. Although the `<A>` tag's `HREF` attribute is not an event handler, it behaves in a similar fashion.

In the next chapter you will see how to evaluate expressions in JavaScript. You will find out that the "location" of the evaluation tool is "`javascript:`". The URL of all JavaScript deferred scripts (functions) starts with `javascript:`, followed by the full name of the function they call. The general syntax of such a link is:

```
<A HREF="javascript:functionName()">any text or images</A>
```

Take a look at Example 4-7 which demonstrates the use of such links.

```
<HTML>
<HEAD>
<TITLE>Calling deferred code from links</TITLE>
<SCRIPT LANGUAGE="JavaScript">
<!--

function alertText() {
     alert("This is text!")
}

function alertImage() {
     alert("This is an image!")
}

// -->
</SCRIPT>
</HEAD>
<BODY>

Click <A HREF="javascript:alertText()">here</A> to see a message.<BR>
Click <A HREF="javascript:alertImage()"><IMG SRC="img4-7.gif" ALT="here"
                 BORDER=0 HEIGHT=43 WIDTH=93></A> to see another message.

</BODY>
</HTML>
```

Example 4-7 (ex4-7.htm). *Calling JavaScript functions from links.*

Figure 4-5 shows the output of the preceding script when the user clicks on the image.

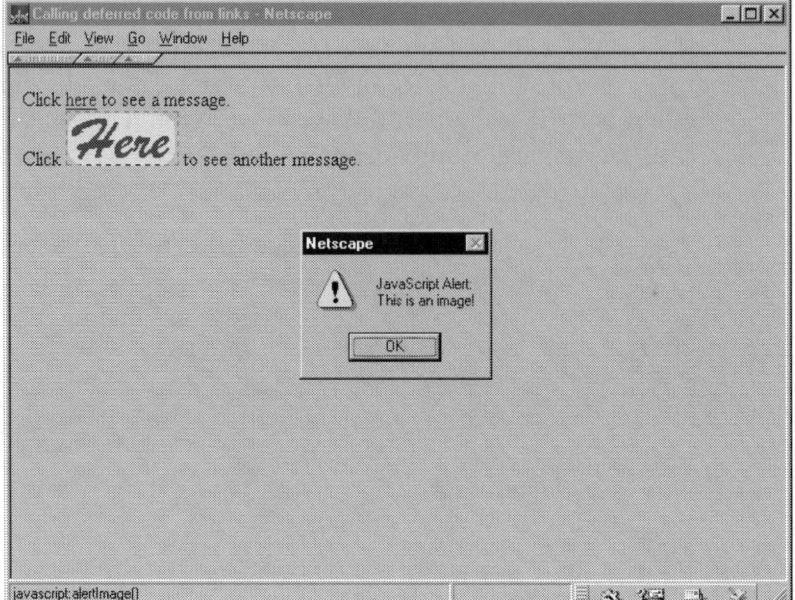

Figure 4-5. *A dialog box generated by a function that was invoked by a link.*

Since "`javascript:`*`functionName`*`()`" is an official URL, you can also use it in image maps. The following example shows how to do this:

```
<HTML>
<HEAD>
<TITLE>Calling deferred code from an imagemap</TITLE>
<SCRIPT LANGUAGE="JavaScript">
<!--

function alertHome() {
     alert("Home")
}

function alertHelp() {
     alert("Help")
}

function alertAbout() {
     alert("About")
}

// -->
</SCRIPT>
</HEAD>
<BODY>

<IMG SRC="img4-8.gif" USEMAP="#bar_map" BORDER=0 ALT="imagemap">
```

```
<MAP NAME="bar_map">
<AREA SHAPE="RECT"     COORDS= "0,0,142,68"
              HREF="javascript:alertHome()">
<AREA SHAPE="RECT"     COORDS= "143,0,254,68"
              HREF="javascript:alertHelp()">
<AREA SHAPE="RECT"     COORDS= "255,0,398,68"
              HREF="javascript:alertAbout()">
</MAP>

</BODY>
</HTML>
```

Example 4-8 (ex4-8.htm). *Functions invoked by an image map's zones.*

There are no special restrictions for JavaScript-based URLs. They behave exactly like standard "http:"-schemed URLs. Therefore, placing the mouse pointer over such a link reveals the URL in the browser's status bar, as shown in Figure 4-6.

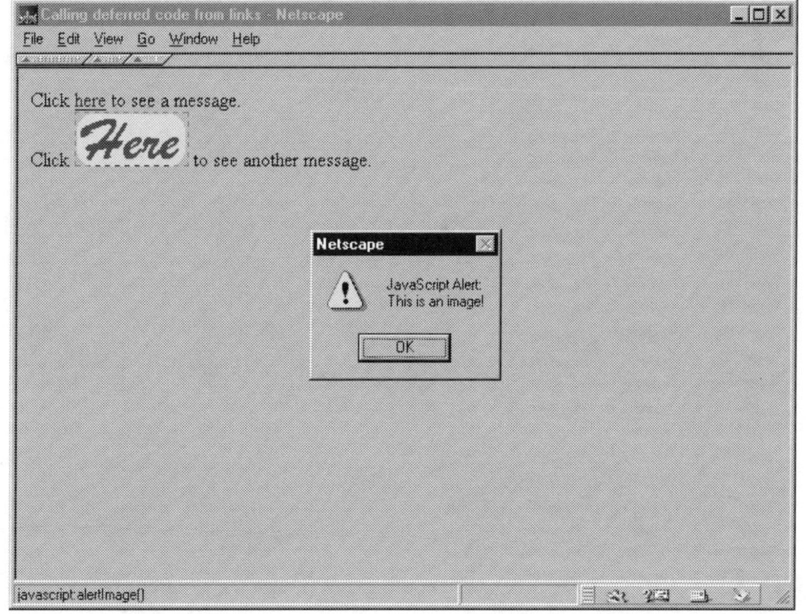

Figure 4-6. *A URL with a "javascript:" scheme displayed in the status bar.*

JavaScript Entities

Netscape Navigator 3.0 introduced a powerful tool that enables a flexible HTML tag creation. You can use any JavaScript value stored in a data structure (such as a variable or a property of an existing object) for an HTML tag attribute. See the following chapter, Basic Declarations and Expressions, for more details.

Summary

In this chapter we discussed basic page layouts and ways to embed JavaScript scripts in HTML. We also learned the basics of functions, function calls, and function definitions. These topics are discussed in detail in following chapters. Finally, we played around with event handlers, which are key elements for enabling user interaction. This introduction will help you understand general browser-related concepts and their effect on JavaScript programmers.

Chapter 5

Basic Declarations and Expressions

"Building" a Script

Writing a JavaScript script is similar in many ways to constructing a building; you need bricks as well as brick-laying instructions. Similarly, JavaScript, like most programming languages, provides variables ("bricks") and instructions ("blueprints") by which to build a script. Once you know how to use both elements, you can write useful programs for various purposes.

Functions are also an important ingredient of JavaScript. Just as all buildings are made of rooms, functions enable you to split a lengthy code into smaller sets of code. Basically, a script is a collection of functions.

Data Types in JavaScript

Every programming language can handle various types of information. For example, a number is a type of information that JavaScript recognizes. Such types of information are known as *data* types. Compared to most programming languages, JavaScript has a small number of data types, but its methods, objects, and other elements help overcome the problem. There are four different data types in JavaScript: numbers, strings, Boolean, and `null` values. As opposed to other languages, a variable data type is not declared explicitly but rather implicitly according to its initial value assignment. Also unique to JavaScript, there is no explicit distinction between integer and real-valued numbers.

All of these data types are specified in Table 5-1.

Table 5-1. Data types in JavaScript.

Type	Description	Examples
Number	Any number without quotes	`42` or `16.3` or `2e-16`
String	A series of characters enclosed in quote marks	`"Hello!"` or `"10"` or `' '` or `""`
Boolean	A logical value	`true` or `false`
Null	A keyword meaning: no value	`null`

The Value Null

The value `null` is often used to initialize variables that do not have any special meaning (see "Variable Declaration" later in the chapter). You assign it to a variable using the standard assignment statement:

```
var name = null
```

The `null` value is special in that it is automatically converted to initial values of other data types. When used as a number it becomes `0`, when used as a string it becomes `""`, and when used as a Boolean value it becomes `false`. Since the source of many JavaScript errors is uninitialized variables, one of the common debugging techniques is to initialize all uninitialized variables, including the meaningless ones, with a `null` value.

JavaScript interpreter uses the `null` value on two occasions: (1) built-in functions return `null` under certain circumstances, and (2) non-existent properties evaluate to `null`. When checking for a `null` value, you should check if it is `false` or if it is equal to `null`.

Variables

Variables are the cornerstone of most programming and scripting languages. They serve as a link between simple words in your script and the computer allocated memory. There is a limit to the amount of memory you can use, but you should not reach that limit. JavaScript applications are not heavy resource demanders, so exceeding available memory is probably an indication of a bug in the browser or a major flaw in your program (such as an unexpected infinite loop).

Because you do not deal directly with the memory allocation, you should think of variables as baskets that contain items. You can put an item in a basket, take it out, or replace it with another. A script that does not use variables is probably useless. It's like picking strawberries and taking them home in the palm of your hand, rather than using a basket—impossible! You need variables to keep data of different types.

Identifiers

Each variable is identified by a *variable name*, also known as an *identifier*. Each variable name is associated with a specific memory location, and the interpreter uses it to determine its location. There are strict rules for naming variables:

- The first character of an identifier must be either a letter (uppercase or lowercase) or an underscore (_).
- All other characters can be letters, underscores, or digits (0-9).
- An identifier cannot be one of the language's reserved words. Reserved words consist of all JavaScript keywords as well as others tokens reserved for future versions.

An identifier length is not limited, and you should take advantage of this feature to select meaningful names. JavaScript is case sensitive (uppercase letters are distinct from lowercase letters). For example, `counter`, `Counter`, and `COUNTER` are names of three different variables. Avoid using such similar identifiers in the same script.

Caution The $ character is not legal in some versions of Netscape and in some other browsers, so it is recommended you avoid using it. Netscape did not designate the $ character as a valid identifier component, so future releases of the browser might not accept it. For example, the following identifiers are accepted by Netscape Navigator 3.0x and 4.0 but not by 2.0x and MSIE 3.0x.

```
$FirstDigit
money$
tenth$cell$10
```

The following identifiers are legal:

```
gameCount
_hamburger
_______
_123456789_
look_at_me
Number16
```

but the following ones are illegal:

```
with // reserved word
^fastTimer // first character is illegal
911phoneNumber // cannot start with a digit
04-825-6408 // first character is illegal
            // "-" is an illegal character
***important*** // * is not a legal character
10_guesses // first character cannot be a digit
```

Naming Conventions

There are a number of generally accepted conventions in JavaScript:

- A variable name is normally written in lowercase letters.
- The variable name indicates its purpose and use in a program.
- In a multiword identifier, either place an underscore between words or capitalize the first letter of each embedded word.

The following are examples of multiword identifiers.

```
all_done // underscores
allDone // capitalized letters
```

Avoid similar variable names. The following script illustrates a poor choice of variable names:

```
digit // current digit
digits // number of digits in the number
```

A much better set of variables is:

```
current_digit // current digit
num_of_digits // number of digits in the number
```

Variable Declaration

Before you use a variable, you need to create it. JavaScript is a loosely typed language, so you do not have to explicitly specify the data type of a variable when you create it. As needed, data types are converted automatically during the course of the script execution.

There are two ways to create a variable. The first type of *declaration* includes the `var` keyword, followed by the name of the variable:

```
var variableName
```

When interpreting this statement, the browser creates a link between the name of the variable and its memory address, so successive references can be done by name. As opposed to most programming languages, declarations are not limited to a specific zone but can be done anywhere throughout the script.

The action of assigning an initial value to a variable is called *initialization*. You give the variable a value using the most common *assignment operator*—the equal sign:

```
var variableName = initialValue
```

You should only use the `var` keyword when you create the variable. When you want to refer to the variable, you only use its name. Assign a value to a variable (after it has been declared) in the following fashion:

```
variableName = anyValue
```

In conclusion, you use `var` only once per variable. A global variable can be created simply by assigning it a value without the `var` keyword. Local variables inside functions, on the other hand, must be declared with the `var` keyword. See Chapter 9, Functions and Variable Scope, for more details on local and global variables.

As in most programming languages, JavaScript allows you to declare numerous variables in the same statement, using a comma to separate them:

```
var variableName1 = initialValue1, variableName2 = initialValue2, …
```


JavaScript Entities

JavaScript entities can be assigned to HTML attributes. This attribute substitution enables creation of more flexible HTML constructions, without the writing overhead of full JavaScript scripts. Note that JavaScript entities are not supported by Netscape Navigator 2.0x and Microsoft Internet Explorer 3.0x.

You are probably familiar with HTML character entities with which you can display a character by its numerical code or name. You precede a name or a number with an ampersand (&) and terminate it with a semicolon (;). Here are a few examples:

```
&gt;
&lt;
&#169;
```

These HTML entities evaluate to the following characters:

> (greater than)
< (less than)
© (copyright)

JavaScript entities also start with an ampersand and end with a semicolon. Instead of a name (as in the first two examples) or a number (as in the third example), you use a JavaScript expression enclosed in curly braces ({ and }). Note that you can use JavaScript entities to assign HTML attributes only. Consider the following HTML document:

```
<HTML>
<HEAD>
<TITLE>JavaScript Entities</TITLE>
<SCRIPT LANGUAGE="JavaScript">
<!-- hide content from old browsers

var fontSize = "+4"
var fontColor = "red"

// end hiding content-->
</SCRIPT>
</HEAD>
<BODY>
<FONT COLOR="&{fontColor};" SIZE="&{fontSize};">
Flexible attributes with JavaScript entities
</FONT>
</BODY>
</HTML>
```

Example 5-1 (ex5-1.htm). *JavaScript entities enable creation of flexible constructs.*

The entity `&{fontColor};` is replaced by the current value of `fontColor` and `&{fontSize};` is replaced by the current value of `fontSize`. Since JavaScript can only use values that are stored in memory at the time of page layout, JavaScript entities should be used only after calling the script that assigns their value. Figure 5-1 shows the result of Example 5-1.

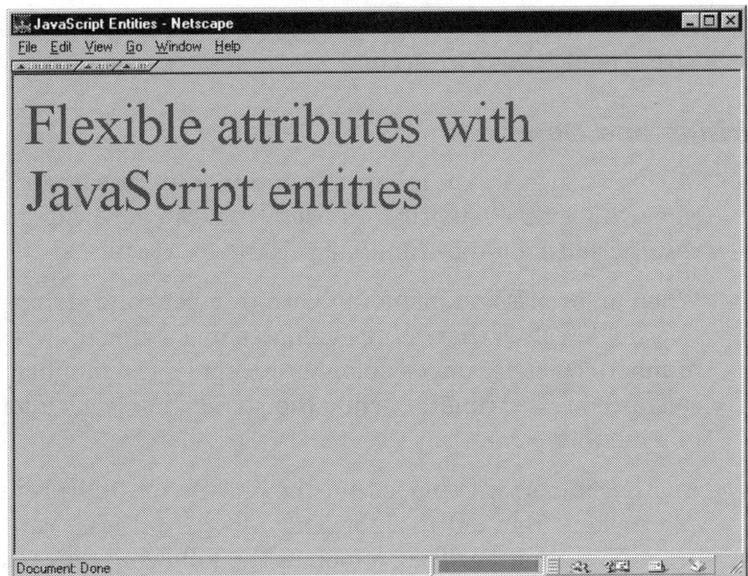

Figure 5-1. A font with attributes specified by JavaScript entities.

Once layout is complete, the display of the page can change only if you reload the page. Even if the value of the JavaScript entity variable changes, the entity itself does not change until you reload the page.

Unlike HTML character entities which can be used in any script statement, JavaScript entities can be used only in a tag statement. Another difference is that, while HTML character entities may substitute for any HTML element, JavaScript ones are limited to HTML attribute substitution only. For example, you cannot specify the entity `"&{text};"` with the variable `text = "<H1>Hi!</H1>"`—it is not a valid value for a tag attribute.

Type Conversion

As mentioned above, data types are converted automatically as needed during the course of script execution. A variable may hold a numeric value at one point of the script and a string at another one. The following statements constitute a valid JavaScript script:

```
var myVar = 12
myVar = "university"
```

The first statement assigns a numeric value to `myVar`, and the second one assigns it a string. Such conversions are not allowed in strictly typed languages such as C++ and Java and, in general, are not recommended in JavaScript either. You should normally assign an initial value to a variable according to its role and keep the same data type throughout the entire script.

Mixing Strings and Numbers

Mixing strings and numbers is sometimes necessary for certain operations. Since this "mixture" is tricky and can generate unexpected results, you should be familiar with its exact rules.

When an expression including both numbers and strings is evaluated to a single value, that value evaluates to a string. Converting it to a number is usually impossible. For example, the number 6 can be easily converted to a string (6), while the string "horse" cannot be converted to a number.

Another important rule is that the JavaScript interpreter evaluates expressions from left to right, and only parentheses can change the order of evaluation. Take a look at the following expressions, numbered by lines.

```
/* 1 */   8 + 8 // 16
/* 2 */   "8" + 8 // "88"
/* 3 */   8 + "8" // "88"
/* 4 */   "8" + "8" // "88"
/* 5 */   8 + 8 + "8" // "168"
/* 6 */   8 + "8" + 8 // "888"
```

All preceding expressions use the string concatenation operator which is also the numeric plus operator. (See Chapter 7, Utilizing JavaScript Operators, for more details.)

The first expression simply adds up two numbers using a numeric format. It uses the standard plus operator and evaluates to the sum of its operands. The second expression is quite different. Its first operand is a string rather than a number. In order to add a number to a string, the number is converted to its matching string and the strings are then concatenated. The third and fourth expressions are similar in that they also include at least one string operand. The fifth expression is a bit more tricky. The first two operands are added up because they are numbers. The expression now evaluates to `16 + "8"` which, as you already know, evaluates to `"168"`. Using parentheses can change the result. For example:

```
8 + (8 + "8") // "888"
```

In this expression the content in the parentheses is evaluated first to `"88"` and the entire expression evaluates to `"888"`. Comparing the sixth expression to the fifth one clearly demonstrates what left-to-right evaluation means. The basic structure of an expression including both numeric and string values is shown in Figure 5-2.

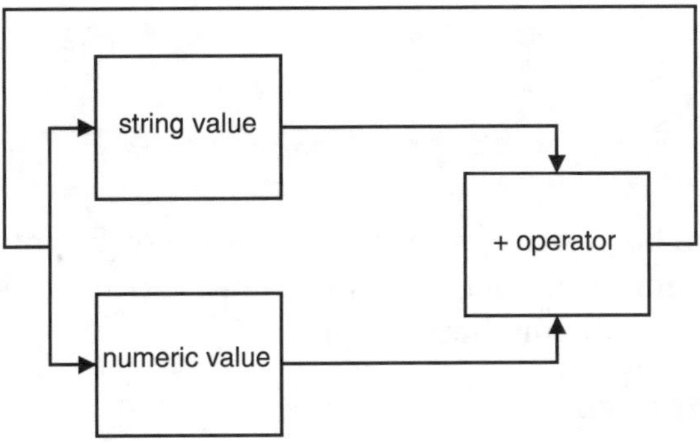

Figure 5-2. *The general syntax of a mixed expression.*

Whenever a string is found during the expression evaluation, the accumulated value thus far is converted to a string. The remaining numeric values on the right-hand side are automatically converted to strings when concatenated to this accumulated value.

If you want to convert a single number to a string, you can use one of the following three methods:

```
var newVar = "" + numericValue
var newVar = new String(numericValue)
var newVar = numericValue.toString()
```

The first method is simple. You use the concatenation operator, which instructs JavaScript to convert the number to a string and then append it to a null string. The other methods are discussed later in the book.

Literals

Literals are fixed values that you literally provide in your application source, and are not variables or any other data structure. They are notations for constant values and therefore do not change throughout the script. A literal gives you a value instead of merely representing possible values.

Unlike C++ and Java, which have five literal types, JavaScript has only four: integer, floating point, Boolean, and string. Character literals are considered strings.

Integer Literals

Integer literals, also called *whole numbers*, are numbers that have no decimal point or fractional part. Here are some integer literals:

```
49
16
0
–18
–42
```

An integer can be positive, negative, or zero. JavaScript, like most other programming languages, supports integers of three types or bases: decimal, octal, and hexadecimal.

Decimal Integers

Decimal integers, also known as base-10 integers, are the common integers we use daily. They are written with the digits: 0, 1, 2, 3, 4, 5, 6, 7, 8, 9. Except for the number 0 itself, a decimal integer cannot have a leading 0 digit. It makes no sense to write the current year as 01997, and, indeed, JavaScript will not evaluate it as 1997.

Octal Integers

Octal integers, also known as base-8 integers, use only eight digits: 0, 1, 2, 3, 4, 5, 6, 7. Octal digits are written with a leading 0 digit (that's a zero, not the letter "o"). If you want to reference the octal integer 12 (equal to 10 in the decimal system), you would have to write it as 012.

Hexadecimal Integers

Hexadecimal integers are commonly used in programming environments because each hexadecimal digit represents four binary bits. See the section "Bitwise Operators" in Chapter 7, Utilizing JavaScript Operators, for more details on internal storage and hexadecimal representations. A hexadecimal number is any sequence of these digits: 0, 1, 2, 3, 4, 5, 6, 7, 8, 9, A, B, C, D, E, F. The integers are called hexadecimal because they are based on 16 different digits. Case sensitivity rules do not apply to numbers, so you can use lowercase letters as well. The prefix for hexadecimal numbers is 0x or 0X.

Hexadecimal numbers might look familiar to HTML authors. In early versions of Netscape Navigator and MSIE, colors were specified in a *hexadecimal triplet* format. Although the latest versions of Netscape Navigator and MSIE let you specify colors by their names, some people continue to use the hexadecimal notation. The following tag sets the background color to the default gray (even for users who changed their default to white):

```
<BODY BGCOLOR="#c0c0c0">
```

You probably know that colors differ in the relative contributions of red, green, and blue. The hexadecimal triplet combines three hexadecimal numbers of two digits each (2 digits = 16 * 16 = 256 possibilities).

Converting from Decimal to Other Bases

You can use a calculator to convert a decimal integer to a different base. But what happens when the calculator is broken?! It is surprisingly simple to do the conversion with a pencil and a piece of paper. You start by dividing the decimal number by the target base (e.g., 2 for binary, 8 for octal, 16 for hexadecimal). Write down the remainder. Now do the same with the quotient, writing the new remainder to the left of that from the previous operation. Keep looping until the quotient is less than the target base. The following table shows the conversion of the decimal number 747 to a hexadecimal notation:

Table 5-2. *A base conversion example.*

Operation and integer quotient	Remainder (decimal)	Remainder (hex)
747 / 16 = 46	11	B
46 / 16 = 2	14	E
no operation	2	2

Take a look at the table's far right column. Reading it bottom up, we get $2EB_{16}$, which is exactly 747_{10}.

The same process converts decimal integers to any base.

Converting from a Specified Base to Decimal

It is equally easy to convert a number from a specified base to a decimal notation. First, let's analyze a number in decimal notation, say 276:

$$276 = (6 * 10^0) + (7 * 10^1) + (2 * 10^2) = 6 + 70 + 200$$

Each digit contributes the value *digit * base*^{digitPlaceFromRight}, where *digit* is the current digit, *digitPlaceFromRight* is the digit's position (starting at the right-hand side 0 position), and *base* is the current base. The number is equal to the sum of all contributed values. Conversion from a given base to a decimal notation uses the same technique, except that each digit is worth its value in decimal notation. Let's convert 1472_8 (octal) to a decimal base:

$$(2 * 8^0) + (7 * 8^1) + (4 * 8^2) + (1 * 8^3) = 2 + 56 + 256 + 512 = 826_{10}$$

We use these techniques to create automatic conversion functions later in the book.

Referring to Octal and Hexadecimal Integers

Octal integers have a leading `0` character. Hexadecimal integers have a leading `0x` or `0X` prefix. Decimal integers are normal integers with no prefixes. So how do we work with these prefixes?

JavaScript refers to all integers as decimal. So if you write `0x2EB`, JavaScript stores the number and refers to it as `747` in decimal notation. The same rule applies also to octal integers. They are stored, displayed, and handled according to their decimal value. The computer obviously stores them as binary numbers, but to the JavaScript programmer it seems as if they are handled in decimal form.

Floating Point Literals

Floating point numbers (sometimes called real) have a fractional part. JavaScript uses a decimal point to distinguish between floating point numbers and integers. Literally, a number such as 16.0 is a floating point number, whereas 16 is an integer one. Additionally, a floating point number may include an exponent specification of the form *e±exp*. Since there is no explicit declaration of data types in JavaScript, the floating point format is implicitly determined by the literals that are assigned to the variables. Here are some floating point numbers, with some explanations:

```
-13.3
0.056
4.2e19 // equal to 4.2 * 10^19
-3.1E12 // equal to -3.1 * 10^12
.1e12 // equal to 0.1 * 10^12
2E-12 // equal to 2 * 10^-12
```

Notice that the exponent specification can be in uppercase or lowercase characters.

Floating point math is much more difficult than integer math and is the source of many bugs. *Overflow* describes the situation in which the exponent of a floating point number exceeds the upper limit. *Underflow* occurs when the exponent is below the lower one. You should avoid calculations that are likely to result in an overflow or an underflow.

A more common problem with floating point numbers is the *roundoff error*. Everyone knows that 5 + 5 is 10, but is 1/3 + 1/3 equal to 2/3? The answer is: not always. Take a look at the following listings to find out why:

1/3 as floating point is 3.333E–1 (rounded-off).

2/3 as floating point is 6.667E–1 (rounded-off).

```
       3.333E-1
+      3.333E-1
---------------
=      6.666E-1
```

As you can see, the result is different from the normal value of 2/3 because 6.666E–1 ≠ 6.667E–1.

Every computer has a similar problem with its floating point. The fraction 0.2, for example, has no exact binary representation. Avoid computing money with floating point numbers, because financial institutions, such as the IRS, tend to be fussy about money and will probably not tolerate an inaccurate payment!

Accuracy is a major problem with floating point numbers. Certain operations, such as subtracting two close numbers, generate inexact results. Some advanced techniques are known to work around such problems, but they are usually targeted for a specific machine, operating system, or browser. Since your scripts need to be compatible with several different browsers, operating systems, and machines, you should avoid getting into trouble with floating point numbers altogether. If your computation involves floating numbers, always round off the result, so it is not influenced by the floating point storage problem. You will also learn to use comparison techniques that take inexact results into consideration. These topics are discussed later.

Boolean Literals

Boolean values, also called *logical values*, are basically `true` or `false`. They are usually used in conditional expressions and statements (presented in Chapter 8, Control Structures). If you are familiar with C++, you probably recognize these terms as 1 and 0, 1 representing `true` and 0 representing `false`. JavaScript officially uses the `true` and `false` values to express Boolean values, but 1 and 0 are acceptable in most situations. The `true` value, or 1, can usually be replaced by any nonzero integer. Avoid using these numeric values as Boolean, because Netscape has not officially recognized this kind of usage and may opt to invalidate it in future versions of the browser. Usage of integer values to represent Boolean ones, as in other programming languages, can cause data type confusion and should not be used at all by novice programmers.

String Literals

String literals are delimited by either single or double quotes. You must terminate the string with the same type of quote you used to open it, so `"Hi'` is not a legal string in JavaScript. Unlike strings in most programming languages and shells, JavaScript does not distinguish between single and double quotes. They serve the exact same purposes. Strings in JavaScript are not subject to variable interpolation, i.e., you cannot embed variables directly in the string and expect them to be replaced by the value they hold. Perl, for example, features variable interpolation (or variable substitution) because variables can be identified by the preceding $ character.

The alternative delimiters q/*string*/ and qq/*string*/ are not supported in JavaScript. You must always use the traditional quotes to delimit strings.

Nested strings are widely used in JavaScript. A nested string consists of a string inside another one. Alternating quotes enables proper interpretation of nested string constructions. The following statement demonstrates how to alternate quote types:

```
document.write("<FONT COLOR='red' SIZE=4>")
```

The `document.write()` statement requires quotes, and so does the `COLOR` attribute of the `<FONT>` tag. You may use single quotes for the string `red` and double quotes for the longer enclosing string. You may also use escaped quotes, as explained below.

Be careful to place the trailing quote at the end of the string. If you forget it, the relevant error will be reported only after JavaScript runs into the end of the file or finds a matching quote character in another line. Fortunately, such errors will be detected immediately as syntax errors on the following line. Sometimes, though, the error message does not give any clue about the runaway string, so paying extra attention when dealing with strings is a profitable strategy.

Strings often include *escape sequences*, also called *escape characters*, *special characters*, or *control characters*. Such sequences have special purposes. For example, "\t" is the tab character. They are usually used to express nonprintable characters or other problematic ones. The following table outlines the escape sequences:

Table 5-3. *Escape sequences in JavaScript.*

Escape sequence	Character	Meaning
\ddd*	0ddd	octal character
\xdd*	0xdd	hexadecimal character
\\	\	backslash
\'	'	single quote
\"	"	double quote
\b	BS	backspace
\f	FF	form feed
\n	NL or LF	new line
\r	CR	carriage return
\t	HT	horizontal tab
\	<new line>	continuation

* The "*d*" character represents a digit.

Be sure to use these inline characters only where needed. You should use the standard HTML tags for line breaks (<BR>) and paragraph breaks (<P>). The carriage return escape sequence creates a new line only in dialog boxes and text area objects. Most of the escape sequences act the same way. Do not expect them to format the look of the page, because layout relies solely on HTML.

Here are some strings that take advantage of escape sequences:

```
"\x2499.99" // $99.99 (the hex value of the $ char is 24)
'c:\\games\\sc2000\\' // c:\games\sc2000\
'Let\'s learn JavaScript...' // Let's learn JavaScript...
"line1\rline2"
```

To see the effect of a carriage return character, try displaying the last string in an alert box.

Making Statements

A *statement* is a line of JavaScript code that includes a keyword. This is the official definition of a statement by Netscape's JavaScript documentation. Most people tend to associate this term with any line of code, with or without a keyword. In this book every line of JavaScript code is a statement. For example, we call the following line a statement, although it does not contain any keywords:

```
yourAge = 16
```

Keywords are words that have special meanings in the language. You cannot use keywords to name elements you created in a script (such as variables, functions, etc.). The list of keywords is the basic vocabulary of the language. The word `if`, for example, is a keyword. You do not have to memorize the list, because you will gradually remember it as you use the words in your scripts. Some keywords do not have any role in the current version of the language, but they will probably be added to a future version. Were they not defined as keywords, people would use them as identifiers, making their scripts incompatible with future versions.

Multiple Statements

The JavaScript interpreter accepts multiple statements on the same line. If you choose to use this method, you must separate the statements with semicolons (;). The last statement of the line does not have to be followed by a semicolon. Such a line looks like this:

```
statement1; statement2; statement3; ...
```

The browser interprets these statements as if they were listed on separate lines:

```
statement1
statement2
statement3
.
.
.
```

Normally, you should not place multiple statements on the same physical line. Multiple statements on one line are difficult to find and make the debugging process difficult.

If it is one of your programming habits, you may terminate all statements with semicolons,

```
statement1;
statement2;
statement3;
.
.
.
```

Nested Statements

In the previous chapter we talked about command blocks. A command block is a unit of statements, enclosed by curly braces. It is very important to understand that a block should be used as a single statement. The statements inside the block are called *nested statements*:

```
{
    nested statement1
    nested statement2
    nested statement3
    .
    .
    .
}
```

command block (one statement)

A loop that includes many statements is actually one statement with many nested statements. This rule applies to functions, `if`-`else` statements, and other language elements.

Simple Assignment Statements

You've already learned how to assign a value to a variable or to initialize it, using the equal assignment operator. As the following piece of code demonstrates, you can also perform calculations when you assign a value:

```
/* 1 */ var answer
/* 2 */ answer = 4 * 2 + 9
/* 3 */ document.write(answer)
```

Line 1 includes the declaration of the variable `answer`. The second line shows how the variable `answer` is assigned the result of a simple mathematical expression. The operators used in this statement are discussed in Chapter 7, Utilizing JavaScript Operators. At this point, the variable holds a value of 17. Referring to the variable `answer` is the same as referring to the number 17. For this reason, the statement on line 3 prints the number 17.

Caution A very common mistake is to use the equal sign for equality check. In Pascal, for example, "=" is an equality test operator, because the basic assignment operator of the language is ":=". However, in JavaScript, like in C++ and Java, "=" (the equal sign operator) is an assignment operator, while "==" (two equal signs) is an equality test operator. See Chapter 7, Utilizing JavaScript Operators, for details on both operators.

Evaluating Expressions

Now that you know how to create a variable, you need to know how to use it. As mentioned earlier, variables hold values of different types. What does "holding a value" mean?

This term refers to expression *evaluation*. A variable always evaluates to its value. When you perform an operation on a variable, you are actually performing the operation on the current value associated with the variable. Let's assume you created a variable named firstNumber using the following statement:

```
var firstNumber = 120 // declaration and initialization
```

At this point, if you refer to the variable firstNumber, its value, 120, is returned. That is, firstNumber is evaluated to 120. The following statement outlines an evaluation of firstNumber:

```
secondNumber = firstNumber * 6
```

The secondNumber variable now holds the value 720, because firstNumber evaluates to 120. Bear in mind that no link between the memory locations of both variables is established. Therefore, secondNumber now holds a value of 720, which does not change even if the value of firstNumber changes. A variable can evaluate to a value of any type (see Table 5-1).

Testing Evaluation

A hidden feature of Netscape Navigator (but not of MSIE 3.0x) enables you to experiment with evaluation in the browser's window. You can reach this window by simply entering `javascript:` in the `Location` box. Another way to do this is by choosing `Open Location` from the File menu. Then type `javascript:` to open the evaluation window.

The evaluation window contains two frames. The field at the bottom frame is used to accept your input and the upper frame displays the Navigator's computation results. To experiment with this tool, enter the following statements at the `javascript typein` field at the bottom:

```
var firstNumber = 120
var secondNumber = firstNumber – 60
firstNumber
secondNumber
var finalAverage = (firstNumber + secondNumber) / 2
finalAverage
secondNumber = firstNumber
finalAverage
finalAverage > secondNumber
```

Before you enter these expressions, try to figure out what they evaluate to. Then type them in the field at the bottom frame, with a carriage return (Enter) after each statement.

After you enter all of the preceding statements, the browser's window should look like the following:

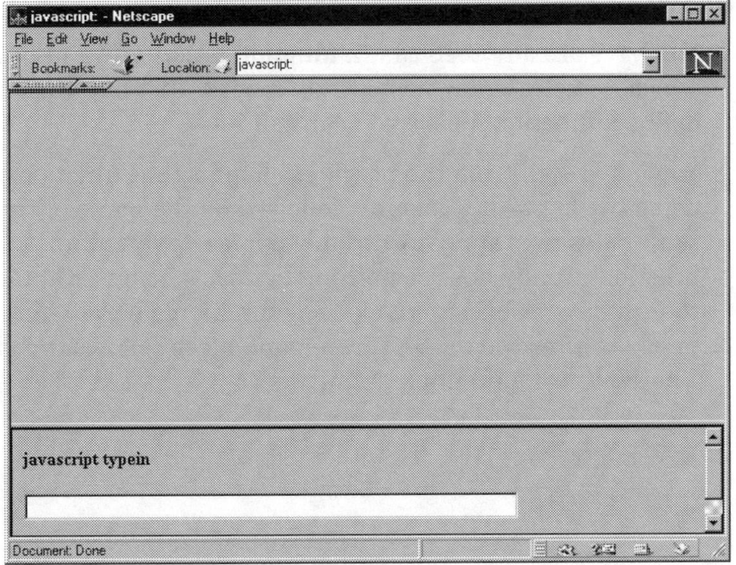

Figure 5-3. *The "`javascript:`" expression evaluation tool.*

Tip You can also use the `mocha:` URL instead of `javascript:`, as shown in Figure 5-4.

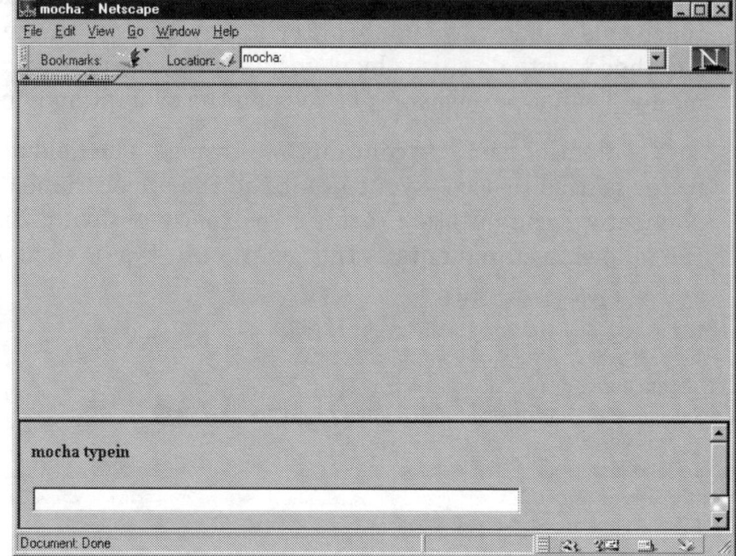

Figure 5-4. *The "mocha:" expression evaluation tool (identical to "javascript:").*

Functions

Function Definition

You have already seen that a function is actually a multiline statement which includes many nested statements. Just like variables, you must define a function before you can call it.

You may recall from the previous chapter that functions are defined using the keyword `function`, followed by the name of the function. The same rules that apply to variable names apply to functions. Since a function usually does something besides storing a value, it is common to include a verb in its name. The function's parameters are written in brackets after the name. A command block follows the parameters. The syntax of a function definition is:

```
function functionName([parameters]) {
    [statements]
}
```

Parameters are local variables that are assigned values when the function is called. At this point, you should always give a name to every parameter.

In a formal syntax specification, the square brackets "[" and "]" usually denote optional elements. Since a function does not have to have parameters or statements, they are both enclosed in such brackets. The curly braces enclosing the function body can be placed anywhere, following the parameters' section. The following functions are valid:

```
function functionName([parameters]) {[statement1]; [statement2]; …}
```

```
function functionName([parameters])
{
     [statement1]
     [statement2]
     .
     .
     .
}
```

The following example demonstrates a function declaration:

```
<HTML>
<HEAD>
<SCRIPT LANGUAGE="JavaScript">
<!-- hide script contents from old browsers

function square(number) {
     document.write("The call passed ",
                    number, // the function's parameter
                    " to the function.<BR>",
                    number, // the function's parameter
                    " square is ",
                    number * number,
                    ".<BR>")
}

// *** add function call

// end hiding contents from old browsers  -->
</SCRIPT>
</HEAD>
<BODY>
</BODY>
</HTML>
```

Example 5-2 (ex5-2.htm). *A function definition (deferred code).*

Example 5-2 does not print anything to the browser's window, nor does it generate any other form of output. The reason is that the function is only defined in the script but is never called. When the browser locates a function, it loads its statements into the memory, ready to be executed later.

Calling Functions

In order to execute the set of statements located in the function block, you must call the function. The syntax of a function call is:

```
functionName([arguments])
```

By adding the statement `square(5)` to Example 5-2, at the specified place, we call the function. The statements in the function are executed, and the following message is output:

```
The call passed 5 to the function.
5 square is 25.
```

You can also call a function from within another function, as the following example demonstrates:

```
<HTML>
<HEAD>
<TITLE>Calling a function from within another function</TITLE>
<SCRIPT LANGUAGE="JavaScript">
<!-- hide script contents from old browsers

function makeBar() {
     var output = "<HR ALIGN='left' WIDTH=400>"
     document.write(output)
}

function makeHeader(text, color, size) {
     var output = "<FONT COLOR='" + color + "' SIZE=" +
                  size + ">" + text + "</FONT>"
     document.write(output)
     makeBar()
}

makeHeader("JavaScript Examples", "red", "+4")

// end hiding contents from old browsers  -->
</SCRIPT>
</HEAD>
<BODY>
</BODY>
</HTML>
```

Example 5-3 (ex5-3.htm). *A function call in a function block.*

Example 5-3 summarizes many of the terms discussed in this chapter. It includes two function definitions. In both functions, the output is assigned to a variable (`output`) and then printed to the client window using the `document.write()` method. Assigning strings to variables before printing them is extremely useful when the string is long (you want to print a lot of data). You can see the result of Example 5-3 in Figure 5-5.

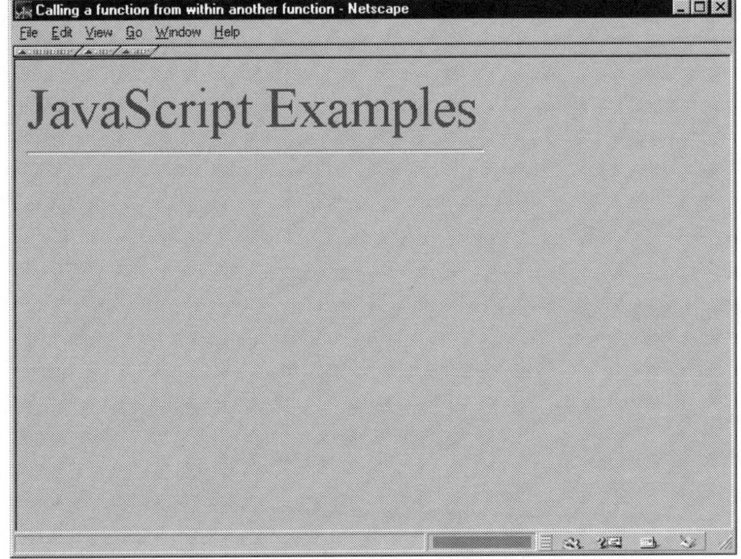

Figure 5-5. *HTML content generated by two JavaScript functions.*

Summary

Variables are the cornerstone of most programming languages. In order to write a script you need to use variables. You've learned how to create variables in JavaScript and how to name them. Functions are another important element in JavaScript. You can use functions to split code into smaller segments. From now on, we will use functions in all of our scripts. Some functions will be general functions that you can add to your personal "library of functions." You can call them from there whenever you need them in your scripts. We will use functions even in short and simple scripts, just to provide you with more experience. This chapter also taught you how to use the hidden `javascript:` and `mocha:` evaluation tools. We also talked about various expression evaluation techniques. You probably still feel that our example scripts are useless, but be patient and you will be amazed to find out what JavaScript can do, and how complex these scripts can get.

Chapter 6

Object-Based Programming

Objects

In a nutshell, an *object* is a programming abstraction that groups data with the code that operates on it. All programs contain data of different types. Variables, as well as functions, were introduced separately in the previous chapter. We defined functions, and we defined variables, but we did not join them in any way. An object encapsulates related data and functions into a single cohesive unit.

Objects are relatively new to the computer programming industry. Traditionally, code and data have been kept apart. For example, in the C language, units of code are called functions, while units of data are known as structures. Functions and structures are not formally connected in C. A C function can operate on numerous data structures, and more than one function can operate on the same structure. In *object-oriented* (OO) and *object-based* programming, code and data are merged into an object, which is a single indivisible "creature."

Figure 6-1 on the following page shows several data structures and related operations—the exact definition of an object. All data is located on the left-hand side of the illustration. Operations are located on the right-hand side. The data is stored as follows:

Table 6-1. *Data structures in Figure 6-1.*

Data Field	Content of Field
`name`	Advanced JavaScript Programming
`reference`	F12345
`day`	Monday
`time`	5 pm - 8 pm
`students`	Name, age, address, telephone, other information

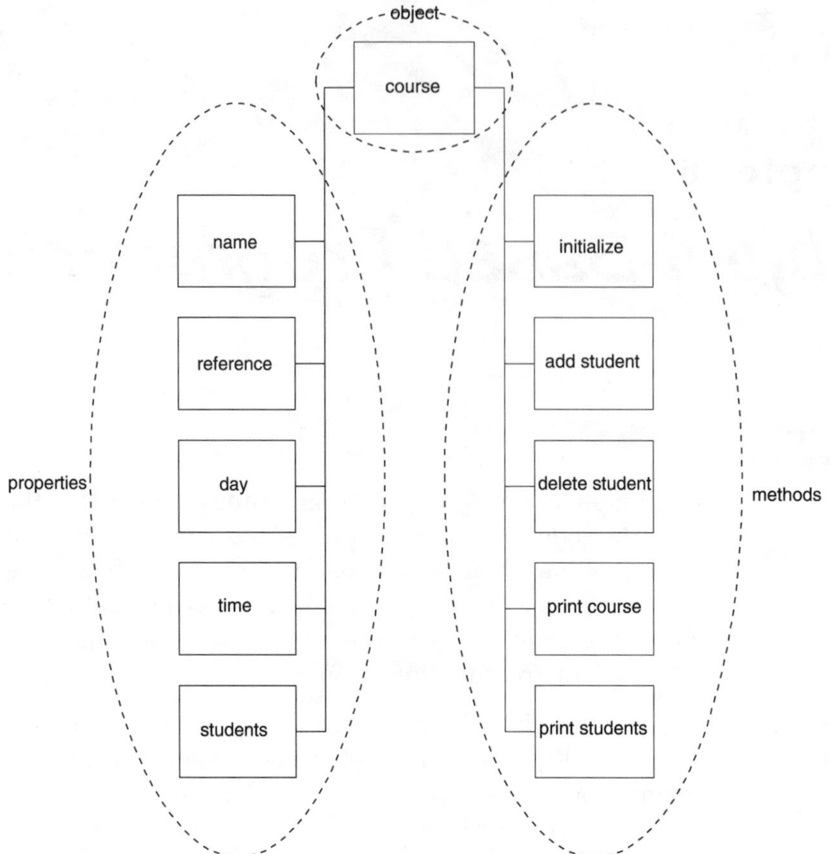

Figure 6-1. *The structure of an object—properties and methods.*

This data is not static. That is, it can change under certain circumstances. For example, if one of the students decides to quit, you must be able to change the data accordingly. The construction should be able to add new students to the course. These actions are illustrated in Figure 6-1, and listed in the following table:

Table 6-2. *Operations in Figure 6-1.*

Operation Name	Processed Data
`initialization`	Basic information (name, reference, day, etc.)
`addStudent`	New student's basic information
`deleteStudent`	Current student's information
`printCourse`	Name and other information regarding the course
`printStudents`	Students' names and other details

As you can see, the operations process the data stored in the object's data structures. The object illustrated in Figure 6-1 is named `course`.

Properties

Any physical object has its own unique characteristics. A car, for example, has a size, a weight, a model, a color, a price, and many other attributes. The full set of attributes distinguish a car from all other objects. These features are called *properties* or *fields* in the OO (object-oriented) vernacular. An object's property stores data related to the object. In Figure 6-1, the properties are the "boxes" on the left-hand side of the illustration.

Properties are usually named according to their meaning. For instance, a property that holds the color of the car would be named `color`. First supported by Netscape Navigator 3.0, it is possible to extend an object by adding new properties to it. Although it is possible to add new properties to an existing object, it is not always possible to modify the value of a static built-in object. For example, the `PI` property of the `Math` object cannot be modified, for obvious reasons.

JavaScript supports two different types of objects:

- *Predefined built-in objects,* such as the `Math` object
- *User-defined objects*, such as the `course` object illustrated in Figure 6-1.

An object can also be a property of another object, thus creating an object hierarchy. We will describe the hierarchical structure later, when we discuss Navigator objects.

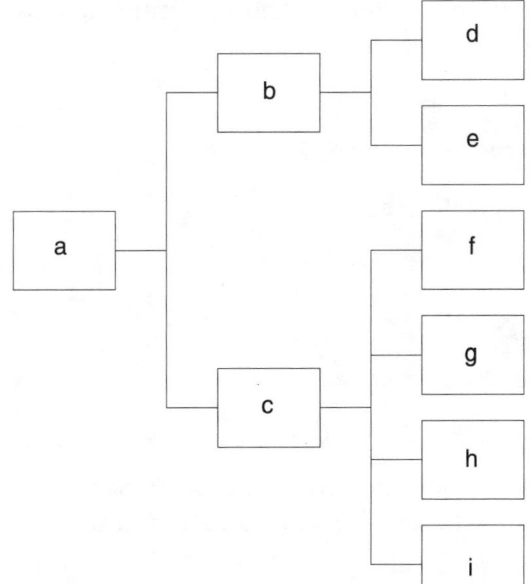

Figure 6-2. *A sample object hierarchy.*

This figure illustrates an object hierarchy, similar to a family tree. a is only an object, while d, e, f, g, h, and i are only properties. b and c are both objects and properties, and therefore, they are located between the other levels of the hierarchy.

Syntax

An object's properties hold its data. You can refer to properties using the following syntax:

```
objectReference.propertyName
```

objectReference is the name of the object that the property belongs to, or any other valid reference to the object. For example, you can assign an object to a variable and then refer to its properties using this variable, followed by the property specification. *propertyName* is the name of the property (data field).

A dot separates each object from its property. A hierarchical object structure, with objects and properties at different levels, uses the same syntax:

```
object1.object2Property1.object3Property2.property3
```

Notice that all the elements in the middle are both objects and properties. Referring again to Figure 6-2, let's assume that the elements of the structure have the following values:

d ⇒ 16
e ⇒ 42
f ⇒ true
g ⇒ "king"
h ⇒ 13
i ⇒ 10

The following statements demonstrate referencing to elements of a hierarchical object structure:

```
var tempVar = ""
tempVar = a.b.d
document.write(tempVar) // prints 16
tempVar = a.b.e
document.write(tempVar) // prints 42
tempVar = a.c.f
document.write(tempVar) // prints true
tempVar = a.c.g
document.write(tempVar) // prints king
tempVar = a.c.h
document.write(tempVar) // prints 13
tempVar = a.c.i
document.write(tempVar) // prints 10
```

Another important concept is that a property belongs to an object, and only to one object. That is, the same location in the memory cannot be associated with two different objects. A property must always be associated with an object. Therefore, the following statements are legal:

```
var d = a.b.d
document.write(d) // prints 16
var e = a.b.e
document.write(e) // prints 42
var f = a.c.f
document.write(f) // prints true
var g = a.c.g
document.write(g) // prints king
var h = a.c.h
document.write(h) // prints 13
var i = a.c.i
document.write(i) // prints 10
```

As you can see, a variable may be named exactly like a property of an object. This is possible because properties are not at the same scope as variables. However, a variable cannot have the same name as an object at the same level. For example, the statement `var a = a.b.d` is not valid (actually it is valid, but the value of `a` is lost). The main object is at the same scope of the variable, because they are not properties of any other object. As a matter of fact, an object is a variable, and two variables that have the exact same name are associated with the same location in memory. The statement `var a = a.b.d` converts `a` to a simple variable containing the value `16`, and not an object. It is generally a good practice to avoid naming variables by an object's property or method, at least until you feel comfortable with objects and properties.

The output of the statement `document.write(a)`, might be "`[object create]`," because that is the object's string equivalent.

Methods

During execution of a JavaScript script, an object may invoke one or more *methods* to accomplish a task. As you know, objects consist of both data (properties) and functions that handle the data. These functions are called methods. Methods enable an object to perform different actions, mostly on its own properties. In Figure 6-1, all methods of the object `course` were located on the right-hand side of the illustration.

Methods are the analogous concept for functions in object-oriented languages. However, they differ from functions in that they have exclusive access to the state of the object, because the object's fields (properties) are in the same scope as its methods.

Most advantages of OOP (object-oriented programming) are associated with methods. JavaScript does not completely support external libraries (other than the `SRC` attribute of the `<SCRIPT>` tag), so the following features apply mostly to built-in objects:

- Because an object encapsulates related data and functions (methods) into a single cohesive unit, it is easy to perform maintenance activities.
- Every language paradigm influences its application design. Therefore, scripts developed in JavaScript often make use of objects. Although you can design your scripts in a traditional procedural way, you will find it a great deal easier to use objects and methods. You will notice the difference between the traditional style and the OO style as soon as you start writing complex scripts.

JavaScript's implementation of objects is not as powerful as that of Java, so some OO programming advantages that apply to Java do not apply to JavaScript.

Syntax

A method can exist at different levels of an object's hierarchy. You can invoke a method using the same syntax you use to reference a property, i.e., the "*dot*" syntax. Methods are actually functions associated with objects. Therefore, they resemble functions in many aspects. A method is called in the following fashion:

```
objectReference.methodName([arguments])
```

`objectReference` is the name of the object, or any other reference. *`methodName`* is the name of the method, and *`arguments`* are the arguments that the method accepts.

Because a method is a function, the name of the method is always followed by a pair of parentheses. This rule applies also to methods that do not accept arguments.

You probably find this syntax familiar. We have been using `document.write([`*`expression`*`])` to print HTML expressions to the page. `write()` is a method belonging to the built-in `document` object.

Using the Array Notation

You can refer to properties and methods using the "dot" syntax or an array notation. In this notation, square brackets replace the dots. For example, the following expression refers to a.b.d:

```
a["b"]["d"]
```

You can use the array notation for both properties and methods. The general syntax is:

```
objectReference["propertyName"]
objectReference["methodName"]([arguments])
```

It is important to understand this alternative syntax, because you cannot always use the traditional dot syntax. For example, the first character of a property name cannot be a digit when using the dot syntax. When you create an array using the built-in Array object, you can only refer to the elements of the array via the array notation (e.g., myArray[0], myArray[99]). You must always use double quotes when you refer to a property of an object that is not an array. Here are some examples for using the array notation to reference methods and properties:

```
document["write"]("hello!")
window["alert"]("howdy!") // note: alert() == window.alert()
Math["PI"]
```

Sometimes you can only use the array notation. Suppose the variable str holds the string "write". You can use the following syntax instead of document.write():

```
document[str]()
```

However, you cannot use document.str() because that is equivalent to document["str"](). Another situation in which you should use the array notation is when you want to name a property not according to the identifier rules. For example, myObject["*"] is possible only with the array notation. When you use the array notation, the value in the square brackets should be a string, because the content is evaluated.

Object Based Versus Object Oriented

Note This explanation is intended mostly for programmers who are familiar with object-oriented environments. Therefore, the basic terms of object-oriented programming will not be explained in this book—they are beyond the scope of this book. Only the most basic differences between JavaScript and full object-oriented languages are introduced here. You will discover many other minor differences as you learn the language. If you are new to object structures, you should skip this explanation altogether.

JavaScript is based on a simple object-oriented paradigm. This paradigm is often called object based, as opposed to object oriented. Classes do not exist in JavaScript (all objects belong to one "class"), nor do packages (because a package groups classes together). The object hierarchy in JavaScript is a containment hierarchy, not an inheritance hierarchy as in Java and C++. That is, an object does not inherit from other objects, but it can be contained by another object if it is a property of that object. Most object-oriented languages require static resolution of objects at compile time. However, an object-oriented language may require dynamic method bindings because polymorphism allows multiple definitions of methods sharing a common name. Calling such polymorphic methods often cannot be resolved until run time. JavaScript is completely based on dynamic binding. That is, object references are checked at run time. There are many other differences between the object paradigm in JavaScript and the one in full object-oriented languages (such as Java and C++).

Summary

This chapter discussed the basics of object-based programming, based on JavaScript's object model. Its purpose is to introduce you to general object-oriented and object-based terminology and to a bit of JavaScript syntax. Every language paradigm heavily influences the design of applications in that language. Therefore, scripts written in JavaScript are typically object-based systems. Procedural scripting is possible in JavaScript, but object-based scripting has many advantages. Because JavaScript has a large set of built-in objects, including very useful methods and properties, a basic understanding of the object structure is necessary. If you are a beginner, and find objects difficult to understand, don't be too concerned. We promise that you will understand these concepts as we move on, mostly by studying examples.

Chapter 7

Utilizing JavaScript Operators

Operator Categories

JavaScript has many operators, most of them borrowed from C and Perl. The wide variety of operators makes it necessary to divide them into the following categories:

- Mathematical operators
- String operators
- Bitwise operators
- Assignment operators
- Relational operators
- Short-circuit logical operators
- More logical operators
- Data type operator
- Void operator

In this chapter we discuss JavaScript's bulk of operators, grouped by the above categories. Operators in each category are divided into two groups:

- *Unary operators*—operators that operate on a single operand
- *Binary operators*—operators that operate on two operands

Mathematical Operators

Mathematical operators, also called *arithmetic operators*, perform basic mathematical operations. Table 7-1 lists the mathematical operators in JavaScript:

Table 7-1. Mathematical Operators

Syntax	Name	Type
+	Addition (plus)	Binary
–	Subtraction (minus)	Binary
*	Multiplication (multiply)	Binary
/	Division (divide)	Binary
%	Modulus (modulo)	Binary
++	Increment	Unary
--	Decrement	Unary
–	Negation	Unary

Arithmetic operators take numeric literals, variables, or properties of existing objects as their operands. They always return a single numeric value, based on their operands' values.

Addition

```
operand1 + operand2
```

The addition operator is a simple mathematical operator. It adds two numbers of any type and evaluates to their sum.

```
-5 + 3 // evaluates to -2
2.4 + 3.6 // evaluates to 6
1.1 + 7.8 // evaluates to 8.9
```

The plus operator is a bit tricky when operands are floating point numbers. This topic is covered later in the book.

Subtraction

```
operand1 - operand2
```

Another simple mathematical operator is the minus one. It subtracts one number from the other.

```
8 - 2 // evaluates to 6
16.3 - 56 // evaluates to -39.7
13.3 - 13.3 // evaluates to 0
```

Multiplication

```
operand1 * operand2
```

The * (multiplication) operator takes two numbers as its operands, and performs the usual arithmetic conversion.

```
4 * 3 // evaluates to 12
```

```
1.2 * 30 // evaluates to 36
20.4 * 6.7 // evaluates to 136.38
```

Division

```
operand1 / operand2
```

The division operator also performs the usual arithmetic conversion. However, since JavaScript is loosely typed, this operator does not act exactly as in C, Perl, and other strictly typed programming languages. In those languages, integer division is different from floating point division in that the result of an integer division is always an integer number. JavaScript, on the other hand, does not explicitly distinguish between integers and real-valued numbers, and therefore, the result of a division operation is not guaranteed to be an integer number. In fact, most of the floating point numbers are the result of a division operator. While debugging a script, it may be helpful to remember that the division operation in JavaScript generates the same value as your pocket calculator. You should also remember that the remainder of a division operation is never discarded.

When the operands are floating point numbers and cannot be represented in binary notation, division expressions often evaluate to inaccurate results. The following code section demonstrates the behavior of JavaScript's division operator:

```
3 / 4 // evaluates to 0.75
3.6 / 0.1 // evaluates to 36
-20 / 4 // evaluates to -5
11.1 / 2.22 // evaluates to 4.999999999999999
```

Modulus

```
operand1 % operand2
```

The modulus operator returns the remainder of a division operation. The division is performed, but only the remainder is kept. The sign of the result is the sign of the quotient. The modulus operator in JavaScript is also different from the one in other programming languages. It operates not only on integers but also on floating point numbers. You should be aware that the modulus operator occasionally returns inaccurate results. The modulus' inaccuracies stem from the division operation which sometimes returns inaccurate results:

```
12 % 5 // evaluates to 2
12.3 % 4 // evaluates to 0.3000000000000007 (inaccuracy)
0 % 99 // evaluates to 0
```

```
12.75 % 4.25 // evaluates to 0
11.1 % 2.22 // evaluates to 2.219999999999999
```

The Nonexistent Integral Division Operator

JavaScript does not feature an integral division (also called `div`) operator. From looking at the list of reserved words, it seems that Netscape does not plan to add it to JavaScript's vernacular in the near future. However, it is easy to create such an operator using simple arithmetic operators. The following function demonstrates this capability:

```
function div(op1, op2) {
     return (op1 / op2 - op1 % op2 / op2)
{
```

The keyword `return` instructs the function to return a value, so the function call itself evaluates to a value, just like an expression consisting of an operator.

Now we can define the newly created `div` syntax:

```
div(operand1, operand2)
```

Here are a few examples:

```
var a = div(23, 3) // a is assigned 7
var b = div(12, 4) // b is assigned 3
```

The function evaluates to the quotient of its arguments, with the remainder discarded. The sign of the result is the sign of the quotient.

Caution Various operations on floating point numbers return inaccurate results. This may seem strange at the moment, but such inaccuracies are a common phenomenon in computers. You should avoid floating point values (if possible), because such inaccuracies often result in unexpected behavior. Above all, debugging scripts that fail to work due to inaccurate calculations is nearly impossible.

Increment

```
operand1++
```

```
++operand1
```

The increment operator is a unary operator, which can be used in either suffix or prefix notations. It increments the operand's value by 1. If used after the operand (suffix), the operator returns the value of the operand before incrementing it. If used before the operand (prefix), the operator returns the value of the operand after incrementing it. Understanding these differences is important when you use such operations as side effects of other statements, such as assignment ones. The following set of statements outlines this concept:

```
var a = 1
var b = ++a // prefix
document.write("a is ", a, ", b is ", b) // a is 2, b is 2
```

The first statement assigns the value 1 to a. The second statement performs two different actions:

- Increments a to 2
- Assigns a's new value to b

The increment operator in suffix notation performs the actions in reverse order, and therefore the results differ. Suffix notation is demonstrated in the following code:

```
var a = 1
var b = a++ // suffix
document.write("a is ", a, ", b is ", b) // a is 2, b is 1
```

b is assigned the value of a, and then a is incremented.

Dual actions in one statement are discussed at the end of this chapter. Generally, you should avoid using such side effects. The previous code would be simpler had it looked like:

```
var a = 1
var b = a
a++
document.write("a is ", a, ", b is ", b) // a is 2, b is 1
```

The increment operator takes only data structures as its operand. That is, you can only use it on a variable or a property of an existing object, but not on a literal.

It is natural to come to a conclusion that incrementing is the same as adding 1 to the value:

```
var a = 1
var b = 1
a++
b = b + 1 // equivalent to b += 1 (see assignment operators)
```

This is true as far as correctness of the script is concerned. It is incorrect if performance is important. The advantage of incrementing is that it is much faster than standard assignment (fourth line in above code section). You should always increment when you want to add 1 to a variable (or to a property of an object). It is not so important when the addition operation is done a few times. You will definitely feel the difference when you have 100,000 addition operations. Another benefit of the incrementing operator is that it is much easier to understand a statement like `countTemp++` than `countTemp = countTemp + 1`.

It is important to remember that Boolean expressions are equivalent to 1 and 0 in certain situations. The following statements show the effect of incrementing Boolean variables:

```
var a = true
var b = false
a++
b++
document.write("a is ", a, ", b is ", b) // a is 2, b is 1
```

Caution Microsoft Internet Explorer 3.0x generates an error when you use prefix notation as an independent statement. The following script segment does not work under MSIE, so use suffix notation to increment a value:

```
var num = 5
++num // error under MSIE
```

Note that this rule does not apply to increment operators in other positions, such as `for` loops. Furthermore, you are free to use both notations as side effects, because the bug only applies to stand-alone statements that increment a value.

Decrement

```
operand1--
```

```
--operand1
```

The decrement operator is similar to the increment operator. It decreases the value of the operand by one, whereas the increment operator increases it by one.

Negation

```
-operand1
```

The negation operator precedes a numeric value (a variable, a property of an existing object, or a numeric literal). By placing this operator before its operand (do not insert any space characters), JavaScript evaluates a positive number as its corresponding negative number, and vice versa. As before, you might think that this operator can be replaced by a statement in which the operand is multiplied by –1. Once again, this is a mistake. Due to the internal structure of the JavaScript interpreter, and the negation operator specifically, negating a numeric value using the negation operator is faster than multiplying it by –1. If you are a traditional Pascal programmer, it might take you a while to get used to the negation and incremental operators, but it is worth the effort!

```
var a = 3
var b = 9
-a + b // evaluates to 6
-b // evaluates to -9
```

String Operators

```
operand1 + operand2
```

The string operator's syntax is identical to that of the addition operator. They differ in the type of operands they operate on. This operator accepts any values as operands, provided that at least one of them is a string. A string is actually an object, so it can be said that the string operator operates on string objects. It joins them together, as in

```
"Ladies " + "and " + "gentlemen"
```

The string operator can operate on more than two operands, but it is still a binary operator, because of the way it works. It *concatenates* the first two strings, then concatenates the third string to the accumulated string, and so on. If one of the operands is not a string, it is automatically *cast* to a string. The string operator is also called a *concatenation operator*.

An expression consisting of numerous string operators evaluates to a single string. Based on that, here are two different statements:

```
document.write("I have " + 2 + " cookies.")
document.write("I have ", 2, " cookies.")
```

At first, you might think that these statements are equivalent. They aren't, because the first one uses the string operator, and the second one uses commas to delimit strings and numbers. They differ more than in style. In the first statement, the expression between the parentheses is evaluated to a single string—"I have 2 cookies." Therefore, the `document.write()` method in this statement prints only one expression. The second statement prints multiple expressions. The literals are not evaluated to a single value as in the first statement but are rather printed independently. Both statements print the exact same HTML to the page, but they do it in different ways. In order to understand how each statement works, take a look at the following sequences of statements. The first sequence is equivalent to the first statement in the previous set, and the second sequence is equivalent to the second statement.

```
// sequence #1
var stringToPrint =  "I have " + 2 + " cookies."
document.write(stringToPrint)
```

```
// sequence #2
document.write("I have ")
document.write(2)
document.write(" cookies.")
```

A common mistake made by beginners and advanced programmers alike is to forget spaces in strings. A space is a character just like any other one. Forgetting a space character is not a severe mistake, because you can easily locate where to add the space. You should use one of the following statements to print two consecutive numbers with a separating space character in between:

```
document.write(16 + " " + 18) // first possibility
document.write(16, " ", 18) // second possibility
```

The first statement is valid because of the automatic casting method used by JavaScript's interpreter.

Tip The plus (+) operator in JavaScript does not convert string operands to numeric values. The reason behind this is that the string concatenation operator and the plus operator use the same character: +. If only one operand is a string, the other is converted to a string value and then the operator concatenates the strings. In Perl, the plus (addition) and minus (subtraction) operators convert their arguments from strings to numeric values if necessary, and return a numeric result. This feature is made possible because the string concatenation operator in Perl is . (dot), not +, which is shared with another operator (addition) in JavaScript. C++ and Pascal feature a function that concatenates strings.

Bitwise Operators

Bitwise operators are the operators used in bit-oriented operations. A bit is the smallest unit of information, usually represented by 0 or 1 specifications. Bit manipulations are used to control the machine at the lowest level. If you plan to program at a higher level, this section may be safely skipped. In JavaScript you won't be using bitwise operators to control the machine at a low level but rather for other purposes such as encrypting and encoding.

Eight consecutive bits form a byte. There are 256 (2^8) byte variations. That is, a byte can be one of 256 eight-bit sequences. For example, 11010001 is one of these 256 possibilities. A byte is represented by a character in programming languages that support character data types, such as C, C++, and Pascal.

Hexadecimal notation is convenient for representing binary data because each hexadecimal digit represents four binary bits. Table 7-2 lists the hexadecimal values from 0 to F along with the equivalent binary values.

Table 7-2. *Hexadecimal and binary equivalence.*

Hexadecimal	Binary	Hexadecimal	Binary
0	0000	8	1000
1	0001	9	1001
2	0010	A	1010
3	0011	B	1011
4	0100	C	1100
5	0101	D	1101
6	0110	E	1110
7	0111	F	1111

Based on the obvious pattern, you should be able to reproduce it blindly.

Bitwise operators enable the scripter to work on individual bits. The bitwise (bit) operators in JavaScript are listed in Table 7-3.

***Table 7-3.** Bitwise operators in JavaScript.*

<table>
<tr><th>Syntax</th><th>Name</th><th>Type</th></tr>
<tr><td>&</td><td>Bitwise AND</td><td>binary</td></tr>
<tr><td>|</td><td>Bitwise OR</td><td>binary</td></tr>
<tr><td>^</td><td>Bitwise XOR (exclusive OR)</td><td>binary</td></tr>
<tr><td>~</td><td>Bitwise NOT</td><td>unary</td></tr>
<tr><td><<</td><td>Left shift</td><td>binary</td></tr>
<tr><td>>></td><td>Right shift</td><td>binary</td></tr>
<tr><td>>>></td><td>Zero-fill right shift</td><td>binary</td></tr>
</table>

Bitwise AND

```
operand1 & operand2
```

The *bitwise AND* operator compares two bits. The only situation in which the result is 1 is when both bits are 1. Here is the truth table for this operator:

***Table 7-4.** Bitwise AND truth table.*

Bit1	Bit2	Bit1 & Bit2
0	0	0
0	1	0
1	0	0
1	1	1

The AND operator, like all other bitwise operators, can take only a numeric value as its operand.

Although you will probably never use bitwise operators, let's learn how the results are calculated. All calculations will be performed in hexadecimal and binary bases, because they are most convenient for the task. Remember that hexadecimal numbers have a "0x" prefix.

Let's take a look at the following numbers, and how the bitwise AND operates on them:

	0x23	00100011_2
&	0x72	01110010_2
=	0x22	00100010_2

```
0x23 & 0x72 // evaluates to 34 (= 0x22 = 22₁₆)
```

The bitwise AND operator is similar to the logical AND operator, which is discussed later in this chapter.

You can use the bitwise AND operator to test whether a number is even or odd. In binary (base 2), the last digit of an odd number is 1, and the last digit of an even number is 0. The following function uses the bitwise AND operator to determine whether the number is odd or even. It returns `true` if `decimalNumber` is even, and `false` if it is odd.

```
function checkEven(decimalNumber) {
    return (decimalNumber & 1 == 0)
}
```

Don't worry if you are not familiar with the "==" equality operator. It is introduced later in this chapter. Come back to this script after we discuss the equality operator.

Bitwise OR

```
operand1 | operand2
```

The OR operator, also known as the *inclusive OR operator*, compares its operands. It returns 1 if at least one of the compared bits is 1. Table 7-5 shows the operator's truth table.

***Table 7-5.** Bitwise OR truth table.*

Bit1	Bit2	Bit1 | Bit2
0	0	0
0	1	1
1	0	1
1	1	1

When operating on bytes:

	0x46	01000110_2
|	0x79	01111001_2
=	0x7F	01111111_2

Bitwise XOR

```
operand1 ^ operand2
```

The *bitwise XOR* (shorthand for *bitwise exclusive OR*) operator returns 1 if only one bit is 1. It results in a 0 if the bits are equal (0 and 0, 1 and 1). Here is the truth table:

Table 7-6. *Bitwise XOR truth table.*

Bit1	Bit2	Bit1 ^ Bit2
0	0	0
0	1	1
1	0	1
1	1	0

Take a look at the following example:

	0x2C	00101100_2
^	0xA3	10100011_2
=	0x8F	10001111_2

The bitwise XOR operator is used in a simple cipher technique called *XORing*, which will be covered later in this book.

Bitwise NOT

The *bitwise NOT* operator returns the reverse of its operand. Therefore, it is also called the *bit flip operator* or the *invert operator*. All 1s are converted to 0s, and all 0s are converted to 1s. Here is the truth table:

Table 7-7. *Bitwise NOT.*

Bit	~Bit
0	1
1	0

For example,

~	70	$00000000000000000000000001000110_2$
=	–71	$11111111111111111111111110111001_2$

Note that this operator refers to all operands (integers) as 32 bits. If they are not 32-bit integers, they are converted for the operation and then converted back to their initial form.

Shift Operators

The *shift operators* take two operands:

- The quantity (value) to be shifted
- The number of bit positions to shift the first operand

Shift operators convert their operands to 32-bit integers, and return a result of the same type as the left operator. There are three shift operators:

- Left shift (<<)
- Right shift (>>)
- Zero-fill right shift (>>>)

Left shift

```
operand1 << operand2
```

The left shift operator shifts the first operand the specified number of bits to the left. All bits that are shifted out (to the left) are discarded. New bits coming in from the right are zeros. In the following example, |___| represents 4 bytes (32 bits):

179 ⇒ 0xB3 ⇒ 10110011_2

179 << 0 ⇒ 00000000000000000000000010110011

179 << 2 ⇒ **00000000000000000000000010110011**

empty space filled with 0s

⇒ **00000000000000000000001011001100**

⇒ 1011001100_2 ⇒ 0x2CC ⇒ 716

You now know that 179 << 2 is 716. You might realize that 179 * 4 is also 716—this is no coincidence. In general, x << n is the same as x * 2^n. Shifting left n places is the same as multiplying by 2^n. This rule applies also to negative numbers—the sign is always preserved. Thus, you can choose between two different methods to multiply by a power of two. Although shifting is faster, it is also less clear to the reader and should be avoided.

Right shift

```
operand1 >> operand2
```

The *right shift operator* is also called *sign-propagating right shift*, because it preserves the sign of the initial operand. Like the left shift operator, the right shift operator shifts the first operand the specified number of bits to the right. Excess bits shifted off the right are discarded. The sign of an integer is stored in the first bit (from the left). In order to preserve the sign, the first bit remains as is. The other 31 bits are shifted to the right. New bits coming in from the left are either 0s or 1s, depending on the sign. If the first bit was a 0, all new bits are 0s, and vice versa. Therefore, if the number was positive, the operation will also return a positive number; if it was negative, the operation evaluates to a negative number. It is important to remember that this operator, like all shift operators, converts the first operand to a 32-bit integer, and after shifting, returns it to its initial representation. Here is a simple example:

176 ⇒ 0xB0 ⇒ 10110000_2

176 >> 0 ⇒ 00000000000000000000000010110000

176 >> 3 ⇒ **0 00000000000000000000000010110000**

⇒ **00000000000000000000000000010110**

⇒ 10110_2 ⇒ 0x16 ⇒ 22

Let's see how this operator works on a negative number, say, –17.

–17 ⇒ $11111111111111111111111111101111_2$

–17 >> 0 ⇒ **11111111111111111111111111101111**

–17 >> 3 ⇒ **1 11111111111111111111111111101111**

⇒ **11111111111111111111111111111101**

⇒ $11111111111111111111111111111101_2$ ⇒ –3

You can refer to the right shift operator as the opposite of the left shift one. While the left shift operator is equivalent to multiplying by a power of 2, the right shift operation is equivalent to dividing by a power of 2. `176 >> 3` is equal to `176 / 2`^{3}. In general, `x << `*n* is the same as *x* `/ 2`^{n}.

Zero-fill right shift

operand1 `>>>` *operand2*

The *zero-fill right shift operator* shifts the first operand the specified number of bits to the right. Like the sign-propagating right shift, the zero-fill right shift discards excess bits that are shifted off to the right. However, the bits shifted in from the left are always zeros. The number's sign is lost because the leftmost bit is always 0. Here is the simple example from the previous section, this time with the zero-fill right shift:

−17 ⇒ $11111111111111111111111111101111_2$

−17 >>> 0 ⇒ **11111111111111111111111111101111**

−17 >>> 3 ⇒ **11111111111111111111111111101111**

⇒ **00011111111111111111111111111101**

⇒ $11111111111111111111111111101_2$ ⇒ 536870909

Don't worry if the bitwise shift operators seem difficult. Chances are you'll never need to use them.

Assignment Operators

operand1 ▯ `=` *operand2*

Assignment operators are binary operators handling arithmetic, string, or bitwise operators. They perform the regular operation (▯) on the operands and assign the result to the first operand. The assignment operators are as follows:

Table 7-8. *Assignment operators.*

Syntax	Name
=	Equals
+=	Add/concatenate by value
–=	Subtract by value
*=	Multiply by value

Syntax	Name
/=	Divide by value
%=	Modulo by value
&=	Bitwise AND by value
|=	Bitwise OR by value
^=	Bitwise XOR
<<=	Left shift by value
>>=	Right shift by value
>>>=	Zero-fill right shift by value

You already know what the simple = assignment operator does—it stores the value of the expression in the data structure. For all the other operators, JavaScript pretends that

```
var1 □ = var2
```

is

```
var1 = var1 □ var2
```

For example:

```
counter =>> 2
```

shifts the value of `counter` two positions to the right, and

```
text += " Gates"
```

attaches the word `Gates` to the end of the string stored in `text`. The same rule applies to all assignment operators listed in Table 7-8.

Since the assignment statements are evaluated from right to left, you can use multiple operators in the same statement. The rule is that the value to the right of the operator is evaluated and then assigned to the variable to the left of the operator.

```
num1 = num2 = num3 = num4 = num5
```

The value of `num5` is assigned to `num4`, the value of `num4` is assigned to `num3`, and so on. After such an operation, all five variables hold the same value.

Relational Operators

```
operand1 _ operand2
```

Relational operators, also called *comparison operators*, compare two values and return a Boolean result. All relational operators are binary, because they compare two values. These operators are often used in conditional statements, covered in Chapter 8, Control Structures. Here is the complete list of JavaScript's relational operators:

Table 7-9. *Relational operators*

Syntax	Name
`==`	equals
`!=`	not equal
`<`	less than
`<=`	less than or equal to
`>`	greater than
`>=`	greater than or equal to

These operators take numeric or string values as their operands. Numeric comparison is usually very simple:

```
2 == 1 // evaluates to false
99.0 == 99 // evaluates to true
2 != 1 // evaluates to true
3 < 2.5 // evaluates to false
2 <= 2 // evaluates to true
9 > 9 // evaluates to false
9 >= -10 // evaluates to false
```

String operands are compared according to the ASCII value of their characters. This comparison is similar to the one by which words are placed in a dictionary. The only difference is that instead of using a single set of letters, JavaScript uses 256 different characters. As you know, each character has a numeric value. This value determines if a character is greater than, equal to, or less than another one.

When you compare multicharacter strings, the first character of the first operand is compared with the first character of the second operand. The second characters are compared only if the comparison of the first ones indicates equality. The process continues until the corresponding characters are not equal, or until the end of one of the strings is reached. Here are some characters and their ASCII values:

0 – 48	A – 65	a – 97
9 – 57	Z – 90	z – 122

You can find the full ASCII table at the end of the book.

Here is an example:

```
"computerA" > "computerB"
"c" == "c"
"o" == "o"
"m" == "m"
"p" == "p"
"u" == "u"
"t" == "t"
"e" == "e"
"r" == "r"
"A" < "B"       ⇒       ("computerA" > "computerB" ⇒ false)
```

Take a look at the following results for a better understanding:

```
"JavaScript" == "javascript" // evaluates to false
"bill" != "bill" // evaluates to false
" " < "  " // ([one space] < [two spaces]) evaluates to true
16 <= "16" // evaluates to true
"luck" > "Work" // evaluates to true!
"XT" >= "pentium pro" // evaluates to false
```

Equality and Inequality

As you can see, the Boolean equality operator (==) is similar to the assignment operator (=). This similarity is the source of many programming errors, not only in JavaScript but also in other languages such as C, C++, and Java. Equality operators are often used in `if-else` statements, where the assignment operator cannot be used. (JavaScript does not allow side effects in a conditional statement.) In this case the interpreter produces a meaningful error saying: "test for equality (==) mistyped as assignment (=)? Assuming equality test." However, in some other situations, both the equality and assignment operators are valid and the browser, rightly so, does not generate any errors. This is the reason why such errors are very difficult to debug. The following example demonstrates a situation in which both operators are acceptable:

```
var i = 1
document.write(i = 2)

var j = 1
document.write(j == 2)
```

The first printing statement prints 2, because an assignment expression evaluates to the assigned value. The second printing statement prints `false` under Netscape Navigator, and 0 on MSIE (MSIE converts the Boolean value `false` to `0` for printing, rather than to `"false"`), because 1 is not equal to 2. In a long script, if you accidentally replaced one operator by the other, you would have a hard time finding the mistake.

Another problem with the equality operator has to do with the way a computer deals with floating point numbers. This problem is especially harsh when you try to store integer numbers in the form of floating point numbers (e.g., 3.0). Depending on the underlying machine, the results may differ. You might find out that `(5. == 5.00)` evaluates to `false`, and `(5.0 == 4.99999999)` evaluates to `true`. Therefore, avoid using equality operators with floating point values. The solution for this problem is presented later in the chapter.

Short-Circuit Logical Operators

Short-circuit logical operators, also called *Boolean operators* or *logical operators*, are binary operators that accept Boolean values as their operands. They group multiple relational expressions together. There are three logical operators:

Table 7-10. *Logical operators.*

Syntax	Name	Type
`||`	logical OR	binary
`&&`	logical AND	binary
`!`	logical NOT	unary

Logical OR

```
operand1 || operand2
```

The *logical OR* operator accepts two Boolean values as its operands, and evaluates to a single Boolean value. It evaluates to `true` if at least one of the operands is `true`; in other words, the only situation in which it evaluates to `false` is when both operands are `false`. Take a look at Table 7-11.

Table 7-11. Logical OR truth table.

Operand1	Operand2	Operand1 || Operand2
true	true	true
true	false	true
false	true	true
false	false	false

Here are a few examples:

```
2 > 1 || 3 < 4 // true
1 == 1 || 99 >= 98 // true
"mouse" > "elephant" || 6 < 5 // true
1 == 2 || 5 <= 4 // false
```

Be careful not to confuse the logical OR operator with the bitwise OR due to their similar meaning and syntax (`||` vs. `|`). The only difference in meaning is that the first handles Boolean operands while the latter handles numeric ones.

The logical OR operator is *short-circuit* evaluated. As you can see from the truth table, if the first operand is `true`, it is certain that the expression will evaluate to `true`. Checking the second operand in such a situation is unnecessary and is avoided by JavaScript.

Logical AND

```
operand1 && operand2
```

The *logical AND* operator is similar to the logical OR operator, except for its truth table:

Table 7-12. Logical AND.

Operand1	Operand2	Operand1 && Operand2
true	true	true
true	false	false
false	true	false
false	false	false

Both operands must be `true` for the expression to evaluate to a `true` value. This operator is similar to the bitwise AND operator, except that the operand types are different, and the logical AND operator operates on the whole operand at once, rather than on a small segment (bit).

Logical AND expressions are also short-circuit evaluated. If the first operand is `false`, the expression will obviously be `false`, so the second operand is not evaluated.

Here are some examples:

```
2 > 1 && 3 < 4 // true
1 == 1 && 99 >= 98 // false
"mouse" > "elephant" && 6 < 5 // false
1 == 2 && 5 <= 4 // false
```

Logical NOT

```
!operand1
```

The *logical NOT* operator is a simple unary operator which accepts a Boolean value and negates it. This operator is similar to the negation operator, which negates a number (changes its sign). It is even more similar to the bitwise NOT operator (~) which converts all 1 bits to 0 bits, and 0 bits to 1 bits. Although the truth table is obvious, here it is for your reference:

Table 7-13. *Logical NOT truth table.*

Operand	!Operand
`true`	`false`
`false`	`true`

Because this is a unary operator, short-circuit evaluation is not relevant.

Here are some examples:

```
!true // evaluates to false
!(2 > 4) // evaluates to true
!(7 == 7) // evaluates to false
!false // evaluates to true
```

Caution Short-circuit evaluation is mostly useful because it makes your scripts more efficient. However, there are times that this method of evaluation is harmful. For example, you finish writing a complicated script and you want to test it. Depending on certain decisions in the script, short-circuit evaluation is performed, and the interpreter ignores the second operand of various expressions.

You might think that the script works perfectly fine, even if there is a data mistype or a syntax error in the second operand. This type of evaluation can mislead you in such situations, but it is unavoidable.

Testing Equality for Floating Point Numbers

We mentioned earlier that the equal operator (==) is not suitable for floating point numbers due to inaccuracy issues. Using logical AND and OR operators you can check if the number is close to the specified value. For example, if you want to evaluate the expression `x == 10.0` you use a *fuzzy comparison* using one of the following expressions, in which ∝ represents a small number (such as 0.001).

```
(x - 10.0) < ∝ || (10.0 - x) < ∝
```

or

```
x > (10.0 - ∝) && x < (10.0 + ∝)
```

More Logical Operators

The *conditional operator* and the *comma operator* are logical operators.

Conditional Operator

```
condition ? trueAlternative : falseAlternative
```

The *conditional operator* is unique because it is trinary (three operands) and because it returns values of all types. It can return a numeric value, a string, a Boolean value, and so on. The first operand is the condition. The condition must be an expression that evaluates to a Boolean value, either `true` or `false`. The second operator holds the value that the operator should return if the condition is `true`. The third operand is the value that the expression evaluates to if the condition is `false`. The conditional operator is often used with an assignment operator. For example:

```
var level = (points > 500) ? "Second Level" : "First Level"
```

The variable `level` is assigned either `"First Level"` or `"Second Level"`, depending on the value of the Boolean expression `points > 500`. If the value of `points` is greater than `500`, the conditional expression evaluates to the string `"Second Level"`, which in turn is assigned to the variable `level`. If the value of `points` does not exceed 500, the string `"First Level"` is assigned to the variable. The first operand (the condition) must be Boolean (a single Boolean value or an expression that evaluates to a single Boolean value). The other operands can be of any type.

Comma Operator

```
operand1, operand2, operand3, ...
```

The *comma operator* is rarely used. You can use it to force the evaluation of a set of expressions. The comma operator is also called a *parameter delimiter* because it does just that. You probably recall that we used the comma operator in functions when we wanted a function to accept multiple arguments.

```
var beerNum = 99
document.write(beerNum, " bottles of beer on the wall")
```

In this example the comma operator delimits the method's arguments.

Here is another example:

```
var a = (b = "Hello", alert("Hi"), "Howdy")
```

The comma operator forces the evaluation of all expressions in the statement. Only the last expression is returned, so the value of `a` would be `"Howdy"`. This statement is equivalent to the following set of statements:

```
b = "Hello"
alert("Hi")
var a = "Howdy"
```

Data Type Operator

```
typeof operand1
```

or

```
typeof (operand1)
```

JavaScript provides an operator to check the data type of its operand. The operand can be either a literal or a data structure such as a variable, a function, or an object. The operator returns the data type. The expression includes the word `typeof` followed by the literal or identifier. Here are some examples:

```
typeof foo == "undefined"        // when foo is undefined
```

```
typeof eval == "function"        // eval is a built-in function
typeof null == "object"          // null is an object
typeof 3.14 == "number"
typeof true == "Boolean"
typeof "a string" == "string"
// all of the expressions are true, of course
```

The `typeof` operator is very useful for debugging. Until strong debugging tools are available, you must do all debugging by hand, and detecting the data type of a structure is sometimes essential.

Void Operator

```
void operand1
void (operand1)
```

or

```
javascript:void operand1
javascript:void (operand1)
```

The `void` operator, like `typeof`, is quite extraordinary. It specifies an expression to be evaluated without returning a value. Take a look at the following script:

```
function foo() {
     alert("Function entered")
     return true
}

alert(foo())
```

The preceding script segment displays two `alert` boxes with the following strings:

- `Function entered`
- `true`

Now take a look at another function and call:

```
function foo() {
     alert("Function entered")
     return true
}

alert(void foo())
```

This script also generates two alerts, but the second one reads "`undefined`," because the `void` operator evaluates the function without returning a value. A more important use of this operator comes with hypertext links, where it is used to evaluate a JavaScript expression.

The expression is evaluated but is not loaded in place of the current document. The following link does nothing because the expression "0" has no effect in JavaScript:

```
<A HREF="javascript:void(0)">Click here to do nothing</A>
```

The following code generates an `alert` box when the link is clicked:

```
<A HREF="javascript:void(alert('Wow'))">Click here to display message</A>
```

The parentheses are optional, so it's up to you to decide on using them. Some scripters specify them in HTML and omit them in JavaScript, with no good reason.

Operator Precedence

You probably remember that 2 + 6 * 9 is 56 and not 72, because multiplication precedes addition. That is exactly the meaning of operator precedence. It is not necessary to remember the precedence rules because parentheses `()` can be used to force evaluation in the desired order. The expressions are evaluated according to the precedence rules. Operators at the same level are evaluated from left to right. The following table will help you when you want to define complex expressions:

Table 7-14. *Operator precedence.*

<table>
<tr><th>Level</th><th>Operators</th><th>Notes</th></tr>
<tr><td>1</td><td>() [] .</td><td>call, member (including typeof and void)</td></tr>
<tr><td>2</td><td>! ~ – ++ ––</td><td>negation, increment</td></tr>
<tr><td>3</td><td>* / %</td><td>multiply/divide</td></tr>
<tr><td>4</td><td>+ –</td><td>addition/subtraction</td></tr>
<tr><td>5</td><td><< >> >>></td><td>bitwise shift</td></tr>
<tr><td>6</td><td>< <= > >=</td><td>relational</td></tr>
<tr><td>7</td><td>== !=</td><td>equality</td></tr>
<tr><td>8</td><td>&</td><td>bitwise AND</td></tr>
<tr><td>9</td><td>^</td><td>bitwise XOR</td></tr>
<tr><td>10</td><td>|</td><td>bitwise OR</td></tr>
<tr><td>11</td><td>&&</td><td>logical AND</td></tr>
<tr><td>12</td><td>||</td><td>logical OR</td></tr>
<tr><td>13</td><td>?:</td><td>conditional</td></tr>
<tr><td>14</td><td>= += –= *= /= %= <<= >>= >>>= &= ^= |=</td><td>assignment</td></tr>
<tr><td>15</td><td>,</td><td>comma</td></tr>
</table>

Expressions

The term *expression* has been mentioned dozens of times throughout this chapter. An expression is any valid set of literals, variables, operators, and other expressions that evaluates to a single value. The value may be a number, a string, or a Boolean value. Conceptually, there are two types of expressions:

- Those that assign a value to a variable (or another data structure)
- Those that have a value

The following are expressions:

```
a = "Shiran"
"Netscape"
256
false
b = true
```

The first type of expression is a bit more difficult to understand. In such expressions, an assignment is performed. The entire specification, including both operands of the assignment operator and the operator itself, is evaluated to the assigned value ("`Shiran`"). Consider the following statement:

```
document.write(x = "Israel")
```

This statement prints `Israel`, because the whole expression evaluates to the assigned value. The next section discusses side effects which take advantage of such expressions.

Side Effects

A *side effect* is an operation performed in addition to the main one. Take a look at the following statements:

```
number = 3
answer = ++number
```

The first line is a simple assignment statement. The second line is a bit more complicated. It performs two actions in the following order:

- Increments `number` (side effect)
- Assigns the value of `number` (4) to `answer` (main operation)

Remembering the order in which the actions take place is not necessary. You could break down the side effect and use two different statements instead:

```
number = 3
number++
answer = number
```

This set of statements is easy to follow. The only "advantage" of the first method is that the code is compact. Compact code is only a holdover from the early days of computing, when storage was expensive, and programmers used various compacting techniques to save disk space. The situation is different today, because the number one rule in programming is to keep programs clear and simple. It comes even before efficiency, especially in simple programs like the ones written in JavaScript (you will not find any 500,000-line scripts in this advanced book).

Other side effects are not related to the increment and decrement operators. Consider the following JavaScript statement:

```
document.write(myName = "Yehuda")
```

You already know that this statement prints `Yehuda`. The assignment operation also takes place in this statement, so `myName` holds the value `Yehuda` after the statement. The assignment operation is the side effect, and the printing action is the main action. The preceding statement should be split into two separate statements:

```
myName = "Yehuda"
document.write(myName)
```

Here are some more "Morse" statements you should avoid (they will keep you busy for a while...):

```
number = 0
answer = (number++ - 2) * (--number - 1)
document.write(number = answer++)
```

This set of statements prints `2`. Let's analyze it:

1.
   - 1.1 `number` is assigned the value `0`.
2.
   - 2.1. `(number++ - 2)` is evaluated to `-2`.
   - 2.2. `number` is incremented to `1`.
   - 2.3. `number` decrements to `0`.
   - 2.4. `(--number - 1)` evaluates to `-1`.
   - 2.5. `answer` is assigned `2` (because `(-1) * (-2)` yields `2`).

3.
   3.1. number is assigned the value of answer (2).
   3.2. The value of number is printed.
   3.3. answer increments to 3.

The final result:

- number holds the value 2.
- answer holds the value 3.
- The number 2 is printed to the document.

The following script is longer, but it is definitely better:

```
number = 0
answer = number – 2
number++
number--
answer *= number – 1
number = answer
document.write(number)
number = amswer
answer++
```

Summary

In this chapter we discussed JavaScript's wealth of operators. Some of them are extremely useful, while others are not used at all. We also discussed various expression forms. In addition, we played around with some side effects. Never use side effects in your programs, because they are hard to follow and difficult to understand. The next chapter will discuss control structures and will show how useful the wide variety of operators is.

Chapter 8

Control Structures

Dialog Boxes

Before we discuss the control structures in JavaScript, we need some basic user-interaction devices. These will allow us to create both useful and helpful examples, for demonstration purposes. Dialog boxes are only introduced in this chapter. They will be presented later in further detail.

JavaScript provides the ability to create small windows called *dialog boxes*. You can create small alert boxes, confirm boxes, and even prompt boxes. These boxes let you generate output and receive input from the user.

Alert Boxes

```
alert(message)
```

An alert box is the most simple dialog box. It enables you to display a short message to the user in a separate window. We have already used these boxes in previous chapters as a simple output mechanism. Take a look at the following script and its corresponding output:

```
alert("Click OK to continue...")
```

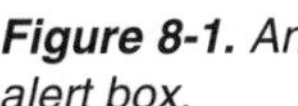
Figure 8-1. *An alert box.*

`alert()` is actually a method of the `window` object. It is not necessary to specify that because `window` is the default object. The same applies to all dialog boxes.

Note Netscape Communications Corp. implemented the "JavaScript Alert:." header for security reasons. It is used to distinguish JavaScript dialog boxes from those created by the operating system, so that the user knows what the source of the message is. JavaScript programmers cannot trick the user into doing something he might not want to do. It also disables the ability to scare the user into giving away personal information. According to JavaScript developers at Netscape, the design of these dialog boxes might change in the future, but Netscape Navigator 2.0x, 3.0x, and 4.0 generate the box in the format illustrated in Figure 8-1. Note that MSIE 3.0 dialog boxes do not include this warning.

You can also display messages using data structures. For example:

```
var message = "Click OK to continue"
alert(message)
```

As you can see, the alert box is often used to pause the execution of a script until the user approves its continuation.

Confirm Boxes

```
confirm(message)
```

Confirm boxes are different from alert boxes in that they evaluate to a value, based on a decision made by the user. Rather than a simple *OK* button, the confirm box includes both *OK* and *Cancel* buttons.

Like the alert box, `confirm` is also a method of the `window` object. This method returns a Boolean value, because there are two options. You can use confirmation boxes to ask the user a yes-or-no question, or to confirm an action. Here is an example and its output:

```
var reply = confirm("OK to continue?")
```

Figure 8-2. *A confirm box.*

`reply` is assigned a `true` value if the user chooses OK, and `false` if the user selects Cancel.

Prompt Boxes

```
prompt(message[, inputDefault])
```

The `prompt()` method displays a prompt dialog box with a message and an input field. You can use these boxes to receive input from the user. It is similar to the confirm box, except that it returns the value of the input field, rather than `true` or `false`. Here is an example:

```
var name = prompt("Enter your name:", "anonymous")
```

Figure 8-3. A prompt box.

The method returns a value of `null` if the user chooses Cancel.

The value of the field is always a string. If the user enters 16 in the form, the string "16" is returned rather than the number 16. When you want to prompt the user for a number, you must convert the input into a numeric value. JavaScript features a built-in function that does this—`parseInt()`. You can use the following statement to ask the user for a number:

```
var number = parseInt(prompt("Enter a number:", 0))
```

or

```
var number = prompt("Enter a number:", 0)
number = parseInt(number)
```

You can see that this function works by using the `typeof` operator for testing:

```
var number = prompt("Enter a number:", 0)
alert(number, " is a ", typeof number) // "... is a string"
number = parseInt(number)
alert(number, " is a ", typeof number) // "... is a number"
```

The input must be of a numeric type, of course (e.g., 99). The `parseInt` function is discussed later in detail, mostly in Chapter 16, Handling Strings.

if Statement

```
if (condition)
    statement
```

The `if` statement lets you put decision making in your scripts. A script without any decisions does the same procedure each time it is executed. Such linear structures limit your scripts to simple algorithms. JavaScript enables decision making using an `if` statement. `if` statements associate a single statement with a `true` condition. That statement is only executed if the conditional expression is `true`, and otherwise it is not executed at all. The condition must evaluate to a Boolean value: `true` or `false`. Numeric values are also acceptable as an alternative to a Boolean condition. `0` is equivalent to `false`, and all other values are equivalent to `true`.

The `if` statement associates a single statement with a `true` condition. A statement can be anything from a simple `document.write()` to a block of statements, using curly braces (`{}`). Some `if` statements require multiple statements, so they use a block in the following form:

```
if (condition) {
    statement1
    statement2
    statement3
    .
    .
    .
}
```

A nested statement can be any legal statement, including an additional `if` statement. Here is a simple example demonstrating the `if` statement:

```
<HTML>
<HEAD>
<TITLE>A simple if statement</TITLE>
<SCRIPT LANGUAGE="JavaScript">
<!--

var age = parseInt(prompt("Please enter your age:", 120))
if (age < 21)
    alert("Sorry, you are too young to enter")

// -->
</SCRIPT>
</HEAD>
```

```
<BODY>
</BODY>
</HTML>
```

Example 8-1 (ex8-1.htm). *A script with one conditional statement.*

At first, the script asks the user for his or her age. The age is stored in numeric format in the variable age. The `if` statement checks if the user's age is less than 21. If so, the expression `age < 21` evaluates to `true`. Because the condition is `true`, the following statement is executed, and an alert box is displayed. Note that if the value of age is greater than or equal to 21, no statements are executed. The remedy to this problem is presented in the next section.

Here is another example using multiple statements associated with a `true` condition:

```
<HTML>
<HEAD>
<TITLE>An if statement with a command block</TITLE>
<SCRIPT LANGUAGE="JavaScript">
<!--

var name = prompt("Enter your name:", "John Doe")

// draw a horizontal rule of the specified width
function drawRule(width) {
     document.write("<HR WIDTH=" + width + "%>")
}

var message = "Click OK if you are using Netscape 3.0 or above"

if (!confirm(message)) {
     document.write("<CENTER><B>")
     document.write("Hello " + name + "!<BR>")
     drawRule(50)
     document.write("Please download the latest ",
                    "version of Netscape Navigator")
     document.write("</B></CENTER>")
}

// -->
</SCRIPT>
</HEAD>
<BODY>
</BODY>
</HTML>
```

Example 8-2 (ex8-2.htm). *A conditional statement associated with a command block.*

Example 8-2 features an `if` statement with a set of statements, grouped together in a command block. Notice the function that prints a horizontal rule of a specified width. In this example, the user must reply to two dialog boxes. If the user responds by clicking Cancel to the prompt dialog box, the page looks like this:

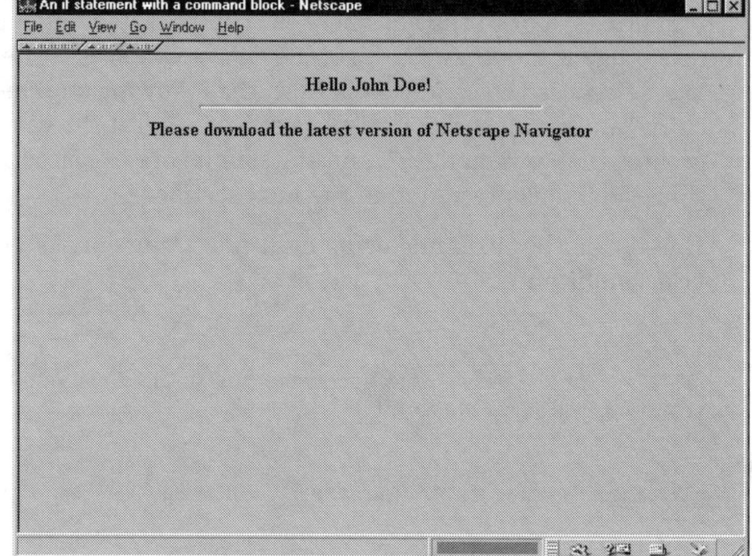

Figure 8-4. *JavaScript-generated HTML content that depends on the user's input.*

else Statement

```
if (condition)
     statement1
else
     statement2
```

You probably felt limited with the structure of the `if` statement, because it only lets you execute a statement when the condition is `true`. The additional `else` statement specifies a statement that is executed when the condition is `false`. This construction covers all possibilities, because a condition can be either `true` or `false`. Here is a script segment extracted from Example 8-1, improved with an `else` statement:

```
var age = parseInt(prompt("Please enter your age:", 120))
if (age < 21)
     alert("Sorry, you are too young to enter")
else
```

```
          alert("Welcome in...")
```

If the user's age is greater than 21, he receives a welcoming message.

You can write these statements with a command block, using one of the following syntax styles:

```
if (condition) {
     statements1
} else {
     statements2
}
```

or

```
if (condition) {
     statements1
}
else {
     statements2
}
```

We prefer the first style, but feel free to choose the second one if you find it more comfortable.

Nested if-else Statements

An `if` statement can execute any legal statement. Obviously, a simple `if` statement meets this requirement. Statements inside a command block are called *nested statements*.

Consider the following function:

```
function testChar(ch) {
     if (ch >= "A" && ch <= "Z")
          alert("An uppercase letter")
     else
          if (ch >= "a" && ch <= "z")
               alert("A lowercase letter")
          else
               alert("Not a letter")
}
```

The function accepts a character (a one-character string) as its argument. If the character is greater than `A` and less than `Z`, it must be an uppercase letter, and an appropriate message is displayed. Only if the character is not an uppercase letter, the execution continues. If it is a lowercase letter, the appropriate message is provided. Once again, only if it is not a lowercase letter (meaning it is not a letter at all) the execution proceeds. No more tests are performed, so the last message is generated.

This function demonstrates simple nested `if-else` statements. Only if the condition is `false` does the execution continue. If, for example, `ch` is `"H"`, only the first expression is evaluated. The message `"An uppercase letter"` is displayed, and the other tests are not performed. The following illustration should help you understand how nested `if-else` statements work (assuming that you do not have any computer programming experience):

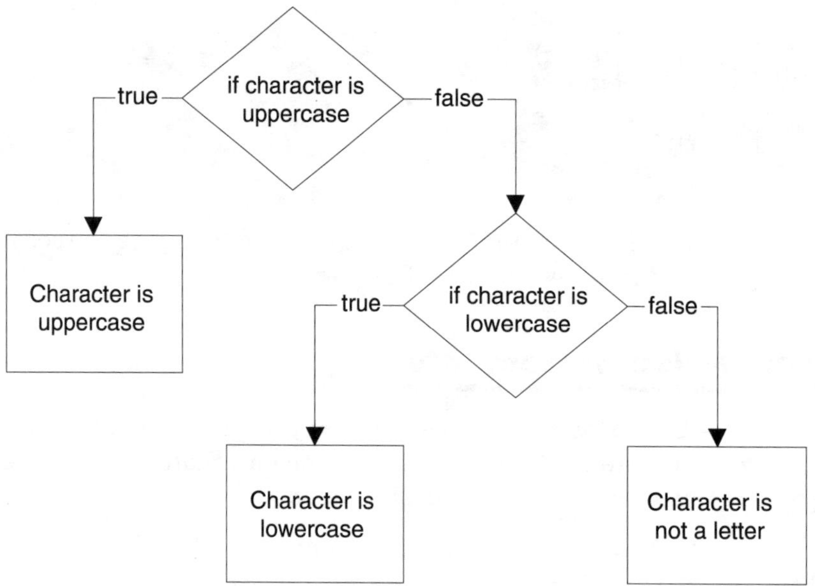

***Figure 8-5.** The structure of nested `if-else` statements.*

Although it is not required, try to put the condition that is most likely to be true as the top condition. If the condition is true, the other tests are not even performed. Such a practice will make your scripts more efficient, especially if the tests are complex.

C++ requires a semicolon after the first statement (*statement1*). Pascal requires that you do not put one there. JavaScript is friendly—it lets you choose.

Note Perl is basically designed as a scripting language used to manipulate files and their contents. Therefore, Perl features some unique statements that make the programming process easier. However, these statements are not vital, because they have simple substitutes using more common statements. For example, the `elsif` statement is a unique feature of Perl, and is not supported by JavaScript. In JavaScript you must use the full `else if...` to create these nested statements. Another statement supported by Perl but not by JavaScript is the `unless` statement. This statement reverses the order of the regular `if` statement; that is, unless the condition is false, the statement block is executed. The following table summarizes most of Perl's conditional statements and their JavaScript equivalents:

Table 8-1. *Conditional statements in Perl versus those in JavaScript.*

Perl	JavaScript

`if (`*condition1*`)`
`{`*statements*`}`
`elsif (`*condition2*`)`
`{`*statements*`}`
`else`
`{`*statements*`}`
	`if (`*condition1*`)`
	`{`*statements*`}`
	`else`
	`if (`*condition2*`)`
	`{`*statements*`}`
	`else`
	`{`*statements*`}`

`unless (`*condition*`)`
`{`*statements*`}`
 	
or
 	
`if (!`*condition*`)`
`{`*statements*`}`
 	
* Followed by an `elsif` or `else` statement.
	`if (!`*condition*`)`
	`{`*statements*`}`
	
	* Followed by an `else` statement.

statement `if` *condition*	`if (`*condition*`)` *statement*
statement `unless` *condition*	`if (!`*condition*`)` *statement*

The Nonexistent Switch Statement

Note JavaScript does not feature a `switch` statement similar to the one in C++. In this section we'll refer to the `switch` statement in C++, and the possible workarounds in JavaScript. When JavaScript supports this statement, it should use the same syntax as in C++.

When your nested `if-else` structures build up, it becomes difficult to get on top of the script. A simple menu system would solve the problem by offering multiple choices or actions.

A `switch` statement in C++ solves the problem. It consists of two parts:

- The declaration of the switch, which is the value to be tested
- A list of cases which associate actions with certain values. A specific action is taken when the switch value matches the value in the corresponding case.

Here is the general syntax of the `switch` statement in **C++**:

```
switch (switchingVariable) {
     case value1 :
          statement1;
          break;
     case value2 :
          statement2;
          break;
     case value3 :
          statement3;
          break;
     default:
          statement4;
}
```

The `break` statement is supported by JavaScript—it is explained later in this chapter.

The `switch` statement starts by comparing the *`switchingVariable`* with the value of *`case1`*. If they match, *`statement1`* is executed, and the `switch` statement is terminated by the `break` statement. If they do not match, testing continues. The testing continues until a `break` statement is reached or until the program drops through the bottom brace.

The switch statement in C++ is similar to the case statement in Pascal. Because JavaScript does not support this statement, you must use nested if-else constructions instead. For example, the preceding switch statement is equivalent to:

```
if (switchingVariable == value1)
    statement1
else
    if (switchingVariable == value2)
        statement2
    else
        if (switchingVariable == value3)
            statement3
        else
            statement4 // default case
```

Loop Statements

Loops are control structures that perform a set of actions more than once. Everyone agrees that a computer can calculate faster than a human. Using loops you can repeat calculations and take advantage of the computer's ability to do them faster. Theoretically, a loop repeats only one statement. However, you already know that a statement can be a block of statements, allowing the repetition of many statements, perhaps the whole program. JavaScript features two basic loop types:

- The for loop
- The while loop

Each loop type has its own advantages. You will learn to choose the most suitable one for your task.

for Statement

Syntax:

```
for ([initialExpression;] [condition;] [operation])
    statement
```

The most commonly used loop is the for one. Because a loop usually repeats more than one statement, you use a command block in the following format:

```
for ([initialExpression;] [condition;] [operation]) {
    statements
}
```

initialExpression is usually a statement or a variable declaration. It should evaluate to a single value and is typically used to initialize a counter variable. This expression may optionally declare new variables with the var keyword.

condition is a condition that is evaluated before each successive pass through the loop. The statement is executed only if the condition evaluates to true.

operation is a statement that is executed after each consecutive pass through the loop's body. It is typically used to update or increment the counter variable, which counts the number of passes through the loop.

Consider the following looping script fragment:

```
var number1 = 1
var number2 = 1

for (var counter = 1; counter <= 10; counter++) {
     document.write(number1 + " ")
     number2 = number2 + number1
     number1 = number2 - number1
}
```

This piece of code prints the first ten numbers of the Fibonacci sequence. The Fibonacci sequence includes the following numbers:

1 1 2 3 5 8 13 21 34 55 89 144 . . . ($f_1 = 1, f_2=1, f_x = f_{x-1} + f_{x-2}$)

Each number is equal to the sum of the two preceding numbers. The first two numbers are both equal to 1.

Take a look at the script. number1 and number2 are initialized to 1, because $f_1 = 1$ and $f_2=1$. The for statement prints the numbers in the Fibonacci sequence. The initial expression of the loop is var counter = 1, which declares the loop counter and initializes its value to 1. The condition counter <= 10 means that the loop executes while the value of counter is less than or equal to 10. Note that the condition is evaluated only at the end of the loop. Incrementing the value of the loop counter is the action in this example, and is typical for for loops. In short, this loop's attributes cause it to execute exactly ten times. The net effect is that it computes and prints the first ten numbers of the Fibonacci sequence.

Understanding the content of the loop is just plain math. After the current number is printed number2 is assigned the sum of its two succeeding numbers in the sequence. number1 should hold the value of number2 before the assignment statement. The following explains how this is done (number2' is the value of number2 before the assignment statement):

```
number1 = number2 - number1 == (number2' + number1) - number1 == number2'
```

Although you do not need to associate a command block with a loop if its body consists of only one statement, it is a common practice in this book.

The counter variable is a regular variable. Its value can change during the execution of the loop.

You can create infinite executing loops with the `for` statement. The `break` statement, which is discussed later, makes such loops meaningful by providing a way to terminate its execution. The basic structure of an infinite loop is:

```
for ( ; ; )
    statement
```

You can also create nested `for` loops. The following loop prints a rectangle of asterisks (25 x 10):

```
for (var i = 1; i <= 10; i++) {
    for (var j = 1; j <= 25; j++) {
        document.write("*")
    }
    document.write("<BR>")
}
```

As you can see, the variables in the preceding example do not have meaningful names. It is common to use such identifiers as loop counters, and most experienced programmers actually do so. Unless the loop counter has a special meaning, name the variable `i`, `j`, `k`, etc.

while Statement

```
while (condition)
    statement
```

The `while` loop continues to loop while the condition (*`condition`*) is true. As opposed to the `for` loop, the loop is not executed at all if the condition is `false` at the beginning. That is, the condition is evaluated before each iteration. *`statement`* can also be a command block, allowing multiple statements.

The following loop calculates `n!` (`n` factorial):

```
var n = parseInt(prompt("Enter a number:", 10))
var nFactorial = 1 // will contain the value of n!
var factor = 1 // the current term by which we must multiply

while (factor <= n) {
      factor++
      nFactorial *= factor
}

alert(n + "! is " + nFactorial)
```

This script asks the user to enter a number. For this example, we assume the user enters a valid number (an integer between 1 and 12). `nFactorial` always holds the product of integers from 1 (or 2) to `factor`. Therefore, the loop is terminated after `nFactorial` is multiplied by `factor`, when `factor` is equal to the original number.

It is possible to create nested `while` loops. For example, you could change the script that printed a rectangle of asterisks so it uses `while` loops instead of `for` loops. You would need to initialize the counter variables before the loop statements, and increment it in the loops' bodies.

You can also use a `while` statement to create an infinite loop in the following fashion:

```
while (1)
      statement
```

or

```
while (true)
      statement
```

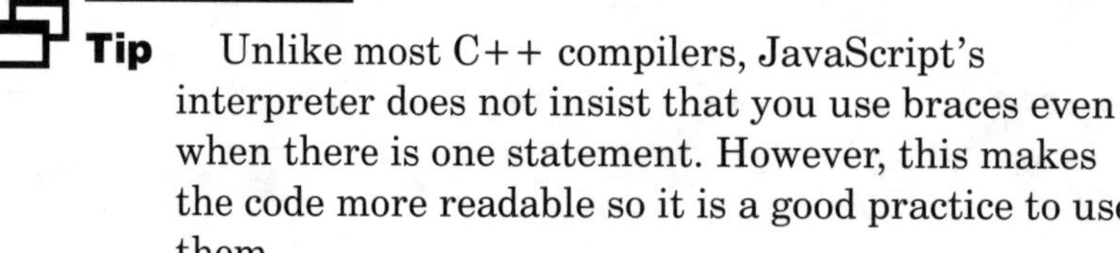

Tip Unlike most C++ compilers, JavaScript's interpreter does not insist that you use braces even when there is one statement. However, this makes the code more readable so it is a good practice to use them.

Although JavaScript does not feature an `until` loop, it is very simple to create one with a `while` statement:

```
while (!condition)
      statement
```

for...in Statement

```
for (variable in object)
     statement
```

So far we have dealt with general loops, typical to all programming languages. The `for...in` loop is quite different. It loops through the existing properties of a given object. It repeats a variable over all of the object's properties.

`variable` is the variable that you repeat over the properties. With each pass through the loop, *`variable`* is set to the current property. *`object`* is the object to which the statement refers. The looping variable is only set to properties of the specified object. Sounds a bit complicated? Take a look at the following script segment:

```
var result = "" // initialize output string

for (curProperty in document) {
     result += "document." + curProperty + "<BR>"
}

document.write(result)
```

The script prints the properties belonging to the `document` object:

```
document.length
document.elements
document.forms
document.links
.
.
.
```

The order in which they are printed depends on the way they are internally stored.

The following function accepts an object and its name. It then iterates over the object's properties and returns an HTML-ready string that lists the property names and their values.

```
function getProps(obj, objName) {
     var result = "" // initialize output string

     for (var i in obj) {
          result += objName + "." + i + " = " + obj[i] + "<BR>"
     }
     result += "<HR>" // add horizontal rule to output string
     return(result) // return output string
}
```

The problem with this function is that it cannot print the properties of a nested object. The remedy for this problem—a recursive function—is presented in Chapter 12, Building and Extending Objects.

This function is a very helpful tool, specifically for debugging scripts dealing with objects. The following statement shows how to invoke the `getProps()` function to list the properties of the built-in `Math` object.

```
document.write(getProps(Math, "Math"))
```

Because the function does not send direct output to the screen, you must use a `document.write()` statement to print the returned value. Notice that the arguments handed to the function in this case are similar: `Math` and `"Math"`. The first argument holds the object reference itself, and the second one holds the name of the object, which is a simple string. Once inside the function, the object is referenced as `obj`, so there is no way to extract its original name automatically.

The `getProps()` function implements the array notation to access properties. We use this notation because the property's name is not a literal but rather a data structure holding a string value. The dot syntax can only be used when the name is in the form of a literal. This rule also applies to methods. Consider the following expressions:

```
var a = "write"

document.write("Test 1 <BR>")
document.a("Test 2 <BR>") // error
document["write"]("Test 3 <BR>")
document[a]("Test 4 <BR>")
```

The second test generates an error, but the rest print the output as we expected, because the dot syntax accepts only literals as its specifications.

break Statement

```
break
```

Normally, a loop executes until the terminating condition is met, but you might want it to terminate earlier if it meets some other condition. The `break` statement does just that; it terminates the loop's execution. In C++, the `break` statement also terminates `switch` statements, but JavaScript does not support this statement yet.

The following script segment demonstrates the `break` statement:

```
for (var i = 0; i < 100; i++) {
    document.write(i + " ")
```

```
        if (i== 50) // additional terminating condition
            break // break out of the loop
}
```

The output of this loop is:

0 1 2 3 4 5 6 7 8 9 . . . 41 42 43 44 45 46 47 48 49 50

As you can see, the loop terminates when i is 50, not when i is equal to 100. That is, it terminates before the condition i < 100 evaluated to false. When i is equal to 50, the condition i == 50 returns true, and the break statement executes, causing the loop to terminate. The break statement lets you place additional terminating conditions at various locations in a loop's command block.

Note that the break statement terminates all loop statements.

Although goto statements are disallowed in modern programming, it is sometimes difficult to perform certain actions without the help of this statement. Unfortunately, JavaScript does not provide that tool, so you must find workarounds even for sophisticated structures. Consider the following control structure:

```
for (i = 1; i <= 10; i++) {
    for (j = 1; j <= 10; j++) {
        for (k = 1; k <= 10; k++) {
            for (l = 1; l <= 10; l++) {

            }
        }
    }
}

/* spot */
```

Suppose you want to terminate the execution of the entire control structure when l, the inner loop's counter, is equal to 5. The problem is that a break statement only terminates the loop in which you place it, not other loops that govern it. Using a goto statement in C++, you could have leaped directly to the desired *spot*. However, JavaScript does not support this statement, so you must find a simple work-around. The following script presents a remedy using an additional variable:

```
var continueLooping = true

for (i = 1; i <= 10; i++) {
    for (j = 1; j <= 10; j++) {
        for (k = 1; k <= 10; k++) {
            for (l = 1; l <= 10; l++) {
```

```
                    if (1 == 5) {
                         continueLooping = false
                         break
                    }
                    if (continueLooping == false) break
               }
               if (continueLooping == false) break
          }
          if (continueLooping == false) break
     }
     if (continueLooping == false) break
}
```

For each pass through the loop, `continueLooping` is evaluated. If it is `false`, the current loop is terminated. `continueLooping` is assigned `false` in the inner loop when the condition `1 == 5` is `true`, and then each loop terminates in turn. Note that it is extremely important to place the `if (continueLooping == false) break` statements immediately after the closing brace of the nested loop, so that the loop terminates when the nested loop terminates, and no other statements are executed in between.

The `break` statement in JavaScript is very important, because it is used to create alternatives to loop statements that do not exist in JavaScript. An important loop type in C++ and Perl is `do…while`. It executes a statement as long as the condition is `true`. Unlike the regular `while` loop, the condition is evaluated at the end of the loop, so the loop executes once without having tested prior to that. However, JavaScript does not feature such a loop. Once again, it will probably be implemented in a future release of the language. For now, you must come up with a simple alternative using the existing statements. Take a look at the following structure:

```
while (1) {
     statements
     if (condition)
          break
}
```

Notice that the preceding script segment is equivalent to the `repeat…until` structure in Pascal, and the `do…until` in Perl, but it doesn't match the `do…while` loop in C++ and Perl. You just have to negate the condition in the following form:

```
while (1) {
     statements
     if (!condition)
          break
}
```

continue Statement

```
continue
```

The `continue` keyword stops the current iteration of a loop, and continues the execution at the top of the loop. The loop continues to execute until the terminating condition is achieved. The "top" of the loop is:

- The *update* expression in `for` loops, such as `++i`
- The *condition* expression in `while` loops

Here is a simple example for the usage of the `continue` statement:

```
var sum = 0 // will hold the sum of the odd numbers

for (var i = 1; i <= 10; ++i) {
     if (i % 2 == 0) // 1: if i is even
          continue  // 2: go to the top of the loop
     sum += i // 3: add i to sum (i is always odd!)
}
```

This example adds up every odd integer from 1 to 10. The easiest way to do that is to increase the counter variable by 2 after each pass through the loop, but we wanted to feature the `continue` statement.

The loop in the preceding script segment is quite simple. It executes while the value of `i` is less than or equal to `10`. Therefore, the loop executes 10 times, once for each integer value of `i`. The first line checks if `i` is an even number, using a simple modulo operation. If the number is even (that is, `i % 2` evaluates to `0`), the expression `i % 2 == 0` evaluates to `true`. In that case, the `continue` statement on the second line is executed, causing the loop to start from the top, at the update expression. The following diagram illustrates the flow of the loop:

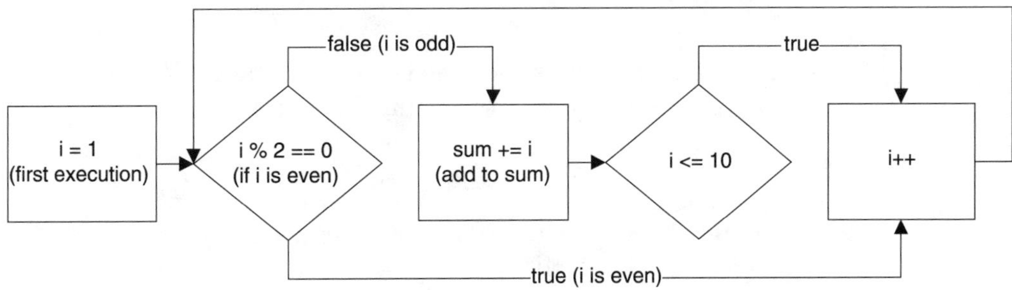

Figure 8-6. The flow of the preceding script segment.

Here is another example using the continue statement:

```
for (i  = 1; i <= 10; ++i) {
     if (i == 5)
          continue
     document.write(i + " ")
}
```

The output is:

```
1 2 3 4 6 7 8 9 10
```

Notice that the 5 is missing, because when i is equal to 5 the loop is sent to the beginning, incrementing i to 6. The continue statement is located before the document.write() statement, so the document.write() method is never invoked when i is 5.

with Statement

```
with (object)
     statement
```

Writing formal addresses to access properties or invoke methods of the same object is often annoying. The with statement establishes a default object for a set of statements. Within the specified set of statements, any property references that do not specify an object are assumed to be governed by the default object defined by the with statement. The same applies to methods belonging to that object.

The with statement is useful only when referring to several properties and methods of the same object, so it should always be followed by a command block:

```
with (object) {
     statements
}
```

We haven't discussed user-defined objects, so take a look at an example where the default object is a built-in one:

```
with (document) {
     write("Notice that the document object is default")
     write("<BR>")
     write("The current background color is " + bgColor)
     // bgColor is normally document.bgColor
}
```

The output is:

```
Notice that the document object is default
The current background color is #c0c0c0
```

You will find this statement useful after learning about built-in and user-defined objects. For now, just remember what it does, and use it with your existing vocabulary if you wish.

You may recall from the beginning of the chapter that the default object throughout the script is the `window` object. You can invoke its methods anywhere without literally specifying that they belong to the current `window` object. For example:

```
alert("STOP")
confirm("OK to proceed?")
prompt("How many cookies would you like?", 12)
```

An alternative syntax specifies the `window` object as in `window.alert("STOP")`. Generally speaking, you can refer to any script as if it were placed in a `with` statement's command block, where the argument specifying the default object is `window`.

```
<SCRIPT LANGUAGE="JavaScript">
<!-- hide code

with (window) {

}

// end hiding code -->
</SCRIPT>
```

You can also implement nested `with` statements. In such cases, several default objects exist simultaneously. The *scope* (where each one exists) is very simple. Inside a command block associated with a `with` statement, you can refer to the properties and methods of the default *`object`*, without specifying their belonging. The following example demonstrates the scope concept:

```
with (object1) {

    // object1 -- default

    with (object2) {

        // object1, object2 -- default

    }

    // object1 -- default
```

```
        with (object3) {

            // object1, object3 -- default

            with (object4) {

                // object1, object3, object4 -- default

            }

            // object1, object3 -- default

        }

        // object1 -- default

    }

    // no default objects (except window)
```

Summary

In this chapter you have learned how to take advantage of the computer's capacity for repetition. At first, we looked at the most simple ways to interact with the user, via JavaScript methods that generate dialog boxes. You should now be familiar with the `if-else` structure, as well as the basic looping statements. We discussed the `continue` and `break` statements that enable flexible loops. By now, you should also know how to use the `for…in` loop and the `with` statement. These are basic object-oriented programming tools.

In addition to all standard control structures in JavaScript, we discussed some statements that are implemented in C++ and Perl but are not supported by JavaScript yet.

Chapter 9

Functions and Variable Scope

Variable Scope and Storage Class

All JavaScript variables have two attributes:

- *Scope*
- *Storage class*

JavaScript implements these characteristics slightly differently from other programming languages.

The scope of a variable describes the area of the script where the variable is valid. You can refer to the variable only in this area—it does not exist elsewhere. The scope of a *global variable* is the entire script. You can access it anywhere between the <SCRIPT> and </SCRIPT> tags and other scripts that are executed after the variable definition (including preceding event handler scripts). In JavaScript, you can declare global variables with or without the keyword `var`. It does not affect the scope of the variable at all.

A *local variable* is declared in a function. It can only be referenced by statements inside that function. Therefore, a global variable may have the same name as a given local variable. In the scope of a local variable (the function where it is defined), only the local variable exists. Outside that function, only the global one exists. A local variable must be declared inside a function using the keyword var. If omitted, the variable is assumed global. The following script segments show how a variable's scope influences various results:

```
// Script 1
function test() {
    age = 43
}

age = 11
```

```
test()
document.write(age + "<BR>")
```

```
// Script 2
function test() {
     var age = 43
}

age = 11
test()
document.write(age + "<BR>")
```

The only difference between these scripts is the statement inside the function. In the second script segment, we use `var` to define the variable `age`, whereas in the first statement, we simply state the desired variable name.

The output of the first script is:

```
43
```

and the output of the second script is:

```
11
```

Take another look at the first script and try following the execution thread. The value 11 is assigned to the global variable `age` and the function is invoked. Notice that the word `var` is not used inside the function. Therefore, the variable `age` in the function is assumed global, and the value 43 is assigned to the global `age`. Therefore, the result is 43.

In the second script, we assign the value 11 to the variable `age`, and then call the function. The `var` word means that the variable `age`, which is defined inside the function, is local. It does not exist beyond the function, so the value of the global variable `age` (the one defined before the function call) is not modified by the assignment statement inside the function. The last statement of the script prints the value of the global variable `age`, because it is the only variable named `age` in that scope. Therefore, the script's output is 11—the global variable's initial value.

Once declared with the `var` keyword, additional statements referring to the variable should not issue that prefix. Here is the previous script with an additional statement inside the function:

```
// Script 2 (additional statement in function)
function test() {
     var age = 43
```

```
        age = 58
}

age = 11
test()
document.write(age + "<BR>")
```

Once again, the output of the script is 11. The variable inside the function is declared with the keyword var. From that point on, the scope of the variable is only the function test(). It does not exist outside the boundaries of that function, so the script's output is the value of the global variable named age, not the local one.

Note that the statement

```
age = 11
```

in the previous script segments is equivalent to

```
var age = 11
```

because the var keyword is optional for global variables.

Here's another script segment that deals with various scopes:

```
function test() {
        age = 5
}

test()
document.write(age + "<BR>")
```

The script's output is 5, because the variable age is declared inside the function as a global one (without var), so its scope is the entire script. The next script generates quite an unexpected output:

```
function test() {
        var age = 5
}

test()
document.write(age + "<BR>")
```

Rather than generating an output, this script generates an error (see Figure 9-1) because age is a local variable, whereas the printing statement is not located in its scope.

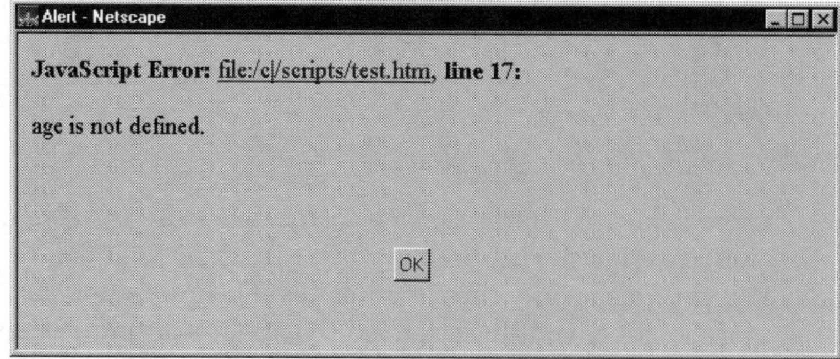
Alert - Netscape
JavaScript Error: file:/c|/scripts/test.htm, line 17:
age is not defined.
OK

Figure 9-1. *An error dialog box that appears when referring to a variable that does not exist (IE shows a similar message).*

The variable's storage class may be either *permanent* or *temporary*. You cannot modify this attribute directly, the way you can declare the variable as `static` in other languages such as C++. The storage class of a variable in JavaScript depends only on its scope. Local variables are temporary, while global variables are permanent. Permanent variables exist throughout the script and even in other scripts. Even after a script has terminated, the global variable remains, and is only discarded when the page unloads. Temporary variables are allocated on the *stack* (a section of memory) when a function is called. The space used by a function's local (temporary) variable is returned to the stack at the end of the function execution. After a local variable "dies," it leaves free memory space for other variables and objects to come.

Avoid declaring large local data structures such as arrays (discussed in the following chapters). If you try to allocate too many temporary variables or extremely large ones, you are likely to receive an error (usually called *stack overflow*). For the same reason, avoid passing large data structures over to a function. It is better to use global variables for such tasks.

Function parameters are identical to local variables. They exist only inside the function, and do not affect any variable outside it. You can refer to function parameters as if they were variables that you declared at the beginning of the function and initialized them with appropriate values. The following script segment demonstrates this:

```
function test(age) {
     age = 5
     document.write(age + "<BR>")
}
test(6)
```

The printed value is 5, because it is assigned to the variable `age` (which is the function's parameter).

JavaScript lacks a few features found in other languages:

- A function's parameter cannot behave as a global variable.
- Nested functions, such as those in Pascal, are not supported. You cannot declare a function inside another one.

Take a look at the following script:

```
/* 1  */  function goFirst(pineapple) {
/* 2  */       var banana = 3
/* 3  */       pineapple = 6
/* 4  */       apple = 4
/* 5  */       goSecond()
/* 6  */       var peach = goThird()
/* 7  */       document.write(apple + "<BR>")
/* 8  */  }

/* 9  */  function goSecond() {
/* 10 */       var apple = 2
/* 11 */       document.write(apple + "<BR>")
/* 12 */  }

/* 13 */  function goThird() {
/* 14 */         var peach = apple
/* 15 */         document.write(peach + "<BR>")
/* 16 */         return peach
/* 17 */  }

/* 18 */  var pineapple = 8
/* 19 */  goFirst(5)
/* 20 */  document.write("apple = " + apple)
/* 21 */  document.write(", pineapple = " + pineapple)
```

As you can see, it is impossible to construct scripts without a deep understanding of variable scopes and storage classes.

The output of the preceding script is:

```
2
4
4
apple = 4, pineapple = 8
```

Table 9-1 keeps track of the variables' values throughout the course of the script execution.

Table 9-1. A classic table to keep track of variable values.

Line number	pineapple	apple	banana	peach
18	8 (g)	-	-	-
1	8 (g) 5 (goFirst)	-	-	-
2	8 (g) 5 (goFirst)	-	3 (goFirst)	-
3	8 (g) 6 (goFirst)	-	3 (goFirst)	-
4	8 (g) 6 (goFirst)	4 (g)	3 (goFirst)	-
10	8 (g) 6 (goFirst)	4 (g) 2 (goSecond)	3 (goFirst)	-
14	8 (g) 6 (goFirst)	4 (g)	3 (goFirst)	4 (goThird)
6	8 (g) 6 (goFirst)	4 (g)	3 (goFirst)	4 (goFirst)
20	8 (g)	4 (g)	-	-

(g) is a shorthand for global, (*functionName*) is a shorthand for local in the function named *functionName*.

This technique is very useful because JavaScript does not have a decent debugger. Make sure you understand every value in the table. If you don't have much programming background, Table 9-1 might seem confusing. However, all you must do to use the table is locate the line where the printing statements are placed and extract the variables' values from the table. For example, suppose you want to find what the statement on Line 11 prints. The last line expressed in the table before Line 11 is Line 10. We are trying to find out what the value of apple is, so you should first check to see if there is a local variable with the corresponding name, because a local variable rules if it exists. As you can see, the value of the local variable apple is 2. Therefore, JavaScript prints that value on Line 11, followed by a line break.

The following script's output is fairly surprising:

```
var num = 4

function funct1() {
     alert(num)
     var num = 2
}

funct1()
```

The output of this script in Netscape Navigator and MS Internet Explorer is illustrated in Figure 9-2 (NN) and Figure 9-3 (MSIE).

Figure 9-2. An alert dialog box displaying the value of a variable that does not exist (Netscape Navigator).

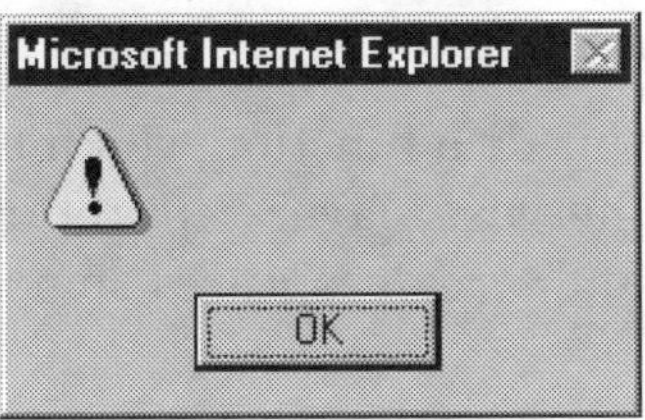

Figure 9-3. An alert dialog box displaying the value of a variable that does not exist (Microsoft Internet Explorer).

The term "undefined" means that a variable does not have a value at the desired point, although it has previously been declared. Generally speaking, JavaScript scans the entire script before any execution begins. During this scan, also called *parsing*, JavaScript evaluates each line of code, testing it for basic syntax errors. It also determines the scope of each variable, regardless of whether it is in a function or not. If it encounters a variable declaration with the keyword `var`, that variable is considered local, even if a global variable with the same name exists. A variable's scope can be either the entire script or just one function. In the preceding script segment, a global variable `num` is declared by initializing it to `4`. The function consists of one local variable declaration. Note that the variable `num` inside the function has no connection to the global variable `num`. The function is executed, as usual, from top to bottom. The first statement instructs JavaScript to display the value of `num`, the local variable inside the function. JavaScript already knows that the local variable is declared inside the function, so it does not generate an error. However, at that point, the variable does not retain any value, so it is undefined.

The following definitions of a function are equivalent:

```
// #1
function functionName {
     [JavaScript statements...]
     var varName = initialValue
     [JavaScript statements...]
}
```

```
// #2
function functionName {
     var varName
     [JavaScript statements...]
     varName = initialValue
     [JavaScript statements...]
}
```

Some scripters find it easier to use the second form. Each form has its own advantages and disadvantages—choose the one most convenient for you. In this book, we use the first syntax, because we prefer to use the `var` keyword in an assignment statement.

If you declare global variables inside a function, you must assign an initial value to the variable; otherwise, JavaScript returns an error. The following script segment and screen captures demonstrate this fact:

```
function foo() {
     // local variable declarations
     var a // without initialization
     var b = 0 // with initialization

     // global variable declarations
     c // without initialization -- error!
     d = 0 // with initialization
}

foo()
```

Alert - Netscape
JavaScript Error: file:/c|/scripts/test.htm, line 19:
c is not defined.
OK

***Figure 9-4.** An error message appears when you attempt to declare a global variable inside a function without initializing it (Netscape Navigator).*

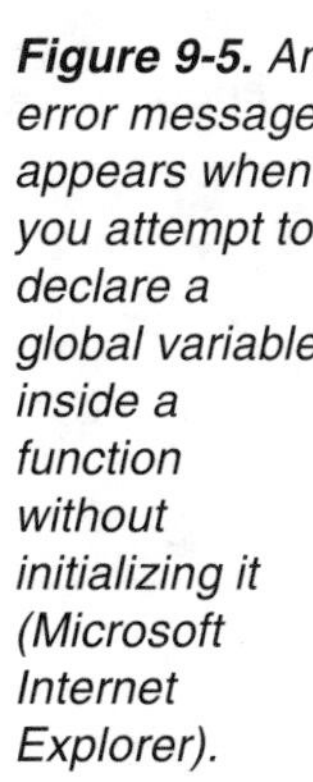

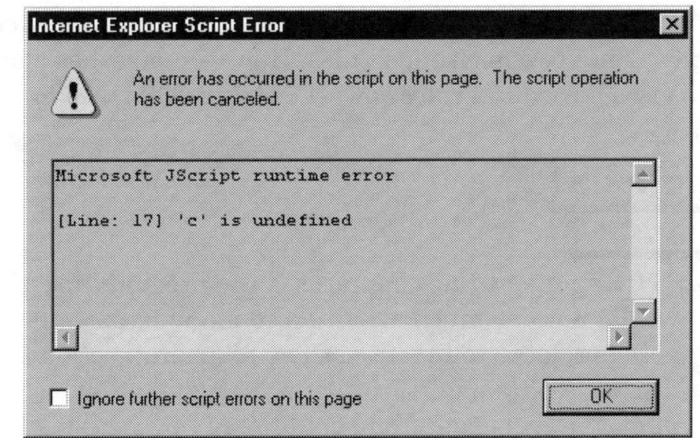

Figure 9-5. *An error message appears when you attempt to declare a global variable inside a function without initializing it (Microsoft Internet Explorer).*

Notice that the variable does not hold an undefined value as it would if the declaration used the `var` keyword—it causes an error instead.

The `var` keyword is used to "officially" declare variables. JavaScript remembers only the scope of variables that are declared in that fashion. It recognizes other variables during the execution of the script, and automatically refers to them as global variables. Although it does not really matter whether or not you use `var` to declare global variables in the main script, it might affect the result of the script under certain circumstances. If you do not use `var` and, when the variable is still undefined, you use it in a value-requiring statement, an error will occur. But this is an easy problem because you get a message about it. The problem with the `var` declaration is that not all statements that require a variable with a meaningful value use the `undefined` string when the variable has no value. The basic `document.write()` statement does not do so on Windows 3.1x, for example. If you try to print the value of an undefined variable with `document.write()` or `document.writeln()` using Netscape Navigator for Windows 3.1x, nothing is printed. It then becomes a real challenge to detect and correct a problem caused by an undefined variable. Note, also, that this bug does not exist on all versions of Netscape Navigator. Take a look at the following HTML script definition:

```
<SCRIPT>
<!--

a = "<HR>"
document.write(a + b + a)
var b

// -->
</SCRIPT>
```

Under Netscape Navigator for Windows 3.1x this immediate script simply prints two horizontal rules. However, on other platforms, it prints two horizontal rules with the string `undefined` in between.

What are Functions?

Note Throughout this chapter and the previous ones, we did not pay much attention to many important details related to functions. The following section discusses parameters, return values, and other important concepts. You should read this section, even if you feel comfortable with functions. A complete understanding of functions will be necessary later when we discuss objects and methods.

Functions group a sequence of statements to perform a specific task or a function. Functions, as opposed to methods, do not belong to an object that encapsulates them with related data. JavaScript features many built-in functions which are presented later in the book. Such functions are predefined.

Defining Functions and Calling Them

We have spoken much about defining functions. The general syntax of a function definition is

```
function functionName([parameters]) {
     statements
}
```

and the form of a function call is

```
functionName(arguments)
```

Function Parameters

Sometimes you want to create a function that accepts values when it is invoked. The function should then be able to use these values to perform a specific task. When you define a function, you should specify the names by which you refer to the custom values handed off to the function from outside. These names must follow the same rules that apply to identifiers in the language.

Parameters act like local variables, so they exist only inside the function where they are defined. Therefore, a parameter may use the same name as a global variable or a local variable in a different function. You can manipulate and modify the value of a parameter as if it were a common variable. There is no need to explicitly declare a parameter inside the function's body as you would with a regular variable.

JavaScript is loosely typed, so you do not specify the data type of the arguments as in C++, Java, Pascal, and other strictly typed programming languages. Both variables and literals can be passed to a function. All parameters in a function definition header should be delimited by the low-precedence comma operator (,). Here is a simple JavaScript function with two parameters:

```
function printName(name, ruleWidth) {
     document.write("<CENTER><H1>" + name + "</H1></CENTER>")
     document.write("<HR WIDTH=" + ruleWidth + "%>")
}
```

You can call this function with a simple function call, such as:

```
printName(prompt("Enter your name:", "John Doe"), 60)
```

Note *Arguments* are the specific values you assign to *parameters*. These terms are sometimes considered exchangeable, even by advanced programmers. It is sometimes difficult to distinguish between them, so you might disagree with some of the terms in this chapter.

Using the Argument Array

JavaScript supports functions that accept a variable number of arguments. The first argument is `functionName.arguments[0]`, the second one is `functionName.arguments[1]`, the third one is `functionName.arguments[2]`, and so on. The number of arguments handed to the function is stored in the `length` property of the `arguments` object; that is:

functionName`.arguments.length`. The following script demonstrates this concept:

```
function calc() {
    document.write("The first argument is ",
        calc.arguments[0], "<BR>")
    document.write("The fourth argument is ",
        calc.arguments[3], "<BR>")
    document.write("There are ", calc.arguments.length,
        " arguments<BR>")
}

var company = "Netscape"
calc(2, 999, "internet", company, 0.0)
```

The script's output is:

```
The first argument is 2
The fourth argument is Netscape
There are 5 arguments
```

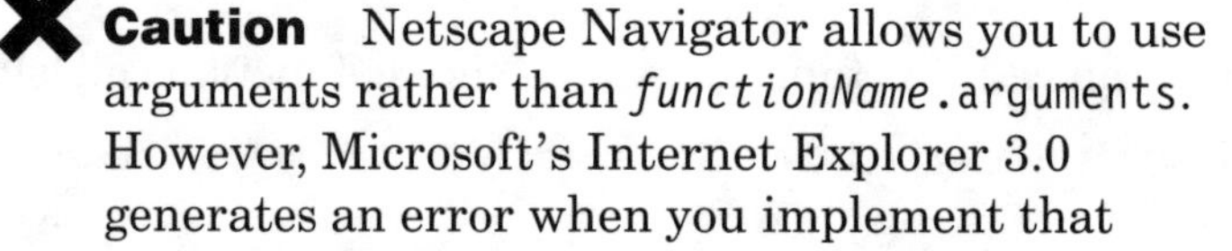

Caution Netscape Navigator allows you to use `arguments` rather than *functionName*`.arguments`. However, Microsoft's Internet Explorer 3.0 generates an error when you implement that shortcut. If you want to be on the safe side, you can use the following statement at the beginning of the function:

```
var args = functionName.arguments
```

You can then use `args` in the regular way (`args[0]`, `args.length`, etc.).

The ability to refer to the arguments passed to the function during the last call of the function often trips up JavaScript scripters. For example, consider the following script:

```
function func() {
  document.write(func.arguments[0] + "<BR>")
}

func("a")
func("b")
func()
func("c")
```

The output of this script is:

```
a
b
b (!)
c
```

The only surprising line is the third one. The argument printed is the one passed to the function during the previous call. The first argument of the current call cannot be printed because there is no such argument. At times, you will receive unexpected results from the `func.arguments.length` property, as well as from the elements of the array itself. See Chapter 13, Arrays, for a possible remedy.

Note, also, that you may only refer to the `arguments` array from within the function.

The scope of the `arguments` object's properties is the current function, so it can only be used inside a function. You can use loop statements to print a list of arguments handed to a function:

```
function createList() {
     var result = ""
     for (var i = 0; i < createList.arguments.length; ++i) {
          result += createList.arguments[i] + "\r"
     }
     alert(result)
}
```

Here is a simple function call:

```
createList("S", "H", "I", "R", "A", "N")
```

When invoked with the preceding statement, the function generates the following dialog box:

Figure 9-6. *An alert dialog box—each line is a distinct argument handed to the function.*

Here is a useful function that creates special alert boxes:

```
<HTML>
<HEAD>
<TITLE>Using the arguments object</TITLE>
<SCRIPT LANGUAGE="JavaScript">
<!-- hide content from old browsers

function specialAlert(verticalLine) {

     // creates an alert box with a short message
     // on the left-hand side.

     var verLength = verticalLine.length // length of string
     var horLines = specialAlert.arguments.length - 1 // total horizontal lines
     var maxLength = (verLength + 1 >= horLines) ? verLength + 1 : horLines
     // assigns the greater value to maxLength
     var text = "\r\r"
     text += "*************************\r"

     for (i = 0; i < maxLength; i++) {
          if (i < verLength)
               text += "**\t" + verticalLine.charAt(i) + "\t**\t"
          else
               if (i == verLength)
                    text += "*************************"
               else
                    text += "\t"
          if (i < horLines)
               text += specialAlert.arguments[i + 1] // exclude first argument
          text += "\r"
     }

     alert(text)

}

specialAlert("Tomer",
             "Tomer Shiran co-authored this JavaScript book.",
             "He worked hard writing the examples.")

// end hiding content from old browsers -->
</SCRIPT>
</HEAD>
<BODY>
</BODY>
</HTML>
```

Example 9-1 (ex9-1.htm). *A simple function that creates uniquely formatted alert boxes.*

Here is the output of Example 9-1:

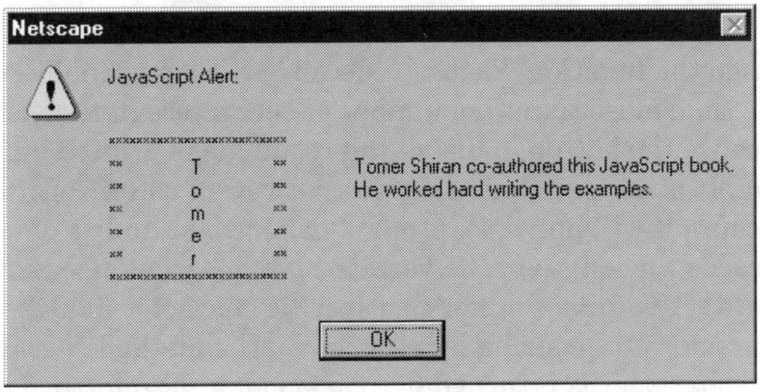

Figure 9-7. A uniquely designed alert box.

First of all, you should be aware that the first argument handed to the function is the string that is displayed vertically, whereas each additional argument represents a single horizontal line in the final layout.

The first portion of the function assigns the number of characters in the vertical line to the variable `verLength`. The `length` property is discussed later in the book. The number of horizontal lines is then assigned to `horLines`. This value is equal to the number of arguments minus 1, because the first argument (vertical line's string) is excluded. The greater of these two values (`verLength` and `horLines`) is assigned to `max`. The variable `text`, that holds the entire string displayed in the alert box, is initialized with two carriage return characters. After a line of asterisks followed by a carriage return is assigned to the variable `text`, the loop begins. The loop is executed `max` times. During each iteration, the following statements are executed:

- If the vertical string is not finished, the next character is printed, with a tab character and two asterisks on both sides. If the vertical string has finished during the previous execution of the loop, the expression

  ```
  i == verLength
  ```

  evaluates to true, and the bottom row of asterisks is assigned to the variable text.

- If additional horizontal lines remain, they are printed following the current row of the rectangle.

After the loop terminates, all that is left is to display the final string in an alert box.

Notice the use of the expression

```
verLength + 1
```

inside the function. We use it because the loop should execute at least one time more than the number of characters in the vertical string, because the bottom panel of the rectangle is printed during that execution. It is not possible to assign that row of asterisks after the loop, because it will not work properly when the number of horizontal lines exceeds the length of the vertical string. Also notice that we use the `charAt()` method to refer to a specific character in a string. The first character of the string is returned by the method `charAt(0)`, the second character is returned by `charAt(1)`, and so forth. The `length` property returns the number of characters in the string. String objects, their methods, and properties are discussed in Chapter 16, Handling Strings.

Creating Functions with Default Arguments

JavaScript does not support functions with default arguments. In C++, these are the values supplied to the parameters in a function's prototype. Calling the following function at the beginning of a function is a simple workaround you can use in JavaScript:

```
function checkDefault(parameter, defaultValue) {
     if (typeof parameter == "undefined")
          return defaultValue
     /* else */
          return parameter
}
```

The appropriate call to this function is:

```
parameterName = checkDefault(parameterName, defaultValue)
```

The parameter is assigned its default value only if the function is called without specifying the required argument. The following function uses this technique to print a row of a given character with an asterisk as the default character, and 30 characters as the default length:

```
function checkDefault(parameter, defaultValue) {
     if (typeof parameter == "undefined")
          return defaultValue
     /* else */
          return parameter
}

function drawLine(character, numOfChars) {
```

```
        character = checkDefault(character, "*")
        numOfChars = checkDefault(numOfChars, 30)
        for (var i = 0; i < numOfChars; i++) {
            document.write(character)
        }
}
```

Here are some function calls and their corresponding output:

```
drawLine() // prints 30 asterisks
```

```
******************************
```

```
drawLine("=") // prints 30 equal signs
```

```
==============================
```

```
drawLine("-", 10) // prints 10 dashes
```

```
----------
```

It is also possible to specify the second argument without providing the first, using an undefined variable (just declare it before with `var`, without initializing it).

Caution Be aware that the preceding `checkDefault()` function is not compatible with Netscape Navigator 2.0x or Microsoft Internet Explorer 3.0x, because they do not support the `typeof` operator. Use the `arguments` array to simulate C++'s default arguments feature. The previous `drawLine()` function would then be as follows:

```
function drawLine(character, numOfChars) {
  args = drawLine.arguments
  if (args.length < 1)
        character = "*"
  if (args.length < 2)
        numOfChars = 30

  for (var i = 0; i < numOfChars; i++) {
        document.write(character)
  }
}
```

If the function receives no arguments, the value of `character` is set to the default "*". If the function received one argument or less, the parameter numOfChars defaults to 30. Because this function uses the arguments array, named parameters are not necessary—you can use the array instead as in the following function definition:

```
function drawLine() {
  args = drawLine.arguments
  if (args.length < 1)
        args[0] = "*"
  if (args.length < 2)
        args[1] = 30

  for (var i = 0; i < args[1]; i++) {
        document.write(args[0])
  }
}
```

Returning a Value

A function can return a value, so it is possible to use a function call as a valid JavaScript value. Use this feature to create general functions for usage by other scripts. For example, you can use a function that accepts a number in one base and returns it in a different representation. This function can be used in creating a base-conversion table, a dialog box, or additional calculations.

Use the following syntax to return a value from within a function:

```
return value
```

The return statement returns a value and terminates the function, similarly to the way break terminates a loop. Take a look at the following function:

```
function sum(op1, op2) {
    return op1 + op2
}

var answer = sum(3, 5)
alert(answer)
```

The value returned by the function is the sum of its arguments. As you can see, the function evaluates to a value. A function may only return one value—either a variable, a literal, or any other valid data structure.

A function with a return value can also generate an output. When you use the function in an expression, it automatically runs, executing all statements until it returns a value that is used in the expression. The preceding function can also display the sum of its arguments inside the function itself, provided that the `alert()` statement precedes the `return` statement (which terminates the function):

```
function sum(op1, op2) {
     var result = op1 + op2
     alert(result)
     return result
}

var answer = sum(3, 5)
```

Be sure that the `return` statement is placed after the statements that should be executed, because it terminates the function, and no additional statements of the function are executed afterwards.

You can use nested `if` constructions without `else` statements, provided that each `if` statement calls a `return` statement, if the condition is `true`. Eliminating the `else` statements does not affect the efficiency of the function, because the function terminates immediately after a true condition is met. The following function converts hexadecimal digits (not numbers) to their equivalent decimal values:

```
function getValue(dig) {
     if (dig == "A") return 10
     if (dig == "B") return 11
     if (dig == "C") return 12
     if (dig == "D") return 13
     if (dig == "E") return 14
     if (dig == "F") return 15
     return dig
     // the return statement terminates the function,
     // so there is no need for else statements
}
```

If the digit is between 0 and 9, none of the conditions evaluate to `true`, so the function returns the same digit it accepts:

```
return dig
```

Recursion

A *recursive* function is usually one that calls itself. It is similar to a loop with or without a terminating condition. Some programming functions lend themselves to recursive algorithms, such as the factorial one. The factorial is a classic recursive algorithm, because it is very obvious. A simple mathematical definition of the factorial operation is:

```
fact(0) = 1
fact(n) = n * fact(n-1)
```

Factorial is commonly represented by the exclamation mark (!).

With this algorithm, let's calculate 3!:

1. `fact(3) = 3 * fact(2)`
2. `fact(2) = 2 * fact(1)`
3. `fact(1) = 1 * fact(0)`
4. `fact(0) = 1`

As you can see, the algorithm works its way down from the given number to zero, so when it gets to `fact(0)` it must work its way back up to the numbers:

We know that `fact(0) = 1`.

```
fact(1) = 1 * fact(0) = 1 * 1 = 1
fact(2) = 2 * fact(1) = 2 * 1 = 2
fact(3) = 3 * fact(2) = 3 * 2 = 6
```

We have reached the desired answer using a recursive algorithm. In JavaScript this is:

```
function fact(num) {
    if (num == 0)
        return 1
    /* else */
        return num * fact(num - 1)
}
```

You can call the function in the following way:

```
var fiveFactorial = fact(5) // 120
```

Notice that the `else` statement is commented because it is not necessary.

The `fact()` function satisfies two rules. First, it has an ending point. Second, it simplifies the problem because `fact(num - 1)` is simpler than `fact(num)`. Recursive functions should always follow these two rules.

Recursive functions have a few advantages:

- Invariably, recursive functions are clearer, simpler, shorter, and easier to understand than their nonrecursive counterparts.
- The program directly reflects the abstract solution strategy (algorithm). The recursive factorial function, for example, uses the common mathematical strategy to solve the problem.

At first, it may seem that recursive functions are more difficult, but they become easier with practice.

Recursion can also be used to compute a value in the Fibonacci sequence (1, 1, 2, 3, 5, 8, 13, ...). The basic algorithm is:

```
getVal(1) = 1
getVal(2) = 1
getVal(place) = getVal(place – 1) + getVal(place – 2)
```

Here is a JavaScript function to calculate the value of the sequence in the specified place:

```
function getVal(place) {
     if (place == 1 || place == 2)
          return 1
     return getVal(place – 1) + getVal(place – 2)
}
```

A call to this function could be:

```
var fibValue7 = getVal(7) // fibValue7 = 13
```

1,	1,	2,	3,	5,	8,	13,	21,	34,	...
1,	2,	3,	4,	5,	6,	7,	8,	9,	...

Note: The bottom row specifies the place; the top row specifies the Fibonacci value at that space.

Notice that we once again left out the unnecessary `else` statement.

Some programmers prefer not to use complex expressions and values returned by other functions with the `return` statement. Instead, they assign those values to variables and then return them:

```
function getVal(place) {
     if (place == 1 || place == 2)
          return 1
     var s1 = getVal(place – 2)
```

```
        var s2 = getVal(place - 1)
        return s1 + s2
}
```

Tracing Values in Recursive Functions

Sophisticated recursion algorithms are often difficult to follow. Many values change, some in the way you expect, while others make surprising "moves." JavaScript still does not have a decent debugger to help us with that, so we must develop our own tools, using output statements to evaluate expressions and variables. With a few additional statements, it is possible to display the values of the variables and parameters throughout the recursive execution. Here is the `getVal()` function with a few additions to track values during the recursion:

```
text = "place\t\ts1\t\ts2\t\tval\r"
text += "=================================================\r"

function getVal(place) {
        if (place == 1 || place == 2)
                return 1
        var s1 = getVal(place - 2)
        var s2 = getVal(place - 1)
        text += place + "\t ||  \t" + s1 + "\t  ||  \t"
        text += s2 + "\t  ||  \t" + (s1 + s2) + "\r"
        return s1 + s2
}

getVal(6)

alert(text)
```

Note that it is legal not to use the value returned by a function (`getVal(6)` in this case). In the preceding script segment a global variable (`text`) is used to store the formatted tracing of the execution course. A self-formatted table is created and displayed in an alert box after the execution terminates. The following values are put in each row of the table:

- The value of the parameter (`place`) in the current function call. The assignment to text is done at the end of the function (after the recursive calls to the function), so the first function in the table is the last to be called.
- The values of `s1`, `s2`, and their sum

The exact output of the preceding script segment (the argument handed over to the function is `6`) is:

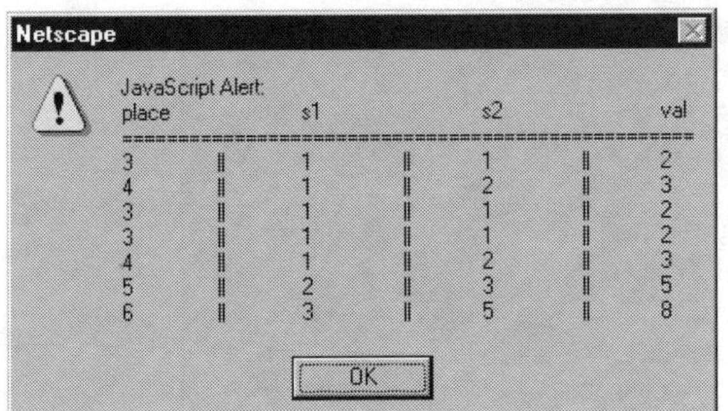

Figure 9-8. A formatted table that helps a scripter trace variables throughout a recursive execution.

From here it is effortless to track all the function calls and the values of the variables during the recursion.

Use recursive algorithms carefully. Do not create functions that call themselves hundreds of times if there is a simple nonrecursive alternative. If you doubt this caution, try crashing your browser or computer by calculating the 100th value of the Fibonacci sequence!

Variables and Recursive Functions

You probably noticed the use of local variables in the previous Fibonacci recursive function. You should regularly use local variables in recursive functions. Make this a habit so you never forget, because it is laborious to detect variable scope-related problems, even when you know the function does not work correctly. This is where variable tracing tables come in handy. Here is the preceding script with the keyword `var` absent:

```
text = "place\t\ts1\t\ts2\t\tval\r"
text += "==================================================\r"

function getVal(place) {
     if (place == 1 || place == 2)
          return 1
     s1 = getVal(place - 2)
     s2 = getVal(place - 1)
     text += place + "\t ||  \t" + s1 + "\t  ||  \t"
     text += s2 + "\t  ||  \t" + (s1 + s2) + "\r"
     return s1 + s2
}

getVal(6)

alert(text)
```

As you could expect, the table's content differs:

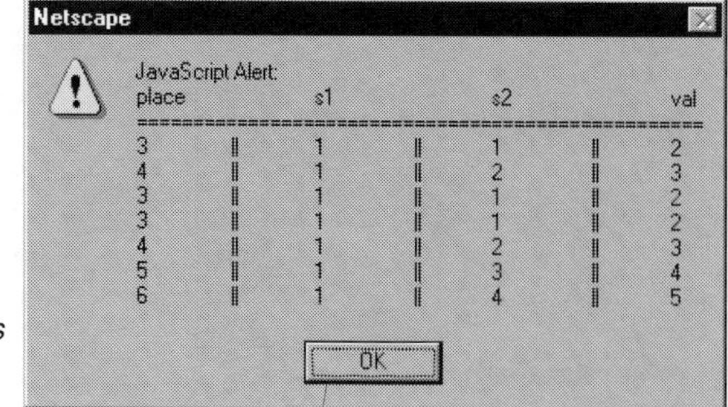

Figure 9-9. *A table that helps the scripter detect variable's scope-related problems.*

An obvious error appears on the sixth line, when the function is called with the value 5. The function returns 4 instead of 5. The seventh line (where `place` is 6) also reflects an error. The function should return 8, not 5. The first mistake encountered appears to be when the function is invoked with the argument 5. The problem there is the variable `s1`, because it holds an incorrect value. The recursive algorithm seems to be fine, so the only possible mistake is with the variables. The exact problem is that the variables are global, not local.

Focus on the call to the function, with the value 5. That function then calls itself with the value 3, and after a few more recursive calls, the correct value is returned to `s1`. Remember that this variable is global. The first function execution (with 5) now calls itself again, this time with the value 4. A few more recursive calls take place, during which the values of `s1` and `s2` are modified. `s1`, like `s2`, is global, so its value is not the same value that was assigned to it in the initial execution of the function (with the argument 5). It holds a value assigned to it by a deeper function call, which is obviously incorrect for the current function. The wrong value of `s1` at this point influences the result. The same problem applies to all function calls with a value greater than 4.

If you do not understand the cause of the problem, use the following script:

```
var text = ""

function getVal(place) {
     if (place == 1 || place == 2)
          return 1
     s1 = getVal(place - 2)

     var tempS1 = s1 // assign correct s1 value to tempS1

     s2 = getVal(place - 1)
```

```
// check if s1 was modified by the preceding statement
     if (tempS1 != s1) {
          text += ">>>\tThere appears to be an error in the "
          text += "current execution of the function (place = "
          text += place + ") --\rthe value of s1 has unexpectedly"
          text += " been modified (" + tempS1 + " => " + s1 + ")\r"
     }


     return s1 + s2
}

getVal(6)

alert(text)
```


The following message explains it all:

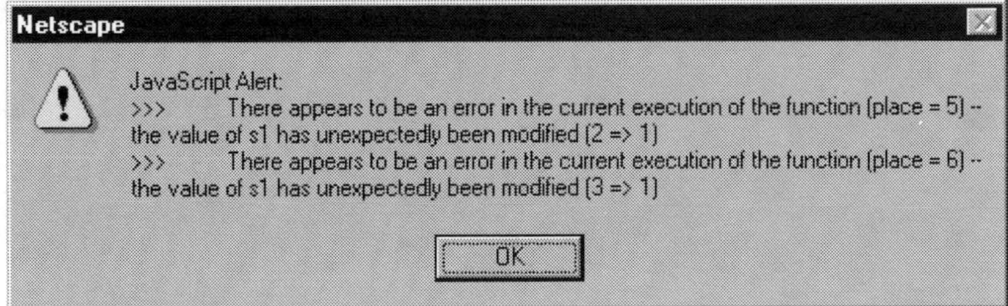

Figure 9-10. *A dialog box that displays a list of errors tracked during the recursive execution.*

Summary

In this chapter we focused on advanced function techniques and variable scope. Failing to pay attention to the variable scope concept results in hours of frustrating work trying to find bugs in simple scripts. After attaining a deeper understanding of variables and their scope, you will find it easy to write scripts with many functions, interleaving local and global variables. This chapter also presented some important matters related to parameters, such as referring to a variable number of arguments. Scripting specially designed dialog boxes took advantage of this feature. Another important concept discussed in the chapter is recursion. We found out how to debug recursive algorithms with a formatted table to trace variables.

Chapter 10

JavaScript by Example—a Review

Height and Weight Calculator

The Task

This script accepts the user's height and weight, and displays a greeting including a comment on the user's weight status. The comment is based on the height and weight measurements of the user, the proportion between them, his or her age and sex, and an overall result. It optionally displays the "scientific" results, including height and weight percentile and their quotient.

The Algorithm

At first, the script asks the user for his or her sex and age (two years is the minimum). If the age exceeds 18, it is converted to 18 in order to fit the pre-entered database. Then, the script asks the user to select the desired measurement system: metric or English. The selected units are reflected in the messages asking the user for his or her height and weight (e.g., "Enter height in centimeters:"). If the user chooses English, the weight and height are converted to the metric system (cm, kg), after which their percentiles are calculated. Based on the user's age, the script finds the height and weight of the 5th and 50th percentiles. Using a simple interpolation, the user's specific height and weight percentiles are calculated. The script checks that the computed percentile is between 1 and 99, and out-of-range results are converted to the nearest valid value (1 or 99). JavaScript displays a comment according to computed percentiles. The script also gives the user an option to view the more "scientific" results, including the actual numeric percentiles and their quotient. The weight and height percentiles were copied from *Compton's Encyclopedia*.

The Script

```
<HTML>
<HEAD>
<TITLE>Body height and weight calculator</TITLE>
<SCRIPT LANGUAGE="JavaScript">
<!--

// Returns the height measurement (50% is
// average...), according to the given
// sex, age, and actual height in cm
////////////////////////////////////////

function getHeight(sex, age, height) {
     height = Math.round(height)
     var height5 = 0
     var height50 = 0
     if (age == 2) {
          height50 = 87
          height5 = 82
     } else
     if (age == 3) {
          height50 = 95
          height5 = 90
     } else
     if (age == 4) {
          height50 = 102
          height5 = 95
     } else
     if (age == 5) {
          height50 = 109
          height5 = 101
     } else
     if (age == 6) {
          height50 = 114
          height5 = 107
     } else
     if (age == 7) {
          height50 = 120
          height5 = 112
     } else
     if (age == 8) {
          height50 = 126
          height5 = 118
     } else
     if (age == 9) {
          height50 = 131
          height5 = 121
```

```
} else
if (age == 10) {
     height50 = 137
     height5 = 127
} else
if (age == 11) {
     height50 = 143
     height5 = 131
} else
if (sex == "f") {
     if (age == 12) {
          height50 = 150
          height5 = 140
     } else
     if (age == 13) {
          height50 = 157
          height5 = 145
     } else
     if (age == 14) {
          height50 = 160
          height5 = 148
     } else
     if (age == 15) {
          height50 = 162
          height5 = 150
     } else
     if (age == 16) {
          height50 = 162
          height5 = 151
     } else
     if (age == 17) {
          height50 = 163
          height5 = 153
     } else
     if (age == 18) {
          height50 = 164
          height5 = 154
     }
} else
if (age == 12) {
     height50 = 150
     height5 = 137
} else
if (age == 13) {
     height50 = 156
     height5 = 142
} else
if (age == 14) {
     height50 = 162
     height5 = 148
} else
if (age == 15) {
```

```
            height50 = 168
            height5 = 155
        } else
        if (age == 16) {
            height50 = 174
            height5 = 160
        } else
        if (age == 17) {
            height50 = 175
            height5 = 165
        } else
        if (age == 18) {
            height50 = 176
            height5 = 165
        }
        var percent = (height - height5) * (50 - 5)
        percent /= (height50 - height5) + 5
        return percent
}

// Returns the weight measurement (50% is
// average...), according to the given
// sex, age, and actual weight in kg
/////////////////////////////////////////

function getWeight(sex, age, weight) {
        weight = Math.round(weight)
        var weight5 = 0
        var weight50 = 0
        if (age == 2) {
            weight50 = 12
            weight5 = 10
        } else
        if (age == 3) {
            weight50 =14
            weight5 = 12
        } else
        if (age == 4) {
            weight50 = 16
            weight5 = 14
        } else
        if (age == 5) {
            weight50 = 18
            weight5 = 15
        } else
        if (age == 6) {
            weight50 = 20
            weight5 = 17
        } else
        if (age == 7) {
            weight50 = 22
            weight5 = 18
```

```
} else
if (age == 8) {
     weight50 = 25
     weight5 = 20
} else
if (age == 9) {
     weight50 = 29
     weight5 = 22
} else
if (sex == "f") {
     if (age == 10) {
          weight50 = 32
          weight5 = 25
     } else
     if (age == 11) {
          weight50 = 37
          weight5 = 27
     } else
     if (age == 12) {
          weight50 = 41
          weight5 = 30
     } else
     if (age == 13) {
          weight50 = 46
          weight5 = 34
     } else
     if (age == 14) {
          weight50 = 50
          weight5 = 38
     } else
     if (age == 15) {
          weight50 = 53
          weight5 = 40
     } else
     if (age == 16) {
          weight50 = 56
          weight5 = 43
     } else
     if (age == 17) {
          weight50 = 57
          weight5 = 45
     } else
     if (age == 18) {
          weight50 = 57
          weight5 = 46
     }
} else
if (age == 10) {
     weight50 = 24
     weight5 = 31
} else
if (age == 11) {
```

```
            weight50 = 35
            weight5 = 27
        } else
        if (age == 12) {
            weight50 = 40
            weight5 = 30
        } else
        if (age == 13) {
            weight50 = 46
            weight5 = 35
        } else
        if (age == 14) {
            weight50 = 51
            weight5 = 38
        } else
        if (age == 15) {
            weight50 = 57
            weight5 = 44
        } else
        if (age == 16) {
            weight50 = 62
            weight5 = 48
        } else
        if (age == 17) {
            weight50 = 67
            weight5 = 53
        } else
        if (age == 18) {
            weight50 = 69
            weight5 = 55
        }
        var percent = (weight - weight5) * (50 - 5)
        percent /= (weight50 - weight5) + 5
        return percent
}

// Creates a comment according to the
// height, weight, age, sex, and a
// computed overall calculation. Also
// displays a disclaimer. It optionally
// displays the "scientific" results
////////////////////////////////////////

function printResult(height, weight, sex, age) {
        var heightAdj = ""
        var weightAdj = ""
        var ageAdj = ""
        var sexAdj = ""
        var gradeAdj = ""
        var grade = 0
        var propWeight = weight / height
        if (height > 70) {
```

```
                heightAdj = "tall"
                grade += 2
            } else
                if (height < 30) {
                    heightAdj = "short"
                    grade += 1
                } else {
                    heightAdj = "medium-height"
                    grade += 3
                }
            if (propWeight > 2) {
                weightAdj = "over-weight"
                grade += 1
            } else
                if (propWeight < 0.5) {
                    weightAdj = "slim"
                    grade += 2
                } else {
                    weightAdj = "medium-weight"
                    grade += 3
                }
            ageAdj = ageInput + "-year-old"
            if (grade >= 5)
                gradeAdj = "great-looking"
            else
                if (grade <= 2)
                    gradeAdj = "awkward-looking"
                else
                    gradeAdj = "fine-looking"
            sexAdj = (sex == "f") ? "female" : "male"
            var finalMessage = "You are a " + heightAdj + ", "
            finalMessage += weightAdj + ", " + gradeAdj + " "
            finalMessage += ageAdj + " " + sexAdj + "."
            alert(finalMessage)
            if (confirm("Are you interested in scientific results?")) {
                scMessage = "height = " + Math.round(height)
                scMessage +="%\rweight = " + Math.round(weight)
                scMessage += "%\rweight/height = " + propWeight
                alert(scMessage)
            } else
                if (grade <= 4)
                    alert("Good idea!")
            var notice = "Thank you for using the JavaScript weight "
            notice += "and height calculator. All calculations are "
            notice += "done according to the child-development graph "
            notice += "in \"Compton's Encyclopedia\". We apologize "
            notice += "if you were insulted by the comments -- that "
            notice += "was not our intention. We used them to demonstrate "
            notice += "various JavaScript scripting techniques."
            alert(notice)
        }
```

```
// converts weight and height from
// English system to metric system.
//////////////////////////////////////////

function convertInput() {
     weightInput *= 0.45359
     heightInput *= 2.54
}

// Global statements to receive input
// and call functions
//////////////////////////////////////////

var sex = prompt("Enter sex ((m)ale or (f)emale):", "")
var ageInput = parseInt(prompt("Enter age in years (minimum = 2):", ""))
ageInput = Math.round(ageInput)
var systemMessage = "Would you like to use the (m)etric system "
systemMessage += "or the (e)nglish one?"
var system = prompt(systemMessage, "m")
var heightUnit = (system == "m") ? "centimeters" : "inches"
var weightUnit = (system == "m") ? "kilograms" : "pounds"
var heightInput = prompt("Enter height in " + heightUnit + ":", "")
heightInput = parseInt(heightInput)
var weightInput = prompt("Enter weight in " + weightUnit + ":", "")
weightInput = parseInt(weightInput)
if (system == "e")
     convertInput()
if (ageInput > 18)
          var age = 18
     else
          if (ageInput < 2)
               var age = 2
          else
          var age = ageInput
var heightPer = getHeight(sex, age, heightInput)
var weightPer = getWeight(sex, age, weightInput)
heightPer = (heightPer < 1) ? 1 : heightPer
heightPer = (heightPer > 99) ? 99 : heightPer
weightPer = (weightPer < 1) ? 1 : weightPer
weightPer = (weightPer > 99) ? 99 : weightPer
printResult(heightPer, weightPer, sex, age)

// -->
</SCRIPT>
</HEAD>
<BODY>
</BODY>
</HTML>
```

Example 10-1. *A script that calculates the user's height and weight percentile.*

Analysis

The script looks rather long, but it is simple and easy to understand, because much of it is pure data and a repeated `if - else` statement.

convertInput()

```
function convertInput() {
     weightInput *= 0.45359
     heightInput *= 2.54
}
```

The `convertInput()` function does not accept any arguments, because it modifies two global variables. The function converts `weightInput` and `heightInput` from the English system to the metric one. `weightInput` is converted to kilograms, and `heightInput` is converted to centimeters. The function does not return any value because both variables are global.

getHeight(sex, age, height)

```
function getHeight(sex, age, height) {
     height = Math.round(height)
     var height5 = 0
     var height50 = 0
     if (age == 2) {
          height50 = 87
          height5 = 82
     } else
     if (age == 3) {
          height50 = 95
          height5 = 90
     } else
     if (age == 4) {
          height50 = 102
          height5 = 95
     } else
     if (age == 5) {
          height50 = 109
          height5 = 101
     } else
     if (age == 6) {
          height50 = 114
          height5 = 107
     } else
     if (age == 7) {
          height50 = 120
          height5 = 112
     } else
     if (age == 8) {
          height50 = 126
```

```
            height5 = 118
        } else
        if (age == 9) {
            height50 = 131
            height5 = 121
        } else
        if (age == 10) {
            height50 = 137
            height5 = 127
        } else
        if (age == 11) {
            height50 = 143
            height5 = 131
        } else
        if (sex == "f") {
            if (age == 12) {
                height50 = 150
                height5 = 140
            } else
            if (age == 13) {
                height50 = 157
                height5 = 145
            } else
            if (age == 14) {
                height50 = 160
                height5 = 148
            } else
            if (age == 15) {
                height50 = 162
                height5 = 150
            } else
            if (age == 16) {
                height50 = 162
                height5 = 151
            } else
            if (age == 17) {
                height50 = 163
                height5 = 153
            } else
            if (age == 18) {
                height50 = 164
                height5 = 154
            }
        } else
        if (age == 12) {
            height50 = 150
            height5 = 137
        } else
        if (age == 13) {
            height50 = 156
            height5 = 142
        } else
```

```
        if (age == 14) {
            height50 = 162
            height5 = 148
        } else
        if (age == 15) {
            height50 = 168
            height5 = 155
        } else
        if (age == 16) {
            height50 = 174
            height5 = 160
        } else
        if (age == 17) {
            height50 = 175
            height5 = 165
        } else
        if (age == 18) {
            height50 = 176
            height5 = 165
        }
        var percent = (height - height5) * (50 - 5)
        percent /= (height50 - height5) + 5
        return percent
}
```


This function accepts three arguments: the user's sex, age, and height. The variable height, holding the user's height, is rounded off to the nearest integer. The height is already represented in centimeters, even if the user chooses to use the English system.

After rounding off the height (age is already an integer, rounded off by a global statement), two new local variables are declared and initialized with the numeric value 0: height50, and height5. The variable height50 is intended to hold the average height measurement for a male or female of the user's specified age. The other variable, height5 holds the height of the 5th percentile. We use an if - else construction to assign these two variables the appropriate values. Each if statement checks if the user's age is equal to the age in the condition expression (e.g., age == 10). The else statements instruct JavaScript to continue executing the if statements in order, as long as the value of age does not match the value against which it is tested. From a quick look at the graph, one can find that males and females have the same height until age 11. Therefore, the first eleven if statements apply to both female and male users. Here is a short section from the function:

```
if (age == 2) {
    height50 = 87
    height5 = 82
```

```
} else
if (age == 3) {
        height50 = 95
        height5 = 90
} else
if (age == 4) {
        height50 = 102
        height5 = 95
} else
...
```

We'll follow this script segment to see what it does. At first, JavaScript checks if age is equal to 2. If it is, the value 87 is assigned to height50, and 82 is assigned to height5. These are the approximate values from the graph. If age is not equal to 2, the expression

```
age == 2
```

evaluates to false, and JavaScript carries out the else statement. An "improper" indentation is used in this script, because the nested if - else statements are extremely deep, and it would be unreasonable to add an additional tab to each statement. The last statement would have been preceded by approximately 17 tabs—impossible!

Another part of the function is the section where the female statistics are different from the male ones:

```
if (age == 11) {
                height50 = 143
                height5 = 131
        } else
        if (sex == "f") {
                if (age == 12) {
                        height50 = 150
                        height5 = 140
                } else
                .
                .
                .
                } else
                if (age == 18) {
                        height50 = 164
                        height5 = 154
                }
        } else
        if (age == 12) {
                height50 = 150
                height5 = 137
        } else
        if (age == 13) {
                height50 = 156
```

```
        height5 = 142
    } else
```

An else statement checks if the user is a female. A true condition instructs JavaScript to execute a command block containing the female-specific if - else segment. JavaScript ignores the command block if the condition is false, i.e., the user is a male. The next area of the function is specific for males. The entire if - else execution terminates after the user's age is matched. The maximum age inside the function is assumed to be 18. If the user enters a higher number, it is converted to 18 in the global section of the script before this function is invoked.

The following graph schematically explains the percentile calculation:

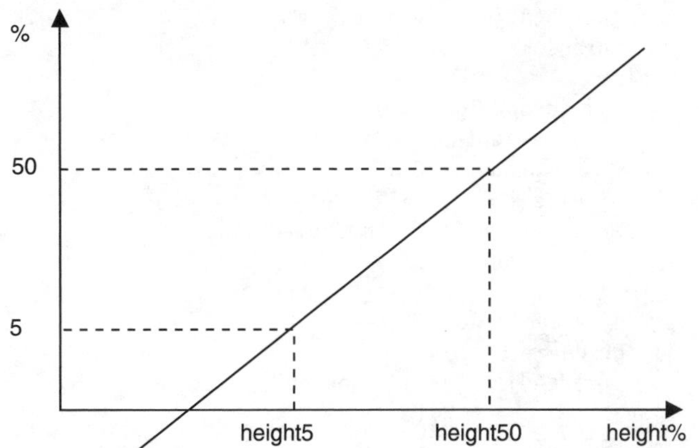

Figure 10-1. *The percentile graph.*

Finding the y (percentile) value of a given x (height) value is a problem you probably solved in one of your geometric analysis classes:

```
percent = (height – height5) * (50 – 5) / (height50 –
height5) + 5
```

The script uses this exact formula.

getWeight(sex, age, weight)

This function is the same as the previous one, except that it deals with the user's weight, instead of his or her height.

printResult(height, weight, sex, age)

```
function printResult(height, weight, sex, age) {
    var heightAdj = ""
    var weightAdj = ""
    var ageAdj = ""
```

```
var sexAdj = ""
var gradeAdj = ""
var grade = 0
var propWeight = weight / height
if (height > 70) {
     heightAdj = "tall"
     grade += 2
} else
     if (height < 30) {
          heightAdj = "short"
          grade += 1
     } else {
          heightAdj = "medium-height"
          grade += 3
     }
if (propWeight > 2) {
     weightAdj = "over-weight"
     grade += 1
} else
     if (propWeight < 0.5) {
          weightAdj = "slim"
          grade += 2
     } else {
          weightAdj = "medium-weight"
          grade += 3
     }
ageAdj = ageInput + "-year-old"
if (grade >= 5)
     gradeAdj = "great-looking"
else
     if (grade <= 2)
          gradeAdj = "awkward-looking"
     else
          gradeAdj = "fine-looking"
sexAdj = (sex == "f") ? "female" : "male"
var finalMessage = "You are a " + heightAdj + ", "
finalMessage += weightAdj + ", " + gradeAdj + " "
finalMessage += ageAdj + " " + sexAdj + "."
alert(finalMessage)
if (confirm("Are you interested in scientific results?")) {
     scMessage = "height = " + Math.round(height)
     scMessage +="%\rweight = " + Math.round(weight)
     scMessage += "%\rweight/height = " + propWeight
     alert(scMessage)
} else
     if (grade <= 4)
          alert("Good idea!")
var notice = "Thank you for using the JavaScript weight "
notice += "and height calculator. All calculations are "
notice += "done according to the child-development graph "
notice += "in \"Compton's Encyclopedia\". We apologize "
notice += "if you were insulted by the comments -- that "
```

```
        notice += "was not our intention. We used them to demonstrate "
        notice += "various JavaScript scripting techniques."
        alert(notice)
}
```

This function is more interesting than the previous ones because it does not have any repeating segment. At the beginning of the function, five adjectives are declared and initialized to an empty string—a clue that they are used to hold string values later in the function. Another variable, `grade`, is declared and initialized to `0`, indicating that it is used to hold a numeric value. It is especially important to assign the value `0` to this variable because it is accumulative, and any other value would generate wrong results. A new variable named `propWeight` is declared and initialized to the user's weight percentile, divided by his or her height percentile. This measure normalizes the person's weight by his or her height, giving a more accurate picture of the person's physical appearance (you can't expect an 8-foot person to be of average weight, can you?!). The following script segment assigns a value to the variable `heightAdj` according to the height percentile computed by the `getHeight()` function:


```
if (height > 70) {
            heightAdj = "tall"
            grade += 2
      } else
            if (height < 30) {
                  heightAdj = "short"
                  grade += 1
            } else {
                  heightAdj = "medium-height"
                  grade += 3
            }
```

Notice that the variable `height`, like `weight`, `sex`, and `age`, is a parameter, so its name is not required to be identical to its counterpart global one.

The preceding script segment assigns one of three values to the variable `heightAdj`: `"tall"`, `"short"`, or `"medium-height"`. If the height percentile is over 70%, the person is considered tall and if it is below 30%, the person is considered short. In all other cases (30% - 70%) the selected adjective is `"medium-height"`. Notice that along with the adjective, a number is added to the variable `grade`, representing the number of points awarded to the given characteristic. For example, a tall person receives two out of three possible points in the height category. Medium-height people receive the maximum three points, whereas short people receive the minimum one point. All of this is done with a nested if - else structure, where each statement is a command block consisting of two nested statements. WeightAdj is assigned similarly.

The adjective describing the person's age is created by concatenating his or her age to the string "-year-old ". Notice the number to string conversion (cast) in this statement.

An overall adjective is assigned to gradeAdj according to the final grade. (Do not take any result as an insult or as medical advice, because it almost never returns a realistic one.)

Finally, the user's sex is assigned to sexAdj, according to his or her input at the beginning.

All adjectives are now ready, so a comment is constructed with the following format:

```
"You are a " + heightAdj + "," + weightAdj + ", " + gradeAdj + ", " +
ageAdj + " " + sexAdj + "."
```

An alert box then displays the sentence. JavaScript displays another alert box with the "scientific" percentile, weight, and height results, if the user wishes to see that information. This is done via an if statement and a confirm() method as its condition.

The last operation in this function is the disclaimer-like message.

Global Statements

```
var sex = prompt("Enter sex ((m)ale or (f)emale):", "")
var ageInput = parseInt(prompt("Enter age in years (minimum = 2):", ""))
ageInput = Math.round(ageInput)
var systemMessage = "Whould you like to use the (m)etric system "
systemMessage += "or the (e)nglish one?"
var system = prompt(systemMessage, "m")
var heightUnit = (system == "m") ? "centimeters" : "inches"
var weightUnit = (system == "m") ? "kilograms" : "pounds"
var heightInput = prompt("Enter height in " + heightUnit + ":", "")
heightInput = parseInt(heightInput)
var weightInput = prompt("Enter weight in " + weightUnit + ":", "")
weightInput = parseInt(weightInput)
if (system == "e")
     convertInput()
if (ageInput > 18)
          var age = 18
     else
          if (ageInput < 2)
               var age = 2
          else
          var age = ageInput
```

```
var heightPer = getHeight(sex, age, heightInput)
var weightPer = getWeight(sex, age, weightInput)
heightPer = (heightPer < 1) ? 1 : heightPer
heightPer = (heightPer > 99) ? 99 : heightPer
weightPer = (weightPer < 1) ? 1 : weightPer
weightPer = (weightPer > 99) ? 99 : weightPer
printResult(heightPer, weightPer, sex, age)
```

At first, JavaScript asks the user to enter his or her sex as a single letter (e.g., "f", "m"). Notice that none of the input values in the script are evaluated, so the user must enter a valid value. Data evaluation is discussed later in the book.

JavaScript then asks the user for his or her age, and converts it to a number (all input from dialog boxes' fields are in the form of strings) with the `parseInt()` function. This built-in function is also discussed later in the book. The user's age is rounded off to the nearest integer.

The user is then prompted to choose the desired measurement system: metric or English. The appropriate values are assigned to `heightUnit` and `weightUnit` (e.g., centimeters, inches, kilograms, pounds) via a conditional expression.

Before calling any function, JavaScript asks the user for his or her height and weight. Each value is converted to a number using the `parseInt()` function.

At this point, the height and weight values are converted to metric units, via `convert()`, if they are in English units. The value of the variable `age` is assigned 18 if it is greater than 18, and 2 if it is less than 2. These values are the limits, and out-of-range values would not work with the `getHeight()` and `getWeight()` functions.

The `getHeight()` and `getWeight()` functions are called in order and return the computed percentile. The percentile is cut to its limits if it is out of range. The minimum percentile is 1; the maximum is 99.

The last statement calls the `printResult()` to print the results as explained earlier.

Output

The height and weight calculator script "listens" and "speaks" only via dialog boxes. Here are a few dialog boxes generated throughout the course of the script's execution:

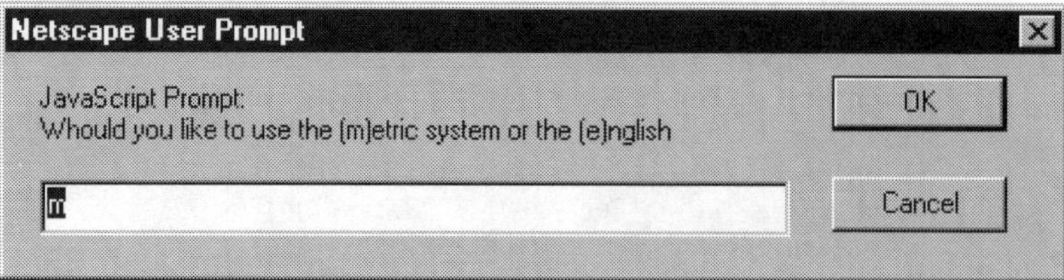

Figure 10-2. A dialog box that prompts the user to enter the desired measurement system.

Figure 10-3. A dialog box that prompts the user to enter his or her weight in kilograms.

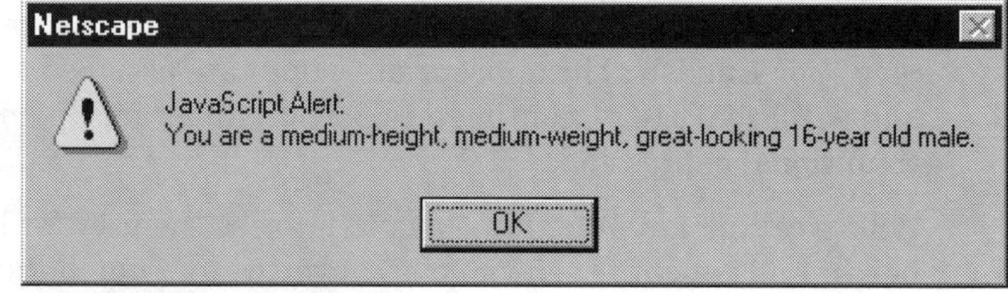

Figure 10-4. A short sentence based on a collection of calculations.

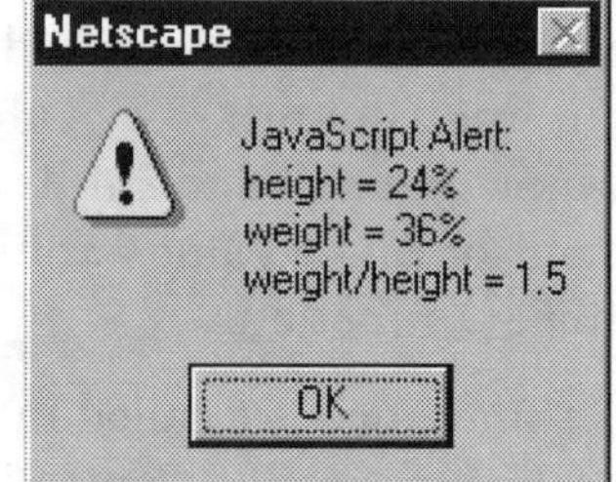

Figure 10-5. The "scientific" results.

Base Converter

Task

This script performs two alternative functions:

- Accepts a number in any base and converts it to a different base, provided by the user
- Accepts a series of numbers and converts them to all even bases between binary (2) and hexadecimal (16)

Note that the script can handle only positive integers.

Algorithm

Note: This script is designed to demonstrate various features of JavaScript. It does not always use the most efficient functions to reach this goal. In addition, as of Netscape Navigator 3.0, this script is totally unnecessary. The reason is that Netscape Navigator 3.0 supports a new method, `toString(`*`radix`*`)`, that enables you to automatically convert a number to any base. For example, `5.toString(2) == "101"`. Some other functions in the script are also unnecessary, such as `power()`, because built-in methods are equivalent to them (in this case, `Math.pow()`).

At first, the script asks the user if he or she wants to create a table or to convert a single value. If the user selects the first function, the number is converted to a decimal base and then to the specified base. If the number is represented in a decimal base, it is directly converted to the desired base. If the number is to be represented in decimal notation, only that conversion is executed. Octal and hexadecimal integers take advantage of their special conventions in JavaScript so their conversion to decimal is automatic. The script functions according to common conversion methods.

Just as a reminder, representation of a number in a system with base N may only consist of digits that are less than (not equal to) N.

Applied to the construction of numbers, the positional principle operates as follows: the sequence of digits *...srqp* is defined to signify a number which is equal to the sum of products involving powers of a number *a*, in which *a* is called the *base* or the *radix*; that is, the position of each of the coefficients `p, q, r, s, ...` is associated, in reverse order, to the representation *srqp* with a zero, first, second, third, ... power of the base *a*. The number of distinct numerals required in this notation is readily seen to be *a*, commonly represented by the known decimal digits, and additional letters from the Latin alphabet. The basic equation for such conversion is:

$$p * a^0 + q * a^1 + r * a^2 + s * a^3 + \ldots$$

Notice that the digits in the original numbers appear in a reverse order.

For example, to find the decimal representation M of 512_8 we use the following calculation:

$$M_{10} = 2 * 8^0 + 1 * 8^1 + 5 * 8^2 = 2 + 8 + 320 = 330_{10}$$

To convert a number in decimal base to base *a* representation, we can use the following division:

$$M_a = [\ldots][((srqp \text{ div } a) \text{ div } a) \% a][(srqp \text{ div } a) \% a][srqp \% a]$$

where each [] represents a digit in the new number.

This equation is schematically presented in Chapter 5, Basic Declarations and Expressions.

The decimal number 330_{10}, will be converted to octal notation as follows:

$$M_8 = [(330 \text{ div } 8) \text{ div } 8) \% 8][(330 \text{ div } 8) \% 8][330 \% 8] = [5][1][2] = 512_8$$

Note that the parentheses are not necessary due to operator precedence rules.

The last accumulated element of the equation is the one containing the expression `[z % a ]` where *z* is smaller than the base, a.

We know now the whole conversion process, so we can represent a number of any base in any other base. If the calculations are not completely clear, you should read them over again and try to use the equations to convert numbers of your choice. Reading the actual function in the script will probably make it clearer.

If the user chooses to create a base conversion table, the user is prompted to enter the highest (last) decimal number in the table, which is also equal to the number of rows + 1 (0 is included). Each value in the table is independently calculated, according to the base conversion methods explained above.

The Script

```
<HTML>
<HEAD>

<TITLE>Base converter</TITLE>

<SCRIPT LANGUAGE="JavaScript">
<!-- hiding content from old browsers

// Simulate the "power of" (^) operator
////////////////////////////////////////////

function power(op1, op2) {
     var result = 1
     for (var i = 1; i <= op2; i++) {
          result *= op1
     }
     return result
}

// Simulate the div (integral division)
// operator
////////////////////////////////////////////

function div(op1, op2) {
     return Math.round(op1 / op2 - op1 % op2 / op2)
}

// Returns a digit (maximum hexadecimal)
// based on its decimal value
////////////////////////////////////////////

function getDigit(val) {
     if (val == 10) return "A"
     if (val == 11) return "B"
     if (val == 12) return "C"
     if (val == 13) return "D"
     if (val == 14) return "E"
     if (val == 15) return "F"
     return val
     // the return statement terminates the function,
     // so there is no need for else statements
}

// Returns the decimal value of a digit
// (maximum hexadecimal)
```

```
/////////////////////////////////////////

function getValue(dig) {
     if (dig == "A") return 10
     if (dig == "B") return 11
     if (dig == "C") return 12
     if (dig == "D") return 13
     if (dig == "E") return 14
     if (dig == "F") return 15
     return dig
     // the return statement terminates the function,
     // so there is no need for else statements
}

// Convert from decimal to specified base
/////////////////////////////////////////

function toBase(num, base) {
     var newNum = (num == 0) ? "0" : ""
     while (num >= 1) {
          newNum = getDigit(num % base) + newNum
          num = div(num, base)
     }
     return newNum
}

// Convert from specified base to decimal
/////////////////////////////////////////

function toDec(num, base) {
     if (base == 8)
          return parseInt("0" + num)
     if (base == 16)
          return parseInt("0x" + num)
     num = "" + num // convert to string by casting
     var numLength = num.length
     // the length property returns the length of a string
     var newNum = 0 // initialization
                // (must be 0 so the sum is not affected)
     var curDigit = ""
     var contributedValueValue = 0
     for (var i = numLength - 1; i >= 0; --i) {
          curDigit = num.charAt(i)
          contributedValue = getValue(curDigit)
          contributedValue *= power(base, numLength - (i + 1))
          newNum += parseInt(contributedValue)
     }
     return newNum
}

// Main function that accepts input and
// calls appropriate functions
```

```
//////////////////////////////////////////

function convert(num, base1, base2) {
     if (typeof num == "string")
          num = num.toUpperCase()
     if (base1 == base2)
          return num
     if (base1 == 10)
          return toBase(num, base2)
     if (base2 == 10)
          return toDec(num, base1)
     return toBase(toDec(num, base1), base2)
}

// Create a conversion table
//////////////////////////////////////////

function drawTable(lastNum) {
     with (document) {
          lastNum = parseInt(lastNum)
          write("<TABLE BORDER=3>")
          write("<TR><TD COLSPAN=8><CENTER><FONT COLOR=purple SIZE=+4>")
          write("Base Converter</FONT></CENTER></TD></TR>")
          write("<TR>")
          for (var k = 2; k <= 16; k = k + 2) {
               write("<TD><CENTER> Base " + k + " </CENTER></TD>")
          }
          write("</TR>")
          for (var i = 0; i <= lastNum; ++i) {
               write("<TR>")
               for (var j = 2; j <= 16; j = j + 2) {
                    write("<TD>" + toBase(i, j) + "</TD>")
               }
               write("</TR>")
          }
          write("</TABLE>")
     }
}

// Gets table's input
//////////////////////////////////////////

function getTableAttributes() {
     var message = "Enter last number to be converted in the table"
     var lastNum = parseInt(prompt(message, 15))
     if (lastNum != 0)
          drawTable(lastNum)
}

// Convert individual numbers, until the
// user selects cancel on the first
// prompt of the loop
```

```
////////////////////////////////////////

function calcNum() {
     while(1) {
          var number = prompt("Enter a number in any base:", 0)
          if (number == null)
               break
          var base1 = prompt("Enter its base:", 10)
          if (base1 == null)
               continue
          base1 = parseInt(base1)
          var base2 = prompt("Enter the desired base:", 16)
          if (base2 == null)
               continue
          base2 = parseInt(base2)
          var outputString = number + " (base " + base1 + ") = "
          outputString += convert(number, base1, base2)
          outputString += " (base " + base2 + ")"
          alert(outputString)
     }
}

// Ask user for conversion device
// (T-table, I-individual values)
////////////////////////////////////////

function mainInput() {
     var message = "Enter (T) to create a table or (V) to "
     message += "calculate a value"
     var chosenDevice = prompt(message, "T")
     if (chosenDevice == "T" || chosenDevice == "t")
          getTableAttributes()
     else
          if (chosenDevice == "V" || chosenDevice == "v")
               calcNum()
          else
               alert("Goodbye!")
}

mainInput()

// end hiding content -->
</SCRIPT>
</HEAD>
<BODY>
</BODY>
</HTML>
```

Example 10-2. *A base converter.*

Analysis

This script demonstrates an output of both HTML and dialog boxes. The HTML output serves the base conversion table, whereas the alert boxes are the output of single-value conversion operations.

power(op1, op2)

```
// Simulate the "power of" (^) operator
////////////////////////////////////////

function power(op1, op2) {
      var result = 1
      for (var i = 1; i <= op2; i++) {
            result *= op1
      }
      return result
}
```

This function returns the value $op1^{op2}$. The function is called with op1 and op2 values as parameters. There are a few restrictions on the value of op2:

- It must be an integer.
- It must not be negative (⇒ positive or 0).

These restrictions are not important for us because all our calculations follow both rules.

The `power()` function uses a loop, although it can be programmed to use recursion as well. The recursive variant is:

```
function power(op1, op2) {
      if (op2 == 0)
            return 1
      else
            return power(op1, op2 - 1) * op1
}
```

This variant works because:

```
power(x, 0) = 1
power(x, y) = power(x, y - 1) * x
```

In its iterative version, the script assigns an initial value of 1 to `result`. It then iterates through a loop, multiplying `result` by the loop's counter value on each iteration, until the counter is equal to the second operator (or parameter). The local variable `result` holds the accumulated result throughout the entire function.

div(op1, op2)

```
// Simulate the div (integral division)
// operator
////////////////////////////////////////

function div(op1, op2) {
      return Math.round(op1 / op2 - op1 % op2 / op2)
}
```

The `div()` function was presented in Chapter 7, Utilizing JavaScript Operators. It simulates the `div` (integral division) operator utilized in many other programming and scripting languages. The calculation is very simple:

```
op1 / op2 - op1 % op2 / op2
```

The first element (`op1 / op2`) is the quotient of the regular division operator. The second term represents the fractional part of the quotient, and therefore it is subtracted from the quotient. The modulo operator returns the remainder of the division as a whole number, so it is divided by the second operand to receive the fractional part of the quotient.

When we first designed this function, this was the only process implemented on the operands. However, we soon found that the function returned strange results, such as 2.9999... . The obvious conclusion was that the division and modulo operators returned inaccurate results. We chose to include the `round` method of the `Math` object (don't worry, it's explained later in the book) to round the result off to the nearest integer. We then had the perfect function, as we had anticipated.

The `div` operation can be simulated with other techniques, such as the `Math.floor()` method, that will be explained later under `Math` object.

getDigit(val)

```
// Returns a digit (maximum hexadecimal)
// based on its decimal value
////////////////////////////////////////

function getDigit(val) {
      if (val == 10) return "A"
      if (val == 11) return "B"
      if (val == 12) return "C"
      if (val == 13) return "D"
      if (val == 14) return "E"
      if (val == 15) return "F"
      return val
```

```
     // the return statement terminates the function,
     // so there is no need for else statements
}

// Returns the decimal value of a digit
// (maximum hexadecimal)
/////////////////////////////////////////
```

This function accepts an integer between 0 and 15, and returns its equivalent hexadecimal (base 16) number. Since there are 16 hex digits, the returned value is always a hexadecimal. The function uses consecutive `if` statements, each one of which, if it evaluates to `TRUE`, can terminate the function. Returning from the middle of the function is preferred, as far as performance is concerned. Many of the possible arguments handed off to this function (all the numbers between 0 and 9) are to be returned without being converted, as their hexadecimal and decimal representations are identical.

At first, the function checks whether the value of the parameter `val` is 10. If it is, the function returns the number's hexadecimal representation, `"A"`. If not, JavaScript continues to the "`B`" statement, and beyond. The process continues until a true condition is met, or until JavaScript has passed all `if` statements without any true condition. It indicates that the value of `val` is not between 10 and 15, meaning it is between 0 and 9. The function returns the exact same value.

getValue(dig)

```
// Returns the decimal value of a digit
// (maximum hexadecimal)
/////////////////////////////////////////

function getValue(dig) {
     if (dig == "A") return 10
     if (dig == "B") return 11
     if (dig == "C") return 12
     if (dig == "D") return 13
     if (dig == "E") return 14
     if (dig == "F") return 15
     return dig
     // the return statement terminates the function,
     // so there is no need for else statements
}
```

The `getvalue()` function may be considered the opposite of `getDigit(value)`, because it accepts a hexadecimal number (actually, it must be a digit), and returns the argument's decimal value. This structure of this function is identical to `getDigit()`'s.

For example, if `dig == "B"`, the function returns 11, which is B's (or b's) decimal representation.

Note that both `getValue()` and `getDigit()` work with systems that do not exceed 16. That is, the maximum base is hexadecimal, so they only work with digits up to "F".

toBase(num, base)

```
// Convert from decimal to specified base
//////////////////////////////////////////

function toBase(num, base) {
     var newNum = (num == 0) ? "0" : ""
     while (num >= 1) {
          newNum = getDigit(num % base) + newNum
          num = div(num, base)
     }
     return newNum
}
```

This function accepts a decimal integer and returns its representation in the specified base. The function uses the algorithm explained earlier in this chapter. At first, the variable newNum is declared and initialized with an empty string. The conditional expression assigns the value "0" to the variable if the value of num is 0. Another version of the same function is as follows:

```
function toBase(num, base) {
     var newNum = ""
     while (num >= base) {
          newNum = getDigit(num % base) + newNum
          num = div(num, base)
     }
     newNum = div(num, base) + newNum
     return newNum
}
```

Referring again to the original version, the variable newNum holds the number in its new representation. It is vital to assign it a string literal so that we can add digits to its left, as explained in the "Algorithm" section.

The main part of this function is the loop. It extracts the appropriate values from the number and concatenates them to the left of the new one. Let's take a look at the loop interior. The variable newNum is assigned the new digit concatenated to the left of the existing value of newNum. The string initialization guarantees that all operations on the new number are string operations, enabling us to "attach" strings or number anywhere. The new digit is `getDigit(num % base)`.

Here is the conversion method explained before:

M_a = [...][((num div base) div base) % base][(num div base) % base][num % base]

Each digit has the format *[aValue % base]*. The first statement in the loop is based on this format. It concatenates the number (`num % base`) with the existing string, from the left. Note that the number is first sent to the `getDigit()` function to be converted to its proper notation. Since the modulo operator returns a value which is smaller than its second operator, no digit will be greater than the maximum digit of that base, `base`.

Look back once again at the equation. Notice the rule related to the value of *aValue*:

```
aValue = theNumber
aValue = theNumber div a
aValue = (theNumber div a) div a
aValue = ((theNumber div a) div a) div a
.
.
.
```

This rule is expressed in the second statement of the loop. The variable `num` is intrinsically divided by the base in every iteration. Its momentary value is always the correct value of *aValue*.

The loop condition is `num >= 1`, because any number less than the base does not need to be converted. The statement `num = div(num, base)` is at the end of the loop, so the value of `num` at the beginning of the next iteration is not the same as it was during the previous one. Since `x div y` always evaluates to 0 when `x < y`, the value of `num` will be equal to 0 if it is less than the value of `base`. The loop condition (`num >= 1`) ensures that the loop will terminate when all digits have been concatenated.

toDec(num, base)

```
// Convert from specified base to decimal
//////////////////////////////////////////

function toDec(num, base) {
     if (base == 8)
          return parseInt("0" + num)
     if (base == 16)
```

```
            return parseInt("0x" + num)
        num = "" + num // convert to string by casting
        var numLength = num.length
        // the length property returns the length of a string
        var newNum = 0 // initialization
                    // (must be 0 so the sum is not affected)
        var curDigit = ""
        var contributedValueValue = 0
        for (var i = numLength - 1; i >= 0; --i) {
            curDigit = num.charAt(i)
            contributedValue = getValue(curDigit)
            contributedValue *= power(base, numLength - (i + 1))
            newNum += parseInt(contributedValue)
        }
        return newNum
    }
```

This function returns the value of num in the specified base. It is based on the algorithm explained earlier in the chapter.

At first, the function checks if the number is an octal or hexadecimal one. If so, it returns the number with a leading prefix (0 or 0x). Note that the parseInt() function converts the concatenated string to an integer in a decimal base, so no prior conversions are needed for octal or hexadecimal numbers. If the base is not octal (8) or hexadecimal (16), an empty string is concatenated to the variable num, converting it to a string, regardless of its original type. The function assigns the number to the local variable numLength via the strings property, length. In JavaScript, all strings, as opposed to numbers, are objects. The length property exists only for strings, so we must convert num to a string before we use it. It is also possible to calculate the number of digits in a number via the modulo operator, but that seems to be longer and more complicated.

You may recall from the "Algorithm" section that the equation used to convert a number in any base to a decimal notation is completely arithmetical. For that, a new variable named newNum is declared and initialized to 0. It holds the value of the computed decimal value.

Two more local variables are declared, curDigit, and contributed-Value; the first one is initialized to an empty string, and the second to 0. The loop section is straightforward and follows the algorithm explained above. The built-in parseInt() function converts its argument to an integer rather than a string (for example, "11" ⇒ 11). The last statement of the function returns the new number.

convert(num, base1, base2)

```
// Main function that accepts input and
// calls appropriate functions
/////////////////////////////////////////

function convert(num, base1, base2) {
       if (typeof num == "string")
              num = num.toUpperCase()
       if (base1 == base2)
              return num
       if (base1 == 10)
              return toBase(num, base2)
       if (base2 == 10)
              return toDec(num, base1)
       return toBase(toDec(num, base1), base2)
}
```


This function accepts a number in base1, and returns its equivalent in base2. Its primary task is to switch between the various function calls that will do the conversion, and to eliminate unnecessary conversions by detecting special cases a priori.

- At first, the function checks if the specified number is a string. If so, it uses the .toUpperCase() method to transform all lowercase letters to uppercase ones. This is required by some of the functions, such as getValue(). It then checks if both bases are the same and returns the original number if they are. If base1, the original base, is 10, the function calls the toBase() function to convert it to the desired base (base2). If the desired base is decimal, the toDec() function is called. If none of these special situations exist, the function converts the number first to decimal and then to the desired base.

getTableAttributes()

```
// Gets table's input
/////////////////////////////////////////

function getTableAttributes() {
       var message = "Enter last number to be converted in the table"
       var lastNum = parseInt(prompt(message, 15))
       if (lastNum != 0)
              drawTable(lastNum)
}
```

The getTableAttributes() function does exactly that. It asks the user for the last decimal number to be displayed in the table. Since the first number is always 0, the number of rows in the table will be greater by 1. If the user clicks **cancel** in the prompt box, the prompt() method evaluates to `null`. As explained in Chapter 5, the `null` value automatically becomes 0 if it is forced to become a number, as is the case with `parseInt()` function. The function checks whether or not the user's input was 0 or **cancel** (**cancel** evaluates to `null`, and `parseInt(null) == 0`). If the input is valid, the function calls the `drawTable` function to create the conversion table.

drawTable(lastNum)

```
// Create a conversion table
/////////////////////////////////////////

function drawTable(lastNum) {
     with (document) {
          lastNum = parseInt(lastNum)
          write("<TABLE BORDER=3>")
          write("<TR><TD COLSPAN=8><CENTER><FONT COLOR=purple SIZE=+4>")
          write("Base Converter</FONT></CENTER></TD></TR>")
          write("<TR>")
          for (var k = 2; k <= 16; k = k + 2) {
               write("<TD><CENTER> Base " + k + " </CENTER></TD>")
          }
          write("</TR>")
          for (var i = 0; i <= lastNum; ++i) {
               write("<TR>")
               for (var j = 2; j <= 16; j = j + 2) {
                    write("<TD>" + toBase(i, j) + "</TD>")
               }
               write("</TR>")
          }
          write("</TABLE>")
     }
}
```

This function prints the conversion table up to the specified number. The table is formatted by regular HTML tags for tables.

The `with(document)` statement enables us to use `write()` rather than `document.write()`. The table consists of eight columns for all even bases between 2 (binary) and 16 (hexadecimal). The `toBase()` function returns the value for each table cell (it uses the main loop's counter as its parameter). Do not try to create extremely large tables, because too many executions of the function take a long time and might crash your browser on weak operating systems such as Windows 3.x.

Notice that the function includes three loops. The first one prints the header of each column (e.g., base 2, base 4, base 6, ...). The second one deals with the vertical dimension of the table. The third one is nested in the second one, and it deals with the horizontal dimension, basically building the rows of the table. This loop terminates after it has constructed the entire row, whereas the second one terminates when the entire table is finished.

The `drawTable()` function lacks efficiency. For example, it converts numbers from decimal notation to decimal notation. You may want to rewrite either this function or the conversion ones.

calcNum()

```
// Converts individual numbers, until the
// user selects cancel on the first
// prompt of the loop
////////////////////////////////////////

function calcNum() {
     while(1) {
          var number = prompt("Enter a number in any base:", 0)
          if (number == null)
               break
          var base1 = prompt("Enter its base:", 10)
          if (base1 == null)
               continue
          base1 = parseInt(base1)
          var base2 = prompt("Enter the desired base:", 16)
          if (base2 == null)
               continue
          base2 = parseInt(base2)
          var outputString = number + " (base " + base1 + ") = "
          outputString += convert(number, base1, base2)
          outputString += " (base " + base2 + ")"
          alert(outputString)
     }
}
```

The `calcNum()` function asks the user for the number he or she wants to convert, its base, and the desired target base. It demonstrates many control structures. The entire function is actually a single loop. The `break` statement converts the `while(1)` loop to a finite one. The `break` statement is executed if the user clicks **cancel** on the first prompt box ("Enter a number ..."). Cancellation of other prompt boxes invokes a `continue` command, sending JavaScript directly to the beginning of the loop. Since any textbox in JavaScript (in a prompt box or a form) is evaluated to a string, all input values need to be converted to numbers (via `parseInt()`), even if the content appears to be numeric. The function then creates a message including the original number-base pair, together with the new one. The message is displayed in an alert box.

mainInput()

```
// Asks user for conversion device
// (T-table, V-individual values)
///////////////////////////////////////

function mainInput() {
     var message = "Enter (T) to create a table or (V) to "
     message += "calculate a value"
     var chosenDevice = prompt(message, "T")
     if (chosenDevice == "T" || chosenDevice == "t")
          getTableAttributes()
     else
          if (chosenDevice == "V" || chosenDevice == "v")
               calcNum()
          else
               alert("Goodbye!")
}
```

This is the main function. It asks the user if he or she wants to create a table or convert a single entry. According to the user's response, an appropriate function is called. It is basically built of a nested `if - else` statement. The logical OR operator is used to test for both uppercase or lowercase input.

Global Statements

The only global statement is the call to the function `mainInput()`.

Output

Here are a few screens generated by the base converter script, demonstrating output via HTML and dialog boxes:

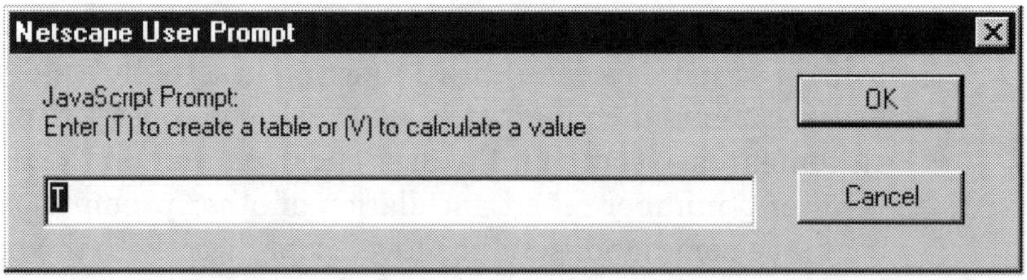

Figure 10-6. *The function displays the main option via an alert box.*

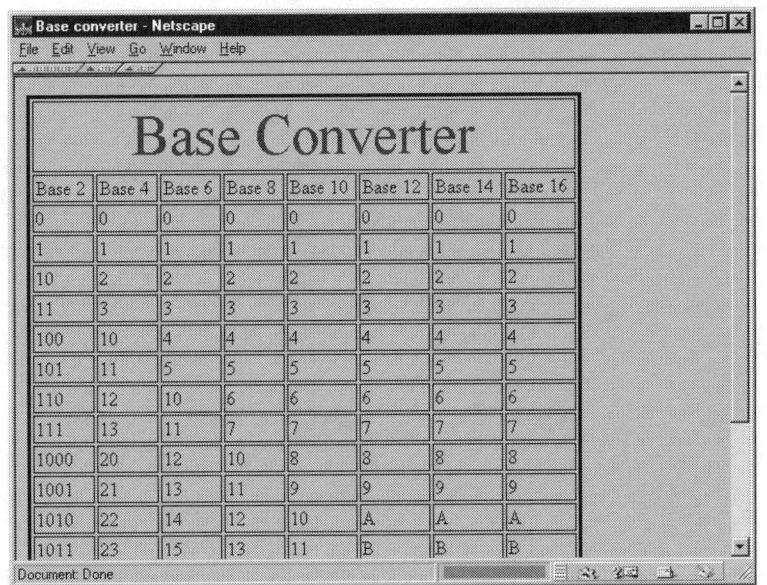

Base Converter

Base 2	Base 4	Base 6	Base 8	Base 10	Base 12	Base 14	Base 16
0	0	0	0	0	0	0	0
1	1	1	1	1	1	1	1
10	2	2	2	2	2	2	2
11	3	3	3	3	3	3	3
100	10	4	4	4	4	4	4
101	11	5	5	5	5	5	5
110	12	10	6	6	6	6	6
111	13	11	7	7	7	7	7
1000	20	12	10	8	8	8	8
1001	21	13	11	9	9	9	9
1010	22	14	12	10	A	A	A
1011	23	15	13	11	B	B	B

Figure 10-7. *A base conversion table made by "pure" JavaScript output.*

Figure 10-8. *The user enters a number in any base.*

Figure 10-9. *The final result.*

Summary

In this chapter, we have explained in detail two complete examples: the Weight and Height Calculator, and the Base Converter. These scripts are a good summary of the first part of the book, and you should take the time to comprehend them in depth. They demonstrate the basic features of the language such as variables, variable scopes, conditional and loop structures, functions, alert boxes, forms, prompts, output techniques, data type conversion, and more. The scripts in the remainder of the book are much more complicated, so make sure your knowledge base is as broad as these scripts entail.

Chapter 11

Events in JavaScript

Events

It was not long ago when static HTML pages ruled the Web. As a matter of fact, such pages still constitute the majority. However, during the last year, many static pages have been replaced by dynamic, interactive, and altogether more exciting pages. HTML provides a limited set of features. When browsing an HTML-based Web page, you can read the text, look at the graphics, or possibly listen to the sound it plays. All of these actions are in the form of "do not touch." You only admire the content of the page, but have no influence on it. Such pages remind us of art masterpieces seen in a museum. You can look at them, maybe take a picture, but you cannot interact with the paintings. For many people the Web experience consists of only visiting pages, without interacting with them. The only interaction experienced is when the user follows a link or clicks somewhere on an image map.

HTML forms are not new to the Web community, but they weren't part of HTML's vernacular in the not-so-distant past. The first browsers did not support forms. You could not use search engines to seek desired information or fill out a survey. Forms have gradually changed the existing model. They add much more interaction to Web pages. HTML forms consist of text fields, buttons, check boxes, and other input devices. They are similar to everyday paper forms you fill out regularly. You have probably filled out a survey in your Web surfing "career," including multiple choice questions, yes-no questions, and open-ended questions. The basic problem with forms is that it takes time to receive a reply. The data entered in the forms is transmitted to the server across the network, processed, and then sent back to the client, your browser. You might find yourself waiting a full minute, maybe even more, just to receive a message such as, "This is not a valid e-mail address. Please enter your e-mail again." You then have to resubmit the form, hoping it will accept the input and set you free. Many games also take advantage of forms. These games are mostly logical ones, because they do not require fast interaction or live processing. A tic-tac-toe CGI game would probably be very boring, because you would have to wait a long time after each move you made. Server-push animations are very slow and annoying, so they are rarely used.

JavaScript is primarily designed to localize all processing. That is, the processing script is loaded by your browser and processes the data entered without any network submission, i.e., all processing is done on the client side. Avoiding network transmission saves time and thus enables fast replies, animation, and other interactions. The script is located on the computer you are using. Therefore, a game written in JavaScript could probably work at the same speed as a game on your hard drive! However, some tasks are just not possible with JavaScript. You cannot search the Web with a client-side JavaScript script because this action requires the use of disk-consuming files, which cannot be transmitted over a slow connection such as a modem. Even a T3 connection would be much too slow for this purpose. The main idea of JavaScript is that you can combine client-side scripts with server-side scripts (usually written in CGI). You can create an e-mail address submission form that checks that the value in the form has an at-sign (@), and only if one is found is the input sent to the server for additional processing. The initial validation is done with JavaScript, and the further processing with server-side applications.

JavaScript enables the designer of an HTML page to take advantage of *events* for automated navigation, client-side processing, and more. Events are signals generated by the browser when various actions occur. You will see later that JavaScript is aware of these events and can react to them. The events supported by JavaScript are listed in Table 11-1.

Event	Description
`abort`	Occurs when the user aborts loading an image.
`blur`	Occurs when focus is removed from a form element (when the user clicks outside the form element). It also occurs when the user removes focus from a browser window.
`click`	Occurs when the user clicks on a link, an image map area, or a form element.
`change`	Occurs when the user changes the value of a form field.
`error`	Occurs if there is an error loading an image.

Event	Description
`focus`	Occurs when the user gives input focus to a form element or a window.
`load`	Occurs when a page or image has finished loading into the browser window.
`mouseOut`	Occurs when the user moves the mouse pointer from inside a link or image map area's bounding box to its outside.
`mouseOver`	Occurs when the user moves the pointer over a hypertext link or an image map area.
`select`	Occurs when the user selects a form field.
`submit`	Occurs when the user submits a form via the "submit" button.
`unload`	Occurs when the user exits a page.

Table 11-1. *Events in JavaScript.*

Not all actions that take place in your browser are events. Events are only actions that occur in the area of the HTML page, such as loading images and selecting form elements. If an action occurs directly in the boundary of the browser's display zone it is an event as well. Take a look at the following page:

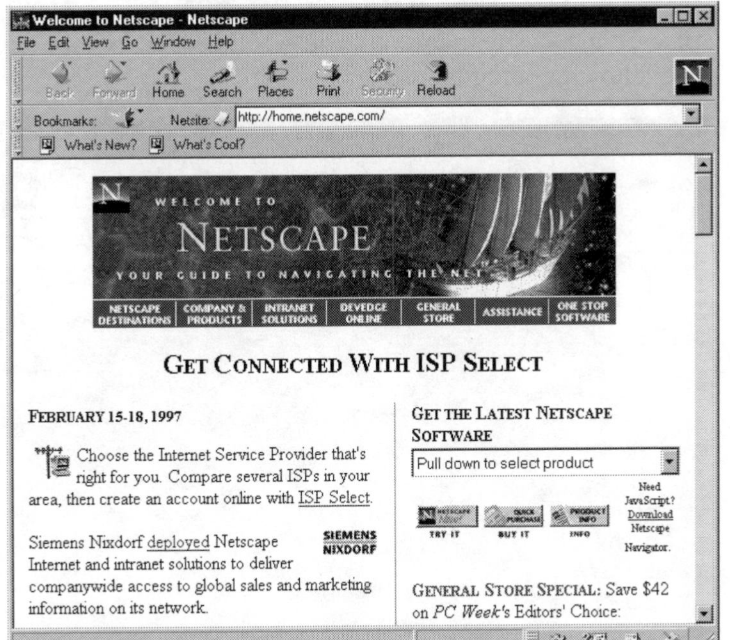

Figure 11-1. *Netscape's homepage displayed in Netscape Navigator's full window.*

You know that this window consists of two parts: the HTML page and the browser. You already know that many actions can occur in the environment illustrated in Figure 11-1. Some are events while others are nonevent actions. The main part of the window is the HTML page, the content window without the surrounding menus and buttons:

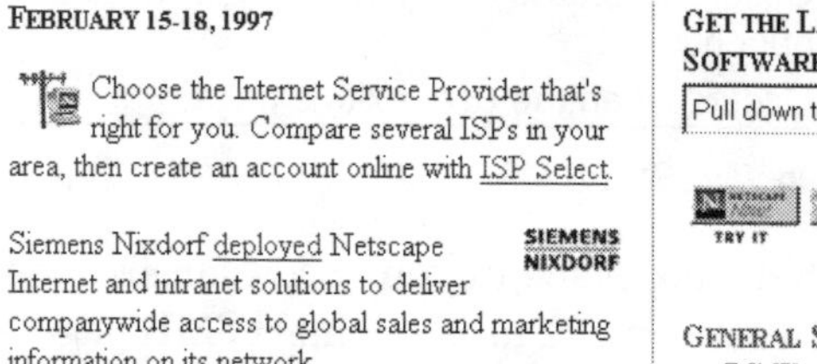

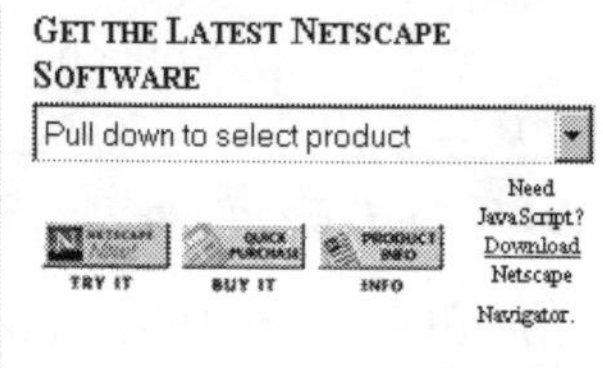

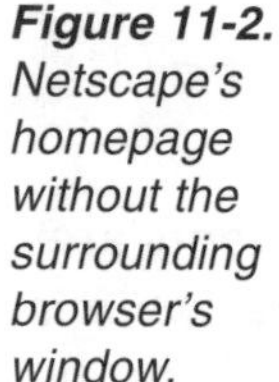
Figure 11-2. Netscape's homepage without the surrounding browser's window.

All actions that take place in the area shown in Figure 11-2 are events. The user loads, unloads, clicks links, and causes many other events in this zone. The second section consists of Netscape Navigator's features, such as the menu bar, the scroll bar, and other elements seen in the following image:

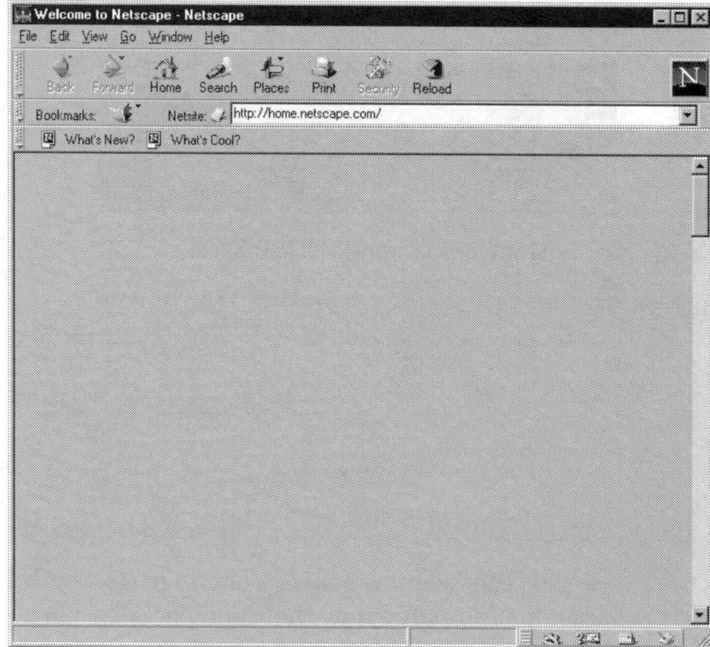

Figure 11-3. Netscape Navigator's window with no content zone.

This window is exactly the same as the one presented in Figure 11-1, except that the HTML page is excluded. No events occur outside of the HTML page. For example, opening Navigator's mail or news window does not generate an event. Scrolling up and down the window does not cause an event either. Even if you change the appearance of an HTML page, you are not triggering an event. It is very important to realize the difference between events and other actions because JavaScript can only handle events, not other actions. Many questions in mailing lists and news groups such as "When do the people at Netscape plan to create an event handler triggered by scrolling...?" show the ignorance of programmers in recognizing what an event is. An event handler can obviously handle only events! Events occur no matter what the size of the HTML page zone is, as long as a page is loaded. Note that future releases of Navigator or Internet Explorer may expand the term of events to the entire window, but that is still in doubt. Netscape Navigator 3.0x made a step towards this when it introduced the ability to automatically scroll via JavaScript, though a corresponding event was not implemented.

Event Handlers

Event handlers correspond to their associated events. They are scripts that execute automatically when events occur. Most deferred JavaScript functions are called by event handlers. You saw earlier that events are actions that do not have any direct influence. They only serve the event handlers. Each event handler is associated with an event.

Event handlers are embedded in documents as attributes of HTML tags to which you assign JavaScript code. The general syntax is:

```
<TAG eventHandler="JavaScript Code">
```

You can use event handlers to embed any JavaScript code. You can place a 500-line script including functions as an event handler tag. You can use more than one event handler with the same HTML tag.

The names of the event handlers are constructed of the word "on" + the name of the event. Here is the full list of supported event handlers:

- onAbort
- onBlur
- onClick
- onChange

- `onError`
- `onFocus`
- `onLoad`
- `onMouseOut`
- `onMouseOver`
- `onSelect`
- `onSubmit`
- `onUnload`

Here is an HTML page that displays the message "Hello" when you load it, and "Goodbye" when you unload it (see Figures 11-4a and 11-4b):

```
<HTML>
<HEAD>
<TITLE>Hello / Goodbye</TITLE>
</HEAD>
<BODY onLoad="alert('Hello')" onUnLoad="alert('Goodbye')">
</BODY>
</HTML>
```

Example 11-1 (ex11-1.htm). *An HTML document with two event handlers as separate attributes of the same tag.*

Figures 11-4a and b*. The output of two event handler scripts attached to the same tag (see Example 11-1).*

Event handlers are not case sensitive. For example, you can use `ONLOAD` instead of `onLoad`. Although event handlers are related to JavaScript, the event handler itself is normally used as an HTML attribute—HTML is not case sensitive. It is still a good practice to use identifier-like naming conventions for event handlers. As you will see later, the official name of an event handler is all lowercase, but in HTML it doesn't matter.

Example 11-2 is a classic script that takes advantage of event handlers.

```
<HTML>
<HEAD>
<TITLE>A link description in the status bar</TITLE>
</HEAD>
```

```
<BODY>
<A HREF="http://www.wordware.com/"
     onMouseOver="window.status = 'Wordware Publishing'; return true"
                    >Wordware</A>
</BODY>
</HTML>
```

Example 11-2 (ex11-2.htm). *An event handler script that displays a short description of a link when the user has the pointer over that link.*

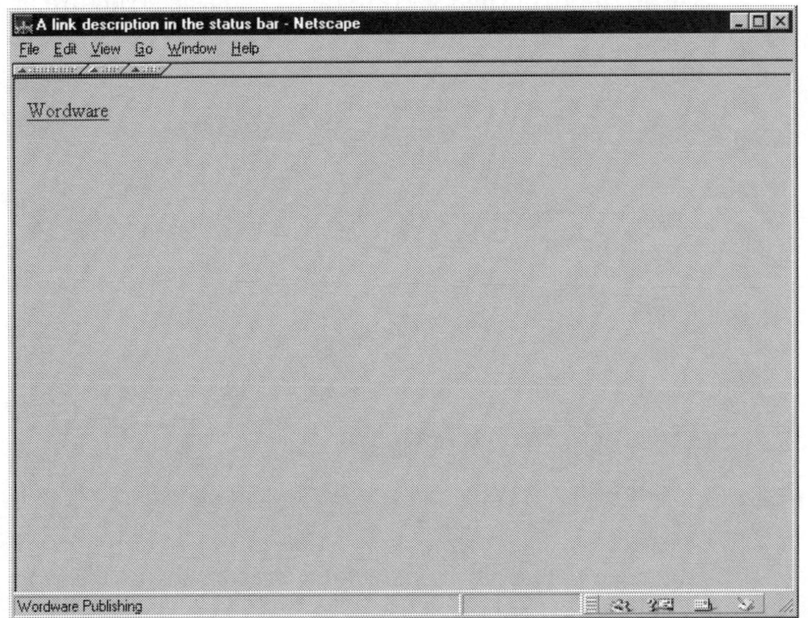

Figure 11-5*. A custom message in the status bar.*

It is sometimes problematic to execute statements directly in an event handler script. For example, if you want to include a long script, placing it in the event handler script makes the HTML page cumbersome, and maintenance becomes difficult. Another case in which difficulties can arise is when you want to correlate a script containing strings—quotation marks—to an event handler. As you can see, the event handler requires quotation marks to delimit the specified JavaScript code from the surrounding HTML content. JavaScript requires alternation of quotation types, single and double, so you will probably find it annoying to write scripts with an emphasis on quotes. Event handlers accept any JavaScript script, as long as it is valid. For that reason, you should associate functions with event handlers. The only statement you need in the event handler script is the function call.

You should normally place all functions at the top of the page, or more accurately, in the `<HEAD>...</HEAD>` portion of the document. This action forces JavaScript to evaluate your functions before it continues laying out the page. With this practice you guarantee that when the browser comes across an event handler in the HTML portion of the page, it will succeed to call the function associated with that event if it occurs. The only restriction is that you do not place any event handlers to pick up events before the JavaScript script in the <HEAD>...</HEAD> portion. Such a restriction applies also to external files implemented via the SRC attribute of the <SCRIPT> tag. The basic structure of such a page is:

```
<HTML>
<HEAD>
<TITLE>The title of the page</TITLE>
<SCRIPT LANGUAGE="JavaScript" [SRC="path.js"]>
<!--

function functionName(parameters) {
     statement1
     statement2
     statement3
     .
     .
     .
}

// -->
</SCRIPT>
</HEAD>
<BODY>
<TAG otherAttributes eventHandler="functionName(arguments)">
</BODY>
</HTML>
```

It is very easy to find the associated functions if you always place their definitions in the <HEAD>...</HEAD> portion of the page. The HTML portion of the page stays as simple as it was before JavaScript was even invented. The only new piece of HTML is the half-line attribute—the event handler. Another important advantage of using functions with event handlers is that you can use the same function many times in the same HTML page. For example, if you have a form with four text fields, you can validate each one of them using the same function, by calling this function upon occurrence of an event which is specific to one of the fields.

You may have noticed that the title is specified before the script tag. Although the title is specified via an HTML tag, it has no event handlers that could possibly invoke a function defined later. You will probably not have any problems if you do not follow this rule, although it is still a good practice, because it contributes to the neat organization of the page and guarantees that you will never have any layout problems.

onLoad and onUnload

Two very important event handlers are onLoad and onUnload. Their corresponding events, load and unload, are triggered by those actions. When the page has finished loading, the load event takes place. When the user exits a page in any way, the unload event occurs. These are the most simple event handlers because they are related to the most basic <BODY> tag, and are specified as attributes of this tag. The following document welcomes the user via an alert box when entering the page, and says goodbye when the user exits, also via an alert box:

```
<HTML>
<HEAD>
<TITLE>onLoad and onUnload event handlers</TITLE>
</HEAD>
<BODY onLoad="alert('Welcome to our page!')" onUnload="alert('Goodbye, and
don\'t forget to come back!')">
</BODY>
</HTML>
```

The onLoad event handler is widely used to call deferred scripts—functions. Placing a function call as the event handler's script enables you to control the timing of the execution, so the script executes only when the page is fully laid out.

onError

The onError event handler expands JavaScript's ability to interact with the user according to errors that occur. This event handler is not supported by Navigator 2.0x or IE 3.0x. It belongs to windows, but also to images. In this section we will only discuss it as associated with windows, because images are discussed later in the book.

An error event occurs when the loading of a window or image causes an error. The onError event handler executes a JavaScript script when such an error occurs.

The onError event handler is extremely useful due to the fact that it can be set to one of three values:

- null — suppresses all error dialogs. Setting window.onerror to null means your users won't see JavaScript errors caused by your own code.

- A function that handles errors — replaces the standard dialog boxes used by JavaScript to report errors.
- Variable that contains `null` or a valid function reference.

The following JavaScript statement disables JavaScript error dialogs:

```
window.onerror = null
```

You should place this statement in its own script directly after the <HEAD> tag to be on the safe side, using the following HTML document structure:

```
<HTML>
<HEAD>
<SCRIPT LANGUAGE="JavaScript">
<!--

window.onerror = null

// -->
</SCRIPT>
</HEAD>
<BODY>
</BODY>
</HTML>
```

The same rule applies to all values you assign to this event handler explicitly.

The following document does not display any error dialog, although an error is encountered. (If you can't fish it out, you may want to review the previous chapters, or just look at the `alert()` method's argument for a clue.)

```
<HTML>
<HEAD>
<SCRIPT LANGUAGE="JavaScript">
<!--

window.onerror = null

// -->
</SCRIPT>
</HEAD>
<BODY>
<SCRIPT LANGUAGE="JavaScript">
<!--

alert(Quotes missing)

// -->
```

```
</SCRIPT>
</BODY>
</HTML>
```

It is a good practice to set the `onError` event handler to `null` when your script runs on a public page. However, it makes no sense when writing the script, because it makes debugging impossible.

Here is another document that disables errors and therefore avoids a stack overflow error from being reported:

```
<HTML>
<HEAD>
<TITLE>Disabling error messages</TITLE>
<SCRIPT LANGUAGE="JavaScript">
<!--

// disable error reports
window.onerror = null

// create an error-generating function (infinite recursion)
function testErrorFunction() {
     testErrorFunction()
}

// -->
</SCRIPT>
</HEAD>
<BODY onload="testErrorFunction()">
</BODY>
</HTML>
```

An error occurs with or without assigning `null` to the event handler. The difference is that no response to the error on the browser's behalf is generated. See "Calling Event Handlers Explicitly" later in this chapter for a discussion on assigning values to event handlers via JavaScript.

Another option is to write a function to handle errors in place of the standard JavaScript error-reporting dialog boxes. The function should accept three arguments:

- The error message
- The URL of the script that caused the error
- The error line number

The function intercepts JavaScript errors. It must return the value `true`.

Here is a classic set of functions and statements for error handling:

```
<HTML>
<HEAD>
<SCRIPT LANGUAGE="JavaScript">
<!--

// assign user-defined function to intercept errors
window.onerror = myOnError

// create array to hold error messages
messageArray = new Array(0)

// create array to hold URLs of errors
urlArray = new Array(0)

// create array to hold line numbers of errors
lineNumberArray = new Array(0)

// error-intercepting function
function myOnError(msg, url, lno) {
     // assign message of current error to the array element following
                    the last element
     messageArray[messageArray.length] = msg

     // assign URL of current error to the array element following the
                    last element
     urlArray[urlArray.length] = url

     // assign line number of current error to the array element
                    following the last element
     lineNumberArray[lineNumberArray.length] = lno

     // return true to intercept JavaScript errors
     return true
}

function displayErrors() {
     // open new browser window to report errors
     errorWindow = window.open('','errors','scrollbars=yes')

     // write header to window
     errorWindow.document.write('<B>Error Report</B><P>')

     // loop to print all error data
     for (var i = 0; i < messageArray.length; ++i) {
          errorWindow.document.write('<B>Error in file:</B> ' +
                         urlArray[i] + '<BR>')
          errorWindow.document.write('<B>Line number:</B> ' +
                         lineNumberArray[i] + '<BR>')
          errorWindow.document.write('<B>Message:</B> ' +
                         messageArray[i] + '<P>')
```

```
        }

        // close data stream
        errorWindow.document.close()
}

// -->
</SCRIPT>
</HEAD>
<BODY>
<FORM>
<INPUT TYPE="button" onClick="displayErrors()" VALUE="display errors">
</FORM>
</BODY>
```

Example 11-3 (ex11-3.htm). *A set of functions to intercept and display a list of errors.*

At first, the function reference is assigned to `window.onerror`. Three arrays are then created; each holds a different piece of data associated with errors that might occur. The length of each array is set to 0, because no errors have occurred thus far. The function that intercepts the JavaScript errors is `myOnError()`. Its arguments are the error message, URL, and line number, respectively.

You do not need to understand the functions at this stage because they use concepts that have not been discussed yet, such as arrays and windows. The only point you should be aware of is that the function returns `true` to instruct JavaScript that it is intended to intercept the standard JavaScript errors. In general, a list of the JavaScript errors generated by the script is printed in another window when the user clicks the button. See the section "Calling Event Handlers Explicitly" for more details on the event handler implementation demonstrated in Example 11-3 (`window.onerror`).

Emulating Events via Methods

We mentioned earlier that each event belongs to a specific object. Some events are associated with more than one object, especially since the release of Netscape Navigator 3.0, which expanded certain events to additional objects. Another characteristic of objects is methods. They are functions that usually work on the data related to that object, the properties. Some methods of objects that include event handlers actually emulate those events. You can use such a method to cause an event to occur. These methods are usually called *event methods*. Although we will discuss these methods in depth later, here are some:

- `blur()`
- `click()`
- `focus()`
- `select()`
- `submit()`

Events generated with these methods are like any other method. Most importantly, they do not invoke their corresponding event handlers.

When you emulate an event, it is important that you do so only after the browser has finished laying out the page, or at least the object (usually a form element) with which the method is associated. The following page generates an error:

```
<HTML>
<HEAD>
<TITLE>Emulating an event of a non-existent (thus far) form</TITLE>
<SCRIPT LANGUAGE="JavaScript">
<!--

document.form1.field1.focus()

// -->
</SCRIPT>
</HEAD>
<BODY>
<FORM NAME="form1" METHOD=POST>
<INPUT TYPE="text" NAME="field1">
</FORM>
</BODY>
</HTML>
```

The error message is:

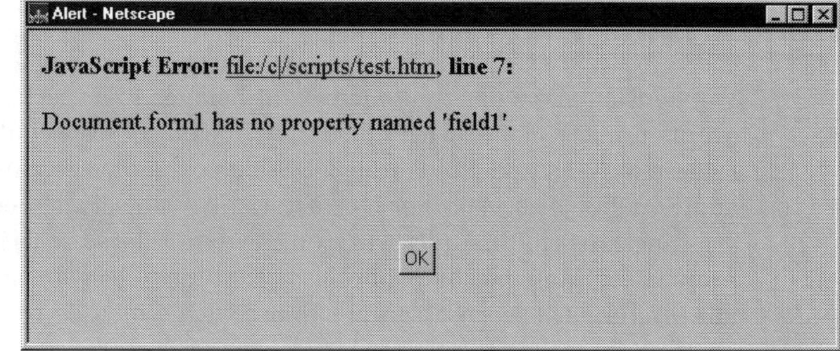
Alert - Netscape
JavaScript Error: file:/c|/scripts/test.htm, line 7:
Document.form1 has no property named 'field1'.
OK

Figure 11-6. *An error generated by a script that attempts to access a non-existent object.*

This error is not guaranteed to be exactly the same on all platforms. Emulating an object's event that has not yet been laid out is just one example that creates such an error. Generally speaking, you cannot refer to any element of a page that has not yet been laid out. A deferred script is allowed to refer to an object laid out after the script, provided that you do not execute that script before the object has been laid out. We will discuss this issue in depth throughout the book.

Calling Event Handlers Explicitly

In Netscape Navigator 3.0x and above you can set an event handler from within a JavaScript script. Here is a short example:

```
<HTML>
<HEAD>
<TITLE>Emulating an event of a non-existent (thus far) form</TITLE>
<SCRIPT LANGUAGE="JavaScript">
<!--

function alert1() {
     alert("This is the first function.")
}

function alert2() {
     alert("This is the second function.")
}

// -->
</SCRIPT>
</HEAD>
<BODY>
<FORM NAME="form1" METHOD=POST>
<INPUT TYPE="button" NAME="button1" VALUE="button1" onClick="alert1()">
</FORM>
<SCRIPT LANGUAGE="JavaScript">
<!--

document.form1.button1.onclick = alert2

// -->
</SCRIPT>
</BODY>
</HTML>
```

Example 11-4 (ex11-4.htm). *You can call a JavaScript script via an event handler.*

Try loading this page and clicking the button. If you are using Navigator 3.0x or 4.0, an alert box displays the message "This is the second function," despite the fact that the event handler associates the `click` event with the first function, `alert1()`. Notice the script placed directly after the form. It associates a different function with the `click` event of `button1` in `form1`.

Note Event handlers are function references as opposed to function calls. Therefore, you must assign `alert2`, not `alert2()`, which is primarily a function call, evaluating to the type and value the function returns. Also, since the event handler HTML attributes are literal function bodies, you cannot use `<INPUT … onClick=alert2>` in the HTML source. You must call the function instead. See Chapter 28, Evaluation and Compilation.

You are probably wondering why we used `onclick` rather than `onClick`. The reason is that JavaScript is case sensitive and understands `onclick` (all lowercase), whereas HTML is case insensitive. In HTML, you may use all lowercase, all uppercase, or any other convention you choose.

Calling event handlers explicitly enables flexible event handlers, because you can modify them anywhere in the script. You can create a customized page, allowing the user to determine what a certain button should do when clicked.

An event handler does not have to exist when you use this technique. The preceding script would work exactly the same if you omitted the event handler specification in the HTML source and used the following line instead:

```
<INPUT TYPE="button" NAME="button1" VALUE="button1">
```

In this case you are actually defining a new event handler to correspond with an event.

Also note that the above method is the only way to assign a function reference to an event handler. You <u>cannot</u> use any of the following structures:

```
<SCRIPT LANGUAGE="JavaScript">
<!--

document.form1.button1.onclick = "alert2()"

// -->
```

```
<SCRIPT LANGUAGE="JavaScript">
<!--

document.form1.button1.onclick = alert2()

// -->
```

```
<SCRIPT LANGUAGE="JavaScript">
<!--

document.form1.button1.onclick = "var counter = 5"

// -->
```

Such attempts to assign statements that are not function references result in an error upon clicking the button:

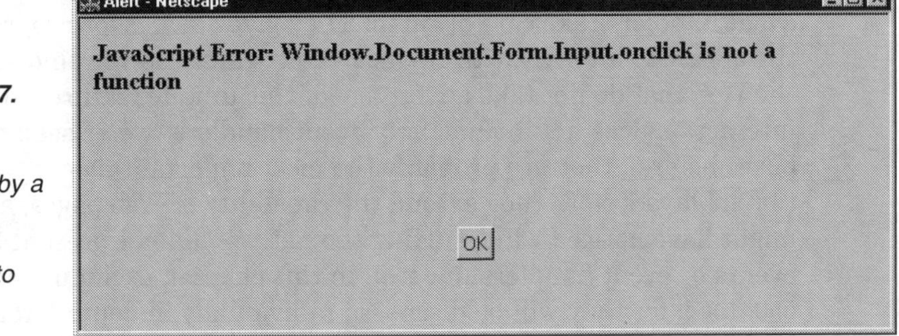
Alert - Netscape
JavaScript Error: Window.Document.Form.Input.onclick is not a function
OK

Figure 11-7. An error message generated by a script that assigns a statement to an event handler.

Cancelling Events

Netscape Navigator 3.0x and 4.0 make it possible to cancel a `click` event, either with a hypertext link or a client-side image map. The `onClick` event handler can return false to cancel the action normally associated with a `click` event. Here is an example:

```
<HTML>
<HEAD>
<TITLE>Cancelling events in onClick</TITLE>
<BODY>
```

```
<A HREF="http://www.netscape.com/" onClick="return confirm('Load
                Netscape home page?')">Netscape</a>

</BODY>
</HTML>
```

Example 11-5 (ex11-5.htm). *Try running this script to cancel the event.*

When you click the hypertext link, a confirm box pops up. If you click OK, the method evaluates to `true`, the event qualifies, and the new page (Netscape's home page) loads. If the user selects Cancel, the method returns `false`, and the new page, associated with the `click` event, does not load.

Summary

In this chapter you discovered events and event handlers. JavaScript is known to add interaction to Web pages, meaning you can respond to actions that the user performs. Events describe such actions, whereas event handlers take care of them. They give JavaScript programmers the ability to interact with the user. Only rarely do you find scripts on the Web that do not take advantage of this unique feature. Although interaction does not include only event handlers (we've seen dialog boxes before), they are probably the most important means of interaction in JavaScript. They extend the capability of Web pages, as you might have noticed while surfing the net. We did not present any events or event handlers in detail in this chapter, excluding `onLoad` and `onUnload`, for they will be discussed individually in depth later in the book. Each event and its corresponding handler has significant features. As you will see later, all events are associated with specific objects, so it is important that you be introduced to these objects before we discuss their event handlers.

Chapter 12

Building and Extending Objects

Creating Instances

Objects are templates by which you create *instances*. For example, suppose you have defined an employee object that includes some methods and properties of an employee, such as his or her social security number and address. This definition has no effect on the script, because no new entity has been changed or created. Only when you apply the object's definition to a specific person, say John Doe, is a new entity created—an instance of that object. The number of instances you create with a single object definition is unlimited. The object definition can be either one you define with a function, or a built-in one. Creating an instance of a built-in object is relatively simple because the object is predefined. As you will see later, you can extend an existing object by adding new properties and methods to it.

You should use the following syntax to create an instance:

```
var name = new constructorFunction([arguments])
```

So, if you want to create an instance of the String object, you can use the following statement:

```
var str1 = new String("Hello!")
```

This statement creates an instance named str1. You can create another instance if you like:

```
var str2 = new String("Hi!")
```

The instances str1 and str2 act similarly to regular variables. You can pass them on to functions as in:

```
function printValue(val) {
     document.write("*** " + val + " ***")
}
printValue(str1)
```

You can also return objects:

```
function printValue(obj) {
     return obj
}
```

Remember that if you create an instance of an object inside a function, it is considered local, i.e., it is visible only inside the function during the function's current execution course. If you declare the instance outside a function, it is preferable that you use the `var` keyword. When you create an instance of an object inside a function without `var`, it is a global structure. Bear in mind that if you create a global instance, or even a simple variable inside a function, you must execute the function before that global data structure exists in the script. From that point on you can refer to it freely anywhere in the document.

When you create an instance of an object via the `new` operator, you are actually declaring a specific data structure according to the object's definition. All properties referenced in the constructor function are accessible as properties of the object's instance.

Note that object definitions (constructor functions) do not take up any memory, because they are abstract units. However, instances are data structures so they do require some RAM space, depending on their exact structure and data.

After you have created an instance of an object, you do not have to use the keyword `new` anymore when referring to that instance. However, if you want one of the instance's properties to be an instance of its own, you must use `new` again to create the new object.

An instance of an object also features its methods. Each instance has a reference to the function playing the role of that method. You do not have to worry about this, because when you refer to the instance's method, you only specify the name of that method. The reference is already defined in the constructor function, so it invokes the corresponding function.

Take a look at the following example:

```
var current = new Date() // the current date
var minutes = current.getMinutes()
var current2 = new Date() // the current date
var minutes2 = current2.getMinutes()
```

As you can see, both instances have methods. A method belongs to a specific instance but not to the general object. Sometimes two different instances of the same object do not have the same methods and properties. This happens when the constructor function includes a conditional statement to determine which methods should be applied to the current instance being defined, or when a single instance of an object is modified afterwards.

Note An object is an abstract definition, whereas an instance is a data structure defined according to an object. Therefore the term "object" differs from "instance." However, instances are commonly referred to as objects. It should be very clear where the term "object" refers to an instance. In this book we often refer to instances as objects, so do not be confused.

Constructor Functions

As you learned earlier, JavaScript supports functions that build custom objects. In order to create such functions you must know how to define properties and methods. A *constructor function* is a simple function that defines the properties and methods of the relevant object type. You can think of built-in objects as objects whose constructor functions are predefined in JavaScript, so you do not need to write them on your own.

A constructor function resembles a cookie cutter. You provide it some dough and it gives the dough the proper shape. The cookie cutter is like the constructor function because they both receive a simple structure and change it according to a specified template.

Defining Object Properties

The keyword `this` is probably the most important word related to objects in JavaScript. It refers to the current object, or instance. Inside a constructor function it refers to the instance for which the function was called. Take a look at the following function:

```
function student(name, age, avgGrade) {
     this.name = name
```

```
        this.age = age
        this.grade = avgGrade
}
```

This function accepts three arguments. It defines an object type of a student in a class. The properties are `name`, `age`, and `grade`, and they are initialized by the values passed on to the function. You can use the following statement to create an instance of this object—a student in a class:

```
var student1 = new student("Sharon", 16, 85)
```

Now you can refer to these properties in the following fashion:

```
alert(student1.name + " is a cute " + student1.age + " - year old.)
```

Figure 12-1. *A simple message built according to the properties of the object.*

It is also possible to add properties to an object once it has been created. Such properties exist only in the specific instance to which they are assigned. The following script segment demonstrates this:

```
function student(name, age, avgGrade) {
        this.name = name
        this.age = age
        this.grade = avgGrade
}


var student1 = new student("Sharon", 16, 85)

student1.sex = "female"
var message = student1.name + " is a cute " + student1.age
message += " - year old "
message += (student1.sex == "female") ? "girl." : "boy."
alert(message)
```

Its output is:

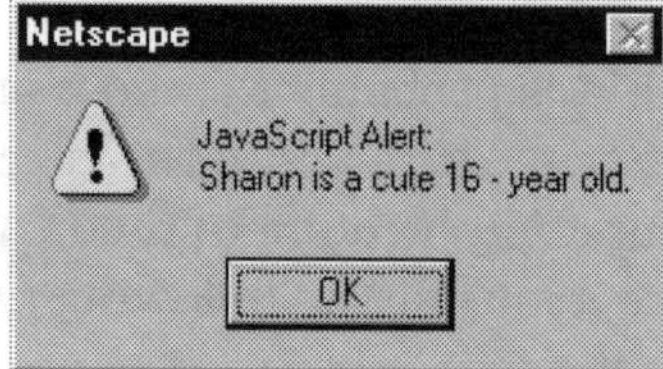

Figure 12-2. *A simple message constructed off an object's properties, including the ones assigned to it after it was constructed.*

The problem with the preceding script is that it adds the new property only to one instance, `student1`. Because constructor functions are just like any other function, you can use valid JavaScript statements in them. Therefore, you can use the following constructor function to add the new property to all instances of the `student` object:

```
function student(name, age, avgGrade, sex) {
     this.name = name
     this.age = age
     this.grade = avgGrade
     this.description = (sex == "female") ? "girl" : "boy"
}
```

Now you can create instances that will include the "girl" or "boy" description:

```
var student2 = new student("Joe", 16, 91, "male")
```

Like before, you can use these properties for many purposes, such as displaying messages:

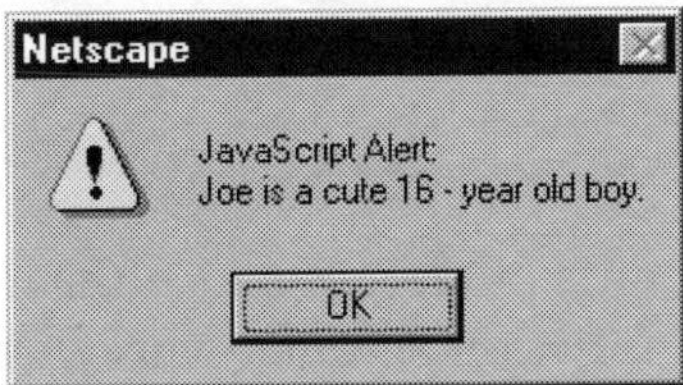

Figure 12-3. *A message generated according to an instance's properties.*

The keyword `this` refers to the calling object. When you use it in a constructor function it refers to the instance that calls the function. For example, if `student2` calls the constructor function `student()`, the keyword `this` inside the function refers to `student2`. Therefore, the statement

```
this.name = name
```

creates a new property of the instance `student2` and initializes it with the corresponding value.

Based on the exact definition of the word `this`, some JavaScript tends to use alternative structures for construction functions. Here is the preceding example in a different form:

```
function student(name, age, avgGrade, sex) {
     obj = this
     obj.name = name
     obj.age = age
     obj.grade = avgGrade
```

```
    obj.description = (sex == "female") ? "girl" : "boy"
}
```

Notice that the calling object, referred to as `this`, is assigned to a variable. This variable must be global because a constructor function's purpose is to create an instance for use outside of that function. A local variable does not have any effect outside the function where it is declared. It is recommended that you do not use this form of constructor functions; it is better to get used to the keyword `this`.

Another key concept to remember is that a constructor function cannot include any direct reference to an existing instance of that object. According to this rule, the following script generates an error:

```
function student(name, age, avgGrade, sex) {
    this.name = name
    this.age = age
    this.grade = avgGrade
    this.description = (sex == "female") ? "girl" : "boy"
    alert("student3 = " + student3.name)

}

var student3 = new student("Kelly", 15, 78, "female")
```

You can only refer to the elements of an instance after it has been created, because the constructor function actually works by returning the calling data structure. You can, however, refer to a specific instance inside a constructor function if it was created by a different constructor function or by a previous call to the current constructor:

```
function student(name, age, avgGrade, sex) {
    this.name = name
    this.age = age
    this.grade = avgGrade
    this.description = (sex == "female") ? "girl" : "boy"
    if (name == "Joe")
        alert("student3 = " + student3.name)

}

var student3 = new student("Kelly", 15, 78, "female")
var student2 = new student("Joe", 17, 91, "male")
```

In this script segment the constructor function checks if the name of the calling object is "Joe." If so, it displays the name of `student3`, which was created earlier by the same function.

Keep in mind that the keyword `this` refers to the calling object. The undercover value of the word `this` is an object. The statement

```
alert(this)
```

prints the string value of the keyword `this` in a constructor function.

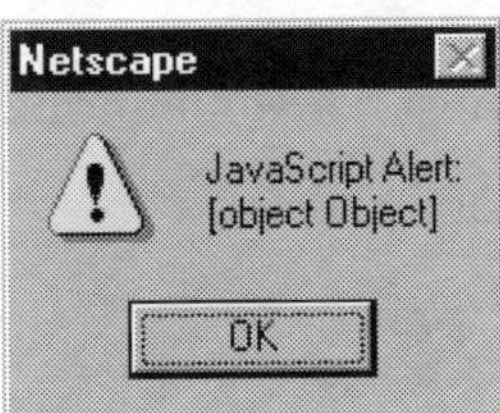

***Figure 12-4.** The undercover value of `this` inside a constructor function.*

You now know how to define properties via constructor functions. If you only want to create one instance of an object, you must also use a constructor function.

To view the properties of an object you can use the function presented in Chapter 8, Control Structures:

```
function getProps(obj, objName) {
     var result = "" // initialize output string

     for (var i in obj) {
          result += objName + "." + i + " = " + obj[i] + "<BR>"
     }
     result += "<HR>" // add horizontal rule to output string
     return(result) // return output string
}
```

To invoke this method use a statement such as:

```
document.write(getProps(student1, "student1"))
```

Note that the arguments are not always the same. For example, if you use this statement from within another function that accepts the instance `student1` as the parameter `person`, you should use the following statement instead:

```
document.write(getProps(person, "student1"))
```

If a property of an object holds a `null` value, it does not exist. Assigning a `null` value to a property will cause the function `getProps()` to count out that property. Keep this in mind, especially when you are debugging a script.

Nested Objects

JavaScript supports *nested objects*. A nested object is an object that is also a property of another object. There are a few ways to create nested objects. We will present the most convenient one.

Take a look at the following script portion:

```
function student(name, age, grade, father, mother) {
     this.name = name
     this.age = age
     this.grade = grade
     this.parents = new parents(father, mother)
}

function parents(father, mother) {
     this.father = father
     this.mother = mother
}

var student1 = new student("Sharon", 16, 85, "Mark", "Stacy")
```

This script consists of two functions. The function `parents()` creates an instance containing two properties, `father` and `mother`. It accepts both values as arguments.

The first function, `student()`, creates a function consisting of four properties. The first three are simple properties like the ones you have seen earlier in this chapter. The fourth property is an instance of an object. This instance is created by the `parents()` function, as described earlier.

You can refer to all elements of an object with the "dot" syntax:

```
student1.name
student1.age
student1.grade
student1.parents.father
student1.parents.mother
```

The property-printing function presented earlier does not fully work properly with nested objects, because it only accesses the object's top-most level. To print the properties of a general object you can use the following recursive function (works only in Netscape Navigator 3.0x, 4.0, and above):

```
function getProps(obj, objName) {
     // initialize accumulative variable
     var result = ""
```

```
        // loop through properties
        for (var i in obj) {
                // if current property is an object call function for it
                if (typeof obj[i] == "object")
                        result += getProps(obj[i], objName + "." + i)
                else
                        result += objName + "." + i + " = " + obj[i] + "<BR>"
        }

        // return final result
        return result
}
```

The function's algorithm is fairly simple. It loops through the properties of the main object. If the current property, represented by `i`, is an object, the function is called once again with the property `obj[i]` as the object, and the property's name attached to object's name with a separating dot (`objName + "." + i`). Each call to the function returns the string listing the properties at the current level. The value returned by a recursive call is assigned to the variable `result` which is local in the calling function. Here is an entire HTML document and its output to help you understand this concept:

```
<HTML>
<HEAD>
<TITLE>Printing properties of nested objects</TITLE>
<SCRIPT LANGUAGE="JavaScript">
<!--

function student(name, age, grade, father, mother) {
        this.name = name
        this.age = age
        this.grade = grade
        this.parents = new parents(father, mother)
}

function parents(father, mother) {
        this.father = father
        this.mother = mother
}

var student1 = new student("Sharon", 16, 85, "Mark", "Stacy")

function getProps(obj, objName) {
        var result = ""
        for (var i in obj) {
                if (typeof obj[i] == "object")
                        result += getProps(obj[i], objName + "." + i)
                else
                        result += objName + "." + i + " = " + obj[i] + "<BR>"
```

```
        }
        return result
}

document.write(getProps(student1, "student1"))

// -->
</SCRIPT>
</HEAD>
<BODY>
</BODY>
</HTML>
```

Example 12-1. *A script that uses the getProps() function to analyze the structure of an object.*

Defining Methods

Objects group data and functions that process that data. Data appears in the form of properties. A method is simply a function associated with an object. Consider the following function:

```
function displayStudent() {
        var result = ""
        result += this.name + " -- "
        result += "a " + this.age + " - year old "
        result += this.grade + "% average student.<BR>"
        result += this.name + "'s parents -- "
        result += this.parents.father + ", " + this.parents.mother
        result += ".<BR>"
        document.write(result)
}
```

You need to include a reference to this function in the constructor function. This is done exactly like you define properties:

```
function displayStudent() {
        var result = ""
        result += this.name + " -- "
        result += "a " + this.age + " - year old "
        result += this.grade + "% average student.<BR>"
        result += this.name + "'s parents -- "
        result += this.parents.father + ", " + this.parents.mother
        result += ".<BR>"
        document.write(result)
}


function student(name, age, grade, father, mother) {
        this.name = name
        this.age = age
        this.grade = grade
```

```
        this.parents = new parents(father, mother)
        this.display = displayStudent
}

function parents(father, mother) {
        this.father = father
        this.mother = mother
}
```

The following statements create an instance and invoke the `display()` method:

```
var student1 = new student("Sharon", 16, 85, "Mark", "Stacy")
student1.display()
```

Notice the extensive use of the keyword `this` inside the function to refer to the object. The main characteristic of a method is that it usually processes the data of its object. You can even create a "constructor method" in the following fashion:

```
function construct(name, val) {
        this[name] = val
}


function student(name, age, grade, father, mother) {
        this.construct = construct
        this.name = name
        this.age = age
        this.grade = grade
        this.parents = new parents(father, mother)
}

function parents(father, mother) {
        this.father = father
        this.mother = mother
}

var student1 = new student("Sharon", 16, 85, "Mark", "Stacy")
student1.construct("boyfriend", "Tom")
```

Notice that the method (`construct()`) refers to the new property via the array notation. You may recall from Chapter 6, Object-Based Programming, that you must use this notation if you wish to use a data value. You can only use the "dot" syntax when you use literals. In this case, `name` is a data structure, not a literal (a literal is a constant value you can see, such as `"boyfriend"`). Now you can use the recursive function presented earlier to view the elements of an object, and to see how it works with methods:

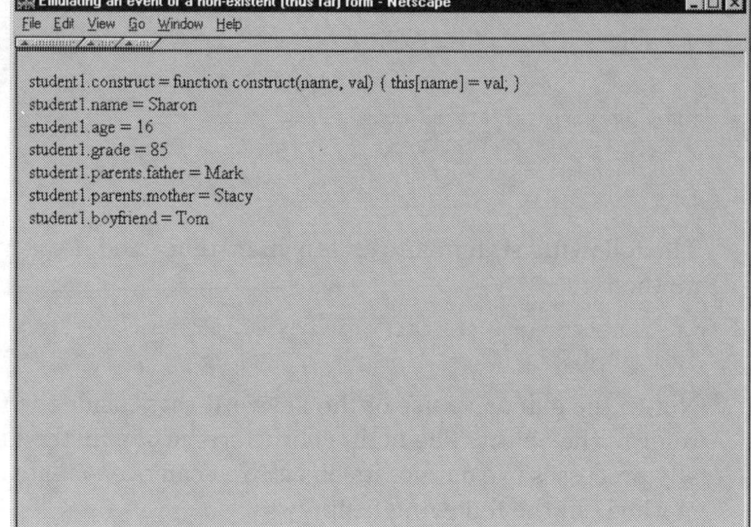

Figure 12-5. *The output of the function getProps() when handed an object consisting of a method.*

Notice that the recursive function works with methods as well as with properties. The statements of the method are placed on the same line. JavaScript automatically adds semicolons to delimit the statement. It also uses a uniform coding scheme if you did not do so originally in the function, as you should.

A method in JavaScript, like a property, belongs only to one instance. You can only invoke it from that instance. All "communication" with an object is done via methods.

The calling object is considered global inside a method. You can modify the object using the word `this`.

Creating Objects—An Example

Let's say you want to create a database-like object structure for a store that sells televisions. Each type of television should be an instance of the same object. The number of televisions of a certain model available in stock should be a property of the object. It should also include the features of that television set. In addition, the object should include two methods: one to be invoked when a customer buys a television set, and another to be invoked when the store owner orders a certain quantity of television sets of a given model.

Example 12-2 demonstrates the most important points.

```
<HTML>
<HEAD>
<SCRIPT LANGUAGE="JavaScript">
```

```
<!--

function television(brand, size, price, num) {
     this.brand = brand     // property
     this.size = size       // property
     this.price = price     // property
     this.num = num         // property
     this.sell = sell       // method
     this.buy = buy         // method
     this.display = display // method
}

function sell(quantity) {
     if (quantity > this.num)
          alert("Not enough " + this.brand + " " + this.size + "\" sets
                              in stock.")
     else
          this.num -= quantity
     if (quantity < 5)
          alert("Order more " + this.brand + " " + this.size + "\" sets
                              urgently.")
}

function buy(quantity) {
     this.num += quantity
}

function display() {
     var result = ""
     result += "<TABLE BORDER=2><TR>"
     result += "<TD WIDTH = 60>" + this.brand + "</TD>"
     result += "<TD WIDTH = 30>" + this.size + "\"</TD>"
     result += "<TD WIDTH = 45>$" + this.price + "</TD>"
     result += "<TD WIDTH = 45>" + this.num + " left</TD>"
     result += "</TR></TABLE>"
     document.write(result)
}

var tel1 = new television("Sony", 27, 1200, 30)
var tel2 = new television("JVC", 20, 650, 20)
var tel3 = new television("Grundig", 14, 420, 45)

tel1.sell(27) // 27 "Sony" television sets sold
tel1.buy(16) // 16 "Sony" television sets ordered (bought)
tel1.display()
tel2.sell(21) // 21 "JVC" television sets sold -- error!
tel2.sell(1) // 1 "JVC" television set sold
tel2.display()
tel3.display()

// -->
</SCRIPT>
```

```
</HEAD>
<BODY>
</BODY>
</HTML>
```

Example 12-2. *A script that stores data using instances of a general object.*

Example 12-2 features three methods:

- `sell()`

  This method modifies the number of television sets of the model number specified in the object. The function's only parameter is one that accepts the number of television sets sold. It checks if there are enough sets in stock, because you cannot sell more than you've got! If there are enough sets of that type in stock, the number is subtracted from the total quantity of that TV available before the transaction. Lastly, the method checks if there are less than five TV sets of that type left. If so, it alerts a message describing that situation.

- `buy()`

  This method simply adds the number of television sets to the `num` property of the object, or instance. The only parameter accepted by the method is the one that accepts the number of television sets bought.

- `display()`

  This method does not accept any arguments. It simply prints all the properties of the current object in a tabular format.

Notice that the first two methods actually change values of the object. This is another example that shows that methods refer to their calling object as global, so all properties of the object modified inside the function (method) are also affected outside the method.

Prototype and Object Extensions

A *prototype* is a property of any object created with the keyword `new`. A prototype resembles the common e-mail address portion of users sharing the same server. Likewise, a prototype belongs to all instances of the object that the prototype belongs to. Prototypes refer not only to properties, but also to an object's methods. Take a look at the following script segment:

```
var str1 = new String("a"), str2 = new String("b")
```

```
function repeat(n, delimiter) {
     var text = ""
     var str = this.toString() // make sure the object is string
     while (n >= 0) {
          text += str
          text += delimiter
          n--
     }
     return text
}

String.prototype.repeat = repeat // String == name of object
                                  // add a repeat() method to String
alert(str1.repeat(5, " ; "))
alert(str1)
alert(str2.repeat(7, " "))
alert(str2.repeat(3))
```

You can see that the function `repeat()` is typical for a method. As a matter of fact, it is implemented as one. The key statement in this script is:

```
String.prototype.repeat = repeat
```

This statement adds a method to all instances of the object (`String`), although they were already created. The word "`prototype`" is constant, and its role is to merely specify that the following property or method is a prototype. It may seem at first that `repeat()` is a method of a nested object. However, `prototype` is not actually a property but a specification. Here are some of the alert boxes generated by the preceding script segment:

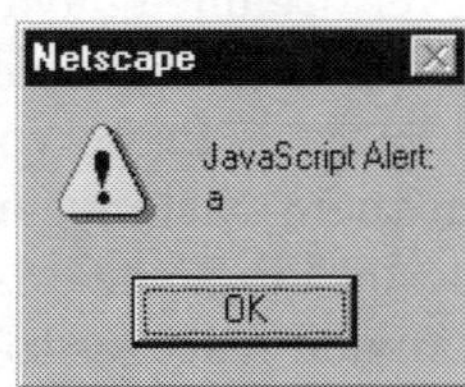

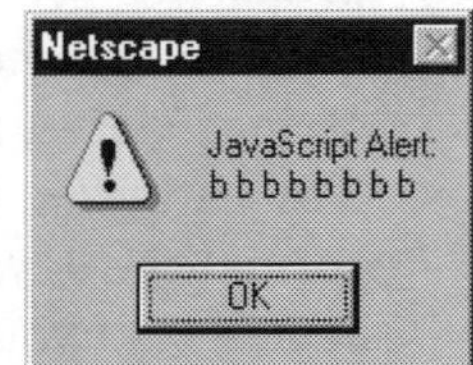

Figures 12-6, 7, and 8. *Object prototypes enable extendible objects in JavaScript.*

It is important to know that object prototypes refer to instances of the object created before the definition of the prototype as well as instances that are created later. The prototype exists only from the moment it is defined. Be sure to refer to such prototype properties and methods only after you have created the prototype. Commenting scripts helps assure that you follow this rule.

Up until now you have seen a method used as a prototype. Obviously, properties can also accomplish this task. In the following script we will look at a property as a prototype of a user-defined object. Here is the script:

```
function car(make, model, year) {
   this.make = make
   this.model = model
   this.year = year
}

var mine1 = new car("Hyundai", "Lantra", 1996)

car.prototype.wheels = 4 // no 3-wheelers please!

var mine2 = new car("Mazda", "Prodigy", 1996)

if (mine1.wheels == 4 && mine2.wheels == 4) // true!
     document.write("Both cars have ", mine2.wheels, " wheels.")
```

The message at the end of the script is printed, because all instances of the car object, whether they are created before the definition of the prototype or after it, consist of a property named wheels, holding the value 4, which is assigned to the prototype. It is practically useless to create a data property prototype without assigning it a value, or at least a default one, because you will need to refer to that property later, and such reference automatically creates the property.

Prototypes are probably more useful with built-in objects, because they can modify the object. You can create outstanding methods and properties you never dreamed JavaScript would support. We use prototypes in many examples in this book, especially ones dealing with strings, dates, and arrays. Prototypes were not supported in Netscape Navigator 2.x, but their existence in Navigator 3.0x (and above) turned the JavaScript language upside down. The revolutionary concept is that you can add features to the language itself, almost as if you were one of JavaScript's developers at Netscape Corp. or Microsoft (although MSIE 3.0x does not support this feature). Note that prototypes can only be added to objects that support instances, as opposed to static objects (such as Math) which do not work with prototypes for obvious reasons.

Summary

In this chapter you learned how to create instances of an object. Instances refer to both user-defined objects as well as to built-in ones. We also discussed constructor functions that build objects or object types. As you will see later in the book, such user-defined objects extend the capabilities of the language and enable structured programming. Lastly, we presented object prototypes—properties of all instances of a certain object type. Although it should be clear by now, do not worry too much about how to use them, as they will be used in many examples later on in the book. Objects are the backbone of JavaScript. Many elements of the language are actually objects, although other languages do not refer to them as such. The classic example for such objects are arrays, discussed later in depth.

Chapter 13

Arrays

What is an Array?

Arrays are data structures, somewhat more complex than simple variables. As a matter of fact, an array in JavaScript is a set of variables with the same name. We use arrays when we want to work with a certain block of data. As a programmer, if you want to process an individual item of an array you need to specify the array name and indicate which array element is being referenced. Specific elements are indicated by an index or a subscript. This way you can have endless variables defined quickly and acted upon either individually or as a group.

If you are constructing a building you need bricks. Naming each brick ("Arthur", "Jordan", ...) is fine for a small number of bricks. Such bricks are known as variables in JavaScript. Sometimes you want to refer to tens, hundreds, or even more bricks. It would be difficult to name each brick separately. A much more convenient naming scheme is "brick 0", "brick 1", "brick 2", "brick 3", and so forth. Arrays allow us to do that with variables. An array is a set of memory locations used to store data. Each item in an array is called an *element*.

Some History

The first version of JavaScript, the one supported by Navigator 2.x, did not feature arrays. This was very strange because whether it is a scripting language like Perl, or a programming language like C++, it must have an explicit array type. JavaScript scripters had no choice but to come up with a simple workaround. Everyone used (and most still use) the following function to create arrays:

```
function createArray(n, init) {
     this.length = n
     for (i = 1 ; i <= n ; i++) {
          this[i] = init
     }
}
```

Some variants of this function did not include the size specification, or did not include the `init` parameter, initializing the array to the same value each time. Not only did JavaScript scripters have to use a custom function just to create an array, no built-in methods or functions were available to deal with such arrays. Sorting arrays became a difficult, inefficient task. Combining arrays was even more difficult. It was obvious that a change needed to be made. And indeed, Netscape Navigator 3.0 introduced a whole new version supporting arrays.

Creating Simple Arrays

Arrays in JavaScript are simple built-in objects. You create an array just like an instance of an object, because that is exactly what it is. The formal name of the object is `Array`—notice the capitalized "A." The general syntax is:

```
var arrayObjectName = new Array()
var arrayObjectName = new Array(arrayLength)
```

`arrayObjectName` is either the name of a new object, an existing variable, or a property of an existing object.

`arrayLength` is the initial length of the array. You can access this value using the length property.

As you can see, specifying the length of the array or the number of elements is not vital. An array is an object like any other object. There is no explicit array type in JavaScript.

Here are some arrays:

```
var day = new Array(31)
var month = new Array(12)
var year = new Array() // number of years "not known"
```

It is unnecessary to understand how arrays correspond with the computer memory because you will not need to use lots of memory in any of your scripts, so let JavaScript do the job for you.

All elements of an array are initially `null`. This is important because such elements do not have any influence on your script. An element with a `null` value actually does not exist. You can prove this to yourself by running the `getProps()` on a new array:

```
function getProps(obj, objName) {
     var result = ""
     for (var i in obj) {
          if (typeof obj[i] == "object")
               result += getProps(obj[i], objName + "[" + i + "]")
          else
               result += objName + "[" + i + "] = " + obj[i] + "<BR>"
     }
     return result
}

var ar = new Array(3)

document.write(getProps(ar, "ar"))
```

This script does not generate any output, because if a property of an object has a `null` value, it does not exist in the computer memory, so it is not recognized.

Strongly typed programming languages require that you specify the number of elements in an array. In such languages all elements of an array must contain values of the same type (`int`, `char`, ...). An array is an explicit data structure in those languages, so it is not an object as in JavaScript. `null` values are not given to the elements of an array. From the moment an array is declared, it takes up the required storage area in memory. It does not matter if you initialized its values or not. Theoretically, if you created an array without specifying the number of elements, it would be as if you created one with zero elements. Extending an array in such languages is usually not possible; therefore you must specify the length in all array declarations.

The `null` value is given by default to each element of an array in JavaScript. When the value is `null`, the element is not stored in the computer's memory. So creating an array with an infinite number of elements is fine in JavaScript. Keep in mind that elements holding a `null` value do not take up space in memory, but they are considered elements in the array, so they are added to the array's `length` property.

With JavaScript, like Perl and unlike C++, it doesn't matter whether the elements of an array are of the same data type. They can be a mix of numbers, strings, Boolean values, objects, and even arrays (which are actually objects).

Referring to an Array's Elements

To use an event you must be able to refer to its elements. Arrays in JavaScript are objects. Like all other objects, they have properties and methods:

```
arrayObjectName.propertyName // ar1.length
arrayObjectName[subscript] // ar1[4]
arrayObjectName.methodName(arguments)
```

In this section we will discuss the second reference, whereas the others are presented later in the chapter.

The *subscript* follows the array name and is enclosed in square brackets. Subscripts are simple integers which start at zero.

Here is a simple array:

```
var ar = new Array(5)
```

This array has five elements: ar[0], ar[1], ar[2], ar[3], ar[4].

After you create an array you can increase its length by specifying a value for the highest subscript element. The following code creates an array of length zero, then assigns a null value to element 99. This changes the length of the array to 100.

```
accounts = new Array() // array of zero elements
accounts[99] = null // array of 100 elements
```

Note that the array does not take up any storage space, even after it is extended.

When referring to an element, the subscript can be either a literal (e.g., 3) or a variable (e.g., num = 3).

An element of an array can be any valid value. It can be a string, a number, a Boolean value, a null value, or even another object. For example, if you want to create an array in which each element is a student object, you can use the following statements:

```
function student() { // constructor function
     // properties not initialized to meaningful value
     this.name = ""
     this.age = ""
     this.grade = ""
}

var size = 35 // num of students in class
var students = new Array(size) // array is defined
```

```
for (var i = 0; i < size; i++) {
     students[i] = new student()
}

students[0].name = "Mark"
students[32].grade = 88
```

At first, the desired size of the array, the number of students in the class, is assigned to the variable `size`. An array of that size is then created. All elements of the array, from `students[0]` to `students[34]`, are then defined using the constructor function `student()`. In this example, all of the elements in the array are of the same type. An array can have elements of different types. Here is an example:

```
function student() { // constructor function
     // properties not initialized to meaningful value
     this.name = ""
     this.age = ""
     this.grade = ""
}

function teacher(name, age) {
     this.name = name
     this.age = age
}

var size = 35 // num of students in class
var students = new Array(size + 1) // array is defined

students[0] = new teacher("Kate", 45)

for (var i = 1; i < size + 1; i++) { // or i <= size
     students[i] = new student()
}

alert("    is the teacher." + students[0].name)
```

In this script segment an array of `size + 1` elements is defined, because the first element, `students[0]`, holds an instance of the `teacher` object.

The output of this script is:

Figure 13-1. *Elements of an array can be of different types.*

The most important rule is that the subscript, or index, starts at zero. Although it might seem quite awkward, use this element like all other elements of the array. It looks better if you start referencing at 0 rather than at 1, like some amateur scripters do.

Creating Dense Arrays

You can construct a *dense* array of two or more elements starting with index (subscript) 0, if you define initial values for all elements. A dense array is one in which each element has a value. They are very popular in many scripting languages, especially in Perl. You can populate an array by specifying the values of its elements:

```
var bb = "baseball"
var sports = new Array("football", bb, "basketball", "soccer")
```

You can refer to the elements of this array with the common syntax:

```
sports[0] == "football"
sports[1] == "baseball"
var val = 2
sports[val] == "basketball"
sports[3] == "soccer"
```

JavaScript for Navigator 3.0 still lacks many features related to arrays that are supported by Perl:

- You cannot assign a list of elements to an array (except when you create it).
- You cannot assign a range to an array.
- You cannot assign elements of one array's values to another array (the resulting array is an *array slice*).

Array Types

JavaScript is a loosely typed language, just like Perl. It is not surprising, therefore, that elements of an array can be of different types. Some elements of a given array can be strings, other can be numbers, Boolean values, and even objects. Basically, there are five types of arrays:

- String arrays
- Number arrays
- Boolean arrays

- Object arrays (including `null` arrays, because `null` is an object)
- Mixed arrays

Sometimes you want to know what type of array you are dealing with. JavaScript does not include any tool to facilitate this. However, using a prototype we can add a property to all arrays (remember, arrays are objects by which you can create instances) which will return the type of the array. Here is the desired method:

```
function getType() {
     var arrayType = typeof this[0]
     for (var i = 1; i < this.length; ++i) {
          if (typeof this[i] != arrayType) {
               arrayType = "mixed"
               break
          }
     }
     return arrayType
}

Array.prototype.getType = getType
```

The following script segment is based on the preceding prototype definition:

```
var ar1 = new Array(3)
ar1[0] = "a"
ar1[1] = "b"
ar1[2] = ""
document.write(ar1.getType()) // string

var ar2 = new Array(2)
ar2[0] = 17
ar2[1] = 15.5
document.write(ar2.getType()) // number

var ar3 = new Array()
document.write(ar3.getType()) // object

var ar4 = new Array(0)
document.write(ar4.getType()) // object

var ar5 = new Array(1)
ar5[9999] = 5
document.write(ar5.getType()) // mixed
```

If you tried out the fifth array, you probably had to wait for a while, because the loop executed 10,000 times! You can use a more efficient function for the same prototype:

```
function getType() {
      var arrayType = typeof this[0]
      for (var i in this) {
            if (typeof this[i] != arrayType) {
                  arrayType = "mixed"
                  break
            }
      }
      return arrayType
}

Array.prototype.getType = getType
```

The improvement in this function is the type of loop used. The `for...in` construct loops only through the existing properties, or elements, not including the `null` ones. The function works just like the previous one. At first, the data type of the first element of the array is assigned to `arrayType`. In every iteration of the loop, if a different type element is found, the value of `arrayType` is changed to "`mixed`" because at least two different data types have been found in the array. Once a "`mixed`" array is detected, the loop is immediately terminated using a `break` statement. The function returns the value held by `arrayType`.

Sometimes you want to refer to all elements of a uniform-type array. The following method is designed to be a prototype of the `Array` object, returning an array of element subscripts where the specified value has been found. Here is the method:

```
function getSubscripts(type) {
      var ar = new Array()
      var arSub = 0
      for (var i = 0; i < this.length; ++i) {
            if (typeof this[i] == type) {
                  ar[arSub] = this[i]
                  ++arSub
            }
      }
      return ar
}

Array.prototype.getSubscripts = getSubscripts
```

You can use the preceding prototype with arrays. For example:

```
var ar1 = new Array(6)
ar1[1] = 5
ar1[2] = 7
ar1[3] = "a"
ar1[4] = 2
ar1[5] = "b"
```

```
var ar1Temp = ar1.getSubscripts("number")
alert("There are " + ar1Temp.length + " numeric values in ar1") // 3
alert("The third number of ar1 is " + ar1Temp[2]) // 2
alert(ar1Temp) // 5, 7, 2 (discussed later in this chapter!)
```

This method returns an array. You can refer directly to the returned array:

```
var ar1 = new Array(6)
ar1[1] = 5
ar1[2] = 7
ar1[3] = "a"
ar1[4] = 2
ar1[5] = "b"
alert("The third number of ar1 is " + ar1.getSubscripts("number")[2])
```

Strings in JavaScript are `String` objects, not arrays. There are many useful methods that operate only on strings, so dealing with strings as arrays of characters, as is often the practice in other languages, is useless and almost impossible.

If you try to print an array, you will see that JavaScript prints the values of all elements in consecutive order, with a delimiting comma in between. You can use a user-defined prototype method to return a string containing all values delimited by a user-provided string:

```
function getList(str) {
     var text = ""
     for (var i = 0; i < this.length - 1; ++i) {
          text += this[i] + str
     }
     text += this[this.length - 1]
     return text
}

Array.prototype.getList = getList

var ar = new Array(5)
ar[1] = 3
ar[3] = "a"
ar[4] = "b b b"
document.write(ar.getList(" ; ")) // null ; 3 ; null ; a ; b b b
```

Notice that the loop in the method executes until `i < this.length - 1`. The reason is that the loop concatenates the delimiter (the method's parameter) after each element of the array. We do not want one placed after the last element, so the last element is concatenated to the accumulated string after the loop terminates.

Array Properties

Although you can add your own properties to the Array object, not all tasks can be achieved by high-level programming via JavaScript. The only built-in property of the Array object is length. When you create an instance of an object (an array), the number of properties (elements) is stored in the length property. You can refer to it as a regular property. We have already seen this property in action earlier in this chapter.

Let's say you want to display some messages, one after the other. You should use an array to store the messages:

```
var messages = new Array()
messages[0] = "message 1"
messages[1] = "message 2"
messages[2] = "message 3"
```

You can then use a loop to display the messages successively:

```
for (var i = 0; i < messages.length; i++) {
     document.write(messages[i] + "<BR>")
}
```

The length property can also be modified; that is, you can change the length of the array by assigning the property a value. Here is an example:

```
var ar = new Array(6)
ar[0] = "Mouse"
ar[1] = 8
ar[2] = 18
ar[3] = true
ar[4] = "Dog"
ar[5] = "Cat"
ar.length = 3
alert(ar[2]) // 18
alert(ar[3]) // null
```

The array consisting of six elements was reduced to three. The last three values were chopped off. Be extra careful when you reduce the size of an array because shifted-off values are unrecoverable.

Array Methods

In this section we will deal with many array methods. We will simulate some array functions in Perl using prototype methods. JavaScript features three built-in methods which we shall also discuss:

- join()
- reverse()
- sort()

In this section we use the getList prototype method, introduced in the section "Array Types," to print arrays.

chop()

The chop method chops off the last character of all strings that are elements of an array. Here it is:

```
function chop() {
     for (var i in this) {
          if (typeof this[i] == "string")
               this[i] = this[i].substring(0, this[i].length - 1)
     }
}

Array.prototype.chop = chop

// EXAMPLE
///////////////////////////////////////////

var line = new Array("red", "green", "blue")
line.chop()
document.write(line.getList(" "))
```

The script's output is:

```
re gree blu
```

The general syntax is:

```
arrayInstance.chop()
```

The substring() method is explained in Chapter 16, Handling Strings.

grep()

The grep method evaluates the expression (*expr*) for each element of the array. It returns another array consisting of those elements for which the expression evaluated to true (the pattern was matched). To understand this method you should know that if string2 is found in string1, string1.indexOf(string2) is not equal to –1. Here is the method:

```
function grep(str) {
     var ar = new Array()
     var arSub = 0
     for (var i in this) {
          if (typeof this[i] == "string" && this[i].indexOf(str) != -1) {
               ar[arSub] = this[i]
               arSub++
          }
     }
     return ar
}

Array.prototype.grep = grep

// EXAMPLE
//////////////////////////////////////////////

var line = new Array("mask", "Mascot", "mine", "amass", "hot")
document.write(line.grep("mas").getList(" "))
document.write("<BR>")
document.write(line.grep("mas").length)
```

The output of this script is:

```
mask amass
2
```

The general syntax is:

```
arrayInstance.grep(expr)
```

An important concept used by this method is short-circuit evaluation. If JavaScript evaluates the first conditional expression (typeof this[i] == "string") to false, the final expression (typeof this[i] == "string" && this[i].indexOf(str) != –1) is obviously false, so the second expression (this[i].indexOf(str) != –1) is not even evaluated. This is critical because the indexOf() method works only with strings, and generates an error otherwise. However, if the current element (this[i]) is not a string, JavaScript does not evaluate the second expression due to short-circuit evaluation.

join()

The join() method is a built-in one in JavaScript. It is equivalent to the same function in Perl. It joins the elements of an array into a single string and separates each element with a given delimiter. This method is exactly like the getList method we created earlier, so we will use it from this point on instead.

Its general syntax is:

```
arrayInstance.join(delimiter)
```

The delimiter is automatically cast to a string if it is not already one.

Here is an example using this method:

```
var line = new Array("a", "b", "c", "d", "e")
document.write(line.join(" : "))
var str = line.join(", ")
document.write("<BR>" + str)
```

Its output is:

```
a : b : c : d : e
a, b, c, d, e
```

pop()

The pop method pops off the last element of an array and returns it. The array size is automatically decreased by one.

The general format is:

```
arrayInstance.pop()
```

This method is not built in, so we need to define it. The following script defines the method as a prototype of the Array object, and demonstrates its use:

```
function pop() {
      var lastElement = this[this.length - 1]
      this.length--
      return lastElement
}

Array.prototype.pop = pop

// EXAMPLE
////////////////////////////////////////////

var names = new Array("Tom", "Mark", "Bart", "John")
var last = names.pop()
document.write(last + "<BR>")
document.write(names.join(" ") + "<BR>")
document.write(names.length)
```

The script's output by rows is:

```
John
Tom Mark Bart
3
```

push()

The push method, not supported by JavaScript, pushes values onto the end of an array, increasing its length. Here is the method declared as a prototype of the Array object type:

```
function push() {
     var sub = this.length
     for (var i = 0; i < push.arguments.length; ++i) {
          this[sub] = push.arguments[i]
          sub++
     }
}

Array.prototype.push = push

// EXAMPLE
////////////////////////////////////////////////

var names = new Array("Tom", "Mark", "Bart", "John")
names.push("Jim", "Richard", "Tim")
document.write(names.join(" "))
```

The output is:

```
Tom Mark Bart John Jim Richard Tim
```

The general syntax is:

```
arrayInstance.push(list)
```

In some situations, this method returns wrong results. The reason is explained in Chapter 9, Functions and Variable Scope. It is also explained later in this chapter in depth.

reverse()

The reverse method transposes the elements of the calling array object. If it was descending, now it is ascending, etc. The last element becomes the first one, and vice versa. This method is a built-in one.

The general syntax is:

```
arrayInstance.reverse()
```

Here are some examples:

```
var names = new Array("Tom", "Mark", "Bart", "John")
```

```
var colors = new Array("red", "orange", "yellow", "green", "blue",
"purple")
document.write("<B>original names: </B>" + names.join(" ") + "<BR>")
names.reverse()
document.write("<B>reversed names: </B>" + names.join(" ") + "<BR>")
document.write("<B>original colors: </B>" + colors.join(" ") + "<BR>")
colors.reverse()
document.write("<B>reversed colors: </B>" + colors.join(" ") + "<BR>")
```

The corresponding output is:

original names: Tom Mark Bart John
reversed names: John Bart Mark Tom
original colors: red orange yellow green blue purple
reversed colors: purple blue green yellow orange red

shift()

The `shift` method is not defined in JavaScript so we will have to create it. It shifts off and returns the first element of an array, decreasing the size of an array by one element. Here is the method along with an example:

```
function shift(str) {
     var val = this[0]
     for (var i = 1; i < this.length; ++i) {
          this[i - 1] = this[i]
     }
     this.length--
     return val
}

Array.prototype.shift = shift

// EXAMPLE
/////////////////////////////////////////////

var line = new Array("aaa", "bbb", "ccc", "ddd", "eee")
document.write(line.shift() + "<BR>")
document.write(line.join(" "))
```

The output is:

```
aaa
bbb ccc ddd eee
```

The general format of this method call (after defining its prototype) is:

```
arrayInstance.shift()
```

splice()

Another method not featured yet by JavaScript is `splice`. It removes and replaces elements in an array. Its general syntax is:

```
arrayInstance.splice(offset, length, list)
```

`offset` is the starting position where elements are to be removed from. The *`length`* is the number of elements to be removed, starting at `offset`. The *`list`* parameter consists of new elements that are designated to replace the removed ones. Here is the method:

```
function splice(offset, length) {
     var ar1 = new Array()
     var ar2 = new Array()
     for (i = 0; i < length; ++i) {
          ar1[i] = this[i + offset]
     }
     for (i = 0; i < this.length - (offset + length); ++i) {
          ar2[i] = this[i + offset + length]
     }
     var args = new Array()
     for (i = 0; splice.arguments[i + 2] != null; ++i) {
          args[i] = splice.arguments[i + 2] // second argument
     }
     j = offset
     for (i = 0; i < args.length; ++i) {
          this[j] = args[i]
          j++
     }
     for (i = 0; i < ar2.length; ++i) {
          this[j] = ar2[i]
          j++
     }
     this.length = j
     // notice that j is one more than subscript of last element
     return ar1
}

Array.prototype.splice = splice
```

This method is more complicated than the previous ones so we shall explain it in depth.

At first, two arrays are declared. Although it is possible to calculate their size, it is completely unnecessary because they will accommodate the proper size as we expand them. The first loop in the function is:

```
for (i = 0; i < length; ++i) {
          ar1[i] = this[i + offset]
}
```

This loop assigns all elements that are to be removed to the array ar1, according to the values of the offset and length parameters. The number of times the loop iterates is exactly the value of length, the number of elements specified to be removed. The array ar1 is populated from the beginning, 0. It is assigned the elements of the calling array (this), starting from offset, because only elements following offset (exactly length of them) are to be removed. When the loop terminates, the array ar1 already consists of elements that should be removed from the calling array. Notice that this array is returned at the end of the function.

Now take a look at the second loop:

```
for (i = 0; i < this.length - (offset + length); ++i) {
        ar2[i] = this[i + offset + length]
}
```

This loop assigns all elements following the removed ones to the array ar2. The loop terminates after it has completed assigning all these elements. this.length - (offset + length) is equal to the number of elements following the removed one. The subscript of the first element following the removed set is offset + length. Subtracting this number from the full length of the calling array gives the number of elements following the removed set.

The next loop is as follows:

```
for (i = 0; splice.arguments[i + 2] != null; ++i) {
        args[i] = splice.arguments[i + 2] // second argument
}
```

The preceding loop assigns all items of list (the third parameter of the method) to the array args. These items are all arguments handed over to the method except for the first two. We use the condition splice.arguments[i + 2] != null to terminate the loop due to some unexpected behavior of the arguments.length property on some platforms. That is, when the function comes across the first null element of the splice.arguments (see Chapter 9, Functions and Variable Scope), it terminates. This action is based on the fact that the method will never be called to replace an element of the calling array by a null one. This concept is explained later in this chapter in depth. The expression i + 2 is used because the needed elements of the arguments array are only the third one (subscript == 2) on. However, the args array created in the function should store the elements starting at subscript 0, so i is used as the subscript of that array.

We now have four arrays:

- this (the calling array)
- args
- ar2
- ar1

Keep in mind that the splice() method needs to modify the calling script. It concatenates the beginning of this array (up to the first removed, exclusively) with args and ar2, in this order. The last portion of the script does just that:

```
j = offset
for (i = 0; i < args.length; ++i) {
     this[j] = args[i]
     j+++
}
for (i = 0; i < ar2.length; ++i) {
     this[j] = ar2[i]
     j++
}
this.length = j
```

At first, j is set to offset, the first value of the array this that should be modified (all the existing elements before should remain at the beginning of the array, as they were before calling the method). The following loops assign elements from the other arrays, args and ar2, respectively, to the calling array (this). The variable j is important because it holds the subscript of the current element of the calling array throughout both loops. At the end, the length of the calling array (now modified) is set to j, so if there were more elements in the original array, they are chopped off.

The last statement of the splice() function returns the removed elements in the form of an array, ar1.

After this long explanation, some examples will surely clear up the method:

```
var cols = new Array("red", "orange", "yellow", "green", "blue", "purple")

var newCols = cols.splice(2, 3, "brown", "black")
document.write(newCols.join(" ") + "<BR>")
document.write(cols.join(" ") + "<BR>")

cols = new Array("red", "orange", "yellow", "green", "blue", "purple")

newCols = cols.splice(0, 1, "brown", "black")
document.write(newCols.join(" ") + "<BR>")
```

```
document.write(cols.join(" ") + "<BR>")

cols = new Array("red", "orange", "yellow", "green", "blue", "purple")

newCols = cols.splice(3, 0, "brown", "black")
document.write(newCols.join(" ") + "<BR>")
document.write(cols.join(" "))
```

The output of this script segment is:

```
yellow green blue
red orange brown black purple
red
brown black orange yellow green blue purple
[blank line]
red orange yellow brown black green blue purple
```

The function will not work if you try to remove elements of the array without inserting new ones.

split()

The `split()` method does the opposite of `join()`. It splits up a string (the object) by some delimiter (space by default) and returns an array. To be accurate, this is a method of the `String` object, not the `Array` one, but because it is closely related to arrays, we chose to discuss it in this section. If the delimiter is not supplied or is not found in the entire string, it returns the string itself. This method is built in so you just have to call it. The general format is:

```
stringName.split(delimiter)
```

Here are some examples:

```
var line1 = "a b c d e f"
var ar1 = new Array()

ar1 = line1.split(" ")
document.write(ar1.join(", ")) // a, b, c, d, e, f
document.write("<BR>")
ar2 = line1.split(";")
document.write(ar2) // a b c d e f
document.write("<BR>")
ar3 = line1.split()
document.write(ar3) // a b c d e f
document.write("<BR>")
ar4 = line1.split("")
document.write(ar4) // [infinite function!]
```

13 Chapter

All of these examples follow the rules explained before, except for the last one, ar4. The statement ar4 = line1.split("") causes an infinite method execution that will eventually crash the browser, or even the operating system, if you are on a 16-bit version of Windows. The reason for this behavior is obvious—JavaScript tries to split the string with an empty string. Everyone knows that an empty string is found an infinite number of times between two characters, and between two empty strings lies another empty string!

sort()

Luckily for us, the sort() method is built into JavaScript. It sorts the elements of an array. It is optional to supply a sorting function. If one is not supplied, the array is sorted lexicographically (comparison order, dictionary order), according to the string conversion of each element. The general syntax of this method is as follows:

```
arrayInstance.sort(compareFunction)
```

If *compareFunction* is not supplied, elements are sorted by converting them to strings and comparing the strings in lexicographic order. For example, "10" comes before "9" in lexicographic order, but numeric comparison puts 9 before 10.

The structure of a comparison function is very specific. First of all, it should have two parameters, one for each element being compared. Secondly, it should return a value. If a and b are the two elements being compared, then:

- If *compareFunction*(a, b) is less than zero (returns a negative number), sort b to a lower index than a.
- If *compareFunction*(a, b) returns zero, leave a and b untouched with respect to each other (if a was before b, it will remain before b, and vice versa).
- If *compareFunction*(a, b) is positive (greater than zero), sort b to a higher index than a.

The basic form of a comparison function is:

```
function compare(a, b) {
     if (a is less than b by some ordering criterion)
          return -1
     if (a is greater than b by the ordering criterion)
          return 1
     // a must be equal to b
     return 0
}
```

The most simple comparison function sorts numbers:

```
function compareNumbers(a, b) {
    return a - b
}
```

JavaScript uses a *stable sort*, so the relative order of a and b does not change if a and b are equal according to the comparison function.

Here are some comparison functions:

```
// 1. Lexicographic -- built-in

// 2. byIncNum (increasing numbers)

function byIncNum(a, b) {
    return a - b
}

// 3. byFirstChar (lexicographic order of first char only)

function byFirstChar(a, b) {
    a += ""
    b += ""
    if (a.charAt(0) < b.charAt(0))
        return -1
    if (a.charAt(0) > b.charAt(0))
        return 1
    return 0
}
```

The following example and its corresponding output in Figure 13-2 should make this topic clear:

```
<HTML>
<HEAD>
<TITLE>Sorting arrays</TITLE>
<SCRIPT LANGUAGE="JavaScript">
<!--

// 1. Lexicographic -- built - in

// 2. byIncNum (increasing numbers)

function incNum(a, b) {
    return a - b
}

stringArray = new Array("house", "hose", "chair")
numericStringArray = new Array("60", "8", "100")
numberArray = new Array(20, 1, 5, -11, 8)
mixedNumericArray = new Array("70", "9", "600", 3, 40, 70, 250)
```

```
function compareNumbers(a, b) {
   return a - b
}

document.write("<U><B>stringArray</B></U><BR>")
document.write("<B>Original array:</B> " + stringArray.join() +"<BR>")
document.write("<B>Sorted by default:</B> " + stringArray.sort() +"<P>")

document.write("<U><B>numberArray</B></U><BR>")
document.write("<B>Original array:</B> " + numberArray.join() +"<BR>")
document.write("<B>Sorted by default:</B> " + numberArray.sort() +"<BR>")
document.write("<B>Sorted with compareNumbers:</B> " + numberArray.sort
                          (compareNumbers) +"<P>")

document.write("<U><B>numericStringArray</B></U><BR>")
document.write("<B>Original array:</B> " + numericStringArray.join()
                          +"<BR>")
document.write("<B>Sorted by default:</B> " + numericStringArray.sort()
                          +"<BR>")
document.write("<B>Sorted with compareNumbers:</B> " + numericString
                          Array.sort(compareNumbers) +"<P>")

document.write("<U><B>mixedNumericArray</B></U><BR>")
document.write("<B>Original array:</B> " + mixedNumericArray.join()
                          +"<BR>")
document.write("<B>Sorted by default:</B> " + mixedNumericArray.sort()
                          +"<BR>")
document.write("<B>Sorted with compareNumbers:</B> " + mixedNumeric
                          Array.sort(compareNumbers) +"<BR>")

// -->
</SCRIPT>
</HEAD>
<BODY>
</BODY>
</HTML>
```

Example 13-1 (ex13-1.htm). *The built-in* `sort` *function is a simple replacement for sorting via pointers (used in many languages that feature pointers).*

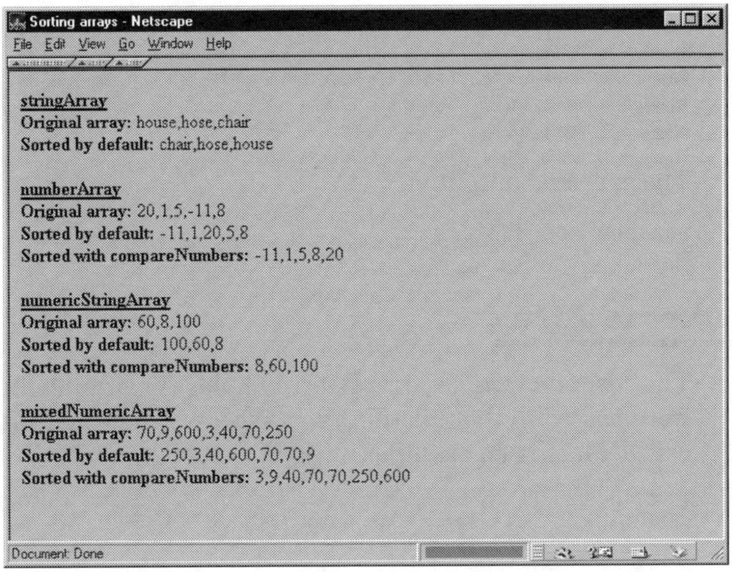
Sorting arrays - Netscape
File Edit View Go Window Help
stringArray
Original array: house,hose,chair
Sorted by default: chair,hose,house
numberArray
Original array: 20,1,5,-11,8
Sorted by default: -11,1,20,5,8
Sorted with compareNumbers: -11,1,5,8,20
numericStringArray
Original array: 60,8,100
Sorted by default: 100,60,8
Sorted with compareNumbers: 8,60,100
mixedNumericArray
Original array: 70,9,600,3,40,70,250
Sorted by default: 250,3,40,600,70,70,9
Sorted with compareNumbers: 3,9,40,70,70,250,600
Document: Done

Figure 13-2. *The arrays sorted by various functions.*

unshift()

The `unshift()` method is actually the opposite of the `shift()` one. It appends a list of elements to the beginning of an array. Here is the method defined as a prototype of the `Array` object type, along with an example to demonstrate it:

```
function unshift() {
     for (var i = 0; i < unshift.arguments.length; ++i) {
          if (unshift.arguments[i] == null)
               break
     }
     // i = number of arguments! (remember ++i is executed during last
                                  loop)
     // i holds the number of arguments
     for (var j = this.length - 1; j >= 0; --j) {
          this[j + i] = this[j]
     }
     // j == -1
     // i == number of arguments
     for (j = 0; j < i; ++j) {
          this[j] = unshift.arguments[j]
     }
}

Array.prototype.unshift = unshift

// EXAMPLE
```

```
/////////////////////////////////////////////

var line = new Array("ccc", "ddd", "eee")
line.unshift("aaa", "bbb")
document.write(line.join(" "))
```

The expected output is:

```
aaa bbb ccc ddd eee
```

The arguments Array

The *functionName*`.arguments` array holds the arguments by order that were passed to the function *functionName* when that function was last called. Here is an example:

```
function func() {
     document.write(func.arguments[2])
}
func(1, 2, 3, 4, 5)
document.write("<BR>")
func()
```

The output of this script is:

```
3
3
```

The second 3 is not an argument passed to the function during the second call, but an argument passed to the function during the first call. It remains an element in the array provided that no argument of a later call replaces it. You can therefore conclude that the *functionName*`.arguments` array has a permanent storage class.

Let's say you want to create a function that accepts string arguments and prints them with a line break after each one. The intuitive function would be:

```
function printList() {
     for (var i = 0; i < printList.arguments.length; ++i) {
          document.write(printList.arguments[i] + "<BR>")
     }
}
```

You can use this function in the following form:

```
printList("message 1", "message 2", "message 3", "message 4")
```

And the output is:

```
message 1
message 2
message 3
message 4
```

You can also use the function twice in a row as in:

```
printList("message 1", "message 2", "message 3", "message 4")
printList("message 5", "message 6", "message 7", "message 8")
```

Once again, the expected output is:

```
message 1
message 2
message 3
message 4
message 5
message 6
message 7
message 8
```

Now let's change the function to the following code:

```
function printList() {
     document.write("There are " + printList.arguments.length + " arguments.")
     document.write("<BR>")
     document.write("The fourth argument is " + printList.arguments[3] + ".")
     document.write("<BR>")
     for (var i = 0; i < printList.arguments.length; ++i) {
          document.write(printList.arguments[i] + "<BR>")
     }
}
```

The function now displays the number of arguments according to the *functionName.arguments.length* property. It also displays the fourth argument, whether or not there are four arguments. Consider the following statements:

```
printList("message 1", "message 2", "message 3", "message 4")
printList("message 5", "message 6", "message 7")
```

The output is:

```
There are 4 arguments.
The fourth argument is message 4.
message 1
message 2
message 3
message 4
```

```
There are 3 arguments.
The fourth argument is message 4. (!!!)
message 5
message 6
message 7
```

Notice that the function prints the fourth argument passed to the function in each call. However, the second call provides only three arguments! The `arguments.length` property holds the correct value, 3. The fourth argument is actually a leftover from the first function call.

As you can see, the `arguments` array does not follow the rules of arrays that are instances of the `Array` object. The following script demonstrates the difference:

```
var ar = new Array("message 1", "message 2", "message 3")
document.write("The array is: " + ar.join(", ") + "<BR>")
document.write("There are " + ar.length + " elements.<BR>")
document.write("The third element is " + ar[2] + ".<BR>")
ar.length = 2
document.write("There are " + ar.length + " elements.<BR>")
document.write("The third element is " + ar[2] + ".<BR>")
```

The output of this script is:

```
The array is: message 1, message 2, message 3
There are 3 elements.
The third element is message 3.
There are 2 elements.
The third element is null.
```

The simple rule regarding arrays is that the last element's subscript is *arrayName*`.length - 1`. When you reduce the size of an array by assigning a smaller number to the `length` property, all elements that were in the range of the array and are now out of range are lost. If you try referring to them, you see that they are `null`. The *functionName*`.arguments` array is different in that its last element has nothing to do with its length.

Note At this stage it is not clear if this is a bug or intentional. Note that this symptom appears in all versions of Navigator 3.0 and MSIE 3.0. To find out if this is a bug you can run the scripts in this section under the latest release of Netscape Navigator or Microsoft Internet Explorer (or any other JavaScript-enabled browser).

Multidimensional Arrays

JavaScript does not feature multidimensional arrays, but they are fairly easy to create via a constructor function.

Up to this point we discussed one-dimensional arrays (1D arrays). Such arrays consist of elements gathered in a row-like structure. They are also known as horizontal arrays. The basic structure of a one-dimensional array is outlined in the following illustration:

0	1	2	3

Figure 13-3. *A one-dimensional array.*

Let's say you want to store a runner's record times in different years and for different distances. If the array is called `curDis`, the record time of 1994 could be put in `curDis[0]`, the record time of 1995 in `curDis[1]`, the record time of 1996 in `curDis[2]`, and so forth. However, you probably noticed that we can only store the record time for a single distance, such as a 400-meter run. It would be easy to store the record times of various runs in this format using a table or spreadsheet-like array. Such arrays are known as two-dimensional (2D) arrays. Figure 13-4 outlines the basic structure of a two-dimensional array:

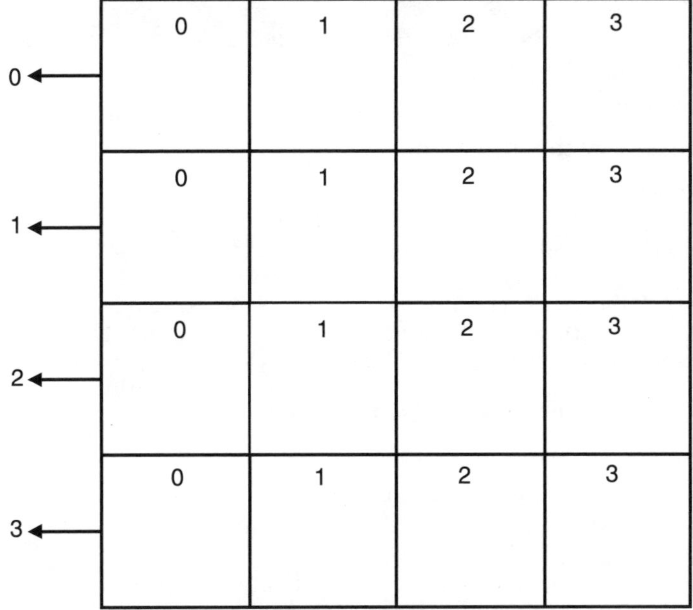

Figure 13-4. *A two-dimensional array.*

JavaScript does not have a built-in two-dimensional array object type. Take a look at the subscripts of the elements. The two-dimensional array is constructed from horizontal arrays (horizontal in the illustration as well) which form an array of their own. That is, the general structure is a regular array of arrays. The main array in the illustration is the vertical one; its subscripts are specified to the left of the arrows.

Note that the dimensions of a multidimensional array do not have to be equal.

The standard reference to elements of a two-dimensional array (2DA) is:

```
ar[1][5]
ar[8][0]
ar[3][3]
```

The first number is the subscript of the first dimension, whereas the second one specifies the subscript of the second dimension.

Creation with a Single Constructor Function

The easiest way to create a two-dimensional array (2DA) is to use a constructor function. Here it is:

```
function Array2D(dim1, dim2) {
      for (var i = 0; i < dim1; ++i) {
            this[i] = new Array(dim2)
      }
      this.length = new Array(dim1, dim2)
}
```

The following script demonstrates the creation and usage of an array created by this function:

```
var ar = new Array2D(4,7)
ar[2][1] = 6
ar[0][0] = "Hello" // this is the "first" element
ar[3][6] = true // this is the "last" element
alert("Length of first dimension is " + ar.length[0])
alert("Length of second dimension is " + ar.length[1])
alert("\"Last\" element: " + ar[ar.length[0] - 1][ar.length[1] - 1])
```

The messages displayed via alert boxes are:

```
Length of first dimension is 4
Length of second dimension is 7
"Last" element: true
```

The constructor function uses a loop. The first array (ar) is not an explicit Array object. It is simply a regular object whose properties are specified using the array notation. The built-in methods of the Array object type do not operate on this array. The loop executes dim1 times, the length of the first dimension. Each property (or element) of the calling object is assigned a "real" array consisting of dim2 elements. Since these are real arrays, you can use the built-in methods and properties of the Array object type. For example, ar[0] is an array of dim2 elements, so you can refer to its elements: ar[0][0], ar[0][1], ar[0][2], etc. The 2DA is actually a one-dimensional array of which all elements are one-dimensional arrays. Therefore, you should be careful not to ruin the structure of the 2DA by assigning values to its main array, such as:

```
ar[3] = "Do not do this to a 2DA!"
```

The preceding constructor method also includes a length property which is an array of two elements. The first element holds the number of elements in the main array (the specified length of the first dimension) while the second element holds the specified length of the second dimension. The example demonstrates this best. Keep in mind that these are static properties. Assigning a value to an element of the length property does not affect the array, but can trip you up when you need the correct values regarding the length of the array's dimensions.

Creation without Constructor Function

It is possible to create a two-dimensional array without a constructor function. This method is based on creating instances of the Array object. Here it is:

```
function addDim2(array1D, dim2) {
     for (var i = 0; i < array1D.length; ++i) {
          array1D[i] = new Array(dim2)
     }
     return array1D
}
```

This function alone means almost nothing, so take a look at a working example:

```
var dim1 = 4
var dim2 = 7
var ar = new Array(dim1)
ar = addDim2(ar, dim2)
ar[2][1] = 6
```

```
ar[0][0] = "Hello" // this is the "first" element
ar[3][6] = true // this is the "last" element
alert("Length of first dimension is " + ar.length)
alert("Length of second dimension is " + ar[0].length)
alert("\"Last\" element: " + ar[ar.length - 1][ar[0].length - 1])
```

At first, the length of the first dimension, 4, is assigned to dim1. The length of the second dimension is then assigned to dim2. A new array, named ar, is created according to the Array object type. Its length is the length of the first dimension of the desired array. The function addDim2 is then called with the array and the length of the second dimension. It returns the final 2DA to the original one-dimensional array, ar. The function is based on a simple loop that assigns an array of dim2 elements to each element of the original one-dimensional array. Since both the first dimension array and the second dimension array are instances of the Array object type, you can refer to the length of each dimension in the following way:

```
ar.length == length of first dimension
ar[0].length == length of second dimension == ar[1].length == ...
```

Note that for the second expression to be true, you must not change the length of the 2DA at any time during the script execution. Otherwise, it does not simulate a 2DA anymore.

Associative Arrays

Associative arrays use strings as subscripts. For example, an element of the array can be:

```
color["yellow"] = "FFFF00"
```

Such arrays group together related data. These arrays are actually objects, except that you use square brackets instead of a dot. Another important difference is that array specification (square brackets) enables you to refer to the value of a variable as the property of method specification rather than the actual literal. For example:

```
var col = "yellow"
color[col] = "FFFF00"
```

Here is another interesting example:

```
var w = "write"
document[w]("Hello!") // prints "Hello!"
```

If you replace the array notation with the regular "dot" specification you receive an error:

```
var w = "write"
document.w("Hello!")
```

The "dot" notation requires the actual literal specified, as it does not evaluate the written value. You can use associative arrays to create nested objects, resembling multidimensional arrays. For example, you can create an associative array where its subscripts are names of students in a class, so each element of the associative array is an object containing fields such as the student's grade, age, and so on.

Note that associative arrays cannot be created as instances of the built-in `Array` object. You must use a constructor function to create one. Here is the example with the students:

```
function studentClass() {
     for (var i = 0; i < arguments.length; ++i) {
          this[studentClass.arguments[i]] = new student()
     }
}

function student() {
     // this.grade = null
     // this.age = null
}

var students = new studentClass("Yehuda", "Yael", "Dikla", "Tomer",
"Carmit", "Alon")
students["Yehuda"].grade = 40
students["Alon"].age = 11
students["Dikla"].grade = "N/A"
alert(students["Dikla"].grade)
```

Creating an associative array is not difficult. Array elements are created according to the names of the students accepted as parameters by the function `studentClass()`. The second function is rather strange—it contains no statements. When you create an instance you can use an "empty" constructor function. You may recall from an earlier discussion that objects may be extended by simply assigning values to them. So, the statement `this[arguments[i]] = new student()` just makes sure each element of the associative array is an object. The global statements later create the properties simply by assigning them values.

Another important concept to remember is that associative arrays are not explicit arrays. You can also refer to them using the "dot" syntax as in:

```
students.Alon.age
```

Suppose you created a database structure listing all the students in a class with their ages and grades. Assume that both fields are fed with the proper values. You can let the user view these values via a prompt dialog box. For example:

```
var grade = students[prompt("Enter name:", "John Doe")].grade
document.write(grade)
```

In this case you must use the array convention because you are prompting the user for the property name. You can use the *dot* notation only when you know the property name. If you use the *dot* notation:

```
students.prompt(...)
```

JavaScript assumes you are referring to a method of the `students` object named `prompt()`, which does not exist at all, of course.

Populating an Associative Array

Creating a dense array is simple when using regular arrays. You simply create the array with the desired values. However, associative arrays require two real values for each element, the key (subscript) and the value. You can create a constructor function to create and populate associative arrays:

```
function AssociativeArray() {
     for (var i = 0; i < arguments.length - 1; i += 2) {
          this[arguments[i]] = arguments[i + 1]
     }
}
```

You can use this function to create associative arrays in the following format:

```
var ar = new AssociativeArray("red", "FF0000", "green", "00FF00",
                              "blue", "0000FF")

document.write("green = " + ar["green"] + "<BR>")
var col = "blue"
document.write("blue = " + ar[col] + "<BR>")
document.write("red = " + ar.red)
```

The relative output of this script is:

```
green = 00FF00
blue = 0000FF
red = FF0000
```

Let's take a look at the constructor function. It accepts the keys of the array elements followed by their corresponding values. Each key must be followed by its own value. The function loops through the arguments and terminates after it has reached the argument before the last one. During each pass through the function, a property of the calling object is created (an "element" in the array lexicon). The key of the property, or element, is the current argument whereas its value is extracted from the following argument. The loop counter is advanced by two after each execution of the block, because each element of the associative array is related to two arguments—its key and its value. Although an associative array is primarily a regular object, this constructor must use square brackets, the array notation, for reference and initialization because the values of the keys (subscripts) are not literals, but rather values stored as parameters.

Splitting a String into an Associative Array

The `split()` method splits a string by a specified delimiter to a real instance of an `Array` object. For example:

```
var str = "a;b;c;d;e;f"
var ar = str.split(";") // ar[0] == "a", ar[1] == "b", ar[2] == "c", ...
```

Let's use the `split()` method to create a function named `associativeSplit()` as a prototype of the `String` object. Here it is:

```
function associativeSplit(del) {
     var tempAr = new Array()
     tempAr = this.split(del)
     var ar = new Obj() // not an array, just an object
     for (var i = 0; i < tempAr.length - 1; i += 2) {
          ar[tempAr[i]] = tempAr[i + 1]
     }
     return ar
}

function Obj() { }

String.prototype.associativeSplit = associativeSplit
```

Notice the use of an empty function to create an object. At first, the function splits the string via the regular method to a regular array. It then loops through the array, using the next element as the key of an element in the associative array and its following element as the value of the same element in the associative array. Upon completion, the function returns the associative array. The function is then declared as a prototype of the built-in `String` object, applying to all strings.

Now take a look at an example:

```
var str = "a b c d e f"
var arl = str.associativeSplit(" ")

document.write(arl.a + "<BR>")
document.write(arl.b + "<BR>")
document.write(arl["c"] + "<BR>")
document.write(arl["d"] + "<BR>")
// document.write(arl[e] + "<BR>")
document.write(arl.f + "<BR>")
```

Note that "associative array" is not a JavaScript term, but rather a regular object. We just prefer to refer to its properties via the array notation.

Summary

In this chapter we learned about arrays in JavaScript. Unlike most languages, array in JavaScript is a regular object, not an explicit data type of its own. We discussed the `Array` object, including its properties and methods. Another important concept brought together in this chapter was constructor functions and prototypes, used mainly to simulate array methods featured by Perl. By now, you should have a grasp on arrays and constructor functions, two very important elements of the language. You should also know how to create and use two-dimensional arrays, as well as multidimensional ones, although they are rarely used. In this chapter we also introduced the term "associative arrays." Such arrays are regular objects with regular properties, but they remind us of associative arrays, widely used in other languages such as Perl. In following chapters we shall look further into JavaScript's object model, while arrays and constructors will serve as the base of some scripts.

Chapter 14

Time and Date in JavaScript

The Date Object

JavaScript includes a `Date` object, borrowed from Java. If you are familiar with other modern programming languages, you probably recall that time and date are stored in explicit type data structures. As explained in Chapter 13, JavaScript tends to implement as many language features as possible. Both dates and times in JavaScript are derived from the `Date` object, which includes a rich set of methods related to derivation of dates and times.

JavaScript treats the `Date` object like a constructor class. To implement the current date or time in your script you must first create a new instance of the object. You can then extract the desired data from that particular instance.

The `Date` object has quite a misleading name because it also includes methods strictly for dealing with time values.

JavaScript handles dates similarly to Java. Many methods are implemented in both languages, resulting in an observable parallelism. All dates are stored as the number of milliseconds since January 1, 1970, 00:00:00.

Creating a Date Instance

Many JavaScript programmers, including book authors, often confuse object-related nomenclature when computing date and time elements as the creation of a `Date` object. The `Date` object is a single built-in object, by which you can create *instances* to store encoded data related to the date and time of a certain moment. The `Date` object is built in, just like the `Array` object discussed in depth in the previous chapter. It acts as a template when creating instances of the object. The most basic assignment statement regarding the Date object is obviously the one that creates an instance according to the default arguments:

```
var dateInstance = new Date()
```

This statement simply assigns an instance of the Date object to the data structure named *dataInstance*. Take a look at the following script:

```
var now = new Date()
alert(now)
```

According to the current time of the operation, the output of the script resembles the following:

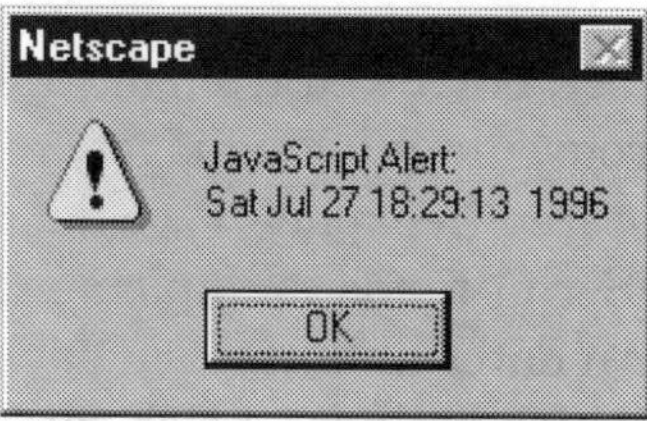

Figure 14-1. *An instance of the* date *object can be displayed to show the current time.*

Although now is an identifier of an instance of the date object, it holds a partial string value at its highest level. That is, if you try to print its value it appears to be a string. However, because it does not belong to the explicit String object, string properties and methods do not apply to it. For example, the following script generates an error because split() is a method of strings only:

```
var nowDate = new Date()
var nowArray = new Array()
nowArray = nowDate.split(" ")
```

You can slightly modify this script to work in the following form:

```
var nowDate = new Date()
var nowArray = new Array()
var nowString = new String(nowDate)
// or: var nowString = nowDate + ""
// or: var nowString = nowDate.toString()
nowArray = nowDate.split(" ")
alert(nowArray.join(" ; "))
```

The script's output is:

Figure 14-2. *An instance of the* `Date` *object can be processed at its highest level by converting it to a string.*

Notice that there are two semicolons near the end of the string. You will see later that the time zone is specified between them.

If you want to refer to an instance of the `Date` object as a string, it is safer to convert it to a string, explicitly:

```
var newObj = new Date()
var str = newObj.toString() // toString method explained later
```

Parameters of the Date Constructor

Until now we created instances of the `Date` object without any arguments; that is, we built the instances according to the default arguments. The default is the current date and time on the client's machine. JavaScript enables you to create `Date` instances of specific dates, which you can later use with date arithmetic.

Whenever you provide arguments to `Date`, pay attention to the following computation algorithms:

- Computers store all dates as the number of milliseconds since January 1, 1970, 00:00:00. As a result, if you try to create an instance of the `Date` object specifying a date before January 1, 1970, 00:00:00, it will probably cause the browser to crash. It is not known yet if and when Netscape and Microsoft will fix this bug in their browsers. Until then, you should always use dates after this 1970 date. If the user is prompted to enter a date, it must be verified so an improper date does not cause the browser to crash. This bug is expected to be solved, or at least modified to return an error whenever you assign such values, but for now you will see an annoying message as the browser crashes under such operations:

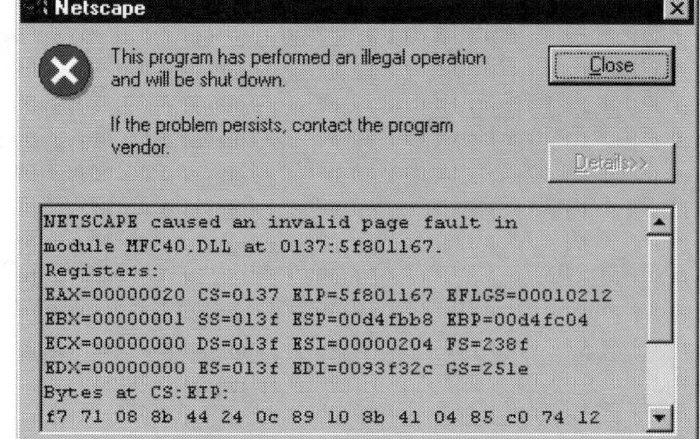

Figure 14-3. *Despite the message, don't call the vendor because this is a known bug. Note that the bug will persist!*

- Similar to the previous bug, some versions of Netscape Navigator crash if you create an instance with a date after 1999. This may seem much more problematic than the pre-1970 bug, because this year is coming closer every day. You have probably heard predictions regarding the computerized world after the year 2000 due to the fact that all two-digit year specifications will have to be fixed. Although the year 2000 may still seem far away (unless you are reading this book after 2000 or a year before), it is important that you make your scripts compatible with future situations. Luckily for us, there is a workaround for this problem: Create such dates with numeric arguments instead of the more intuitive string format. Note also that this bug exists in Netscape Navigator 2.0 but is apparently fixed in Navigator 3.0.

You can use an argument of the following format to create a date other than the current one:

Month day, year hours:minutes:seconds

Here is an example that creates an instance of a date that occurred in the past:

```
var Xmas95 = new Date("December 25, 1995 13:30:00")
```

You can also create an instance according to a set of integers of the following format:

year, month, day, hour, minute, seconds

Here is an example using this format:

```
var Xmas95 = new Date(95,11,25,9,30,0)
```

One important concept is the requirement of year, month, and day specification in both formats (string and integers). If you omit the hours, minutes, or seconds they are set by default to zero. Nonetheless, omitting any of the first three arguments results in an error and even crashes the browser under some operating systems.

Macs are one day in the future

A bug in Netscape Navigator 2.0x on the Macintosh platform causes instances of the Date object representing the current date to be approximately one day in the future. Since the number of people using this browser is small, you might want to ignore it (we prefer to do that). However, if you are still concerned, you can use the following function to solve the problem:

```
function fixDate(date) {
     var base = new Date(0)
     var skew = base.getTime()
     if (skew > 0)
          date.setTime(date.getTime() - skew)
}
```

You then pass all instances to this function in the following fashion:

```
var now = new Date()
fixDate(now)
```

Date Numeric Conventions

Dates in JavaScript, as acquired from Java, use integers to specify values that succeed each other. For example, the first day of a month is 1, the second is 2, the third is 3, and so on. The numbers used are not always so obvious. Most date attributes are actually zero-based; that is, they start at zero. For example, the first minute of an hour is 0, the second one is 1, the third minute is 2, and so on. This behavior is clearly the result of array structure influence. In all modern programming languages, including Perl, C++, and also Java, the first element of an array is normally the one which has a subscript, or index, of 0. JavaScript, which was born of Java, also implemented this rule, as you have seen in the previous chapter. The following table summarizes the numeric conventions of each attribute of a `Date` instance:

***Table 14-1.** Ranges of date attributes.*

Date attribute	Range
seconds	0 - 59
minutes	0 - 59
hours	0 - 23
day	0 - 6
date	1 - 31
month	0 - 11
year	number of years since 1900 (e.g., 97)

Most importantly, when referring to client-side JavaScript, the date and time refer to the client side. All values are the ones passed to the script by the browser. As you might know, especially if you are a Mac or Windows environment programmer, all applications on your computer have access to the machine clock, including the current time and date. If the system clock is not set to the current time and date, JavaScript will use these incorrect values in the script, possibly surprising the user. However, unlike computers from about ten years ago, most computers today come with the correct local time, enabling the user to be worry-free regarding the current time setting. You should assume, then, that the clock is set to the correct local settings.

Date Method Categories

JavaScript provides JavaScript scripters with a handful of methods to deal with instances of the `Date` object. As you have seen, `Date` instances are not very useful at their top level. However, extracting and manipulating their data makes them one of the most important elements of the language.

The whole bulk of methods may seem dazzling if you approach them at once. Therefore, we have chosen to divide them into four groups, according to their operation:

- `get` methods
- `set` methods
- `to` methods
- `parse` methods

The first type of method is by far the most useful one. get methods return an integer corresponding to the attribute of the instance you desire. You can "get" the year number, the month number, the hour one, and so on. set methods enable you to modify the value of a certain attribute of an existing instance. These methods accept integer values rather than returning them. You actually "set" the values of attributes with these statements. to methods convert the date into a string according to arguments passed over to the method. You can then take advantage of the string format with string methods and properties, such as the method split(). parse methods simply interpret date strings.

get Methods

getYear()

The getYear() method returns the current year stored in an instance of the Date object type. Years are represented in integers, specifying the year of the 20th century. For example, this book was written in 97, not 1997. If you ask the user to enter a certain year, you must specify that the two-digit format is necessary, or validate the input instead. The latter is demonstrated in the following script segment:

```
var now = new Date()
var year = now.getYear()
while (1) {
     var guessYear = parseInt(prompt("Enter current year:", ""))
     if (guessYear > 1900)
          guessYear -= 1900
     if (guessYear == year) {
          alert("That's right!")
          break
     } else
          alert("Wrong answer! Try again...")
}
```

The current year (based on the system clock) is extracted from the instance now, created according to default arguments (current time and date). A loop without a terminating condition is executed next. The user is asked to enter the current year, according to his or her knowledge! If the user enters the year using the four-digit convention, it is reduced to the two-digit one, via an if statement. Another if statement checks if the user entered the correct year. If so, the proper message is displayed, and the loop is broken up with a break statement. Otherwise, a message informs the user that his or her input was incorrect, and the loop iterates once more. You will often find the first `if` statement in the form of a conditional operation:

```
guessYear = (guessYear > 1900) ? guessYear - 1900 : guessYear
```

The `if` statement is undoubtedly better in this situation because it is clearer. As a matter of fact, it is also simpler and shorter (count the number of characters in each!). When the year 2000 arrives, you will probably need to find a workaround, or more likely, you won't be programming in JavaScript.

getMonth()

The `getMonth()` method extracts and returns the month of its calling object. Months range from January to December, or more accurately, from 0 to 11. Here is a simple example demonstrating this method as well as an array instance:

```
var now = new Date()
var month = now.getMonth()

var ar = new Array(12)
ar[0] = "January"
ar[1] = "February"
ar[2] = "March"
ar[3] = "April"
ar[4] = "May"
ar[5] = "June"
ar[6] = "July"
ar[7] = "August"
ar[8] = "September"
ar[9] = "October"
ar[10] = "November"
ar[11] = "December"

var message = "It is now " + ar[month] + ", my favorite.<BR>"
document.write(message)
```

The current month is extracted from the `now` instance which holds the attributes of the current time (after the statement has executed). A static array is then created to hold all months' names (as strings), matching each name to its corresponding number in JavaScript, starting at zero. This obviously fits the default array structure, featuring the first index as zero. Therefore, no math needs to be done, and the current month, by name, is used to construct a message, obviously a string. The message is then printed as plain HTML.

Warning: The `getMonth` attribute returns an incorrect value (off by one) on some versions of Navigator. (MSIE works fine.)

getDate()

Called by a `Date` object, the `getDate()` method returns the date as an integer between 1 and 31. For some unknown reason, the first day is not zero. The reason might be that the last date of a specific month varies from the last date of another month, making calculations somewhat more difficult to understand. Here is an example:

```
var now = new Date()
var year = now.getYear()
var month = now.getMonth()
var date = now.getDate()

if (date < 10)
     var lastDigit = date
else
     var lastDigit = date % 10
var exp = ""

// determine suffix
if (lastDigit == 1)
     suf = "st"
else
     if (lastDigit == 2)
          suf = "nd"
     else
          if (lastDigit == 3)
               suf = "rd"
          else
               suf = "th"

// array for name of month
var ar = new Array(12)
ar[0] = "January"
ar[1] = "February"
ar[2] = "March"
ar[3] = "April"
ar[4] = "May"
ar[5] = "June"
ar[6] = "July"
ar[7] = "August"
ar[8] = "September"
ar[9] = "October"
```

```
ar[10] = "November"
ar[11] = "December"

var formDate = date + suf

// build full date such as "May 5th, 1997"
var totalDate = ar[month] + " " + formDate + ", 19" + year

document.write(totalDate)
```

This script segment combines all methods learned up to now to display a nicely formatted date. At first, all needed attributes of the previously created instance of the `Date` object are received and assigned to their corresponding variables (e.g., year, month, date). The last digit of the date (1 - 31) is then assigned to the variable `lastDigit`. According to the value of `lastDigit`, the proper suffix is assigned to `suf` via a nested `if - else` statement. For the digit 1, the suffix is "st" (1st); for the digit 2, the suffix is "nd" (2nd); for the digit 3, it is "rd" (3rd); for all other digits, it is "th" (5th, 6th, ...). Note that the last `else` statement associates the "th" suffix with all digits other than 1, 2, and 3. Even the ones ending with a 0 apply to this suffix. An array of month names is created as before. The current date is then combined with its suffix to create a string such as "27th". This string, along with all the other desired values, is used to build a complete date format, such as "April 24th, 1997." The full string is printed.

getDay()

This method returns the day of the week as an integer between 0 and 6. The day of the week is calculated according to the other attributes, so this method does not have a corresponding `setDay()` method. Here is an example:

```
ar = new Array(7)
ar[0] = "Sunday"
ar[1] = "Monday"
ar[2] = "Tuesday"
ar[3] = "Wednesday"
ar[4] = "Thursday"
ar[5] = "Friday"
ar[6] = "Saturday"

var birthday = new Date("January 3, 1978")
var day = birthday.getDay()
alert("You were born on " + ar[day])
```

getHours()

The `getHours()` function returns the number of hours since midnight. That is, it returns the current hour according to the 24-hour clock. Note that the range is 0 - 23, from midnight (0) to 11 PM (23). Here is an example:

```
var now = new Date()
var hour = now.getHours()
var text = ""

if (hour < 12)
     text = "morning"
else
     if (hour < 16)
          text = "afternoon"
     else
          if (hour < 20)
               text = "evening"
          else
               text = "night"
document.write("Good " + text + "!")
```

This script segment prints a short greeting according to the time of the day. For example, if it is between 12:00 (noon) and 16:00 (4 PM), it prints "Good afternoon!" It is based on a nested `if - else` construct.

getMinutes()

The `getMinutes()` method returns the minute attribute of a `Date` instance. The integer returned is always between 0 and 59. Here is a short example to demonstrate the method:

```
var now = new Date()
var minute = now.getMinutes()
var hour = now.getHours()
var text = "Don't you have an appointment for " + (hour + 1)
text += ":00 ?"
if (minute > 49)
     document.write(text)
```

At first, the message containing the nearest hour is built. For example, if it is currently 15:55, the message is built with the nearest hour, 16:00. The message is printed if the current time is less than ten minutes from the next hour. Note that if it is 23:59 the hour is presented as 24:00, not 00:00.

getSeconds()

This method returns the seconds of a given Date instance, between 0 and 59. The following example takes advantage of this rapidly changing attribute to display a "randomly" chosen image out of ten different ones:

```
var now = new Date()
var second = now.getSeconds()
var num = second % 10

var image = new Array()
image[0] = "img1.gif"
image[1] = "img2.gif"
image[2] = "img3.gif"
image[3] = "img4.gif"
image[4] = "img5.gif"
image[5] = "img6.gif"
image[6] = "img7.gif"
image[7] = "img8.gif"
image[8] = "img9.gif"
image[9] = "img10.gif"

var img = "<IMG SRC=\"" + image[num] + "\"HEIGHT=100 WIDTH=100>"
document.write(img)
```

The modulo operator is used to reduce the 60 different numbers to just ten.

> Note that some of the methods use a plural form, while others use a singular form. The plural ones are getHour**s**(), getMinute**s**(), and getSecond**s**(). Remember that the plural ones are the ones associated with time units that are smaller than or equal to hours. All others use a singular form.

getTimezoneOffset()

This method returns the time zone offset in minutes for the current locale. The time zone offset is the difference between local time and Greenwich Mean Time (GMT). Daylight savings time prevents this value from being a constant. The returned value is an integer representing the difference in minutes. The following script shows how to use the user's time zone offset to figure out where he or she lives:

```
if (confirm("Are you in the United States?")) {
     var now = new Date()
     var curOffset = now.getTimezoneOffset()
     curOffset /= 60 // convert from minutes to hours
     var zone = ""
     var prep = ""

     if (curOffset == 8) {
          zone = "west coast"
          prep = "on"
     }
     else
          if (curOffset == 7) {
               zone = "mid - west"
               prep = "in"
          }
          else
               if (curOffset == 6) {
                    zone = "mid - east"
                    prep = "in"
               }
               else {
                    zone = "east coast"
                    prep = "on"
               }
     alert("I think you live " + prep + " the " + zone + "!")
}
else
     alert("Sorry, this script is intended for U.S. residents only")
```

The script starts by asking the user if he or she lives in the United States. If not, a message is displayed. Otherwise, the following command block is executed. The area in the United States is determined according to the difference in hours between the local time zone and the GMT. The preceding preposition (e.g., "in", "on") is determined as well in the `if - else` construct. JavaScript then builds an appropriate message based on the current location of the user as well as the proper preposition.

getTime()

The `getTime()` method returns the number of milliseconds since January 1, 1970 00:00:00. Here is an example that calculates the number of seconds passed since the beginning of the century:

```
var now = new Date()
var milliseconds70 = now.getTime()
var seconds70 = milliseconds70 / 1000

var seconds00 = 70 * 365 * 24 * 60 * 60
```

```
// years * days * hours * minutes * seconds
// leap years and additional seconds not counted

var totalSeconds = seconds00 + seconds70
document.write("Approximately " + totalSeconds + " seconds have passed in
the 20th century!")
```

`seconds70` holds the number of seconds since 1970. `seconds00` holds the number of seconds from 1900 to 1970 (approximately).

set Methods

setYear()

This method sets the year attribute of a given `Date` instance. The following example computes the day of the current date last year:

```
var now = new Date()
var year = now.getYear()
now.setYear(year + 1)

ar = new Array(7)
ar[0] = "Sunday"
ar[1] = "Monday"
ar[2] = "Tuesday"
ar[3] = "Wednesday"
ar[4] = "Thursday"
ar[5] = "Friday"
ar[6] = "Saturday"

document.write("Last year, the current day was " + ar[now.getDay()])
```

At first, an instance of the current date is created, and the current year is assigned to the variable `year`. The year attribute of the instance, `now`, is set to one year behind. The day attribute is then extracted from the modified instance, and a message is built based on that day, transformed to a string (via the array).

setMonth()

Sets the month attribute of a given instance of the `Date` object. The following script sets the month attribute of the current date to May:

```
var now = new Date()
now.setMonth(4)
```

setDate()

This method sets the date attribute of a given instance of the Date object. The following script prints the day on which the first day of the month occurred:

```
var now = new Date()
now.setDate(1)

ar = new Array(7)
ar[0] = "Sunday"
ar[1] = "Monday"
ar[2] = "Tuesday"
ar[3] = "Wednesday"
ar[4] = "Thursday"
ar[5] = "Friday"
ar[6] = "Saturday"

document.write("The first day of the month occurred on " +
                          ar[now.getDay()])
```

setHours()

This method sets the hour attribute of a given instance of the Date object. Here is an example:

```
var obj = new Date("December 4, 1995 18:50:59") // JS press release
obj.setHours(obj.getHours() - 2)
alert(obj.getHours()) // 16
```

setMinutes()

This method sets the minutes of a given date instance. Here is a simple example:

```
var obj = new Date("December 4, 1995 18:50:59") // JS press release
obj.setMinutes(obj.getMinutes() - 1)
alert(obj.getMinutes()) // 49
```

setSeconds()

The setSeconds method sets the seconds of a given instance of the Date object type. The following example demonstrates its usage:

```
var obj = new Date("December 4, 1995 18:50:59") // JS press release
obj.setSeconds(obj.getSeconds() - 9)
alert(obj.getSeconds()) // 50
```

setTime()

This method sets the number of milliseconds since January 1, 1970 00:00:00. It actually modifies all fields of its calling object. Here is an example:

```
var obj = new Date()
obj.setTime(867999600000)
var date = obj.getDate()
var month = obj.getMonth()

if (date < 10)
     var lastDigit = date
else
     var lastDigit = date % 10
var exp = ""

// determine suffix
if (lastDigit == 1)
     suf = "st"
else
     if (lastDigit == 2)
          suf = "nd"
     else
          if (lastDigit == 3)
               suf = "rd"
          else
               suf = "th"

// array for name of month
var ar = new Array(12)
ar[0] = "January"
ar[1] = "February"
ar[2] = "March"
ar[3] = "April"
ar[4] = "May"
ar[5] = "June"
ar[6] = "July"
ar[7] = "August"
ar[8] = "September"
ar[9] = "October"
ar[10] = "November"
ar[11] = "December"

var text = ar[month] + " " +date + suf
alert(text) // July 4th (setTime modifies the entire instance)
```

to Methods

toGMTString()

This method converts a date to a string, using the Internet GMT conventions. The conversion is done according to the operating system's time zone offset and returns a string value that is similar to the following form:

```
Tue, 30 Jul 1996 01:03:46 GMT
```

The exact format depends on the platform. Here is a simple example:

```
var now = new Date()
var ar1 = now.toGMTString().split(" ")
document.write("The current time in Greenwich is " + ar1[4])
```

A sample output of this script segment is:

```
The current time in Greenwich is 01:08:21
```

toLocaleString()

This method returns the date in the form of a string, using the current locale's conventions.

If you are trying to pass a date using `toLocaleString`, be aware that different locales assemble the string in different ways. Using methods such as `getHours`, `getMinutes`, and `getSeconds` will give more portable results. The following example demonstrates it:

```
var now = new Date()
var ar1 = now.toLocaleString().split(" ")
document.write("The current time is " + ar1[1])
```

The script's output is:

```
The current time is 18:12:51
```

The general format of the converted string is:

MM/DD/YY HH:MM:SS

parse Methods

parse()

The `parse` method accepts a date string in the IETF standard and converts it to the number of milliseconds since January 1, 1970 00:00:00. The IETF standard date representation is:

DayAbb, *date MonthAbb year HH*:*MM*:*SS TimeZoneAbb*

An example for this standard is "Mon, 25 Dec 1995 13:30:00 GMT." This method also understands the continental U.S. time zone abbreviations such as PST (Pacific Standard Time) and EST (Eastern Standard Time). However, time zones outside the United States (and their equivalent in Canada, for instance) do not have a standard abbreviation accepted by JavaScript. For such time zones the offset must be specified; that is, you must specify the difference in hours and minutes between the local time zone and Greenwich Mean Time. For example, in "Mon, 25 Dec 1995 13:30:00 GMT+0430," GMT+0430 is shorthand for 4 hours, 30 minutes west of the Greenwich meridian. If you do not specify a time zone, the local time zone is assumed, according to the settings of the clock in the operating system. If your time zone is not set correctly, you should change it in the control panel, both on Macs and Windows-based machines. GMT is also known as Universal Coordinate Time, or UTC.

The `parse` method is a static one. It does not belong to a specific instance of the `Date` object, but to the object type itself. Therefore, it is always used as `Date.parse()`. Here is an example for this method:

```
var aDate = "Aug 27 1985"
var birthday = new Date()
birthday.setTime(Date.parse(aDate))
```

UTC()

The `UTC()` method takes a comma-delimited list and returns the number of milliseconds since January 1, 1970 00:00:00, Greenwich Mean Time (GMT, UTC). This is also a static method, so it is called along with the general `Date` object. You cannot use this method to refer to a specific date in the local time zone, because it constantly refers to the Universal Coordinate Time (GMT, UTC). For example, the following statement creates a date object using GMT instead of local time, as it would if the method was not used:

```
gmtDate = new Date(Date.UTC(96, 11, 1, 0, 0, 0))
```

The general syntax of the method is:

```
Date.UTC(year, month, day [, hrs] [, min] [, sec])
```

All attributes should be specified as integers.

Time-Related Methods of Other Objects

setTimeout()

The `setTimeout()` method evaluates an expression after a specified number of milliseconds have elapsed. Its general syntax is:

```
timeoutID = setTimeout(expression, msec)
```

timeoutID is an identifier used to identify the current timeout.

expression is a string expression or property of an existing object. It is normally a simple statement that is to be executed after the specified time has ticked off.

msec is a numeric value, a numeric string, or a property of an existing object in millisecond units.

The `setTimeout()` method evaluates an expression after a specified amount of time. Take a look at the following example:

```
<HTML>
<HEAD>
<TITLE>setTimeout() method</TITLE>
<SCRIPT LANGUAGE="JavaScript">
function displayAlert() {
   alert("5 seconds have elapsed since the button was clicked.")
}
</SCRIPT>
</HEAD>
<BODY>
<FORM>
Click the button on the left for a reminder in 5 seconds;
click the button on the right to cancel the reminder before
it is displayed.
<P>
<INPUT TYPE="button" VALUE="5-second reminder"
   NAME="remind_button"
   onClick="timerID = setTimeout('displayAlert()',5000)">
</FORM>
</BODY>
</HTML>
```

When you click the button, the event handler's script sets a timeout. The timeout specifies that after 5,000 milliseconds, or five seconds, the function `displayAlert()` is called. Therefore, five seconds after you click the button an alert box is displayed.

This method does not repeatedly execute the specified statement. That is, it does not execute it every five seconds, for example. When the time limit specified has ticked down, the statement is executed and the timeout does not exist anymore. `SetTimeout()` is a method of the window or frame object, depending on the basic structure of the HTML document it is used in.

It is common to use the `setTimeout()` method for creating a pause between two consecutive calls to a user-defined recursive function.

The `setTimeout()` method is probably one of the most difficult to use, because it requires a deep understanding of the language. Take a look at the following script:

```
function alertNumbers(num) {
        if (num > 10)
                return
        alert(num)
         val = ++num
        timerID = setTimeout("alertNumbers(val)", 3000)
}

alertNumbers(0)
```

This script segment pops up an `alert` box every three seconds. The displayed message is a number. The first `alert` box displays the number 0. After three seconds another one displays the number 1. This process continues until the number 10. If you attempt to print the number to the document rather than displaying it in a window (box), an error is generated. The reason for such an error is that by writing to the document after a delay you are trying to change the layout, which has been completed. Another important point is that if the expression provided to the `setTimeout()` method is a function call, as in this example, and the function requires an argument, then it must a global variable. Local variables do not work, because `setTimeout()` is a method of a frame or the `window` object (`window` is the default value if no object is specified). Nonetheless, you can use a literal as the argument. Bear in mind that `setTimeout()` requires a string-encapsulated expression. You can embed a local variable in this expression as follows:

```
var cmd = "foo(" + num + ")"
timerID = setTimeout(cmd, 2000) // or any other time
```

> Note that the identifier for the timeout does not have to be `timerID`. You can use any valid identifier, even your name if you wish.

clearTimeout()

This method, also belonging to the `window` object, cancels a timeout that was set with the `setTimeout()` method. It is also a method of the frame or window object, so it is discussed later in detail. At this point, it is important that you know how to use it to cancel a timeout. Its general syntax is:

```
clearTimeout(timeoutID)
```

`timeoutID` is a timeout setting that was returned by a previous call to the `setTimeout()` method. It must be exactly the same as the one used in the `setTimeout()` method, because it actually identifies the timeout's settings according to it.

The `setTimeout()` method sets a timeout; that is, it executes a statement after a specified amount of time. If you want to cancel the time "bomb" during its ticking, you clear it via this method. If you want to change the amount of time set by the `setTimeout()` method, you must clear it and then set a new timeout. Here is the previous example enriched by the `clearTimeout()` method:

```
<HTML>
<HEAD>
<TITLE>setTimeout() and clearTimeout() methods</TITLE>
<SCRIPT LANGUAGE="JavaScript">
function displayAlert() {
   alert("5 seconds have elapsed since the button was clicked.")
}
</SCRIPT>
</HEAD>
<BODY>
<FORM>
Click the button on the left for a reminder in 5 seconds;
click the button on the right to cancel the reminder before
it is displayed.
<P>
<INPUT TYPE="button" VALUE="5-second reminder"
   NAME="remind_button"
   onClick="timerID=setTimeout('displayAlert()',5000)">
<INPUT TYPE="button" VALUE="Clear the 5-second reminder"
```

```
   NAME="remind_disable_button"
   onClick="clearTimeout(timerID)">
</FORM>
</BODY>
</HTML>
```

Time and Date Examples

Times and dates are widely used in scripts to achieve many goals and to create various effects. In this section, we shall introduce a few useful scripts that exercise the concepts learned in this chapter.

A Simple Digital Clock

The time and date methods are useful for computing time values in JavaScript scripts. The following example shows how to use such values to create an attractive graphical clock on an HTML page:

```
<HTML>
<HEAD>
<TITLE>
JavaScript clock
</TITLE>
</HEAD>
<BODY>
<!-- JavaScript immediate script -->
<SCRIPT LANGUAGE="JavaScript">
<!--

// Copyright 1997 -- Tomer Shiran

// image files needed:
// *******************
// dg0.gif
// dg1.gif
// dg2.gif
// dg3.gif
// dg4.gif
// dg5.gif
// dg6.gif
// dg7.gif
// dg8.gif
// dg9.gif
// dgam.gif
// dgpm.gif
// dgc.gif
// Any set of digit images (0-9), an "am" image,
// a "pm" image, and a colon image, respectively,
```

```
// will work with this script.

// instructions:
// *************
// Place all image files in a folder / directory.
// Add this script, including all comments, to
// the desired HTML document. The HTML file must
// be located in the same directory as the image
// files.

document.write(setClock())

function setClock() {
     // initialize accumulative HTML variable to empty string
     var text = ""

     // set standard convention for digit and punctuation images
     var openImage = "<IMG SRC=\"" + getPath(location.href) + "dg"
     var closeImage = ".gif\" HEIGHT=21 WIDTH=16>"

     // initialize time-related variables with current time settings
     var now = new Date()
     var hour = now.getHours()
     var minute = now.getMinutes()
     now = null
     var ampm = ""

     // validate hour values and set value of ampm
     if (hour >= 12) {
          hour -= 12
          ampm = "pm"
     } else
          ampm = "am"
     hour = (hour == 0) ? 12 : hour

     // add zero digit to a one-digit minute as spaceholder
     if (minute < 10)
          minute = "0" + minute // do not parse this number!

     // convert minute and hour values to strings
     minute += ""
     hour += ""

     // assign image tags according to the value of hour
     for (var i = 0; i < hour.length; ++i) {
          text += openImage + hour.charAt(i) + closeImage
     }

     // assign image tag of colon separator to text variable
     text += openImage + "c.gif\" HEIGHT=21 WIDTH=9>"

     // assign image tags according to the value of minute
```

```
        for (var i = 0; i < minute.length; ++i) {
            text += openImage + minute.charAt(i) + closeImage
        }

        // assign am / pm image tag to text variable
        text += openImage + ampm + closeImage

        // return accumulative HTML string
        return text
}

function getPath(url) {
        lastSlash = url.lastIndexOf("/")
        return url.substring(0, lastSlash + 1)
}

// -->
</SCRIPT>
</BODY>
</HTML>
```

Example 14-1 (ex14-1.htm). *A simple graphical clock based on time and date methods.*

Here is a screen shot of the script's output:

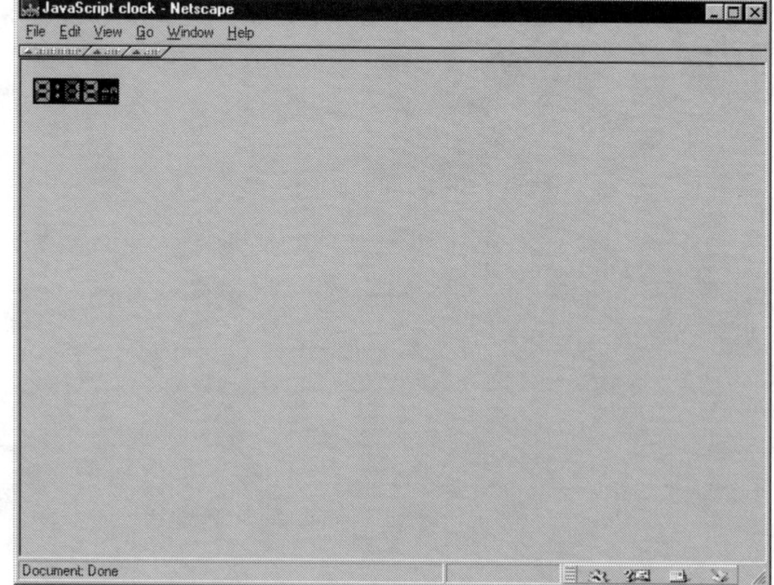

Figure 14-4. *With just a few images and a script you can create a graphical clock with the current time on an HTML page.*

The first part of the script is built of comments including a copyright notice, the needed images, and some instructions. It is important to add these comments to every public-domain script because it is often difficult to guess what a script does and what additional objects are needed, such as images.

The function `getPath()` accepts the URL of the current document. This includes all portions of the URL, including "http://..." and the name of the file. The function returns the URL up to the filename, not including the filename but including the last slash. For example, consider the following URL:

http://www.netscent.com/index.html

Upon acceptance of this string, the function would return:

http://www.netscent.com/

At this point, pay no attention to the statements inside functions. These are explained later on in the book. For now just understand what the functions do.

The first function in the script, `setClock()`, actually creates the clock, from top to bottom. Notice that each portion of the function is explained by a comment. Take a look at the following statements, taken directly from the function:

```
var openImage = "<IMG SRC=\"" + getPath(location.href) + "dg"
var closeImage = ".gif\" HEIGHT=21 WIDTH=16>"
```

In this script segment, two constant-like variables are declared and initialized a meaningful value. The first is assigned the opening structure of an `<IMG>` tag in HTML. Note that `location.href` is the current URL of the document. Notice also the use of escape sequences (`\"`). If the URL is http://www.netscent.com/index.html, then the value assigned to `openImage` is `<IMG SRC="http://www.netscent.com/dg`. The value assigned to `closeImage` is independent of local influences such as the URL of the document. It simply assigns the value `.gif\" HEIGHT=21 WIDTH=16>`. The `HEIGHT` and `WIDTH` attributes are based on the actual height and width of the digit images used to display the time.

Here is the following portion of the script:

```
var now = new Date()
var hour = now.getHours()
var minute = now.getMinutes()
now = null
var ampm = ""
```

This section has two important tasks:

1. It assigns the local hour to hour.
2. It assigns the minute attribute of the current time to minute.

There is obviously no need to explain how, but if you do not remember, read through this chapter once again.

The following script segment simply modifies the value of hour according to the regular conventions used in the United States and other countries using 12-hour clock systems. First of all, noon is considered PM. Furthermore, midnight is written 12:00, not 0:00.

Take a look at the following statement:

```
if (minute < 10)
    minute = "0" + minute // do not parse this number!
```

This statement makes sure that the minute attribute holds a two-digit number. That is, if it is originally a one-digit number, a leading "0" digit is placed. Notice that this digit is actually a string. Attempting to parse this string with a function such as parseInt() would convert it to a numeric type, causing its value to change, because it is written in octal notation (leading 0). It must keep the string value throughout the entire script.

The following two statements in the script cast the value of minute and the value of hour to strings by concatenating an empty string to them. This is important, because string properties, which can only be used on strings, are used later on in the script.

The following statement is a loop:

```
for (var i = 0; i < hour.length; ++i) {
    text += openImage + hour.charAt(i) + closeImage
}
```

The loop executes hour.length times. That is, if hour is a two-digit number, the loop executes twice, once for each digit. During each execution, an image tag corresponding to the current digit in the string, the value of hour, is being concatenated to text. For example, if the value of hour is 12, the loop's command block executes twice. During the first execution, the following string is assigned to text:

```
text += '<IMG SRC="http://www.netscent.com/dg1.gif" HEIGHT=21
WIDTH=16>'
```

During the second pass through the loop, this equivalent statement is executed:

```
text += '<IMG SRC="http://www.netscent.com/dg2.gif" HEIGHT=21
WIDTH=16>'
```

If the value of `hour` is a one-character string, the loop obviously executes only once.

The following statement in the script is:

```
text += openImage + "c.gif\" HEIGHT=21 WIDTH=9>"
```

This statement simply assigns the tag associated with the colon image. Notice that `closeImage` is not concatenated in this statement because this image's `WIDTH` attribute is different from the other images.

The following loop is exactly like the one described earlier associated with the variable `hour`. It only differs in that it relates to the variable `minute`.

The AM or PM image tag is assigned to `text`, according to the value of `ampm`.

The final statement inside the function instructs JavaScript to return the value of `text`, the accumulative string of all the HTML tags needed to print the clock. The returned value is printed to the document by a global statement—`document.write(text)`.

Digital Date

This example is similar to the previous one, except that it displays a set of images associated with the current date, rather than the time. It is based on the same functions, so we shall spare the explanation. Refer to the comments inside the script for some short explanations. Here is the script:

```
<HTML>
<HEAD>
<TITLE>
JavaScript date
</TITLE>
</HEAD>
<BODY>
<!-- JavaScript immediate script -->
<SCRIPT LANGUAGE="JavaScript">
<!--

// Copyright 1997 -- Tomer Shiran

// image files needed:
// ******************
// dg0.gif
```

```
// dg1.gif
// dg2.gif
// dg3.gif
// dg4.gif
// dg5.gif
// dg6.gif
// dg7.gif
// dg8.gif
// dg9.gif
// dgp.gif
// Any set of digit images (0-9), and a period
// image (.) will work with this script.

// instructions:
// *************
// Place all image files in a folder / directory.
// Add this script, including all comments, to
// the desired HTML document. The HTML file must
// be located in the same directory as the image
// files.

document.write(setDate())

function setDate() {
    // initialize accumulative HTML variable to empty string
    var text = ""

    // set standard convention for digit and punctuation images
    var openImage = "<IMG SRC=\"" + getPath(location.href) + "dg"
    var closeImage = ".gif\" HEIGHT=21 WIDTH=16>"
    // initialize time-related variables with current date settings
    var now = new Date()
    var month = now.getMonth()
    var date = now.getDate()
    var year = now.getYear()
    now = null

    // convert integer value of month to standard range
    month++ // 0 - 11 => 1 - 12

    // convert minute and hour values to strings
    month += ""
    date += ""
    year += ""

    // assign image tags associated with month to text variable
    for (var i = 0; i < month.length; ++i) {
        text += openImage + month.charAt(i) + closeImage
    }

    // assign image tag of period separator to text variable
    text += openImage + "p.gif\" HEIGHT=21 WIDTH=9>"
```

```
        // assign image tags associated with date to text variable
        for (var i = 0; i < date.length; ++i) {
              text += openImage + date.charAt(i) + closeImage
        }

        // assign image tag of period separator to text variable
        text += openImage + "p.gif\" HEIGHT=21 WIDTH=9>"

        // assign image tags associated with year to text variable
        for (var i = 0; i < year.length; ++i) {
              text += openImage + year.charAt(i) + closeImage
        }

        // return accumulative HTML string
        return text
}

function getPath(url) {
        lastSlash = url.lastIndexOf("/")
        return url.substring(0, lastSlash + 1)
}

// -->
</SCRIPT>
</BODY>
</HTML>
```

Example 14-2 (ex14-2.htm). *A simple graphical output of the current local date.*

Here is the output of this script:

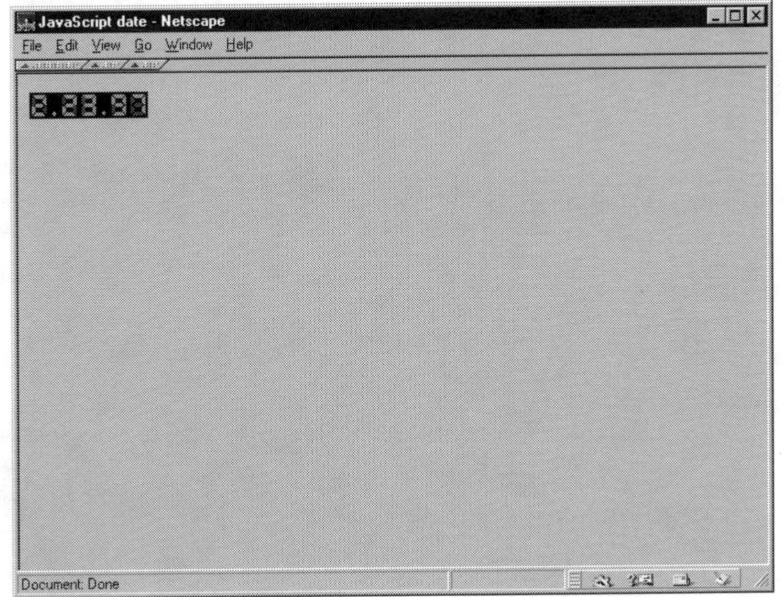

Figure 14-5. *No CGI, no Java, just a JavaScript script used to generate such an effect.*

Calendar

The next example outputs a monthly calendar. Before we discuss the code, take a look at a sample output of the function:

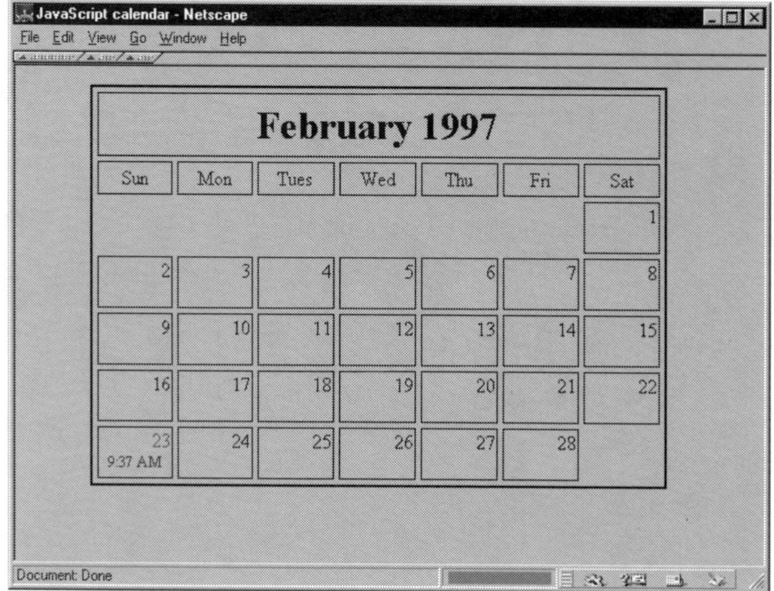

Figure 14-6. A calendar based on HTML tables printed via JavaScript.

Now take a look at the script itself:

```
<HTML>
<HEAD>
<TITLE>
JavaScript calendar
</TITLE>
</HEAD>
<BODY>
<!-- JavaScript immediate script -->
<SCRIPT LANGUAGE="JavaScript">
<!--

// Copyright 1997 -- Tomer Shiran

setCal()

function getTime() {
     // initialize time-related variables with current time settings
     var now = new Date()
     var hour = now.getHours()
     var minute = now.getMinutes()
     now = null
     var ampm = ""
```

```
        // validate hour values and set value of ampm
        if (hour >= 12) {
            hour -= 12
            ampm = "PM"
        } else
            ampm = "AM"
        hour = (hour == 0) ? 12 : hour

        // add zero digit to a one-digit minute
        if (minute < 10)
            minute = "0" + minute // do not parse this number!

        // return time string
        return hour + ":" + minute + " " + ampm
    }

    function leapYear(year) {
        if (year % 4 == 0) // basic rule
            return true // is leap year
        /* else */ // else not needed when statement is "return"
            return false // is not leap year
    }

    function getDays(month, year) {
        // create array to hold number of days in each month
        var ar = new Array(12)
        ar[0] = 31 // January
        ar[1] = (leapYear(year)) ? 29 : 28 // February
        ar[2] = 31 // March
        ar[3] = 30 // April
        ar[4] = 31 // May
        ar[5] = 30 // June
        ar[6] = 31 // July
        ar[7] = 31 // August
        ar[8] = 30 // September
        ar[9] = 31 // October
        ar[10] = 30 // November
        ar[11] = 31 // December

        // return number of days in the specified month (parameter)
        return ar[month]
    }

    function getMonthName(month) {
        // create array to hold name of each month
        var ar = new Array(12)
        ar[0] = "January"
        ar[1] = "February"
        ar[2] = "March"
        ar[3] = "April"
        ar[4] = "May"
```

```
        ar[5] = "June"
        ar[6] = "July"
        ar[7] = "August"
        ar[8] = "September"
        ar[9] = "October"
        ar[10] = "November"
        ar[11] = "December"

        // return name of specified month (parameter)
        return ar[month]
    }

    function setCal() {
        // standard time attributes
        var now = new Date()
        var year = now.getYear()
        var month = now.getMonth()
        var monthName = getMonthName(month)
        var date = now.getDate()
        now = null

        // create instance of first day of month, and extract the day it occurs on
        var firstDayInstance = new Date(year, month, 1)
        var firstDay = firstDayInstance.getDay()
        firstDayInstance = null

        // number of days in current month
        var days = getDays(month, year)

        // call function to draw calendar
        drawCal(firstDay + 1, days, date, monthName, 1900 + year)
    }

    function drawCal(firstDay, lastDate, date, monthName, year) {
        // constant table settings
        var headerHeight = 50 // height of the table's header cell
        var border = 2 // 3D height of table's border
        var cellspacing = 4 // width of table's border
        var headerColor = "midnightblue" // color of table's header
        var headerSize = "+3" // size of tables header font
        var colWidth = 60 // width of columns in table
        var dayCellHeight = 25 // height of cells containing days of the week
        var dayColor = "darkblue" // color of font representing week days
        var cellHeight = 40 // height of cells representing dates in the calendar
        var todayColor = "red" // color specifying today's date in the calendar
        var timeColor = "purple" // color of font representing current time

        // create basic table structure
        var text = "" // initialize accumulative variable to empty string
        text += '<CENTER>'
        text += '<TABLE BORDER=' + border + ' CELLSPACING=' + cellspacing + '>'
                                   // table settings
```

```
text +=   '<TH COLSPAN=7 HEIGHT=' + headerHeight + '>' // create table
                                                          header cell
text +=        '<FONT COLOR="' + headerColor + '" SIZE=' + headerSize +
                                  '>' // set font for table header
text +=             monthName + ' ' + year
text +=        '</FONT>' // close table header's font settings
text +=   '</TH>' // close header cell

// variables to hold constant settings
var openCol = '<TD WIDTH=' + colWidth + ' HEIGHT=' + dayCellHeight + '>'
openCol += '<FONT COLOR="' + dayColor + '">'
var closeCol = '</FONT></TD>'

// create array of abbreviated day names
var weekDay = new Array(7)
weekDay[0] = "Sun"
weekDay[1] = "Mon"
weekDay[2] = "Tues"
weekDay[3] = "Wed"
weekDay[4] = "Thu"
weekDay[5] = "Fri"
weekDay[6] = "Sat"

// create first row of table to set column width and specify week day
text += '<TR ALIGN="center" VALIGN="center">'
for (var dayNum = 0; dayNum < 7; ++dayNum) {
    text += openCol + weekDay[dayNum] + closeCol
}
text += '</TR>'

// declaration and initialization of two variables to help with tables
var digit = 1
var curCell = 1

for (var row = 1; row <= Math.ceil((lastDate + firstDay - 1) / 7); ++row) {
    text += '<TR ALIGN="right" VALIGN="top">'
    for (var col = 1; col <= 7; ++col) {
        if (digit > lastDate)
            break
        if (curCell < firstDay) {
            text += '<TD></TD>'
            curCell++
        } else {
            if (digit == date) { // current cell represent today's date
                text += '<TD HEIGHT=' + cellHeight + '>'
                text += '<FONT COLOR="' + todayColor + '">'
                text += digit
                text += '</FONT><BR>'
                text += '<FONT COLOR="' + timeColor + '" SIZE=2>'
                text += '<CENTER>' + getTime() + '</CENTER>'
                text += '</FONT>'
                text += '</TD>'
```

```
                } else
                    text += '<TD HEIGHT=' + cellHeight + '>' + digit +
                                                        '</TD>'
                digit++
            }
        }
        text += '</TR>'
    }

    // close all basic table tags
    text += '</TABLE>'
    text += '</CENTER>'

    // print accumulative HTML string
    document.write(text)
}

// -->
</SCRIPT>
</BODY>
</HTML>
```

Example 14-3 (ex14-3.htm). *A calendar based on HTML tables printed via JavaScript.*

Let's follow the script step by step, explaining the task of every function.

getTime()

This function simply returns a string representing the current local time in the following format:

> *hours* : *minutes AM/PM*

Note that there are no spaces between any characters. The function is based on the same algorithm as the first part of `setClock()` in Example 14-1. Refer to the explanation regarding that example for further insights.

leapYear(year)

This function returns `true` if the current year is a leap year. Otherwise it returns `false`. The basic rule used for the decision is that a leap year occurs every four years, in the same year of the summer Olympic games. More exactly, if the year is divisible by 4, it is a leap year. Therefore, the modulo operator suits the case perfectly. If `year % 4` is zero, the year is divisible by 4, meaning the current year is a leap year. Otherwise, the year is not divisible by 4, so `false` is returned. An obvious call to this function is:

```
if (leapYear(current year))
      // is a leap year
else
      // is not a leap year
```

Another possibility is to use the returned value in a conditional statement, or operation (?:).

Note that the parameter of the function must accept an integer value, which is reasonable when computing years.

getDays(month, year)

This function accepts two arguments: a month and a year. An array of 12 elements is then created. The array is an instance of the built-in `Array` object. Therefore, the keyword `new` is used. Each element of the array represents the number of days in its corresponding month. `ar[0]` holds the number of days in January (31); `ar[11]` holds the number of days in December. The array is simply assigned the proper data, according to the constant number of days in each month. However, the number of days in February is not constant. In leap years there are 29 days in February, whereas in all other years there are 28 days. The function `leapYear()` is used to decide if the specified year is a leap one. This situation is a typical one for a conditional operator, because one of two values is to be assigned to a variable depending on the value of the condition (the Boolean value returned by the function `leapYear()`). Notice the extensive use of comments. They help you understand the script.

The value returned by the function is equal to the number of days in the month passed over to the function upon calling. For example, if the value of `month` is 0 (as passed to the function), the value `ar[0] == 31` is returned by the function.

Note that both arguments must be integers. The month must be specified as an integer between 0 and 11, 0 representing January, and 11 representing December.

getMonthName(month)

This function accepts the integer value of a certain month (0 - January, 11 - December) and returns the full name of the function, obviously in the form of a string. This function, like its preceding one, uses an instance of the `Array` object to store constant values. The name of the desired month is retrieved from the array by its index (subscript).

setCal()

At first, the function creates a new instance of the Date object, holding the attributes of the current local time. The current year is assigned to year via the method getYear(), and the current month is assigned to month via the method getMonth(). The name of the month, returned by getMonthName(), is assigned to monthName. After the current date is assigned to date, the instance now is assigned null, a good JavaScript programming practice.

The following statement of the function is:

```
var firstDayInstance = new Date(year, month, 1)
```

It creates a new instance of the Date object; this time it is for the first day of the current month. Therefore, the value 1 is used to specify the date. This obviously influences the day of the week on which the date occurred. This value is assigned to firstDay in the following statement. The instance firstDayInstance is then assigned null. This script segment computes the day of the week (Sunday, Monday, Tuesday, etc.) on which the month started. Another possible way to achieve this goal is to create an instance of the current date as usual:

```
var firstDayInstance = new Date() // not first day yet!
```

You then need to set the date to 1, via the setDate() method. You should use the following statement to do so:

```
firstDayInstance.setDate(1)
```

The next portion of the function consists of only one statement. It assigns days the number of days in the current month.

The last statement of the function draws the calendar. Here it is:

```
drawCal(firstDay + 1, days, date, monthName, 1900 + year)
```

The arguments are:

1. Integer value of the first day of the month + 1. That is, 1 for Sunday, 2 for Monday, 3 for Tuesday.
2. The number of days in the specified month.
3. The specified date.
4. The name of the specified month (e.g., "January," "February," "March").
5. The specified year, as a four-digit integer (e.g., 1997, 1998).

drawCal(firstDay, lastDate, date, monthName, year)

This function's main task is to print the calendar table. Before it does so, the HTML structure of the table must be constructed.

The first part of the function assigns values to attributes associated with the final format of the table. Such attributes are the size of cells, font colors, and more. Here is the full list, including the variable names and their roles:

Table 14-2. *Variables in* `drawCal()` *and their role in the final format of the calendar.*

Variable	Role
`headerHeight`	The height of the table header's cell. The header cell is the cell containing the name of the month and the year in a large font. The height is specified in pixels.
`border`	The table's border. You should already know that HTML tables have a `BORDER` attribute. This attribute specifies the three-dimensional height of the border.
`CellSpacing`	The width of the border. A table border's width can also be set in HTML. This value is the distance between the inner line of the border and its outer line.
`HeaderColor`	The color of the header's font. This is the color of the font in the largest cell of the table at the top of the calendar.
`HeaderSize`	The size of the header's font (see role of `headerHeight`).
`ColWidth`	The width of the table's columns. This is actually the width of each cell, or the width of the widest cell in each column.
`DayCellHeight`	The height of the cell containing the names of the days ("Sunday," "Monday," "Tuesday," etc.)
`dayColor`	The color of the font representing the days of the week.
`CellHeight`	The height of all the regular cells in the table containing the dates of the month.
`TodayColor`	The color specifying the current date in the calendar.
`TimeColor`	The color of the font used with the current time, located in the cell of the current date.

The following portion of the function creates the basic table structure, including all general HTML tags referring to the outline of the table. Notice how the variables are implemented in the script. Now take a look at the following two statements of the script:

```
var openCol = '<TD WIDTH=' + colWidth + ' HEIGHT=' + dayCellHeight + '>'
openCol += '<FONT COLOR="' + dayColor + '">'
var closeCol = '</FONT></TD>'
```

These are the tags used to create each of the cells containing the day names. For example, the syntax for "Sunday" using the default values of the variables is:

```
<TD WIDTH=60 HEIGHT=25><FONT COLOR="midnightblue"></FONT></TD>
```

Here are the next two portions of the function for reference:

```
// create array of abbreviated day names
      var weekDay = new Array(7)
      weekDay[0] = "Sun"
      weekDay[1] = "Mon"
      weekDay[2] = "Tues"
      weekDay[3] = "Wed"
      weekDay[4] = "Thu"
      weekDay[5] = "Fri"
      weekDay[6] = "Sat"

      // create first row of table to set column width and specify week day
      text += '<TR ALIGN="center" VALIGN="center">'
      for (var dayNum = 0; dayNum < 7; ++dayNum) {
            text += openCol + weekDay[dayNum] + closeCol
      }
      text += '</TR>'
```

In the first segment, a regular array is created. It is then assigned the abbreviated names of the days. This array enables us to refer to each name via a number. The following portion, where a cell is created for each day, takes advantage of this referencing method. A new day is printed on every iteration of the loop. Note that the tags associated with the beginning and the end of the table's current row are not located inside the loop. A new row with all day names is started before the loop. The current row is terminated after the tags related to the cell of "Sat" are assigned to `text`.

The following portion of the function is:

```
var digit = 1
var curCell = 1
```

You will see the role of these variables later in the function.

By now, all tags associated with the table's header and the column headers have been assigned to the accumulative string variable `text`. The remaining part of the function assigns the tags associated with all table's cells. As you know, the calendar is a rectangular table. Therefore, we prefer to use a nested loop structure to refer to its cells. If you want to practice your skills, try replacing this structure with a single loop, using the modulo operator to compute the location of new table rows.

The more difficult part of the loop is its terminating condition. Here it is again:

```
row <= Math.ceil((lastDate + firstDay - 1) / 7)
```

The `Math` object and its `ceil()` method are explained in Chapter 15, JavaScript Math. For now, you should just know that `Math.ceil(`*`num`*`)` evaluates to the nearest integer to *`num`* that is equal to or greater than *`num`* (rounding up). Here are some examples:

```
Math.ceil(15.15) == 16
Math.ceil(16) == 16
Math.ceil(16.0001) == 17
```

You may recall from the previous function, `setCal()`, that the value passed over to the parameter `firstDay` is between 1 and 7, not 0 and 6. Therefore 1 is subtracted from `firstDay` in this expression. `Math.ceil((lastDate + firstDay - 1) / 7)` represents the minimum number of rows needed in the calendar, or table. The number of cells in the calendar (not including the main header, column headers, and cells after the last day in the month) is `lastDate + firstDay - 1`, because `lastDate` is equal to the number of days in the month, and `firstDay - 1` is equal to the number of cells before the first date. The value is divided by 7, to get the exact minimum number of rows needed. However, the loop must execute a whole number of times. Therefore, the `Math.ceil()` method is needed. Other, more simple, calendars just use five rows for every month, no matter what. However, this simple rule of five rows per month fails when (a) the first day of a non-leap year February occurs on Sunday, meaning only four lines are needed, and (b) the first day of a 31-day month is on Friday or Saturday, meaning six rows are needed. Although these situations seldom occur, you must take them into account. If the row computation is replaced by a simple 5 in this script, a month such as February 1987 does not appear properly. Here is a screen shot of this special occurrence, where the script justifiably uses the complex expression (`Math.ceil((lastDate + firstDay - 1) / 7)`):

JavaScript calendar - Netscape

File Edit View Go Window Help

February 1987						
Sun	Mon	Tues	Wed	Thu	Fri	Sat
1	2	3	4	5	6	7
8	9	10	11	12	13	14
15	16	17	18	19	20	21
22	23 10:43 AM	24	25	26	27	28

Document: Done

Figure 14-7. *February 1987—only 28 cells (4 rows) needed—every thing looks fine.*

Now, here is the output of the script using five rows (notice the width of the bottom border, representing an empty table row):

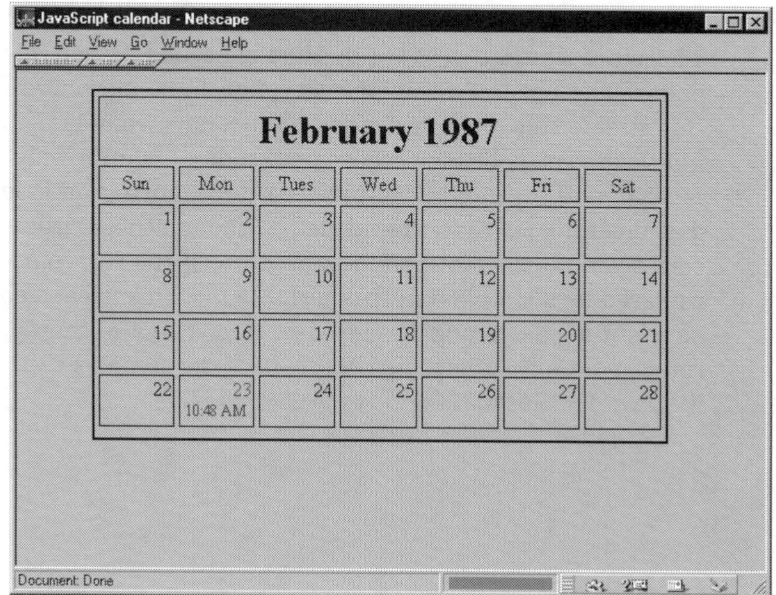

Figure 14-8. *February 1987—only 28 cells (4 rows) needed—the bottom border is doubled in width.*

The nested loop is not nearly as difficult, because it always executes seven times, once for each day of the week. Throughout the entire loop construct, including inner and outer loops, `digit` holds the current cell to be created. The variable `curCell` holds the accumulative number of cells in the table created (assigned) thus far. This variable is only needed until the cell of the first day of the month is created, and is not handled afterwards; that is, after the first day of the month, it is not incremented anymore.

The string `<TD></TD>` is used to create blank cells, used as placeholders. These are only needed before the first day of the month, because the loop is terminated via a `break` statement after the last day of the month, and the remaining place in the line is filled in the same way as blank cells (placeholders). Each execution of the inner loop creates the current cell of the table. There are basically two types of cells:

- A cell representing the current day, which uses a special font color and displays the time inside the cell
- All other cells

The HTML tags used are obvious and are not dealt with in depth here.

There are two statements outside the inner loop but inside the containment loop. The first one creates a new table row and the second one ends the current row. Each execution of the inner loop (seven executions or its command block) is responsible for the creation of an entire row, or a partial one if it is the last row and the last day of the month is encountered before the last cell of the row—in this case the loop is terminated via a `break` statement. The term "create" refers to the concatenation of the proper strings and values and assignment to the variable `text`.

The last, but definitely not least, statement of the function is the one that actually prints the table to the HTML document. Up to that statement, the HTML document was stored as a string in the variable `text`.

Random Quotes

The finale for this chapter is a simple, yet interesting script to display a different message each time the page is loaded. Yes, only with JavaScript. Here is the script:

```
<HTML>
<HEAD>
<TITLE>Random quote</TITLE>
<SCRIPT LANGUAGE="JavaScript">
<!--

function getMessage() {
```

```
        // create array of Murphy's laws
        var ar = new Array(20)
        ar[0] = "Nothing is as easy as it looks."
        ar[1] = "Everything takes longer than you think."
        ar[2] = "Anything that can go wrong will go wrong."
        ar[3] = "If there is a possibility of several things going wrong, the one
                 that will cause the most damage will be the one to go wrong."
        ar[4] = "If there is a worse time for something to go wrong, it will
                 happen then."
        ar[5] = "If anything simply cannot go wrong, it will anyway."
        ar[6] = "If you perceive that there are four possible ways in which a
                 procedure can go wrong, and circumvent these, then a fifth
                 way, unprepared for, will promptly develop."
        ar[7] = "Left to themselves, things tend to go from bad to worse."
        ar[8] = "If everything seems to be going well, you have obviously
                 overlooked something."
        ar[9] = "Nature always sides with the hidden flaw."
        ar[10] = "Mother nature is a bitch."
        ar[11] = "It is impossible to make anything foolproof because fools are
                 so ingenious."
        ar[12] = "Whenever you set out to do something, something else must be
                 done first."
        ar[13] = "Every solution breeds new problems."
        ar[14] = "Trust everybody ... then cut the cards."
        ar[15] = "Two wrongs are only the beginning."
        ar[16] = "If at first you don't succeed, destroy all evidence that
                 you tried."
        ar[17] = "To succeed in politics, it is often necessary to rise above
                 your principles."
        ar[18] = "Exceptions prove the rule ... and wreck the budget."
        ar[19] = "Success always occurs in private, and failure in full view."

        var now = new Date()
        var sec = now.getSeconds()
        alert("Murphy's Law:\r" + ar[sec % 20])
}

// -->
</SCRIPT>
</HEAD>
<BODY onLoad="getMessage()">
</BODY>
</HTML>
```

Example 14-4 (ex14-4.htm). *A script to display a random message each time the page is loaded.*

The first statement in the function creates an array, an instance of the built-in `Array` object. The array includes 20 elements, starting from `ar[0]` and ending with `ar[19]`. Each element is assigned a string, or to be exact, a Murphy law. An instance of the `Date` object, `now`, is then created. The number of seconds in the current time is retrieved from now via the getSeconds() method. As you know, the value of sec is an integer between 0 and 59, with a random possibility for each. In total there are 60 consecutive integers. Due to this fact, the expression sec % 20 returns an integer between 0 and 19, with an equal chance for each, because 60 is divisible by 20 (60 / 20 = 3!). The ability to create a random number between 0 and 19 using this technique enables us to randomly choose a Murphy law from the array. The selected Murphy law is displayed by an alert box.

The most important part of the script to pay attention to is the use of an event handler to respond to the load event—onLoad. When the event handler is triggered (when the page has completed loading), the function getMessage() is called to display an alert message as described earlier. Just so you can get a feel for the script, here is a sample output:

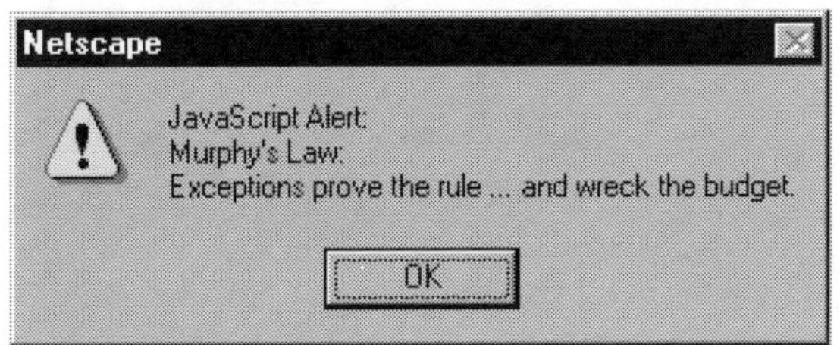

Figure 14-9. A Murphy's law chosen from a list of 20 is displayed.

Also notice the use of an escape sequence, the carriage return character (\r).

Summary

In this chapter we discussed date- and time-related concepts in JavaScript. Such concepts are based on the Date object. We learned about this built-in object, the only one in JavaScript without any properties. After a deep look through the object, we saw how its instances can be created and used in scripts. By now, you should have enough tools to create interesting scripts of various types. As we look further into the language in the following chapters, you will be able to grasp the power of JavaScript to enhance HTML documents. In this chapter you have seen that without much effort, you can add a graphical digital clock to any page. This may seem amazing, but the best is yet to come, including animated clocks, and more.

Chapter 15
JavaScript Math

Math in JavaScript

Computers are well known for their ability to perform complex calculations at extreme speeds. All programming languages include features, constants, functions, and other math elements that unleash the mathematical power of the computer. Likewise, JavaScript includes many features related to math, enabling JavaScript scripters to invoke numeric calculations in our scripts.

Math in JavaScript is based on two general elements of the language:

- Mathematical operators
- The built-in `Math` object

Mathematical operators should be clear by now, because they were discussed in Chapter 7, Utilizing JavaScript Operators. However, you are not yet familiar with the `Math` object. In this chapter we shall take a look into this object, including its properties and methods. We shall also take a look at some possible usages of this object.

The Math Object

JavaScript's `Math` object provides many arithmetic and trigonometric functions. Most of these are functions you probably already know. These functions expand the mathematical ability of JavaScript beyond the basic arithmetic operators.

Although JavaScript does not feature classes as Java does, built-in objects resemble classes in many ways. You already know how to create instances of dynamic objects, such as `Date`. Instances are created according to dynamic objects. Some objects in JavaScript are static ones. That is, they act like a single instance. You can refer directly to the object's methods and properties. This is different from dynamic objects such as `Date`. Recall that to retrieve the current year, you must first create an instance of the object, and then refer to the instance's methods.

JavaScript's `Math` object is a static one. Its properties are actually basic constants, such as PI (π) and the square root of 2. Its methods are mathematical functions, such as `pow()` (power), `sin()`, `cos()`, and others. These methods and properties are encapsulated in an object because objects are meant to be entities constructed of related data and functions—a good definition of math. As a general rule, JavaScript prefers to organize its functions and constants in its structured object model, to enable simple reference and maintenance. The requirements from mathematical functions and constants led JavaScript's developers to create a built-in object related to mathematics—`Math`.

To access elements of the `Math` object, you do not need to create an instance. You access them via messages sent directly by the `Math` object itself. For example, the PI constant is a property of the `Math` object, and can be accessed via the following syntax:

```
var pi = Math.PI
```

The reason that the `Math` object is static is that mathematical constants and functions never change. For example, the value of PI will not change, nor will any trigonometric function.

The `Math` object implementation is inspired by the `Math` class in Java. Despite this parallelism, you will find that JavaScript offers fewer methods.

Constants

Constants are defined with the full precision of floating point numbers in JavaScript. All constants in JavaScript are properties of the `Math` object. In this section we shall outline these properties for your reference and understanding. Notice that all properties are specified with capital letters, although this convention is not common in the mathematical community. All properties refer to well-known constants (read your math books if you don't remember!); that is, they do not change. Therefore, these properties are read-only ones, and accessing them for the purpose of modification results in a JavaScript error.

E

A very important constant in mathematics is Euler's constant. Its approximate value is 2.718281828459045. It is rounded off to 15 digits after the decimal point. For your reference, the equation is:

$e^{i\pi} + 1 = 0$

In JavaScript you refer to it via a capital E; that is, `Math.E`.

LN2

Another constant featured as a property of the `Math` object is the natural logarithm of 2. Its approximate value is 0.6931471805599453. A defining equation is:

$e^{LN2} = 2$

JavaScript refers to this number as `LN2`. Because it is a property of the `Math` object, you should specify them together as in `Math.LN2`.

You can use the `pow` method to assure that the preceding equation is true:

```
document.write(Math.pow(Math.E, Math.LN2))
```

Because both Euler's constant and the natural logarithm of 2 are approximate, the output of this statement is also an approximate:

```
1.9999999999999998
```

LN10

The natural logarithm of 10 is also featured as a property of the static `Math` object. Its value, as stored in its corresponding property, is 2.302585092994046. Once again, you can understand this value via an equation:

$e^{LN10} = 10$

In JavaScript this value is referred to as `Math.LN10`.

Once more, here is a JavaScript statement to define the natural logarithm of 10:

```
document.write(Math.pow(Math.E, Math.LN10))
```

Since both Euler's constant and the natural logarithm of 10 are approximate, the output of this statement is also an approximate:

```
10.000000000000002
```

LOG2E

Another important constant in the math arena is the base-2 logarithm of Euler's constant. Its approximate value is 1.4426950408889634. In math that is:

$$2^{LOG2E} = e$$

As you can see, you refer to this constant in JavaScript as `Math.LOG2E`. Here is a simple statement to confirm the value:

```
document.write(Math.pow(2, Math.LOG2E) - Math.E)
```

This time the output is apparently exact:

```
0
```

LOG10E

The base-10 logarithm is also widely used in complex mathematical calculations. Its value in JavaScript is approximately 0.4342944819032518. The following equation demonstrates the definition of the constant:

$$10^{LOG10E} = e$$

As you can see, the equation is built according to one of the basic logarithm rules. In JavaScript, log base-10 of Euler's constant is a property of the `Math` object: `Math.LOG10E`.

Here is a simple script for confirmation:

```
document.write(Math.pow(10, Math.LOG10E) - Math.E)
```

Once again, the output is exact:

```
0
```

PI

Probably the most known value among all constants featured by JavaScript is `pi`. Its approximate value, as enabled by the precision limits of real numbers in JavaScript, is 3.141592653589793. As before, here is an equation to demonstrate this value:

$$\pi = 4(1 - 1/3 + 1/5 - 1/7 + 1/9 - \ldots)$$

As you could expect, you refer to pi in JavaScript as `Math.PI`. For example, to obtain the circumference of a circle you can use the following function:

```
function circumference(diameter) {
     if (typeof diameter == "number" && diameter >= 0)
          return Math.PI * diameter
}
```

Note that the function does not return a value if the diameter is not a number or is not positive.

SQRT1_2

The square root of 0.5, as stored in JavaScript's object model, is 0.7071067811865476. You can also reach this value by calculating the square root of 0.5 (using the `sqrt()` method of the `Math` object), but accessing an existing property is somewhat faster and more obvious than calculating it via an execution of a method.

You refer to this property as `Math.SQRT1_2`. The reason an underscore is used for the property name is that the name of a property must follow the identifier rules which allow only letters, numbers, and underscores in the middle of a name.

Here is an obvious statement to confirm that the value is correct:

```
document.write(Math.pow(Math.SQRT1_2, 2))
```

The not-so-obvious output is:

```
0.5000000000000001
```

SQRT2

The square root of 2 is also a well-known constant. Its approximate value is 1.4142135623730951. You refer to it as `Math.SQRT2`. You can use the following statement to ensure the value:

```
document.write(Math.pow(Math.SQRT2, 2))
```

As you could expect, the result is not an exact one:

```
2.0000000000000004
```

Math Methods

Constant values make up only a fraction of the entire strength of mathematical implementation in JavaScript. To harness the power of the `Math` object you have to familiarize yourself with the set of methods available.

JavaScript tends to organize functions and values in object structures to enable easy reference and simple understanding. For this reason, all functions related to math are implemented as methods of the `Math` object.

The methods of the `Math` object can be divided into two categories, each one related to a different branch of mathematics:

- Arithmetic methods
- Trigonometric methods

All methods of the `Math` object are specified in lowercase letters, as opposed to constants which are properties of this object, and are specified in uppercase letters.

Arithmetic Methods

We use the term "arithmetic methods" to describe all methods that do not relate in any way to trigonometric math.

abs()

You can calculate the absolute value of any number, integer or floating point via this method. The absolute value of a number is its corresponding positive number; that is, if the number is positive, its absolute value is the number itself, whereas if it is negative, its absolute value is the same number with a + sign instead of a –. You can simulate this method easily:

```
function abs(num) {
      if (num < 0)
            return -num
      return num
}
```

For example, the absolute value of –5 is 5. The absolute value of 5 is also 5. In JavaScript you can calculate the absolute value of a number via the method `Math.abs()`. This method returns the absolute value of its argument. You can use this method to compute the absolute value of only one argument. If you call the method with more than one, only the absolute value of the first is returned.

If you want the corresponding negative value of a number, as opposed to the positive value, you can negate the returned value. For example:

```
var neg1 = -Math.abs(-3.7)
var neg2 = -Math.abs(3.7)
```

You can use the Math.abs() for many purposes, not only in mathematical algorithms.

ceil()

The Math.ceil() method accepts a single numeric argument and returns the next integer greater than or equal to the argument (rounding up). Therefore, the returned value is never less than the argument. Here are a few examples:

```
Math.ceil(16) == 16
Math.ceil(16.01) == 17
Math.ceil(-15.01) == -15
```

Let's say you need to fit num1 cars into parking lots, where each parking lot has space for num2 cars. You can use the Math.ceil() method along with a function to calculate the minimum number of parking lots:

```
function getNumLots(num1, num2) {
     return Math.ceil(num1 / num2)
}
```

The reason why we need to use this method in the above function is that you can only use a whole parking lot, not a fractional part; that is, we are trying to calculate the minimum number of parking lots needed, not the exact space.

exp()

This method returns Euler's constant to the power of the specified argument ($e^{argument}$). It is approximately equivalent to the following function:

```
function exp(num) {
     return Math.pow(Math.E, num)
}
```

You refer to this function as Math.exp(). Here is an example:

```
document.write(Math.exp(4))
```

Its output is:

```
54.598150033144236
```

floor()

The Math.floor() method returns the greatest integer less than or equal to the value passed to it. This is equivalent to integral division when dealing with non-negative numbers. It is also equivalent to rounding down to the nearest integer. Here are a few expressions, each evaluating to true:

```
Math.floor(16) == 16
Math.floor(16.01) == 16
Math.floor(-15.01) == -16
```

log()

This method returns the natural logarithm of the argument passed to it. For example, the natural log (base e) of e (Euler's constant) is 1. You can confirm it via the following statement:

```
document.write(Math.log(Math.E))
```

And indeed, the output is 1.

max(), min()

Both of these methods accept two numeric arguments. `max()` returns the greater of two numbers, whereas `min()` returns the lesser of the two. Here is a function that prints the lesser of two numbers followed by the greater:

```
function printInOrder(num1, num2) {
     document.write(Math.min(num1, num2) + ", " + Math.max(num1, num2))
}
```

The following function call prints the string "`-5, 1`" to the document:

```
printInOrder(1, -5)
```

Here are a few true expressions to demonstrate the basic `min()` and `max()` methods:

```
Math.max(1, 2) == 2
Math.min(2, Math.abs(-2)) == 2
Math.min(2, -2) == -2
```

pow()

Given two numeric arguments, this method returns the first one to the power of the second. Here are a few true expressions demonstrating the method:

```
Math.pow(10, 2) == 100
Math.pow(0.5, 0.5) == 0.7071067811865476
Math.pow(Math.SQRT2, 4) == 4.000000000000001
```

random()

This method returns a random number between 0 and 1. It is obviously a floating point number. The returned number's precision is usually 16 digits after the decimal point (or less, if last digits were chosen to be 0). Here is a simple example:

```
for (var i = 0; i < 5; ++i) {
     document.write(Math.random() + "<BR>")
}
```

The output of this loop depends on the output of random() and it is guaranteed that your results will not be the same as the following:

```
.924853870611902
.8248305636609181
.9539277224126104
.9806934571332098
.7639888801207115
```

This method is mostly used to create random integer numbers between x and y. Suppose x is 0 and y is a given number. You should multiply the value that random() returns by y and then round it off. For example, to generate a random number between 0 and 37 you can use the following expression:

```
Math.round(Math.random() * 37)
```

If you want an integer between 15 and 37 you can create a random integer between 0 and 22 and then add 15. Be very careful when attempting to create random numbers.

round()

The Math.round() method returns the nearest integer to the argument. If the argument's decimal part is equal to 0.5, the number is rounded upwards. Here are a few true expressions to demonstrate the method:

```
Math.round(3.7) == 4
Math.round(4.5) == 5
Math.round(16.1) == 16
Math.round(0) == 0
```

sqrt()

This method returns the square root of the argument. For example:

```
Math.sqrt(4) == 2
```

```
Math.sqrt(0) == 0
Math.sqrt(0.25) == 0.5
```

If the argument is a negative number, the method returns zero, which happens to be the wrong answer. It would be better if an error was generated instead, because this wrong answer can go undetected.

Trigonometric Methods

Trigonometric methods are obviously those that deal with trigonometry.

You should also know how to convert an angle from degrees to radians, and vice versa. Here is the basic conversion table:

Table 15-1. *Degree-radian conversion table.*

Degrees	Radians
360	2π
270	1.5π
180	π
90	0.5π

All angles in JavaScript are measured by radians, so the conversion table should help you visualize the size of an angle in radians.

cos()

The `Math.cos()` method accepts one argument, the angle of a triangle. It returns the cosine of that value, which must be specified in radians. The following statement prints "–1":

```
document.write(Math.cos(Math.PI))
```

acos()

The `Math.acos()` method also accepts one argument. It returns the arc cosine of the argument in radians; that is, it accepts the cosine of a certain value and returns that value—the opposite of the `Math.cos()` method. Therefore, the following statement prints the value of `PI`:

```
document.write(Math.acos(-1))
```

sin()

The Math.sin() function returns the sine of its argument. Keep in mind that the argument must be in radian units. Here is a statement that prints "1":

```
document.write(Math.sin(0.5 * Math.PI))
```

asin()

The Math.asin() method accepts one argument and returns its arc sine in radians. The following statement prints half the value of pi:

```
document.write(Math.asin(1))
```

tan()

The Math.tan() method returns the tangent of its argument, which is equal to the quotient of the value's sine and cosine. Take a look at the following script segment:

```
var val = 0.25 * Math.PI
document.write("sine = " + Math.sin(val) + "<BR>")
document.write("cosine = " + Math.cos(val) + "<BR>")
document.write("tangent = " + Math.tan(val))
```

The output of these statements in Netscape Navigator is:

```
sine = .7071067811865475
cosine = .7071067811865476
tangent = .9999999999999999
```

From this script you can learn:

- The sine of ¼ * pi is equal to its cosine which is also equal to the square root of ½.
- The cosine and sine methods sometimes return inaccurate results.

Take extra caution regarding the second concept—inaccuracy. The following statements:

```
var val = 0.25 * Math.PI
if (Math.tan(val) == 1)
    do_this
else
    do_that
```

should be replaced by:

```
var val = 0.25 * Math.PI
if (Math.tan(val) > 0.99 && Math.tan(val) < 1.01)
```

```
        do_this
else
        do_that
```

Inaccuracy is more obvious in this case, because the result differs even from browser to browser. The following is the output received from Microsoft Internet Explorer:

```
sine = 0.707106781186547
cosine = 0.707106781186548
tangent = 1
```

Notice that the sine and cosine values differ. Also notice that Internet Explorer appends a leading zero digit to all numbers between –1 and 1 (not inclusive).

atan()

As you could expect, the `Math.atan()` method returns the arc tangent of its argument. For example, the following returns one-fourth of the value of `pi`:

```
document.write(Math.atan(1))
```

atan2()

The `Math.atan2()` returns the angle (theta component) of the polar coordinate (r, theta) that corresponds to the specified Cartesian coordinate. You probably know that the normal `x`, `y` coordinates of a point are called Cartesian coordinates. Another measurement system is the polar one. You need to specify the point's radius (distance from the pole) and angle (theta component). The `Math.atan2()` method actually returns the arc tangent of `x/y` in the range $-\pi$ to π. A quick way to get the value of π via this method is to say:

```
var pi = Math.atan2(1, 1) * 4
```

First of all, `atan2(1, 1)` is equal to `atan(1)`, which is $\frac{1}{4}\pi$ in radians. So `atan2(1, 1)` is equal to π. In general, `atan2(a, a) * 4` is equal to π, because `a/a` is always 1.

The Number Object

The Number object is a built-in JavaScript object, very similar to the Math object in that it encapsulates several primitive numeric values. It is different from the Math object in that Number object is a dynamic one requiring a creation step, while Math object is a static one, not requiring any instantiation.

The primary use for the Number object is to access its constant properties, including the largest and smallest representable numbers, positive and negative infinity, and the Not-a-Number value. You can also use the Number object to create numeric objects that you can add properties to. It is unlikely that you will need to use the Number object, and it is given here for sake of completion.

To create a Number object, use the following statement:

```
numberObjectName = new Number()
```

where numberObjectName is either the name of a new object or a property of an existing one. To access Number's properties, use the following format:

```
numberObjectName.propertyName
```

where numberObjectName is either the name of an existing Number object or a property of an existing object. PropertyName is one of the properties listed below:

MAX_VALUE

This is the maximum numeric value representable in JavaScript. The MAX_VALUE property has a value of approximately 1.79E+308. Values larger than MAX_VALUE are represented as "infinity." Because MAX_VALUE is a constant, it is a read-only property of Number. The following code demonstrates the use of MAX_VALUE. The code multiplies two numeric values. If the result is less than or equal to MAX_VALUE, the func1 function is called; otherwise, the func2 function is called:

```
if (num1 * num2 <= Number.MAX_VALUE)
   func1()
else
   func2()
```

MIN_VALUE

The MIN_VALUE property is the number closest to zero, not the most negative number, that JavaScript can represent. MIN_VALUE has a value of approximately 2.22E–308. Values smaller than MIN_VALUE ("underflow values") are converted to zero. Because MIN_VALUE is a constant, it is a read-only property of Number. The following code divides two numeric values. If the result is greater than or equal to MIN_VALUE, the func1 function is called; otherwise, the func2 function is called.

```
if (num1 / num2 >= Number.MIN_VALUE)
   func1()
else
   func2()
```

NaN

Unquoted literal constant NaN is a special value representing Not-A-Number. Since NaN always compares unequal to any number, including NaN, it is usually used to indicate an error condition for a function that should return a valid number. Notice, then, that you cannot check for Not-a-Number value by comparing to Number.NaN. Use the isNaN() function instead. Because NaN is a constant, it is a read-only property of Number. In the following code segment, dayOfMonth is assigned NaN if it is greater than 31, and a message is displayed indicating the valid range:

```
if (dayOfMonth < 1 || dayOfMonth > 31) {
   dayOfMonth = Number.NaN
   alert("Day of Month must be between 1 and 31.")
}
```

NEGATIVE_INFINITY

This is a special numeric value representing negative infinity. This value is represented as "–Infinity." This value resembles an infinity in its mathematical behavior. For example, anything multiplied by NEGATIVE_INFINITY is NEGATIVE_INFINITY, and anything divided by NEGATIVE_INFINITY is zero. Because NEGATIVE_INFINITY is a constant, it is a read-only property of Number.

The following code extract checks a number for NEGATIVE_INFINITY and calls a different function if it is:

```
if (smallNumber == Number.NEGATIVE_INFINITY)
   func1()
else
```

```
        func2()
```

POSITIVE_INFINITY

This is a special numeric value representing infinity. This value is represented as " Infinity." This value resembles an infinity in its mathematical behavior. For example, anything multiplied by POSITIVE_INFINITY is POSITIVE_INFINITY, and anything divided by POSITIVE_INFINITY is zero. Because POSITIVE_INFINITY is a constant, it is a read-only property of `Number`.

The following code extract checks a number for POSITIVE_INFINITY and calls a different function if it is:

```
if (bigNumber == Number.POSITIVE_INFINITY)
   func1()
else
   func2()
```

Number Methods

The `Number` object has no specific methods. You can still use the generic methods `eval()`, `toString()`, and `valueOf()`, which are applicable to every object.

Math-Related Functions

Although the functions presented in this section are also discussed later in the book, it is important that you attain a basic understanding, so do not skip the following explanation. These functions are used in examples later in the chapter.

parseInt()

This built-in function accepts a numeric string of an integer and returns its corresponding numeric value. The following example is worth a thousand words:

```
var numStr = "99"
document.write("The initial " + typeof numStr + " is " + numStr)
document.write("<BR>")
var num = parseInt(numStr)
document.write("The converted " + typeof num + " is " + num)
```

The script's output is:

```
The initial string is 99
The converted number is 99
```

The data types are not provided to the `document.write()` method as literals, but as values. Note that the `parseInt()` function accepts a string and returns an integer. If a noninteger numeric string is given to the function, it returns the nearest integer, as a number (as opposed to a string).

parseFloat()

This function is exactly the same as its preceding one, except that it does not round off any number. It converts the numeric string to a number, without changing the numeric value at all. You should use this function with floating point numeric strings, or when you are not sure what type of number is being used.

eval()

The `eval()` function is both powerful and useful. For now, you just need to know that upon acceptance of a string representing a numeric value or mathematical expression, it returns the value which the expression evaluates to. The following script segment prints "13":

```
var str = "6 + 7"
document.write(eval(str))
```

The function returns a number, not a string. Note that this function acts differently on Netscape Navigator than it does on Microsoft Internet Explorer. An example for such different behavior is seen in the following statement, which works fine under Internet Explorer, but generates an error under Navigator:

```
var str = "+7"
document.write(eval(str))
```

However, it works fine when the sign is minus (–) rather than plus (+).

Math Examples

Creating a Curve

Although JavaScript does not correspond very well with custom-created graphics, it is possible to create simple graphs, plots, and curves. In this section we shall plot a sine curve using JavaScript. First take a look at the script's output:

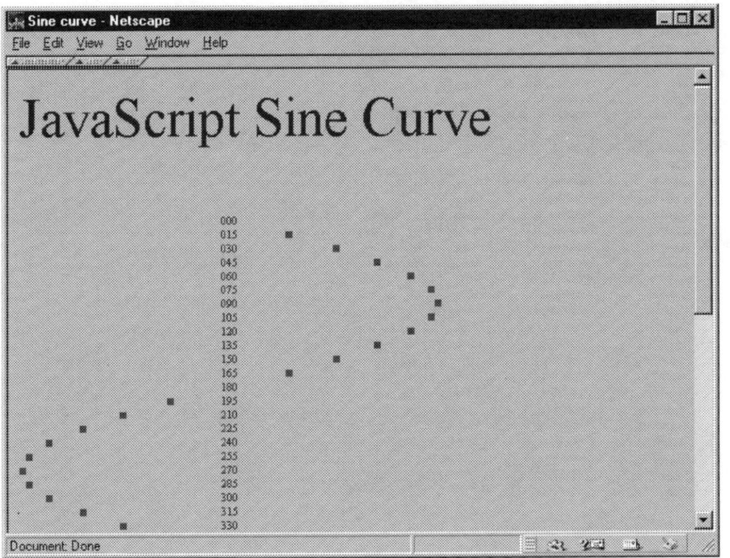

Figure 15-1. *A sine curve.*

Now take a look at the script itself:

```
<HTML>
<HEAD>
<TITLE>Sine curve</TITLE>
</HEAD>
<BODY >
<FONT COLOR="blue" SIZE=+4>JavaScript Sine Curve</FONT><BR><BR>
<SCRIPT LANGUAGE="JavaScript">
<!--

function drawBlank(num) {
     // draw num blank dots
     for (var i = 0; i < num; ++i) {
          document.write("<IMG SRC='blank.gif' HEIGHT=6 WIDTH=6>")
     }
}

function drawDot() {
     document.write("<IMG SRC='dot.gif' HEIGHT=6 WIDTH=6>")
}

function getRadian(deg) {
     // return deg in radians
     return Math.PI * deg / 180
}

function getSpot(deg) {
     // convert from degrees to radians
     var rad = getRadian(deg)
```

```
	// assign sine to variable
	var sine = Math.sin(rad)

	// return spot in graph
	return Math.round(sine * 30)
}

function get3DigitNum(num) {
	// convert num to string
	num += ""

	// assign number of digits in num to variable
	var length = num.length

	// add preceding zero digits to reach three digits
	for (var i = 0; i < 3 - length; i++) {
		num = "0" + num
	}

	// return four-digit number
	return num // do not parse number!
}

function printDeg(deg) {
	// print degree in green font
	document.write("<FONT COLOR='purple' SIZE=1>" + get3DigitNum(deg)
			+ "</FONT>")
}

function drawLine(deg) {
	// assign spot (-30 to 30)
	var spot = getSpot(deg)

	// if sine is negative
	if (spot < 0) {
		// draw blank images up to spot, not inclusive
		drawBlank(30 + spot)

		// draw dot image
		drawDot()

		// draw remaining images until axis
		drawBlank(-spot - 1) // 30 - ((30 + spot) + 1)

		// print current degree
		printDeg(deg)
	} else
		// if sine is positive
		if (spot > 0) {
			// draw 30 blank images = left of axis
			drawBlank(30)
```

```
                // print current degree
                printDeg(deg)

                // draw blank images up to spot, not inclusive
                drawBlank(spot - 1)

                // draw dot image
                drawDot()
            } else {
                // draw 30 blank images = left of axis
                drawBlank(30)

                // print current degree
                printDeg(deg)
            }
        // move to next line
        document.write("<BR>")
}

function drawCurve(lastDeg, jump) {
        // loop through plot vertically
        for (var deg = 0; deg <= lastDeg; deg += jump) {
            drawLine(deg)
        }
}

drawCurve(720, 15)

// -->
</SCRIPT>
</BODY>
</HTML>
```

***Example 15-1 (ex15-1.htm).** A simple script to plot the sine curve.*

The script is intentionally divided into many short functions for better understanding by the reader. We shall analyze each function to see how it works.

drawBlank(num)

```
function drawBlank(num) {
    // draw num blank dots
    for (var i = 0; i < num; ++i) {
        document.write("<IMG SRC='blank.gif' HEIGHT=6 WIDTH=6>")
    }
}
```

This function uses a `for` loop to print the transparent image the number of times indicated by `num`. Note that the transparent (blank) image's height and width are both equal to 6.

drawDot()

```
function drawDot() {
     document.write("<IMG SRC='dot.gif' HEIGHT=6 WIDTH=6>")
}
```

This function simply draws the dot image.

getRadian(deg)

```
function getRadian(deg) {
     // return deg in radians
     return Math.PI * deg / 180
}
```

This function accepts a number (actually the size of an angle in degrees) and returns it in radians. The conversion is based on a simple linear equation.

getSpot(deg)

```
function getSpot(deg) {
     // convert from degrees to radians
     var rad = getRadian(deg)

     // assign sine to variable
     var sine = Math.sin(rad)

     // return spot in graph
     return Math.round(sine * 30)
}
```

This function accepts the size of an angle in degrees and returns its sine value multiplied by 30. At first, it assigns the radian measurement of the angle to the local variable `rad`. It then assigns the sine of that angle to the local variable `sine`. The function then multiplies the sine by 30 and returns the rounded-off value of that number. The reason for the multiplication by 30 is that the sine of any angle is a value between –1 and 1. The curve we are plotting generally consists of 30 images, transparent or not, at each side of the center axis. If you enlarge this number, the horizontal width of the curve becomes large. As you can see, 30 images looks good. By multiplying a value between –1 and 1 by 30, we receive a value between –30 and 30. By rounding it off using the `Math.round()` method, the function returns an integer between –30 and 30.

Note that the plot acts like a 2D array, because it consists of rows of images.

get3DigitNum(num)

```
function get3DigitNum(num) {
     // convert num to string
     num += ""

     // assign number of digits in num to variable
     var length = num.length

     // add preceding zero digits to reach three digits
     for (var i = 0; i < 3 - length; i++) {
          num = "0" + num
     }

     // return three-digit number
     return num // do not parse number!
}
```

This function accepts any single-digit, double-digit, or triple-digit number, and returns a triple-digit number, appending preceding 0 digits when needed. At first, it converts the number to a string, required for the use of the `length` property. A string type is also required because numbers with leading 0 digits are considered octal. The length, or the number of digits in the original number, is assigned to the local variable `length`. The following statement is a loop whose command block is executed once for each digit missing to complete a triple-digit number. For example, if the number consists of two digits, the loop's command block is executed once (3 – 2 = 1, 1 – 0 = 1).

printDeg(deg)

```
function printDeg(deg) {
     // print degree in green font
     document.write("<FONT COLOR='purple' SIZE=1>" + get3DigitNum(deg)
                    + "</FONT>")
}
```

This function accepts a number, converts it to a triple-digit number, and prints it in a purple font.

drawLine(deg)

```
function drawLine(deg) {
     // assign spot (-30 to 30)
     var spot = getSpot(deg)

     // if sine is negative
     if (spot < 0) {
          // draw blank images up to spot, not inclusive
          drawBlank(30 + spot)
```

```
            // draw dot image
            drawDot()

            // draw remaining images until axis
            drawBlank(-spot - 1) // 30 - ((30 + spot) + 1)

            // print current degree
            printDeg(deg)
        } else
            // if sine is positive
            if (spot > 0) {
                // draw 30 blank images = left of axis
                drawBlank(30)

                // print current degree
                printDeg(deg)

                // draw blank images up to spot, not inclusive
                drawBlank(spot - 1)

                // draw dot image
                drawDot()
            } else {
                // draw 30 blank images = left of axis
                drawBlank(30)

                // print current degree
                printDeg(deg)
            }
        // move to next line
        document.write("<BR>")
}
```

The rounded-off sine value multiplied by 30 is assigned to the variable `spot`. The function is basically divided into three sections, of which only one is executed. The first deals with a situation in which the sine value is negative, the second deals with positive sine values, and the third deals with the remaining situations; that is, when the sine is zero.

When the sine (sine multiplied by 30) is negative, `30 - spot` transparent images are printed. For example, if the value of `spot` is –20, 10 transparent images are printed. The dot image is printed after these transparent images. The function then prints `–spot - 1` transparent images, up to the center axis. So far `30 + spot` transparent images were printed, as well as one more image representing the dot on the curve. In total, there are `31 + spot` images. Remember that each side of the axis consists of 30 images, so `30 - (31 + spot)` images still need to be printed; that is -`spot - 1`. The current degree is then printed via a call to the function `printDeg()`.

When the sine of the current angle is positive, 30 transparent images are printed to fill up the left side of the center axis. The current degree is then printed to continue the vertical span of the axis. Then `spot - 1` images are printed, up to the place where the dot on the curve needs to be placed. The dot image is then printed.

When the sine of the current angle is zero, a row of 30 transparent images is printed, followed by the current angle in degrees.

The last statement of the function appends a line break to the document, opening a new row of images.

drawCurve(lastDeg, jump)

```
function drawCurve(lastDeg, jump) {
     // loop through plot vertically
     for (var deg = 0; deg <= lastDeg; deg += jump) {
          drawLine(deg)
     }
}
```

This function accepts two arguments. The first parameter, `lastDeg`, accepts the last value included in the curve; that is, the last angle whose sine appears. The second argument specifies the difference between each two angles.

Global Statements

The script includes only one global statement, a function call. It calls the `drawCurve()` function with the desired arguments.

General Plotting Utility

Note This script is not compatible with Microsoft Internet Explorer at this stage, although it probably will be in future releases of the browser. It is compatible with Netscape Navigator 3.0 and above.

As you can see it is not difficult to plot a specific curve in JavaScript using two different images. The following example enables you to plot the curve of almost any function:

```
<HTML>
<HEAD>
<TITLE>Plot</TITLE>
</HEAD>
<BODY >
<SCRIPT LANGUAGE="JavaScript">
<!--

function root(a, b) {
     // return b to the root of a
     return Math.pow(b, 1 / a)
}

function logab(a, b) {
     // return log base-a of b
     return Math.log(b) / Math.log(a)
}

function factorial(a) {
     // set recursion termination condition
     if (a == 0)
          return 1
     return a * factorial(a - 1)
}

function startWizard() {
     // create array to hold messages
     var ar = new Array()

     ar[0] = "\r\rWelcome to the ultimate JavaScript function plotter!\r\r"
     ar[0] += "Press OK to continue, or CANCEL to exit the wizard...\r\r"

     ar[1] = "\r\rYou can plot almost any function you wish with this
                                   script.\r"
     ar[1] += "The plotter supports common arithmetic and trigonometric
                                   functions.\r"
     ar[1] += "It also supports widely used mathematical constants.\r"
     ar[1] += "For a list of the supported functions press OK...\r\r"

     ar[2] = "\r\r"
     ar[2] += "abs(val) = absolute value of val\r"
     ar[2] += "acos(val) = arc cosine of val\r"
     ar[2] += "asine(val) = arc sine of val\r"
     ar[2] += "atan(val) = arc tangent of val\r"
     ar[2] += "atan2(val) = angle (theta component) of the polar "
     ar[2] += "coordinate (r,theta) that corresponds to the specified "
     ar[2] += "cartesian coordinate (x,y).\r"
     ar[2] += "ceil(val) = next integer greater than or equal to val\r"
     ar[2] += "cos(val) = cosine of val\r"
     ar[2] += "exp(val) = Euler's constant to the power of val\r"
     ar[2] += "factorial(val) = val factorial (val!)\r"
     ar[2] += "floor(val) = next integer less than or equal to val\r"
```

```
    ar[2] += "log(val1, val2) = logarithm base-val1 of val2\r"
    ar[2] += "loge(val) = natural logarithm of val\r"
    ar[2] += "max(val1, val2) = greater of val1 and val2\r"
    ar[2] += "min(val1, val2) = lesser of val1 and val2\r"
    ar[2] += "pow(val1, val2) = val1 to the power of val2\r"
    ar[2] += "root(val1, val2) = val1-root of val2\r"
    ar[2] += "round(val) = val rounded off to the nearest integer\r"
    ar[2] += "sin(val) = sine of val\r"
    ar[2] += "sqrt(val) = square root of val\r"
    ar[2] += "tan(val) = tangent of val\r"
    ar[2] += "\r* all trigonometric functions deal with radians only
                        *\r\r"
    ar[2] += "Click OK to view the supported constants...\r\r"

    ar[3] = "\r\r"
    ar[3] += "e = Euler's constant\r"
    ar[3] += "ln2 = Natural log of 2\r"
    ar[3] += "ln10 = Natural log of 10\r"
    ar[3] += "log2e = log base-2 of Euler's constant\r"
    ar[3] += "log10e = log base-10 of Euler's constant\r"
    ar[3] += "pi = pi (3.14...)\r"
    ar[3] += "sqrt1_2 = square root of 0.5\r"
    ar[3] += "sqrt2 = square root of 2\r"
    ar[3] += "\r\rEnjoy the plotter...\r\r"

    for (var i = 0; i < ar.length; ++i) {
        if (!confirm(ar[i]))
            break
    }
}

function drawBlank(num) {
    // draw num blank dots
    for (var i = 0; i < num; ++i) {
        document.write("<IMG SRC='blank.gif' HEIGHT=4 WIDTH=4>")
    }
}

function drawDot(x, y) {
    // print dot image
    document.write("<A HREF=\"javascript:alert(\'X = " + x + ",
                    Y = " + y +
        "\')\"><IMG SRC='dot.gif' HEIGHT=4 WIDTH=4 BORDER=0></A>")
}

function replaceSpecialSequence(str) {
    // replace all specified sequences by other sequences
    str = str.split("cos").join("Math.cos")
    str = str.split("sin").join("Math.sin")
    str = str.split("tan").join("Math.tan")
    str = str.split("acos").join("Math.acos")
    str = str.split("asin").join("Math.asin")
```

```
        str = str.split("atan").join("Math.atan")
        str = str.split("pi").join("Math.PI")
        str = str.split("ln2").join("Math.LN2")
        str = str.split("ln10").join("Math.LN10")
        str = str.split("log2e").join("Math.LOG2E")
        str = str.split("log10e").join("Math.LOG10E")
        str = str.split("sqrt1_2").join("Math.SQRT1_2")
        str = str.split("sqrt2").join("Math.SQRT2")
        str = str.split("abs").join("Math.abs")
        str = str.split("ceil").join("Math.ceil")
        str = str.split("exp").join("Math.exp")
        str = str.split("floor").join("Math.floor")
        str = str.split("loge").join("Math.log")
        str = str.split("max").join("Math.max")
        str = str.split("min").join("Math.min")
        str = str.split("pow").join("Math.pow")
        str = str.split("round").join("Math.round")
        str = str.split("log").join("logab")
        str = str.split("sqrt").join("Math.sqrt")
        str = str.split("e").join("Math.E")

        // return string
        return str
    }

    function splitFunc(func) {
        // exclude "y =" from func
        var expr = func.substring(func.indexOf("=") + 1, func.length)

        // replace regular trigonometric functions with JavaScript convention
        expr = replaceSpecialSequence(expr)

        // split argument to *global* array, excluding "x" chars
        funcArray = expr.split("x")
    }

    function getInput() {
        // ask user for function via prompt box
        var input = prompt('Enter function (example: "y = x * x +
                           sin(x) - 5"):', '')

        // if user enters value in field
        if (input) {
            // split function to global array
            splitFunc(input)

            // print function to document
            document.write("<TT><H1><B>" + input + "</B></H1></TT><BR>")

            // return true to indicate that user entered a value
            return true
        }
```

```
        // generate alert box to display error message
        alert("Error in input...")

        // return false to indicate cancellation
        return false
    }

    function yVal(xVal) {
        // build expression with xVal instead of x in original equation
        var expr = funcArray.join(xVal)

        // return evaluated expression
        return eval(expr)
    }

    function makeArray(min, max, dif) {
        // create properties of array-like object
        for (var i = min; i <= max; i += dif) {
            this[i] = yVal(i)
        }
    }

    function printUnit(num) {
        // print number in specified font and size, inside a table cell
        document.write("<FONT SIZE=1 COLOR='purple'>" + num + "</FONT>")
    }

    function drawCurve() {
        for (var x = minX; x <= maxX; x += dif) {
            // print openning table attributes and cell to hold current unit
            document.write("<TABLE BORDER=0><TR><TD WIDTH=90>")

            // print current number on axis
            printUnit(x)

            // close table cell and open new one
            document.write("</TD><TD>")

            // assign Y value to variable
            var y = ar[x]

            // get y value as integer from 1 to 100
            var ySpot = (y - minY) / (maxY - minY) * 100

            // draw transparent images
            drawBlank(ySpot - 1)

            // draw dot on curve
            drawDot(x, y)

            // close cell, row, and table (new line is automatic)
```

```
                document.write("</TD></TR></TABLE>")
            }
        }

        function main() {
            // start wizard
            startWizard()

            // get input from user; if user cancels function is terminated
            if (!getInput())
                return

            // accept minimum X value from user and assign to global variable
            minX = prompt("Enter minimum value on X axis:", "")

            // if user pressed "cancel" terminate function
            if (!minX)
                return

            // accept maximum X value from user and assign to global variable
            maxX = prompt("Enter maximum value on X axis:", "")

            // if user pressed "cancel" terminate function
            if (!maxX)
                return

            // assign difference between numbers on X axis global variable
            dif = prompt("Enter difference between each value on X axis:", "")

            // if user pressed "cancel" terminate function
            if (!dif)
                return

            // convert all input to numbers, replacing special sequences
            maxX = eval(replaceSpecialSequence(maxX))
            minX = eval(replaceSpecialSequence(minX))
            dif = eval(replaceSpecialSequence(dif))

            // create global array and assign Y values via function call
            ar = new makeArray(minX, maxX, dif)

            // assign maxY and minY (global variables) property of ar
            maxY = ar[minX]
            minY = ar[minX]

            // determine maximum and minimum Y values
            for (var i in ar) {
                if (ar[i] < minY)
                    minY = ar[i]
                else
                    if (ar[i] > maxY)
                        maxY = ar[i]
```

```
        }

        // draw the final curve
        drawCurve()
}

main()

// -->
</SCRIPT>
</BODY>
</HTML>
```

Example 15-2 (ex15-2.htm). *A general function plotter.*

When you load the page, the "wizard" pops up. It is not exactly the Microsoft-like wizard, but it's probably the most you can do in JavaScript. The wizard displays the basic features and usage instructions via a few confirm boxes. Here are two of them:

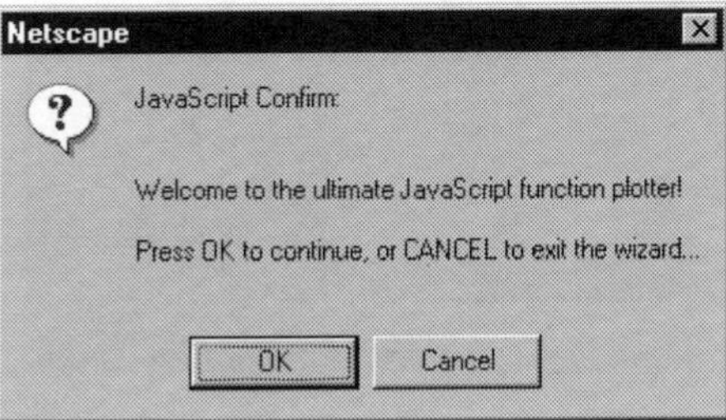

Figure 15-2. *The first confirm box presented by the wizard displays a welcome message.*

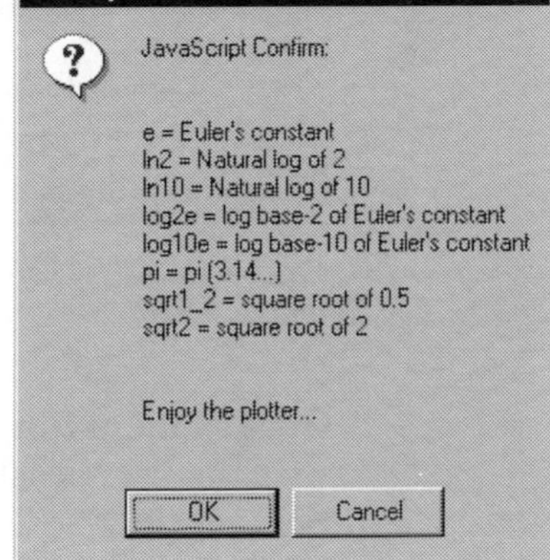

Figure 15-3. *The last confirm box presented by the wizard summarizes the supported constants and their specification.*

If the user presses Cancel on any of the confirm boxes, the wizard is terminated, and the actual plotting application begins. The first output of the plotter is a confirm box requesting the function, which may be constructed out of JavaScript's supported mathematical functions, constants, and operators. Here is the prompt box:

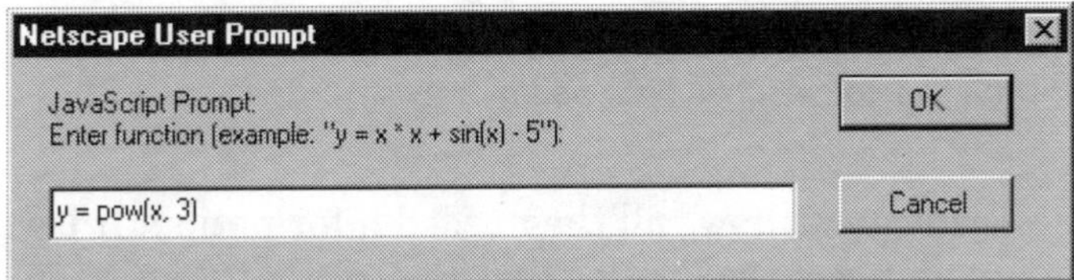

Figure 15-4. *The user is requested to enter any function consisting of any supported elements.*

If the user selects Cancel, an alert box displays an error message. Otherwise, the execution continues, and JavaScript asks the user to enter the minimum value on the X axis. Here is the prompt box:

__Figure 15-5.__ The user is requested to enter the minimum value on the X axis.

Cancellation of this box results in the termination of the script. If the user selected OK, the execution continues, and another prompt box is presented:

__Figure 15-6.__ The user is requested to enter the maximum value on the X axis.

Once again, if the user pressed Cancel, the script is terminated. Otherwise the user is asked to enter the difference between two consecutive ticks on the X axis (e.g., if the user wants to see –4, –2, 0, 2, 4, 6, then the difference is 2).

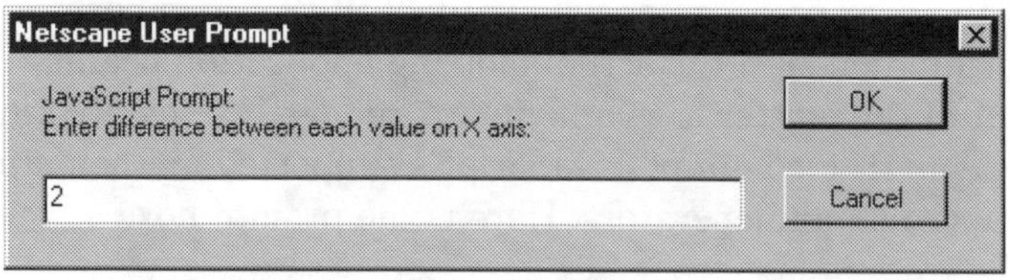

Netscape User Prompt
JavaScript Prompt:
Enter difference between each value on X axis:
2
OK
Cancel

__Figure 15-7.__ The user is requested to enter the difference between two consecutive ticks on the X-axis.

The script now knows all the needed information. It is ready to plot the function's curve. Notice that Figure 15-4, Figure 15-5, Figure 15-6, and Figure 15-7 all contained sample values entered by the user. Based on these entered values, the final output of the script is:

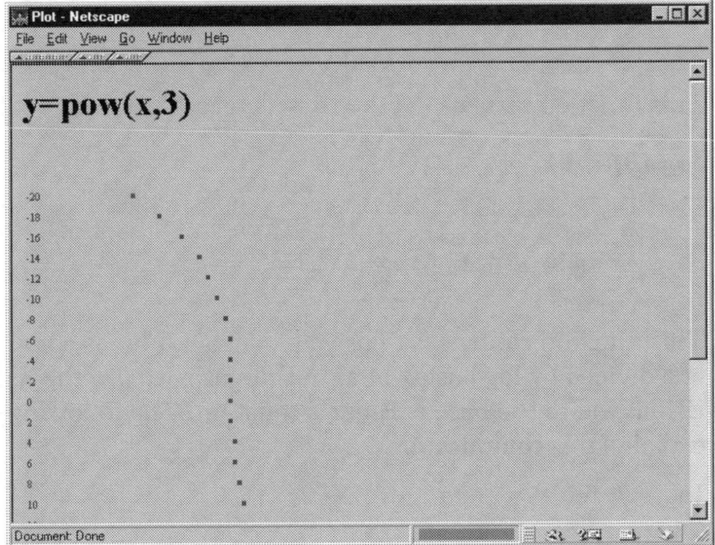

Figure 15-8. *The script plots the function's curve.*

First of all, notice that the X axis is the vertical one. With some modification of the script you can swap the X axis with the Y axis (the unseen horizontal axis). The script automatically fits the script to a constant width, so you should not have to scroll horizontally under normal circumstances (a reasonable window width). However, this automatic setting requires that you plot functions whose Y values are proportional. For example, if you enter data to plot a curve consisting of one Y value equal to 10,000, and the other values under 100, the single Y value (10,000) will be placed on the right, whereas all the other values will seem to be on the same spot. There is another feature to solve this problem. You can click on a point to view its coordinates via an alert box. The following alert box was generated when we clicked on the point whose X value is –16 (see Figure 15-8).

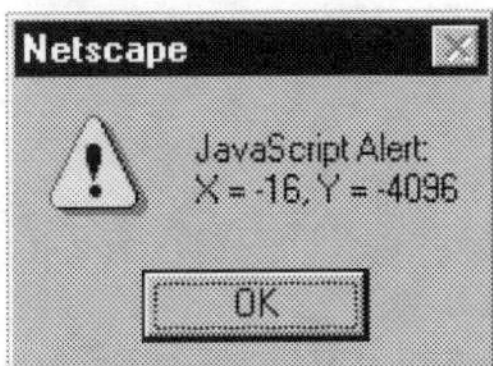

Figure 15-9. *You can view the exact coordinates of a point in the plot by clicking on its image.*

Now that we know exactly what the script does, let's see how it does that by analyzing each function.

root(a, b)

```
function root(a, b) {
     // return b to the root of a
     return Math.pow(b, 1 / a)
}
```

This function returns $\sqrt[a]{b}$, which is equal to $b^{1/a}$.

logab(a, b)

```
function logab(a, b) {
     // return log base-a of b
     return Math.log(b) / Math.log(a)
}
```

This function returns log base-a of b. This value is equal to log base-x of b divided by log base-x of a. In this case, we use the natural logarithm, where the base is Euler's constant. The following statement explains this computation:

$\log_e b / \log_e a = \log_a b$

factorial(a)

```
function factorial(a) {
     // set recursion termination condition
     if (a == 0)
          return 1
     return a * factorial(a - 1)
}
```

This function returns a factorial (a!). Its algorithm is recursive. For more information on this specific function see Chapter 9.

startWizard()

```
function startWizard() {
     // create array to hold messages
     var ar = new Array()

     ar[0] = "\r\rWelcome to the ultimate JavaScript function plotter!\r\r"
     ar[0] += "Press OK to continue, or CANCEL to exit the wizard...\r\r"

     ar[1] = "\r\rYou can plot almost any function you wish with
                         this script.\r"
     ar[1] += "The plotter supports common arithmetic and trigonometric
                         functions.\r"
     ar[1] += "It also supports widely used mathematical constants.\r"
     ar[1] += "For a list of the supported functions press OK...\r\r"

     ar[2] = "\r\r"
     ar[2] += "abs(val) = absolute value of val\r"
```

```
        ar[2] += "acos(val) = arc cosine of val\r"
        ar[2] += "asine(val) = arc sine of val\r"
        ar[2] += "atan(val) = arc tangent of val\r"
        ar[2] += "atan2(val) = angle (theta component) of the polar "
        ar[2] += "coordinate (r,theta) that corresponds to the specified "
        ar[2] += "cartesian coordinate (x,y).\r"
        ar[2] += "ceil(val) = next integer greater than or equal to val\r"
        ar[2] += "cos(val) = cosine of val\r"
        ar[2] += "exp(val) = Euler's constant to the power of val\r"
        ar[2] += "factorial(val) = val factorial (val!)\r"
        ar[2] += "floor(val) = next integer less than or equal to val\r"
        ar[2] += "log(val1, val2) = logarithm base-val1 of val2\r"
        ar[2] += "loge(val) = natural logarithm of val\r"
        ar[2] += "max(val1, val2) = greater of val1 and val2\r"
        ar[2] += "min(val1, val2) = lesser of val1 and val2\r"
        ar[2] += "pow(val1, val2) = val1 to the power of val2\r"
        ar[2] += "root(val1, val2) = val1-root of val2\r"
        ar[2] += "round(val) = val rounded off to the nearest integer\r"
        ar[2] += "sin(val) = sine of val\r"
        ar[2] += "sqrt(val) = square root of val\r"
        ar[2] += "tan(val) = tangent of val\r"
        ar[2] += "\r* all trigonometric functions deal with radians
                          only *\r\r"
        ar[2] += "Click OK to view the supported constants...\r\r"

        ar[3] = "\r\r"
        ar[3] += "e = Euler's constant\r"
        ar[3] += "ln2 = Natural log of 2\r"
        ar[3] += "ln10 = Natural log of 10\r"
        ar[3] += "log2e = log base-2 of Euler's constant\r"
        ar[3] += "log10e = log base-10 of Euler's constant\r"
        ar[3] += "pi = pi (3.14...)\r"
        ar[3] += "sqrt1_2 = square root of 0.5\r"
        ar[3] += "sqrt2 = square root of 2\r"
        ar[3] += "\r\rEnjoy the plotter...\r\r"

        for (var i = 0; i < ar.length; ++i) {
             if (!confirm(ar[i]))
                  break
        }
}
```

This function is responsible for the wizard. At first, an array is created as an instance of the `Array()` object. Four different messages are assigned to the array as elements. The first is stored in `ar[0]`, the second in `ar[1]`, and so on. Note that the assigned strings are very long, so the assignment operator concatenates them by assigning them, one after the other, to the element of the array. The function uses a `for` loop to print the messages to the confirm boxes. If the user presses

Cancel, the confirm box evaluates to `false`, and the `break` statement is executed, causing the loop to terminate immediately.

drawBlank(num)

```
function drawBlank(num) {
     // draw num blank dots
     for (var i = 0; i < num; ++i) {
          document.write("<IMG SRC='blank.gif' HEIGHT=4 WIDTH=4>")
     }
}
```

This function prints the transparent image `num` times, `num` being handed to the function as its sole argument. The image is repeatedly printed via a simple `for` loop.

drawDot(x, y)

```
function drawDot(x, y) {
     // print dot image
     document.write("<A HREF=\"javascript:alert(\'X = " + x + ", Y = " +
          y + "\')\"><IMG SRC='dot.gif' HEIGHT=4 WIDTH=4 BORDER=0></A>")
}
```

This function basically prints the dot image, but it prints it as a hypertext link. The URL specified as the link is a JavaScript statement. When the user clicks the image, an alert box is displayed, presenting the coordinates of that dot. The coordinates are given to this function as arguments. For example, if the arguments are –5 and 10, then the following string is printed to the document:

```
<A HREF="javascript:alert('X = -5, Y = 10')"><IMG SRC='dot.gif'
HEIGHT=4 WIDTH=4 BORDER=0></A>
```

Decoding this string is a good exercise for escaping quotes.

You may recall that a hypertext link's URL can be a JavaScript statement, provided that the statement is preceded by "`javascript:`".

replaceSpecialSequence(str)

```
function replaceSpecialSequence(str) {
     // replace all specified sequences by other sequences
     str = str.split("cos").join("Math.cos")
     str = str.split("sin").join("Math.sin")
     str = str.split("tan").join("Math.tan")
     str = str.split("acos").join("Math.acos")
     str = str.split("asin").join("Math.asin")
     str = str.split("atan").join("Math.atan")
     str = str.split("pi").join("Math.PI")
     str = str.split("ln2").join("Math.LN2")
```

```
        str = str.split("ln10").join("Math.LN10")
        str = str.split("log2e").join("Math.LOG2E")
        str = str.split("log10e").join("Math.LOG10E")
        str = str.split("sqrt1_2").join("Math.SQRT1_2")
        str = str.split("sqrt2").join("Math.SQRT2")
        str = str.split("abs").join("Math.abs")
        str = str.split("ceil").join("Math.ceil")
        str = str.split("exp").join("Math.exp")
        str = str.split("floor").join("Math.floor")
        str = str.split("loge").join("Math.log")
        str = str.split("max").join("Math.max")
        str = str.split("min").join("Math.min")
        str = str.split("pow").join("Math.pow")
        str = str.split("round").join("Math.round")
        str = str.split("log").join("logab")
        str = str.split("sqrt").join("Math.sqrt")
        str = str.split("e").join("Math.E")

        // return string
        return str
}
```

This function matches certain strings in the argument and replaces them by other strings. Here is an example:

```
str = str.split("max").join("Math.max")
```

The string is split into an array where the substring `max` is the delimiter, and the elements are joined back to a string with a delimiter, `Math.max`. The final result is that, wherever the string `max` appears in the main string (`str`), it is replaced by the string `Math.max`. This is important because the string must be constructed as a valid JavaScript expression (the `eval()` function evaluates a string consisting of a valid JavaScript expression). The same process is done with all supported constants and mathematical functions. The function `factorial()` remains untouched, because its reference in the script is also `factorial()`.

An important concept to notice is that the order in which substrings are replaced is vital. For example, you cannot replace the `sqrt` substring with `Math.sqrt` before you replace `sqrt2` with `Math.SQRT2`, because the result would be that the substring `sqrt2` is replaced by `Math.sqrt2`, which is not `Math.SQRT2`. The function must first replace subscripts that contain other subscripts that need to be replaced.

After all desired substrings are replaced, and provided the user entered a function in a valid format, the function returns the formatted string, which is now a valid JavaScript expression.

splitFunc(func)

```
function splitFunc(func) {
     // exclude "y =" from func
     var expr = func.substring(func.indexOf("=") + 1, func.length)

     // replace regular trigonometric functions with JavaScript convention
     expr = replaceSpecialSequence(expr)

     // split argument to *global* array, excluding "x" chars
     funcArray = expr.split("x")
}
```

This function accepts one parameter—the function. As you know, the general format of the function is `y=f(x)`. At first, the function assigns everything after the equal sign to the local variable `expr`. It then sends the value of `expr` to the function `replaceSpecialSequence()` and accepts a string in return in which the special substrings were replaced (see explanation about that function). A global array, `funcArray`, is created by assigning it a value without using the keyword `var`. The string stored in the variable `expr` is split into the `funcArray` array, using the character `x` as a delimiter. Let's say the function's argument is `y = x * sin(x)`. The variable `expr` is assigned `x * sin(x)`. This value is sent to the function `replaceSpecialSequence()`, and the string `x * Math.sin(x)` is assigned to `expr`. This string is split by `x` to the global array, `funcArray`. Its elements are now:

```
funcArray[0] == " "
funcArray[1] == " * Math.sin("
funcArray[2] == ")"
```

getInput()

```
function getInput() {
     // ask user for function via prompt box
     var input = prompt('Enter function (example: "y = x * x + sin(x) –
                              5"):', '')
     // if user enters value in field
     if (input) {
          // split function to global array
          splitFunc(input)

          // print function to document
          document.write("<TT><H1><B>" + input + "</B></H1></TT><BR>")

          // return true to indicate that user entered a value
          return true
     }

     // generate alert box to display error message
```

```
        alert("Error in input...")

        // return false to indicate cancellation
        return false
}
```

This function is responsible for prompting the user for the function he or she wants to plot. At first, the function, as entered by the user in a prompt box, is assigned to the local variable input. If the user entered a value and selected OK, the following command block is executed. This command block consists of a call to the function splitFunc(). It also includes a statement that prints the function to the document as a bold level-1 header. After the Boolean value true is returned to indicate that the user entered a value and pressed OK, the function is terminated. If the user selected Cancel, the command block is not executed, so the execution continues immediately after the block. An error message is displayed in an alert box, and the value false is returned.

yVal(xVal)

```
function yVal(xVal) {
        // build expression with xVal instead of x in original equation
        var expr = funcArray.join(xVal)

        // return evaluated expression
        return eval(expr)
}
```

This function accepts a value representing the x coordinate of a dot on the curve and returns its corresponding y coordinate. The first statement declares a local variable, expr. It joins the elements of the global array funcArray back to a string, with the value of xVal between each two. Refer back to the function splitFunc() and read the example given (y = x * sin(x)). The values of the elements of the array are the following:

```
funcArray[0] == " "
funcArray[1] == " * Math.sin("
funcArray[2] == ")"
```

The function yVal() joins these elements using the value of xVal as a glue between each two. Let's say the value of xVal is 5. The constructed string assigned to expr in this case is:

```
" 5 * Math.sin(5)"
```

The function returns the evaluated value of this string. For the preceding string, the value returned is:

```
" 5 * Math.sin(5)" == -4.794621373315692
```

makeArray(min, max, dif)

```
function makeArray(min, max, dif) {
    // create properties of array-like object
    for (var i = min; i <= max; i += dif) {
        this[i] = yVal(i)
    }
}
```

makeArray() is a constructor function. It creates an object consisting of properties only. The names of the properties are the x values of the points that are to be drawn on the curve. Their value is the corresponding y coordinates of the points. The function accepts three arguments, which are all entered by the user via prompt boxes outside this function. The function creates the properties of the calling instance via a loop. The loop counter starts at min, and is incremented by dif after iteration. The loop continues as long as its counter is less than or equal to max. The corresponding y coordinate of each x coordinate is retrieved by the function yVal().

printUnit(num)

```
function printUnit(num) {
    // print number in specified font and size, inside a table cell
    document.write("<FONT SIZE=1 COLOR='purple'>" + num + "</FONT>")
}
```

This function accepts a numeric value, and prints it in the specified font color and size.

drawCurve()

```
function drawCurve() {
    for (var x = minX; x <= maxX; x += dif) {
        // print opening table attributes and cell to hold current unit
        document.write("<TABLE BORDER=0><TR><TD WIDTH=90>")

        // print current number on axis
        printUnit(x)

        // close table cell and open new one
        document.write("</TD><TD>")

        // assign Y value to variable
        var y = ar[x]

        // get y value as integer from 1 to 100
        var ySpot = (y - minY) / (maxY - minY) * 100
```

```
            // draw transparent images
            drawBlank(ySpot - 1)

            // draw dot on curve
            drawDot(x, y)

            // close cell, row, and table (new line is automatic)
            document.write("</TD></TR></TABLE>")
      }
}
```

This function does not accept any argument. It is responsible for printing the curve. To understand this function you must first understand how each row of the bitmap is printed. The entire row is placed inside an HTML table. The x value, or unit, is printed in the first cell of the table. This cell's width is fixed in order to preserve uniformity across rows. The second, and last, cell of the table is located on the same row, and contains all the images, both the transparent ones as well as the dot one. The dot image is obviously the last image on the second cell of every row. Note that the left cell (the first in each table) is wide enough to hold almost any number.

The entire function is built of a single loop, which iterates through the points that are to be placed on the curve. See the explanation on the function makeArray() for information on the loop's algorithm. At first, the function prints the opening <TABLE>, <TR>, and <TD> tags. The border of the table is set to zero, so it is not seen. The width of the cell is set to 90 pixels. The value in the first cell is printed by the printUnit() function. The current cell of the table is then closed, and a new one is opened. The y value of the current point, which is stored as a property in the global object ar, is assigned to the local variable y for the sake of convenience. The minimum and maximum y coordinates of the whole curve are already stored in the global variables minY and maxY, respectively. A simple linear equation is used to convert the current y coordinate to a value between 1 and 100, where the minimum y coordinate in the entire curve is 1, and the maximum is 100. This value is assigned to the local variable yspot. The following statement calls the function drawBlank() to print ySpot - 1 transparent images, which is equal to the number of images up to ySpot, the spot where the dot image is placed. The function drawDot() is called with the current coordinates to print the current dot, or bullet, on the imaginary curve. The current cell and row of the table are closed, and so is the table. When closing the table, a line break is automatically appended.

main()

The name of this function is an inspiration from the C++ language, where the function `main()` is executed automatically. In JavaScript you have to call `main()` to draw the graph.

At first, the function calls the `startWizard()` function to execute the wizard. The function `getInput()` is then executed. If it evaluates to `false`, meaning the user pressed Cancel when asked to enter a function, the function is terminated. Otherwise, execution continues. The function asks the user to enter additional information, including the minimum and maximum `x` coordinates and the difference between two consecutive ticks on the X axis. If the user selects Cancel on any of these requests, the function is terminated immediately, without executing any additional statements. After the user enters the values (and presses OK), the data is sent to the function `replaceSpecialSequence` from which a string is returned and converted to a number with the `eval()` function.

The following statement creates a global array-like object and assigns values by its constructor function, `makeArray()`.

The function now needs to find the minimum and the maximum `y` coordinates of the curve. First, it assigns each variable, `maxY` and `minY`, an existing `y` coordinate. A `for…in` loop then iterates through the properties of the `ar` object, and if it finds a value less than the current `minY` or greater than the current `maxY`, it updates that value.

The last statement of the function draws the curve itself.

Global Statements

The only global statement is a call to the `main()` function.

Summary

In this chapter you learned about math usage in JavaScript. We have mostly discussed the `Math` object and its properties and methods. Among the methods discussed are the arithmetic and trigonometric ones. Arithmetic methods are found in almost every JavaScript script, whereas trigonometric methods are rather rare. You also grasped the basics of some built-in functions that are closely related to JavaScript. These functions are discussed later in depth, so do not worry if you do not understand them very well. To spice things up, we have also shown some interesting examples related to math, one involving curve plotting. If you understood all scripts, or at least the curve plotting one, you are surely on the right track. However, don't worry if they seem very difficult at this stage, because knowledge comes by practice. In the following chapters we shall continue to learn about JavaScript's unique object model, including built-in objects and browser objects.

Chapter 16

Handling Strings

String Indexing

Strings are constructed from a variable number of characters. They are very similar to arrays which are constructed of elements as well. The elements of an array are placed in a certain order, where each element has its index, or subscript. The index determines the position of the element in the array. Strings are characters chained in a certain order as well. Each character has its position, or index. The indexing of strings, like that of arrays, is zero-based. The index of the first character of a string is 0, the index of the second one is 1, that of the third one is 2, and so on.

Characters

JavaScript, unlike most languages, does not include an explicit character (`char`) data type. A character is simply a string constructed of only one character. Characters of a string must be visual. That is, each symbol that appears in a string is a character. However, not all characters that appear in the ASCII table can be characters of a string, because some are not visual. An escape sequence is a sequence of characters that represents a single special character, which is usually difficult to enter via the keyboard. For example, take a look at the following string:

```
"car\'s wheel"
```

It appears as if the string contains 12 characters (c, a, r, \, ', s, , w, h, e, e, l). However, when you print the string you can see only 11 characters (c, a, r, ', s, , w, h, e, e, l). Therefore, the string consists of 11 characters. The fourth character is an apostrophe, not a backslash, because the sequence "\'" is shorthand for an apostrophe.

Creating Strings

String is a very special built-in object, because of the way you can create it. All strings belong to the built-in object String, so you can create strings as instances of the String object:

```
var str = new String("Hello!")
```

The general syntax is:

```
stringObjectName = new String(string)
```

stringObjectName is the name of the string object you are creating. *string* is any string, including strings that were not created via the String constructor. Strings created via this constructor function are considered objects. If you test their data type using the typeof operator you will find that they are objects, not strings. However, all the string properties and methods work on such objects.

Another way to create a string is by simply quoting a sequence of characters. If you want to use it as an object, you can follow the identifier by the desired property or method.

Netscape first implemented strings as objects (created via the constructor) in Netscape Navigator 3.0. Microsoft included this feature in version 3.0 of its browser as well. Although it is rarely used, creating strings with the constructor is sometimes essential. Netscape implemented this feature due to a bug that disabled passing scripts among the browser's window and frames. In Navigator 2.0, you had to concatenate an empty string as a workaround for the bug. Generally speaking, you should create a string via the String constructor whenever your script involves windows or frames. These topics are covered later in the book.

String Length

The String object combines many methods and one property, length. This property reflects the length of its calling object. Here are a few examples:

```
var str1 = "abc"
var str2 = "a b c"
var str3 = "\"abc\""
document.write(str1.length + "<BR>")
document.write(str2.length + "<BR>")
document.write(str3.length)
```

The output of this script is:

```
3
5
5
```

The index of a string's last character is equal to its length (number of characters) minus one. The string's length is the index of the non-existing character following the string's last character.

HTML Formatting Methods

You have seen a great amount of HTML formatting throughout the book. You can print HTML tags by combining strings to receive the desired tag and attribute values. Here is an example:

```
var openBold = "<B>"
var closeBold = "</B>"
var message = "Something"
document.write("<B>Something</B>")
```

The result of this script is that the string "Something" is printed in bold. JavaScript provides methods to simplify this process. For example, you can create the exact same output using the following statement:

```
document.write("Something".bold())
```

The following table lists all these methods along with the HTML they generate:

Table 16-1. *HTML formatting methods.*

Method Name	Example	Returned Value
anchor	"text".anchor("anchorName")	<A NAME="anchorName"> text</A>
big	"text".big()	<BIG>text</BIG>
blink	"text".blink()	<BLINK>text</BLINK>
bold	"text".bold()	<BOLD>text</BOLD>
fixed	"text".fixed()	<TT>text</TT>
fontcolor	"text".fontcolor("red")	<FONT COLOR="red"> text</FONT>
fontsize	"text".fontsize(–1)	<FONT SIZE=–1>text</FONT>
italics	"text".italics()	<I>text</I>
link	"text".link("URL")	<A HREF="URL">text</A>
small	"text".small()	<SMALL>text</SMALL>
strike	"text".strike()	<STRIKE>text</STRIKE>

Method Name	Example	Returned Value
sub	"text".sub()	_{text}
sup	"text".sup()	^{text}
toLowerCase	"TexT".toLowerCase()	text
toUpperCase	"TexT".toUpperCase()	TEXT

The following screen shows the rendering of the word `text` using each of the above methods:

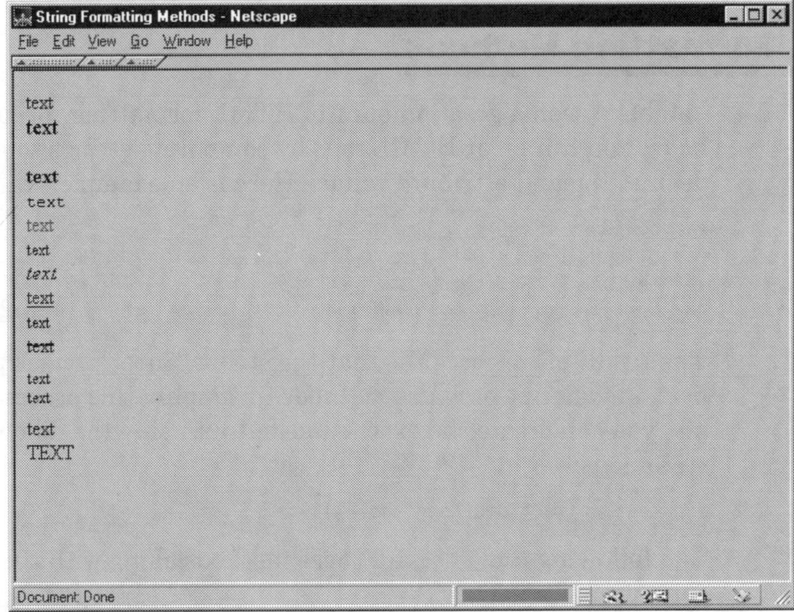

Figure 16-1. *The `String` methods return formatted HTML.*

You can "chain" methods together in order to apply more than one formatting conversion. For example, if you want an italic bold uppercase string, you can use the following expression: `toUpperCase().bold().italics()`. The evaluation here is done from left to right. The following list outlines the stages of the evaluation, where the calling string is the literal `"text"`:

```
"text".toUpperCase().bold().italics()

"TEXT".bold().italics()

"<B>TEXT</B>".italics()

"<I><B>TEXT</B></I>"
```

The value processed by a specific method is the accumulative value returned by the expression to the left of the method; that is, the expression that is implemented as the calling object, or string. Therefore, you must make sure that the expression to the left of a method returns a value which is valid for that method.

HTML text formatting tags usually consist of two tags that enclose the text. The nested structure is very clear in HTML, because a set of tags can enclose another set of tags. In the previous example, the `<I></I>` set encloses the `<B></B>` set. When creating HTML via JavaScript's `String` methods, keep in mind that the far-left specified method appears as the inner set of tags when formatted to HTML, whereas the far-right method is responsible for the outer set of tags.

General String Methods

As you already know, the `String` object packs many methods. Those that convert strings to constant HTML formats (and listed above) are only some of the methods JavaScript offers. In this section, we shall take a look at the rest of the `String` methods.

charAt()

This method returns the character whose index is equal to the argument of the method. The characters of a string are indexed from 0 to `length - 1`. The general syntax is:

```
anyString.charAt(index)
```

Here is an example:

```
var pres = "Kennedy"
document.write(pres.charAt(1))
```

This script segment prints the character "e", because it is the second character in the string. You can also call this method with a literal as in the following example:

```
document.write("Kennedy".charAt(1))
```

You can print the characters of a string via a simple loop:

```
var str = "I am a string!"
for (var i = 0; i < str.length; ++i) {
     document.write(str.charAt(i))
}
```

At first, a string literal is assigned to the variable `str`. The loop then iterates `length` times. It starts at 0, and ends at `str.length - 1` (notice the less than operator, not less than or equal to). The i-indexed character is printed in the ith iteration of the loop. Since the command block is executed once for each integer value of `i`, each character of the string is printed once and only once. The output of the preceding script segment is actually the string itself, printed one character at a time (no, you cannot notice the difference!).

indexOf()

This method returns the index of the first occurrence of the specified substring in the calling string object, starting the search at the beginning of the string. An example will surely clear things up:

```
var str = "ababa"
document.write(str.indexOf("ba"))
```

This script's output is the number 1. The first occurrence of the substring "`ba`" in the calling string object is at the second character whose index is 1. The search for the specified substring starts at index 0, the beginning of the string. However, you can also instruct JavaScript to start the search at a different index, somewhere in the middle of the string. The following script segment prints the number 3:

```
var str = "ababa"
document.write(str.indexOf("ba", 2))
```

The general syntax of this method is:

```
stringName.indexOf(searchValue, [fromIndex])
```

Note that *fromIndex* must be an integer between 0 and the string's length minus 1. *SearchValue* does not have to be a string. The following script prints 8:

```
var str = "August 27, 1985"
document.write(str.indexOf(7))
```

If the index to start looking for the substring is not specified, the default value is used, 0.

If the specified substring is not found in the entire string, the method returns one less than the base, –1. This method is equivalent to the `index` function in Perl.

lastIndexOf()

This method is identical to the indexOf method, except that it returns the index of the last occurrence of the specified value, rather than the first occurrence. Its syntax is, therefore, the same:

```
stringName.lastIndexOf(searchValue, [fromIndex])
```

The following script prints the number 3:

```
var str = "a/b/c"
document.write(str.lastIndexOf("/"))
```

See the indexOf method for more details on this method.

substring()

Strings are constructed of characters. The substring() method returns a set of characters within its calling String object. Its general syntax is:

```
stringName.substring(indexA, indexB)
```

stringName is any string. *indexA* and *indexB* are both integers between 0 and *stringName*.length – 1. *indexA* is the index of the first character in the substring, whereas *indexB* is the index of the last character in the substring plus 1. The following script assigns the string "bc" to the variable seg:

```
var str = "abcd"
var seg = str.substring(1, 3)
```

Notice that the length of the substring is *indexA* – *indexB*.

The substring whose arguments are 0 and *stringName*.length is equal to the string itself (*stringName*).

This method is similar to its equivalent in Perl, the function substr. Nonetheless, it is important to point out the differences. First of all, since Perl does not support objects, the plain substr() function accepts the string itself as the first argument and *indexA* as the second one. However, the third argument is not *indexB*, but the length of the substring. Another difference is that when you call the function with a negative value as the offset (*indexA*), the substring starts that far from the end of the string. In JavaScript, though, a negative index is equivalent to a zero index, the first character of the string. JavaScript prototypes enable us to reproduce the substr function in Perl as a JavaScript method using the following script segment:

```
function substr(offset, length) {
```

```
        if (offset < 0)
            offset = this.length + offset
        return this.substring(offset, offset + length)
}

String.prototype.substr = substr
```

You can use this method with any string in the following way:

```
var str = "abcd"
document.write(str.substr(-3, 2))
```

This statement prints the string "bc".

escape & unescape

JavaScript provides us with some built-in functions that deal with strings, such as escape and unescape. Before we can present these functions, we must discuss the ISO Latin-1 character set. The ISO Latin-1 (8859-1) is the standard set of characters used over the Internet. This standard also serves as the basis for the ANSI character set of MS-Windows, but, naturally, Microsoft extended and improved the set. However, only the ISO Latin-1 characters are guaranteed to be supported on a Web site. You already know the standard coding scheme of the ISO Latin-1 character set through HTML, which enables you to display a character by its number or name, as an entity. For example, the character © can be displayed on a page via two different expressions:

- ©
- ©

The first expression is based on the character code in the ISO Latin-1 character set. The second method is based on the name given to the character. With only a few exceptions, almost all platforms are compatible with the glyphs of ISO Latin-1 (ISO-8859-1). If you are interested in character sets, or ISO-8859-1, search the Web for more information. The ISO-8859-1 character table can be found at the end of the book.

Now back to JavaScript. The escape function returns the ASCII encoding of an argument in the ISO Latin-1 character set. The general syntax is:

```
escape(string)
```

Like all methods, you can pass it a variable, a property of an existing object, or a plain string literal. The `escape()` function is not a method associated with any object, but is a part of the language itself. The value returned by the escape function is the string argument, where all nonalphanumeric characters are replaced by a string in the form of "%*xx*", *xx* being the ASCII encoding of a character in the argument.

The `unescape()` function is responsible for the opposite conversion. That is, it converts the string from nonalphanumeric ASCII encoding to ISO Latin-1 characters. Its syntax is similar:

```
unescape(string)
```

The following example demonstrates the conversion in both directions:

```
var str1 = "My phone # is 123-456-7890"
var str2 = escape(str1)
var str3 = unescape(str2)
document.write("After escape: " + str2 + "<BR>")
document.write("After unescape: " + str3)
```

The script's output is self-explanatory:

```
After escape: My%20phone%20%23%20is%20123-456-7890
After unescape: My phone # is 123-456-7890
```

Number-to-String Conversion

Occasionally, you need to convert a number to a string. For example, if you want to compute the number of digits in a number, you can convert it to a string and use the `length` property, which applies to strings only. In this section we shall take a look at a few ways to convert a number into a string.

Empty String Concatenation

The most obvious way to convert a number to a string is by concatenating an empty string to the number. Here is an example of such conversion:

```
var num = 987
num += ""
```

You can also make sure that the value of the variable is a string using the `typeof` operator in the following way:

```
var num = 987
document.write("num is a " + typeof num + "<BR>")
num += ""
```

```
document.write("num is a " + typeof num)
```

The expected output of this script segment is:

```
num is a number
num is a string
```

You can also convert the number to a string and assign the numeric string to another variable, or, even better, do both operations in one statement:

```
var num = 987
var numericString = num + ""
```

This script results in two different variables; the first holds a pure numeric value whereas the second one, `numericString`, holds a string type. The side of the variable to which the empty string is concatenated has no importance:

```
var num = 987
var numericString = "" + num
```

If you concatenate several different literals, where some are numbers and other are strings, the expression evaluates to a string. Here is an example:

```
var str = 99 + " bottles of beer on the wall"
```

However, scripts become tricky when you concatenate more than two values or literals, especially when the first few are numbers. Here is a tricky expression:

```
var str = 50 + 49 + " bottles of beer on the wall"
```

JavaScript evaluates from left to right. The accumulated value is converted to a string only when a string value or literal is encountered in the expression. In the preceding example, JavaScript adds `49` to `50` in the regular mathematical way, so `50 + 49` evaluates to 99, which is then concatenated to the following string. So the value of `str` in this case is "`99 bottles of beer on the wall`." The following statement demonstrates a slightly different situation:

```
var str = "bottles of beer on the wall -- " + 50 + 49
```

Like always, evaluation is done from left to right. The string, `bottles of beer on the wall --` , is concatenated with `50` and evaluates to `bottles of beer on the wall -- 50`. This value in turn is concatenated with the number `49`, and evaluates to `bottles of beer on the wall -- 5049`, which is certainly not the value we want. A simple workaround is to enclose the numeric operation in parentheses in the following form:

```
var str = "bottles of beer on the wall -- " + (50 + 49)
```

The parentheses instruct JavaScript to evaluate the enclosed expression first, so the value of `str` in this case is `bottles of beer on the wall -- 99`.

String Instance Construction

Another way to convert a number to a string is by providing the number to the `String()` constructor function, which returns a regular `String` object. Here is a simple example to demonstrate this:

```
var num = 987
num = new String(num)
```

The data type of the variable `num` in this case is not a string, but an object. As mentioned earlier, strings created via the `String()` constructor are regular objects. However, you can still use any property or method associated with strings on such objects.

A more obvious way to convert a number to a string via the constructor function is to assign the new string, or object, to a new variable in the following form:

```
var num = 987
var numericString = new String(num)
```

The toString() Method

The `toString()` method belongs to all objects. Its general syntax is:

```
objectName.toString([radix])
```

`objectName` is the object to convert to a string, whereas *`radix`* is the base to use for representing numeric values when the calling object is a number. The following example prints the string equivalents of the numbers 0 through 9 in decimal and binary:

```
for (x = 0; x < 10; x++) {
   document.write("Decimal: ", x.toString(10), " Binary: ",
                                 x.toString(2), "<BR>")
}
```

The loop's output is:

```
Decimal: 0 Binary: 0
Decimal: 1 Binary: 1
Decimal: 2 Binary: 10
```

```
Decimal: 3 Binary: 11
Decimal: 4 Binary: 100
Decimal: 5 Binary: 101
Decimal: 6 Binary: 110
Decimal: 7 Binary: 111
Decimal: 8 Binary: 1000
Decimal: 9 Binary: 1001
```

All objects, numbers included, have a `toString()` method. If an object has no string value, the method returns "`[object` *`type`*`]`", where *type* is the object type (e.g., `Date`, `Array`, `Object` (user defined), `Image`). When used with an array, `toString()` joins the array elements and returns one string where elements are separated by commas. This operation is exactly like the `join()` method which concatenates the elements with a specified delimiter, possibly a comma.

For functions, `toString()` decompiles the function back into a canonical source string. Take a look at the following script segment:

```
function foo() {
     var a = 5
     alert(a)
     document.write("wow")
}

document.write(foo.toString())
```

The script's output is:

```
function foo() { var a = 5; alert(a); document.write("wow"); }
```

String-to-Number Conversion

Mathematical operators, for example, accept numeric strings as operands and handle them fine. Here is an example for such an operation:

```
var num1= "7"
var num2 = "2"
var result = num1 - num2
document.write(result)
```

This script prints 5, just as if both variables were assigned a plain numeric value rather than a numeric string (we use the term *numeric string* to characterize a string that encloses a number, such as "911"). An operation consisting of numeric string operands returns a plain numeric value, not a string. Therefore, you can theoretically convert a numeric string to a number by performing an arithmetical operation on it. If you want, you can even use a function to execute the conversion in the following form:

```
function convert(val) {
  return val - 0
}
var num = "911"
num = convert(num)
```


Note that you cannot use the plus (+) operator because it is also a string concatenation operator in JavaScript. If you are not sure whether or not a value is a numeric string or a number, always convert it. It's better to stay on the safe side than to spend hours searching for such errors. Conversion via mathematical operations is somewhat annoying, because it looks like a workaround. Therefore JavaScript provides us with a few conversion functions, each with its own attributes.

parseInt() and parseFloat()

These two functions were briefly discussed in Chapter 15, JavaScript Math. They are built-in functions, so they do not belong to any object. They convert their argument from a numeric string to a number. If the argument is a string but not a numeric one, the function returns zero. The `parseFloat()` function is more general, because it works with floating point numbers as well as integers. The `parseInt()` function works with integers only, and returns a rounded-off value when called with a floating point numeric string. Both functions return the value they are given if it is a plain number, not a numeric string. Therefore, if you are not sure whether a value is a number or a numeric string, simply send it to the function.

If a certain value in the script has a chance to be a floating point number, use `parseFloat`. It will also work if the value is an integer.

Here are a few expressions to demonstrate these functions, along with returned values:

```
parseInt("16") // 16
parseInt("16.33") // 16
parseFloat("16") // 16
parseFloat("16.33") // 16.33
parseInt("Howdy!") // 0
```

These functions are very useful when accepting input from the user via forms or prompts, because they always return a string, even if it represents a number.

Note that both functions return zero when the argument is a Boolean value. Therefore, if you want to check if the user canceled a `prompt` box by pressing the Cancel button, you must evaluate the condition before parsing the value. Here is an example:

```
var num = prompt("Enter a number between 0 and 9:")
if (num = false)
     alert("You must enter a value to continue.")
else
     num = parseInt(num)
```

A common but mistaken practice is to parse the value immediately. The result is that you cannot check if the user canceled the box, because he or she might have entered the number 0, which is parsed to the same value as a Boolean value.

Checking if a Value is a Number or Not

The `isNaN()` function evaluates an argument to determine if it is not a number, or "NaN." Netscape Navigator 2.0 supports this function on Unix platforms only, but Navigator 3.0 fully implements it on all platforms.

The functions `parseFloat()` and `parseInt()` return "`NaN`" when they evaluate a value that is not a number or a numeric string. "`NaN`" is not a number in any string. If "`NaN`" is passed on to arithmetic operations, the result is also "`NaN`." The `isNaN()` returns a Boolean value, according to the argument. Bear in mind that MSIE 3.0 does not support this feature—`parseFloat()` and `parseInt()` both return 0 if their argument is neither a string nor a numeric string.

"`NaN`" is not a string, nor is it a data type of its own. It is primarily a number! You can prove that to yourself via the following statement:

```
alert(typeof parseInt("something"))
```

The following construct demonstrates how to implement the `isNaN` function (with the `parseFloat()` function for the sake of the example):

```
var floatValue = parseFloat(valueToBeConvertedToFloat)

if isNaN(floatValue) {
     functionToBeCalledIfFloat()
} else {
     functionToBeCalledIfNotFloat()
}
```

The `isNaN()` function is not as important as `parseInt` and `parseFloat`, but we have discussed it here for completeness.

Evaluating Text Expressions

JavaScript supports evaluation and execution of text expressions via the `eval()` method. Here are some examples:

```
var str = "5 + 2"
var num = eval(str)
alert(num)

var al = "alert('This is an evaluated string.')"
eval(al)
```

This script segment pops up two alerts. The first one displays the number 7, because the expression "`5 + 2`" evaluates to 7. The second call to the `eval()` function does not cause it to return a value, but to execute the statement encapsulated in a string.

You can also use the `eval()` function to convert strings representing numbers to regular numbers.

The `eval()` function accepts any valid JavaScript piece of code in the form of a string. You can store an entire script as a string and then hand it over to this function. The classic example for the function is to let the user enter a mathematical expression in a form field or a `prompt` box, and to display the result. Here is a simple example:

```
var inp = prompt("Enter mathematical expression", "")
alert(inp + " = " + eval(inp))
```

String Handling Examples

In this section we focus on scripts that take advantage of the various built-in functions as well as the elements of the `String` object in JavaScript.

String Enciphering

The following script prompts the user for a short string. It then asks for a numeric key. The key has 63 possible values—all integers from 1 to 63. The ciphering technique used in this script is known as XORing, because it is primarily based on the bitwise XOR (exclusive OR) operator. The numeric value of each character of the input string, or password, is mixed with the numeric key value. A reversed process can be used to convert the enciphered string back to the original one. Since the conversion simply swaps the same two characters according to the key, the same JavaScript script is used as the decoder and the encoder. Enough theory—let's get to the point! Here is the script:

```
<HTML>
<HEAD>
<TITLE>Enciphering</TITLE>
<SCRIPT LANGUAGE="JavaScript">
<!--

// create list of valid characters
var list = "0123456789abcdefghijklmnopqrstuvwxyz._~ABCDEFGHIJKLMNOPQRSTU
                                        VWXYZ"

function encipher() {
      // prompt user for string
      var str = prompt("Enter string:", "")

      // terminate function if user selects CANCEL
      if (!str)
            return

      // check that each character of input string is valid
      for (var i = 0; i < str.length; ++i) {
            if (list.indexOf(str.charAt(i)) == -1) {
                  alert("script terminated -- invalid character found")
                  return
            }
      }

      // prompt user for key
      var key = prompt("Enter key (1-63):", "")

      // terminate function if user selects CANCEL
      if (!key)
            return

      // convert key to integer (number)
      key = parseInt(key)

      // alert enciphered string
      alert(encode(str, key))
}

function encode(str, key) {
      // initialize accumulative string variable
      var code = ""

      // encipher all characters
      for (var i = 0; i < str.length; ++i) {
            var ind = list.indexOf(str.charAt(i))
            var converted = list.charAt(ind ^ key)
            code += converted
```

```
        }

        // return enciphered value
        return code
}

encipher()

// -->
</SCRIPT>
</HEAD>
<BODY>
</BODY>
</HTML>
```

Example 16-1 (ex16-1.htm). *A simple ciphering script.*

> **Warning:** Do not count on this script for securing your data. An average high school graduate can beat the system within a few minutes. (If you read the chapter about operators you should be able to do so yourself.)

The first global statement initializes the variable `list` with a string consisting of all supported characters.

encipher()

At first, the function prompts the user for the string he or she wants to encode. It is stored in the variable `str`. If the value of the variable is a Boolean false, the function, and actually the script itself, is terminated. The motivation behind terminating the function is that a Boolean `false` value can only be the result of the user pressing Cancel. A `for` loop is then used to check that all characters of the string are also located in the string held by `list`. The loop iterates through every character of the input string. Take a look at the condition used to test if the character is supported:

```
list.indexOf(str.charAt(i)) == -1
```

`str.charAt(i)` is the character for which the loop's block is currently being executed. The variable `i` starts at 0, the index of the string's first character, and is incremented each time until it is equal to the index of the string's last character. Suppose the current character is "t." The condition looks like this then:

```
list.indexOf("t") == -1
```

If the character "t" is not found in the string `list`, the method `indexOf()` whose argument is "t" returns –1—exactly the number against which the returned value is tested.

If a character is not valid (not found in `list`), a message is displayed and the function is terminated, indirectly causing the script's execution to end.

The function then asks the user to enter the key number, which must be an integer between 1 and 63. Because this is just an example, the input value is not tested. If the user clicks Cancel, the function is terminated. Otherwise the function continues, and the key number is converted from a numeric string to a number via the `parseInt()` function. The encoded string, which is returned by the function `encode()`, is displayed.

encode(str, key)

At first, an empty string is assigned to the variable `code`. A loop is used to replace every character of the input string by another character. The index of the current character (the one whose index in `str` is equal to the loops counter, `i`) in the `list` string is assigned to the variable `ind`. The bitwise OR operator is given the key number and the value of `ind` as operands. The character whose index in `list` is equal to the value returned by the bitwise OR operation is the one used to replace the current character in the new string, so it is assigned to the variable that holds the encoded string. The new string is returned by the function.

Global Statements

The only global statement is the one that calls the `encipher` function.

Summary

Strings are one of the most important data types in JavaScript. JavaScript tends to organize its elements in the form of objects, so all string-related functions and data are grouped together to form the `String` object. In this chapter we discussed the methods of the `String` object, as well as its single property, `length`. Because strings are direct or indirect (based on the way you create them) instances of this object, you can create prototypes to extend the object's capabilities. The JavaScript example provided at the end of the chapter gives a clear view of the `String` object's strength. We did not provide many examples in this chapter because string manipulation and handling can be found in almost every example further on in this book.

Chapter 17

Browser Objects

Browser objects are special objects that correspond to elements of a page. These objects exist on all pages, even if the page is "empty." Each browser object corresponds to one element of the page. For example, the `location` object consists of all the properties related to the current URL of the document. Browser objects are also known as *Navigator objects*, but that term is specific to Netscape's browser. Some even refer to them as built-in objects, but this term is completely mistaken, because built-in objects are another explicit type of objects (`Date`, `Array`, `Math`, `String`).

Although browser objects exist on all pages, they consist of nested objects that are largely content-dependent. Browser objects are the only type of objects in JavaScript that feature event handlers as a part of their structure. Although these objects are only referred to using JavaScript, they are not created via JavaScript but by HTML.

The Object Hierarchy

You may recall that objects often consist of properties that are also objects. The term *nested objects* is usually used to characterize such child objects. The nested structure of an object is also known as its *hierarchy*. The highest-level object is the one that does not have any parent object. Browser objects are classic examples for hierarchy usage, because they are deeply nested. The browser object structure is fairly complex, so it is difficult to remember each and every property at the bottom of the tree. Nonetheless, it is important to study the upper section of the hierarchy. Figure 17-1 shows the upper part of the browser object hierarchy. The `window` object is the topmost object in the entire structure. Everything you script in JavaScript refers to elements of the browser's window, whether or not it appears in the page itself. Normally, it is not necessary to specify the `window` object when you refer to its properties. For example, the `document` object is a property of `window`, but you say `document.write` rather than `window.document.write`. The implementation of the `window` object as the default object throughout the script is influenced by the fact that it is solely the topmost level of the hierarchy. Once you establish a mental model of the browser hierarchy and script these objects a few times, the structure will become second nature to you.

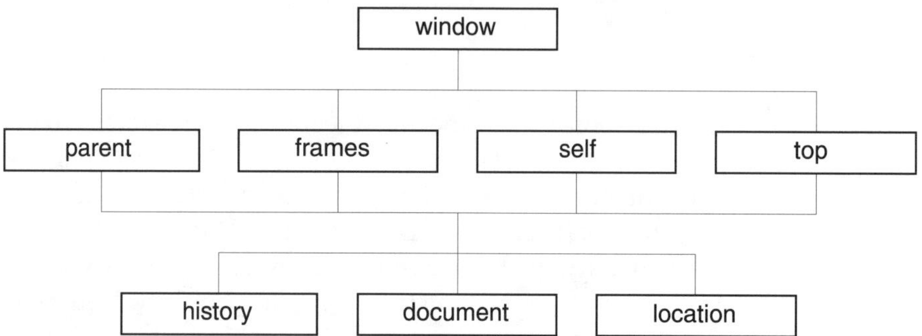

Figure 17-1. *The browser object hierarchy.*

Creating Browser Objects

As you know, you do not create browser objects via JavaScript. JavaScript is only the high-level scripting language used to refer to these objects. Browser objects existed even when the most popular browser was Mosaic or Navigator 1.0, but they were not originally implemented to facilitate interaction with the user. Since there was no way to refer to these objects, they were not stored in memory in these earlier versions.

The topmost browser objects are established when the HTML document loads in the Java- or JavaScript-enhanced browser. JavaScript lets us handle browser objects via their properties, methods, and event handlers.

Bear in mind that browser objects exist in memory as they are created by the browser. You can refer to a browser object via JavaScript only if the specified object has been laid out already. Otherwise, JavaScript will generate an error reporting that the object does not have any properties. At that moment, it is true that the object does not have properties, because the elements of the object haven't been laid out yet.

Keep in mind that browser objects are visible objects. For example, a form's field is a browser object, and it is visible. Because browser objects are actually made of HTML, they include event handlers that enable a response to actions by the user, who is interacting with those elements of the page.

The Topmost Objects

The `window` object is standing alone at the top of the browser hierarchy. The properties of this object are, therefore, very rudimentary. In this section we shall outline the most important properties of the `window` object.

window

This object is the top-level object of the hierarchy. It contains properties that apply to the entire window. For example, the status bar of the browser is a property of this object. It also includes a property which is actually the object itself. Sounds strange? Not really. You will find out more about this reference when we discuss windows and frames. When the document features frames, there can be several `window` objects in a single HTML document. Frames actually divide the page into "child" windows, so each frame has its own browser object hierarchy. You must be careful with such child windows because they can cause a collision due to the fact that several `window` objects have a shared property. For example, there is only one status bar in the browser, no matter which page you load (unless you open a window without a status bar). However, there can be many `window` objects in action on that page, each one of them optionally referring to the same status bar. You will learn more about the `window` object later in the book.

document

By far the most useful property of the `window` object is the `document` object. It contains properties for the current page loaded in the window. The properties of this object are content-dependent because each and every page has its own outline and elements. Almost everything in the page is a property of the document object, including links, images, forms and their elements, anchors, and more. Because each frame is a window (`window` object), it contains a `document` object as well. Even the background and the title are properties of this object. As a matter of fact, the `document` object is so complex that it is divided into several chapters in this book, each dealing with different properties of this object.

history

The `history` object is also a property of the `window` object. It contains properties of the URLs the user has previously visited. This information is stored in a history list, and is accessible through the browser's menu. If the document consists of child documents in frames, each frame has its own history list, or `history` object. This object also contains methods enabling you to send the user's browser to a URL found in the history list.

location

The `location` object contains properties of the current URL. Although you may think of URLs as simple standard structures, they are far from being that. There are many types of protocols, and various sections in every URL. There are also optional sections in the URL such as anchor names and queries.

The following image summarizes all the browser objects:

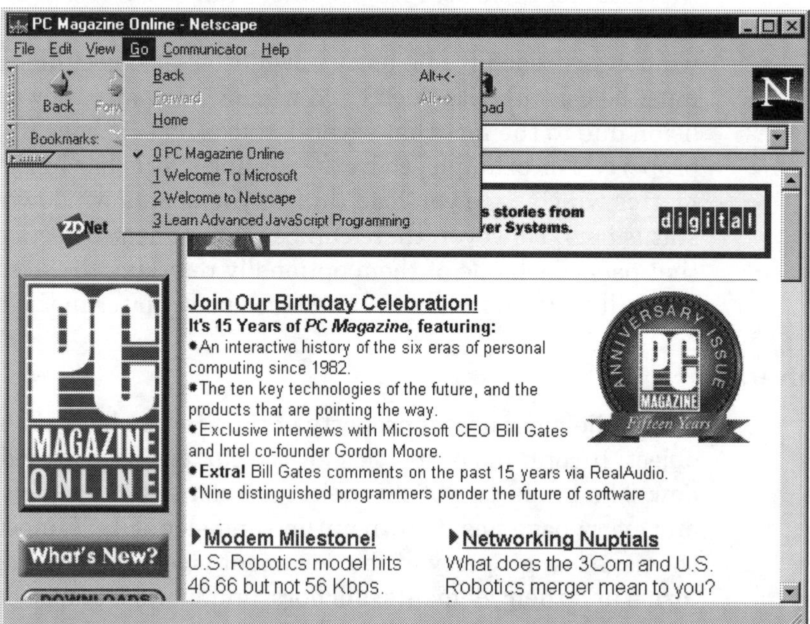

Figure 17-2. A standard Web page.

In Figure 17-2 you can see the various top-level browser objects, except for those that deal with frames. Study the image carefully so you know the role of every object.

Summary

In this short chapter we have introduced browser object as a very important model. Mastering browser objects is the key to success in JavaScript, because JavaScript is primarily designed to enable interaction with the user via these objects. Although we did not discuss any specific browser object, you should have a clear picture of the hierarchical structure. In the following chapters we discuss various concepts related to browser objects, including their methods, properties, and event handlers. Browser objects are not dealt with specifically in these chapters, but rather they are presented as the key to many JavaScript topics.

[illegible]

Summary

[illegible]

Chapter 18

Utilizing the Status Bar

The Status Bar

The status bar is found at the bottom of the browser's window. It exists in all browsers, including Navigator and IE. It normally displays the current status of the document being loaded. The status bar is present in every window, unless the window is opened by a script that explicitly disables the status bar. Figure 18-1 shows the status bar.

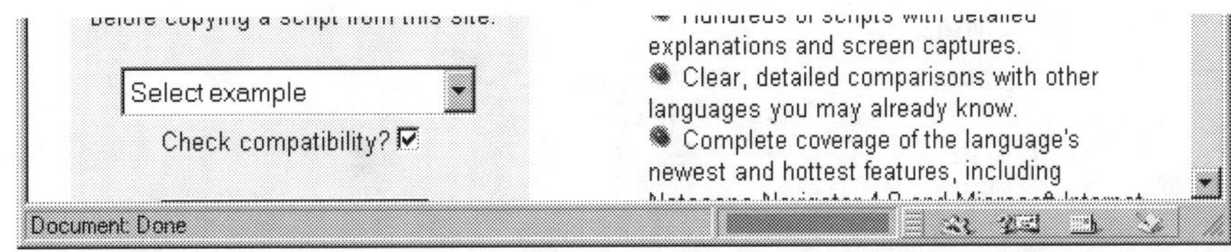

Figure 18-1. *The status bar shows the current status of the document in the window.*

The status bar is the gray bar at the bottom that shows the string "Document: Done."

In terms of JavaScript, the status bar is a direct property of the `window` object. In multiple-frame documents each frame has a property representing the status bar, but you should only reference one of them to avoid an unwanted collision. The status bar in JavaScript is generally represented by the `status` property `window.status`. You can also refer to the status bar of the current window via `self.status`, because `self` is actually a property of the `window` object that is the `window` object itself.

Note You can also refer to the status bar as `status` instead of `window.status`. However, we shall stick with the latter for clarity.

Never try to read the content of the status bar, because such action usually generates an error, both in Navigator and IE. Setting the value of the status bar is permitted, with some restrictions.

Writing to the Status Bar

You should avoid writing to the status bar via an immediate script because it normally does not work. Nonetheless, deferred scripts are used to assign values to this property. A string is written to the status bar by assigning a value to its property which represents it in JavaScript. The following document does not write anything to the status bar because it is an immediate script:

```
<HTML>
<HEAD>
<TITLE>status bar</TITLE>
</HEAD>
<BODY>
<SCRIPT LANGUAGE="JavaScript">
<!--

window.status = "You cannot see this!"

// -->
</SCRIPT>
</BODY>
</HTML>
```

Even if you use a function and the `onLoad` event handler to write something to the status bar, it does not work, because another property fills that purpose (`window.defaultStatus`, discussed later in this chapter). You can assign values to `window.status` via buttons, links, and every other event that is triggered by the user. For example, to have a message displayed when the user clicks a button you can use the following form:

```
<HTML>
<HEAD>
<TITLE>status bar</TITLE>
<SCRIPT LANGUAGE="JavaScript">
```

```
<!--

function showMessage() {
    window.status = "Fascinating!"
}

// -->
</SCRIPT>
</HEAD>
<BODY>
<FORM>
<INPUT TYPE="button" VALUE="show message" onClick="showMessage()">
</FORM>
</BODY>
</HTML>
```

Example 18-1 (ex18-1.htm). *You can display a string in the status bar as a reaction to a user-initiated event such as a button click.*

Here is a screen capture to show the effect:

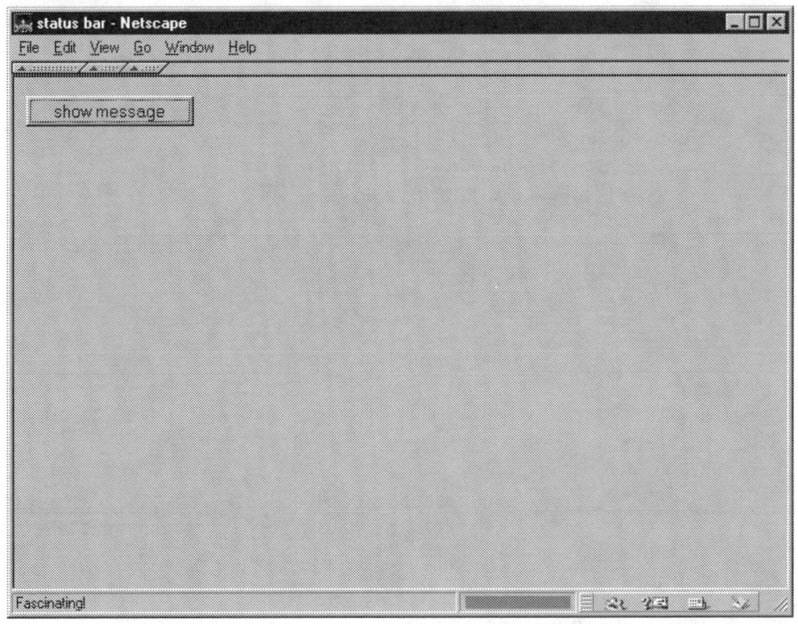

Figure 18-2. *A custom string in the status bar.*

You have probably noticed a fad that developed on Web pages during the last year. When you place the mouse's pointer over a link, it displays a short description in the status bar rather than the URL. A description is usually much more meaningful than a URL. The event handler that is triggered when the user places the mouse's pointer over a link is `onMouseOver`. The event handler should always return the

Boolean value `true` after the message is placed in the status bar. The only correct way to assign a message corresponding to a link in the status bar is to use the following syntax for the link:

```
<A HREF="URL" onMouseOver="window.status = 'any string'; return true">
```

Don't forget to return `true`—it's essential. The following statement creates a link to Netscape's site and displays a short message when you place the pointer over it:

```
<A HREF="http://www.netscape.com" onMouseOver="window.status = 'Get a
                    copy of Navigator'; return true">Netscape</A>
```

If you tried it out, you probably noticed that the message remains in the status bar until the page is unloaded or another string is assigned to replace it.

Take a look at the following example:

```
<HTML>
<HEAD>
<TITLE>status bar</TITLE>
<SCRIPT LANGUAGE="JavaScript">
<!--

function showMessage(txt) {
     window.status = txt
     setTimeout("clearMessage()", 2500)
}

function clearMessage() {
     window.status = ""
}

// -->
</SCRIPT>
</HEAD>
<BODY>
<A HREF="http://www.netscape.com" onMouseOver="showMessage('Get a
                    copy of Navigator'); return true">Netscape</A>
</BODY>
</HTML>
```

Example 18-2 (ex18-2.htm). *A script that displays the string in the status bar for 2.5 seconds.*

The `setTimeout()` method is a possible replacement for the need to return `true`. This script is very simple. When the user places the pointer over the link, the function `showMessage()` is called with the desired string. The string is assigned to the `status` property, and the function `clearMessage()` is called to clear the status bar after 2.5 seconds, by replacing the current message with an empty string.

A much better way to erase a string written by `onMouseOver` from the status bar is to implement the `onMouseOut` event handler. This event handler serves as an attribute of a link or client-side image map area, and it is triggered when the mouse pointer leaves an area or link from inside that area (see Chapter 23, Links, Anchors, and Image Maps). This outside movement enables us to assign an empty string to the status bar when the user removes the pointer from the link.

Here is another example:

```
<A HREF="http://www.netscape.com" onMouseOver="window.status = 'Get a
                    copy of Navigator'; return true" onMouseOut="window.
                    status = ''; return true">Netscape</A>
```

Setting a Default Value to Status Bar

You have seen that it is possible to write one-line strings to the status bar via the `status` property. It is also possible to set a default value to the status bar. This value is kept in the status bar as long as no value is written to it by the `status` property. The general syntax of this property is `window.defaultStatus` or `defaultStatus`. When using this property with an event handler, you must return `true`.

Take a look at the following example:

```
<HTML>
<HEAD>
<TITLE>status bar</TITLE>
<SCRIPT LANGUAGE="JavaScript">
<!--

function statusSetter() {
   window.defaultStatus = "Click the link for the Netscape homepage"
   window.status = "Netscape homepage"
}

// -->
</SCRIPT>
</HEAD>
<BODY>
<A HREF="http://www.netscape.com" onMouseOver = "statusSetter();
                          return true">Netscape</A>
</BODY>
</HTML>
```

Example 18-3 (ex18-3.htm). *Sets a default value to the status bar.*

When you load the page in the browser, you see one link. At that moment, the status bar does not contain any string (it might contain a string to report that the page has been loaded). When you place the pointer over the link, the message "Netscape homepage" is written to the status bar. When the pointer is taken off the link, the string is replaced by another string—"Click the link for the Netscape homepage." This is a nice alternative to using the onMouseOut event handler.

Banners

Banners are classic JavaScript scripts. They were and still are an attractive addition to any Web page. The original banners appeared in the status bar, scrolling several messages in sequence. Some prefer to place the banner in a text box, because they feel that status-bar-based banners are annoying to the common surfer. Banners are sometimes very unsteady, their speed is not uniform, and they blink at times. There is no workaround to make them better. But, all in all, they are still a lot of fun. In this section we shall take a look at a few different banner-like scripts, most of which were created exclusively for this book.

T-banner

The T-banner simulates a typewriter. It displays each message by typing it in, one character at a time. It seems as if someone is typing the message at a certain speed, deleting it upon completion. First, take a look at the script:

```
<HTML>
<HEAD>
<TITLE>T-Banner</TITLE>
<SCRIPT LANGUAGE="JavaScript">
<!--

// set speed of banner (pause in milliseconds between characters)
var speed = 100 // decrease value to increase speed (must be positive)

// set pause between completion of message and beginning of following one
var pause = 1000 // increase value to increase pause

// set initial values
var timerID = null
var bannerRunning = false

// create global array
```

```
var ar = new Array()

// assign the strings to the array's elements
ar[0] = "Welcome to our JavaScript page"
ar[1] = "We hope you enjoy the T-Banner script"
ar[2] = "It is designed to be more stable than regular banners"
ar[3] = "Don't forget to check out our other scripts"

// set index of first message to be displayed first
var currentMessage = 0

// set index of last character to be displayed first
var offset = 0

// stop the banner if it is currently running
function stopBanner() {
     // if banner is currently running
     if (bannerRunning)
          // stop the banner
          clearTimeout(timerID)

     // timer is now stopped
     bannerRunning = false
}

// start the banner
function startBanner() {
     // make sure the banner is stopped
     stopBanner()

     // start the banner from the current position
     showBanner()
}

// type in the current message
function showBanner() {
     // assign current message to variable
     var text = ar[currentMessage]

     // if current message has not finished being displayed
     if (offset < text.length) {
          // if last character of current message is a space
          if (text.charAt(offset) == " ")
               // skip the current character
               offset++

          // assign the up-to-date to-be-displayed substring
          // second argument of method accepts index of last char plus one
          var partialMessage = text.substring(0, offset + 1)

          // display partial message in status bar
          window.status = partialMessage
```

```
            // increment index of last character to be displayed
            offset++ // IE sometimes has trouble with "++offset"

            // recursive call after specified time
            timerID = setTimeout("showBanner()", speed)

            // banner is running
            bannerRunning = true
        } else {
            // reset offset
            offset = 0

            // increment subscript (index) of current message
            currentMessage++

            // if subscript of current message is out of range
            if (currentMessage == ar.length)
                // wrap around (start from beginning)
                currentMessage = 0

            // recursive call after specified time
            timerID = setTimeout("showBanner()", pause)

            // banner is running
            bannerRunning = true
        }
    }

// -->
</SCRIPT>
</HEAD>
<BODY onLoad="startBanner()">
</BODY>
</HTML>
```

Example 18-4 (ex18-4.htm). *The T-banner.*

Global Statements

```
// set speed of banner (pause in milliseconds between characters)
var speed = 100 // decrease value to increase speed (must be positive)

// set pause between completion of message and beginning of following one
var pause = 1000 // increase value to increase pause

// set initial values
var timerID = null
var bannerRunning = false

// create global array
```

```
var ar = new Array()

// assign the strings to the array's elements
ar[0] = "Welcome to our JavaScript page"
ar[1] = "We hope you enjoy the T-Banner script"
ar[2] = "It is designed to be more stable than regular banners"
ar[3] = "Don't forget to check out our other scripts"

// set index of first message to be displayed first
var currentMessage = 0

// set index of last character to be displayed first
var offset = 0
```

At first, the speed of the banner is set to 100. This is equal to the pause between each character of a message in milliseconds. The pause (in milliseconds) between the completion of a message (string) and its deletion is assigned to the variable `pause`. The identifier for the current timeout is assigned `null`, because no timeout is set yet. The current state of the banner (`false` because it is not running yet) is assigned to the variable `bannerRunning`. An array is then created to hold the strings that are to be displayed as banner messages. The first string is assigned to the first element of the array, `ar[0]`, and so on. The number `0` is assigned to `currentMessage` because the first message displayed is `ar[0]`. The index of the last character displayed at a given moment in the status bar is assigned to the global variable `offset`. It is set to zero because the first appearance of the banner consists of only one character—the first one—whose index is zero.

stopBanner()

```
// start the banner
function startBanner() {
     // make sure the banner is stopped
     stopBanner()

     // start the banner from the current position
     showBanner()
}
```

This function is called to stop the banner. If the banner is running, the current timeout is cleared. The variable `bannerRunning` is set to `false` because the banner is stopped.

startBanner()

```
// start the banner
function startBanner() {
     // make sure the banner is stopped
```

```
          stopBanner()

          // start the banner from the current position
          showBanner()
}
```

This function calls the `stopBanner` function to make sure the banner is stopped, and then calls the function `showBanner` to start running the T-banner.

showBanner()

```
// type in the current message
function showBanner() {
     // assign current message to variable
     var text = ar[currentMessage]

     // if current message has not finished being displayed
     if (offset < text.length) {
          // if last character of current message is a space
          if (text.charAt(offset) == " ")
               // skip the current character
               offset++

          // assign the up-to-date to-be-displayed substring
          // second argument of method accepts index of last char plus one
          var partialMessage = text.substring(0, offset + 1)

          // display partial message in status bar
          window.status = partialMessage

          // increment index of last character to be displayed
          offset++ // IE sometimes has trouble with "++offset"

          // recursive call after specified time
          timerID = setTimeout("showBanner()", speed)

          // banner is running
          bannerRunning = true
     } else {
          // reset offset
          offset = 0

          // increment subscript (index) of current message
          currentMessage++

          // if subscript of current message is out of range
          if (currentMessage == ar.length)
               // wrap around (start from beginning)
               currentMessage = 0

          // recursive call after specified time
```

```
            timerID = setTimeout("showBanner()", pause)

            // banner is running
            bannerRunning = true
        }
}
```

The current message is assigned to the local variable `text`. The function then continues in one of two directions. The first is selected if the current message is still being displayed; that is, if the index of the last character that was displayed of the current message is the last character or less. In that case the expression `offset < text.length` evaluates to `true`. If the last character to be displayed during this pass through the function is a space, the value of `offset` is incremented, and no time is wasted on typing the space character. The substring that needs to be displayed during the current iteration is assigned to the local variable `partialMessage`. Since the second argument of the `substring` method is the index of the last character plus one, it is set to be `offset + 1`. The current substring is displayed in the status bar, and the value of `offset` is incremented. The function is called once more after `speed` milliseconds.

When the end of the current message has been reached, another execution path is taken. In this case the variable `offset` is assigned zero, the index of the first character of a string. To allow posting of the next message in the array, the index of the array element holding the current message is incremented. If the new value of `currentMessage` is out of range, it is set to zero, so the following message is the first one. The function is called recursively after `pause` milliseconds. This time the function should take the first route, because the message is only at its beginning.

Event Handlers

The `startBanner` function is called when the document has finished loading by the `onLoad` event handler.

R-banner

While T stands for type, typewriter, or Tomer, R probably stands for random, denoting the flavor of this special banner. The messages appear by popping up various characters of the message in a random order. Another special effect involved in this banner is the scrolling motion from right to left. This effect is being achieved by simply letting each character that pops up take a three-character space. Take a look at the script now:

```
<HTML>
<HEAD>
<TITLE>R-Banner</TITLE>
<SCRIPT LANGUAGE="JavaScript">
<!--

// set speed of banner (pause in milliseconds between addition of
                    new character)
var speed = 10 // decrease value to increase speed (must be positive)

// set pause between completion of message and beginning of following one
var pause = 1500 // increase value to increase pause

// set initial values
var timerID = null
var bannerRunning = false

// create array
var ar = new Array()

// assign the strings to the array's elements
ar[0] = "Welcome to our JavaScript page"
ar[1] = "We hope you enjoy the R-Banner script"
ar[2] = "It is designed to be more stable than regular banners"
ar[3] = "Don't forget to check out our other scripts"

// assign index of current message
var message = 0

// empty string initialization
var state = ""

// no value is currently being displayed
clearState()

// stop the banner if it is currently running
function stopBanner() {
     // if banner is currently running
     if (bannerRunning)
          // stop the banner
          clearTimeout(timerID)

     // banner is now stopped
     bannerRunning = false
}

// start the banner
function startBanner() {
     // make sure the banner is stopped
```

```
        stopBanner()

        // start the banner from the current position
        showBanner()
    }

    // assign state a string of "0" characters of the length of the
                      current message
    function clearState() {
        // initialize to empty string
        state = ""

        // create string of same length containing 0 digits
        for (var i = 0; i < ar[message].length; ++i) {
            state += "0"
        }
    }

    // display the current message
    function showBanner() {
        // if the current message is done
        if (getString()) {
            // increment message
            message++

            // if new message is out of range wrap around to first message
            if (ar.length <= message)
                message = 0

            // new message is first displayed as empty string
            clearState()

            // display next character after pause milliseconds
            timerID = setTimeout("showBanner()", pause)

            // banner is now running
            bannerRunning = true
        } else {
            // initialize to empty string
            var str = ""

            // build string to be displayed (only characters selected
                                   thus far are displayed)
            for (var j = 0; j < state.length; ++j) {
                str += (state.charAt(j) == "1") ? Ar[message].charAt(j)
                                   : "      "
            }

            // partial string is placed in status bar
            window.status = str

            // add another character after speed milliseconds
```

```
            timerID = setTimeout("showBanner()", speed)

            // banner is now running
            bannerRunning = true
        }
    }

    function getString() {
        // set variable to true (it will stay true unless proven otherwise)
        var full = true

        // set variable to false if a free space is found in string
                              (a not-displayed char)
        for (var j = 0; j < state.length; ++j) {
            // if character at index j of current message has not been
                              placed in displayed string
            if (state.charAt(j) == 0)
                full = false
        }

        // return true immediately if no space found (avoid infinitive
                              loop later)
        if (full)
            return true

        // search for random until free space found (broken up via
                              break statement)
        while (1) {
            // a random number (between 0 and state.length - 1 ==
                              message.length - 1)
            var num = getRandom(ar[message].length)

            // if free space found break infinitive loop
            if (state.charAt(num) == "0")
                break
        }

        // replace the 0 character with 1 character at place found
        state = state.substring(0, num) + "1" + state.substring(num + 1,
                              state.length)

        // return false because the string was not full (free space was
                              found)
        return false
    }

    function getRandom(max) {
        return Math.round((max - 1) * Math.random())
    }

    // -->
    </SCRIPT>
```

```
</HEAD>
<BODY onLoad="startBanner()">
</BODY>
</HTML>
```

Example 18-5 (ex18-5.htm). *An R-banner.*

Global Statements

```
// set speed of banner (pause in milliseconds between addition of
                         new character)
var speed = 10 // decrease value to increase speed (must be positive)

// set pause between completion of message and beginning of following one
var pause = 1500 // increase value to increase pause

// set initial values
var timerID = null
var bannerRunning = false

// create array
var ar = new Array()

// assign the strings to the array's elements
ar[0] = "Welcome to our JavaScript page"
ar[1] = "We hope you enjoy the R-Banner script"
ar[2] = "It is designed to be more stable than regular banners"
ar[3] = "Don't forget to check out our other scripts"

// assign index of current message
var message = 0

// empty string initialization
var state = ""

// no value is currently being displayed
clearState()
```

At first, the number 10 is assigned to the variable `speed`, representing the pause in milliseconds between the popping up of two consecutive characters in the current message. A longer pause is assigned to the variable `pause`, representing the number of milliseconds between the completion of the current message and its deletion. A null value is assigned to the global variable `timerID` and the Boolean value `false` is assigned to the variable `bannerRunning`. Predefined messages are stored in an array. The variable `message` is assigned zero, the index of the first element of the array to be displayed, `ar[0]`.

The second section of the global statement section consists of only two statements, but they are important for understanding the entire script. The first statement in this section assigns an empty string to the global variable `state`. The `clearState()` function is called next. It modifies the value of the global variable `state`, by assigning it *n* "0" characters, where *n* is the length of the current message. The variable `state` is basically constructed of 0s and 1s. Suppose the first character is a 0. That means that the first character of the current message has not been popped up yet. The same applies to the second character and all the following ones. Therefore, the string starts off at all 0s, and the message is finished when all characters are 1s.

stopBanner()

See explanation of this function in the T-banner.

startBanner()

See explanation of this function in the T-banner.

clearState()

See the section "Global Statements" for information regarding this function.

getRandom(max)

This simply returns an integer between 0 and `max - 1` (see explanation of `Math.random()`).

getString()

```
function getString() {
     // set variable to true (it will stay true unless proven otherwise)
     var full = true

     // set variable to false if a free space is found in string (a
                                   not-displayed char)
     for (var j = 0; j < state.length; ++j) {
          // if character at index j of current message has not been
                                   placed in displayed string
          if (state.charAt(j) == 0)
               full = false
     }

     // return true immediately if no space found (avoid infinitive
                                   loop later)
     if (full)
          return true
```

```
        // search for random until free space found (broken up via
                                 break statement)
        while (1) {
                // a random number (between 0 and state.length - 1 ==
                                 message.length - 1)
                var num = getRandom(ar[message].length)

                // if free space found break infinitive loop
                if (state.charAt(num) == "0")
                        break
        }

        // replace the 0 character with 1 character at place found
        state = state.substring(0, num) + "1" + state.substring(num + 1,
                                 state.length)

        // return false because the string was not full (free space
                                 was found)
        return false
}
```

At first, the variable `full` is initialized to `true`. An infinite loop (terminated by the `break` statement) is employed to go over all 0 and 1 characters of the `state` string. If a 0 character is found, the variable `full` is changed to `false`. It is not mandatory to break up the loop (as done above in `getString()`) when a free space, or 0, is found, because efficiency is not a concern in a random banner.

The remaining part of the function is executed only if a free space is available.

An infinite loop generates a new random index every iteration and checks if the space at that index is taken up. The loop continues to execute as long as the space at the random index is taken up. When a free space is finally found, the loop breaks up, returning the index `num` of the free space.

The value of `state` is updated by replacing the 0 character at index `num` with a 1 character. The function returns `false` upon termination, indicating that the message was not completed.

showBanner()

Like in the T-banner script, this function is the main one.

The function `getString()`is called to update the value of `state` and to check if the message has been completed. If it has, the current message is updated to the following one by incrementing the value of message, representing the index of the array's element where the current message is. If the new value is out of range, it is reset to the initial zero value. The function clearState() is called to set up the variable state, as explained above in the "Global Statements" section. The function is then called recursively after pause milliseconds.

In an ordinary case in which the message is not complete yet, the special display effects are generated. An empty string is assigned to the local variable str, ready to accumulate characters for display. A for loop iterates through the characters of the string ar[message]. If there is a 1 at the same index of the string state, the character from ar[message] is appended to the end of str. An alternative string is appended if a 0 character is found in the string state. The only way to create a right-to-left scrolling effect is to use a fairly long alternative string of a few spaces. Since a space has a very small horizontal span (characters are not uniform in width), a single-space alternative string will create a friendly left-to-right movement! Using an empty alternative string squeezes the string and creates a different right-to-left movement. The built-up string is placed in the status bar, and the function is called recursively after a pause of speed milliseconds.

Event Handlers

When the document is completely loaded, the startBanner() function is called by the onLoad event handler.

N-banner

The N(normal)-banner scrolls from right to left in the status bar. You have probably seen hundreds of these banners on the Web. Here is a script to implement such a banner:

```
<HTML>
<HEAD>
<TITLE>N-Banner</TITLE>
<SCRIPT LANGUAGE="JavaScript">
<!--

function scrollBanner(seed) {
     // set pause in milliseconds between each movement
     var speed = 10

     // assign one-space string to variable (space pads left side
                              of status bar)
     var str = " "

     // create global array
```

```
var ar = new Array()

// assign the strings to the array's elements
ar[0] = "Welcome to our JavaScript page. "
ar[1] = "We hope you enjoy the N-Banner script. "
ar[2] = "It is designed to be more stable than regular banners. "
ar[3] = "Don't forget to check out our other scripts. "

// join all messages to one string variable with no delimiter
var total = ar.join("")

// if message has not yet reached the left side of the status bar
if (seed > 0) {
     // assign string of seed spaces to variable
     for (var i = 0; i < seed; ++i) {
          str += " "
     }

     // append message to end of output string
     str += total

     // message moved one position to the left
     seed--

     // assign expression containing recursive call with literal
                    argument in form of string
     var cmd = "scrollBanner(" + seed + ")"

     // place computed message in status bar
     window.status = str

     // recursive call after speed milliseconds
     timerID = setTimeout(cmd, speed)
} else
     // if a substring of the total message still remains in
                    status bar
     if (-seed < total.length) {
          // assign part of message that has not slid off the left
          str += total.substring(-seed, total.length)

          // message has moved one position to the left
          seed--

          // assign expression containing recursive call with
                    literal argument in form of string
          var cmd = "scrollBanner(" + seed + ")"

          // place computed message in status bar
          window.status = str

          // recursive call after speed milliseconds
          timerID = setTimeout(cmd, speed)
```

```
            } else {
                  // assign a one-space string to status bar
                  window.status = str

                  // recursive call after speed milliseconds at initial
                                    position
                  timerID = setTimeout("scrollBanner(100)", speed)
            }
}

// -->
</SCRIPT>
</HEAD>
<BODY onLoad="scrollBanner(100)">
</BODY>
</HTML>
```

Example 18-6 (ex18-6.htm). *A regular N-banner.*

A major advantage of this banner is that is does not include any global statements and it includes only one function. Many other styles have been used to create this type of banner.

scrollBanner(seed)

The banner's speed and messages are specified as in the previous banners. A single-space string is assigned to the variable `str`. It pads the left side of the status bar by leaving a space between the border and the far left side of the message. Since this banner scrolls the messages one after the other, all messages are combined to a single string via the `join()` method of the `Array` object.

The function accepts one argument, which is assigned to the parameter `seed`. The value of `seed` determines the message's distance from the left side of the status bar. Space characters are used as space-holders. It is common to start the banner 100 spaces from the left, so the function is initially called with the value of 100.

The function chooses one of three routes. The first is selected if the value of `seed` is positive; that is, if the message has not reached the left panel of the status bar. In this case, a loop is used to concatenate a string of `seed` space characters to the variable `str`. The entire message is then concatenated to `str`. Note that if a string placed in the status bar exceeds the maximum length of the bar, the excess characters are not displayed. After concatenating the entire message to the accumulative string, the value of `seed` decrements, creating a scrolling effect on the next iteration. A recursive call is constructed in a string in the following form:

```
var cmd = "scrollBanner(" + seed + ")"
```

Suppose the value of seed is 50. The value of cmd is then "scrollBanner(50)". A literal is used here because local variables or parameters cannot be evaluated by setTimeout as arguments of a function. The accumulative string is then placed in the status bar, and the function is called recursively, following a pause of speed milliseconds.

The second route is taken if part of the message has been dropped to the left, but some of it still remains in the status bar. This state is checked via the following expression:

```
-seed < total.length
```

If the absolute value of seed exceeds the message's length, this expression evaluates to false. It means that the length of the message that has gone out of range to the left is greater or equal to the length of the message, meaning that no part of the message actually remains in the status bar. If this expression evaluates to true, only part of the message has gone past the left barrier.

If the expression above evaluates to true, the substring total.substring(-seed, total.length) is concatenated to the variable str. This substring represents the part of the message that has not gone overboard (|seed| is equal to the number of characters disposed). The remaining part of the command block is identical to the one used when the first route of the function is taken.

The third route that can be taken by the function is the most simple one. It places the value of str, a single-space string, in the status bar. It then calls the function recursively with the initial argument of 100.

Summary

This chapter introduced status bar programming. We saw how to display link-related messages in the status bar, as well as default values. We emphasized one of JavaScript's pioneer scripts, the banner. We discussed some unique banners developed exclusively for this book, as well as other common banners. In terms of JavaScript, we have discussed two properties of the window object, status and defaultStatus. Besides enabling fun stuff like banners, the status bar can be used as an additional output device for displaying critical values while debugging the script.

Chapter 19

URLs and JavaScript

A Crash Course in URLs

JavaScript features several properties and methods related to URLs. Before discussing JavaScript's support, a general description of URLs is in order.

A URL is a Uniform Resource Locator, a standard way to specify the location of an electronic resource. Its definition is derived from concepts introduced by the World Wide Web Global Information Initiative; it has been in use since 1990. URLs make Internet resources available to different Internet protocols. When surfing the net, you often run into URLs in your browser's "location" box. Such URLs usually start with "http:", but other protocols such as FTP and Gopher are also supported. Even e-mail addresses can be specified as URLs.

A URL is a very convenient, succinct way to direct people and applications to a file or other electronic resource.

General URL Syntax

In general, URLs are written as follows:

```
<scheme>:<scheme-specific-part>
```

A URL includes the name of the scheme being used, followed by a colon and a string. The characters supported as schemes are lowercase letters, "a" to "z", and the characters plus ("+"), period ("."), and hyphen ("-"). For resiliency, programs should treat uppercase letters as lowercase ones. For example, both HTTP and http should be accepted. Examples of schemes are "http," "ftp," "gopher," and "news." The scheme instructs the application or person how to treat that specific resource.

Most schemes include two different types of information:

- the Internet machine where the resource resides
- the full path to that resource

Such schemes are usually separated from the machine address by two slashes ("//"), whereas the machine address is separated from the full path via only one slash ("/"). Therefore, the common format is:

```
scheme://machine.domain/full-path-of-file
```

As an exercise, let's take a look at a simple URL:

```
http://www.geocities.com/SiliconValley/9000/index.html
```

The URL's scheme is "http," for the HyperText Transfer Protocol. The Internet address of the machine is "`www.geocities.com`," and the path to the specific file is "`SiliconValley/9000/index.html`." You will find that the path portion sometimes ends with a slash. This indicates that the path is pointing to a directory rather than a file. In this case, the server returns either a directory listing of all the files or a default file, if one is available. The default filename is either "`index.html`" or "`home.html`," but other variants are also used.

The URL Schemes

HyperText Transfer Protocol (HTTP)

HTTP is the Internet protocol specifically designed for use with the World Wide Web, and therefore is most often seen by Web surfers. Its general syntax is:

```
http://<host>:<port>/<path>?<searchpart>
```

The *host* is the Internet address of the WWW server, such as `www.geocities.com`, and the *port* is the port number to connect to. In most cases the port can be omitted along with the colon delimiter, and it defaults to the standard "80." The *path* tells the server which file is requested. The *searchpart* is very important. It may be used to pass information on to the server, often to an executable CGI script. It can also be referenced by other languages, including JavaScript as you will soon find out. Another frequently used character is the pound sign ("#"). It is used for referencing a named anchor. Anchors are often used on Web pages to enable linking from one section of the page to another one.

File Transfer Protocol (FTP)

FTP is commonly used for distributing and transmitting files over the Internet. Its general syntax is:

```
Ftp://<user>:<password>@<host>:<port>/<cwd1>/<cwd2>/.../
<cwdN>/<name>;type=<typecode>
```

When contacting a site providing anonymous login, the *user* and *password* may be omitted, including the separating colon and the following at symbol. The *host* and *port* are exactly the same as in the HTTP URL specification. The "<cwd1>/<cwd2>/.../<cwdN>" refers to the series of "change directory" (cd in Unix) commands a client must use to move from the main directory to the directory in which the desired file resides. Since most servers use Unix operating systems, you can print the working (current) directory by typing *pwd* at the command line. The name is the desired file's full name, as it is recognized by the operating system. The portion ";type=<typecode>" allows you to specify the transmission mode (ASCII vs. binary). Most systems are not configured to work properly with this trailing specification, and some are even misled by it.

Gopher Protocol (Gopher)

The Gopher protocol is not important for JavaScript scripters. Its syntax is very similar to HTTP's:

```
gopher://<host>:<port>/<gopher-path>
```

Electronic Mail (Mailto)

The Mailto URL scheme is different from the previous three schemes in that it does not identify the location of a file but rather someone's e-mail address. Its syntax differs widely as well:

```
mailto:<account@site>
```

The *account@site* is the Internet e-mail address of the person you wish to mail to. Most WWW browsers, including the leaders, Navigator and IE, support this scheme when encoded in an HTML document.

Usenet News (News)

The News URL scheme allows you to refer to Usenet newsgroups or specific articles in such a newsgroup. The syntax is either one of the following:

```
news:<newsgroup-name>
news:<message-id>
```

The *newsgroup-name* is the Usenet's newsgroup name (e.g., `comp.lang.javascript`) from which all title articles will be retrieved by the browser (a maximum number may be specified in the browser setup). *message-id* corresponds to the Message-ID of a specific article to obtain. It is found in the article's header information.

Host-Specific File Names (File)

The File URL scheme indicates a file which can be obtained by the client machine. The syntax for the File scheme is:

```
file://<host>:<path>
```

The *host* is the fully qualified domain name of the system, and the *path* is the hierarchical directory path to the required file. Leave *host* empty or specify "localhost" to refer to the client's local files.

JavaScript Statements (javascript)

The JavaScript URL scheme is quite different. Its general syntax is:

```
javascript:<valid-javascript-statement-expression-command>
```

This scheme evaluates the expression after the colon. If the expression can be evaluated to a string, a new page is opened and the string displayed. If the expression is undefined, a new page does not open.

Other Schemes

There are probably over ten other schemes that are far beyond the scope of this book. Bear in mind that we are dealing with JavaScript, so we only focus on schemes that might be needed in a script.

location Object

The `location` object represents a complete URL. Therefore, it is a property of the `window` object. As always, specifying the `window` object when referring to a property or a method of `location` is optional. Each property of the `location` object represents a different portion of the URL. The following syntax of a URL shows the relationship between the object's properties:

```
protocol//hostname:port pathname search hash
```

The location object belongs to the window containing the JavaScript script. Single-frame pages have only one `location` object. However, pages that use multiple frames consist of a `window.location` (`location`) object for each frame, as well as one for the main frameset document. For example, a page with two frames consists of three URLs, and a `location` object is available for each.

Because `window` is a default object in scripts, you can use `location` rather than `window.location`. However, if you use this object to specify an event handler script, you must specify the full `window.location`. Due to the scoping of static HTML objects in JavaScript, a call to `location` without specifying an object name is equivalent to `document.location`, which is currently a synonym for `document.URL`. You should avoid `document.location` because it will not be supported in the future.

location Properties

As you know, the `location` object consists of both properties and methods. The methods were added later, debuting in Navigator 3.0. In this section we shall take a look at the object's properties, basing the discussion on the previous section, "A Crash Course in URLs."

href

The `href` property is the most popular one in HTML scripting. The identifier "href" stands for hypertext reference. This property supplies a string of the entire URL of the calling `window` object. This property is for both reading and setting. By assigning a string to this property, you can change the URL of the page in the window. For example, if you want to load Netscape's homepage when the user clicks a button, you can use the following syntax:

```
<HTML>
<SCRIPT LANGUAGE="JavaScript">
<!--

function load() {
    location.href = 'http://www.netscape.com'
}

// -->
</SCRIPT>
<FORM>
<INPUT TYPE="button" VALUE=" load page " onClick="load()">
```

```
</FORM>
</HTML>
```

You can also retrieve the full URL of the current window (the current `window` object to be exact) by reading the URL value. For example, if you want the full URL of the current file, not including the filename itself, you can use the following script segment:

```
var url = location.href
var lastSlash = url.lastIndexOf("/")
var partialURL = url.substring(0, lastSlash + 1)
```

For example, if an HTML document with these three statements is located at <URL:http://www.geocities.com/SiliconValley/9000/links.html>, `partialURL` is the string `http://www.geocities.com/SiliconValley/9000/`. The problem with this script is that it is not guaranteed to work on a client computer running Windows and MSIE. The reason is that MS chose to stick to the regular Windows' backslash-based path syntax instead of the Unix slash-based one.

Because `href` is the most popular among the `location` object's properties, it is also the default one. That is, you can specify `location or window.location` in place of `location.href` or `window.location.href`.

Take a look at the following script:

```
var location = "Ben"
```

This statement does not generate any error because `location` is not a reserved word. However, it deletes the `location` object inside the function in which `location` is assigned. Since `location` is not a browser object but rather a simple variable, it is fully accessible from outside the function.

Microsoft Internet Explorer and Netscape Navigator deal differently with the `location.href` property, and with the `location` object in general. The following document segment stresses the difference:

```
<HTML>
<HEAD>
<TITLE>location test</TITLE>
</HEAD>
<SCRIPT LANGUAGE="JavaScript">
<!--

function load() {
     location.href = "http://www.microsoft.com"
     alert(location.href)
}
```

```
// -->
</SCRIPT>
<BODY onLoad="load()">
</BODY>
</HTML>
```

Suppose this file is located at <URL:http://www.geocities.com>. When Netscape Navigator loads a page, it holds the loaded URL in a cell somewhere in memory. Only when another page has begun loading (data is being transferred) is the value of that cell modified to match the new URL. When you read the value of `location.href`, you are reading the value of that cell. However, when you assign it a string representing another URL, the value held in that cell does not change immediately. Only if and when the page at the specified URL is found on the server is the value of the cell updated. Microsoft's browser differs in this case. When the user assigns a string to `location.href`, it automatically updates the corresponding cell in memory. Therefore, if you display the value of the property `location.href` immediately after you assign it a value, the assigned value appears. In Navigator, on the other hand, the original URL is still displayed because the file at the new URL has not been found yet. Let's sum things up. The displayed value of the preceding script on each of the leading browsers is as follows:

- Netscape Navigator—`http://www.geocities.com`
- Microsoft Internet Explorer—`http://www.microsoft.com`

Depending on your browser, the value of `location.href` may be encoded with ASCII equivalents of nonalphanumeric characters. Such characters appear as a percent sign ("`%`") followed by the ASCII code of that character. The most commonly encoded character is the space, "`%20`." You can run such URLs under the `unescape()` function to convert them to ISO Latin-1 format.

Suppose you have an HTML file named `foo.html` located in a certain directory, better known as a folder on Macs and Windows95. Loading the full path of this directory in the browser should normally show the listing of all the directory's files, provided that a default filename supported by the server is not included in that directory. You can use the following script to allow the user to view the listing of the files just by clicking a button:

```
<HTML>
<HEAD>
<TITLE>Directory listing</TITLE>
</HEAD>
<SCRIPT LANGUAGE="JavaScript">
```

```
<!--

function getListing() {
     var url = location.href
     var lastSlash = url.lastIndexOf("/")
     location.href = url.substring(0, lastSlash + 1)
}

// -->
</SCRIPT>
<BODY>
<FORM>
<INPUT TYPE="button" VALUE=" view directory listing "
onClick="getListing()">
</FORM>
</BODY>
</HTML>
```

There is no need to go over this script because its backbone was already explained. It strips off the filename and loads the string as the new URL. Once again, MSIE has problems with this script on PCs, due to the backslash versus slash URL specification differences. Here is a screen capture of a directory listing retrieved by clicking on the button:

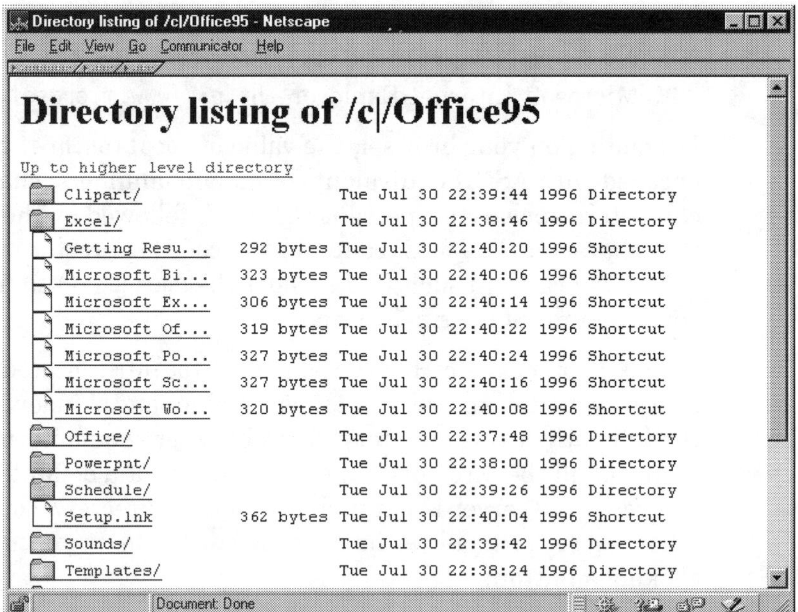

Figure 19-1. *A sample directory listing.*

hash

An anchor is a mark for other data to point to. It enables you to create a link to a specific place somewhere in a given Web page. Suppose you have a Web page that provides information on various VCR models of different brands. A user who is looking for specific information on Sony VCRs should not be penalized by having to scroll through other makes, say JVCs. Therefore, you can create a named anchor somewhere near the name Sony. An anchor is created using the following syntax:

```
<A NAME="sony1">Sony VCRs</A>
```

The text "Sony VCRs" appears on the page as normal, but it serves as an anchor. You can direct the user to "Sony VCRs" section via a simple link to the anchor, in the following fashion:

```
<A HREF="#sony1">Get information on Sony VCRs</A>
```

In this case, the link's URL is the anchor's name preceded by a hash mark (#). When the user clicks on the link "Get information on Sony VCRs," the browser automatically "scrolls" down to the anchor named "sony1" (you can't see the "scrolling" of course). You can also direct the user to that anchor from within another page. For example, suppose the full URL of the VCR page is <URL:http://www.vcr.com/information/index.html>. Now, let's say you want to provide a link from the page <URL:http://www.electronics.com/VCRlinks/new.html> to the page containing information on VCRs, and, in particular, to the Sony section. You can accomplish this task by including the URL of the VCR file, as well as the Sony anchor name, somewhere in the electronics file:

```
<A HREF=" http://www.vcr.com/information/index.html#sony1">Get
information on Sony VCRs</A>
```

This form enables you to specify the document URL as well as the specific anchor name. By specifying only the anchor name, it is assumed that the anchor resides in the current document, just as if you specify a filename without a full path, it is assumed to reside in the same directory as the HTML document. Such URL references are known as relative or partial ones.

When you click on a link to a URL containing a named anchor reference, the new URL, or location, consists of the hash mark (#) followed by the anchor name. This portion of the URL is considered a part of the URL, just like the path or filename. After linking to an anchor, user-initiated scrolling does not affect the URL (or the location.href value).

JavaScript provides a property for the current anchor reference in the URL. This property is named hash (location.hash), because anchor references are stored in a hash table. You can assign a string to location.hash in order to direct the browser to a specified anchor within the current page. Like the href property, hash is also readable. You should use this property only when dealing with local anchors residing within the current document. Suppose the following document is saved as an .html file on a server, or even on your computer:

```
<HTML>
<HEAD>
<TITLE>status bar</TITLE>
<SCRIPT LANGUAGE="JavaScript">
<!--

function loadPage() {
   location.href = "http://www.geocities.com/SiliconValley/
                    9000/index.html"
   location.hash = "authors"
}

// -->
</SCRIPT>
</HEAD>
<BODY onLoad="loadPage()">
</BODY>
</HTML>
```

The function loadPage() (called via the onLoad event handler) attempts to load the page <URL:http://www.geocities.com/SiliconValley/9000/index.html>. Since the browser does not wait until the page is loaded, the function continues to execute, advancing to the following statement. However, this statement also attempts to modify the URL of the page by specifying an anchor, via the location.hash property. Since the anchor resides on the current page, it is loaded immediately. The anchor is not found on the current page because it is on the page that was loaded before. By trying to allocate an anchor, the onLoad event handler is triggered, executing the function once again. The encountered loop is obviously infinite, and continues until the user presses the big red "stop" button. It is very important to remember not to assign location.hash separately from location.href. You must assign them at the same statement:

```
function loadPage() {
   location.href =
"http://www.geocities.com/SiliconValley/9000/index.html#authors"
}
```

When attempting to modify multiple properties of `href`, you should assign the property `href` instead, as it refers to a complete URL, including anchor references, search specifications, and all other properties of the `location` object. In general, the `location.hash` property is the only one that can be assigned separately to adjust the current anchor referencing position within the current document. Also, bear in mind that a page reload will follow the property assignment.

A common problem for beginners is that the value of the `hash` property seems to be inconsistent at times. For example, `location.hash` evaluates to an empty string if no anchor is referenced. If an anchor is specified, though, both the hash mark (#) and the anchor name are part of this property. When changing the value of an anchor, do not include the hash mark.

The following HTML document will clear up this matter:

```
<HTML>
<HEAD>
<TITLE>location.hash property</TITLE>
<SCRIPT LANGUAGE="JavaScript">
<!--

function goNext(nextAnchor) {
    location.hash = nextAnchor
}

// -->
</SCRIPT>
</HEAD>
<BODY>
<A NAME="anchor1">Top</A>
<BR>
<FORM>
<INPUT TYPE="button" VALUE="advance" onClick="goNext('anchor2')">
</FORM>
<BR>
<HR>
<BR>
<A NAME="anchor2">Middle</A>
<BR>
<FORM>
<INPUT TYPE="button" VALUE="advance" onClick="goNext('anchor3')">
</FORM>
<BR>
```

Chapter 19

```
<HR>
<BR>
<A NAME="anchor3">Bottom</A>
<BR>
<FORM>
<INPUT TYPE="button" VALUE="advance" onClick="goNext('anchor1')">
</FORM>
</BODY>
</HTML>
```

Example 19-1 (ex19-1.htm). *A script that jumps to anchors without using common links.*

In order to observe the effect of the script in Example 19-1, you must resize the browser window to make it smaller than the full document (the scroll bar should appear), because referencing a named anchor has no effect if the anchor is already in view. By clicking each of the four buttons on the page, the focus is placed on a corresponding anchor and on a different button. Clicking the fourth button scrolls the page to the first anchor and to the beginning of the page. Since HTML does not support linking form buttons to anchors, you must use JavaScript to accomplish such a task.

host

The `location.host` property is not commonly used, but we shall cover it for completeness. This property represents the `<host>:<port>` part of a URL, not only the <host> (see `location.hostname`). When the scheme is `file` and the file is local, this property is an empty string. When no port is specified, the value of `location.host` is equal to `location.hostname`, or `<host>`. Suppose the complete URL of a page is `<URL:http://www.geocities.com:80/SiliconValley/9000/index.html>`. The value of `location.host`, if queried on that page, is `www.geocities.com:80`. This value is always equal to the expression `location.hostname + ":" + location.port`. The colon is included only when a port is explicitly specified. The basic rule is that if the browser's "location" box does not include the port, it is not part of the `location.host` string.

Since "80" is considered the default port, the following function displays the full `<host>:<port>` portion of the URL:

```
function alertHost() {
     var colonIndex = location.host.lastIndexOf(":")
     var port = (colonIndex == -1) ? ":80" : ""
     alert("The complete host specification is: " + location.host + port)
}
```

If you call this function from the page <URL:http://www.geocities.com/SiliconValley/9000/index.html>, the value displayed in the alert box is www.geocities.com:80. The same value is displayed if the page is loaded directly via the full host specification: <URL:http://www.geocities.com:80SiliconValley/9000/index.html>.

hostname

The location.hostname property is almost identical to location.host, except that it does not include the port number if specified in the URL. That is, it consists of only the <host> portion of the complete URL (see the section "A Crash Course in URLs"). The location.hostname is simply the Internet address of the hosting machine. This property evaluates to www.geocities.com on the following two URLs:

```
<URL:http://www.geocities.com/SiliconValley/9000/index.html>
<URL:http://www.geocities.com:80/SiliconValley/9000/index.html>
```

pathname

The pathname component of the URL consists of a directory structure, relative to the hosting server's root volume. In terms of http, this is the <path> portion of the URL. If the file is located in the root directory of the server, the pathname property evaluates to a single slash ("/"), followed by the complete filename. The pathname property always includes the name of the file where the script is located. This property returns a nonstandard value in MSIE. When the file is on the client's computer, backslashes are used in place of slashes to separate directory names in the path.

For example, if the complete URL of the hosting document is <URL:http://www.geocities.com/SiliconValley/9000/index.html>, the value of location.pathname is "/SiliconValley/9000/index.html".

port

As expected, the location.port property holds the port number, or the <port> portion of the general URL syntax. These days, few Web sites require an explicit specification of the port number as part of their URL. When a port is not specified, it defaults to the standard "80," which is not part of the location.port property. If you intend to construct a URL from the values of the port and the hostname properties, remember to separate them with a colon.

protocol

The protocol component of a URL is more commonly known as the scheme (<scheme>). The `location.protocol` property holds the scheme component of the document's URL, followed by a colon. The scheme component should normally be "http:", but other schemes are also supported. For more information on most popular schemes, see the section "A Crash Course in URLs," at the beginning of the chapter.

You can display the "mocha:" or "javascript:" protocols by loading one of them as the URL of the document and then typing "`alert(location.protocol)`". You can also try loading the following strings as URLs instead:

- `javascript:alert(location.protocol)`
- `mocha:alert(location.protocol)`

See Chapter 5 for more information on these specific protocols (javascript: and mocha:).

search

When you submit a form, you sometimes find that the URL of the retrieved document is followed by a question mark (?) and an encoded string. For example, a typical "Yahoo" search looks like `"http://search.yahoo.com/bin/search?p=perl+book&a=n"`. The value of `location.search` is precisely that, including the question mark. Each part of the search specification (`?p=perl+book&a=n`) is usually delimited by an ampersand (&), as seen in the above string. Nonalphanumeric characters are encoded and replaced by their corresponding two-digit ASCII code, preceded by a percent sign (%). If text fields or text areas consist of space characters, then they are replaced by plus operators (+). The string following the question mark is known as the *search query,* although it does not serve as a query submitted to a search engine.

The `location.search` property may seem distant to you, but it is truly one of the most important properties supported by JavaScript. The reason for its great importance is that you can make use of it for various purposes that are not related to CGI scripts or search engines.

First of all, remember that if a search query is specified (including the question mark), the URL of the page is actually the string preceding the query. For example, you can load Intel's homepage via the URL `http://www.intel.com/index.htm?Intel+home+page` rather than the standard URL for that page, `http://www.intel.com/index.htm`. Since

Intel's page does not use any search queries, a query specification serves as a decoration only. You can load every page on the Web by entering its regular URL followed by any search query. This feature enables the usage of search queries in JavaScript. For example, you can prompt the user for his or her name, and pass it on to all other pages on your site as a search query. Along with "Cookies" (explained in Chapter 24, Implementing Cookies), the `location.search` property serves as a way to store permanent data acquired from an outside resource. The following example consists of two pages, "page1.html" and "page2.html":

```
<HTML>
<HEAD>
<TITLE>User first name input</TITLE>
</HEAD>
<BODY>
<SCRIPT LANGUAGE="JavaScript">
<!--

var usernm = prompt("Enter your first name:", "")
location.href = "page2.html?" + usernm

// -->
</SCRIPT>
</BODY>
</HTML>
```

page1.html

```
<HTML>
<HEAD>
<TITLE>User first name output</TITLE>
</HEAD>
<BODY>
<SCRIPT LANGUAGE="JavaScript">
<!--

function getQuery() {
     var query = location.search.substring(1, location.search.length)
     return query
}

alert("I know your name -- " + getQuery())

// -->
</SCRIPT>
</BODY>
</HTML>
```

page2.html

The script on “page1.html” prompts the user for his or her first name, and then, using a search query preceded by a question mark, loads “page2.html” with the input first name. The script on “page2.html” calls a function that strips off the question mark, returns the bare query, and then displays the user’s first name. The `location.search` property serves as a convenient way to pass small pieces of information between documents, as shown in this example.

Example 19-2 demonstrates the use of this property in a more complex script:

```
<HTML>
<HEAD>
<TITLE>Matches game</TITLE>
</HEAD>
<BODY>
<SCRIPT LANGUAGE="JavaScript">
<!--

// return the current search query excluding question mark
function stripQuery() {
     // assign value of location.search and length to local variables
     var search = location.search
     var length = search.length

     // if no query specified
     if (search == "")
          // return number of matches at beginning of game
          return "25"

     // strip question mark off string
     var query = search.substring(1, length)

     // return the stripped-off query
     return query
}

// print the desired row of match images
function placeMatches(num) {
     // place num matches via loop
     for (var i = 1; i <= num; ++i) {
          document.write('<A HREF="' + getURL(i, num) + '">
                         <IMG SRC="match.gif" BORDER=0></A>')
     }
}

// return computed URL for match image link
function getURL(pos, num) {
     // assign position of match in row from right
     var distance = num – pos + 1
     // e.g., 19th match among 20 in row, 20–19+1 = 2nd match from right
```

```
        // if the match is not one of the last three in row
        if (distance > 3)
             // link does not do anything
             return "javascript:alert('Choose one of last three matches')"
        // else not required because return statement terminates function

        // return number of matches needed in following load of page
        return "ex19-2.htm?" + (num - 4)
}

// number of matches to be displayed
var num = parseInt(stripQuery())

// assign instructions to variable
var instructions = ""
instructions += "The objective of the game is to force the other player "
instructions += "(the computer) to pick up the last match. On each turn "
instructions += "you may pick up some matches, but only 1, 2, or 3. The "
instructions += "computer does the exact same on its turn. Play smart, "
instructions += "or else you will be devastated."

// if no query specified
if (num == 25)
        // display instructions
        alert(instructions)


// if only one match remains
if (num == 1) {
        // print the match image and a link to enable a new game
        document.write('<IMG SRC="match.gif"><BR><BR><A HREF="ex19-
                                 2.htm">Play again?</A>')

        // tell the human he / she lost
        alert("I win -- come back when you improve!")
} else
        // impossible condition
        if (num < 1)
             // tell the user he / she cheated
             alert("You cheated!")
        else
             // place the required number of matches
             placeMatches(num)

// -->
</SCRIPT>
</BODY>
</HTML>
```

Example 19-2 (ex19-2.htm). *A simple game.*

Let's explain the rules of the game in Example 19-2. The game starts when the user first loads the page and 25 matches are displayed in a row. The user must pick up one, two, or three matches by clicking on the corresponding match. For example, to pick up only one match, the user must click on the far-right match. Clicking on the second match from the right is equivalent to picking up two matches, and the same applies to three. After the user picks up some matches, the computer plays its turn, following the same rules as the user. The objective of the game is to force the other player to pick up the last match. That is, the one who picks up the last match loses the game.

We designed this game to prove that computers are smarter than humans, because you cannot win. The real reason that it is impossible to defeat the computer is that the user makes the first move. The number of matches selected by the computer is equal to four minus the number of matches selected by the user. For example, if the user picked up two matches, the computer also picks up two. If the user selected three matches, the computer goes with one. Finally, if the user selects one match, the computer selects three. Therefore, each dual move (user and computer sequence) ends up with four matches lifted. After six dual moves, 24 (4 * 6) matches have been removed, and only one remains. It is then the user's turn, which means that the computer records another victory.

The `stripQuery()` function is very simple and has already been discussed in this chapter. It returns the search query, without the question mark. If no query is specified, then the user has not begun the game, and the returned string is defaulted to "`25`."

The `placeMatches()` function is also very simple. It accepts the number of matches to be printed and uses a loop to print the corresponding number of `match.gif` images. Each image is also a hypertext link, where the specified URL is retrieved by `getURL()` function, based on the index of the current match (a positive integer `i`) and the total number of matches that are placed (`num`).

The function `getURL()` accepts the index of a given match as well as the total number of matches to be placed. The match's index corresponding to the far-right match is assigned to the variable `distance`. For example, if there are 25 matches, and the value of `pos` is 23, the value assigned to `distance` is 25 – 23 + 1 = 3. If the assigned value is greater than three, the data of the given match indicates that it is not one of the last three matches in the row, so the returned URL is a JavaScript `alert` statement (using the "javascript:" scheme, or protocol). The function is terminated if the given match is not one of the last three, so the remaining portion applies only to matches that are one of the last three in the row. In this case, the returned URL is the bare URL of the document with a search query equal to the remaining number of matches (the current number of matches minus four, because the computer always completes the user's move to four—see explanation of algorithm).

The global statements are also a very important part of the script. At first, the query of the current page is converted from a numeric string to a number and then assigned to the variable `num`. If the value of `num` is 25, the game has just begun, and the instructions are displayed in the form of an `alert` box. If the value of `num` is 1, the game is over (the computer wins), and a corresponding message is displayed, followed by a link to restart the game by loading the current document without a query. If the value of `num` is less than 1, an impossible state has been encountered, meaning that the user has tried to cheat or override the script by modifying the search query and an `alert` box reports this finding. The game is currently under way for all other values of `num`, so the function `placeMatches()` is called to place the matches according to the given situation.

Search Utilities

You may have noticed that multiengine search utilities are beginning to rule the Web. For example, you can use one form to search Infoseek, AltaVista, and Yahoo. There are basically two ways to create such search interfaces:

- via server-side CGI scripts
- via client-side JavaScript scripts

Since CGI is beyond the scope of this book, we are going to discuss just the second method. JavaScript is a very flexible cross-platform language. You can perform a specific task with many completely different scripts. For example, you can put a long script in your page to enable a multiengine search interface. You can also place a form in the page to submit the query to another page, which contains the script. You can even call a function located in an external script to do the work.

You have probably been exposed to advanced HTML for quite a while, so you should know how forms submit. There are generally two submission methods:

- get
- post

The get method calls a specified file along with the content of the form's fields. The ACTION attribute specifies the name of the document or script to be called when the form is submitted. Take a look at the following form:

```
<FORM METHOD="get" ACTION="file1.html">
<INPUT TYPE="text" SIZE=50 NAME="userid">
<INPUT TYPE="text" SIZE=30 NAME="passwd">
<INPUT TYPE="submit" VALUE="submit form">
</FORM>
```

This construct creates a form with three elements. The first two are simple text boxes, or fields. The latter is a submit button, which triggers the submission. That is, when the user clicks the button, the form is submitted according to the ACTION of the METHOD. Suppose the user enters "input of first box" in the first field, and "input of second box" in the second field, and then clicks the "submit form" button. The form is submitted. In this case the method is "get," so the browser "gets" the specified file, "file1.html." Nevertheless, the file is retrieved including a search query. The full URL retrieved by the browser in this case is <URL:file1.html?**userid=**input+of+first+box&**passwd=** input+of+second+box>. Notice that each value in the search query is separated by an ampersand. In addition, the value entered by the user in each field, or the element's value in general, is preceded by the element's name followed by an equal sign (=). The constructed URL is loaded, and the search query can be used if the loaded file is an HTML document with a JavaScript script. Now let's take a look at an actual example:

```
<HTML>
<HEAD>
<TITLE>Multiple engine search</TITLE>
</HEAD>
<BODY>
<FORM METHOD="get" ACTION="ex19-3b.htm">
  <STRONG><FONT SIZE=+1>Search</FONT> the Web for information
                        about:</STRONG>
  <BR>
  <INPUT TYPE="text" SIZE=40 MAXLENGTH=80 VALUE="" NAME="query">
  <BR>
  <STRONG>via the </STRONG>
  <SELECT NAME="engine" ALIGN="right">
    <OPTION VALUE="altavista" SELECTED>AltaVista
    <OPTION VALUE="excite">Excite
    <OPTION VALUE="infoseek">Infoseek
```

```
      <OPTION VALUE="lycos">Lycos
      <OPTION VALUE="magellan">Magellan
      <OPTION VALUE="yahoo">Yahoo
    </SELECT>
    <STRONG>engine. Click </STRONG>
    <INPUT TYPE="submit" VALUE="search">
  </FORM>
  </BODY>
  </HTML>
```

Example 19-3a (ex19-3a.htm). *The search interface can be added to any page.*

This form is a bit more complex than the previous one we have explained. It consists of two value-contributing elements, a field (text box) and a `SELECT` object, enabling the user to choose an option from a list. The value of the selected `OPTION` is the contributed value of the `SELECT` element. Take a look at the following image which demonstrates a possible user input:

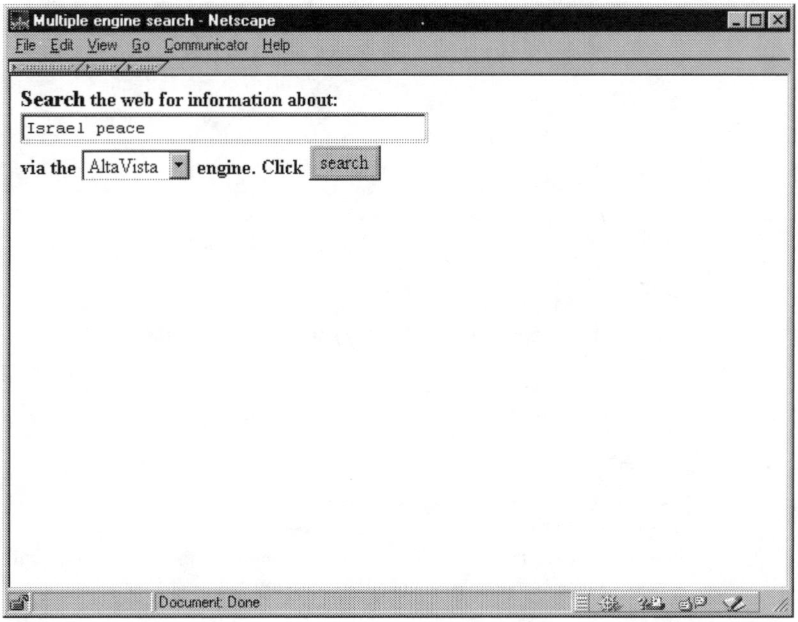

Figure 19-2. *A sample input.*

For the output demonstrated in Figure 19-2, the loaded URL is `<URL:ex19-3b.htm?query=Tomer+JavaScript&engine=infoseek>`. The name of the text box element is "query" which is the first substring of the loaded URL's search query. The value in this case is "`Tomer JavaScript`," where all space characters are replaced by plus signs—this is the common encoding. The submitted form includes the

SELECT object as well. Its name is "engine" and it follows the delimiting ampersand. Its value is the selected OPTION, "infoseek." You now understand all the components of the retrieved URL, so we can go on to analyze the script itself.

First of all, here is the source for <URL:ex19-3b.htm>:

```
<HTML>
<HEAD>
<TITLE>Please wait</TITLE>
<SCRIPT LANGUAGE="JavaScript">
<!--

// create object of all prefixes
var prefix = new prefixObject()

// create object of query prefixes
function prefixObject() {
        // lycos prefix
        this.lycos = "http://www.lycos.com/cgi-bin/pursuit?query="

        // altavista prefix
        this.altavista = "http://www.altavista.digital.com/
                                cgi-bin/query?pg=q&q="

        // infoseek prefix
        this.infoseek = "http://guide-p.infoseek.com//Titles?qt="

        // yahoo prefix
        this.yahoo = "http://av.yahoo.com/bin/search?p="

        // magellan prefix
        this.magellan = "http://searcher.mckinley.com/searcher.cgi?query="

        // excite prefix
        this.excite = "http://www.excite.com/search.gw?search="
}

// execute search
function callSearch() {
        // create array to hold search engine and search query
        var queryArray = location.search.split("=")

        // assign search query
        var query = queryArray[1].substring(0, queryArray[1].indexOf("&"))

        // assign search engine
        var engine = queryArray[2]

        // load the desired page to display search results
        location.href = prefix[engine] + query
```

```
}

// -->

</SCRIPT>
</HEAD>
<BODY BGCOLOR="white" onLoad="timerID = setTimeout('callSearch()', 3000)">
<CENTER>
<BR>
<B>P<FONT SIZE=-1>LEASE </FONT>W<FONT SIZE=-1>AIT...</FONT></B>
<BR>
<BR>
Click the button to terminate search...
<FORM>
<INPUT TYPE="button" VALUE="terminate search"
onClick="clearTimeout(timerID)">
</FORM>
</CENTER>
</BODY>
</HTML>
```

Example 19-3b (ex19-3b.htm). *The script that interprets the user's input and calls the appropriate search engine.*

The script consists of only two functions. The first one, `prefixObject()`, is a constructor. It creates an object whose properties are the query prefixes for the supported search engines. A query prefix is the URL by which a query can be submitted to a search engine. The prefix is followed by the encoded inquiry (e.g., the user's keywords). For example, you can look up the keywords "Tomer JavaScript" in Infoseek by loading `<URL:http://guide-p.infoseek.com//Titles?qt=Tomer+JavaScript>`. Each search engine has its own unique prefix, so the prefix for each of the supported engines must be explicitly specified. The constructor function `prefixObject()` assigns each prefix to a property, named according to the search engine with which the prefix is associated. For example, Infoseek's prefix is assigned to a property named `infoseek` in the following fashion:

```
this.infoseek = "http://guide-p.infoseek.com//Titles?qt="
```

If you know the prefixes, you can easily extend the script to support additional search engines. It is not difficult to find such a prefix—just run a normal search on the desired engine and then extract the desired prefix. Since prefixes are sufficient for most engines, suffixes are only occasionally used. Search engines' prefixes are subject to change and should be maintained by the script owner (Webmaster).

The global variable prefix is an instance of this object, so its properties are the search engines' prefixes.

The callSearch() function is also very simple. At first, it assigns the encoded user input (keywords) to the variable query. It also assigns the selected search engine to the variable engine. The expression prefix[engine] is equal to the selected search engine's prefix, because the values of the form's OPTIONs (see Example 19-3a) are equivalent to the names of the properties used in this script. The expressions stored in prefix[engine]and query are combined to construct the full desired URL. The combined string is then loaded as the new URL via assignment to the location.href property. See Chapter 16, Handling Strings, and Chapter 13, Arrays, for more information on string and array handling.

You have probably noticed that the function is not called as an immediate script. It is called via the onLoad event handler, which delays the execution until the page has finished loading. In this case, a setTimeout statement is used to delay the execution another three seconds, giving the user a chance to terminate the process. This is extremely important, especially if the user is surfing in "reverse" using the Back button.

A form consisting of a single button is used to clear the timeout via the clearTimeout() method, which is handed the identifier of the initial timeout. The user can click this button to terminate the search process before the specified search engine is actually called.

location Methods

The location object (window.location) also consists of a several methods. These methods are not supported by Microsoft Internet Explorer 3.0 or Netscape Navigator 2.0x. They will surely be supported in future releases of MSIE and are already featured in Navigator 3.0.

reload

The location.reload method forces a reload of the window's current document. Its general syntax is:

```
location.reload([true])
```

Specifying the Boolean value true as the method's optional argument forces an unconditional HTTP GET of the document from the server. An unconditional GET retrieves a document directly from the server, ignoring the content of the browser's cache, which might already contain the desired data from that document. Therefore, `true` specification should not be used unless you have reason to believe that either disk or memory cache is broken, or the server has a new version of the document. If such a version is available, you must force an unconditional HTTP GET because the version of the document stored in cache is different from the new version on the server. This situation is common to CGI-generated documents.

The `reload()` method simply reloads the document its URL stored in `location.href`. It uses the same policy as the "reload" or "refresh" button. Microsoft has opted to label the button "refresh" rather than "reload," but will probably keep the same method names. The exact reload policy depends on the cache handling menu option. In Netscape Navigator, the user sets the default value of this policy by choosing Network Preferences from the Options menu, and specifying Verify Documents on the Cache tab of the Preferences dialog box.

The `reload()` method does not force a transaction with the server under normal conditions. However, if the user has set the preference to "Every Time," the request is an unconditional GET using an "if-modified-since" HTTP header. HTTP headers are passed to the browser when a document is retrieved from the server. It contains important information regarding the current document. If the user sets the preference to "Every Time," the browser checks the transmitted HTTP header to see if the document has been updated according to the "last-modified time" property. If it has, the document cannot be loaded from the cache which holds a previous version of the file. In short, `reload()` will bring the cache's version unless the user has specified "Every Time" and (&&) the document has changed on the server since the last time it was loaded and saved in the cache. Since its size is limited, the cache might lose a document version that has not been reloaded for a long time. In this case, the document needs to be fully loaded from the server, even if it has not been changed since the previous load.

In event handlers, you must specify `window.location.reload()` instead of simply using `location.reload()`. Due to the static objects' scoping in JavaScript, a call to `location` without specifying an object name is equivalent to a call to `document.location`, which is a synonym for `document.URL`. This concept is explained later in the chapter in greater detail.

You have probably experienced situations in which you leave your computer connected to a host and go out for a break, then come back to find that the connection has been dumped. The usual cause is that the host (server) has disconnected you because you have not transmitted any data via the server for a long time. You can overcome this problem by periodically reloading a JavaScript document from the server. Next time you go out for lunch, load the following document in the browser's window:

```
<HTML>
<HEAD>
<TITLE>stay connected</TITLE>
</HEAD>
<!-- 200000 milliseconds == 200 seconds -->
<BODY onLoad="timerID = setTimeout('window.location.reload(true)',
                                   200000)">
</BODY>
</HTML>
```

Example 19-4 (ex19-4.htm). *A simple HTML document keeps the connection alive.*

The `onLoad` event handler is used to call the `reload()` method. A `setTimeout()` method delays the reload procedure for 200,000 milliseconds, or 200 seconds, from the moment the document is completely loaded. Since it is used in the form of an event handler, the `reload()` method must be fully specified, including the `window` object reference. The `true` argument forces the transaction with the server.

replace

The `replace()` method is also a property of the `location`, or `window.location`, object. It overwrites the current history entry with the specified URL. The current history entry is the most recent URL added to the history list, or the URL of previous page loaded. This is the URL that is retrieved when the user presses Back, provided that the "forward" button is dimmed out. The general syntax of the `replace()` method is as follows:

```
location.replace("URL")
```

After the `replace()` method is used, the user cannot navigate to the previous URL via the Back button. Once again, bear in mind that event handlers require a full method specification.

Suppose you want the user to load page B by clicking a link on page A. Instead of using a plain hypertext link, you can invoke this method to load page B (using the URL of page B as the argument). Once page B has loaded, the user cannot return to page A via the Back button.

Another Location—document.location (document.URL)

So far, any reference to the `location` object defaulted to `window.location`. But, there is another `location` in JavaScript—`document.location`. To avoid confusion, Netscape decided to change `document.location` to `document.URL`. Although Navigator 3.0 supports both references, Netscape has announced that the `document.location` property reference will not be supported by future releases. Microsoft's Internet Explorer 3.0 supports only `document.location`. In this chapter, we are following Netscape's decision to use `document.URL`.

The property `document.URL` holds the complete URL of the current document. In contrast to `window.location(.href)`, it is a read-only value. It does not know windows from frames but just the document that contains the script and the reference to this property. Keep in mind that the URL belongs to the document, not to the window. Therefore, when a window consists of multiple documents including frame structures, a single frame's `document.URL` is different from `window.location(.href)`, from any other frame's `document.URL`, and from the main frame set's `document.URL`.

If you want to load a new document into the browser's window, you have to use the write-enabled `window.location (==window.location.href)`. If you want the URL of a specific frame, you should use `document.URL`. You can also use this property to retrieve the URL of the window if the document does not have frames and you are sure you do not want to change the URL (to load another page).

Since `document.location` is still in use (especially with MSIE 3.0), you must be very careful when using the `location` property. If you are not a very experienced scripter or do not fully understand the object scoping in JavaScript, it is a good practice to always specify the calling object, `window` or `document`. When you refer to `location` in a script, it defaults to `window.location`, because `window` is the default object inside scripts. However, when you specify the bare `location` in an event handler script, the calling object defaults to `document`; that is, `location` defaults to `document.location`.

> **Important rule:**
>
> Although the `href` property is the default one, always use `location.href` to refer to the URL of the window. If you follow this rule, trying to specify `location.href` for a document will generate an easy-to-fix error. If you just use `location` rather than `location.href`, it will be accepted by both windows and documents and you will have a hard time debugging the problem.

Summary

In this chapter we discussed JavaScript's URLs. At first, we introduced common URL terms, including the various supported schemes (`http`, `ftp`, `gopher`, etc.). We then presented the `window.location` object with all its properties and methods. The `href` property is used to link documents to each other. We have also discussed a URL-processing-based multiple-engine search utility. We have introduced another URL-related element, the `document.URL` property, also known as `document.location`. You should be mastering URL handling by now, because we will move on to more advanced URL-related concepts, such as frames, later in the book.

Chapter 20

Using the History List

What is a History List?

As you surf the Web, you will load many different pages, each with its own URL. The browser maintains a list of the most recent URLs, which can be viewed with ease in both Navigator and IE, as demonstrated in the following figures:

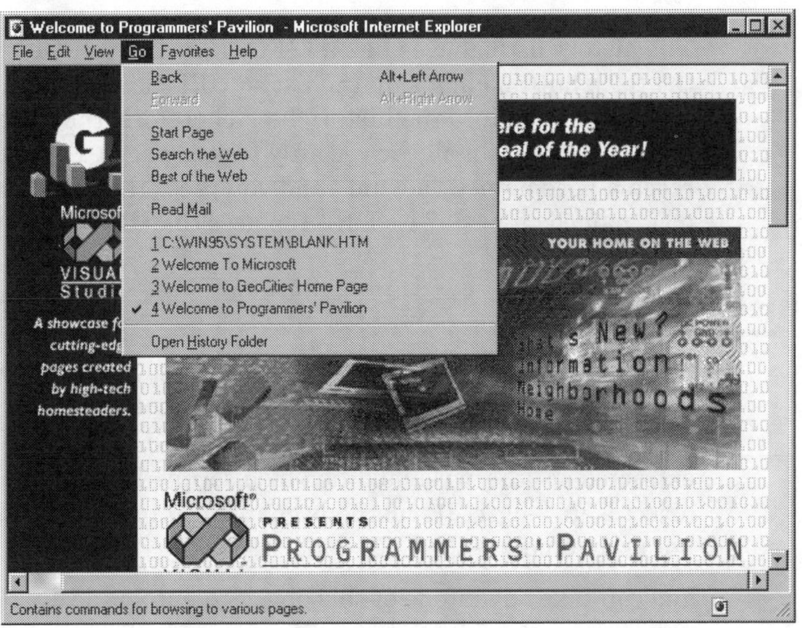

Figure 20-1.
IE's history list.

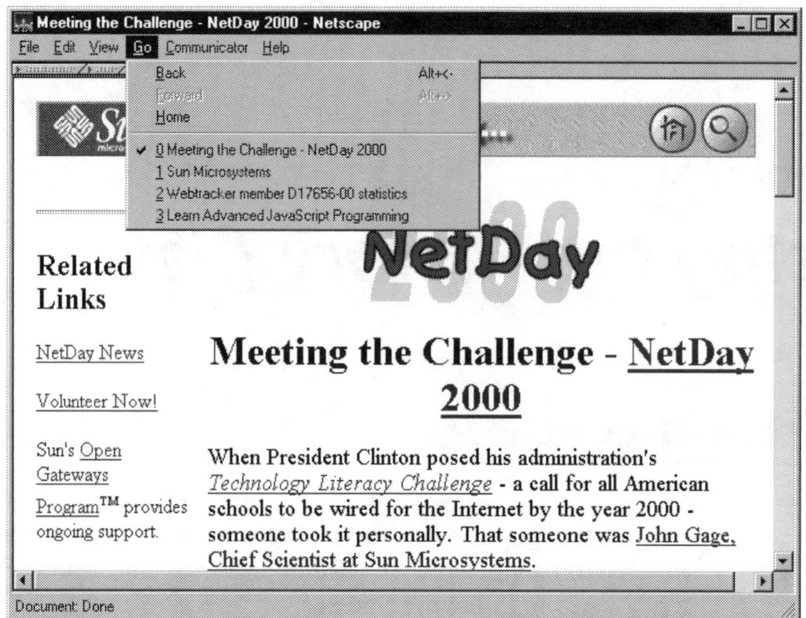

Figure 20-2. Navigator's history list.

The history list behaves like a LIFO (Last In First Out) queue, where the Back button climbs up the list so URLs loaded by the Back button are not entered into the history list. Therefore, the history list does not always contain all the recently visited pages. For example, if you reach a page named "a.html" and you press the Back button to load a page named "b.html," its URL replaces the URL of "a.html."

The history Object

The history list is represented in JavaScript by the `window.history` object. This object lets you deal with the history list but not with its exact data. That is, actual URLs maintained in that list cannot be extracted or otherwise modified by a script. The only property of this object is its length. Its methods enable you to load the list's entries but not to manipulate the URL explicitly.

You can take advantage of this object to automatically navigate the user's browser backwards, as if possessed by spirits. Another possible application is to create the equivalent of the browser's Back button directly in the document.

Since the `history` object is a property of the topmost `window` object, you have the option to refer to it as `window.history` or simply `history`.

History List Length

You can access the number of entries in the history list via the history.length property. It works exactly like the strings' and arrays' length property. You can use this property to find how many pages the user has visited lately:

```
// display message according to number of entries
if (history.length > 10)
     alert("You've already accessed " + history.length + " Web
                           pages this session")
else
     alert("You've only accessed " + history.length + " Web pages
                           this session")
```

This script displays an alert message which depends on the number of entries in the history list.

History List Entry Indexing

Like in arrays, each entry of the history list has an index, which differentiates it from the other elements of the list. However, the indexing method is quite different from character indexing in strings, or element indexing in arrays. As opposed to these indexing algorithms, the history list indexing scheme does not feature a minimum value. The index of the document currently loaded into the browser's window is 0. The index of the document that was loaded before the current document, the one that can be reached by pressing the Back button, is –1. The document before that is indexed at –2, and so on. Similarly, documents that were first loaded after the current document are indexed positively. The index of the first document loaded after the current one, the one that can be retrieved via the Forward button, is 1. The following one is indexed at 2, and so on. The complete index resembles an axis with no limit at both ends.

The history list is dynamic (changes rapidly) because whenever the page in the browser's window is replaced by a new document, the current entry becomes the previous one, and a new document takes its place. The desired shifting in terms of indexing is performed automatically by the browser, so you don't have to worry about it.

Since most people tend to surf different places at different times, the content of the history list almost never repeats itself. You might think that by creating a very structured site, you can control the way the user surfs your site and thus be able to forecast the content of the history list. This is generally impossible, and you should not even try to do it.

history Methods

You can implement the history object's methods in your script to enable the user to navigate among the list's URLs. You cannot access the string value of any URL, but you can load any of them into the browser's window.

back

This method performs the same action as the Back button in the browser's toolbar. It loads the most recent entry in the history list—the entry with index –1. The following HTML tags can be used to create a Back button in a Web page:

```
<FORM>
<INPUT TYPE="button" VALUE="Back" onClick="history.back()">
</FORM>
```

forward

The history.forward method is equivalent to the Forward button in the browser's toolbar. It loads the entry with index 1. It is less useful than the preceding method because the current document is usually the most recent in the list, so there is no URL that can be loaded when this method is invoked. You must take special precautions when using this method, because it normally does not have any effect. It should be used only when you are sure that you have full control over the user's navigational path. The following sequence creates a Forward button for a Web page:

```
<FORM>
<INPUT TYPE="button" VALUE="Back" onClick="history.back()">
</FORM>
```

go

The go method is also one of those less useful methods featured in JavaScript. It enables you to load a history list entry in the browser's window. You must have full control over the user's navigating path in order to implement this method for useful purposes.

This method accepts one argument. The most basic argument is the index of the history list that you want to retrieve. This can be any integer number which has a corresponding history list entry. If the argument is 0, the current page is loaded, or better said, reloaded. For example, the following call is equivalent to invoking the `history.back()` method:

```
history.go(-1)
```

When you want to jump back to the entry with index –1, use `history.go(-1)` rather than `history.back()`, because, among other reasons, you can just change the argument in order to jump back a few steps instead of only one. The same applies to `history.forward()`, which is equivalent to the following call:

```
history.go(1)
```

Also bear in mind that this method does not return any value but causes immediate navigation.

Alternatively, you can specify one of the URLs as the argument of this method. A portion of the desired URL is also sufficient, provided that it is a unique substring of only one entry. In both cases, the specified string (literal or value) is compared against all entries, and the one whose URL includes the specified substring will be loaded.

Unfortunately, you cannot extract the URL, just load it. The following script segment retrieves Netscape's homepage (www.netscape.com or home.netscape.com) if it is resident in the history list:

```
<FORM>
<INPUT TYPE="button" VALUE="Go" onClick="history.go('netscape.com')">
</FORM>
```

The following call reloads the current document:

```
history.go(0)
```

Netscape Navigator 3.0x and above provide an explicit and more advanced method for reloading documents: `location.reload()`.

Security Aspects of the history Object

It would be very useful to be able to extract and process URLs which reside in the history list. For security reasons, this functionality has been excluded thus far. First of all, nobody should use the back door to know where the user has been and, secondly, data can be easily submitted from the client to the server via e-mail. Netscape has solved the e-mail breach of security by displaying a warning whenever an e-mail is sent (other than that sent explicitly by the user from the mail window). Netscape's solution is not foolproof since the user might have disabled this warning, might not pay attention, or might ignore it altogether. Figure 20-3 shows the warning:

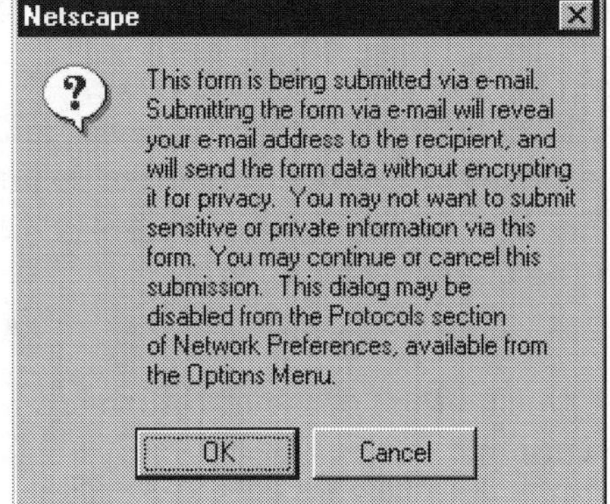

Figure 20-3. *A warning generated when the user submits a form via JavaScript or a Submit button.*

The problem with the history list's entries is that they contain complete URLs. A URL may contain extremely confidential information, especially in the form of a search query. For example, the user might have recently submitted a form with a field containing a credit card number. The form may have loaded another page with a search query containing the credit card number.

Credit card numbers or other secure information may be revealed and gleaned by malicious individuals.

Summary

This chapter focused on JavaScript's `window.history` object. Since this object is not important and does not have many uses, we kept the discussion short. The most important property of the object is the `go` method. Besides having a unique functionality of its own, the `go` method can replace all other `history` methods. Because it is closely related to URLs, the history-related function `replace` is discussed in the previous chapter. The following chapters describe various concepts of JavaScript's object model.

Chapter 21

The document Object—Colors, Output, and Properties

The document Object

The `document` object is a property of the `window` object. Every `window` object, whether it is a full browser window, a frame, or a JavaScript-generated window, has a `document` property. The `document` object encapsulates everything that exists in the content region of the browser's window or frame. It is the parent object of the Web page's content, including links, anchors, colors, titles, and so forth. The `document` object's properties are spread over the entire HTML document. Some are commonly placed in the Head portion, while others are normally found in its Body portion. The `document` object does not consist of any event handlers. You might have thought that `onLoad`, `onUnload`, and `onError` belong to this object, but they are actually properties of the `window` object.

Not all `document` object's properties are HTML-driven content. For example, the `lastModified` property provides the date on which the document was last modified, even though this date is not provided explicitly in the document but rather in the document's unseen header.

The `document` object groups many content-related properties, such as text color, background color, and others. It also includes more complex properties which are actually objects, such as forms, links, and image maps.

The title Property

The document's title is set by default to its complete URL. Most Web page authors replace this title with their own text. It is specified in the <TITLE></TITLE> tag pair in the Head portion. The title, which usually appears in the title bar, also identifies the browser in the operating system's environment. When the Web page includes frames, the title bar displays the title of the document which contains the frameset. Documents providing the content of the frames may include their own titles, but they don't affect the title bar.

The document's title can be scripted via JavaScript as well. Its general reference is `document.title`. If the document does not make up the main browser window, the reference must be preceded by the specific `window` to which the document belongs. The title of a frame document is also accessible via JavaScript, using the same procedure.

The `document.title` property cannot be set by just any JavaScript script, but only during construction of the entire document. You can use the `title` property in many different ways. Suppose you want your document to have a large header containing the document's title. Here is such a page's outline:

```
<HTML>
<HEAD>
<TITLE>Tomer Shiran's Home Page</TITLE>
</HEAD>
<BODY>
<SCRIPT LANGUAGE="JavaScript">
<!--

document.write("<CENTER><H1>" + document.title + "</H1></CENTER>")

// -->
</SCRIPT>
</BODY>
</HTML>
```

If you do not include the <TITLE></TITLE> tag pair, the title defaults to the complete URL of the document, including any search query, if one is specified. If you place the <TITLE></TITLE> tag pair without text in between, the title still defaults to the URL. If the text between the opening and closing tags does not include any characters but one or more space characters, the document is assumed untitled, and `document.title` remains an empty string, or a space-filled string in the case of Microsoft Internet Explorer. The property `document.title` never evaluates to the URL, unless you specifically write the URL between the <TITLE></TITLE> tags.

Because the value of the title bar also identifies the browser application in the operating system environment, neither Netscape nor Microsoft have made it possible to explicitly modify it. Since it would not make any sense to identify an application as scrolling text, for example, the value of the title bar can be assigned only via the `document.title` property.

Colors

JavaScript supports several Web page color properties, such as background colors and activated link colors. They are all constructed by the same method. There are generally two ways to construct color specifications:

- Netscape color names
- hexadecimal triplets

The tendency among Web page designers is to use Netscape color name specification, which is more intuitive and easier to maintain. For example, you can set the document's background color in the following fashion:

```
<BODY BGCOLOR="white">
```

Before Netscape implemented such color names, and Microsoft followed suit, the only way to specify a color was via hexadecimal triplets. These are still supported, so you can set the background color to white, for instance, in the following way:

```
<BODY BGCOLOR="#ffffff">
```

As you can see, the triplet is constructed of three two-digit hexadecimal numbers. They represent the red, green, and blue elements of the color descriptor. In total, there are approximately 17 million combinations, which is equal to the number of colors supported by a typical Macintosh or SVGA color display. However, Netscape uses a much more limited color cube. The cube consists of all the combinations of 00, 33, 66, 99, CC, and FF for each of the color descriptors. The result is 216 (6 * 6 * 6) distinct colors. The cube occasionally varies. On Macs, it includes the full 256-color palette. On X-Windows systems, if more than 40 (256-216) colors are already in use, the cube is minimized to only 125 (5 * 5 * 5) colors. For now, we shall base our discussion on the standard 216-color cube. Many more colors that are the result of dithering, or mixing, are beyond the standard cube.

An HTML document may consist of several color specifications. The following script segment demonstrates them:

```
<BODY
     [BGCOLOR="#backgroundColor"]
     [TEXT="#foregroundColor"]
     [LINK="#unfollowedLinkColor"]
     [ALINK="#activatedLinkColor"]
     [VLINK="#followedLinkColor"]>
</BODY>
```

All color attributes are scripted via JavaScript as properties of the `document` object.

bgColor

The `document.bgColor` property is expressed as a hexadecimal RGB triplet or as one of the string literals listed at the end of the book. This property is the JavaScript reflection of the BGCOLOR attribute of the <BODY> tag. You can change the background color at any time, even via a deferred script. If you express the color as a hexadecimal RGB triplet, you must use the format *rrggbb* (case insensitive).

The `bgColor` property is a commonly scripted property. You can set it to create fade effects, color cubes, and so forth, as will be demonstrated in this chapter. The following script creates a Netscape color cube and sets the background color to the one the user selected from the cube. Here is the script:

```
<HTML>
<HEAD>
<TITLE>Netscape color cube</TITLE>
</HEAD>
<BODY>
<SCRIPT LANGUAGE="JavaScript">
<!--

// create 6-element array
var hex = new Array(6)

// assign non-dithered descriptors
hex[0] = "FF"
hex[1] = "CC"
hex[2] = "99"
hex[3] = "66"
hex[4] = "33"
hex[5] = "00"
```

```
// accept triplet string and display as background color
function display(triplet) {
     // set color as background color
     document.bgColor = '#' + triplet

     // display the color hexadecimal triplet
     alert('Background color is now ' + triplet)
}

// draw a single table cell based on all descriptors
function drawCell(red, green, blue) {
     // open cell with specified hexadecimal triplet background color
     document.write('<TD BGCOLOR="#' + red + green + blue + '">')

     // open a hypertext link with javascript: scheme to call
                                display function
     document.write('<A HREF="javascript:display(\'' + (red +
                                green  + blue) + '\')">')

     // print transparent image (use any height and width)
     document.write('<IMG SRC="place.gif" BORDER=0 HEIGHT=12  WIDTH=12>')

     // close link tag
     document.write('</A>')

     // close table cell
     document.write('</TD>')
}

// draw table row based on red and blue descriptors
function drawRow(red, blue) {
     // open table row
     document.write('<TR>')

     // loop through all non-dithered color descripters as green hex
     for (var i = 0; i < 6; ++i) {
          drawCell(red, hex[i], blue)
     }

     // close current table row
     document.write('</TR>')
}

// draw table for one of six color cube panels
function drawTable(blue) {
     // open table (one of six cube panels)
     document.write('<TABLE CELLPADDING=0 CELLSPACING=0 BORDER=0>')

     // loop through all non-dithered color descripters as red hex
     for (var i = 0; i < 6; ++i) {
          drawRow(hex[i], blue)
```

```
          }

          // close current table
          document.write('</TABLE>')
          }

     // draw all cube panels inside table cells
     function drawCube() {
          // open table
          document.write('<TABLE CELLPADDING=5 CELLSPACING=0 BORDER=1><TR>')

          // loop through all non-dithered color descripters as blue hex
          for (var i = 0; i < 6; ++i) {
               // open table cell with white background color
               document.write('<TD BGCOLOR="#FFFFFF">')

               // call function to create cube panel with hex[i] blue hex
               drawTable(hex[i])

               // close current table cell
               document.write('</TD>')
          }

          // close table row and table
          document.write('</TR></TABLE>')
     }

     // call function to begin execution
     drawCube()

     // -->
     </SCRIPT>
     </BODY>
     </HTML>
```

Example 21-1 (ex21-1.htm)*. A Netscape color cube.*

This script basically prints tables. Each table cell contains a transparent image which defines the size of the cell. Each cell is also assigned a background color which determines the color that fills that cell. When you click on the image, the hexadecimal triplet is displayed via an `alert` box, and the background color is set to the selected color.

The main outline of the cube is a table with one row and six cells (columns). Each cell contains a table of all non-dithered colors with a given blue descriptor. There are six tables in total, one for each of the non-dithered colors: 00, 33, 66, 99, CC, FF. Since there are six non-dithered hexadecimal values, each table is 6 x 6: Each row presents a red hexadecimal value and each column represents a green one.

The final output can be viewed in the following screen:

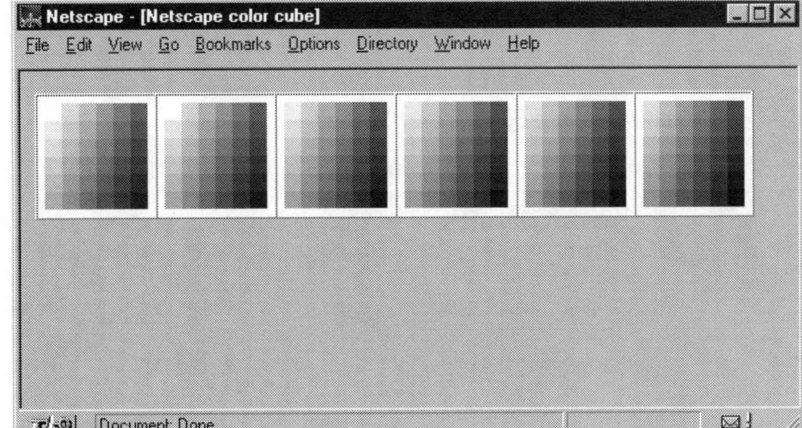

Figure 21-1. Sorry folks, graphics in the book are limited to black and white.

Now let's analyze the script itself.

Global Statements

```
// create 6-element array
var hex = new Array(6)

// assign non-dithered descriptors
hex[0] = "FF"
hex[1] = "CC"
hex[2] = "99"
hex[3] = "66"
hex[4] = "33"
hex[5] = "00"
```

A six-element array is created as an instance of the `Array` object. The elements of the array are assigned the six values from which the 216 non-dithered colors, which are supported on all platforms, can be combined. The `drawCube()` function call at the end of the script is also global.

display(triplet)

```
// accept triplet string and display as background color
function display(triplet) {
     // set color as background color
     document.bgColor = '#' + triplet

     // display the color hexadecimal triplet
     alert('Background color is now ' + triplet)
}
```

This function's single argument is a six-character string representing the hexadecimal RGB triplet of a color. The document's background color is set, and an `alert` dialog box displays the selected color's exact RGB triplet.

drawCell(red, green, blue)

```
// draw a single table cell based on all descriptors
function drawCell(red, green, blue) {
     // open cell with specified hexadecimal triplet background color
     document.write('<TD BGCOLOR="#' + red + green + blue + '">')

     // open a hypertext link with javascript: scheme to call
                         display function
     document.write('<A HREF="javascript:display(\'' + (red + green  +
                         blue) + '\')">')

     // print transparent image (use any height and width)
     document.write('<IMG SRC="place.gif" BORDER=0 HEIGHT=12
     WIDTH=12>')

     // close link tag
     document.write('</A>')

     // close table cell
     document.write('</TD>')
}
```

This function accepts three arguments: the red, green, and blue descriptors. It creates a table cell with the combined triplet as the background color. The content of each cell is a gif89 transparent image, `place.gif`. The image's height and width specification determines the size of each cell. Each image is also a hypertext link to a "`javascript:`"-scheme URL, which calls the `display()` function. The argument to this function is a hexadecimal triplet which is also used for the cell's background. Note that all global array's descriptors are strings, so the plus sign is used to concatenate the three double-digit hexadecimal values.

drawRow(red, blue)

```
// draw table row based on red and blue descriptors
function drawRow(red, blue) {
     // open table row
     document.write('<TR>')

     // loop through all non-dithered color descriptors as green hex
     for (var i = 0; i < 6; ++i) {
          drawCell(red, hex[i], blue)
     }
```

```
        // close current table row
        document.write('</TR>')
}
```

This function accepts the red and blue descriptors and prints a table row. The content of the table is created by six calls to the `drawCell()` function, passing the red and blue descriptors "as is" and a different green descriptor (from the global `hex` array) on each call.

drawTable(blue)

```
// draw table for one of six color cube panels
function drawTable(blue) {
        // open table (one of six cube panels)
        document.write('<TABLE CELLPADDING=0 CELLSPACING=0 BORDER=0>')

        // loop through all non-dithered color descriptors as red hex
        for (var i = 0; i < 6; ++i) {
                drawRow(hex[i], blue)
        }

        // close current table
        document.write('</TABLE>')
}
```

This function is very similar to the `drawRow()` function. The only difference is that it draws a 6 x 6 table, instead of a 6 x 1 row. It calls the `drawRow()` function six times, each time with a different red descriptor. All table attributes are set to 0 in order to avoid boundaries between the cells, making the impression of gradually changing colors across the cube.

drawCube()

```
// draw all cube panels inside table cells
function drawCube() {
        // open table
        document.write('<TABLE CELLPADDING=5 CELLSPACING=0  BORDER=1><TR>')

        // loop through all non-dithered color descripters as blue hex
        for (var i = 0; i < 6; ++i) {
                // open table cell with white background color
                document.write('<TD BGCOLOR="#FFFFFF">')

                // call function to create cube panel with hex[i] blue hex
                drawTable(hex[i])

                // close current table cell
                document.write('</TD>')
        }
```

```
     // close table row and table
     document.write('</TR></TABLE>')
}
```

Unlike all other functions, this one does not accept any arguments. It creates the outline table of a single six-cell row with a white background color. The function calls `drawTable()` six times, once for each given blue descriptor. Setting the `CELLPADDING` attribute to a positive number separates the tables between themselves.

Another classic example that takes advantage of the ability to set background colors via JavaScript is a script that creates a fade-in or fade-out effect when the page is loaded or unloaded. Here is the script:

```
<HTML>
<HEAD>
<TITLE>Fade in and out</TITLE>
<SCRIPT LANGUAGE="JavaScript">
<!--

// convert decimal value (0 - 255) to hexadecimal
// (use .toString(16) method supported by IE)
function toHex(dec) {
     // create list of hex characters
     var hexCharacters = "0123456789ABCDEF"

     // if number is out of range return limit
     if (dec < 0)
          return "00"
     if (dec > 255)
          return "FF"

     // decimal equivalent of first hex character in converted number
     var i = Math.floor(dec / 16)

     // decimal equivalent of second hex character in converted number
     var j = dec % 16

     // return hexadecimal equivalent
     return hexCharacters.charAt(i) + hexCharacters.charAt(j)
}

// set background color to specified descriptors
function setbgColor(red, green, blue) {
      document.bgColor = "#" + toHex(red) + toHex(green) + toHex(blue)
}

// fade from start to end descriptors (increase step to increase
                              transition speed)
function fade(sred, sgreen, sblue, ered, egreen, eblue, step) {
```

```
        // loop to create fade effect
        for(var i = 0; i <= step; ++i) {
            // set current red descriptor
            var red = Math.floor(sred * ((step - i) / step) + ered *
                                (i / step))

            // set current green descriptor
            var green = Math.floor(sgreen * ((step - i) / step) + egreen *
                                (i / step))

            // set current green descriptor
            var blue = Math.floor(sblue * ((step - i) / step) + eblue *
                                (i / step))

            // set background color according to descriptors
            setbgColor(red, green, blue)
        }
    }

    // -->
    </SCRIPT>
    </HEAD>
    <BODY onLoad="fade(0, 0, 0, 255, 255, 255, 64)" onUnload="fade(255,
                                255, 255, 0, 0, 0, 64)">
    <H1>Hello net!</H1>
    </BODY>
    </HTML>
```

***Example 21-2 (ex21-2.htm)**. A script to create a fade effect.*

The script gradually changes the document's background color from a given color to another specified color. It works with any colors represented in a hexadecimal triplet format. Let's analyze the script.

toHex(dec)

```
// convert decimal value (0 - 255) to hexadecimal
// (use .toString(16) method supported by IE)
function toHex(dec) {
    // create list of hex characters
    var hexCharacters = "0123456789ABCDEF"

    // if number is out of range return limit
    if (dec < 0)
        return "00"
    if (dec > 255)
        return "FF"

    // decimal equivalent of first hex character in converted number
    var i = Math.floor(dec / 16)
```

```
        // decimal equivalent of second hex character in converted number
        var j = dec % 16

        // return hexadecimal equivalent
        return hexCharacters.charAt(i) + hexCharacters.charAt(j)
}
```

This function accepts a single argument representing a decimal number, normally between 0 and 255. It converts it to its hexadecimal equivalent. At first, a list of the hexadecimal digits is assigned to the string variable `hexCharacters`. It returns the minimum 00 string, if the decimal argument is less then 0, and the maximum `FF`, if the decimal argument is greater than 255, "FF"'s equivalent in hex representation. The value `Math.floor(dec / 16)` is equal to the decimal representation of the first hexadecimal digit in the converted number. The value `Math.floor(dec % 16)` is equal to the decimal value of the second hex digit of the converted number. The hexadecimal value of a decimal number between 0 and 15 is that `hexCharacter's` character, the index of which is equal to the decimal number.

setbgColor(red, green, blue)

```
// set background color to specified descriptors
function setbgColor(red, green, blue) {
      document.bgColor = "#" + toHex(red) + toHex(green) + toHex(blue)
}
```

This function accepts three RGB descriptors and assigns the color combination to the `document.bgColor` property, setting the document's background color. The arguments are in decimal notation, so first they are converted to hex numbers.

fade(sred, sgreen, sblue, ered, egreen, eblue, step)

```
// fade from start to end descriptors (increase step to increase
                                    transition speed)
function fade(sred, sgreen, sblue, ered, egreen, eblue, step) {
      // loop to create fade effect
      for(var i = 0; i <= step; ++i) {
            // set current red descriptor
            var red = Math.floor(sred * ((step - i) / step) + ered *
                                    (i / step))

            // set current green descriptor
            var green = Math.floor(sgreen * ((step - i) / step) + egreen *
                                    (i / step))

            // set current green descriptor
            var blue = Math.floor(sblue * ((step - i) / step) + eblue *
                                    (i / step))
```

```
            // set background color according to descriptors
            setbgColor(red, green, blue)
        }
}
```

This function is responsible for the fade effect. It accepts seven arguments: The first three represent the RGB descriptors of the initial background color, the next three represent the RGB values of the target one, and the last argument determines the speed of the fade. The function consists of a single loop which iterates from 0 to `step` in increments of one. The RGB descriptors of the current background are computed and assigned to local `variables` on each iteration of the `loop`. A computed red, green, or blue color is a weighted average between the initial color value and the target one. During the first iteration, `step - i` is equal to `step`, so the initial color descriptor is actually multiplied by 1 in the expression `Math.floor(s`*`col`*` * ((step - i) / step)`. Since `i` is 0, the descriptor of the target color is multiplied by 0 in the expression `e`*`col`*` * (i / step)` where *`col`* is `red`, `green`, or `blue`. Therefore, the background color is set to the initial color during the first pass, and to the target color during the last pass. The last statement in the loop actually sets the background color by passing the computed descriptors to `setbgColor()`.

Event Handlers

It is common to use the fading effect with the `onLoad` and `onUnload` event handlers. If you prefer to use it with both, it is recommended that you generate the reversed transition for each.

fgColor

The `document.fgColor` property represents the color of the document text (foreground color). It reflects the `<BODY>` tag's `TEXT` attribute. The property is expressed as a hexadecimal RGB triplet or as one of the supported color names. When you assign it a triplet, the crosshatch mark (#) is optional.

Setting a value to the `fgColor` property is equivalent to setting a value to the `<BODY>` tag's `TEXT` attribute, enclosing the entire text with the `<FONT COLOR="`*`setColor`*`"></FONT>` tag pair, or using the `String` object's `fontcolor` method.

alinkColor

The `document.alinkColor` property is JavaScript's reflection of the `<BODY>` tag's `ALINK` attribute. It is a string specifying the color of an active link (after the mouse button is pressed down over a link but before it goes back up). The string must represent the hexadecimal RGB triplet of a color or one of the supported color names.

Aside from a few exceptions, you cannot set the value of this property after the page has finished loading, because there is no way to modify a page's content after it has been laid out.

linkColor

The `document.linkColor` property is JavaScript's reflection of the `<BODY>` tag's `LINK` attribute. It specifies the color of the document's hypertext links which the user has not visited yet. The color must be represented in the form of a hexadecimal RGB triplet or one of the supported color names. As explained above, you cannot set this property after the HTML source has gone through the layout stage. You can still read the property's value at any time via an immediate script or a deferred one.

vlinkColor

The `document.vlinkColor` property is JavaScript's reflection of the `<BODY>` tag's `VLINK` attribute. The color must be represented in the form of a hexadecimal RGB triplet or one of the supported color names. This property represents the color of already-followed hypertext links. You can set it as long as the HTML source has not been through layout yet.

Output Methods and Streams

write and writeln

The `document.write` method displays any number of expressions in a document window. Expressions to be printed can be of any type, including numerics, strings, and logicals.

This method prints its arguments to the plain HTML document window. It does not append any external character to the printed arguments. The method `document.write`, also accessible as `window.document.write`, can be used from either a plain script (`<SCRIPT LANGUAGE="JavaScript">…</SCRIPT>`) or from an event handler.

Bear in mind that event handler scripts are executed only after the HTML source has been through layout. The `write()` method implicitly opens a new document of *mimeType* `text/html` if you do not explicitly invoke a `document.open()` method prior to the `document.write()` call.

The `writeln()` method acts exactly like the `write()` method, except that it appends a new line character to the end of the output. HTML generally ignores this character, but certain tags, such as `<PRE>`, welcome it:

```
<PRE>
one
two
three
<PRE>
```

After interpretation, the Web page appears as:

```
one
two
three
```

You can create the same output via JavaScript in the following fashion:

```
document.write("<PRE>")
document.writeln("one")
document.writeln("two")
document.writeln("three")
document.write("</PRE>")
```

Data Streams

The `document.open()` method opens a stream to collect the output of `write()` and `writeln()` methods. Its general syntax is:

```
document.open(["mimeType"])
```

mimeType specifies the type of document which is one of the following:

```
text/html
text/plain
image/gif
image/jpeg
image/x-bitmap
plugIn
```

plugIn is any two-part plug-in supported by the user's browser.

Generally speaking, if the *mimeType* is text or image, the stream is opened to layout which is generated by instructions from the browser.

Otherwise, the stream is opened to a target plug-in which you have to make sure understands the data you provide. Since document is a property of window, document.open() or window.document.open() opens a stream specific to the document in the target window. If a document already exists in the target window, the open method clears it. If you do not specify *mimeType* as the method's argument, the most common one, text/html, is assumed. Note that you should never use this method to open a stream in the document which includes the JavaScript method itself. It is always used to open data streams to documents in other windows.

After you complete supplying data to the opened stream, you should close it via the document.close() method. Its syntax is simply the following:

```
document.close()
```

This method primarily closes a stream opened with the document.open() method. If not explicitly closed by the script, all font style tag pairs are closed implicitly. For example, if you provide a <BIG> tag but do not provide a closing </BIG> tag later, JavaScript provides it automatically. The close() method also stops the "meteor shower" in the Netscape icon or the rotation of the IE icon, and displays "Document: Done" in the status bar.

The document.close() method is extremely important because it instructs the browser's interpreter to display the data stream. If you do not invoke it, the output might not have any influence on the content of the page.

Since we have not discussed windows yet, this discussion seems a bit theoretical. We will refer back to these methods later, when the subject of windows will be dealt with in depth.

Another related method is document.clear(). Clearing a document via this method clears all HTML outputs in that document and resets the object model corresponding to that document. Normally, since JavaScript automatically clears the old document when you open a new stream, you don't have to clear a document prior to its opening or rewriting. The only case in which you should clear a document is after you close the stream to it. Since the method document.clear() is not functioning in many Netscape versions, you can clear a document by opening it, writing a line break to it, and then closing it. Look at the following example:

```
windowReference.document.open("text/html")
```

```
windowReference.document.write("<BR>")
windowReference.document.close()
```

For some reason, this clearing method requires writing at least one character to the stream. The line break is used here because it is transparent to the user.

Summary

In this chapter we discussed several properties and methods of the `document` object. We focused on colors, and naturally on hexadecimal triplets that define them. We learned how to script the various document colors such as background color, link color, and so forth. Two interesting examples dealing with colors were also analyzed. We have discussed other properties and methods as well. We have presented the basic output methods, `document.write()` and `document.writeln()`, as well as data streams. Data streams and document clearing play an important role in scripting windows and frames, as will be explained later.

Chapter 22

Forms

What are HTML Forms?

HTML forms, consisting of buttons, menus, and text boxes, are the means by which the client computer can gather information from the user. Forms are supported by almost all browsers so Web page authors can take them for granted. Search engines, for example, accept their input using simple HTML forms that submit the user's entry to the server.

Form tags are part of the HTML 2.0 standard and are supported by all JavaScript-enabled browsers. This is one of the reasons why forms are heavily supported by JavaScript. As will be explained later, JavaScript provides a convenient means of form content manipulation and validation through the use of a client-side application. You should be aware that Microsoft Internet Explorer still lacks many of the form properties and methods supported by Netscape Navigator, but is quickly catching up.

JavaScript Form Reference

JavaScript enables you to interact with the user via forms. You must know how forms are referenced in order to implement them in scripts. A form in terms of JavaScript is a plain object. It has properties, methods, and even event handlers. There are quite a few possible references from which you may choose. In this section we shall outline all of these possibilities so you will have the freedom to select the most convenient method.

forms Array

Suppose you have an HTML document which includes several forms, each defined by a regular `<FORM>…</FORM>` tag pair. You can refer to each form by its index in the `forms` array. The `forms` array is a property of the `document` object so it is referred to as `document.forms`. The object representing the first form in the page is `document.forms[0]`. The second form is `document.forms[1]`, the third one is `document.forms[2]`, and so forth. The `forms` array includes an entry for each of the document's forms (`<FORM>` tag), in source order. The general reference to a form is as follows:

```
document.forms[index]
```

As with all of JavaScript's arrays, the `forms` one includes a `length` property representing the number of forms on the page. The last form in the document, therefore, is:

```
document.forms[document.forms.length - 1]
```

Elements in the `forms` array can be set only by the HTML document and, hence, they are read-only for JavaScript. The following statement, for example, has no effect:

```
document.forms[0] = "work hard"
```

The string value of a form is `<object` *`nameAttribute`*`>`, where *`nameAttribute`* is the NAME attribute of the form.

Form Name

You can refer to a form by its name, rather than by its index:

```
document.formName
```

In order to take advantage of this referencing method, you have to explicitly assign a name to the form, via the NAME attribute.

Note: The term *reference* is used to describe an object's scripting protocol. A single object can be referenced via different but equivalent protocols.

Form Object

HTML Syntax

All forms are plain HTML tags. The top-level tags are the <FORM>…</FORM> tag pair. All form elements must be placed within these tags, or else they are not interpreted correctly. The general syntax of the <FORM> tag is as follows:

```
<FORM
    [NAME="formName"]
    [TARGET="windowName"]
    [ACTION="serverURL"]
    [METHOD="get" | "post"]
    [ENCTYPE="encodingType"]
    [onSubmit="handlerText"]
    [onReset="handlerText"]>
</FORM>
```

The attributes are:

- METHOD—specifies how to submit the form. It can be either GET or POST. The latter is more popular because it enables the client to send a greater amount of data to the processing script. Nonetheless, GET is much easier to use and is also suitable for JavaScript scripts. If a form is returned with GET, the data is placed in the QUERY_STRING environment variable. POST, on the other hand, instructs the client to pass the data to the server via its operating system's standard input method.
- ACTION—specifies the URL of the server-side script that processes the data submitted by the form. This attribute is necessary only when the processing script resides on the server. In this case, the script will be written in either C or Perl and will adhere to the CGI (Common Gateway Interface) protocol. The URL scheme must be HTTP.
- NAME—specifies the name of the form. This attribute is seldom used because it does not have any effect when using a server-side script. When using client-side JavaScript, though, it is recommended you name the form for much easier referencing. Since a form's name will be mostly used by JavaScript's scripts, it is also preferred to use the JavaScript's identifier naming standards.
- ENCTYPE–specifies the MIME type of the submitted data such as "text/plain" for plain text. The default MIME encoding of the data sent is "application/x-www-form-urlencoded."

- TARGET—specifies the window to which form responses go to. This attribute instructs the browser to display the server responses in the specified window rather than in the default window where the form resides. The specified value cannot be a JavaScript reference to a window—it must be a plain HTML frame or a window reference.

Although the <FORM>...</FORM> tag pair represents an HTML form, you can still place any other valid HTML tags within it. Mixing tables with forms, for example, is often used to enable simple layout. Although syntactically valid, nesting a form inside another form does not make any sense and you should avoid doing it.

Note: Microsoft Internet Explorer allows you to place form elements outside the <FORM>...</FORM> tag pair. You should avoid using such elements because they are not accessible via a full object hierarchy. They are accessible, though, via JavaScript's `this` scheme (see explanation on this keyword later in this chapter).

Event Handlers

onSubmit

A `submit` event occurs when a form is submitted, an event reflected by the `onSubmit` event handler. This attribute is a must, or else there won't be any response to the form's submission.

The `onSubmit` event handler is an attribute of the <FORM> tag because its action relates to the entire form, not only to its Submit button. A form can be submitted in several ways; the Submit button is only one of many.

The `submit` event occurs immediately upon clicking the Submit button, pressing Enter, or via any other method. Since JavaScript triggers the event prior to sending the data to the server, the event handler's script is executed before the form's data is actually submitted to the server for further processing. Timing is very important here. For example, suppose you ask the user to send you comments by filling a text area box in a form you place on your page. One would want to thank the user by replacing his comments in the text area box with a "Thank

You" notice. You cannot use the onSubmit event handler to do that because the "Thank You" notice will replace the user's input before it would have a chance to be submitted to the server. The net effect would be that you will receive the "Thank You" notice instead of the user's comments. One way to work around the problem is to use an alert box instead of overwriting the form's text area box.

The onSubmit event handler is commonly used to validate the content of a form's element. Client-side form validation is gaining popularity because, rather than waiting for a server-side CGI script to respond, the user receives an immediate response regarding invalid entries. Let's say you have a form with a text box in which the user is asked to type his or her e-mail address. You can use a simple JavaScript script that will make sure (upon submission) that the user's entry is a string containing an "at" sign (@), which is a must for all e-mail addresses.

You can use the onSubmit event handler not only to validate the form's elements but also to cancel its submission altogether. The form's submission is aborted when the event handler returns a false value, as in the following example:

```
<FORM NAME="form1" onSubmit="return false">
```

Obviously, this example is not very useful because it disables the form submission unconditionally. Usually, a function validates the form and returns a true or false value accordingly. You can use the following structure to cancel or proceed with the form submission, according to the value returned by the function:

```
<FORM NAME="form1" onSubmit="return checkData()">
```

The following example shows how to create a form with a text area box and a Submit button which e-mails you the contents of the text area after prompting the user for confirmation:

```
<SCRIPT LANGUAGE="JavaScript">
<!--

function proceedSubmission() {
    return confirm("Click OK to mail this information")
}

// -->
</SCRIPT>
<FORM ACTION="mailto:yshiran@iil.intel.com" METHOD="post" ENCTYPE=
            "text/plain" onSubmit="return proceedSubmission()">
<TEXTAREA NAME="inputField" COLS=40 ROWS=10></TEXTAREA><BR>
<INPUT TYPE="submit" VALUE="mail it!">
</FORM>
```

The Boolean value returned by the onSubmit event handler is actually the result of a confirm box presented to the user. Although some elements of this form are discussed later, you should be aware that, in order to receive the form's content as plain, unscrambled e-mail, you need to assign a "text/plain" value to the ENCTYPE attribute.

onReset

Another event handler of the <FORM> tag is onReset. A reset event usually occurs when the user clicks the Reset button. Except for the triggering event, the onReset event handler behaves like the onSubmit event handler.

The following example asks the user to confirm the resetting process before executing it:

```
<FORM ACTION="mailto:yshiran@iil.intel.com" METHOD="post"
ENCTYPE="text/plain" onReset="return confirm('Click OK to reset form to
default status')">
<TEXTAREA NAME="input" COLS=40 ROWS=10></TEXTAREA><BR>
<INPUT TYPE="reset" VALUE="reset it!">
</FORM>
```

A page containing the preceding form appears in the following image:

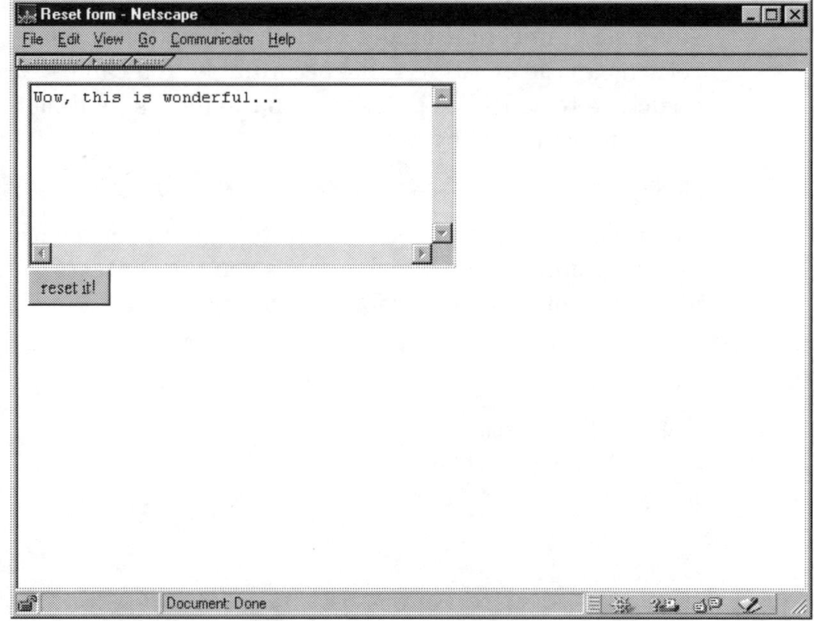

Figure 22-1*. A simple text area and a Reset button (both covered later in this chapter).*

After clicking the Reset button, the following dialog box appears:

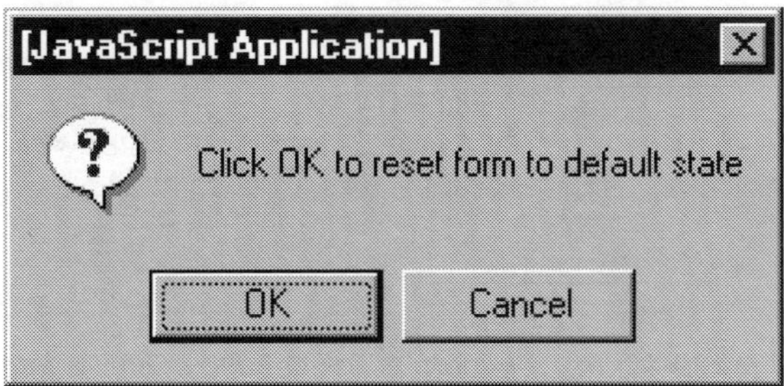

Figure 22-2. A confirm box asking the user for his or her confirmation to reset the form to its default state.

Note: The onReset event handler was first implemented in Navigator 3.0x.

Methods

submit()

The submit() method submits a form much the same way as the Submit button. The submit() method sends data back to the HTTP server either via GET or POST submission schemes. The general syntax is as follows:

```
formName.submit()
```

formName is the exact reference of the form object. You can invoke this method when the user clicks a given hypertext link. Take a look at the following example:

```
<HTML>
<HEAD>
<TITLE>hypertext link submission</TITLE>
<SCRIPT LANGUAGE="JavaScript">
<!--

function submitForm(sub) {
     document.forms[sub].submit()
}

function proceedSubmission() {
     return confirm("Click OK to mail this information")
}

// -->
```

```
</SCRIPT>
</HEAD>
<BODY>
<FORM METHOD="post" ACTION="mailto:yshiran@iil.intel.com" ENCTYPE=
                "text/plain" onSubmit="return proceedSubmission()">
<TEXTAREA NAME="inputField" COLS=40 ROWS=10></TEXTAREA><BR>
<A HREF="thanks.htm" onClick="submitForm(0)">Mail it!</A>
</FORM>
</BODY>
</HTML>
```

Example 22-1 (ex22-1.htm)*. A hypertext link used to submit a form just like a submit button.*

In Example 22-1 the form is submitted by the `submitForm` function which is invoked via the `onClick` event handler of a link object (links and image maps are discussed in Chapter 23, Links, Anchors, and Image Maps). After prompting the user for confirmation via the `onSubmit` event handler, the form, referenced as `document.forms[0]` (it is the first and only form in the page), is submitted through its `submit()` method. Example 22-1a shows the file thanks.htm which displays the "Thank You" notice referenced in Example 22-1:

```
<HTML>
<HEAD>
<TITLE>Thank you</TITLE>
</HEAD>
<BODY>
Thank you very much for your feedback
</BODY>
</HTML>
```

Example 22-1a (thanks.htm)*. The thank-you message displayed after submitting the mail in Ex. 22-1.*

Note: The `submit` method is broken in many versions of Navigator and Internet Explorer. Test every new release before usage.

reset()

The `reset()` method resets a given form and is equivalent to clicking the Reset button. Its syntax and usage is exactly the same as the `submit` method. See the `onReset` event handler for more information on resetting a form.

Properties

action

The action property reflects the value of the <FORM> tag's ACTION attribute. Its value is the URL of a CGI or LiveWire application on the server which needs to execute upon submission. If no explicit URL for the server-side application is specified, the value of action in Navigator 3.0 defaults to the URL of current document (the one containing the form), while Microsoft Internet Explorer, on the other hand, defaults the property to an empty string.

The *formReference*.action property can also be assigned a value by JavaScript. You can take advantage of this feature to modify the form's behavior after the page has been laid out, according to the user's preferences.

In general, you can assign the form's properties by JavaScript, instead of HTML attributes. Take a look at the following form example:

```
<FORM NAME="form1" METHOD="post" ACTION="http://www.foo.com/trash.cgi">
...
</FORM>
```

An alternative to this construct is the following combination of HTML and JavaScript:

```
<FORM NAME="form1" METHOD="post">
...
</FORM>
<SCRIPT LANGUAGE="JavaScript">
<!--

document.form1.action = "http://www.foo.com/trash.cgi"

// -->
</SCRIPT>
```

This example is just to demonstrate how you can assign a property. In practice, HTML is much preferred, for reasons explained later in this chapter.

Notice that Netscape Navigator and MSIE 3.0 deal differently with relative URLs. The following statement, executed as part of a form layout:

```
document.forms[0].action = "bla.cgi"
```

yields different values of document.forms[0].action in Netscape Navigator and IE:

```
bla.cgi // IE
http://currentDirectoryPath/bla.cgi // Netscape Navigator
```

elements

The `elements` property is an array of objects corresponding to the form elements. It is a property of any form and is referenced as *formReference*`.elements`.

As you already know, since all form objects are elements of the `document.forms` object, it is possible to refer to a specific form within a document if you know its index in relationship to the other forms in the document. Similarly, a specific form's elements are elements of the `elements` array. The first element of this array is a reference to the first form element (`button`, `checkbox`, `hidden`, `password`, `radio`, `reset`, `select`, `submit`, `text`, or `textarea` object), the second entry is a reference to the second form element, and so on, in source order. For example, if a form has one text box and three radio buttons, you can reference these elements as *formReference*`.elements[0]`, *formReference*`.elements[1]`, *formReference*`.elements[2]`, and *formReference*`.elements[3]`.

Like the `forms` array, the `elements` array is an alternative to referencing by name. Some programmers prefer to use array reflection, whereas others prefer to trace elements by their names. It is convenient to implement the `elements` array when a form contains many elements that are related to indexes. A form with ten text boxes which accepts ten telephone numbers, for example, should be referenced via the `elements` array. Such referencing will allow you to use a loop to iterate through the ten different elements.

Usually, though, you will use forms to collect data fields of different meanings which are not similar to each other as the phone numbers in the previous example. In such cases, referencing by name is much more convenient and easier to understand, follow, and maintain. You can easily redesign the physical layout of the form or even add new elements in the middle while keeping the old references. If you use the `elements` array, on the other hand, any layout modification causes the indexes to shift, invalidating all previous references.

The number of elements in a form is *formReference*`.elements.length`. Therefore, the last element in a form is reflected by the *formReference*`.elements[formReference.elements.length - 1]` entry.

Elements in the `elements` array are read-only, so the following statement, for example, has no effect:

```
formReference.elements[0] = "do not do this"
```

The first few elements of the `elements` array represent the form elements. The following property, `length`, reflects the number of form elements. You would expect the list to end here, but Netscape added all forms properties to the `elements` array, starting at this index. In general, although we explain it here in detail, you should avoid referencing a form object's properties through its `elements` property. This feature is not documented and is not supported by IE.

Suppose a form element evaluates to `foo`. Then, the following references all evaluate to `foo`:

```
document.forms[0].elements[0].value
document.forms[0].elements.elements[0].value
document.forms[0].elements.elements.elements[0].value
```

These bizarre references are possible due to the fact that an `elements` object contains all the properties of its form, in addition to the form's elements. A form, say `document.forms[0]`, can also have a property named `name` reflecting the value of the `NAME` attribute of the corresponding `<FORM>` tag. You can also reference this property in Navigator using one of the following known methods:

```
document.forms[0].name
document.forms[0].elements.name
document.forms[0].elements.elements.name
```

You may recall from Chapter 8 that the `for...in` loop statement provides the capability to list an object's properties, top to bottom. The following function can be used to list the properties of a typical `elements` object by name (not index):

```
function printElements(form, formString) {
     // initialize output string
     var result = ""

     for (var i in form.elements) {
          result += formString + ".elements." + i + " = " +
                                        form.elements[i] + "\r"
     }

     alert(result)
}
```

You can use this function by invoking it with a specific form's reference and a name. Consider the following simple HTML form:

```
<FORM NAME="form1" ACTION="http://www.yourserver.com/filename.cgi"
                                      METHOD="post">
<INPUT TYPE="text" NAME="num1" VALUE="bla">
<INPUT TYPE="hidden" NAME="num2" VALUE="foo">
<TEXTAREA NAME="num3">wow</TEXTAREA>
</FORM>
```

The preceding `printElements()` function returns the following output when provided with the arguments `document.forms[0]` and `"document.forms[0]"`:

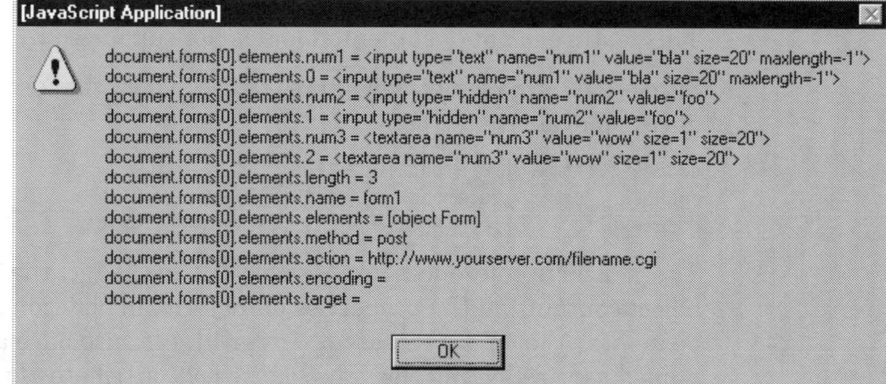

Figure 22-3. *A list of a typical elements object's properties.*

Notice that the first four lines list the exclusive properties of the `elements` object. The following lines represent properties of `elements` which are identical to those of the form itself, `document.forms[0]` in this case. Theoretically, you can reference all forms properties of a given form as properties of its `elements` object.

If you think this wealth of referencing methods is confusing, you are right. The best way to get out of it is to stick to some standards. Suppose you have a form in a document which is referenced as `document.forms[`*`index`*`]`, `document.`*`formName`*, or *`formReference`*. The following objects include all forms properties:

```
formReference
formReference.elements
```

The `elements` property of *`formReference`* is just another interface to the same object. Since Netscape originally documented the above two objects as different ones (and still does), it is common to refer to *`formReference`* when accessing a form's general properties and to *`formReference`*`.elements` when accessing the properties of the form's elements. Theoretically, you can also access the first element of the form by:

```
formReference[0]
```

As you already know, any form element object can be referenced by its name. For example, a `text` object whose name is "field1" in the first form of a page can be accessed as follows:

```
document.forms[0].field1
```

When two or more elements have the same name, they form an array in which the indices are determined according to their layout order. For example, if there are three `text` objects in one form, all named `inputField`, you can reference these elements in the following fashion:

```
document.forms[0].inputField[0]
document.forms[0].inputField[1]
document.forms[0].inputField[2]
```

encoding

The content of a form is encoded before it is submitted to the server. There are various types of encoding, or MIME encoding, some suitable for files, while others are suitable for plain text or other purposes. The encoding method is initially specified by assigning it to the `<FORM>` tag's `ENCTYPE` attribute. The default encoding method is `application/x-www-form-urlencoded`, but others such as `multipart/form-data` and `text/plain` are also available.

Every HTML form has a MIME encoding specification, even if it is not explicitly shown. The value of JavaScript's *formReference*`.encoding` is initially the value assigned to the HTML `ENCTYPE` attribute. This property is not read-only, so it can be set at any time, even after layout has been completed. Setting encoding overrides the `ENCTYPE` attribute and instructs the browser (primarily Navigator) to use the new MIME encoding method. For your reference, the general syntax of this property is as follows:

```
formReference.encoding
```

If no value is specified as the `ENCTYPE` attribute of a form, it is defaulted to `application/x-www-form-urlencoded`. Nevertheless, the value of *formReference*`.encoding` remains an empty string.

method

The METHOD attribute of a <FORM> tag accepts either a "get" or a "post" value. JavaScript reflects the value of this attribute in the form of a method property. You can use this property like all other form properties. It can be read or set at any time, even after layout has been completed. The term "method," in this case, has no relation whatsoever to the object-oriented interpretation of the word (a function associated with an object).

The *formReference*.method property is when the client-side JavaScript script interacts with a specific server-side CGI or LiveWire application. In this case, you can set the method property along with other form-related properties to modify the form's layout "on-the-fly." The general syntax to reference this property is:

```
formReference.method
```

The default value of the HTML METHOD attribute is get. The value of the JavaScript method property, however, has no default and stays empty.

target

When you "surf the Web," you often encounter HTML forms that submit data to the server and return a result, such as a list of sites or a simple "Thank You" page. Since most forms serve as a means to interact with the user, you will seldom find forms that submit to the server and do not respond. Furthermore, even forms that just receive input from the user and submit it to a server-side script are expected to respond and give the user an indication that the content of the form was correctly submitted.

Most server-side applications return a new HTML page in the same window as the form. Sometimes, however, you intend to receive the results in a different window or frame. You can specify the target of the returned page by setting the TARGET attribute of the <FORM> tag. This value is reflected by JavaScript's target property, which belongs to the form object. The general syntax for referencing this property is:

```
formReference.target
```

This property can be both read and set at any time, even after the page has been laid out. Despite the fact that the TARGET attribute defaults to the current window or frame's HTML document, the JavaScript's target property does not default to any string.

The value of the JavaScript's `target` property, like the HTML's `TARGET` attribute, can be either a window or a frame name. In addition to these obvious values, there are several common references: `_top`, `_parent`, `_self`, and `_blank`. These values will be covered again when we discuss frames and windows and, for detailed information, you may also refer to HTML documentation. It may seem convenient to assign `window` or `frame` objects to this property, but unfortunately it only accepts HTML specifications.

Element Types

Netscape Navigator version 3.0 and up enables you to retrieve a given element's type. Each and every form element (button, radio, text area, etc.) features a `type` property which reflects the type of that form element. As usual in JavaScript syntax, the `type` property follows the element reference. For example, you can access the type of the first element of the first form in the following fashion:

```
document.forms[0].elements[0].type
```

Table 22-1 lists the various form elements with their corresponding types:

HTML element	Value of type attribute
`INPUT TYPE="button"`	`"button"`
`INPUT TYPE="checkbox"`	`"checkbox"`
`INPUT TYPE="file"`	`"file"`
`INPUT TYPE="hidden"`	`"hidden"`
`INPUT TYPE="password"`	`"password"`
`INPUT TYPE="radio"`	`"radio"`
`INPUT TYPE="reset"`	`"reset"`
`INPUT TYPE="submit"`	`"submit"`
`INPUT TYPE="text"`	`"text"`
`SELECT`	`"select-one"`
`SELECT MULTIPLE`	`"select-multiple"`
`TEXTAREA`	`"textarea"`

All values listed in the right column are plain strings representing the element type.

Using `this` with Event Handlers

When you call a function via an event handler you may refer to the form element which triggered the event handler, such as a `text` object or a button. The following script segment demonstrates this concept:

```
<SCRIPT LANGUAGE="JavaScript">
<!--

function process() {
      document.forms[0].elements[0].value = "thank you"
}

// -->
</SCRIPT>
<FORM>
<INPUT TYPE="text" NAME="myField" VALUE="email..." onChange="process()">
</FORM>
```

At this point, it is not so important to understand what exactly this script does. The `INPUT TYPE="text"` definition creates a simple text box in which the user can enter a value. The text box (or `text` object) is assigned the string `"email..."` as its default value (the form comes up with this text inside the box). The `onChange` event handler captures a `change` event which occurs when the user changes the value of the `text` object and clicks outside of it. When such an event occurs, the function `process` is invoked and assigns the string `"thank you"` to that `text` object's `value` property. Notice that a full object path specification, from the `document` browser object downwards, is used to access the `text` object. Such referencing has two disadvantages:

- The path is fairly long and complex.
- If you change the position or the name of either a form or an element, the path must be modified to reflect this change, making the maintenance very difficult.

The answer to this problem is using the keyword `this` to refer to the "current" object. For example, you can simplify the preceding code by implementing the `this` reference in the following way:

```
<SCRIPT LANGUAGE="JavaScript">
<!--

function process(callingElement) {
      callingElement.value = "thank you"
}

// -->
</SCRIPT>
<FORM>
<INPUT TYPE="text" NAME="myField" VALUE="email..." onChange=
                                           "process(this)">
</FORM>
```

Using the above scheme, you can change the element's position, name, or any other optional attribute (other than the event handler) and the script will still work without any modifications. The keyword this refers to the element providing the event handler. In this case, the value of this is equal to document.forms[0].elements[0]. When the function process is called, the value assigned to the callingElement parameter is this, so callingElement.value is equivalent to document.forms[0].elements[0].value.

The keyword this within an event handler script refers to the form element which the event handler belongs to. For example, the keyword this in an event handler that belongs to the first element of the first form in a document can be safely replaced by document.form[0].element[0].

Using the object this is very convenient when you use a single function to refer to different form elements.

You can also use this in an event handler script for purposes other than a function's argument. You can also hand any property of the this object to a function, as demonstrated by the following script segment:

```
<SCRIPT LANGUAGE="JavaScript">
<!--

function display(str) {
     alert(str)
}

// -->
</SCRIPT>
<FORM>
<INPUT TYPE="text" NAME="myField1" VALUE="d" onChange=
                         "display(this.value)">
<INPUT TYPE="text" NAME="myField2" VALUE="f" onChange=
                         "display(this.value)">
</FORM>
```

Note: Object, property, and method references can be passed as function arguments. Just like assigning any other value, they can be assigned to a variable as well. For example, you can use the following script segment instead of a window.document.write statement:

```
var obj = window.document
obj.write("Cool<BR>")
```

Be careful not to enclose an object reference by quotation marks—it is not a string.

Until now, the special object `this` was used as a substitute for a form element's full path. JavaScript also allows you to reference a form from an element's event handler script via the `form` property of `this` object. The previous source can be rewritten in the following form:

```
<SCRIPT LANGUAGE="JavaScript">
<!--

function process(callingElement) {
    callingElement.elements[0].value = "thank you"
}

// -->
</SCRIPT>
<FORM>
<INPUT TYPE="text" NAME="myField" VALUE="email..."
onChange="process(this.form)">
</FORM>
```

The object representing the form is equivalent to `document.forms[0]`.

Generally speaking, every form element includes a `form` property which enables a reverse access; that is, ability to reach the form from its element (although the element is really the form's property). Therefore, you can use any one of the following expressions to access the first element of the first form in a given document:

```
document.forms[0].elements[0]
document.forms[0].elements[0].form.elements[0]
document.forms[0].elements[0].form.elements[0].form.elements[0]
```

You will probably never use this property independently in a script, because you can always refer to a form directly as a property of a window's `document` object. However, such a reference is used a lot with forms, because an event handler's script references the event handler as `this`, and the `form` property enables you to reference the form through a back door.

Note: Microsoft Internet Explorer 3.0 does not properly support the use of `this` in all form element event handlers. Double-check every script that uses this object.

In addition to event handlers associated with form elements, you can also use `this` with event handlers of the `<FORM>` tag. In this case, `this` represents the object encompassing the entire form (such as `document.forms[0]`). Suppose you want to call a function from an `onSubmit` event handler. You can use the following outline to hand an object reference representing the form object to the function:

```
<FORM ... onSubmit="functionName(this)">
```

In this case, the expression `this.form` has no logical meaning.

Utilizing the form Property

In this chapter we discuss the various objects reflecting HTML form elements. Each form element is a direct property of the form to which it belongs. Take a look at the following example:

```
<FORM NAME="myForm">
<INPUT TYPE="text" NAME="myField" SIZE=10> <!-- discussed later -->
</FORM>
```

In this simple example, the `text` object may be referenced as `document.myForm.myField`. This top-to-bottom hierarchy enables you to access any form element object if you already have an access to the form object itself. However, you may encounter a situation in which you pass a form element object to a function, for instance, and you want to reference the form object through a back door. JavaScript enables you to do so with the `form` property. For example, suppose you have a variable `myField` which holds a form element object. (For now, simply ignore how the object was assigned to the variable.) Assume the variable is named `objRef` and the object reference was explicitly assigned to it by the following statement:

```
var objRef = document.myForm.myField
```

Bear in mind that you do not have this statement in the script—all you have is the variable `objRef`, and you are attempting to reference the form object, `myForm`. You can use the `form` property to do so:

```
var formObjRef = objRef.form
```

form is a property of every form element object, with no exceptions. It is very convenient to invoke a function from an event handler with this as an argument. For example, consider the following script segment:

```
<SCRIPT LANGUAGE="JavaScript">
<!--

function getValue(otherElement) {
     alert(otherElement.form.elements[1].value)
}

// -->
</SCRIPT>
<FORM>
<INPUT TYPE="button" VALUE="click me" onClick="getValue(this)">
<INPUT TYPE="text" VALUE="Bill Clinton" SIZE=10>
</FORM>
```

The first text object (form element) invokes the getValue function with this object as the argument. The function is designed to print the value of the second element, elements[1]. The only relation between the value handed to the function (the object representing the first form element) and the second form element is that they are both "children" of the same "parent." The function accepts the object reflecting the first element, so it must access the second element through the common parent, the form object. Therefore, the correct syntax must include the form property (which is an object as well):

```
firstElement.form.secondElement
```

The form property acts like a connector in this case. If you implement a function that references various elements of a form, you may want to initially use this.form as the function's argument. You should then use the following code in place of the preceding script segment:

```
<SCRIPT LANGUAGE="JavaScript">
<!--

function getValue(form) {
     alert(form.elements[1].value)
}

// -->
</SCRIPT>
<FORM>
<INPUT TYPE="button" VALUE="click me" onClick="getValue(this.form)">
<INPUT TYPE="text" VALUE="Bill Clinton" SIZE=10>
</FORM>
```

Text Object

HTML Syntax

A text object is defined by the following plain HTML syntax:

```
<INPUT
    TYPE="text"
    NAME="textName"
    [VALUE="contents"]
    [SIZE="integer"]
    [MAXLENGTH="integer"]
    [onBlur="handlerStatement"]
    [onChange="handlerStatement"]
    [onFocus="handlerStatement"]
    [onSelect="handlerStatement"]>
```

The NAME attribute enables you to assign this HTML object a name which identifies it in both server-side queries and JavaScript scripts. The VALUE attribute accepts the initial string that should appear in the box when the page loads. Not only is this string the initial one in the text box, it is also the default string. When you reset the form via a Reset button or the reset() method, this string reappears in the text box. The SIZE attribute is essential because it determines the size (in characters) of the text box. The MAXLENGTH attribute specifies the maximum input length allowed in this field. If the user enters a string that is longer than MAXLENGTH, only the first MAXLENGTH characters are entered. This option is especially handy when requesting a specific string, such as a password, which is naturally limited to a given length. The following script segment demonstrates the use of the text object in an HTML document:

```
Processor: <INPUT TYPE="text" NAME="comp" SIZE=15 MAXLENGTH=20
VALUE="Pentium Pro">
```

If implemented correctly within <FORM>…</FORM> tags, this text box should appear as follows:

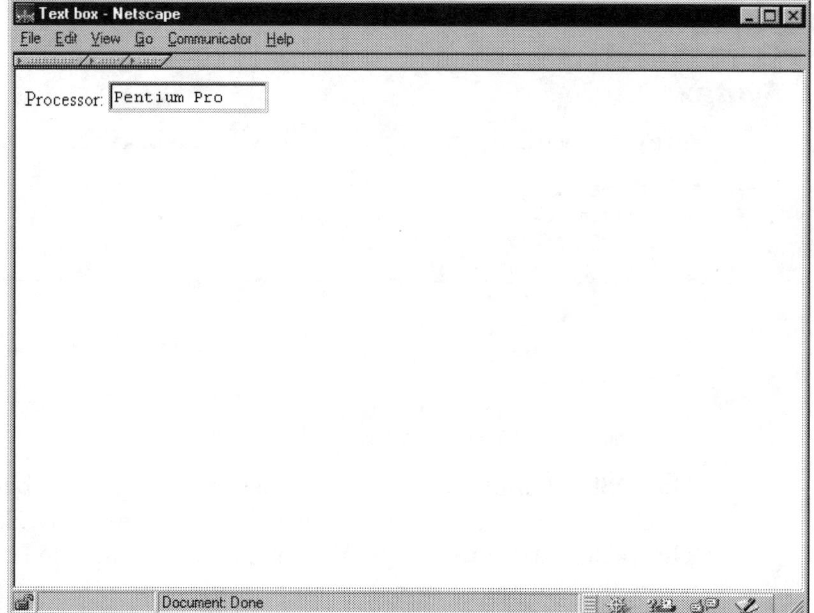

***Figure 22-4**. A simple text box with an initial (default) value.*

Notice that a `text` object can hold a maximum of one line. You can use a `textarea` object to display multiple lines.

JavaScript Access

There are basically four ways to access a `text` object via JavaScript:

```
[window.]document.formName.textName
```

```
[window.]document.formName.elements[index]
```

```
[window.]document.forms[index].textName
```

```
[window.]document.forms[index].elements[index]
```

You already know that a form can be accessed through its name or via the `forms` object when the form's index is known. Similarly, you can access a form's element by its name or through the `elements` array if the element's index is known.

The preceding expressions show how to access a `text` object by itself. Usually, you will not access the `text` object, but rather its properties, methods, or event handlers.

Event Handlers

The text object is a very convenient means for both input and output. A text object has a wealth of event handlers you can use.

onBlur

A blur event occurs when a text field loses focus. A field gains focus when the user clicks inside the text box, and the focus is lost when the user clicks outside the box, anywhere on the page. The onBlur event handler executes JavaScript code when a blur event occurs. Take a look at the following form and function:

```
<SCRIPT LANGUAGE="JavaScript">
<!--

function checkInput(element) {
     if (element.value == "")
          alert("Please enter a value!")
}

// -->
</SCRIPT>
<FORM>
<INPUT TYPE="text" NAME="myField" VALUE="" onBlur="checkInput(this)">
</FORM>
```

An alert dialog box informs the user that he or she must enter a value in the text box if the box is left empty. The dialog box is displayed only if the user first accesses the field and then exits it without entering any value.

onChange

A change event occurs when a blur event occurs and the value of the text object has been modified. The onChange event handler, also defined as an HTML tag attribute, executes JavaScript code when a change event occurs.

The onChange event handler is probably the most commonly used among other event handlers related with the text object (box or field). You can use this event handler when validating data entered by the user. That is, when the user modifies the text box content, a function is invoked to validate the changes. Validation via JavaScript instead of CGI or LiveWire saves precious network transmission time.

In order to demonstrate the onBlur event handler, a simple form element and a corresponding function have been implemented. The problem with this example is that the value of the text box is validated whenever it loses focus. However, it is generally better to validate the form only after changes are made. Therefore, the onChange event handler is superior for such tasks. The previous example is much better in the following version:

```
<SCRIPT LANGUAGE="JavaScript">
<!--

function checkInput(element) {
     if (element.value == "")
          alert("Please enter a value!")
}

// -->
</SCRIPT>
<FORM>
<INPUT TYPE="text" NAME="myField1" VALUE="" onChange="checkInput(this)">
</FORM>
```

The following dual rule is very important in order to fully understand this event handler:

- A blur event naturally takes place whenever a change event occurs.
- A change event takes place only when a blur event occurs and the value of the text object has been modified and gained focus.

onFocus

A focus event occurs when a field receives input focus by tabbing on the keyboard or clicking with the mouse. The onFocus event handler obviously executes a prespecified code when a focus event occurs.

In addition, a focus event occurs in Microsoft Internet Explorer when the page loads. This behavior is unique to Microsoft's browser (3.0 and up), but you have to take it into account if you are committed to support both browsers.

The following script scrolls a "T-banner" in a text object. It starts when the user clicks somewhere inside the text box (text object), triggering the onFocus event handler. Here is the script:

```
<HTML>
<HEAD>
<TITLE>T-Banner</TITLE>
<SCRIPT LANGUAGE="JavaScript">
<!--

// set speed of banner (pause in milliseconds between characters)
var speed = 100 // decrease value to increase speed (must be positive)
```

```
// set pause between completion of message and beginning of following one
var pause = 1000 // increase value to increase pause

// set initial values
var timerID = null
var bannerRunning = false

// create global array
var ar = new Array()

// assign the strings to the array's elements
ar[0] = "Welcome to our JavaScript page"
ar[1] = "We hope you enjoy the T-Banner script"
ar[2] = "It is designed to be more stable than regular banners"
ar[3] = "Don't forget to check out our other scripts"

// set index of first message to be displayed first
var currentMessage = 0

// set index of last character to be displayed first
var offset = 0

// stop the banner if it is currently running
function stopBanner() {
        // if banner is currently running
        if (bannerRunning)
                // stop the banner
                clearTimeout(timerID)

        // timer is now stopped
        bannerRunning = false
}

// start the banner
function startBanner() {
        // make sure the banner is stopped
        stopBanner()

        // start the banner from the current position
        showBanner()
}

// type in the current message
function showBanner() {
        // assign current message to variable
        var text = ar[currentMessage]

        // if current message has not finished being displayed
        if (offset < text.length) {
                // if last character of current message is a space
                if (text.charAt(offset) == " ")
```

```
                                // skip the current character
                                offset++

                        // assign the up-to-date to-be-displayed substring
                        // second argument of method accepts index of last
                                    character plus one
                        var partialMessage = text.substring(0, offset + 1)

                        // display partial message in text field
                        document.bannerForm.bannerField.value = partialMessage

                        // increment index of last character to be displayed
                        offset++ // IE sometimes has trouble with "++offset"

                        // recursive call after specified time
                        timerID = setTimeout("showBanner()", speed)

                // banner is running
                bannerRunning = true
        } else {
                        // reset offset
                        offset = 0

                        // increment subscript (index) of current message
                        currentMessage++

                        // if subscript of current message is out of range
                        if (currentMessage == ar.length)
                                // wrap around (start from beginning)
                                currentMessage = 0

                        // recursive call after specified time
                        timerID = setTimeout("showBanner()", pause)

                // banner is running
                bannerRunning = true
        }
}

// -->
</SCRIPT>
</HEAD>
<BODY>
<FORM NAME="bannerForm">
<INPUT TYPE="text" NAME="bannerField" VALUE="Click here..." SIZE=50
                    onFocus="if (!bannerRunning) { startBanner() }">
</FORM>
</BODY>
</HTML>
```

***Example 22-2**. A T-banner starts in a text box when the user clicks in the box.*

You can find a detailed explanation of this script in Chapter 18. Only new features will be covered here.

First of all, notice the form named bannerForm in the HTML body. The form consists of only one element, a text object. The name of this object is bannerField. Its size is set to 50 characters, and its default value is the string "Click here...". The onFocus event handler is provided. When the user clicks inside the text box, a focus event occurs and startBanner() function is invoked to start the scrolling. Notice that this statement is executed only if the banner is not running. The variable bannerRunning holds the banner's current state and is already true when the page loads.

The only difference between the original status-bar-based T-banner script in Chapter 18 and the text-box-based one in Example 22-2 is that the property window.status is replaced by document.bannerForm.bannerField.value, which is the reference to the text object's content-reflecting property.

onSelect

A select event occurs when the user selects part of the text within a text field. The onSelect event handler enables you to respond to such an event.

Here is the general syntax for implementing this event handler:

```
<INPUT TYPE="text" VALUE="" NAME="valueField" onSelect="selectState()">
```

Since the select event is rather rare and insignificant, this event handler is not commonly used. It was also broken in some versions of Navigator.

Methods

blur()

You already know what a blur event is. You can explicitly blur a text object using the object's blur() method, which removes focus from the field. This method deselects any text that might be selected in the field and removes the text insertion pointer from the field. At this point, no fields or form elements are focused. A manual way to blur a text object is to hit Tab, which advances focus to the next field in order and removes it from the current field (blurring it). However, the JavaScript blur() method only removes focus from its object, without giving focus to any other field in the form or in the page.

A read-only text field is a classic example for using the `blur()` method. The algorithm to create such a field is very simple. When the user explicitly gives focus to a field in order to write in it, an event handler (`onFocus`) invokes the `blur()` method to instantly remove the focus. Here is a read-only text field example:

```
<INPUT TYPE="text" NAME="myField" VALUE="" SIZE=15 onFocus="this.blur()">
```

You can consider the expression `onFocus="this.blur()"` an attribute of a read-only `<INPUT TYPE="text">` element.

focus()

The `focus()` method focuses on a `text` object (or other form element object which is described later in this chapter). Focusing on a form element usually means that the window scrolls until the text field is viewable and the cursor is positioned at the beginning of the text in the field.

Although not mandatory, it is a good practice to give focus to a `text` object before accessing it. It will have a positive contribution to the script's robustness.

When the page contains many fields, you can use the script-driven `focus()` method to emphasize one of them, thus "attracting" the user to it. The `focus()` method resembles the camera's focus: It emphasizes a specific object and prepares it for further use.

The following HTML tag can be used to maintain focus on a `text` object (it may be useful if you have multiple `text` objects and the user is allowed to modify only one of them):

```
<INPUT TYPE="text" NAME="myField" VALUE="" SIZE=15 onBlur="this.focus()">
```

When the text field loses focus, a `blur` event occurs, the `onBlur` event handler is triggered, and focus is given once again to the field.

The `focus()` method usually belongs to `text` objects (fields), but, as will be explained later in this chapter, other kinds of objects use it as well.

select()

The most useful method of the `text` object is the `select()` one. When you select a field via JavaScript, the entire text in the field is selected. Since this method is broken in Microsoft Internet Explorer 3.0, the focus here will be on Netscape Navigator.

Due to a bug, or rather a feature, in Navigator on some platforms, you must give a focus to a text field before selecting it. Suppose you have a document with one form that contains one element, a `text` object. The following script segment is needed in order to select that text field via JavaScript:

```
document.forms[0].elements[0].focus()
document.forms[0].elements[0].blur()
```

The `select()` method is extremely useful and very convenient when validating a form on the client side. For example, let's say you have a form which accepts inputs from the user for several elements and validates each element in turn before submitting the data to the server. The most basic way to report an error is to display a message in an alert dialog box. More sophisticated error reporting includes automatic preparation of the form for the user's corrections. Such preparation can be implemented by playing the `focus() + select()` method concert. When the script encounters a text field that contains invalid data, you can direct the cursor to that field and automatically highlight the interior text. The user can then write the new, correct value without even having to delete the invalid entry. Sounds quite complicated on the programmer's behalf, but it is actually very simple. The following script and form demonstrate a simple validation and handy error reporting:

```
<HTML>
<HEAD>
<TITLE>Simple form validation</TITLE>
</HEAD>
<SCRIPT LANGUAGE="JavaScript">
<!--

function checkName(field) {
     if (field.value == "") {
          alert("Value is required")
          field.focus()
          field.select()
     } else
          if (field.value.split(" ").length < 2) {
               alert("Enter full name")
               field.focus()
               field.select()
          }
}

function checkEmail(field) {
     if (field.value.indexOf("@") == -1) {
          alert("Enter a valid e-mail address")
```

```
                    field.focus()
                    field.select()
            }
    }

    // -->
    </SCRIPT>
    </HEAD>
    <BODY>
    <FORM>
    Full name: <INPUT TYPE="text" NAME="userName" VALUE="" SIZE=15 onChange=
                                  "checkName(this)">
    <BR>
    Email address: <INPUT TYPE="text" NAME="email" VALUE="" SIZE=15 onChange=
                                  "checkEmail(this)">
    </FORM>
    </BODY>
    </HTML>
```

Example 22-3*. A simple form validation and error handling script.*

The form in Example 22-3 includes two `text` objects: the user's full name and e-mail address. The element (`text` field) object is passed as an argument to the two different event handler functions. The `value` property reflects the current string in the text field.

`checkName()` checks that the value of its calling object (text field) is not empty and that it contains exactly two words (with a separating space). If one of these rules is violated, an appropriate message is displayed, and the calling element (the `userName text` object) is focused and selected, indicating the invalid text field.

`checkEmail()` checks if the value of its calling `text` object contains an "at" character (`@`). If one is not found, an appropriate message is displayed, and the calling element (the `email text` object) is focused and selected. The text within the field is highlighted by the `select()` method of the second `text` object in the form. As you can see, the script conveniently uses `this` for all references to the form element objects. Also notice that the field checking is done per every mouse click anywhere inside the window.

Properties

defaultValue

The `defaultValue` property is a string indicating the default value of a `text` object. The default value is initially assigned to the `VALUE` attribute of the HTML tag, reflected also by JavaScript's `defaultValue` property. Setting this property in JavaScript overrides the initial HTML values. You can set and read the defaultValue property at any time, even after layout has been completed. Since it reflects the field's default value only (the one seen when the page loads or after resetting the form), this property cannot be used to dynamically update the text in the field.

If the HTML attribute VALUE is not specified, defaultValue defaults to an empty string, as if explicitly specifying VALUE="". Also note that Microsoft Internet Explorer 3.0 does not support this property.

The following script segment demonstrates a simple use of the defaultValue property to reset only a specific form element (a text object in this case), rather than resetting the entire form with the Reset button or the reset() method. Note that this script uses the value property which is discussed later. Here it is:

```
<SCRIPT LANGUAGE="JavaScript">
<!--

function resetField(sub) {
     document.forms[0].elements[sub].value = document.forms[0]
                                .elements[sub].defaultValue
}

// -->
</SCRIPT>
<FORM NAME="fields">
<INPUT TYPE="text" NAME="field1" VALUE="enter first" SIZE=15>
<A HREF="javascript:resetField(0)">reset</A><BR>
<INPUT TYPE="text" NAME="field2" VALUE="enter second" SIZE=15>
<A HREF="javascript:resetField(1)">reset</A><BR>
<INPUT TYPE="text" NAME="field3" VALUE="enter third" SIZE=15>
<A HREF="javascript:resetField(2)">reset</A><BR>
</FORM>
```

Since we haven't discussed buttons yet, this script uses links for invoking JavaScript functions. A link is not a form element, so you cannot refer to this or this.form inside the resetField() function. To work around this problem, each link is identified by the index of the corresponding text object and is handed to the function as an argument. The first link, for example, is responsible for resetting the first text object in the form, so it hands a 0 to the resetField() function. Instead of resetting the form element, the function sets the current value of the corresponding text field to its default value.

name

It is generally a good practice to name every form element, and especially the text objects. Names are mandatory for CGI scripts which use them for field identification and value extraction. Since it allows a more logical and convenient access to JavaScript text objects, identifying text objects by names contributes significantly to the script's robustness and ease of maintenance. All names, therefore, should be meaningful and adhere to JavaScript's naming conventions.

The name property initially reflects the value of the HTML's NAME attribute. Changing the value of this property overrides the initial HTML setting. By assigning a new string to the name property, you can set the name of a text object at any time.

Do not confuse this property with the text that appears in the field. A field's content is represented by the VALUE attribute, rather than the NAME attribute. Hence, if you modify the value of name, you will notice no change in the page's appearance.

You should recall that a form element can be referenced by its index or by its name. If a form contains multiple elements with identical names, they form an array. Although this situation is especially common to radio buttons, as you will see later in this chapter, you may encounter it with text objects as well. The following example demonstrates the use of such arrays to handle complex forms:

```
<HTML>
<HEAD>
<TITLE>Form element arrays</TITLE>
<SCRIPT LANGUAGE="JavaScript">
<!--

function correctName() {
     for (var i = 0; i < document.fields.username.length; ++i) {
          var field = document.fields.username[i]
          field.value = field.value.charAt(0).toUpperCase() + field
                              .value.substring(1, field.value.length)
     }
}

function checkEmail() {
     for (var i = 0; i < document.fields.email.length; ++i) {
          var field = document.fields.email[i]
          if (field.value.indexOf("@") == -1) {
               alert("Error in email address!")
               field.focus()
               field.select()
               return
```

```
                    }
                }
            }

            // -->
            </SCRIPT>
            </HEAD>
            <BODY>
            <FORM NAME="fields">
            Employee #1: <INPUT TYPE="text" NAME="username" VALUE="first name" SIZE=10>
            <INPUT TYPE="text" NAME="username" VALUE="last name" SIZE=10>
            <INPUT TYPE="text" NAME="email" VALUE="email" SIZE=10><BR>
            Employee #2: <INPUT TYPE="text" NAME="username" VALUE="first name" SIZE=10>
            <INPUT TYPE="text" NAME="username" VALUE="last name" SIZE=10>
            <INPUT TYPE="text" NAME="email" VALUE="email" SIZE=10><BR>
            Employee #3: <INPUT TYPE="text" NAME="username" VALUE="first name" SIZE=10>
            <INPUT TYPE="text" NAME="username" VALUE="last name" SIZE=10>
            <INPUT TYPE="text" NAME="email" VALUE="email" SIZE=10><BR>
            <P>
            <A HREF="javascript:checkEmail()">Check email addresses</A>.
            <A HREF="javascript:correctName()">Correct names</A>.
            </FORM>
            </BODY>
            </HTML>
```

***Example 22-4**. A form validation script based on arrays reflecting elements with identical names.*

In order to understand this listing you must be aware of the page's initial appearance:

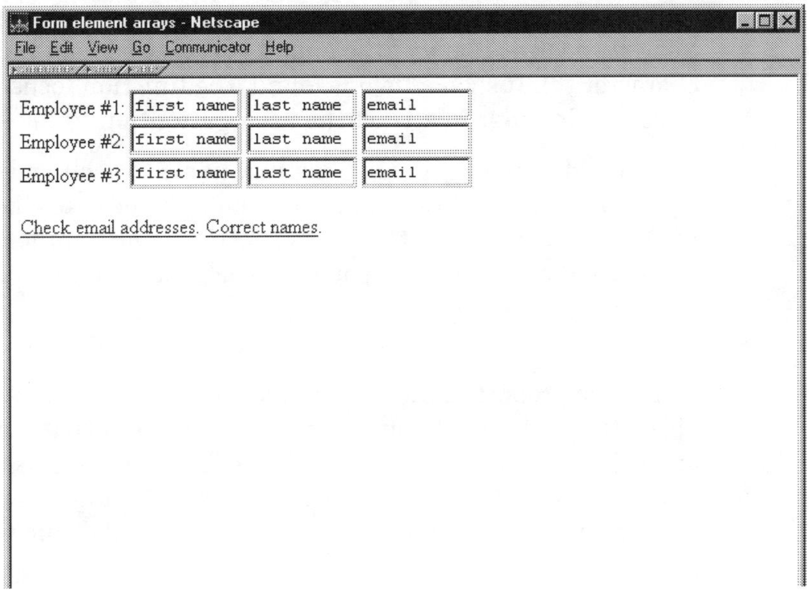

Form element arrays - Netscape

File Edit View Go Communicator Help

Employee #1: first name | last name | email

Employee #2: first name | last name | email

Employee #3: first name | last name | email

Check email addresses. Correct names.

***Figure 22-5**. A form that collects data about several people.*

As you can see, this form is divided into nine text objects. All six text objects for entering first and last names are named username. The value of document.forms[0].elements[0].name, for example, is equal to the string "username". The three text objects for entering e-mail addresses are named email.

There are basically two element groups, username and email. Since all form elements are named fields, you can reference these two groups as arrays, via the following syntax:

```
document.fields.username
document.fields.email
```

Both arrays have a length property, representing the number of elements sharing the given name. The length and elements of the username array, for example, can be referenced as follows:

```
document.fields.username.length // number of name-related elements
document.fields.username[0] // first First Name object
document.fields.username[1] // first Last Name object
document.fields.username[2] // second First Name object
document.fields.username[3] // second Last Name object
document.fields.username[4] // third First Name object
document.fields.username[5] // third Last Name object
```

The same syntax is also used to reference elements of the email array. Take another look at the script in Example 22-4. It includes two functions, one for handling name input fields and one for e-mails. The first function, correctName(), loops through all username elements and capitalizes their first letters. The second function uses the same technique to alert the user if any of the e-mail addresses do not include the "at" character (@). If such a field is found, the function focuses on and selects it, in order to attract the user's attention to the invalid field.

You should normally assign a distinct name to each and every form element. Example 22-4 demonstrates that in some cases, however, it is much more convenient to reuse a specific name in order to enable a loop-based processing of elements which share similar characteristics.

value

The value property reflects the current text located in a given text object (field). It is not equivalent to any HTML attribute. You can read and set this property at any time. The field's content is updated immediately upon setting. Although we have been using this property throughout this chapter, here is another example which shows how to reference the value attribute of the first element of the first form in a page:

```
document.forms[0].elements[0].value
```

Password Object

HTML Syntax

Another possible value for the TYPE attribute is password. It is similar to the text option except that, instead of displaying the user's input, it responds to any typed character with a predefined single character, such as an asterisk (*). The general syntax of this object is as follows:

```
<INPUT
     TYPE="password"
     NAME="passwordName"
     [VALUE="contents"]
     [SIZE="integer"]
     [MAXLENGTH="integer"]
     [onBlur="handlerStatement"]
     [onChange="handlerStatement"]
     [onFocus="handlerStatement"]
     [onSelect="handlerStatement"]>
```

The value property is an asterisk character (or any other character chosen by the browser). The additional properties are identical to those of the text input type. Here is a simple password box code:

```
Password: <INPUT TYPE="password" NAME="pswrd" SIZE=15 MAXLENGTH=20
VALUE="">
```

Here is the appearance after typing a six-character string in the text box, "bgates" for example:

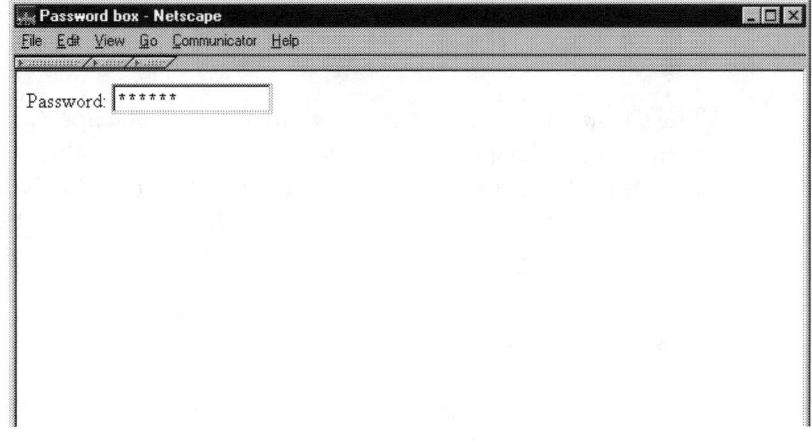

***Figure 22-6**. A password box after typing in a six-letter string.*

The value of the password box is the typed-in string, not the shown asterisks. The value is hidden so it cannot be seen by someone standing behind the user.

JavaScript Access

Like all other elements, there are four ways to access a `password` object via JavaScript:

```
[window.]document.formName.passwordName
```

```
[window.]document.formName.elements[index]
```

```
[window.]document.forms[index].passwordName
```

```
[window.]document.forms[index].elements[index]
```

All methods and element references adhere to one of these alternatives.

Event Handlers

The `password` event handlers are identical to those of the `text` object in all aspects. Refer to earlier discussion in this and other chapters.

Properties and Methods

The `password` object's methods are identical to those of the `text` object:

- `focus`
- `blur`
- `select`

The `password` object's properties are:

- `defaultValue`
- `name`
- `value`

The `password` object was not very useful in Netscape Navigator 2.0 because JavaScript was not allowed to access its value. Starting with versions 3.0, JavaScript on Navigator and IE can freely access the `value` attribute as if it is a `text` object. In terms of JavaScript, the `password` object is identical to the `text` object. The only difference is that the value of the password field is never displayed.

Textarea Object

HTML Syntax

Multiple lines of text can be entered into a form via text areas which are defined by the <TEXTAREA>...</TEXTAREA> tag pair. You should always name a text area and specify its size. The general syntax of the <TEXTAREA> tag is as follows:

```
<TEXTAREA
    NAME="textareaName"
    ROWS="integer"
    COLS="integer"
    WRAP="off | virtual | physical"
    [onBlur="handlerStatement"]
    [onChange="handlerStatement"]
    [onFocus="handlerStatement"]
    [onSelect="handlerStatement"]>
    textToDisplay
</TEXTAREA>
```

The attributes are:

- NAME—specifies the name (label) of the text area element. It is very difficult to work with unnamed text areas, so always name your text areas according to JavaScript naming conventions.
- ROWS—specifies the number of text rows in the text area. Since Netscape Navigator and Microsoft Internet Explorer use different size fonts in text fields, you cannot set the text area size in pixels by setting ROWS.
- COLS—specifies the number of text columns in the text area. It is equal to the number of characters in one text line.

Here is a capture of a text area in Netscape Navigator:

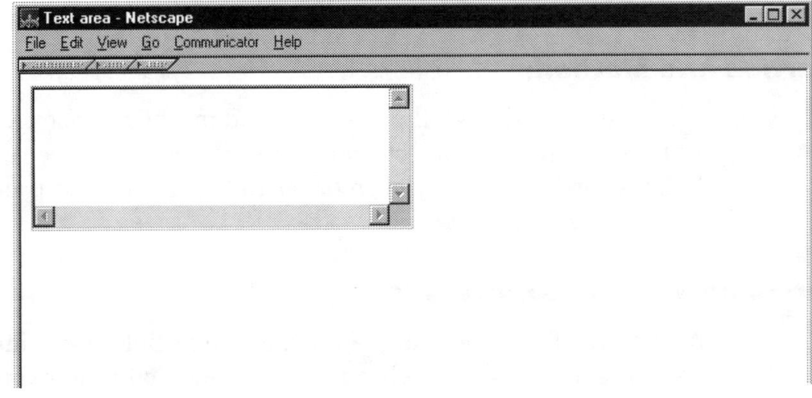

Figure 22-7*. A simple text area with no initial value.*

It is possible to initialize the text area by placing text between the <TEXTAREA> and </TEXTAREA> tags in the following fashion:

```
<TEXTAREA NAME="comments" COLS=35 ROWS=5>
Write any comments regarding this page here.
Don't forget to mention your e-mail address.
</TEXTAREA>
```

Carriage return characters are interpreted as new lines in this text zone. Netscape Navigator enables you to write HTML tags in the text area by simply placing the script between the opening and closing TEXTAREA tags. MSIE 3.0 does not support this feature, though, so you should avoid using it altogether.

Another attribute accepted by the <TEXTAREA> tag is WRAP. It can be set to one of the following values:

- OFF—do not wrap lines (default value).
- VIRTUAL—wrap lines on the screen but refer to them as one line otherwise.
- PHYSICAL—insert actual line breaks (CR characters) in the string.

JavaScript Access

There are four ways to access a textarea object via JavaScript:

```
[window.]document.formName.textareaName
```

```
[window.]document.formName.elements[index]
```

```
[window.]document.forms[index].textareaName
```

```
[window.]document.forms[index].elements[index]
```

Event Handlers

The textarea object's event handlers are identical to those of the text object.

Properties and Methods

Like event handlers, all properties and methods are exactly the same as those of the text object and password object. Please refer to previous listings for the text object in order to learn about its properties, methods, and event handlers.

Inserting new line Characters

A text area field is actually a multiline text field. Printing output to a textarea object is somewhat more complicated than printing to a text object due to the extra complication of new line insertion. This is especially important when the WRAP attribute is set to off and you are interested in avoiding a long horizontal text span.

Since the new line character is not uniform across different platforms, inserting a new line is not as simple as inserting any other printable character. The new line character on Unix- and Macintosh-based machines is "\n", while Windows operating systems require the "\r\n" pair. The simplest way to work around the problem is to test the actual platform and insert the corresponding new line character. Here is a function that automatically returns the correct string for the user's platform:

```
function getNL() {
      if (navigator.appVersion.lastIndexOf('Win') != -1)
            return "\r\n"
       /* else */
            return "\n"
}
```

You can assign the new line character in the following fashion:

```
var NL = getNL()
```

Now, you can use the function's return value to place a multiple-line text in a textarea object. Here is a simple example:

```
document.forms[0].elements[0].value = "line 1" + NL + "line 2"
```

Important note: Netscape Navigator 3.0 supports "\n" as a new line character on all platforms. However, Microsoft Internet Explorer 3.0 requires a platform-dependent new line character.

Handling textareas By Line

In general, you cannot deal with specific lines of textarea content. The following function overcomes this deficiency by assigning the text to an array, line by line:

```
function getLines(textareaReference) {
      var str = escape(textareaReference.value)

      var ar = str.split("%0D%0A") // "%0D%0A" <=> "\r\n"

      if (ar.length == 0)
```

```
        ar = str.split("%0A") // "%0A" <=> "\n"

    for (var i = 0; i < ar.length; ++i) {
        ar[i] = unescape(ar[i])
    }

    return ar
}
```

The function is a bit tricky. It first encodes the textarea's value via the escape function and assignes the "escaped" string to a local variable, str. You may recall that after escape, any nonalphanumeric characters are represented in a "%*XX*" format. The escape sequence "\n" is represented as "%0A" (zero + A) whereas "\r" is converted to "%0D" (zero + D). The entire encoded string is then spliced with the split() method, using either the "%0D%0A" or the "%0A" string as the delimiter. The "trick" is to use the second delimiter ("%0A") only after the first one ("%0D%0A") fails to split the text. At the end, each element of the ar array is decoded back by the unescape function. The final array of lines is returned.

Hidden Object

HTML Syntax

A hidden form field is one that is not displayed on an HTML page. It is used for passing unique identification values upon submission. Since the user cannot modify or interact with a hidden element, the initial value given when the page loads stays the same throughout the life of the page. The hidden object, then, is not useful for the user but rather for the programmer. On a large Web site, a server-side application can use a hidden object to distinguish between different forms submitted to the server.

Except that it is not viewable, you should basically treat the hidden element exactly like the text type. The element's general syntax is:

```
<INPUT
    TYPE="hidden"
    NAME="hiddenName"
    [VALUE="textValue"]>
```

The NAME property specifies the name of the hidden object whereas VALUE specifies the value of the field. Although not viewable, they are part of the form's content, as any other element type's attributes.

JavaScript Access

There are four ways to reference a hidden object:

```
[window.]document.formName.hiddenName
```

```
[window.]document.formName.elements[index]
```

```
[window.]document.forms[index].hiddenName
```

```
[window.]document.forms[index].elements[index]
```

Event Handlers

Since a hidden object cannot be seen on a page, no events can be associated with it, and hence there is no support for event handlers for hidden objects.

Properties and Methods

Since all methods associated with form element objects emulate events, a hidden object does not have any methods.

A hidden object does not feature any event handlers either, but it does have several properties which you can access via JavaScript. The object's properties are:

- defaultValue
- name
- value

These properties are equivalent to those of the text, password, and textarea objects. You can read and set the value property, for example, at any time. The value property can be used to earmark forms submitted to the server for identification by a server-side application.

Button Object, Submit Object, Reset Object

HTML Syntax

The most precise input event is a button click. Submit, reset, and button objects are all buttons which feature identical properties and attributes. The general syntax of a button is as follows:

```
<INPUT
     TYPE="button" | "submit" | "reset"
     NAME="buttonName"
     VALUE="buttonText"
     [onClick="handlerText"]>
```

Figure 22-8 shows a simple example of a Windows 95-style button:

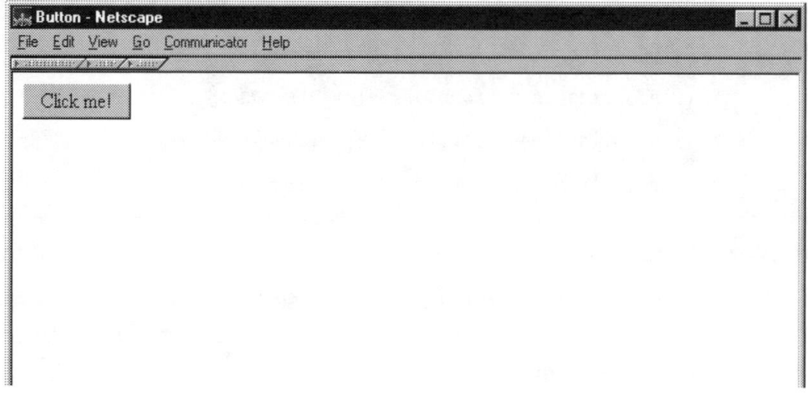

***Figure 22-8**. A Windows 95-style button.*

Although a plain button (`<INPUT TYPE="button">`) does not have any explicit meaning in HTML, it is extremely useful in JavaScript scripts. A submit button plays a very important role in all forms that are submitted to a server. A reset button resets the form in which it is located.

A button's style depends on the client's platform. Macintosh buttons, for example, are different from Windows 95 buttons. The only control you have over a button's appearance is by determining its label, initially defined by the `VALUE` attribute. Since the button size is solely determined by the label string, you can only modify its width, by padding it with spaces on both ends. This "sophisticated" technique may be very annoying, but it is the only way to explicitly control a button's size.

A submit button's syntax differs from plain buttons and reset buttons only in the value assigned to the `TYPE` attribute `"submit"`. This button is primarily designed for server-side applications. When the user clicks such a button, the form's data is sent to the URL specified in the `<FORM>` tag's `ACTION` attribute. A reset button's `TYPE` is `"reset"` and, when clicked, it resets the entire form. A plain button (with no HTML meaning) is defined by assigning `"button"` to the `TYPE` attribute.

JavaScript Access

The four ways you can reference a button via JavaScript are:

```
[window.]document.formName.buttonName
```

```
[window.]document.formName.elements[index]
```

```
[window.]document.forms[index].buttonName
```

```
[window.]document.forms[index].elements[index]
```

Event Handlers

All button objects (button, reset, and submit) are associated with a single event, and therefore support only one event handler. This event handler is probably the most important of all form-related event handlers.

onClick

A button, by definition, has only one designation—to be clicked. Its event handler, therefore, responds only to a `click` event. Such an event occurs when the user presses the button and then releases it while the pointer is still atop the button. The event does not take place immediately when the user presses the button, in order to give the user a chance to cancel the clicking action by releasing it outside the button area.

You can use this event handler also with Submit and Reset buttons. The `onClick` event handler script is executed prior to performing the built-in action associated with a button. You can use this event, for example, to compute a certain expression and assign its value to the `value` property of an existing form element object.

The general syntax for this event handler is as follows:

```
<INPUT TYPE=... onClick="handlerScript">
```

Netscape Navigator 3.0 features a new option to cancel a `click` event. This can be done by having the event handler return `false`, much the same way you cancel a form's submission or resetting. The canceled action is the one defined by the button (or other objects that support this event handler). Canceling a `click` event of a Submit button, for example, cancels the form's submission.

Example 22-5 demonstrates the usage of the `onClick` event handler for invoking a function that handles other elements of the form:

```
<HTML>
<HEAD>
<TITLE>Expression evaluator</TITLE>
<SCRIPT LANGUAGE="JavaScript">
<!--

function compute(form) {
    form.result.value = eval(form.expression.value)
}

// -->
</SCRIPT>
```

```
</HEAD>
<BODY>
<FORM>
<INPUT TYPE="text" NAME="expression" VALUE="" SIZE=15> =
<INPUT TYPE="text" NAME="result" VALUE="" SIZE=8 onFocus="this.blur()">
<P>
<INPUT TYPE="button" NAME="computeButton" VALUE="compute" onClick=
                                  "compute(this.form)">
<INPUT TYPE="button" NAME="clear" VALUE="clear result" onClick=
                                  "this.form.result.value = ''">
</FORM>
</BODY>
</HTML>
```

***Example 22-5**. A simple expression evaluation script.*

Before we discuss this short script, it is essential that you know how the page looks. Figure 22-9 shows the initial appearance.

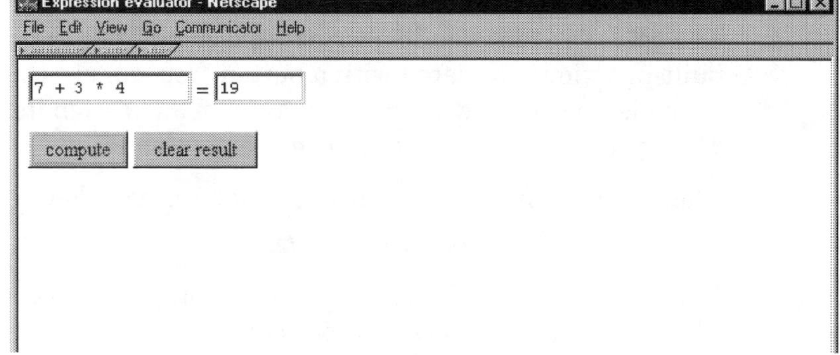

***Figure 22-9**. A form with four elements: a simple numeric evaluation utility.*

The user types any numeric expression (such as 4 + 6 * 15) in the upper left field, and, after pressing **compute**, the result appears in the upper right field. The "clear result" button deletes the value in that field.

As you can see, the form contains four elements. The first two are `text` objects—each with its own unique attributes. The first button, named `computeButton`, uses an `onClick` event handler to call the `compute` function with the object reflecting the entire form. The second button provides the only means for clearing the result field (the upper right one). The `onClick` event handler of this object is a single, immediate statement. Its `onFocus` event handler creates a read-only field by calling the `blur` method.

Since the entire form object is assigned to `compute`'s `form` parameter, the property `form.result.value` refers to the content of the top right `text` object, whereas `form.expression.value` refers to the text inside the first field. The text in the first field is evaluated, and the numeric result becomes its value. If the left field contains the expression "`5 * 3 – 2`", for example, then `eval` returns 13 which is placed in the second `text` object by assigning 13 to its `value` property.

Methods

click()

A button's `click()` method simulates the user's action of clicking that button. It causes the same action as would a human click, except that the button's `onClick` event handler is not triggered. Since their only usefulness is in triggering the `onClick` event handler, this method is not useful for `TYPE="button"` buttons. On some platforms, a visual border effect is created when invoking this method.

You will probably never need to use this method, but here is an example for your reference:

```
document.forms[0].elements[0].click()
```

Properties

name

A button's `name` property is an exact reflection of the `NAME` attribute and is read-only. In order to respond correctly to an event, the `onClick` event handler function commonly uses this property to figure out which button was clicked. Here is an example of how to reference this property:

```
var buttonName = document.forms[0].elements[0].name
```

value

A button's value is the visual label you give the button by assigning it to the `VALUE` attribute of the `<INPUT>` tag. All form elements defined by `<INPUT>` tag feature this attribute. As far as buttons are concerned, the length of the string determines the button's size. The `VALUE` attribute can be more than one word, and should generally be enclosed by quotation marks.

The `VALUE` attribute is reflected in JavaScript by the `value` property. Although it is unlikely you will ever need to extract the property's value, its modification may be useful. Suppose you have a single button on a Web page, and you want its label to change whenever the user clicks the button. You can implement such behavior by modifying the `value` property as a response to the `click` event. Netscape Navigator 3.0 enables explicit JavaScript setting of event handlers, so you can even modify the event handler's script along with the button's label, to create a "new" button on the fly (without reloading the page). Example 22-6 uses these features to create a simple stopwatch.

```
<HTML>
<HEAD>
<TITLE>stopwatch (timer)</TITLE>
<SCRIPT LANGUAGE="JavaScript">
<!--

// set initial values
var timerRunning = false
var timerID = null

// create instance of Date object representing current time
var initial = new Date()

// start timer
function start() {
     // set the button's label to "stop"
     document.forms[0].general.value = "stop"

     // assign the stop function reference to the button's onClick
                                   event handler
     document.forms[0].general.onclick = stop

     // ask if the user wants to reset the timer
     if (confirm("Would you like to reset the timer?"))
          // set global variable to new time
          initial = new Date()

     // assign milliseconds since 1970 to global variable
     startTime = initial.getTime()

     // make sure the timer is stopped
     stopTimer()

     // run and display timer
     showTimer()
}

// set button to initial settings
function stop() {
     // set the button's label to "start"
     document.forms[0].general.value = "start"

     // assign the start function reference to the button's onClick
                                   event handler
     document.forms[0].general.onclick = start
```

```
          // stop timer
          stopTimer()
     }

     // stop timer
     function stopTimer() {
          // if the timer is currently running
          if (timerRunning)
               // clear the current timeout (stop the timer)
               clearTimeout(timerID)

          // assign false to global variable because timer is not running
          timerRunning = false
     }

     function showTimer() {
          // create instance of Date representing current timer
          var current = new Date()

          // assign milliseconds since 1970 to local variable
          var curTime = current.getTime()

          // assign difference in milliseconds since timer was cleared
          var dif = curTime - startTime

          // assign difference in seconds to local variable
          var result = dif / 1000

          // if result is not positive
          if (result < 1)
               // attach an initial "0" to beginning
               result = "0" + result

          // convert result to string
          result = result.toString()

          // if result is integer
          if (result.indexOf(".") == -1)
               // attach ".00" to end
               result += ".00"

          // if result contains only one digit after decimal point
          if (result.length - result.indexOf(".") <= 2)
               // add a second digit after point
               result += "0"

          // place result in text field
          document.forms[0].display.value = result

          // call function recursively immediately (must use setTimeout
                                        to avoid overflow)
```

```
        timerID = setTimeout("showTimer()", 0)

        // timer is currently running
        timerRunning = true
}

// -->
</SCRIPT>
</HEAD>
<BODY>
<FORM>
<INPUT TYPE="text" NAME="display" VALUE="" onFocus="this.blur()">
<INPUT TYPE="button" NAME="general" VALUE="start" onClick="start()">
</FORM>
</BODY>
</HTML>
```

Example 22-6. *A simple timer with an adjusting button.*

Look through the script for a few minutes, and make sure you understand the recursive flow and the handling of time-related features. Since most of the features in this script should be well known to you by now, we'll just cover the new and difficult ones.

Take a look at the following statements from the `start()` function:

```
// set the button's label to "stop"
document.forms[0].general.value = "stop"

// assign the stop function reference to the button's onClick
                                  event handler
document.forms[0].general.onclick = stop
```

The first statement adjust the button's label by assigning it a new value—`stop`. The second statement assigns a function reference (no parentheses because it is a function reference, not a function call) to the button's `onClick` event handler. Notice that the event handler must be specified in lowercase letters. These statements convert the Start button to a Stop button. The following statements from the `stop()` function convert the Stop button back to a Start button, on the fly:

```
// set the button's label to "start"
document.forms[0].general.value = "start"

// assign the start function reference to the button's onClick
                                  event handler
document.forms[0].general.onclick = start
```

Notice that the button is labeled Stop when the timer is running and is labeled Start otherwise.

The form in Example 22-6 consists of two elements. The first one is a read-only `text` object (set via an event handler), whereas the second one is a simple button.

Setting the value of a button is somewhat problematic. First, the button size is not adjusted to the new label, so any excess text is dropped on both sides. Another problem is that since the button label is centered, you do not have control over its alignment with other buttons of different form elements. If you initialize a button to a very long string via its HTML attribute (try assigning a string with many spaces to `VALUE`), you can even run a T-banner on the button!

Checkbox Object

HTML Syntax

A check box is a small box which reflects an "on" or "off" state. An HTML check box is a form element that closely resembles a check box on a paper form. If a mark is placed in the box, the current state is considered `true`. If the check box is unchecked, the current state is `false`.

Check boxes are used a lot in server-based forms. If a box is checked, it is included in the submitted data, whereas if it is empty it is excluded from the data submitted to the server. Since a check box is an individual form element which is not grouped with other elements, you should apply a distinct name to every check box in a form. The user can check or uncheck a text box at any time after the page has been laid out.

The general syntax of a check box is as follows:

```
<INPUT
     TYPE="checkbox"
     NAME="checkboxName"
     VALUE="checkboxValue"
     [CHECKED]
     [onClick="handlerText"]>
```

Both the `NAME` and `VALUE` attributes specify internal values which are not displayed on the page. In order to label a check box, you should simply place the label directly after the check box, so it appears as if connected to the object. The following piece of code demonstrates this trick:

```
Select all the computers used at your business:
<P>
<INPUT TYPE="checkbox" NAME="PC">PC
<P>
<INPUT TYPE="checkbox" NAME="Mac">Macintosh
<P>
<INPUT TYPE="checkbox" NAME="Unix">Unix (X-Windows)
```

The output page is the following:

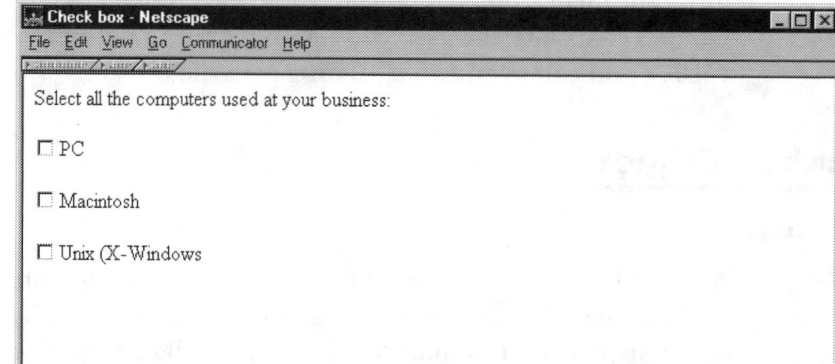

Figure 22-10*. A few check boxes.*

In order to create a check box that is initially checked, you simply specify the `CHECKED` attribute, without assigning it any value. Its presence determines the initial state of the check box when the page loads.

A JavaScript check box provides a wide variety of functionality, but you should not use it as a regular button (supporting, for example, an `onClick` event handler); rather use it only as a "yes"/"no" selection interface. You can, however, use the `click` event to trigger a side-effect statement. It is important to recognize that a check box is primarily a toggle switch.

JavaScript Access

There are basically four ways to reference a check box:

```
[window.]document.formName.checkboxName
```

```
[window.]document.formName.elements[index]
```

```
[window.]document.forms[index].checkboxName
```

```
[window.]document.forms[index].elements[index]
```

Event Handlers

onClick

Since a check box responds to only the `click` event, the `checkbox` object does not support event handlers other than `onClick`. Use this event handler when you want to invoke a function or execute a statement immediately when the user clicks a check box. A `click` event occurs when the user clicks a check box, regardless if it is checked or empty.

Again, be extremely conservative when using this event handler. A check box should be used only for "yes"/"no" voting interface.

Methods

click()

The `checkbox` object supports only the `click()` method, which is equivalent to manually clicking the check box. You can use this method to implement a nonmodifiable check box, for example, by clicking the check box whenever the user clicks it, thus always reversing the user's action and leaving the check box untouched. Here is how to define such a "read-only" check box:

```
<INPUT TYPE="checkbox" onClick="this.click()">
```

Another useful implementation of this method is to open an invisible connection between two or more check boxes. Here is an example script that always keeps two check boxes at the same state (checked or unchecked):

```
<SCRIPT LANGUAGE="JavaScript">
<!--

function connectMe(destination) {
     document.forms[0].elements[destination].click()
}

// -->
</SCRIPT>
</HEAD>
<BODY>
<FORM>
<INPUT TYPE="checkbox" onClick="connectMe(1)"> Number 1<BR>
<INPUT TYPE="checkbox" onClick="connectMe(0)"> Number 2
</FORM>
```

Each check box's `onClick` event handler invokes the `connectMe()` function with the target check box's index as the argument. The second check box's event handler, for example, calls connectMe() with a 0 value because it is connected to the first check box (its index is 0). The connectMe() function simply emulates a click event for the form element at the given index.

The click() method does not trigger the onClick event handler so you should not worry about the script getting into an infinite loop here. You can generalize the connectMe() function to handle an array of check boxes with a for loop.

Properties

checked

The check box's Boolean property checked reflects the button's current state. A true value means that the specified check box is checked, whereas a false one represents an unchecked box. Of the properties supported by the checkbox object, this property is both the simplest and the most useful. You can read and adjust this property at any time, even after layout has been completed.

Checking and unchecking a check box is accomplished by simply assigning the corresponding Boolean value to the object's checked property. The following statement unchecks a box:

```
document.forms[0].elements[0].checked = false
```

Since a check box can be set to any of the two possible states regardless of the current one, you do not have to use an if statement to determine the current state and then invoke the action accordingly. Be aware that setting the state of a check box by assigning checked is much more efficient than probing the current state and calling the check box's click() method.

Example 22-7 demonstrates the use of the checked property in a simple game. It features both reading the checked property as well as setting it. The objective of the game is to check as many boxes as possible within 20 seconds (20,000 milliseconds). The accumulated number of currently checked boxes is displayed in a text object at the top. When time is over, all check boxes become read-only, and a start button is placed at the bottom for restarting the game.

```
<HTML>
<HEAD>
<TITLE>Checkbox game</TITLE>
<SCRIPT LANGUAGE="JavaScript">
<!--
```

```
// assign initial values to global variables
var total = 0
var play = false

// react to a click in a checkbox (element == clicked checkbox object)
function display(element) {
     // assign instance of Date object representing current time
     var now = new Date()

     // if the game has not started yet
     if (!play) {
          // game starts now
          play = true

          // milliseconds since 1970 for time at beginning
          startTime = now.getTime()
     }

     // if more than 20 seconds have passed since startTime was last set
     if (now.getTime() - startTime > 20000) {
          // reject modification (make "read-only")
          element.checked = !element.checked

          // terminate function
          return
     }

     // if the clicked check box is now checked
     if (element.checked)
          // increment total
          total++
     else
          // decrement total
          total--

     // display total in text object
     element.form.num.value = total
}

function restart(form) {
     // set global variables back to initial values
     total = 0
     play = false

     // uncheck all 100 check boxes
     for (var i = 1; i <= 100; ++i) {
          // uncheck current check box
          form.elements[i].checked = false
     }
}
```

```
// -->
</SCRIPT>
</HEAD>
<BODY>
<SCRIPT LANGUAGE="JavaScript">
<!--

// immediate script (executed before the other script because it
                                  is deferred)

document.write("<FORM><CENTER>")
document.write('<INPUT TYPE="text" VALUE="0" NAME="num" SIZE=10 onFocus=
                                  "this.blur()"><BR>')
document.write("<HR SIZE=1 WIDTH=40%>")

// use loop to create a 10 x 10 square of check boxes
for (var i = 0; i < 10; ++i) {
     for (var j = 0; j < 10; ++j) {
          // write check box with "display(this)" as event handler script
          document.write('<INPUT TYPE="checkbox" onClick=
                                  "display(this)">')
     }
     document.write("<BR>")
}

document.write("<HR SIZE=1 WIDTH=40%>")

// create button to call restart function to restart game
document.write('<INPUT TYPE="button" VALUE="restart" onClick=
                                  "restart(this.form)">')

document.write("</CENTER></FORM>")

// -->
</SCRIPT>
</BODY>
</HTML>
```

***Example 22-7**. A game demonstrating the use of check boxes.*

The global statements in the `<HEAD>...</HEAD>` portion define the variable `total` that holds the accumulated number of checked check boxes and the variable `play` that holds a Boolean indication as to whether the game is currently being played (timer is running) or not.

Since its statements are all immediate ones, the first script segment to be executed is the one within the `<BODY>...</BODY>` portion of the page. That script simply prints the HTML interface of the game: a `text` object, 100 check boxes, a button, and two horizontal rules. All check boxes have an onClick event handler that calls the display() function with the checkbox object itself (this) as an argument.

The display() function accepts one argument—the triggered checkbox object. First, an instance of the Date object, representing the time at which the display() function was called, is assigned to the local variable now. The next segment of the function checks if the game is already being played. If not, play is set to true and the number of milliseconds since 1970 is assigned to the global variable startTime. If the difference between the current time and that at the beginning of the game is greater than 20 seconds, the property checked of the calling checkbox is reversed (rejecting user's attempts to continue playing after time is out), and the function terminates immediately. The rest of the function deals with a normal event of the user clicking the check box. The total number of checkboxes is incremented if the calling check box is currently checked, and is decremented if the check box is currently unchecked. The total number of checked check boxes is assigned to element.form.num.value, the text object's value property.

The restart() function simply resets all global variables and checkbox states to their initial settings.

Note: Instead of using the click() method to restrict modification of a check box, you should simply return the box's state to its previous one. That is, set it to true if it was false and vice versa. A general "read-only" check box uses the following syntax:

```
<INPUT TYPE="checkbox" onClick="this.checked =
!this.checked">
```

defaultChecked

A check box definition may include a CHECKED specification to signal that the default state of the check box is "on," or true. If you do not specify this HTML attribute, it defaults to false. You can access a check box's default state via JavaScript's defaultCheck property. You can set defaultCheck at any time, thus overriding the CHECKED attribute. Use the following statement to reset a check box's state to its default:

```
this.checked = this.defaultChecked
```

`this` is the specific check box you want to reset.

name

A `checkbox` object's `name` property reflects the `NAME` attribute of the `<INPUT>` element definition. It is a read-only property, so you cannot modify it. You should be as descriptive as possible when choosing a `NAME` attribute, especially for server-side applications which access the box's value only through its name. If your form is primarily for JavaScript processing, you can use the `NAME` attribute to mimic the functionality of a second `VALUE` attribute.

value

The `value` property initially reflects the `VALUE` attribute of the `<INPUT>` definition, but it can be adjusted via JavaScript script at any time.

Just like a `text` object's string value, the `value` property represents the `checkbox` object's value, and as such is very important for forms processed by the server. By setting the `value` attribute, you explicitly affect the content of the form submitted to the server.

Although you can accomplish many tasks without using the `value` property, it is sometimes very convenient to use this property instead. The following example demonstrates how to use a check box list to print all operating systems which your business uses:

```
<HTML>
<HEAD>
<TITLE>Checkbox value property</TITLE>
<SCRIPT LANGUAGE="JavaScript">
<!--

function displayList(list) {
    var total = ""

    for (var i = 0; i < list.length; ++i) {
        if (list[i].checked)
            total += list[i].value + "\r"
    }

    if (total == "")
        alert("No OS selected!")
    else
        alert(total)
```

```
}

// -->
</SCRIPT>
</HEAD>
<BODY>
<FORM>
<INPUT TYPE="checkbox" VALUE="DOS / Windows" NAME="computer">DOS /
                                    Windows 3.1x<BR>
<INPUT TYPE="checkbox" VALUE="Windows 95" NAME="computer">Windows 95<BR>
<INPUT TYPE="checkbox" VALUE="Macinstosh" NAME="computer">Macintosh<BR>
<INPUT TYPE="checkbox" VALUE="Unix" NAME="computer">Unix<BR>
<INPUT TYPE="button" VALUE="display list"
onClick="displayList(this.form.computer)">
</FORM>
</BODY>
</HTML>
```

First of all, notice that the form consists of four check boxes and one button. The button's `onClick` event handler invokes the `displayList()` function, passing the `computer` form element as an argument. Since there are four elements matching that name, `this.form.computer` is actually an array of four check box elements. A check box's `VALUE` attribute specifies the operating system associated with that check box.

The `displayList()` function is based on a simple `for` loop which concatenates the `checkbox values` inside the local variable `total`, inserting new line characters as delimiters. When the loop terminates, `local` holds a list of all the operating systems that the user had checked. If the value of `total` is an empty string, the user did not check any of the boxes, and an appropriate message is displayed. Otherwise, the list of the checked operating systems is displayed in an `alert` box.

Radio Object

HTML Syntax

A radio button provides an interface to select an option among multiple choices. Unlike check boxes which are rectangular in shape, radio buttons are circular ones. Another difference between the two types of buttons is that radio buttons belong to a group of buttons and are not independent. A group of radio buttons behaves exactly like the station buttons on your old car radio. It has two possible states: one button is pressed (ON) or all buttons are released (OFF). When a button is pressed, the currently pressed button is automatically released.

All buttons of the same group share the same name. In fact, the identical name is an indication to the browser to restrict the number of checked radio buttons to one. Clicking a button automatically deselects the currently selected button of the same group. The general syntax of a single radio button is as follows:

```
<INPUT
    TYPE="radio"
    NAME="groupName"
    VALUE="buttonValue"
    [CHECKED]
    [onClick="handlerText"]>
```

Keep in mind that you should only use this type of button to enable a single selection among multiple choices. The following construct, for example, provides the means to choose a computer type out of three options:

```
What computer do you most often use:
<P>
<INPUT TYPE="radio" NAME="computers" VALUE="unix">Unix (X-Windows)
<P>
<INPUT TYPE="radio" NAME="computers" VALUE="pc">PC
<P>
<INPUT TYPE="radio" NAME="computers" VALUE="mac">Macintosh
```

When implemented correctly within a form, this group of elements appears as outlined below:

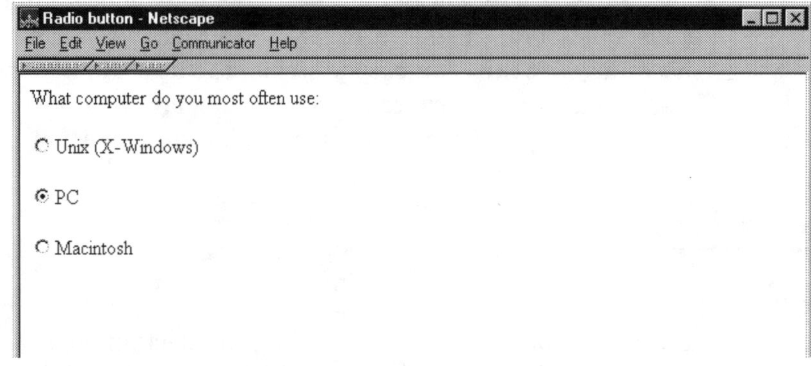

***Figure 22-11**. A group of radio buttons (only one can be selected).*

JavaScript Access

Although a radio button is a simple form element, its reference is an unusual one. You can reference a radio button group via one of the following expressions:

```
[window.]document.formName.radioGroupName
```

```
[window.]document.formName.elements[ElementIndex]
```

```
[window.]document.forms[FormIndex].radioGroupName
```

```
[window.]document.forms[FormIndex].elements[ElementIndex]
```

As explained at the beginning of this chapter, elements with the same names are combined and indexed into a single array. Therefore, the above references are actually arrays, where each element is a single radio button. Hence, the four ways to reference a specific radio button are as follows:

```
[window.]document.formName.radioGroupName[ButtonIndex]
```

```
[window.]document.formName.elements[ElementIndex][ButtonIndex]
```

```
[window.]document.forms[FormIndex].radioGroupName[ButtonIndex]
```

```
[window.]document.forms[FormIndex].elements[ElementIndex][ButtonIndex]
```

You can look up the number of radio buttons in a group by accessing the group's `length` attribute. For more details, check the section about the `name` property of the `text` object.

Internet Explorer does not work perfectly well with the `radio` object, so be sure to test your script with both browsers.

When a radio button group consists of only one radio button, it is not considered a group. Therefore, you cannot access the array, and references such as the following ones are not valid:

```
[window.]document.formName.radioGroupName[index]
[window.]document.formName.radioGroupName.length
```

Instead, you must access the radio button directly, without an array:

```
[window.]document.formName.radioButtonName
```

The difference in referencing a single button and a multiple-button group complicates scripts quite a bit. If the radio buttons are created with plain HTML, you obviously know if the number of radio buttons is greater than one and access them accordingly. If the radio buttons are automatically generated by a script, then you have to add a counter that will indicate if the number of buttons is greater than one.

Event Handlers

onClick

A `radio` object supports only one event handler—the `onClick` event. When the user checks (fills) a radio button, a `click` event occurs, and the specified statements are executed. See the listings for the checkbox object for more details, syntax, and examples.

Methods

click()

The click() method emulates a button click on the calling radio object. It does not, however, trigger the button's onClick event handler. Example 22-8 demonstrates the use of this method to create a "Christmas lights" effect.

```
<HTML>
<HEAD>
<TITLE>Blinking lights</TITLE>
</HEAD>
<BODY onLoad="animate()">
<SCRIPT LANGUAGE="JavaScript">
<!--

// create row of radio buttons
lay(20)

// set index of lamp to start animation
var current = 0

// set speed (pause in milliseconds between each movement)
var speed = 100

function lay(num) {
     // assign "greater than" character to variable
     var gt = unescape("%3e")

     // open form
     document.write("<FORM NAME='animation'" + gt)

     // use loop to lay radio buttons down (all buttons in same group)
     for (var i = 0; i < num; ++i) {
          document.write("<INPUT TYPE='radio' NAME='lamps'" + gt)
     }

     // close form
     document.write("</FORM" + gt)
}

function animate() {
     // click next radio button
     document.animation.lamps[current].click()

     // if radio button is the last one reset variable to 0
                         (otherwise increment)
```

```
        current = (current == document.animation.lamps.length - 1) ? 0
                                      : ++current

        // recursive call after speed milliseconds
        timerID = setTimeout("animate()", speed)
}

// -->
</SCRIPT>
</BODY>
</HTML>
```

***Example 22-8**. A radio button animation.*

The function `lay()` prints a form with a given number of `radio` objects. Notice a very important technique to encode the greater than character. This character (">") is assigned to the variable `gt` via the `unescape()` function. You may recall from Chapter 3, Writing Your First Script, that Netscape uses a different HTML comment than other browsers. While standard browsers terminate a comment with a greater-than character (">"), Navigator uses a three-character string ("-->") instead. Therefore, if a greater than character is really placed in the script, it terminates the comment that hides the script from browsers which do not support JavaScript (specified by the `<SCRIPT>` tag). When creating a JavaScript-powered Web page, you should be sure to use this technique whenever possible, especially to close HTML tags that are printed via `document.write`. You can also use less than operators instead of greater than ones, simply by reversing the order of the operands of a conditional statement. If your page is based on JavaScript, though, you may choose to disregard other browsers because they probably won't be able to display the page anyway. Nevertheless, if you are using JavaScript only to add some special effects, you should use this technique to make it clearly viewable with any browser, even with those that do not feature JavaScript. Yahoo, for example, used this technique to create a "Yahoo Remote" for its page. The button that launched this JavaScript device was printed by a script, so browsers without JavaScript didn't even see the button. Had the greater than character not been escaped, the whole page (not just one button) would have been scrambled for users without JavaScript-enabled browsers.

Back to the `lay()` function. It is important to name the form for later access—`animation` is chosen. A simple `for` loop is executed to print `num` (the parameter) `radio` objects named `lamps` (belong to the same group). Notice that all HTML tags are printed in the following fashion:

```
document.write("<TAG ATTRIBUTES" + gt)
```

As explained before, the value of gt is a greater than character (a one-character string). See the preceding section for a complete explanation on the motivation for this encoding.

The second function, animate(), is responsible for the actual animation. A global variable, current, is already defined and initialized to 0. The function's main task is to invoke the click() method associated with the radio object of index current. Note that all radio objects are elements of a unique array—document.animation.lamps. The second statement handles the boundary case when the checking loop needs to advance from the last button of the row to the first one (wraparound). The expression current == document.animation.lamps.length - 1 evaluates to true when the value of current is equal to the index of the last element in the document.animation.lamps array (the last radio button). In this case, current is set to 0, forcing the first button on the row to be checked next. In all other cases, the value of current is incremented, advancing the checked radio button. Note that when a radio button belonging to a group is clicked, any previously selected button is deselected. The last statement of the function recursively calls itself after a pause of speed milliseconds (speed is a global variable).

Properties

checked

The checked property evaluates to a Boolean value. If its calling radio object is checked (highlighted), the value of checked is true; otherwise it is false. Due to the structure of a radio object group, the checked property of a single radio object in a group is always true.

You can set the value of checked in order to modify the radio object's display. Since all buttons of a group can be deselected, setting a checked property to false simply deselects the calling radio object, without causing any side effects to the other buttons. Checking an empty radio object, however, does deselect any previously highlighted member of the group. See the listings for the checkbox object for full coverage of this property.

defaultChecked

The defaultChecked property reflects the HTML CHECKED attribute. Refer to the section about the checkbox object for further details.

name

The name property initially reflects the NAME attribute in the HTML definition. See the listings for the checkbox object's name property for a complete explanation.

value

The value property initially corresponds to the VALUE attribute of a radio button HTML tag, but it can be adjusted to any valid string. Once again, refer to the listings for the checkbox object for the syntax and a full description.

Select Object

HTML Syntax

Scrolling menus are a flexible means of input you can use on your forms. The <SELECT> tag is used to create various types of scrolling menus. This is the common way to enable the user to select an option from a list.

The <SELECT> tag is specified by a <SELECT>...</SELECT> pair. You should always specify the menu's name in the following fashion:

```
<SELECT NAME="anyName">
```

It is preferred to use a name that meets the JavaScript identifier naming conventions. As you might expect, the interior of the <SELECT>...</SELECT> portion includes the list's options. An option is specified in the following form:

```
<OPTION VALUE="optionValue">optionText
```

For example, the following element creates a simple menu of computer firms:

```
<SELECT NAME="comp">
<OPTION VALUE="http://www.microsoft.com/">Microsoft
<OPTION VALUE="http://home.netscape.com/">Netscape
<OPTION VALUE="http://www.sun.com/">Sun
</SELECT>
```

The following image shows two identical menus; the first is in its initial state and the second one is opened by the user:

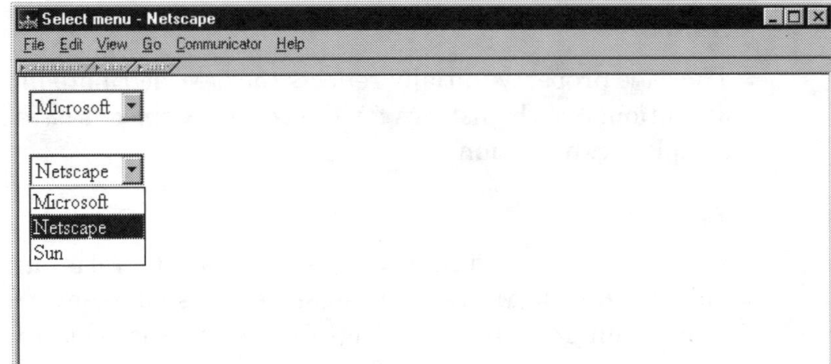

Figure 22-12. *Two identical <SELECT> menus: a closed one and an opened one.*

You can use the SELECT attribute (no value is necessary) to automatically select a default option when the page loads. For example, the following script creates a menu as shown in Figure 22-13, where the default option (which is also the value that appears highlighted in the box) is "Sun":

```
<SELECT NAME="comp">
<OPTION VALUE="http://www.microsoft.com/">Microsoft
<OPTION VALUE="http://home.netscape.com/">Netscape
<OPTION VALUE="http://www.sun.com/" SELECTED>Sun
</SELECT>
```

The text in the box is not the VALUE attribute specified inside the <OPTION> tag, but is rather the string placed outside the <OPTION> tag. The string has no effect other than being the menu label.

The main advantage of this menu is that, due to its pop-up configuration, it does not take up much space on the page. Its disadvantage is that the user can select only one option. To work around this deficiency, you can specify the MULTIPLE attribute, but, since all options are laid out instead of popping up, you lose the space advantage (no free lunch!). Here is a simple example:

```
<SELECT NAME="comp" MULTIPLE>
<OPTION VALUE="http://www.microsoft.com/">Microsoft
<OPTION VALUE="http://home.netscape.com/">Netscape
<OPTION VALUE="http://www.sun.com/" SELECTED>Sun
</SELECT>
```

Figure 22-13 outlines the construct used for such menus:

Figure 22-13*. A <SELECT> menu that enables the user to select numerous options.*

You can select multiple options by holding the Shift button down and selecting or deselecting options from the menu. The Control key can also be held in order to select each option individually. These keys are commonly used in all major operating systems.

The complete syntax for the `select` object is as follows:

```
<SELECT
     NAME="selectName"
     [SIZE="integer"]
     [MULTIPLE]
     [onBlur="handlerText"]
     [onChange="handlerText"]
     [onFocus="handlerText"]>
     <OPTION VALUE="optionValue" [SELECTED]>textToDisplay
     [...<OPTION VALUE="optionValue" [SELECTED]>textToDisplay]
</SELECT>
```

You should recognize all attributes except for the event handlers, which are explained later.

JavaScript Access

```
[window.]document.formName.selectName
```

```
[window.]document.formName.elements[index]
```

```
[window.]document.forms[index].selectName
```

```
[window.]document.forms[index].elements[index]
```

You can access a specific option in a `select` object by appending an `options` property to its reference (one of the above). This property is actually an array of options, starting at index 0. You can reference, for example, the first option of a `select` object in the following fashion:

```
[window.]document.formName.selectName.options[0]
```

The `options` array is discussed later as one of the `select` object's properties.

Event Handlers

onBlur

A `blur` event occurs when a `select` object loses focus. The `onBlur` event handler's script executes upon a `blur` event. There are a few ways to generate a `blur` event:

- Select an option from the list and then click outside the `select` object, either on the page's body or in another form element.
- Select an option from the menu and then send the browser's window to the background. The new window you focus on may be a different browser window or a window associated with any foreign application.

This event handler is not very useful, because it relies on the user to remove focus from the object, which is not that intuitive.

onFocus

A `focus` event associated with a `select` object occurs when the user gives it a focus; that is, when the user attempts to select an option from the menu, but before the menu pops up or modifies the currently selected option. The `onFocus` event handler responds to a `focus` event. When the user clicks somewhere inside the `select` object, you can, for example, pop up an alert box with user instructions for that particular menu. The following source demonstrates this suggestion:

```
<FORM>
<SELECT NAME="comp" onFocus="alert('Simply select the desired home')">
<OPTION VALUE="http://www.microsoft.com/">Microsoft
<OPTION VALUE="http://home.netscape.com/">Netscape
<OPTION VALUE="http://www.sun.com/" SELECTED>Sun
</SELECT>
</FORM>
```

onChange

A `change` event associated with a `select` object occurs when the user changes the selected option. Unlike `change` events associated with other objects, the `select` object does not have to lose focus in order to generate the event. The `onChange` event handler executes when a `change` event occurs.

The onChange event handler is commonly used for exchanging information with the user. We will demonstrate this event handler in later examples, when we discuss the select object's methods and properties.

Methods

blur, focus

The only explicit methods of the select object are blur() and focus(). See the listings for the text object at the beginning of this chapter for complete coverage of these methods.

Properties (select object)

The select object features various properties, but the most useful are actually properties of the options array, as you will find out later. In this section we shall discuss only the properties that directly belong to the select object.

length

You can access the number of options in a select object through the length property. Since this value is also referenced as the length property of the options array, you have the freedom to choose whose length to use. Since length is known to be a standard property of all arrays in JavaScript, we personally prefer referencing length via the options array. Netscape Navigator accepts any of the following references to the number of options in the select object:

```
selectName.length
selectName.options.length
selectName.options.options.length
selectName.options.options.options.length
.
.
.
```

Microsoft Internet Explorer 3.0 accepts only the first two, but, since the third one does not make any sense, you should avoid using it anyway.

The value of the length property should not be assigned by a script. It is dynamic, so it changes whenever an option is added to the corresponding select object.

name

The name property reflects the NAME attribute of the <SELECT> tag. You can modify this property freely. Adjusting it via a script overrides the initial HTML setting. The following script segment shows how to display the name property ("products") via an alert dialog box:

```
<SCRIPT LANGUAGE="JavaScript">
<!--

function sayName(selectObject) {
     alert(selectObject.name)
}

// -->
</SCRIPT>
<FORM>
<SELECT NAME="products" onChange="sayName(this)">
<OPTION VALUE="sny">Sony
<OPTION VALUE="jvc">JVC
<OPTION VALUE="tsh">Toshiba
</SELECT>
</FORM>
```

options

You can reference the options in a select object by the options object. Generally speaking, this array contains an entry for each option (<OPTION>) in a select object (<SELECT>). Suppose the first element of the first form in a document is a select object with three options. These options can be referenced in JavaScript as:

```
document.forms[0].elements[0].options[0]
document.forms[0].elements[0].options[1]
document.forms[0].elements[0].options[2]
```

As always, the length of the array, which is equal to the number of options in the given select object, is stored in the array's length property. In the preceding examples that would be:

```
document.forms[0].elements[0].options.length
```

Elements of the options array are read-only. Although it does not generate a JavaScript error, assigning a value to any of the elements has no effect.

The bare-bones *selectObject*.options reference evaluates to the full HTML syntax used to create the specified *selectObject*.

Note that you can also access the properties of the select object as if they were direct properties of the options array.

selectedIndex

The selectedIndex property is an integer specifying the index of the selected option in a select object. Options in a select object are indexed in the order of definition, i.e., in the same order they are entered in the options array. You can also set the value of selectedIndex in a script to immediately update the state (the selected option) of a select object.

The selectedIndex property is not useful with MULTIPLE select object because it can only refer to the first selected option in the list. You can work around this problem by using the selected property of the options array and a simple loop. See the listings for this property for further details.

Example 22-9 demonstrates the selectedIndex property. Although we have not discussed the value property yet, its role is obvious. If needed, refer to its description later in this chapter.

```
<HTML>
<HEAD>
<TITLE>URL option</TITLE>
<SCRIPT LANGUAGE="JavaScript">
<!--

function loadPage(list) {
     location.href = list.options[list.selectedIndex].value
}

// -->
</SCRIPT>
</HEAD>
<BODY>
<FORM>
<SELECT onChange="loadPage(this)">
<OPTION VALUE="http://www.cnn.com/">CNN
<OPTION VALUE="http://www.msnbc.com/">MSNBC
<OPTION VALUE="http://www.usatoday.com/">USA TODAY
</SELECT>
</FORM>
</BODY>
</HTML>
```

Example 22-9*. A URL picker.*

When the user selects an option in the select object, the loadPage() function is invoked by the onChange event handler, passing the select object as an argument. The URL associated with each option is stored as the option's VALUE attribute, or value property in terms of

JavaScript. The selected option is `list.options[list.selectedIndex]` because `list.selectedIndex` is an integer representing the index of the selected option. The `value` property is used to access the URL of the `selected` object, which is then assigned to `location.href`, in order to load that page to the browser window. You may prefer to use a button in place of the `onChange` event handler:

```
<HTML>
<HEAD>
<TITLE>URL option with button</TITLE>
<SCRIPT LANGUAGE="JavaScript">
<!--

function loadPage(list) {
     location.href = list.options[list.selectedIndex].value
}

// -->
</SCRIPT>
</HEAD>
<BODY>
<FORM>
<SELECT>
<OPTION VALUE="http://www.cnn.com/">CNN
<OPTION VALUE="http://www.msnbc.com/">MSNBC
<OPTION VALUE="http://www.usatoday.com/">USA TODAY
</SELECT>
<INPUT TYPE="button" VALUE="load page"
onClick="loadPage(this.form.elements[0])">
</FORM>
</BODY>
</HTML>
```

***Example 22-10**. Another version of the URL picker—this one uses a button.*

The only difference between Example 22-10 and Example 22-9 is that in Example 22-10 the event handler is attached to a `button` object, while in Example 22-9 it is attached to a `select` object. In order to avoid changing the function, we have modified the argument handed to the function to keep passing the `select` object. The expression `this.form` references the form and `elements[0]` references the `select` object which is the first element in the form.

Properties (options array)

An element in the `options` array reflects a `select` object's option defined by the `<OPTION>` tag in HTML. Properties of the `options` array are properties of specific options in a `select` object.

defaultSelected

The defaultSelected property evaluates to a Boolean value. If the specified option is defined with a SELECTED attribute (<OPTION ... SELECTED>), the value of defaultSelected is true. Otherwise, it is false.

DefaultSelected initially reflects whether the SELECTED attribute is used within an <OPTION> tag. Setting the defaultSelected property via a script overrides the initial HTML setting.

In a select object without a MULTIPLE specification you can only have one option selected by default. Therefore, setting the defaultSelected property of a given option to true clears any previous default selections, including those set with SELECTED. Nevertheless, if you set defaultSelected in a select object defined with the MULTIPLE attribute, previous default selections are not cleared.

index

The index property of a single option in a select object is the number identifying the position of the object in the selection list, starting from zero. Under normal circumstances, there is no justification for the existence of the index property, because in order to reference an option, you need to know its index:

```
document.selectObject.options[indexValue]
```

and when you reference the index property, you supposedly know the index already:

```
document.selectObject.options[indexValue].index
```

length

See the listings for this property in the preceding section—"Properties (select object)."

selected

The selected property is a Boolean value specifying the current selection state of an option in a select object. Its general syntax is as follows:

```
selectName.options[index].selected
```

If an option in a select object (*selectName*.options[*index*]) is selected, the selected property evaluates to true. Otherwise, it evaluates to false. You can set this property at any time, affecting immediately the display of the select object.

The selected and defaultSelected properties are very useful. Suppose you want to create a button by which the user can reset the select object. Using the reset button is not desirable because it resets the entire form, not just the select object. You can solve the problem by using a simple JavaScript function to revert the select object to its default state. Here is the function that the button should invoke:

```
<HTML>
<HEAD>
<TITLE>Reset select object</TITLE>
<SCRIPT LANGUAGE="JavaScript">
<!--

function setDefault(selectName) {
     for (var i = 0; i < selectName.options.length; ++i) {
          selectName.options[i].selected = selectName
                              .options[i].defaultSelected
     }
}

// -->
</SCRIPT>
</HEAD>
<BODY>
<FORM>
<SELECT NAME="myMenu" MULTIPLE>
<OPTION> First option
<OPTION SELECTED> Second option
<OPTION> Third option
<OPTION> Fourth option
<OPTION SELECTED> Fifth option
</SELECT>
<INPUT TYPE="button" VALUE="reset menu"
onClick="setDefault(this.form.myMenu)">
</FORM>
</BODY>
</HTML>
```

Example 22-11. *A simple function resets a select object.*

The setDefault() function works with any type of select object, whether it is a multiple one or not. It simply loops through the options of the select object and sets the selected property of each to its defaultSelected property, reverting all options to their default selection state. The value handed to the function is the select object, referenced as this.form.myMenu. Figure 22-14 displays the select object when the page loads or after clicking the button to reset it.

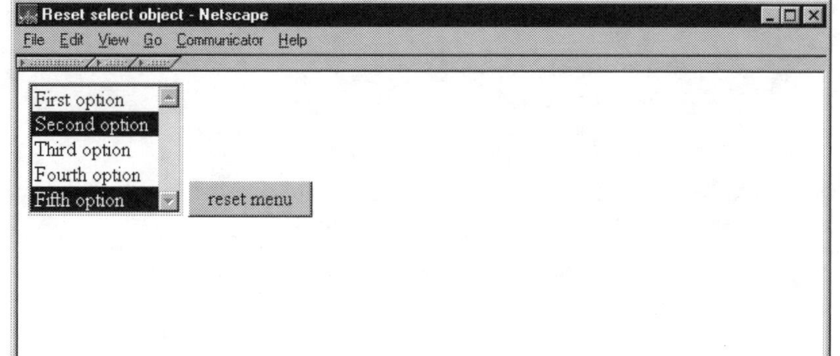

***Figure 22-14**. A multiple select object with a private reset button.*

Note: Microsoft Internet Explorer does not fully support the `select` object. The entire discussion is based on Navigator 3.0 because it simply does not work for Microsoft's browser. As you can see, Microsoft has focused on the user interface of its browser but did not pay much attention to script-level access via JavaScript. The average Web surfer does not feel the disadvantages because Web content providers use only features that are supported by both browsers.

text

There is no HTML attribute that defines the option's label. Take a look at Example 22-11. The strings "First option," "Second option," and so forth are not specified in any HTML attribute as you could expect. They are simply appended to the `<OPTION>` definitions.

The `text` property can be set at any time, immediately affecting the display. Example 22-12 demonstrates the use of this property. When the user selects an option from the list, that option is automatically placed at the top of the list, shifting all other options downwards. See the listings for the `value` property if it is not completely clear.

```
<HTML>
<HEAD>
<TITLE>Swapping options</TITLE>
<SCRIPT LANGUAGE="JavaScript">
<!--
```

```
var choiceIndex = -1

function swap(opt1, opt2) {
     var tempText = opt1.text
     var tempValue = opt1.value
     var tempDefault = opt1.defaultSelected

     opt1.text = opt2.text
     opt1.value = opt2.value
     opt1.defaultSelected = opt2.defaultSelected

     opt2.text = tempText
     opt2.value= tempValue
     opt2.defaultSelected = tempDefault
}

function shift(selectName) {
     if (choiceIndex == -1) {
          choiceIndex = selectName.selectedIndex
          swap(selectName.options[choiceIndex], selectName.options[0])
     } else {
          swap(selectName.options[choiceIndex], selectName.options[0])
          choiceIndex = selectName.selectedIndex
          swap(selectName.options[choiceIndex], selectName.options[0]
     }

     selectName.options[0].selected = true
}

// -->
</SCRIPT>
</HEAD>
<BODY>
<FORM>
<SELECT onChange="shift(this)">
<OPTION VALUE="val1"> First option
<OPTION VALUE="val2" SELECTED> Second option
<OPTION VALUE="val3"> Third option
<OPTION VALUE="val4"> Fourth option
<OPTION VALUE="val5"> Fifth option
</SELECT>
</FORM>
</BODY>
</HTML>
```

***Example 22-12**. You can swap options in a select object by swapping their values.*

When the user selects an option from the `select` object, the top option is swapped back to its original position and then the selected option is swapped with the top option that the first swap yielded.

At first, when the page loads and the `select` object has not been through layout yet, the global variable `choiceIndex` is initialized to –1. Since the index of an option in a `select` object is always non-negative, –1 is used to indicate that this is the first execution and that the current state of the `select` object is its initial one.

The `swap()` function accepts two options associated with a `select` object and simply swaps them by swapping their three properties:

- `text`
- `value`
- `defaultSelected`

You cannot directly swap two options because the `options` array is a read-only one.

The `shift()` function accepts one argument—a `select` object. If the value of `choiceIndex` is –1 then `choiceIndex` is assigned the index of the selected option, and the selected option is swapped with the option at the top of the list (index is 0). Since `choiceIndex` is a global variable, its value will stay intact until the next invocation of the `shift()` function. When the value of `choiceIndex` is not –1, the function runs a different set of statements. First, it swaps the option at the top of the menu with option number `choiceIndex`. Since `choiceIndex` has not been set yet during the current execution of the function, it holds the index of the option that the user selected on the previous round. That is, the function simply returns the `select` object to the state that preceded the previous function's execution. The following two statements are identical to those executed when the value of `choiceIndex` is –1. It is unnecessary to specify these statements twice. Instead, you may conditionally execute the first statement (if `choiceIndex` is not –1) and then unconditionally execute the other two.

value

The `value` property initially reflects the `VALUE` attribute of an `<OPTION>` definition. You can override the initial setting at any given time by assigning this property a value. We have seen this property in action before. For working examples, see the listings for the `defaultSelected` property of the `select` object and the preceding listings for the `text` property.

The Option Object—Adding Options Using the Option Constructor

JavaScript for Netscape Navigator 3.0 enables you to explicitly create options via the `Option` constructor. Options you create are instances of the `Option` object. The syntax for creating an option is as follows:

```
var optionName = new Option([optionText, optionValue, defaultSelected,
selected])
```

Here is a brief explanation of the arguments you should normally hand to the constructor function:

- *optionText*—a string representing the option's `text` property.
- *optionValue*—a string representing the option's `value` property.
- *defaultSelected*—a string representing the option's `defaultSelected` property.
- *selected*—a string representing the option's `selected` property.

See the listings for each of these properties for more details. You can add an option to an existing `select` object in the following fashion:

```
selectName.options[index] = optionName
```

After you create an option and add it to a `select` object you must refresh the document. You can do that via JavaScript using the following statement:

```
history.go(0)
```

You can also refresh a document using the browser control options, in two ways:

1. By clicking in the Location box and pressing **Enter**.
2. By selecting **Refresh** from the View menu.

You can also delete an option from a `select` object, by assigning it a `null` value. The general syntax is as follows:

```
selectName.options[index] = null
```

Once again, you must refresh the document via `history.go(0)` in order to see the updated appearance of the `select` object.

An option created as an instance of the `Option` object includes the same properties as an option which is associated with a `select` object.

Example 22-13 demonstrates the use of the `Option` constructor to create a nested `select` object structure.

```
<HTML>
<HEAD>
<TITLE>Nested select structure</TITLE>
<SCRIPT LANGUAGE="JavaScript">
<!--

var menu = new Array(3)

for (var i = 0; i < menu.length; ++i) {
     menu[i] = new Array()
}

menu[0][0] = new Option("Option 1-1", "", true, true)
menu[0][1] = new Option("Option 1-2")
menu[0][2] = new Option("Option 1-3")
menu[0][3] = new Option("Option 1-4")
menu[0][4] = new Option("Option 1-5")

menu[1][0] = new Option("Option 2-1", "", true, true)
menu[1][1] = new Option("Option 2-2")
menu[1][2] = new Option("Option 2-3")

menu[2][0] = new Option("Option 3-1", "", true, true)
menu[2][1] = new Option("Option 3-2")
menu[2][2] = new Option("Option 3-3")
menu[2][3] = new Option("Option 3-4")

function updateSub(index, subMenu) {
     // delete all options in submenu
     for (var j = 0; j < subMenu.options.length; ++j) {
          subMenu.options[j] = null
     }

     // add options to submenu
     for (var k = 0; k < menu[index].length; ++k) {
          subMenu.options[k] = menu[index][k]
     }

     history.go(0)
}

// -->
</SCRIPT>
</HEAD>
<BODY>
<FORM>

<SELECT NAME="main" onChange= "updateSub(this.selectedIndex,
                                this.form.sub)">
<OPTION SELECTED> Option 1
<OPTION> Option 2
```

```
<OPTION> Option 3
</SELECT>

<SELECT NAME="sub">
<SCRIPT LANGUAGE="JavaScript">
<!--

for (var ind = 0; ind < menu[0].length; ++ind) {
     document.write("<OPTION> Option 1-" + (ind + 1))
}

// -->
</SCRIPT>
</SELECT>

</FORM>
</BODY>
</HTML>
```

Example 22-13. *"Nested" select objects connected via JavaScript.*

When the page first loads, two `select` objects are created. The first one includes three options and is not modified at any stage. The second one is a dynamic `select` object, i.e., its options and length change. The script in the `<HEAD>…</HEAD>` portion of the page defines a two-dimensional array. The first index is of the first `select` object (an integer from 0 to 2). The second index is an integer between 0 and the index of the last option of the second `select` object. The number of options in the second `select` object depends on the option selected from the first `select` object.

Sounds difficult, but it's not! First you must understand what the script does. When the user selects an option from the first menu (`select` object), the second `select` object is updated with the corresponding option list. For example, if the second option in the main menu is selected, the script uses its index (1) to determine the array of elements (`menu[1]`) that should constitute the options of the second `select` object. For the sake of the example, we used `text` properties to identify the structure (1-1, 0-3, etc.).

When the user first loads the page, the first `select` object is laid out according to its HTML definition, while the second `select` object is generated via a JavaScript `for` loop which iterates over the `menu[0]` array and writes out its elements.

The first `select` object includes an `onChange` event handler that invokes the `updateSub()` function, passing, as arguments, the form and the selected index. The function is based on two loops. The first one deletes the current options of the second menu by assigning each a `null` value. The second loop adds new options to the second menu, according to the elements of the selected `menu` array. Notice that we did not add properties for all options, but rather only for the first option of each `menu` array (a `value`, a `default` property, and a `defaultSelected` property). The elements of the `menu` array are obviously instances of the `Option` object. The document is refreshed by `history.go(0)`.

An instance of the `Option` object has the same structure as an element of a `select` object's `element` array. Both objects include the same properties and none have methods.

FileUpload Object

HTML Syntax

A file upload element of an HTML form enables the user to supply a local file as input. This feature is fairly new and is not supported by MSIE 3.0. Generally speaking, its syntax is as follows:

```
<INPUT
    TYPE="file"
    NAME="fileUploadName">
```

Note that *fileUploadName* is not the name of the file, but rather the name of the form element that enables the user to supply the file.

JavaScript Access

The regular syntax is as follows:

```
[window.]document.formName.fileUploadName
```

```
[window.]document.formName.elements[index]
```

```
[window.]document.forms[index].fileUploadName
```

```
[window.]document.forms[index].elements[index]
```

Event Handlers

JavaScript for Netscape Navigator 3.0 still does not support any event handlers for this object. Look for `onBrowse` in future releases.

Methods

This object does not provide any methods either.

Properties

The `file upload` object combines two meaningless properties:

name

The `name` property initially reflects the `NAME` attribute of the HTML definition. You may set its value at any time.

value

This read-only property reflects the current value of the file upload element's field—the name of the file to upload.

Summary

You deserve a reward if you had the motivation to read through this lengthy chapter. We believe that you have already been rewarded with the knowledge to implement interactive forms including their event handlers. Forms are a convenient means of collecting user's input without producing annoying dialog boxes. Some form elements such as `text` objects and `textarea`s also come in handy when you need to display changing output, such as a clock or a banner. Don't worry if you do not remember every single method and property of the objects discussed in this chapter. This book will serve as an easy-to-use reference when you actually need to create a JavaScript-powered form. At this point, you should know the basics of and how to use form elements in JavaScript, and the properties, methods, and event handlers of `text` objects and regular buttons.

Chapter 23

Links, Anchors, and Image Maps

Defining a Link

Assuming you know what a link is, here is the general HTML syntax:

```
<A HREF="locationOrURL"
     [NAME="anchorName"]
     [TARGET="windowName"]>
     linkText
</A>
```

The HREF attribute defines the document or anchor to which you are linking. The NAME attribute specifies a tag that becomes an available hypertext target within the current document. If this attribute is present, the link object is also an anchor object. The TARGET attribute specifies the window where the linked document should load (e.g., a name of a window, a name of a frame, a special literal frame name such as _top, _parent, _self, and _blank).

You can create a link with a plain HTML tag as shown above, but you can also use JavaScript for that. The following script segment demonstrates how to create a link with JavaScript:

```
document.write(linkText.link(hrefAttribute))
```

The preceding statement uses the link() method of the String object. See Chapter 16, Handling Strings, for instructions on using this method.

Another obvious way to create a link with JavaScript is by printing the plain HTML syntax via document.write in the following form:

```
document.write('<A HREF="locationOrURL" [NAME="anchorName"]
[TARGET="windowName"]>linkText</A>')
```

Although this syntax works on a JavaScript-enabled browser, it contains several flaws that will spoil the appearance of the page when viewed with a browser that does not support JavaScript. The problem is that greater than (>) characters in a script terminate code hiding. (See "Problems with Code Hiding" in Chapter 3 for details on a workaround technique.)

Defining an Anchor

The plain HTML definition of an anchor is as follows:

```
<A [HREF=locationOrURL]
     NAME="anchorName"
     [TARGET="windowName"]>
     anchorText
</A>
```

The attributes are the same as those of a link.

You can also use the `String` object's `anchor()` method to create an anchor using the following format:

```
text.anchor(nameAttribute)
```

Defining an Image Map (area)

The general syntax of a client-side image map is as follows:

```
<MAP NAME="mapName">
     <AREA
          [NAME="areaName"]
          COORDS="x1,y1,x2,y2,..." | "x-center,y-center,radius"
          HREF="location"
          [SHAPE="rect" | "poly" | "circle" | "default"]
          [TARGET="windowName"]>
</MAP>
```

The first `NAME` attribute specifies the name of the image map that contains various areas, whereas the second one specifies the name of a single area in the image map. An image map can consist of any number of areas. The `COORDS` attribute specifies the coordinates of a specific area in a map. This attribute consists of either four coordinates, if the area is defined as a rectangle (an x and y for the top left and bottom right corners), or three coordinates, if the area is a circle (x and y for the center and the radius). HREF specifies the URL of the document to load when the user clicks the area. Any area of the image map that does not have this attribute does not act as a hypertext link. You can use any scheme (protocol) for the location, including a JavaScript statement via javascript:. The SHAPE attribute determines the shape of an area in an image map. If not specified, the shape defaults to rect. TARGET specifies the window or frame in which the destination document is loaded. See the section on link definition for additional information regarding this attribute.

links Array

The only way to reference a link object in your code is by using the links array. This array is similar to the forms array. It is also a property of the document object, so you can access this array in the following fashion:

```
[window.]document.links
```

This links array contains an entry for each Link (<A HREF="...">) and Area (<AREA HREF="...">) object in the document. Suppose you have a document containing three links, for example. You can reference these links using the following syntax:

```
document.links[0]
document.links[1]
document.links[2]
```

These references can equally apply to a document with three Area objects (within a single or multiple image maps), as well as for a document with two links and one image map area. The total number of qualifying links and image map areas is reflected by the length property of the array:

```
document.forms.length
```

This is probably the most useful link-related property. Elements in the links array are obviously read-only, but assigning a value to a given element does not cause an error—it simply doesn't work.

anchors Array

You can reference the anchors in your code via the anchors array. This array contains an entry for each <A> tag containing a NAME attribute in a document, in source order. If a document contains three named anchors, for example, these anchors are reflected as document .anchors[0], document.anchors[1], and document.anchors[2]. You can use this array in one of two ways, exactly like you use the links array or the forms array:

```
document.anchors[index]
document.anchors.length
```

Each element of the document.anchors array holds a null value and does not feature any methods or properties. The value of document.anchors[0], for example, is null, regardless of whether there are anchors in the document. The anchors array does not play a role in any script, but its length property occasionally does. If you use a systematic naming scheme for all anchors in a document, you can take advantage of the length property (document.anchors.length). Suppose a document contains a variable number of anchors. You can name these anchors anchor0, anchor1, anchor2, and so forth, or, alternatively, Tomer0, Tomer1, and Tomer2, if you so desire. The latter anchors would use the following syntax:

```
<A … NAME="Tomer0" …></A>
<A … NAME="Tomer1" …></A>
<A … NAME="Tomer2" …></A>
```

Take a look at the following function:

```
function goAnchor(num) {
     if (num >= document.anchors.length)
          alert("Anchor does not exist!")
     else
          location.hash = "Tomer" + num
}
```

This function accepts an existing anchor's index and scrolls the page to that anchor by assigning its name to the location.hash property. It also demonstrates a possible usage of the anchors array, or its length property, to be exact. See Chapter 19, URLs and JavaScript, for details on the location.hash property.

Link and Area Event Handlers

Anchors do not feature any event handlers, but links and image map areas do provide them. Some of the event handlers are very useful, so it is important that you know how to use them.

Calling Event Handlers Explicitly

Since the `document.links` array holds an entry for every link and image map area in a document, it is fairly straightforward to explicitly call an event handler for a specific link or area by assigning it to the corresponding array element. You can use the following statement to explicitly call the event handler `doSomething()` for the first link or area (whichever is first in source order):

```
document.links[0].onmouseover = doSomething
```

onClick

You can add an `onClick` event handler in the following fashion:

```
<A … onClick="validJavaScriptCode">
<AREA … onClick="validJavaScriptCode">
```

A `click` event associated with a `Link` object or an `Area` object occurs when the user clicks the content of the link, which can be plain text, an image, and so forth. In the case of an `Area` object, the link content is (usually) a portion of an image.

The JavaScript statements you specify for the `onClick` event handler are executed prior to loading the URL defined by the `HREF` attribute. They can be used to do any last-minute preparations.

Usually, you simply want a link or image map area to execute a JavaScript code when the user clicks it. You can accomplish this task by simply using a URL based on a `javascript:` scheme with the `HREF` attribute. When the user clicks it, the following link calls a function named `register`:

```
<A HREF="javascript:register()">Register Profile</A>
```

If you wish to create a link that does not respond at all to a link but still enables `onMouseOver` and `onMouseOut` event handlers, you can use the `void` operator (only compatible with Netscape Navigator 3.0 and above):

```
<A HREF="javascript:void(0)">Register Profile</A>
```

onMouseOver

A mouseOver event occurs each time the mouse pointer moves into an object or an area, from outside that object or area. Upon this event, the onMouseOver event handler executes a JavaScript code. The syntax of a general script to accomplish it is as follows:

```
<A ... onMouseOver="validJavaScriptCode">
<AREA ... onMouseOver="validJavaScriptCode">
```

If the mouse moves from one area of a client-side image map to another, it is the onMouseOver event handler of the destination area (the one you are moving to) that is being triggered.

Instead of having its URL displayed by default in the status bar whenever the user places the mouse over it, this event handler is often used to display a message associated with a link. (You must return true from the event handler.) The following link, for example, displays "Cool shareware stuff" in the status bar, when the user places the mouse over the link labeled "Jumbo":

```
<A HREF="http://www.jumbo.com" onMouseOver="window.status = 'Cool
                               shareware stuff'; return true">Jumbo</A>
```

If you prefer to use a function, you should return true in the following fashion:

```
<SCRIPT LANGUAGE="JavaScript">
<!--

function displayStatus(str) {
      window.status = str
      return true
}

// -->
</SCRIPT>
<A HREF="http://www.jumbo.com" onMouseOver="return displayStatus('Cool
                               shareware stuff')">Jumbo</A>
```

Alternatively, you may choose to explicitly return a true value by adding a statement to the event handler code.

onMouseOut

A mouseOut event occurs each time the mouse pointer leaves an area within a client-side image map or a link, from inside that area or link. The onMouseOut event handler executes a JavaScript code upon this event.

If the mouse moves from one area to another in a client-side image map, the onMouseOut event handler of the source area is triggered, and the onMouseOver event handler of the destination area is triggered.

If you want an area to use the onMouseOut or the onMouseOver event handler, you should specify the HREF attribute of the <AREA> tag. Nice effects can be achieved by an in-concert usage of the onMouseOver and the onMouseOut event handlers. Upon placing the pointer over a link or over an image map area, for example, you can display a message in the status bar, and then, instead of waiting for an arbitrary number of seconds, you can delete it immediately upon the removal of the mouse pointer. The following code demonstrates how to implement such an effect:


```
<A HREF="http://www.jumbo.com" onMouseOver="window.status = 'Cool
                shareware stuff'; return true" onMouseOut="window.status
                = ''; return true">Jumbo</A>
```

Note that a similar effect can be achieved with an image map area instead of a link. Example 23-1 demonstrates both onMouse event handlers, for a client-side image map. First, take a look at the image map in Figure 23-1:

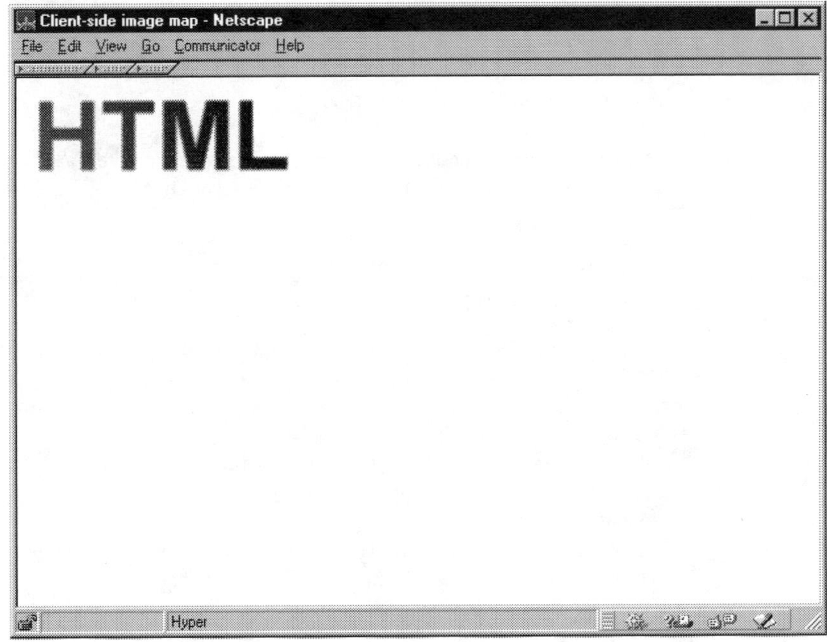

***Figure 23-1**. The image used for the client-side image map.*

When the user clicks the "H" area, the word "Hyper" is displayed in an alert box. When he or she clicks the "T" area, "Text" is displayed, and so forth with "Markup" and "Language." When the mouse pointer is over a certain letter, the corresponding word ("Hyper," "Text," "Markup," "Language") is displayed in the status bar. When the mouse pointer is removed from the image map, the status bar is blanked (only in Navigator 3.0 and above). Now, take a look at the listings of Example 23-1 to find out how this example works.

```
<HTML>
<HEAD>
<TITLE>Client-side image map</TITLE>
</HEAD>
<BODY BGCOLOR="#ffffff">
<IMG SRC="img23-1.gif" HEIGHT=69 WIDTH=214 ALT="HTML" BORDER=0
                    USEMAP="#html_map">
<MAP NAME="html_map">
<AREA
    NAME="H"
    COORDS="0, 0, 55, 69"
    HREF="javascript:alert('Hyper')"
    SHAPE="rect"
    onMouseOver="window.status = 'Hyper'; return true"
    onMouseOut="window.status = ''; return true">
<AREA
    NAME="T"
    COORDS="56, 0, 101, 69"
    HREF="javascript:alert('Text')"
    SHAPE="rect"
    onMouseOver="window.status = 'Text'; return true"
    onMouseOut="window.status = ''; return true">
<AREA
    NAME="M"
    COORDS="102, 0, 161, 69"
    HREF="javascript:alert('Markup')"
    SHAPE="rect"
    onMouseOver="window.status = 'Markup'; return true"
    onMouseOut="window.status = ''; return true">
<AREA
    NAME="L"
    COORDS="161, 0, 214, 69"
    HREF="javascript:alert('Language')"
    SHAPE="rect"
    onMouseOver="window.status = 'Language'; return true"
    onMouseOut="window.status = ''; return true">
</MAP>
</BODY>
</HTML>
```

***Example 23-1**. JavaScript to handle the image map areas.*

First, notice the HTML tag that creates the image:

```
<IMG SRC="img23-1.gif" HEIGHT=69 WIDTH=214 ALT="HTML" BORDER=0
                USEMAP="#html_map">
```

Except for the last one, all attributes are self-explanatory. USEMAP specifies the name of the image map definition (<MAP>) for the image, preceded by a hash character. The image map definition itself uses the following opening tag:

```
<MAP NAME="html_map">
```

You should set the name of the map as shown above, or else the image won't be able to refer to it. There are basically four areas in Figure 23-1's image map, one for each letter of the "HTML" banner. Since, except for the triggered message and coordinates, all four areas are alike, only one will be discussed here. Let's take a look at the last area:

```
<AREA
    NAME="L"
    COORDS="161, 0, 214, 69"
    HREF="javascript:alert('Language')"
    SHAPE="rect"
    onMouseOver="window.status = 'Language'; return true"
    onMouseOut="window.status = ''; return true">
```

First, notice that this area is defined as a rectangle (SHAPE="rect"). The *x* and *y* coordinates of the upper left corner are 161 and 0, respectively. Coordinates are measured in pixels starting at (0, 0), the first pixel in the image. The *x* and *y* coordinates of the bottom right corner are 214 and 69, respectively, which are the HEIGHT and WIDTH attributes of the image. When the user places the mouse pointer over this area, the status bar displays the string "Language" (for "L") (the string is assigned to the status bar property), and, as required by Navigator, the Boolean value true is returned. When the user removes the mouse from this area, the status bar is blanked (assigned an empty string). Since the onMouseOver event handler of the destination area immediately overtakes the onMouseOut operation of the source area, the user usually won't notice this interim state when moving the pointer to one of the adjacent image map areas. When the user removes the mouse pointer from this area to outside of the entire image, the status bar is cleared and remains empty, until either a different value is explicitly assigned to the status bar, or the mouse moves back into the image map area. When the user clicks this area, the location specified in HREF is loaded, and, since the value of this attribute is a JavaScript statement preceded by the javascript:

scheme, it does not load a new document but rather pops up an alert dialog box with the string Language.

Link and Area Properties

Location-Equivalent Properties

Most of the properties that belong to a Link or an Area object (document.links[*index*]) are associated with the URL of the HREF definition. These are all properties of the window.location object, to which a full chapter is dedicated. Only a short description of each property will be given here. The only way to reference a property of a Link or an Area object is to use the following syntax:

```
document.links.propertyName
```

Note that links do not have any methods.

Here is the equivalence list between the properties of document.links and those of window.location:

- hash specifies an anchor name in the URL.
- host specifies the *hostname*:*port* portion of the URL.
- hostname specifies the host and domain name, or IP address, of a network host.
- href specifies the entire URL.
- pathname specifies the *url-path* portion of the URL.
- port specifies the communications port that the server uses for communications (80 by default).
- protocol specifies the beginning of the URL, including the colon (also known as the scheme).
- search specifies a query.

target

The target property initially reflects the TARGET property of the <A HREF="..."> or <AREA HREF="..."> HTML definitions. Setting the value of this property overrides the initial definition.

The target property (document.links[*index*].target) cannot be assigned a JavaScript expression or variable.

Referring Documents

When a user clicks a link in one document and causes a new page to load in the same or other window, the calling document is known as the *referring document*. When a user arrives at a page via a link from another page (and not from his or her bookmark, history list, friends, etc.), the URL of the referring page is reflected in the new page as a read-only property, `document.referrer`. You should also know that a referring document is also called the *source document*, whereas the new page the referrer document links to is known as the *destination document*.

The property `document.referred` is very useful for tracking a user's movement inside a large site you maintain by yourself. It is not helpful at all if the user surfs to foreign pages, so, unless *Playboy* provides a link to your page, you won't be able to greet the user with a message such as "Naughty boy—*Playboy* is for grown-ups only!"

Suppose you have a page on your site, C.html, that is linked from two different pages, A.html and B.html. Let's say A.html includes important copyright information on a shareware product available on C.html, and B.html provides important instructions on installing the software package. You can use the following JavaScript script on C.html to check where the user came from and to print a link to the third page:

```
<SCRIPT LANGUAGE="JavaScript">
<!-- begin JavaScript *immediate* script

// assign greater than character without literally displaying it
var gt = unescape("%3E")

if (document.referred.indexOf("A.html") == -1)
     document.write('<A HREF="A.html"' + gt + 'Copyright notice</A' + gt)
if (document.referred.indexOf("B.html") == -1)
     document.write('<A HREF="B.html"' + gt + 'Installation
                                instructions</A' + gt)

// -->
</SCRIPT>
```

This script prints links to the documents the user has not come from. It prints A.html it the user has not come from A.html, B.html if the user has not come from B.html, or both links if the user has apparently arrived from a different document or not from a link at all.

Summary

In this chapter, we discussed the `Link`, `Area`, and `Anchor` objects. You learned that the only way to reference one of these objects is by either `document.links` or `document.anchors`. There are three important concepts you should remember from this chapter:

- The `javascript:` protocol specifies a JavaScript statement for the `HREF` attribute of a link or image map area.
- The `onMouseOver` event handler of links and image map areas can execute a JavaScript statement. When the user places the mouse pointer over the link, it is an indication for his or her interest in it, so displaying related information in the status bar may be very helpful in such a scenario.
- The `onMouseOut` event handler is also an attribute of a link or image map area. Its usage is similar to that of `onMouseOver` event handler.

Chapter 24

Implementing Cookies

Maintaining a State

When you create a Web site, you normally expect the user to load HTML documents, view them, navigate from one page to another, and so on. Occasionally, it is important to enable the Web page to maintain a *state*. That is, the page "remembers" certain actions executed by the user during previous sessions.

A classic example of maintaining a given *state* is a Shopping Cart application, as implemented, for example, in Netscape's On-Line Store. The user travels from one product review to the other, via simple HTML links. When he or she comes across an interesting product, clicking a button puts the selected product's data in a "Shopping Cart." The Shopping Cart, which is sometimes displayed visually on the page, is basically a name for a storage mechanism. Since it is not possible to store the data for each user on the server, the data is kept on the client side, in what is called a Shopping Cart.

Cookies

Cookies are a general mechanism which server-side applications (such as CGI) and client-side JavaScript scripts can use to store textual data on the client side for the purpose of retrieving it later. The term *cookies* was initially used by Netscape, the pioneer in this area, and was later adopted by other browsers such as Microsoft IE. The name *cookies* does not have any significant meaning.

Cookies are tidbits of information, stored in a browser-dependent format on the client machine. Netscape Navigator, for example, holds all cookies in a regular text file named `cookies.txt` (in the directory where Navigator is installed), whereas MSIE 3.0 stores cookies in multiple files, located in a user-provided directory.

Cookies and HTTP

The connection established between the server and the client uses a HyperText Transfer Protocol (HTTP). Although this protocol is very complicated at the implementation level, it is fairly easy to understand at the conceptual one. When a user requests a page, an *HTTP request* is sent to the server, specifying the user's exact request with some additional attributes. As a user, you are not aware of any data sent to the server as a result of your request. Among all elements, an HTTP request includes a header that defines the most important attributes, such as the URL of the requested page. An HTTP request includes all valid cookies as well (explained later in this chapter).

When the server replies to the client's request, it returns an *HTTP response* which also features a header. This header contains important information about the file being returned, such as its MIME types (discussed later in the book).

The general syntax of an HTTP header is as follows:

```
Field-name: Information
```

When the server returns an HTTP object to the client, it may also transmit some state information for the client, to store as cookies. Since a cookie is basically simple text, the server-side script does not have the ability to abuse the client machine in any way. In addition to its textual value, a cookie contains several attributes, such as the range of URLs for which the cookie is valid. Any future HTTP requests from the client to one of the URLs in the above range will transmit back to the server the current cookie's value on the client.

Setting an HTTP Cookie

An HTTP cookie is introduced to the client in an HTTP request, usually by a CGI script, using the following syntax:

```
Set-Cookie: NAME=VALUE; expires=DATE; path=pathName;
domain=DOMAIN_NAME; secure
```

The attributes are as follows:

name=value

name is the name of the cookie by which you can reference it later. Notice that the only way to access the cookie is by this name. *value* is the regular string to be stored as a cookie. It is recommended that the string be encoded using the "*%XX*" style (equivalent to JavaScript's escape function's output). Generally speaking, the *name=value* is the only required attribute of the `Set-Cookie` field.

expires=*date*

`expires` is an optional attribute which specifies the expiration date of the cookie. The cookie will no longer be stored or retrieved beyond that date. The date string is formatted as follows:

Wdy, *DD-Mon-YYYY HH*:*MM*:*SS* GMT

You will see later that this date format is equivalent to the value returned by the `toGMTString()` date's method. If `expires` is not specified, the cookie will expire when the user's session ends.

domain=*domainName*

When searching for valid cookies, Navigator compares the `domain` attributes of each cookie to the Internet domain name of the host from which the URL will be retrieved. If there is a tail match, then the cookie will go through a full path matching. "Tail matching" means that the `domain` attribute is matched against the tail of the fully qualified domain name of the host. A domain attribute of "ac.il", for example, would tail match "mis.study.ac.il" as well as "mba.haifa.ac.il".

The `domain` attribute makes sure that only hosts within the specified domain can set a cookie for the domain. Domains must have at least two or three periods, to avoid collision between domains of the form ".com", ".edu", etc. There are seven common top-level domains that require at least two periods in their *domain name*: "com", "edu", "net", "org", "gov", "mil", and "int". All other domains require at least three periods in their *domainName*.

The default value of `domain` is the host name of the server which generated the cookie response.

path=*pathName*

path specifies a subset of URLs in a domain for which a cookie is valid. After domain matching, the pathname component of the URL is compared with the path attribute, and, if successful, the cookie is considered valid and is sent along with the URL requests. The path "/foo", for example, would match "/foobar" and "/foo/bar/html". The path "/" is the most general one. If the path is not specified, it is assumed to be the same path as the document specified in the cookie's header.

secure

If a cookie is marked secure, it will only be transmitted across a secured communication channel between the client and the host. Currently, secured cookies will only be sent to HTTP servers. If secure is not specified, the cookie will be sent over unsecured channels.

Getting an HTTP Cookie

When a script (client-side or server-side) requests a URL from an HTTP server, the browser will match the URL against all cookies, and if any of them matches, a line containing the name and value pairs of all matching cookies will be included in the HTTP request. The format is straightforward:

```
Cookie: name1=value1; name2=value2 ...
```

Notice that the Cookie field in a request header contains only the names and values of all valid cookies. The Set-Cookie field in the response header includes additional attributes such as expiration date. These attributes are not actually part of the cookie, but rather are used to determine if a specific cookie is valid for the purpose of entering the HTTP request header.

Notes and Limitations

The only way to overwrite a cookie is by creating another cookie with the same name and path as an existing one. Creating a cookie with the same name but with a different path than that of an existing one will add an additional cookie. The only way to instantly delete a cookie is by overwriting it with an expired cookie. A cookie may be deleted by the browser before its expiration date but only if the number of cookies exceeds its internal limit.

When sending cookies to a server, all cookies with more specific path mapping should be sent before cookies with less-specific path mapping. If both are sent, the cookie "name1=foo" with a path mapping of "/", for example, should be sent after the cookie "name1=foo2" with a path mapping of "/bar".

There are several extremely important limitations on the size and number of cookies a client can store at any given time:

- The client can hold up to 300 cookies.
- A cookie can be up to 4KB, including its name and values. Cookies that exceed this length are trimmed to fit, so remember to keep within this length.
- A maximum of 20 cookies per server or domain are allowed.

A client is not expected to exceed these limits. The oldest cookies are deleted in case this rule is violated.

Proxy servers should propagate the Set-Cookie header to the client, regardless of whether the response was 304 ("not modified") or 200 ("OK"). Proxy servers work fine with cookies.

Examples

Here are some sample exchanges from Netscape documentation which are designed to illustrate the use of cookies.

First Transaction Sequence Example

Client requests a document and receives in the response:

```
Set-Cookie: CUSTOMER=WILE_E_COYOTE; path=/; expires=Wednesday, 09-Nov-99
23:12:40 GMT
```

When client requests a URL in the path "/" on this server, it sends:

```
Cookie: CUSTOMER=WILE_E_COYOTE
```

Client requests a document and receives in the response:

```
Set-Cookie: PART_NUMBER=ROCKET_LAUNCHER_0001; path=/
```

When client requests a URL in the path "/" on this server, it sends:

```
Cookie: CUSTOMER=WILE_E_COYOTE; PART_NUMBER=ROCKET_LAUNCHER_0001
```

Client receives:

```
Set-Cookie: SHIPPING=FEDEX; path=/foo
```

When client requests a URL in the path "/" on this server, it sends:

```
Cookie: CUSTOMER=WILE_E_COYOTE; PART_NUMBER=ROCKET_LAUNCHER_0001
```

When client requests a URL in the path "/foo" on this server, it sends:

```
Cookie: CUSTOMER=WILE_E_COYOTE; PART_NUMBER=ROCKET_LAUNCHER_0001;
SHIPPING=FEDEX
```

Second Transaction Sequence Example

Assume all mappings from above have been cleared.

Client receives:

```
Set-Cookie: PART_NUMBER=ROCKET_LAUNCHER_0001; path=/
```

When client requests a URL in the path "/" on this server, it sends:

```
Cookie: PART_NUMBER=ROCKET_LAUNCHER_0001
```

Client receives:

```
Set-Cookie: PART_NUMBER=RIDING_ROCKET_0023; path=/ammo
```

When client requests a URL in the path "/ammo" on this server, it sends:

```
Cookie: PART_NUMBER=RIDING_ROCKET_0023; PART_NUMBER=ROCKET_LAUNCHER_0001
```

Note that there are two attributes named "PART_NUMBER" due to the two different paths, "/" and "/ammo".

Cookies and JavaScript

Setting and getting cookies with a server-side application relies on HTTP headers. You cannot set a cookie or retrieve one after the page has loaded. However, a JavaScript script is a client-side application and thus enables you to process cookies at any time, without contacting the server.

The `cookie` property of the `document` object reflects all cookies that are valid for the Web page hosting the script; that is, `document.cookie` is equivalent to the `Cookie` field in the HTTP request header.

In the same way you set a cookie via the `Set-Cookie` field in an HTTP response header, you can do so with JavaScript, by assigning a value to `document.cookie`.

Cookie Functions

You should have noticed that we neither demonstrated nor emphasized the usage of cookies with JavaScript. The reason for this is that it is difficult and almost useless to explicitly deal with the `document.cookie` property. Furthermore, there are only three defined actions related to cookies:

- Retrieving the value of a cookie according to its name
- Setting a cookie to a desired attribute
- Deleting a cookie

We have written several functions that you may find useful, whenever you want to perform one of the above actions. All functions are self-explanatory and are fully commented:


```
// Boolean variable specified if alert should be displayed if
                            cookie exceeds 4KB
var caution = false

// name - name of the cookie
// value - value of the cookie
// [expires] - expiration date of the cookie (defaults to end of
                            current session)
// [path] - path for which the cookie is valid (defaults to path of
                            calling document)
// [domain] - domain for which the cookie is valid (defaults to domain
                            of calling document)
// [secure] - Boolean value indicating if the cookie transmission
                            requires a secure transmission
// * an argument defaults when it is assigned null as a placeholder
// * a null placeholder is not required for trailing omitted arguments
function setCookie(name, value, expires, path, domain, secure) {
     var curCookie = name + "=" + escape(value) +
          ((expires) ? "; expires=" + expires.toGMTString() : "") +
          ((path) ? "; path=" + path : "") +
          ((domain) ? "; domain=" + domain : "") +
          ((secure) ? "; secure" : "")
     if (!caution || (name + "=" + escape(value)).length <= 4000)
          document.cookie = curCookie
     else
          if (confirm("Cookie exceeds 4KB and will be cut!"))
               document.cookie = curCookie
}

// name - name of the desired cookie
// * return string containing value of specified cookie or null if
                            cookie does not exist
```

```
function getCookie(name) {
     var prefix = name + "="
     var cookieStartIndex = document.cookie.indexOf(prefix)
     if (cookieStartIndex == -1)
          return null
     var cookieEndIndex = document.cookie.indexOf(";", cookieStartIndex
                         + prefix.length)
     if (cookieEndIndex == -1)
          cookieEndIndex = document.cookie.length
     return unescape(document.cookie.substring(cookieStartIndex +
                         prefix.length, cookieEndIndex))
}

// name - name of the cookie
// [path] - path of the cookie (must be same as path used to
                         create cookie)
// [domain] - domain of the cookie (must be same as domain used to
                         create cookie)
// * path and domain default if assigned null or omitted if no
                         explicit argument proceeds
function deleteCookie(name, path, domain) {
     if (getCookie(name)) {
          document.cookie = name + "=" +
          ((path) ? "; path=" + path : "") +
          ((domain) ? "; domain=" + domain : "") +
          "; expires=Thu, 01-Jan-70 00:00:01 GMT"
     }
}

// date - any instance of the Date object
// * you should hand all instances of the Date object to this
                         function for "repairs"
// * this function is taken from Chapter 14, Time and Date in JavaScript,
                         in "Learn Advanced JavaScript Programming"
function fixDate(date) {
     var base = new Date(0)
     var skew = base.getTime()
     if (skew > 0)
          date.setTime(date.getTime() - skew)
}
```

Read through the functions and comments so you understand how to use them. The most basic demonstration of these functions is a script that counts the number of times a user has visited the page that hosts the code:

```
<HTML>
<HEAD>
<TITLE>Remember number of visits</TITLE>
<SCRIPT LANGUAGE="JavaScript">
<!--
```

```
// Boolean variable specified if alert should be displayed if
                         cookie exceeds 4KB
var caution = false

// name - name of the cookie
// value - value of the cookie
// [expires] - expiration date of the cookie (defaults to end of
                         current session)
// [path] - path for which the cookie is valid (defaults to path of
                         calling document)
// [domain] - domain for which the cookie is valid (defaults to domain of
                         calling document)
// [secure] - Boolean value indicating if the cookie transmission
                         requires a secure transmission
// * an argument defaults when it is assigned null as a placeholder
// * a null placeholder is not required for trailing omitted arguments
function setCookie(name, value, expires, path, domain, secure) {
     var curCookie = name + "=" + escape(value) +
          ((expires) ? "; expires=" + expires.toGMTString() : "") +
          ((path) ? "; path=" + path : "") +
          ((domain) ? "; domain=" + domain : "") +
          ((secure) ? "; secure" : "")
     if (!caution || (name + "=" + escape(value)).length <= 4000)
          document.cookie = curCookie
     else
          if (confirm("Cookie exceeds 4KB and will be cut!"))
               document.cookie = curCookie
}

// name - name of the desired cookie
// * return string containing value of specified cookie or null if
                         cookie does not exist
function getCookie(name) {
     var prefix = name + "="
     var cookieStartIndex = document.cookie.indexOf(prefix)
     if (cookieStartIndex == -1)
          return null
     var cookieEndIndex = document.cookie.indexOf(";", cookieStartIndex +
                         prefix.length)
     if (cookieEndIndex == -1)
          cookieEndIndex = document.cookie.length
     return unescape(document.cookie.substring(cookieStartIndex +
                         prefix.length, cookieEndIndex))
}

// name - name of the cookie
// [path] - path of the cookie (must be same as path used to create
                         cookie)
// [domain] - domain of the cookie (must be same as domain used to
                         create cookie)
```

```
// * path and domain default if assigned null or omitted if no
                          explicit argument proceeds
function deleteCookie(name, path, domain) {
     if (getCookie(name)) {
          document.cookie = name + "=" +
          ((path) ? "; path=" + path : "") +
          ((domain) ? "; domain=" + domain : "") +
          "; expires=Thu, 01-Jan-70 00:00:01 GMT"
     }
}

// date - any instance of the Date object
// * you should hand all instances of the Date object to this function
                          for "repairs"
// * this function is taken from Chapter 14, Time and Date in JavaScript,
                          in "Learn Advanced JavaScript Programming"
function fixDate(date) {
     var base = new Date(0)
     var skew = base.getTime()
     if (skew > 0)
          date.setTime(date.getTime() – skew)
}

var now = new Date()
fixDate(now)
now.setTime(now.getTime() + 365 * 24 * 60 * 60 * 1000)
var visits = getCookie("counter")
if (!visits)
     visits = 1
else
     visits = parseInt(visits) + 1
setCookie("counter", visits, now)
document.write("You have been here " + visits + " time(s).")

// -->
</SCRIPT>
</HEAD>
</HTML>
```

***Example 24-1**. A simple cookie-based counter.*

Bear in mind that this script does not emulate a regular counter that counts the number of visitors to a given site. Because cookies are stored on the client side, they can only be used to count the number of visits by a specific client. At first, an instance of the `Date` object reflecting the current date is assigned to the variable `now`. The instance is then handed to the `fixDate()` function in order to fix it for Mac computers (see Chapter 14, Time and Date in JavaScript). The `now.setTime(now.getTime() + 365 * 24 * 60 * 60 * 1000)` statement sets the cookie expiration date to one year in the future. This expiration date is used later when setting the cookie. The script gets a cookie named "`counter`" and retrieves the number of `visits` from it. If there is no cookie by the specified name, the variable `visits` is initialized to one; otherwise, the number of `visits` in the cookie is incremented by one. The script then writes the new number of `visits` back to the cookie by `setCookie()`. The last statement of the script informs the user how many visits the user had in the current page.

The following script is similar to the preceding one, but it asks the user for his or her name and "remembers" it. Here is the script:

```
<HTML>
<HEAD>
<TITLE>Remember user's name</TITLE>
<SCRIPT LANGUAGE="JavaScript">
<!--

// Boolean variable specified if alert should be displayed if
                          cookie exceeds 4KB
var caution = false

// name - name of the cookie
// value - value of the cookie
// [expires] - expiration date of the cookie (defaults to end of
                          current session)
// [path] - path for which the cookie is valid (defaults to path of
                          calling document)
// [domain] - domain for which the cookie is valid (defaults to domain
                          of calling document)
// [secure] - Boolean value indicating if the cookie transmission
                          requires a secure transmission
// * an argument defaults when it is assigned null as a placeholder
// * a null placeholder is not required for trailing omitted arguments
function setCookie(name, value, expires, path, domain, secure) {
     var curCookie = name + "=" + escape(value) +
          ((expires) ? "; expires=" + expires.toGMTString() : "") +
          ((path) ? "; path=" + path : "") +
          ((domain) ? "; domain=" + domain : "") +
          ((secure) ? "; secure" : "")
     if (!caution || (name + "=" + escape(value)).length <= 4000)
          document.cookie = curCookie
     else
          if (confirm("Cookie exceeds 4KB and will be cut!"))
               document.cookie = curCookie
}

// name - name of the desired cookie
// * return string containing value of specified cookie or null if
                          cookie does not exist
```

Chapter 24

```
function getCookie(name) {
      var prefix = name + "="
      var cookieStartIndex = document.cookie.indexOf(prefix)
      if (cookieStartIndex == -1)
            return null
      var cookieEndIndex = document.cookie.indexOf(";", cookieStartIndex
                          + prefix.length)
      if (cookieEndIndex == -1)
            cookieEndIndex = document.cookie.length
      return unescape(document.cookie.substring(cookieStartIndex +
                          prefix.length, cookieEndIndex))
}

// name - name of the cookie
// [path] - path of the cookie (must be same as path used to
                          create cookie)
// [domain] - domain of the cookie (must be same as domain used to
                          create cookie)
// * path and domain default if assigned null or omitted if no
                          explicit argument proceeds
function deleteCookie(name, path, domain) {
      if (getCookie(name)) {
            document.cookie = name + "=" +
            ((path) ? "; path=" + path : "") +
            ((domain) ? "; domain=" + domain : "") +
            "; expires=Thu, 01-Jan-70 00:00:01 GMT"
      }
}

// date - any instance of the Date object
// * you should hand all instances of the Date object to this
                          function for "repairs"
// * this function is taken from Chapter 14, Time and Date in JavaScript,
                          in "Learn Advanced JavaScript Programming"
function fixDate(date) {
      var base = new Date(0)
      var skew = base.getTime()
      if (skew > 0)
            date.setTime(date.getTime() - skew)
}

var now = new Date()
fixDate(now)
now.setTime(now.getTime() + 31 * 24 * 60 * 60 * 1000)
var name = getCookie("name")
if (!name)
      name = prompt("Please enter your name:", "John Doe")
setCookie("name", name, now)
document.write("Hello " + name + "!")

// -->
</SCRIPT>
```

```
</HEAD>
</HTML>
```

***Example 24-2**. A script that remembers the user's name and displays a greeting each time.*

The differences between this script and the previous one are confined to the last five statements of the script. In the current script, the name of the cookie is "`name`" and it is the user's `name` that is being retrieved from it. Notice that the variable to which you assign the value of `getCookie()` does not have to be named as the cookie name, as is done here. If the cookie is not found, the user is prompted for his or her name. The script then sets the cookie with the user's name and prints a personalized welcome message.

Examples 24-1 and 24-2 were rather simple, because they only set and read a cookie. Example 24-3 demonstrates using cookies in a slightly different way. It creates a calendar that enables the user to enter reminders for specific days of the month. This reminder calendar stores the data for the entire month, even if the user turns off his or her computer. Since there are up to 31 days in a month, and since you are limited to 20 cookies per domain or server, the script stores all reminders in a single cookie, with special delimiting sequences. Assuming a reminder does not exceed 100 characters, storing 31 values takes up 31 * 100, or 3100 characters, which is less than the 4KB upper limit. Here is the script:

```
<HTML>
<HEAD>
<TITLE>
JavaScript calendar
</TITLE>
</HEAD>
<BODY>
<SCRIPT LANGUAGE="JavaScript">
<!--

//
// Cookie functions to store and retrieve cookies
//

// Boolean variable specified if alert should be displayed if
                             cookie exceeds 4KB
var caution = false

// name - name of the cookie
// value - value of the cookie
```

```
// [expires] - expiration date of the cookie (defaults to end of
                        current session)
// [path] - path for which the cookie is valid (defaults to path of
                        calling document)
// [domain] - domain for which the cookie is valid (defaults to domain
                        of calling document)
// [secure] - Boolean value indicating if the cookie transmission
                        requires a secure transmission
// * an argument defaults when it is assigned null as a placeholder
// * a null placeholder is not required for trailing omitted arguments
function setCookie(name, value, expires, path, domain, secure) {
    var curCookie = name + "=" + escape(value) +
        ((expires) ? "; expires=" + expires.toGMTString() : "") +
        ((path) ? "; path=" + path : "") +
        ((domain) ? "; domain=" + domain : "") +
        ((secure) ? "; secure" : "")
    if (!caution || (name + "=" + escape(value)).length <= 4000)
        document.cookie = curCookie
    else
        if (confirm("Cookie exceeds 4KB and will be cut!"))
            document.cookie = curCookie
}

// name - name of the desired cookie
// * return string containing value of specified cookie or null if
                        cookie does not exist
function getCookie(name) {
    var prefix = name + "="
    var cookieStartIndex = document.cookie.indexOf(prefix)
    if (cookieStartIndex == -1)
        return null
    var cookieEndIndex = document.cookie.indexOf(";", cookieStartIndex
                        + prefix.length)
    if (cookieEndIndex == -1)
        cookieEndIndex = document.cookie.length
    return unescape(document.cookie.substring(cookieStartIndex +
                        prefix.length, cookieEndIndex))
}

// name - name of the cookie
// [path] - path of the cookie (must be same as path used to create cookie)
// [domain] - domain of the cookie (must be same as domain used to
                        create cookie)
// * path and domain default if assigned null or omitted if no
                        explicit argument proceeds
function deleteCookie(name, path, domain) {
    if (getCookie(name)) {
        document.cookie = name + "=" +
        ((path) ? "; path=" + path : "") +
        ((domain) ? "; domain=" + domain : "") +
        "; expires=Thu, 01-Jan-70 00:00:01 GMT"
    }
```

```
}

// date - any instance of the Date object
// * you should hand all instances of the Date object to this function
                        for "repairs"
// * this function is taken from Chapter 14, Time and Date in JavaScript,
                        in "Learn Advanced JavaScript Programming"
function fixDate(date) {
     var base = new Date(0)
     var skew = base.getTime()
     if (skew > 0)
          date.setTime(date.getTime() - skew)
}

function initCookie(monthName) {
     // initializes cookie with the following format:
     // ^1^^2^^3^^4^...^30^^31^

     // initialize accumulative variable
     var text = ""
     for (var i = 1; i <= 31; ++i) {
          text += "^" + i + "^"
     }

     var now = new Date()
     fixDate(now)

     // set time to one month (31 days) in the future
     now.setTime(now.getTime() + 1000 * 60 * 60 * 24 * 31)

     setCookie(monthName + "Calendar", text, now)
}

function getSpecificReminder(num, monthName) {
     var prefix = "^" + num + "^"
     var totalCookie = getCookie(monthName + "Calendar")
     var startIndex = totalCookie.indexOf(prefix, 0)
     var startData = totalCookie.indexOf("^", startIndex + 1) + 1
     if (num == 31)
          var endData = totalCookie.length
     else
          var endData = totalCookie.indexOf("^", startData)

     return totalCookie.substring(startData, endData)
}

function setSpecificReminder(num, monthName, newValue) {
     var prefix = "^" + num + "^"
     var totalCookie = getCookie(monthName + "Calendar")
     var startIndex = totalCookie.indexOf(prefix, 0)
     var startData = totalCookie.indexOf("^", startIndex + 1) + 1
          if (num == 31)
```

```
            var endData = totalCookie.length
        else
            var endData = totalCookie.indexOf("^", startData)
        var now = new Date()
        fixDate(now)

        // set time to one month (31 days) in the future
        now.setTime(now.getTime() + 1000 * 60 * 60 * 24 * 31)

        setCookie(monthName + "Calendar", totalCookie.substring(0, startData)
        + newValue + totalCookie.substring(endData, totalCookie.length), now)
    }

    function getInput(num, monthName) {
        if (!getCookie(monthName + "Calendar"))
            initCookie(monthName)
        var newValue = prompt("Enter reminder for current date:",
                        getSpecificReminder(num, monthName))
        if (newValue) // user did not cancel
            setSpecificReminder(num, monthName, newValue)
    }

    function getTime() {
        // initialize time-related variables with current time settings
        var now = new Date()
        var hour = now.getHours()
        var minute = now.getMinutes()
        now = null
        var ampm = ""

        // validate hour values and set value of ampm
        if (hour >= 12) {
            hour -= 12
            ampm = "PM"
        } else
            ampm = "AM"
        hour = (hour == 0) ? 12 : hour

        // add zero digit to a one-digit minute
        if (minute < 10)
            minute = "0" + minute // do not parse this number!

        // return time string
        return hour + ":" + minute + " " + ampm
    }

    function leapYear(year) {
        if (year % 4 == 0) // basic rule
            return true // is leap year
        return false // is not leap year
    }
```

```
function getDays(month, year) {
     // create array to hold number of days in each month
     var ar = new Array(12)
     ar[0] = 31 // January
     ar[1] = (leapYear(year)) ? 29 : 28 // February
     ar[2] = 31 // March
     ar[3] = 30 // April
     ar[4] = 31 // May
     ar[5] = 30 // June
     ar[6] = 31 // July
     ar[7] = 31 // August
     ar[8] = 30 // September
     ar[9] = 31 // October
     ar[10] = 30 // November
     ar[11] = 31 // December

     // return number of days in the specified month (parameter)
     return ar[month]
}

function getMonthName(month) {
     // create array to hold name of each month
     var ar = new Array(12)
     ar[0] = "January"
     ar[1] = "February"
     ar[2] = "March"
     ar[3] = "April"
     ar[4] = "May"
     ar[5] = "June"
     ar[6] = "July"
     ar[7] = "August"
     ar[8] = "September"
     ar[9] = "October"
     ar[10] = "November"
     ar[11] = "December"

     // return name of specified month (parameter)
     return ar[month]
}

function setCal() {
     // standard time attributes
     var now = new Date()
     var year = now.getYear()
     var month = now.getMonth()
     var monthName = getMonthName(month)
     var date = now.getDate()
     now = null

     // create instance of first day of month, and extract the day
                        on which it occurs
     var firstDayInstance = new Date(year, month, 1)
```

```
        var firstDay = firstDayInstance.getDay()
        firstDayInstance = null

        // number of days in current month
        var days = getDays(month, year)

        // call function to draw calendar
        drawCal(firstDay + 1, days, date, monthName, 1900 + year)
    }

    function drawCal(firstDay, lastDate, date, monthName, year) {
        // constant table settings
        var headerHeight = 50 // height of the table's header cell
        var border = 2 // 3D height of table's border
        var cellspacing = 4 // width of table's border
        var headerColor = "midnightblue" // color of table's header
        var headerSize = "+3" // size of table's header font
        var colWidth = 60 // width of columns in table
        var dayCellHeight = 25 // height of cells containing days of the week
        var dayColor = "darkblue" // color of font representing weekdays
        var cellHeight = 40 // height of cells representing dates
                        in the calendar
        var todayColor = "red" // color specifying today's date in the
                        calendar
        var timeColor = "purple" // color of font representing current time

        // create basic table structure
        var text = "" // initialize accumulative variable to empty string
        text += '<CENTER>'
        text += '<TABLE BORDER=' + border + ' CELLSPACING=' + cellspacing
                        + '>' // table settings
        text +=    '<TH COLSPAN=7 HEIGHT=' + headerHeight + '>' // create
                        table header cell
        text +=       '<FONT COLOR="' + headerColor + '" SIZE=' + headerSize
                                + '>' // set font for table header
        text +=          monthName + ' ' + year
        text +=       '</FONT>' // close table header's font settings
        text +=    '</TH>' // close header cell

        // variables to hold constant settings
        var openCol = '<TD WIDTH=' + colWidth + ' HEIGHT=' + dayCellHeight
                        + '>'
        openCol += '<FONT COLOR="' + dayColor + '">'
        var closeCol = '</FONT></TD>'

        // create array of abbreviated day names
        var weekDay = new Array(7)
        weekDay[0] = "Sun"
        weekDay[1] = "Mon"
        weekDay[2] = "Tues"
        weekDay[3] = "Wed"
        weekDay[4] = "Thu"
```

```
weekDay[5] = "Fri"
weekDay[6] = "Sat"

// create first row of table to set column width and specify week day
text += '<TR ALIGN="center" VALIGN="center">'
for (var dayNum = 0; dayNum < 7; ++dayNum) {
    text += openCol + weekDay[dayNum] + closeCol
}
text += '</TR>'

// declaration and initialization of two variables to help with tables
var digit = 1
var curCell = 1

for (var row = 1; row <= Math.ceil((lastDate + firstDay - 1) / 7);
                ++row) {
    text += '<TR ALIGN="right" VALIGN="top">'
    for (var col = 1; col <= 7; ++col) {
        if (digit > lastDate)
            break
        if (curCell < firstDay) {
            text += '<TD></TD>';
            curCell++
        } else {
            if (digit == date) { // current cell represents
                                today's date
                text += '<TD HEIGHT=' + cellHeight + '>'
                text += '<FONT COLOR="' + todayColor + '">'
                text += '<A HREF="javascript:getInput(' + digit +
                    ', \'' + monthName + '\')"onMouseOver
                    ="window.status = \'Store or retrieve data
                    for ' + monthName + ' ' + digit + '\';
                    return true"><FONT COLOR="' + todayColor +
                    '">' + digit + '</FONT></A>'
                text += '<BR>'
                text += '<FONT COLOR="' + timeColor + '" SIZE=2>'
                text += '<CENTER>' + getTime() + '</CENTER>'
                text += '</FONT>'
                text += '</TD>'
            } else
                text += '<TD HEIGHT=' + cellHeight + '><A HREF=
                    "javascript:getInput(' + digit + ', \'' +
                        monthName + '\')" onMouseOver="window.
                        status = \'Store or retrieve data for
                        ' + monthName + ' ' + digit + '\';
                        return true">' + digit + '</A></TD>'
            digit++
        }
    }
    text += '</TR>'
}
```

24 Chapter

```
        // close all basic table tags
        text += '</TABLE>'
        text += '</CENTER>'

        // print accumulative HTML string
        document.write(text)
}

setCal()

// -->
</SCRIPT>
</BODY>
</HTML>
```

***Example 24-3**. A cookie-based reminder calendar.*

The setCal() function creates the calendar. The calendar is created by the same functions as those in Example 14-3 (Chapter 14, Time and Date in JavaScript). The only difference is the following:

```
if (digit == date) { // current cell represents today's date
        text += '<TD HEIGHT=' + cellHeight + '>'
        text += '<FONT COLOR="' + todayColor + '">'
        text += '<A HREF="javascript:getInput(' + digit + ', \'' + monthName +
                 '\')" onMouseOver="window.status = \'Store or retrieve
                 data for ' + monthName + ' ' + digit + '\'; return true">
                 <FONT COLOR="' + todayColor + '">' + digit + '</FONT></A>'
        text += '<BR>'
        text += '<FONT COLOR="' + timeColor + '" SIZE=2>'
        text += '<CENTER>' + getTime() + '</CENTER>'
        text += '</FONT>'
        text += '</TD>'
} else
        text += '<TD HEIGHT=' + cellHeight + '><A HREF="javascript:getInput('
                 + digit + ', \'' + monthName + '\')" onMouseOver="window
                 .status = \'Store or retrieve data for ' + monthName + ' '
                 + digit + '\'; return true">' + digit + '</A></TD>'
```

This statement differs from its corresponding one in Example 14-3 in that, instead of writing the date as a plain number, it makes each number a link that invokes the getInput() function, using the javascript:getInput() URL. The exact syntax of the URL is as follows:

```
javascript:getInput(digit, monthName)
```

The first argument is the digit that serves as a link (an integer from 1 to 28, 29, 30, or 31). The second argument is a string—the full name of the current month reflected by the calendar. Figure 24-1 outlines the links that trigger the getInput() function, when clicked:

Figure 24-1. A reminder calendar where each date is a link to the `getInput()` function.

Note that when the user places the mouse pointer over a link, a related message is assigned to the status bar. We will only discuss the functions that are responsible for the cookie handling and storage because the functions that create the calendar are discussed in Chapter 14, Time and Date in JavaScript.

getInput(num, monthName)

```
function getInput(num, monthName) {
     if (!getCookie(monthName + "Calendar"))
          initCookie(monthName)
     var newValue = prompt("Enter reminder for current date:",
getSpecificReminder(num, monthName))
     if (newValue) // user did not cancel
          setSpecificReminder(num, monthName, newValue)
}
```

The `getInput()` function, in general, reads the reminder from the cookie, asks the user to modify it or enter it for the first time, and then saves the reminder back to the cookie. First, it gets the reminder text from the cookie, the name of which is composed of the name of the current month and the "`Calendar`" string. The name selection algorithm prevents mixing cookies between different months or different applications. If the cookie is not found, the function `initCookie()` is called to create a cookie with empty reminders, one for each day of the month. The script then prompts the user for a reminder, displaying the old one in the form's input field. Notice that the reminder is displayed in the field of a prompt dialog box by specifying the value returned by `getSpecificReminder()`, as the second argument for the `prompt()` method. If the user did not press **Cancel** as a response to the request form, the new information is saved in the cookie by the `setSpecificReminder()` function. Figure 24-2 outlines the method used to display a reminder and enable modification.

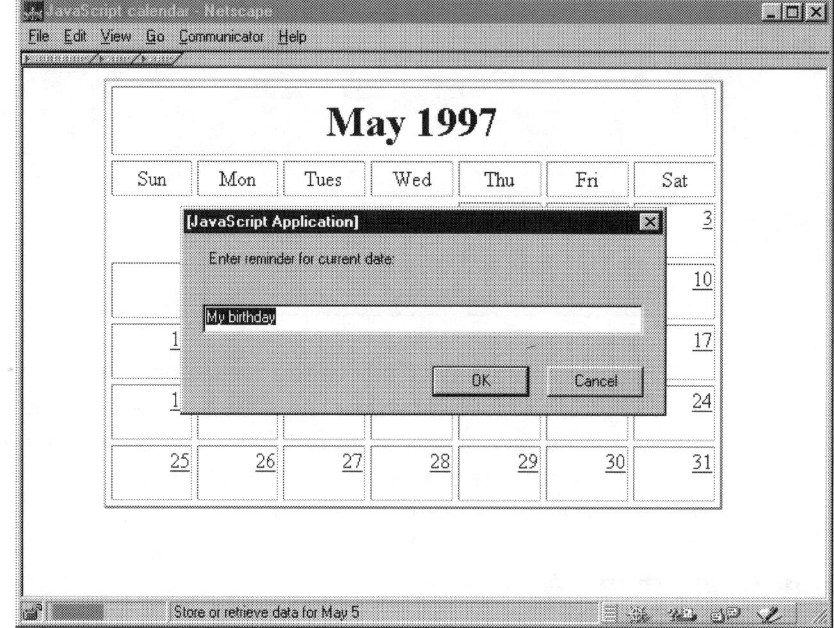

Figure 24-2*. The date "January 3rd" already consisted of a reminder so when clicking on it, the text is displayed in the box, giving an option to modify it.*

initCookie(monthName)

```
function initCookie(monthName) {
    // initializes cookie with the following format:
    // ^1^^2^^3^^4^...^30^^31^

    // initialize accumulative variable
    var text = ""
    for (var i = 1; i <= 31; ++i) {
        text += "^" + i + "^"
    }

    var now = new Date()
    fixDate(now)
```

```
        // set time to one month (31 days) in the future
        now.setTime(now.getTime() + 1000 * 60 * 60 * 24 * 31)

        setCookie(monthName + "Calendar", text, now)
}
```

The initCookie() function creates a cookie with empty reminders, one for every day of the month. The cookie's text is a string concatenation of all 31 reminders, delimited by " ^ " from each other. The function first builds the empty string, fixes the date for Mac computers, computes the time, and finally sets the cookie, saving the empty reminders, date, and time in it.

getSpecificReminder(num, monthName)

```
function getSpecificReminder(num, monthName) {
        var prefix = "^" + num + "^"
        var totalCookie = getCookie(monthName + "Calendar")
        var startIndex = totalCookie.indexOf(prefix, 0)
        var startData = totalCookie.indexOf("^", startIndex + 1) + 1
        if (num == 31)
                var endData = totalCookie.length
        else
                var endData = totalCookie.indexOf("^", startData)

        return totalCookie.substring(startData, endData)
}
```

This function retrieves the specific reminder of the month from the cookie. It first builds the "search key" in prefix. It is built of a "^" followed by the day number of the month and then yet another "^". After getting the cookie and reading the string into totalCookie string object, the function searches for the position of the relevant reminder, according to prefix "search key," yielding the startIndex position. Looking for the next "^" skips over the number of the day itself and leaps onto the string index of the reminder's first character, startData. The last character of the reminder is found via a search for the next "^" character or by reaching the end of the cookie. Once the startData and endData are known, the substring between these two indices is returned. Note that because the indexing relies on "^" characters, that character should not be provided by the user in a reminder text.

setSpecificReminder(num, monthName, newValue)

```
function setSpecificReminder(num, monthName, newValue) {
        var prefix = "^" + num + "^"
        var totalCookie = getCookie(monthName + "Calendar")
        var startIndex = totalCookie.indexOf(prefix, 0)
```

```
        var startData = totalCookie.indexOf("^", startIndex + 1) + 1
            if (num == 31)
            var endData = totalCookie.length
        else
            var endData = totalCookie.indexOf("^", startData)
        var now = new Date()
        fixDate(now)

        // set time to one month (31 days) in the future
        now.setTime(now.getTime() + 1000 * 60 * 60 * 24 * 31)

        setCookie(monthName + "Calendar", totalCookie.substring(0,
                startData) + newValue + totalCookie.substring
                (endData, totalCookie.length), now)
}
```

As in `setSpecificReminder()`, the first section determines the indices of the first and last character of the relevant reminder (`startData` and `endData`, respectively). An instance of the `Date` object is then created and fixed for Mac computers. The expiration date is then computed to one month in the future. The last statement of the function sets the cookie. The first parameter is the name of the cookie, while the second one is the reminder string, composed of the substring before the new reminder (all previous days are not modified), the `newValue` of the current day, and the rest of the old string (all following days are not modified as well). The expiration date is handed to the function as the last argument.

Outliner

As you have seen in this chapter, you can use JavaScript to store data in the form of client-side cookies. The *outliner* is another example for using cookies. It is an exploding/collapsing structure used to store an index or table of contents. The user can expand (explode) or collapse items in the outline. Outliners were very popular in Windows 3.1x and are also present in many applications. An outliner written in JavaScript enables the user to take advantage of the structure for convenient navigation among many Web pages and anchors. The main topics of a Web site are the topmost items in the outline, while the more detailed items are usually deeply nested. It is very difficult to explain exactly what an outliner is, so stick with the saying "A picture is worth a thousand words."

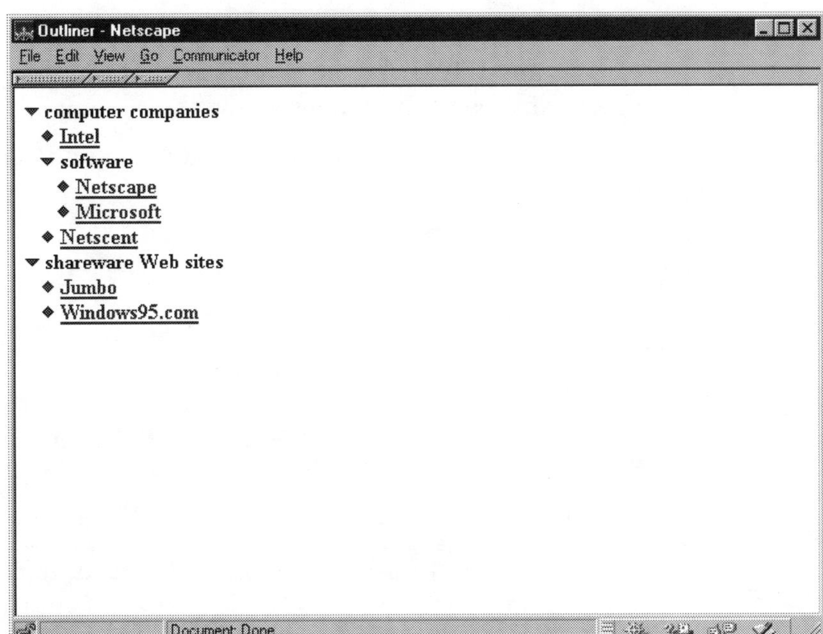

***Figure 24-3**. A fully exploded (expanded) outline.*

Figure 24-3 illustrates a fully expanded outline. When the user clicks the downwards triangle to the left of "software," the icon becomes a triangle facing right. The "Netscape" and "Microsoft" items then disappear, because their parent was collapsed. The basic idea should be clear. You can toggle a single item (only if it is a parent) between two different states (either expanded or collapsed).

Before we discuss the script itself, it is important that you understand exactly what the script does and how it differs from other JavaScript outliners available. Because an outliner script can easily be reproduced with custom items, all outliner scripts were written by the most advanced scripters. Nevertheless, we believe that you have enough background and experience in JavaScript to understand this script, and maybe even to write something similar on your own. Compared to other variants you might find on the Web, our outliner script has the following advantages:

- You can use any HTML tag for an item. You can use colored text, hypertext links, and even small images.
- The current state of the outline structure is stored in the form of a cookie, so it is safe, even if you leave the page.
- You can use as many nested items as you wish. Some outline designs limit you to two levels, which is very restrictive.

- The outliner design is not limited to frame documents. Since you can use any HTML for the text of an item, you can target any link to any frame or window you wish.

First, study the script (Example 24-4) and try to understand as much as you can:

```
<HTML>
<HEAD>
<TITLE>Outliner</TITLE>
<SCRIPT LANGUAGE="JavaScript">
<!--

// Boolean variable specified if alert should be displayed if cookie
                    exceeds 4KB
var caution = false

// name - name of the cookie
// value - value of the cookie
// [expires] - expiration date of the cookie (defaults to end of current
                    session)
// [path] - path for which the cookie is valid (defaults to path of
                    calling document)
// [domain] - domain for which the cookie is valid (defaults to domain of
                    calling document)
// [secure] - Boolean value indicating if the cookie transmission requires
                    a secure transmission
// * an argument defaults when it is assigned null as a placeholder
// * a null placeholder is not required for trailing omitted arguments
function setCookie(name, value, expires, path, domain, secure) {
     var curCookie = name + "=" + escape(value) +
          ((expires) ? "; expires=" + expires.toGMTString() : "") +
          ((path) ? "; path=" + path : "") +
          ((domain) ? "; domain=" + domain : "") +
          ((secure) ? "; secure" : "")
     if (!caution || (name + "=" + escape(value)).length <= 4000)
          document.cookie = curCookie
     else
          if (confirm("Cookie exceeds 4KB and will be cut!"))
               document.cookie = curCookie
}

// name - name of the desired cookie
// * return string containing value of specified cookie or null if
                    cookie does not exist
function getCookie(name) {
     var prefix = name + "="
     var cookieStartIndex = document.cookie.indexOf(prefix)
     if (cookieStartIndex == -1)
          return null
     var cookieEndIndex = document.cookie.indexOf(";", cookieStartIndex +
                    prefix.length)
```

```
     if (cookieEndIndex == -1)
          cookieEndIndex = document.cookie.length
     return unescape(document.cookie.substring(cookieStartIndex +
                         prefix.length, cookieEndIndex))
}

// name - name of the cookie
// [path] - path of the cookie (must be same as path used to create cookie)
// [domain] - domain of the cookie (must be same as domain used to
                    create cookie)
// * path and domain default if assigned null or omitted if no explicit
                    argument proceeds
function deleteCookie(name, path, domain) {
     if (getCookie(name)) {
          document.cookie = name + "=" +
          ((path) ? "; path=" + path : "") +
          ((domain) ? "; domain=" + domain : "") +
          "; expires=Thu, 01-Jan-70 00:00:01 GMT"
     }
}

// date - any instance of the Date object
// * you should hand all instances of the Date object to this function
                    for "repairs"
// * this function is taken from Chapter 14, Time and Date in JavaScript,
                    in "Learn Advanced JavaScript Programming"
function fixDate(date) {
     var base = new Date(0)
     var skew = base.getTime()
     if (skew > 0)
          date.setTime(date.getTime() - skew)
}

// constructor function to create an entry (parent or child)
function item(parent, text, depth) {
     this.parent = parent // is this item a parent?
     this.text = text // text for link (may include HTML)
     this.depth = depth // nested depth
}

// constructor function to create array (compatible with all browsers)
function makeArray(length) {
     this.length = length // length of array (integer)
}

// create items of outline
function makeDatabase() {
     outline = new makeArray(9) // create global object

     // create items in outline
     outline[0] = new item(true, 'computer companies', 0)
```

```
        outline[1] = new item(false, '<A HREF="http://www.intel
                   .com">Intel</A>', 1)
        outline[2] = new item(true, 'software', 1)
        outline[3] = new item(false, '<A HREF="http://www.netscape
                   .com">Netscape</A>', 2)
        outline[4] = new item(false, '<A HREF="http://www.microsoft
                   .com">Microsoft</A>', 2)
        outline[5] = new item(false, '<A HREF="http://www.netscent
                   .com">Netscent</A>', 1)
        outline[6] = new item(true, 'shareware Web sites', 0)
        outline[7] = new item(false, '<A HREF="http://www.jumbo
                   .com">Jumbo</A>', 1)
        outline[8] = new item(false, '<A HREF="http://www.windows95
                   .com">Windows95.com</A>', 1)

        // determine current state of each item and assign to state properties
        setStates()

        // set image for each item (only items with true state)
        setImages()
}

function setStates() {
        // assign current cookie to local variable
        var storedValue = getCookie("outline")

        // if desired cookie not found (null)
        if (!storedValue) {
                // set states to default if no cookie found
                for (var i = 0; i < outline.length; ++i) {
                        // only topmost level is visible by default
                        if (outline[i].depth == 0)
                                outline[i].state = true
                        else
                                outline[i].state = false
                }
        } else {
                // extract current states from cookie (0 => false, 1 => true)
                for (var i = 0; i < outline.length; ++i) {
                        if (storedValue.charAt(i) == '1')
                                outline[i].state = true
                        else
                                outline[i].state = false
                }
        }
}

function setImages() {
        // loop through all elements of the outline "array" (object)
        for (var i = 0; i < outline.length; ++i) {
                if (outline[i].state)
                        if (outline[i].parent) // outline[i] is a parent
```

```
                    if (outline[i + 1].state) // outline[i] is exploded
                         outline[i].pic = '<A HREF="javascript:toggle(' +
                         i + ')"><IMG SRC="exploded.gif" BORDER=0></A>'
                    else // outline[i] is collapsed
                         outline[i].pic = '<A HREF="javascript:toggle(' +
                         i + ')"><IMG SRC="collapsd.gif" BORDER=0></A>'
               else // outline[i] is only a child (not a parent)
                    outline[i].pic = '<IMG SRC="child.gif" BORDER=0>'
     }
}

// change from expanded to collapsed and vice versa
function toggle(num) {
     // loop starts at item following argument
     // terminate loop when:
     //   a) last element of outline "array" reached
     //   b) current item (outline[i]) is not deeper than toggled item
                         (outline[num])
     for (var i = num + 1; i < outline.length && outline[i].depth >=
                         outline[num].depth + 1; ++i) {
          // if current item (outline[i]) is a direct child of
                         outline[num]
          if (outline[i].depth == outline[num].depth + 1)
               outline[i].state = !outline[i].state // toggle state
     }

     // store new states in cookie
     setStorage()

     // reload page
     history.go(0)
}

function setStorage() {
     // initialize local variable to empty string
     var text = ""

     // loop through all properties of outline "array"
     for (var i = 0; i < outline.length; ++i) {
          // use "1" character to represent true state, and "0" for
                              false state
          text += (outline[i].state) ? "1" : "0"
     }

     // create cookie named "outline" with "binary" string
     setCookie("outline", text)
}

// update database
makeDatabase()

// -->
```

```
</SCRIPT>
</HEAD>
<BODY>
<SCRIPT LANGUAGE="JavaScript">
<!--

// use <PRE> to enable indentation via spaces
document.write('<PRE><H4>')

// loop through elements of outline "array"
for (var i = 0; i < outline.length; ++i) {
     // if current item's state is true
     if (outline[i].state) {
          // place three spaces for each nesting (depth * 3 spaces)
          for (var j = 0; j < outline[i].depth * 3; ++j) {
               document.write('   ')
          }

          // follow indentation with picture, another space, text, and
                                  new line
          document.write(outline[i].pic, ' ', outline[i].text, '<BR>')
     } else {
          // current item's state is false (skip all its children)
          var previous = i
          for (var k = i + 1; k < outline.length && outline[k].depth >=
                                  outline[previous].depth; ++k) {
               ++i
          }
     }
}

// end <PRE> to return to normal formatting
document.write('</H4></PRE>')

// -->
</SCRIPT>
</BODY>
</HTML>
```

***Example 24-4 (ex24-4.htm)**. The outliner script includes deferred script and immediate script.*

A quick look at Example 24-4 is enough to conclude that the script uses cookies. Our set of cookie-related functions is embedded in the script. Although not all are invoked, we feel that you should always provide all the functions, regardless of whether you require all of them. Also notice that the HTML document includes two scripts—one in the <HEAD>…</HEAD> portion and one in the <BODY>…</BODY> one. The first script is responsible for setting up the outline-style table and contents, and for performing the calculations and manipulations. The second script simply interprets the data and prints it to the Web page. First let's take a look at the script in the <HEAD>…</HEAD> portion.

item(parent, text, depth)

```
// constructor function to create an entry (parent or child)
function item(parent, text, depth) {
     this.parent = parent // is this item a parent?
     this.text = text // text for link (may include HTML)
     this.depth = depth // nested depth
}
```

The constructor function `item()` accepts three arguments and creates three properties with the same names as the function's parameters: `parent`, `text`, and `depth`. The first parameter (and property), `parent`, accepts a Boolean value indicating whether or not the item is a parent. An item is considered a parent only if it has children, or nested items. In Figure 24-3, "Software" is a parent, but "Microsoft" is not. The function's second argument, `text`, accepts an HTML-valid string such as `<A HREF="http://www.jumbo.com">Jumbo</A>` for the "Jumbo" entry in Figure 24-3. You can use virtually any HTML-valid string such as plain text, a link (as in the "Jumbo" example), or even a small image. The last argument, `depth`, is the depth of the item being created, i.e., it specifies how deep the item is nested. The topmost level item's `depth` property is 0, whereas its children's `depth` property is 1, and so forth.

24 Chapter

makeArray(length)

```
// constructor function to create array (compatible with all browsers)
function makeArray(length) {
     this.length = length // length of array (integer)
}
```

This function is an alternative to the built-in `Array()` constructor of Navigator and MSIE. We decided to write an array-constructor on our own in order to make the script compatible with all JavaScript-enabled browsers, and for didactic purposes. We used JavaScript's support for adding properties to an object, to explicitly create `length`, which holds the number of elements in the array, or the number of its properties (not counting `length` itself), to be exact.

makeDatabase()

```
// create items of outline
function makeDatabase() {
```

```
        outline = new makeArray(9) // create global object

        // create items in outline
        outline[0] = new item(true, 'computer companies', 0)
        outline[1] = new item(false, '<A HREF="http://www.intel
                             .com">Intel</A>', 1)
        outline[2] = new item(true, 'software', 1)
        outline[3] = new item(false, '<A HREF="http://www.netscape
                             .com">Netscape</A>', 2)
        outline[4] = new item(false, '<A HREF="http://www.microsoft
                             .com">Microsoft</A>', 2)
        outline[5] = new item(false, '<A HREF="http://www.netscent
                             .com">Netscent</A>', 1)
        outline[6] = new item(true, 'shareware Web sites', 0)
        outline[7] = new item(false, '<A HREF="http://www.jumbo
                             .com">Jumbo</A>', 1)
        outline[8] = new item(false, '<A HREF="http://www.windows95
                             .com">Windows95.com</A>', 1)

        // determine current state of each item and assign to state properties
        setStates()

        // set image for each item (only items with true state)
        setImages()
}
```

This function creates the main array used for the outline structure. Notice that the `outline` array is declared without the keyword `var` and thus is global. Try adding `var` to this statement to find out how important "one small word" can be. The next portion of this function deals with the properties (elements) of the `outline` array. Each property becomes an instance of the `item` object. The order of the elements in the array is very important. An item's children should immediately follow the item, so the order in the `outline` array is the order in which the entries appear, from top to bottom, in a fully expanded table of contents.

The function then calls `setStates()` and `setImages()`.

setStates()

```
function setStates() {
        // assign current cookie to local variable
        var storedValue = getCookie("outline")

        // if desired cookie not found (null)
        if (!storedValue) {
                // set states to default if no cookie found
```

```
            for (var i = 0; i < outline.length; ++i) {
                // only topmost level is visible by default
                if (outline[i].depth == 0)
                    outline[i].state = true
                else
                    outline[i].state = false
            }
        } else {
            // extract current states from cookie (0 => false, 1 => true)
            for (var i = 0; i < outline.length; ++i) {
                if (storedValue.charAt(i) == '1')
                    outline[i].state = true
                else
                    outline[i].state = false
            }
        }
    }
```


The `setStates()` function adds a `state` property to all properties of the `outline` object (array). If no cookie by the name of "`outline`" is found, the default states are used, i.e., the entire outline structure is collapsed, and only the topmost level is viewable. If the desired cookie is found, the current states are extracted. The cookie is basically a string of "`0`" and "`1`" characters, the first representing a `false` state, and the latter representing a `true` one. The first character of the string is associated with the first element of the array (`outline[0].state`), and so on. An item's state determines whether or not that item's parent is expanded. Therefore, on a two-level outline-style table of contents, if an item has a true state it is viewable.

setImages()

```
    function setImages() {
        // loop through all elements of the outline "array" (object)
        for (var i = 0; i < outline.length; ++i) {
            if (outline[i].state)
                if (outline[i].parent) // outline[i] is a parent
                    if (outline[i + 1].state) // outline[i] is exploded
                        outline[i].pic = '<A HREF="javascript:toggle
                                (' + i + ')"><IMG SRC="exploded.gif"
                                BORDER=0></A>'
                    else // outline[i] is collapsed
                        outline[i].pic = '<A HREF="javascript:toggle
                                (' + i + ')"><IMG SRC="collapsd.gif"
                                BORDER=0></A>'
                else // outline[i] is only a child (not a parent)
                    outline[i].pic = '<IMG SRC="child.gif" BORDER=0>'
        }
    }
```

This function loops through all elements of the `outline` object and assigns an image to the `pic` property of each element whose `state` is `true`. Note that this property is an extension to the original instance of the `item` object. If an element is a parent, there are two possible images—one to represent an expanded item, and the other to reflect a collapsed one. Notice that if the Boolean expression `outline[i + 1].state` is true, `outline[i]` is expanded. You may recall that an element's `state` property is `true` if its parent is expanded (by definition). Since `outline[i]` is surely a parent in this case (`if (outline[i].parent)…`), `outline[i + 1]` is its child. If `outline[i + 1]`'s current state is `false`, the image representing a collapsed item is chosen. If `outline[i]` is not a parent at all, there is only one option for the image—the one representing a child item. The immediate conclusion from this function is that in order to use the outliner, you must have three images:

- exploded.gif
- collapsd.gif
- child.gif

toggle(num)

```
// change from expanded to collapsed and vice versa
function toggle(num) {
     // loop starts at item following argument
     // terminate loop when:
     //   a) last element of outline "array" reached
     //   b) current item (outline[i]) is not deeper than toggled
                    item (outline[num])
     for (var i = num + 1; i < outline.length && outline[i].depth >=
                    outline[num].depth + 1; ++i) {
          // if current item (outline[i]) is a direct child of
                         outline[num]
          if (outline[i].depth == outline[num].depth + 1)
               outline[i].state = !outline[i].state // toggle state
     }

     // store new states in cookie
     setStorage()

     // reload page
     history.go(0)
}
```

When the user clicks an image (exploded.gif or collapsd.gif), the item associated with it either collapses or explodes, depending on its current status. The `toggle()` function accepts an integer reflecting the index of the item whose icon the user clicked, and then toggles the state property of all the item's direct children. By definition, when an item has no children with a true state, the item is collapsed, and when all children of an item have a true state, the item is expanded. Therefore, toggling the state property of the selected item's children toggles that item's current status (exploded or collapsed). After all manipulations, the function invokes the setStorage() function to store the current status in a cookie, overwriting any previous cookie used for the outliner. After the cookie is written, the function reloads the page via the history.go() method, with the argument 0 to indicate that the **current** page should be loaded. We chose to use go(0) rather than reload() because:

1. It works with all JavaScript-compatible browsers.
2. It is perfect for refreshing a document, which is exactly what the script does.

setStorage()

```
function setStorage() {
     // initialize local variable to empty string
     var text = ""

     // loop through all properties of outline "array"
     for (var i = 0; i < outline.length; ++i) {
          // use "1" character to represent true state, and "0" for
                                   false state
          text += (outline[i].state) ? "1" : "0"
     }

     // create cookie named "outline" with "binary" string
     setCookie("outline", text)
}
```

The setStorage() function creates a string with binary characters (0s and 1s). The first character of the string is associated with the first element of the outline array, and so forth. The character "0" indicates that the value of the item's state property is false, and a "1" character means that the item's state property is true. The last statement of this function sets the cookie via the setCookie() function, using "outline" as the name and the accumulative string as the value. No path or expiration date is specified, so the cookie is specific to the creating page and expires at the end of the user's current session.

Global Statements

The only global statement in the first script is the one invoking the makeDatabase() function. The second script, on the other hand, consists of global statements only and is responsible for printing the outline-style table of contents. The <PRE>...</PRE> tags are important because they enable us to use regular spaces for indentation.

The most important statement in the second script is the loop itself, which iterates through all elements of the global outline array (created by the makeDatabase() function in the first script). Each indentation level consists of three spaces and can be configured to any other integer for customized indentation. The topmost level items are not indented at all ($0 * 3 = 0$), the second level is indented by 3 spaces ($1 * 3 = 3$), the third level by 6 spaces ($2 * 3 = 6$), and so on. Note that an item is only printed if the value of its state property is true (by definition, if it is false, its parent is collapsed so you are not supposed to see the item). Each printed item consists of its small image (outline[i].pic), followed by one space and its text (outline[I].text). A new line (<BR>) is appended to each item. When an element whose state property is false is encountered, i is incremented the desired amount of times, until its index is that of the next item at its level or a higher one. It passes over all items at lower levels because they do not appear.

Summary

In this chapter you have learned the fundamentals and usage of cookies, one of the most powerful features of JavaScript. It enables the programmer of a Web page to store information in one session and retrieve it later in another one. We have provided three important functions by which you can get a cookie, set a cookie, and delete a cookie. All operations, as well as storage, are handled on the client side. Cookies are transparent to the server. The client imposes two limitations on cookies: maximum 20 cookies per server or domain, 4KB each. We have shown several scripts in this chapter: one that uses cookies to remember the number of visits to a Web site, one that uses cookies to store the user name, and one which uses cookies to remember a user's reminder for every day of the month. We also included an advanced collapsing/expanding outline-style table of contents which uses cookies as well.

Chapter 25

Images and Graphics

Defining Images in HTML

The syntax to define an image in HTML is as follows:

```
<IMG
     [NAME="imageName"]
     SRC="Location"
     [LOWSRC="Location"]
     [HEIGHT="Pixels" | "Value"%]
     [WIDTH="Pixels" | "Value"%]
     [SPACE="Pixels"]
     [BORDER = "Pixels"]
     [ALIGN = "left" | "right" |"top" | "absmiddle" | "absbottom"
               |"texttop" | "middle"  | "baseline" | "bottom" ]
     [ISMAP]
     [USEMAP="Location#MapName"]
     [onAbort="handlerText"]
     [onError="handlerText"]
     [onLoad="handlerText"]>
```

The attributes are:

NAME="*imageName*" specifies the name of the image object.

SRC="*Location*" specifies the URL of the image to be displayed in the document.

LOWSRC="*Location*" specifies the URL of a low-resolution version of the image to be displayed in the document. When this argument is provided, Navigator loads this smaller image first, and then replaces it with the larger image specified by SRC. Loading a low-resolution version first gives the user an impression of a shorter turnaround time.

HEIGHT="*Pixels*" | "*Value*"% specifies the height of the image, either in pixels or as a percentage of the window height. If necessary, Navigator scales the image to fit the space specified by this attribute.

`WIDTH="Pixels" | "Value"%` specifies the width of the image, either in pixels or as a percentage of the window width. If necessary, Navigator scales the image to fit the space specified by this attribute.

`HSPACE="Pixels"` specifies the margin in pixels between the left and right edges of the image and the surrounding text. This attribute applies only to images that use "left" or "right" as the value of the `ALIGN` attribute.

`VSPACE="Pixels"` specifies the margin in pixels between the top and bottom edges of the image and the surrounding text. This attribute applies only to images that use "left" or "right" as the value of the `ALIGN` attribute.

`BORDER="Pixels"` specifies the width in pixels of the image border. You can suppress the border by setting its value to 0. If, however, it appears within an anchor, users will not see the colored border indicating a hyperlink.

`ALIGN` specifies the alignment of the image in relation to the surrounding text. Images that are aligned as `left` or `right` float into the next available space on the left or right side of the page, respectively, while text fills the empty space next to the image. The rest of the `ALIGN` values specify the alignment of the image with respect to a line of text in which it is placed (no filling). If omitted, `bottom` is used, which means that the bottom of the image is aligned with the line of text.

`ISMAP` specifies the image as a server-side image map.

`USEMAP="Location#MapName"` specifies the image as a client-side image map. This attribute must specify the URL of the file that contains the map definition, followed by a # symbol, and then the name of the map. For example, `USEMAP="http://www.HomeWorld.com/maplist.html#area-map"`. The URL can be omitted if the image map specifications reside in the same document as the reference.

Creating an Instance of Image Object

The `Image` object enables you to create instances that reflect a given image in any supported format (usually gif or jpeg). Since this object is not featured by Netscape Navigator 2.0x and Microsoft Internet Explorer 3.0, scripts that use it under these browsers will crash. By introducing movement and animation, the `Image` object immensely increased JavaScript's capabilities. You can take advantage of this object to create an animation, for example, with full control over timing and order of events. You can also create animation-based games such as Tetris, MineSweeper, and so forth.

The primary incentive to use the Image object is to accelerate image displaying in the browser window. Instead of waiting for the image to be transmitted from the server to the client when the display is needed, it is loaded and stored in the browser's cache ahead of time, and displayed immediately upon request. In order to use the Image object you must create an instance associated with a given image. The general syntax is as follows:

```
var imageName = new Image([width, height])
```

width is the width of the image in pixels, whereas *height* is its height. An instance of the Image object can be associated with one image at any given time. In order to associate an instance with an existing image you must assign it a source in the following fashion:

```
var imageName = new Image([width, height])
imageName.src = "imageLocation"
```

imageLocation is the full URL of the image. The second statement in the preceding script segment assigns a value to the instance's src property. The browser will retrieve the image from the server and will keep it in the cache until needed. Note that the width and height attributes are optional.

The images Array

When you create an HTML document you usually include several images (defined by the <IMG> definition). JavaScript features an array that reflects all images in a document—document.images. Each element of the array reflects an existing image. The first image in a document, for example, is document.images[0]. Obviously, the total number of images in a document is stored in the length property—document.images.length. Using the array within a deferred script ensures that all images have been loaded and the array reflects all images of a document.

An alternative way to reference an image is by its name, which is defined by the NAME attribute of the <IMG> HTML tag. See Example 25-5 for further details and explanations.

The size and position of an image in a document are set when the document is displayed in the browser window, and cannot be changed.

Therefore, when creating an animation, you should generally use images of the same height and width. You can only change the image itself by setting the `src` and `lowsrc` properties. (See the listings for `src` and `lowsrc` in the previous section, "Defining Images in HTML.")

Consider the following HTML document:

```
<HTML>
<HEAD>
<TITLE>images</TITLE>
<SCRIPT LANGUAGE="JavaScript">
<!--

function swapImages(a, b) {
     var asource = document.images[a].src
     document.images[a].src = document.images[b].src
     document.images[b].src = asource
}

// -->
</SCRIPT>
</HEAD>
<BODY>
<IMG SRC="bla.gif" HEIGHT=60 WIDTH=70>
<IMG SRC="foo.gif" HEIGHT=60 WIDTH=70><P>
<FORM>
<INPUT TYPE="button" VALUE="swap" onClick="swapImages(0, 1)">
</FORM>
</BODY>
</HTML>
```

***Example 25-1**. A button enables the user to swap two given images.*

When the user clicks the button, the `swapImages()` function is invoked with two arguments: 0 and 1. The `src` property of the image whose index is the first argument is assigned to the local variable `source`. The `src` property of the second image is assigned to the `src` property of the first image, and the `src` property of the second image is assigned the previous `src` property of the first image, stored locally in `asource`.

The `document.images` array is a read-only one—you cannot explicitly assign a value to any of its elements. Nevertheless, you can assign values to properties of an array element, as the preceding example demonstrates with the `src` property.

As mentioned earlier, an animation should consist of images of the same size. Example 25-2 demonstrates a simple animation with seven images of identical dimensions.

```
<HTML>
<HEAD>
<TITLE>images</TITLE>
<SCRIPT LANGUAGE="JavaScript">
<!--

var pause = 250

var on = new Array()
on[0] = new Image(12, 12)
on[1] = new Image(12, 12)
on[2] = new Image(12, 12)
on[3] = new Image(12, 12)
on[4] = new Image(12, 12)
on[5] = new Image(12, 12)
on[6] = new Image(12, 12)

for (var i = 0; i < 7; ++i) {
     on[i].src = "1" + i + ".gif"
}

timerID = setTimeout("", 0)

function animate(num, imageIndex) {
     document.images[imageIndex].src = on[num].src
     num = (num == on.length - 1) ? 0 : (++num)
     var str = "animate(" + num + ", " + imageIndex + ")"
     timerID = setTimeout(str, pause)
}

// -->
</SCRIPT>
</HEAD>
<BODY onLoad="timerID = setTimeout('animate(1, 0)', pause)">
<IMG SRC="&{on[0].src};" HEIGHT="&{on[0].height};" WIDTH="&{on[0].width};">
</BODY>
</HTML>
```

Example 25-2*. A simple animation with images of identical size.*

The script consists of a few immediate statements as well as a deferred code. First, an array named on is created to store the images of the animation. Each element is actually an instance of the Image object.

Take a look at the following statement:

```
timerID = setTimeout("", 0)
```

This statement sets the value of timerID to null, but it does not explicitly assign that value. This syntax is useful with MSIE 3.0 because it generates an error if you use the `clearTimeout()` with a variable that holds a `null` value. This is not so important in Example 25-2 because `clearTimeout()` is not used. Furthermore, the preceding example does not work at all under MSIE 3.0, because that browser does not support the `Image` object.

```
function animate(num, imageIndex) {
     document.images[imageIndex].src = on[num].src
     num = (num == on.length - 1) ? 0 : (++num)
     var str = "animate(" + num + ", " + imageIndex + ")"
     timerID = setTimeout(str, pause)
}
```

The `animate()` function accepts two arguments. The first specifies the index of the first image in the animation according to the `on` array. Take a look at the following statement from `animate()`, which is the most important one:

```
document.images[imageIndex].src = on[num].src
```

The current image that appears in the document at the `imageIndex` index of the `document.images` array is replaced by the image in the `on` array, whose index is equal to the first argument handed to the function. The second statement in this function sets the value of `num` to 0 if the current value exceeds the index of the last entry in the `on` array. Otherwise, it increments the value of `num`, so the following image is displayed during the next execution of the function.

Properties

Instances of the `Image` object feature many properties, some of which are more useful than others. You can also add more properties by creating prototypes. This section describes each property in depth.

border

An image's border appears only when the image is used in a hypertext link and when the value of the `BORDER` attribute is set to a positive integer. The general reference is as follows:

```
imageName.border
```

where *imageName* is either the name of an `Image` object's instance or an element in the `document.images` array. The `border` property is a read-only one. The following function displays the image's border if it is not 0:

```
function checkBorder(theImage) {
     if (theImage.border == 0)
          alert('The image has no border!')
     else
          alert('The image's border is ' + theImage.border)
}
```

complete

This property is a Boolean value that indicates whether Navigator has completed its attempt to load an image. The general specification is as follows:

```
imageName.complete
```

where *imageName* is either the name of an `Image` object's instance or an element in the `document.images` array.

The `complete` property does not work properly on some platforms, so check it first on all platforms.

height

The `height` property specifies the height of an image, either in pixels or as a percentage of the window's total height. The general syntax is as follows:

```
imageName.height
```

where *imageName* is either the name of an `Image` object's instance or an element in the `document.images` array. The `height` property reflects the `HEIGHT` attribute of the `<IMG>` tag. For images created with the `Image()` constructor, the value of the height property is the actual height, not the displayed height. The `height` property is a read-only one.

The script in Example 25-3 shows how an alert box can display, upon clicking a button, the height, width, and space figures of an image.

```
<HTML>
<HEAD>
<TITLE>images</TITLE>
<SCRIPT LANGUAGE="JavaScript">
<!--

function showImageSize(theImage) {
     alert('height=' + theImage.height +
          '; width=' + theImage.width +
          '; hspace=' + theImage.hspace +
          '; vspace=' + theImage.vspace)
```

```
}

// -->
</SCRIPT>
</HEAD>
<BODY>
<IMG SRC="bla.gif" HEIGHT=60 WIDTH=70 VSPACE=30 HSPACE=10>
<FORM>
<INPUT TYPE="button" VALUE="show image size" onClick=
                            "showImageSize(document.images[0])">
</FORM>
</BODY>
</HTML>
```

Example 25-3*. A script to display the height, width, and space around an image.*

hspace

The hspace property specifies the margin in pixels between the left and right edges of an image and the surrounding text. The general syntax is as follows:

```
imageName.hspace
```

where *imageName* is either the name of an Image object's instance or an element in the document.images array. The hspace property reflects the HSPACE attribute of the <IMG> tag. For images created with the Image()constructor, the value of the hspace property is 0. The hspace property is a read-only one. The script in Example 25-3 shows how an alert box can display, upon clicking a button, the height, width, and space figures of an image.

lowsrc

lowsrc is a string specifying the URL of a low-resolution version of an image to be displayed in a document. The general syntax is as follows:

```
imageName.lowsrc
```

where *imageName* is either the name of an Image object's instance or an element in the document.images array. The lowsrc property initially reflects the LOWSRC attribute of the <IMG> tag. Navigator loads the smaller image specified by lowsrc and then replaces it with the larger image specified by the src property. You can change the lowsrc property at any time.

The script in Example 25-4 lets the user display one image out of three available ones. There are two images ready for each of the three selections: low resolution and high resolution. When loading the requested selection, the low-resolution image is loaded first and then the high-resolution one:

```
<HTML>
<HEAD>
<TITLE>Aircrafts</TITLE>
<SCRIPT LANGUAGE="JavaScript">
<!--

function displayImage(lowRes, highRes) {
   document.images[0].lowsrc = lowRes
   document.images[0].src = highRes
}

// -->
</SCRIPT>
</HEAD>
<BODY>
<FORM NAME="imageForm">
<B>Choose an image:</B>
<BR><INPUT TYPE="radio" NAME="imageChoice" VALUE="image1" CHECKED
   onClick="displayImage('img1l.gif','img1h.gif')"> IMAGE 1
<BR><INPUT TYPE="radio" NAME="imageChoice" VALUE="image2"
   onClick="displayImage('img2l.gif', 'img2h.gif')"> IMAGE 2
<BR><INPUT TYPE="radio" NAME="imageChoice" VALUE="image3"
   onClick="displayImage('img3l.gif', 'img3h.gif')"> IMAGE 3
<BR>
<IMG NAME="firstImage" SRC="img1h.gif" LOWSRC="img1l.gif" ALIGN="left"
                    VSPACE="10"><BR>
</FORM>
</BODY>
</HTML>
```

***Example 25-4**. A script to display one of three images; low-resolution images are loaded first.*

name

The *imageName*.name property reflects the NAME attribute of the <IMG> HTML definition. The name property is a read-only one. Similar to forms, you can use an image's name to reference it. If the first image in a document is defined by the following syntax, for instance, you can reference it as document.myImage as well as document.images[0]:

```
<IMG SRC="myPicture.gif" NAME="myImage">
```

src

scr specifies the URL of an image to be displayed in a document. The general syntax is as follows:

```
imageName.src
```

where *imageName* is either the name of an Image object's instance or an element in the document.images array. The src property will be used in almost all this chapter's examples. Consider the following statement:

```
var myImage = new Image()
```

An instance of the Image object, named myImage, is created with the Image() constructor. When you create an instance of the Image object in this fashion, it is not associated with any image. In order to associate it with an existing image you must assign a value to its src property, in the following method:

```
myImage.src = "myPicture.gif"
```

You can use either a full or relational URL. When you associate an image with an instance, in this fashion, the image is cached. Since it is already stored on the client side (where normally the cache is), the user does not have to wait for the image to be received from the server when you decide to display the image. When you adjust the src property of an element from the document.images array (or an image that is viewable on the page), the image immediately changes to the image at the new URL.

vspace

This property is a string specifying the margin in pixels between the top and bottom edges of an image and the surrounding text. The general syntax is as follows:

```
imageName.vspace
```

where *imageName* is either the name of an Image object's instance or an element in the document.images array. The vspace property reflects the VSPACE attribute of the <IMG> tag. For images created with the Image()constructor, the value of the vspace property is 0. The vspace property is a read-only one. The script in Example 25-3 shows how an alert box can display, upon clicking a button, the height, width, and space figures of an image.

width

width is a string specifying the width of an image either in pixels or as a percentage of the window width. The general syntax is as follows:

```
imageName.width
```

where *imageName* is either the name of an Image object's instance or an element in the document.images array. The width property reflects the WIDTH attribute of the <IMG> tag. For images created with the Image() constructor, the value of the width property is the actual, not the displayed, width of the image. The width property is a read-only one. The script in Example 25-3 shows how an alert box can display, upon clicking a button, the height, width, and space figures of an image.

Event Handlers

onAbort

An abort event occurs when the user aborts the loading of an image (for example, by clicking a link or the Stop button). The onAbort event handler executes a JavaScript code when an abort event occurs. In Example 25-5 (based on 25-4), an onAbort handler belonging to an Image object displays a message when the user aborts the image's loading:

```
<HTML>
<HEAD>
<TITLE>Aircrafts</TITLE>
<SCRIPT LANGUAGE="JavaScript">
<!--

function displayImage(lowRes, highRes) {
   document.images[0].lowsrc = lowRes
   document.images[0].src = highRes
}

// -->
</SCRIPT>
</HEAD>
<BODY>
<FORM NAME="imageForm">
<B>Choose an image:</B>
<BR><INPUT TYPE="radio" NAME="imageChoice" VALUE="image1" CHECKED
   onClick="displayImage('img1l.gif', 'img1h.gif')"> IMAGE 1
<BR><INPUT TYPE="radio" NAME="imageChoice" VALUE="image2"
   onClick="displayImage('img2l.gif', 'img2h.gif')"> IMAGE 2
<BR><INPUT TYPE="radio" NAME="imageChoice" VALUE="image3"
   onClick="displayImage('img3l.gif', 'img3h.gif')"> IMAGE 3
```

```
<BR>
<IMG NAME="onAbort" SRC="img1h.gif" LOWSRC="img1l.gif" ALIGN="left"
              VSPACE="10" onAbort="alert('You didn\'t get to see the
              image!')"><BR>
</FORM>
</BODY>
</HTML>
```

***Example 25-5**. The previous script with onAbort event handler.*

onError

An `error` event occurs when the loading of an image causes an error. The `onError` event handler executes a JavaScript code when an `error` event occurs.

The `onError` event handler can be assigned a `null` value to suppress all error dialogues. When you set *`imageName`*`.onerror` to `null`, your user won't see any JavaScript errors caused by the image.

An `error` event occurs only when a JavaScript syntax or runtime error occurs, and not when a Navigator error occurs. If you try to set *`imageName`*`.src = 'notThere.gif'`, for instance, and `notThere.gif` does not exist, the resulting error message is a Navigator error message, and an `onError` event handler would not intercept that message.

In the following `<IMG>` tag, the `onError` event handler calls the function `badImage` if errors occur when the image loads:

```
<SCRIPT LANGUAGE="JavaScript">
<!--

function badImage(theImage) {
     alert('Error: ' + theImage.name + ' did not load properly.')
}

// -->
</SCRIPT>
<IMG NAME="imageBad2" SRC="orca.gif" ALIGN="left" BORDER=2
onError="badImage(this)">
```

onLoad

The `onLoad` event handler is triggered when an image is displayed. Do not confuse displaying an image with loading one. You can load several images and then, by setting the instance's `src` property, you can display them one by one, in the same `Image` object instance. If you change a displayed image this way, the `onLoad` event handler executes every time an image is displayed, not only when the image is loaded into memory.

If you specify an onLoad event handler for an Image object that displays a looping gif animation (multi-image gif), each loop of the animation triggers the onLoad event, and the event handler executes once for each loop.

By repeatedly setting the src property of an image's JavaScript reflection, you can use the onLoad event handler to create a JavaScript animation.

Demonstration 1: Up-to-date Digital Clock

The following JavaScript script displays a digital clock on your page, updated every minute. The clock includes two digits for the hour, delimiting colon, two digits for the minute, and am/pm subscript:

```
<HTML>
<HEAD>
<TITLE>
JavaScript clock
</TITLE>
</HEAD>
<BODY>
<!-- JavaScript immediate script -->
<SCRIPT LANGUAGE="JavaScript">
<!--

// Copyright 1997 -- Tomer Shiran

// create array of all digit images
var digit = new Array()
digit[0] = new Image(16, 21)
digit[1] = new Image(16, 21)
digit[2] = new Image(16, 21)
digit[3] = new Image(16, 21)
digit[4] = new Image(16, 21)
digit[5] = new Image(16, 21)
digit[6] = new Image(16, 21)
digit[7] = new Image(16, 21)
digit[8] = new Image(16, 21)
digit[9] = new Image(16, 21)
digit[10] = new Image(16, 21) // am
digit[11] = new Image(16, 21) // pm
digit[12] = new Image(9, 21) // colon
digit[13] = new Image(9, 21) // blank

// assign sources to digit image objects (0 - 9)
```

```
for (var i = 0; i < 10; ++i) {
     digit[i].src = getPath(location.href) + "dg" + i + ".gif"
}

// assign sources to other image objects
digit[10].src = getPath(location.href) + "dgam.gif"
digit[11].src = getPath(location.href) + "dgpm.gif"
digit[12].src = getPath(location.href) + "dgc.gif"
digit[13].src = getPath(location.href) + "dgb.gif"

// set initial time values to impossible ones
var hour1 = getHour(0)
var hour2 = getHour(1)
var minute1 = getMinute(0)
var minute2 = getMinute(1)
var ampm = getAmpm()
var colon = false

// get array substring of first clock image in document.images array
var start = document.images.length // number of images in document

// print initial clock
var openImage = "<IMG SRC=\"" + getPath(location.href) + "dg"
var closeImage = ".gif\" HEIGHT=21 WIDTH=16>"
document.write(openImage + hour1 + closeImage)
document.write(openImage + hour2 + closeImage)
document.write(openImage + "c.gif\" HEIGHT=21 WIDTH=9>")
document.write(openImage + minute1 + closeImage)
document.write(openImage + minute2 + closeImage)
document.write(openImage + ((ampm == 10) ? "am" : "pm") + closeImage)

var timerID = null
var timerRunning = false

update()

function setClock() {
     if (getHour(0) != hour1) { // not getHours()!
          hour1 = getHour(0)
          document.images[start].src = digit[hour1].src
     }
     if (getHour(1) != hour2) { // not getHours()!
          hour2 = getHour(1)
          document.images[start + 1].src = digit[hour2].src
     }
     colon = !colon
     if (!colon)
          document.images[start + 2].src = digit[13].src
     else
          document.images[start + 2].src = digit[12].src
     if (getMinute(0) != minute1) { // not getMinutes()!
          minute1 = getMinute(0)
```

```
			document.images[start + 3].src = digit[minute1].src
		}
		if (getMinute(1) != minute2) { // not getMinutes()!
			minute2 = getMinute(1)
			document.images[start + 4].src = digit[minute2].src
		}
		if (getAmpm() != ampm) {
			ampm = getAmpm()
			document.images[start + 5].src = digit[ampm].src
		}
		timerID = setTimeout("setClock()",1000)
		timerRunning = true
	}

	function update() {
		stopClock()
		setClock()
	}

	function stopClock() {
		if (timerRunning)
			clearTimeout(timerID)
		timerRunning = false
	}

	function getHour(place) {
		var now = new Date()
		var hour = now.getHours()
		if (hour >= 12)
			hour -= 12
		hour = (hour == 0) ? 12 : hour
		if (hour < 10)
			hour = "0" + hour // do not parse number!
		hour += ""
		return parseInt(hour.charAt(place))
	}

	function getMinute(place) {
		var now = new Date()
		var minute = now.getMinutes()
		if (minute < 10)
			minute = "0" + minute // do not parse number!
		minute += ""
		return parseInt(minute.charAt(place))
	}

	function getAmpm() {
		var now = new Date()
		var hour = now.getHours()
		if (hour >= 12)
			return 11 // pm
		/* else */
```

```
        return 10 // am
}

function getPath(url) {
    lastSlash = url.lastIndexOf("/")
    return url.substring(0, lastSlash + 1)
}

// -->
</SCRIPT>
</BODY>
</HTML>
```

Example 25-6*. An updating clock.*

Global Statements

The script starts by creating the `digits` array, holding 14 instances of the `Image` object, for the digits 0 through 9, AM, PM, colon, and blank symbols. All images are 21 pixels high and 16 pixels wide, except for the colon and the blank images which are thinner (9 pixels):

```
// create array of all digit images
var digit = new Array()
digit[0] = new Image(16, 21)
digit[1] = new Image(16, 21)
digit[2] = new Image(16, 21)
digit[3] = new Image(16, 21)
digit[4] = new Image(16, 21)
digit[5] = new Image(16, 21)
digit[6] = new Image(16, 21)
digit[7] = new Image(16, 21)
digit[8] = new Image(16, 21)
digit[9] = new Image(16, 21)
digit[10] = new Image(16, 21) // am
digit[11] = new Image(16, 21) // pm
digit[12] = new Image(9, 21) // colon
digit[13] = new Image(9, 21) // blank
```

Since the artistic representation of each symbol is given in a gif format, we assign a gif filename to the `src` property of each element of the `digit` array. The gif files are located in the same directory as the URL, and the naming algorithm is based on concatenating the "`dg`" substring to the characters represented by the image (0-9, am, pm). The colon symbol is denoted by a "c" character, and the "blank" one by a "b."

```
// assign sources to digit image objects (0 - 9)
for (var i = 0; i < 10; ++i) {
    digit[i].src = getPath(location.href) + "dg" + i + ".gif"
```

```
}

// assign sources to other image objects
digit[10].src = getPath(location.href) + "dgam.gif"
digit[11].src = getPath(location.href) + "dgpm.gif"
digit[12].src = getPath(location.href) + "dgc.gif"
digit[13].src = getPath(location.href) + "dgb.gif"
```

Then, we find the current time and store it in six variables, four digits for the hour and minute, one for the ampm value, and one Boolean variable for the blinking colon. After initializing the time variables, the script turns off the colon, ready to be turned on next time:

```
// set initial time values to current time
var hour1 = getHour(0)
var hour2 = getHour(1)
var minute1 = getMinute(0)
var minute2 = getMinute(1)
var ampm = getAmpm()
var colon = false
```

We need to probe and remember the number of images already displayed in the document:

```
// get array substring of first clock image in document.images array
var start = document.images.length // number of images in document
```

When the page is loaded, the script displays the clock. Since JavaScript does not support image creation, all images are constructed via HTML:

```
// print initial clock
var openImage = "<IMG SRC=\"" + getPath(location.href) + "dg"
var closeImage = ".gif\" HEIGHT=21 WIDTH=16>"
document.write(openImage + hour1 + closeImage)
document.write(openImage + hour2 + closeImage)
document.write(openImage + "c.gif\" HEIGHT=21 WIDTH=9>")
document.write(openImage + minute1 + closeImage)
document.write(openImage + minute2 + closeImage)
document.write(openImage + ((ampm == 10) ? "am" : "pm") + closeImage)
```

The `timerID` variable, which holds the elapsed time before the next clock updating, is initialized to `null` before the clock starts running. For the same reason, the `timerRunning` variable is set to `false`. The function `update()` starts the infinite loop of running the clock:

```
var timerID = null
var timerRunning = false

update()
```

setClock()

```
function setClock() {
     if (getHour(0) != hour1) { // not getHours()!
          hour1 = getHour(0)
          document.images[start].src = digit[hour1].src
     }
     if (getHour(1) != hour2) { // not getHours()!
          hour2 = getHour(1)
          document.images[start + 1].src = digit[hour2].src
     }
     colon = !colon
     if (!colon)
          document.images[start + 2].src = digit[13].src
     else
          document.images[start + 2].src = digit[12].src
     if (getMinute(0) != minute1) { // not getMinutes()!
          minute1 = getMinute(0)
          document.images[start + 3].src = digit[minute1].src
     }
     if (getMinute(1) != minute2) { // not getMinutes()!
          minute2 = getMinute(1)
          document.images[start + 4].src = digit[minute2].src
     }
     if (getAmpm() != ampm) {
          ampm = getAmpm()
          document.images[start + 5].src = digit[ampm].src
     }
     timerID = setTimeout("setClock()",1000)
     timerRunning = true
}
```

This function retrieves the current value of each digit (and symbol) in the clock and updates only the necessary images, i.e., only those digits that have been changed since the previous iteration. The blinking colon effect is accomplished by simply reversing the value of `colon`. Notice that the index of the `images` array is an offset from the last image of the document, not counting the clock's images. The variable `timerID` is now modified to recursively execute the function `setClock()`, after 1000 milliseconds.

update()

```
function update() {
     stopClock()
     setClock()
}
```

The function `update()` stops the clock and then restarts it.

stopClock()

```
function stopClock() {
     if (timerRunning)
          clearTimeout(timerID)
     timerRunning = false
}
```

This function clears the time out and sets the `timerRunning` variable to `false`, indicating that the timer is not running because no time out is set.

getHour(place)

```
function getHour(place) {
     var now = new Date()
     var hour = now.getHours()
     if (hour >= 12)
          hour -= 12
     hour = (hour == 0) ? 12 : hour
     if (hour < 10)
          hour = "0" + hour // do not parse number!
     hour += ""
     return parseInt(hour.charAt(place))
}
```

The `getHour()` function has been mentioned a lot before. It finds the digit in `place` position of a two-digit hour representation. Notice the computation to convert a 24-hour military time notation to AM/PM 12-hour notation. Pay attention, also, to the concatenation of a null string to force the conversion to a string, needed for the `charAt()` method. The returned value is converted back to integer format.

getMinute(place)

```
function getMinute(place) {
     var now = new Date()
     var minute = now.getMinutes()
     if (minute < 10)
          minute = "0" + minute // do not parse number!
     minute += ""
     return parseInt(minute.charAt(place))
}
```

This function is similar to the `getHour()` function. See the listings for that function.

getAmpm()

```
function getAmpm() {
     var now = new Date()
     var hour = now.getHours()
     if (hour >= 12)
          return 11 // pm
     /* else */
          return 10 // am
}
```

The getAmpm() function returns 11 if the current time is PM, and 10 if it is AM. Notice that, since a return statement immediately terminates a function, the else keyword is not needed here and is commented out.

getPath(url)

```
function getPath(url) {
     lastSlash = url.lastIndexOf("/")
     return url.substring(0, lastSlash + 1)
}
```

The script's last function, getPath(), extracts the full URL of the document's directory (or folder). It simply finds the last slash in the URL and returns the substring, starting at the beginning of the URL and ending at its last slash.

Demonstration 2: LED Sign

You have probably seen LED signs in airports, bulletin boards, street signs, etc. Our LED sign displays a given number of messages, one after the other, and returns to the first one when the list is exhausted. Each character is built of on and off dots, where each dot (or light) is a small 5 x 5 gif image.

```
<HTML>
<HEAD>
<TITLE>LED sign</TITLE>
</HEAD>
<BODY>
<SCRIPT LANGUAGE="JavaScript">
<!--

// set messages (specify backslash in double form (i.e, \\)
var messages = new Array()
messages[0] = "welcome to our page"
messages[1] = "free scripts available"
```

```
messages[2] = "new:scripts by request"
messages[3] = "this site is updated..."
messages[4] = "almost every day"
messages[5] = "we are now working..."
messages[6] = "on a revolutionary..."
messages[7] = "javascript book!!!"
messages[8] = "contact us for more info"

// number of milliseconds to pause between two messages
var pause = 3000

// set normal spacing between two characters (no whitespace in between)
var space = 1

// set height and width of each character
var height = 5
var width = 3

// create object of all supported characters in font
var letters = new letterArray()

// initialize image variables
var on = new Image(5, 5)
var off = new Image(5, 5)

// set image URLs
on.src = "on.gif"
off.src = "off.gif"

// get number of images already laid out in page
var imageNum = document.images.length

// compute width of board
//var boardWidth = longest * (width + space) - space

// set maximum message length in images
var boardWidth = 0
for (var i = 0; i < messages.length; ++i) {
     var lengthWithNoSpaces = messages[i].split(" ").join("").length
     var numberOfSpaces = messages[i].length - lengthWithNoSpaces
     var currentBoardWidth = lengthWithNoSpaces * (width + space) -
                        space + numberOfSpaces * space * 2
     if (boardWidth < currentBoardWidth)
          boardWidth = currentBoardWidth
}

// sign is currently not running
var running = false
var timerID = null

function letterArray() {
     this.a = new Array(height)
```

```
this.a[0] = " * "
this.a[1] = "* *"
this.a[2] = "***"
this.a[3] = "* *"
this.a[4] = "* *"

this.b = new Array(height)
this.b[0] = "** "
this.b[1] = "* *"
this.b[2] = "** "
this.b[3] = "* *"
this.b[4] = "** "

this.c = new Array(height)
this.c[0] = "***"
this.c[1] = "*  "
this.c[2] = "*  "
this.c[3] = "*  "
this.c[4] = "***"

this.d = new Array(height)
this.d[0] = "** "
this.d[1] = "* *"
this.d[2] = "* *"
this.d[3] = "* *"
this.d[4] = "** "

this.e = new Array(height)
this.e[0] = "*** "
this.e[1] = "*  "
this.e[2] = "***"
this.e[3] = "*  "
this.e[4] = "***"

this.f = new Array(height)
this.f[0] = "***"
this.f[1] = "*  "
this.f[2] = "***"
this.f[3] = "*  "
this.f[4] = "*  "

this.g = new Array(height)
this.g[0] = "***"
this.g[1] = "*  "
this.g[2] = "***"
this.g[3] = "* *"
this.g[4] = "***"

this.h = new Array(height)
this.h[0] = "* *"
this.h[1] = "* *"
this.h[2] = "***"
```

```
this.h[3] = "* *"
this.h[4] = "* *"

this.i = new Array(height)
this.i[0] = "***"
this.i[1] = " * "
this.i[2] = " * "
this.i[3] = " * "
this.i[4] = "***"

this.j = new Array(height)
this.j[0] = "  *"
this.j[1] = "  *"
this.j[2] = "  *"
this.j[3] = "* *"
this.j[4] = "***"

this.k = new Array(height)
this.k[0] = "* *"
this.k[1] = "* *"
this.k[2] = "** "
this.k[3] = "* *"
this.k[4] = "* *"

this.l = new Array(height)
this.l[0] = "*  "
this.l[1] = "*  "
this.l[2] = "*  "
this.l[3] = "*  "
this.l[4] = "***"

this.m = new Array(height)
this.m[0] = "* *"
this.m[1] = "***"
this.m[2] = "***"
this.m[3] = "* *"
this.m[4] = "* *"

this.n = new Array(height)
this.n[0] = "* *"
this.n[1] = "***"
this.n[2] = "***"
this.n[3] = "***"
this.n[4] = "* *"

this.o = new Array(height)
this.o[0] = "***"
this.o[1] = "* *"
this.o[2] = "* *"
this.o[3] = "* *"
this.o[4] = "***"
```

```
this.p = new Array(height)
this.p[0] = "** "
this.p[1] = "* *"
this.p[2] = "** "
this.p[3] = "*  "
this.p[4] = "*  "

this.q = new Array(height)
this.q[0] = "***"
this.q[1] = "* *"
this.q[2] = "* *"
this.q[3] = "***"
this.q[4] = "***"

this.r = new Array(height)
this.r[0] = "** "
this.r[1] = "* *"
this.r[2] = "** "
this.r[3] = "* *"
this.r[4] = "* *"

this.s = new Array(height)
this.s[0] = "***"
this.s[1] = "*  "
this.s[2] = "***"
this.s[3] = "  *"
this.s[4] = "***"

this.t = new Array(height)
this.t[0] = "***"
this.t[1] = " * "
this.t[2] = " * "
this.t[3] = " * "
this.t[4] = " * "

this.u = new Array(height)
this.u[0] = "* *"
this.u[1] = "* *"
this.u[2] = "* *"
this.u[3] = "* *"
this.u[4] = "***"

this.v = new Array(height)
this.v[0] = "* *"
this.v[1] = "* *"
this.v[2] = "* *"
this.v[3] = "* *"
this.v[4] = " * "

this.w = new Array(height)
this.w[0] = "* *"
this.w[1] = "* *"
```

```
this.w[2] = "***"
this.w[3] = "***"
this.w[4] = "***"

this.x = new Array(height)
this.x[0] = "* *"
this.x[1] = "* *"
this.x[2] = " * "
this.x[3] = "* *"
this.x[4] = "* *"

this.y = new Array(height)
this.y[0] = "* *"
this.y[1] = "* *"
this.y[2] = "***"
this.y[3] = " * "
this.y[4] = " * "

this.z = new Array(height)
this.z[0] = "***"
this.z[1] = "  *"
this.z[2] = " * "
this.z[3] = "*  "
this.z[4] = "***"

this['!'] = new Array(height)
this['!'][0] = " * "
this['!'][1] = " * "
this['!'][2] = " * "
this['!'][3] = "   "
this['!'][4] = " * "

this[':'] = new Array(height)
this[':'][0] = "   "
this[':'][1] = " * "
this[':'][2] = "   "
this[':'][3] = " * "
this[':'][4] = "   "

this['.'] = new Array(height)
this['.'][0] = "   "
this['.'][1] = "   "
this['.'][2] = "   "
this['.'][3] = "   "
this['.'][4] = " * "

this['='] = new Array(height)
this['='][0] = "   "
this['='][1] = "***"
this['='][2] = "   "
this['='][3] = "***"
this['='][4] = "   "
```

```
this['='] = new Array(height)
this['='][0] = "   "
this['='][1] = "***"
this['='][2] = "   "
this['='][3] = "***"
this['='][4] = "   "

this['+'] = new Array(height)
this['+'][0] = "   "
this['+'][1] = " * "
this['+'][2] = "***"
this['+'][3] = " * "
this['+'][4] = "   "

this['-'] = new Array(height)
this['-'][0] = "   "
this['-'][1] = "   "
this['-'][2] = "***"
this['-'][3] = "   "
this['-'][4] = "   "

this['/'] = new Array(height)
this['/'][0] = "  *"
this['/'][1] = "  *"
this['/'][2] = " * "
this['/'][3] = "*  "
this['/'][4] = "*  "

this['\\'] = new Array(height)
this['\\'][0] = "*  "
this['\\'][1] = "*  "
this['\\'][2] = " * "
this['\\'][3] = "  *"
this['\\'][4] = "  *"

this['\\'] = new Array(height)
this['\\'][0] = "*  "
this['\\'][1] = "*  "
this['\\'][2] = " * "
this['\\'][3] = "  *"
this['\\'][4] = "  *"

this['"'] = new Array(height)
this['"'][0] = "* *"
this['"'][1] = "* *"
this['"'][2] = "* *"
this['"'][3] = "   "
this['"'][4] = "   "

this["'"] = new Array(height)
this["'"][0] = " * "
```

```
this["'"][1] = " * "
this["'"][2] = " * "
this["'"][3] = "   "
this["'"][4] = "   "

this['('] = new Array(height)
this['('][0] = "  *"
this['('][1] = " * "
this['('][2] = " * "
this['('][3] = " * "
this['('][4] = "  *"

this[')'] = new Array(height)
this[')'][0] = "*  "
this[')'][1] = " * "
this[')'][2] = " * "
this[')'][3] = " * "
this[')'][4] = "*  "

this['*'] = new Array(height)
this['*'][0] = "   "
this['*'][1] = "***"
this['*'][2] = "***"
this['*'][3] = "***"
this['*'][4] = "   "

this['?'] = new Array(height)
this['?'][0] = "** "
this['?'][1] = "  *"
this['?'][2] = " * "
this['?'][3] = "   "
this['?'][4] = " * "

this['0'] = new Array(height)
this['0'][0] = " * "
this['0'][1] = "* *"
this['0'][2] = "* *"
this['0'][3] = "* *"
this['0'][4] = " * "

this['1'] = new Array(height)
this['1'][0] = " * "
this['1'][1] = " * "
this['1'][2] = " * "
this['1'][3] = " * "
this['1'][4] = " * "

this['2'] = new Array(height)
this['2'][0] = "***"
this['2'][1] = "  *"
this['2'][2] = "***"
this['2'][3] = "*  "
```

```
        this['2'][4] = "***"

        this['3'] = new Array(height)
        this['3'][0] = "***"
        this['3'][1] = "  *"
        this['3'][2] = "***"
        this['3'][3] = "  *"
        this['3'][4] = "***"

        this['4'] = new Array(height)
        this['4'][0] = "* *"
        this['4'][1] = "* *"
        this['4'][2] = "***"
        this['4'][3] = "  *"
        this['4'][4] = "  *"

        this['5'] = new Array(height)
        this['5'][0] = "***"
        this['5'][1] = "*  "
        this['5'][2] = "***"
        this['5'][3] = "  *"
        this['5'][4] = "** "

        this['6'] = new Array(height)
        this['6'][0] = "** "
        this['6'][1] = "*  "
        this['6'][2] = "***"
        this['6'][3] = "* *"
        this['6'][4] = "***"

        this['7'] = new Array(height)
        this['7'][0] = "***"
        this['7'][1] = "  *"
        this['7'][2] = " * "
        this['7'][3] = "*  "
        this['7'][4] = "*  "

        this['8'] = new Array(height)
        this['8'][0] = "***"
        this['8'][1] = "* *"
        this['8'][2] = "***"
        this['8'][3] = "* *"
        this['8'][4] = "***"

        this['9'] = new Array(height)
        this['9'][0] = "***"
        this['9'][1] = "* *"
        this['9'][2] = "***"
        this['9'][3] = "  *"
        this['9'][4] = "***"
}
```

```
function drawBlank() {
     // assign greater than symbol to variable
     var gt = unescape("%3e")

     document.write('<TABLE BORDER=2 CELLPADDING=8' + gt + '<TR' + gt +
                    '<TD BGCOLOR ALIGN="center" VALIGN="center"' + gt)

     // print entire board of off images
     for (var y = 0; y < height; ++y) {
          for (var x = 0; x < boardWidth; ++x) {
               document.write('<IMG SRC="' + off.src + '" HEIGHT=5
                              WIDTH=5' + gt)
          }
          document.write('<BR' + gt)
     }
     document.write('</TD' + gt + '</TR' + gt + '</TABLE' + gt)
}

function setLight(state, x, y) {
     // set a specific light in sign to on (true) or off (false)
     if (state)
          document.images[computeIndex(x, y)].src = on.src
     else
          document.images[computeIndex(x, y)].src = off.src
}

function drawLetter(letter, startX) {
     // draws a letter at the given x coordinate
     for (var x = 0; x < width; ++x) {
          for (var y = 0; y < height; ++y) {
               setLight(letters[letter][y].charAt(x) == "*", startX +
                                   x, y)
          }
     }
}

function drawSpace(startX) {
     // create a small space between each two characters
     for (var x = 0; x < space; ++x) {
          for (var y = 0; y < height; ++y) {
               setLight(false, startX + x, y)
          }
     }
}

function computeIndex(x, y) {
     // compute the document index of an image in the sign, based on the
                              x-y coordinates
     return (y * boardWidth + x) + imageNum
}

function floodBoard(startX) {
```

Chapter 25

```
          // set all lights from startX to off
          for (var x = startX; x < boardWidth; ++x) {
               for (var y = 0; y < height; ++y) {
                    setLight(false, x, y)
               }
          }
     }

     function drawMessage(num) {
          // initialize variable to current message
          var text = messages[num]

          // initialize two counters (j - current character in message,
                                      i - current x coordinate)
          var i = 0
          var j = 0

          while (1) {
               if (text.charAt(j) != " ") {
                    // draw current letter
                    drawLetter(text.charAt(j), i)

                    // increment i by the constant width of an image
                    i += width
               } else {
                    // add an extra space (do not advance j yet)
                    drawSpace(i)
                    i += space
               }

               // if j is less than index of last character
               if (j < text.length - 1) {
                    drawSpace(i)
                    i += space
               } else // j is the index of the last character (last character
                                      already printed)
                    break

               // increment j by one because one letter was printed
               ++j
          }

          // flood the remaining piece of the sign (turn it off)
          floodBoard(i)

          // if message printed this time was not the last one in the array
          if (num < messages.length - 1)
               // val *must* be a global variable for use with the timeout
               val = ++num
          else
               val = 0 // start cycle over again
```

```
        // recursive call after waiting 3 seconds (some of the time already
                            passed during printing)
        timerID = setTimeout("drawMessage(val)", pause)
    }

    function startSign() {
        running = true

        // wait 3 seconds and then call function to print first message
        drawMessage(0)
    }

    function stopSign() {
        if(running)
            clearTimeout(timerID)
        running = false
    }

    // open form
    document.write('<FORM>')

    // create initial sign (all signs are off)
    drawBlank()

    document.write('<INPUT TYPE="button" VALUE="start" onClick="startSign()">')
    document.write('<INPUT TYPE="button" VALUE="stop" onClick="stopSign();
    floodBoard(0)">')
    document.write('</FORM>')

    // -->
    </SCRIPT>
    </BODY>
    </HTML>
```

Example 25-7*. A JavaScript-only LED sign.*

Global Statements

The script starts by filling the message array with nine messages:

```
// set messages (specify backslash in double form (i.e, \\)
var messages = new Array()
messages[0] = "welcome to our page"
messages[1] = "free scripts available"
messages[2] = "new:scripts by request"
messages[3] = "this site is updated..."
messages[4] = "almost every day"
messages[5] = "we are now working..."
messages[6] = "on a revolutionary..."
messages[7] = "javascript book!!!"
messages[8] = "contact us for more info"
```

Note that all messages must be written in lowercase.

The definition of the following variables are documented inline:

```
// number of milliseconds to pause between two messages
var pause = 3000

// set normal spacing between two characters (no whitespace in between)
var space = 1

// set height and width of each character
var height = 5
var width = 3

// create object of all supported characters in font
var letters = new letterArray()

// initialize image variables
var on = new Image(5, 5)
var off = new Image(5, 5)
```

The on and off `Images` represent the on and off lights. The artistic presentations of these dots are stored in `on.gif` and `off.gif`:

```
on.src = "on.gif"
off.src = "off.gif
```

As in Demonstration 1, we load all images to the browser before we start to display the LED sign:

```
// get number of images already laid out in page
var imageNum = document.images.length
```

The next section computes the length of the longest message by multiplying the number of nonblank characters by the combined width of a normal character and an intercharacter space, and then adding the width of blanks. The number of nonblank characters is computed by first splitting the message on blanks, then joining the pieces, and finally extracting the concatenated length:

```
// set maximum message length in images
var boardWidth = 0
for (var i = 0; i < messages.length; ++i) {
     var lengthWithNoSpaces = messages[i].split(" ").join("").length
     var numberOfSpaces = messages[i].length - lengthWithNoSpaces
     var currentBoardWidth = lengthWithNoSpaces * (width + space) -
                         space + numberOfSpaces * space * 2
     if (boardWidth < currentBoardWidth)
          boardWidth = currentBoardWidth
}
```

After setting the `running` variable to `false` and `timerID` to `null` (see Demonstration 1), we define the dots of each character of the alphabet by the function `letterArray()`.

letterArray()

`letterArray()`is a constructor function. The general syntax to create an instance of this object is as follows:

```
var instanceName = new letterArray()
```

This object has many properties but no methods. Each property represents a single character supported by the script. For example, the "A" character is defined as follows:

```
      this.a = new Array(height)
      this.a[0] = " * "
      this.a[1] = "* *"
      this.a[2] = "***"
      this.a[3] = "* *"
      this.a[4] = "* *"
```

Notice that each property is defined as an array of five three-character strings. You will see how to use an instance of this object later in the chapter.

drawBlank()

```
function drawBlank() {
      // assign greater than symbol to variable
      var gt = unescape("%3e")

      document.write('<TABLE BORDER=2 CELLPADDING=8' + gt + '<TR' + gt +
                    '<TD BGCOLOR ALIGN="center" VALIGN="center"' + gt)

      // print entire board of off images
      for (var y = 0; y < height; ++y) {
            for (var x = 0; x < boardWidth; ++x) {
                  document.write('<IMG SRC="' + off.src + '" HEIGHT=5
                              WIDTH=5' + gt)
            }
            document.write('<BR' + gt)
      }
      document.write('</TD' + gt + '</TR' + gt + '</TABLE' + gt)
}
```

The next function, `drawBlank()`, draws the border around the LED sign and then covers the entire board with off dots (gif images). Notice that the board's width and height are stored in global variables and thus are not passed as arguments to the `drawBlank()` function. Also, notice how `unescape()` is used for avoiding the ">" literal. (See the section "Problems with Code Hiding" in Chapter 3, Writing Your First Script.)

setLight(state, x, y)

```
function setLight(state, x, y) {
     // set a specific light in sign to on (true) or off (false)
     if (state)
          document.images[computeIndex(x, y)].src = on.src
     else
          document.images[computeIndex(x, y)].src = off.src
}
```

The `setLight()` function accepts three arguments. The first one is either a Boolean value or a binary digit (0 or 1). The second parameter accepts the *x* coordinate of the light, and the third specifies its *y* coordinate. For example, the following statement replaces the second image from the left and third from the top of the LED sign, with an on image, regardless of which image is currently displayed there:

```
setLight(true, 1, 2)
```

It is correct to define this function as one that turns on or off a specific light in the LED sign.

drawLetter(letter, startX)

```
function drawLetter(letter, startX) {
     // draws a letter at the given x coordinate
     for (var x = 0; x < width; ++x) {
          for (var y = 0; y < height; ++y) {
               setLight(letters[letter][y].charAt(x) == "*", startX +
                                                            x, y)
          }
     }
}
```

This function accepts two arguments:

- the letter that it is supposed to draw
- the X coordinate of the letter in the entire LED sign

This function reads the letter's coordinates by scanning the appropriate properties of the `letters` object. Figure 25-1 illustrates the direction in which the scanning is performed.

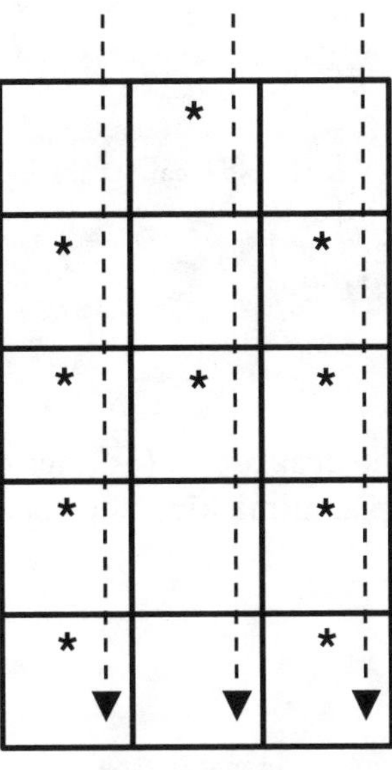

Figure 25-1*. The letter "A," like all other characters, is scanned from top to bottom and from left to right (column by column).*

The LED sign is updated by adding characters consecutively, creating the effect of a top-to-bottom, left-to-right motion. You can notice that motion even in a static picture, as in Figure 25-2.

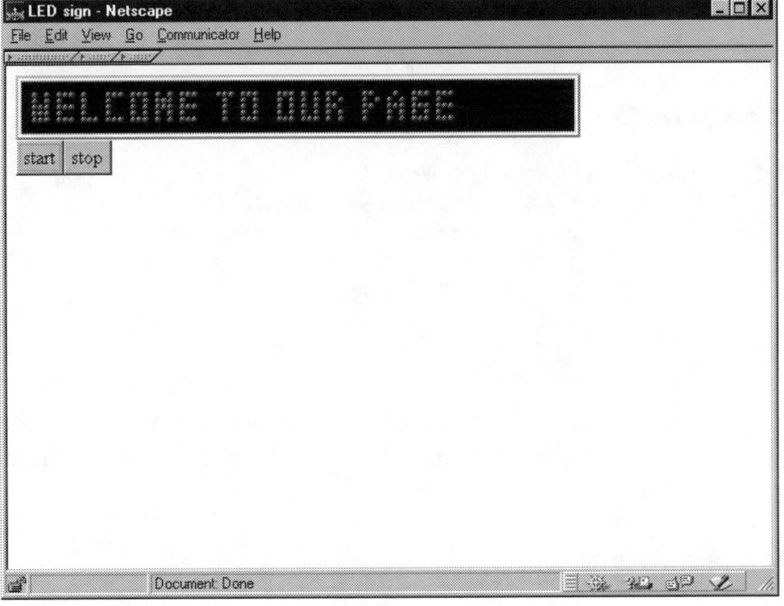

Figure 25-2*. An LED sign.*

drawSpace(startX)

```
function drawSpace(startX) {
     // create a small space between each two characters
     for (var x = 0; x < space; ++x) {
          for (var y = 0; y < height; ++y) {
               setLight(false, startX + x, y)
          }
     }
}
```

This function is very similar to the `drawLetter()` function. It simply creates `space` columns of off images, mimicking the space characters of the message.

computeIndex()

```
function computeIndex(x, y) {
     // compute the document index of an image in the sign, based on
                              the x-y coordinates
     return (y * boardWidth + x) + imageNum
}
```

The `computeIndex()` function accepts *x* and *y* coordinates of a dot and returns the corresponding index of the image in the `document.images` 1D array.

floodBoard(startX)

```
function floodBoard(startX) {
     // set all lights from startX to off
     for (var x = startX; x < boardWidth; ++x) {
          for (var y = 0; y < height; ++y) {
               setLight(false, x, y)
          }
     }
}
```

The function `floodBoard()` sets all dots (images) to the right of a given coordinate, one column at a time, from top to bottom and from left to right.

drawMessage(num)

```
function drawMessage(num) {
     // initialize variable to current message
     var text = messages[num]
```

```
    // initialize two counters (j - current character in message,
                           i - current x coordinate)
    var i = 0
    var j = 0

    while (1) {
          if (text.charAt(j) != " ") {
                // draw current letter
                drawLetter(text.charAt(j), i)

                // increment i by the constant width of an image
                i += width
          } else {
                // add an extra space (do not advance j yet)
                drawSpace(i)
                i += space
          }

          // if j is less than index of last character
          if (j < text.length - 1) {
                drawSpace(i)
                i += space
          } else // j is the index of the last character (last character
                                 already printed)
                break

          // increment j by one because one letter was printed
          ++j
    }

    // flood the remaining piece of the sign (turn it off)
    floodBoard(i)

    // if message printed this time was not the last one in the array
    if (num < messages.length - 1)
          // val *must* be a global variable for use with the timeout
          val = ++num
    else
          val = 0 // start cycle over again

    // recursive call after waiting 3 seconds (some of the time already
                           passed during printing)
    timerID = setTimeout("drawMessage(val)", pause)
}
```

The next function, `drawMessage()`, is probably the most important but is still straightforward. After initializing some variables, the `while` statement loops over the message characters and displays them by the `drawLetter()` or the `drawSpace()` functions. After the message is exhausted, the rest of the board is flooded with off dots. The function ends, after determining the index of the next message to be displayed

Chapter 25

(either next or first one), by recursively calling itself after a pause of pause milliseconds. See the online documentation for more details.

startSign()

```
function startSign() {
     running = true

     // wait 3 seconds and then call function to print first message
     drawMessage(0)
}
```

This function simply sets the value of the global variable running to true, indicating that the ticker has started, and then invokes the draw-Message() function to actually start displaying the first message (0).

stopSign()

```
function stopSign() {
     if(running)
          clearTimeout(timerID)
     running = false
}
```

This function stops the LED ticker by clearing the last time out via the clearTimeout() method. Reflecting the status of the banner, the value of running is set to false. Note that the stopSign() function does not clear the current LED sign display.

More Global Statements

```
// open form
document.write('<FORM>')

// create initial sign (all signs are off)
drawBlank()

document.write('<INPUT TYPE="button" VALUE="start" onClick="startSign()">')
document.write('<INPUT TYPE="button" VALUE="stop" onClick="stopSign();
                    floodBoard(0)">')
document.write('</FORM>')
```

The second segment of global statements at the end of the script creates the form where the Start and Stop buttons reside (they are form elements). We then define the buttons and their onClick event handler script. Notice that the Stop button event handler includes two function calls, one to stop the LED sign and the other to clear (flood) it. It is important to open the form before the drawBlank() function creates the LED sign, because the <FORM> tag starts a new line with some vertical space from the HTML elements above it. In order to assure that the buttons touch the border of the LED sign, we include the LED sign in the form itself.

Many people ask us how to get rid of the buttons and make the LED sign start on its own. You simply need to delete the lines that open and close the form, as well as the lines that define the buttons:

```
1. document.write('<FORM>')
2. document.write('<INPUT TYPE="button" VALUE="start"
   onClick="startSign()">')
3. document.write('<INPUT TYPE="button" VALUE="stop"
   onClick="stopSign(); floodBoard(0)">')
4. document.write('</FORM>')
```

You should then use an onLoad event handler to start the LED sign when the document finishes loading:

```
<BODY onLoad="startSign()">
```

Demonstration 3: Netris Deluxe

"Netris Deluxe" is the name of our JavaScript-only Tetris game. The Netris Deluxe script is approximately 1,000 lines of code, including comments, and we suggest you read its entire description. Although we have more efficient versions, we decided to include the original version, because it demonstrates a larger variety of JavaScript features and concepts. First, take a look at the script and find functions you are familiar with:

```
<HTML>
<HEAD>
<TITLE>Tetris</TITLE>
<SCRIPT LANGUAGE="JavaScript">
<!--

// array to hold number of shapes used from each type
var statistics = new Array(7)
for (var shapeNum = 0; shapeNum < 7; ++shapeNum) {
     statistics[shapeNum] = 0
}

// set pause to false
var paused = false

// game is currently running
var timerRunning = false
```

```
// no shape currently falling
var shape = -1

// timer is not running
var timerID = null

// initialize image variables for seven shapes
var on = new Array()
on[0] = new Image(12, 12)
on[1] = new Image(12, 12)
on[2] = new Image(12, 12)
on[3] = new Image(12, 12)
on[4] = new Image(12, 12)
on[5] = new Image(12, 12)
on[6] = new Image(12, 12)

// create a transparent block
var off = new Image(12, 12)

// set image URLs
on[0].src = "10.gif"
on[1].src = "11.gif"
on[2].src = "12.gif"
on[3].src = "13.gif"
on[4].src = "14.gif"
on[5].src = "15.gif"
on[6].src = "16.gif"
off.src = "0.gif"

// get number of images already laid out in the page
var firstImage = document.images.length

// create initial screen
drawScreen()

// array of screen (10 x 19)
var ar = new Array()
for (var i = 0; i < 10; ++i) {
     ar[i] = new Array(19)
     for (var j = 0; j < 19; ++j) {
          ar[i][j] = 0
     }
}

// draw initial empty screen
function drawScreen() {
     with (document) {
          // center entire game
          write('<CENTER>')

          // start main table
```

```
write('<TABLE BORDER=1 CELLPADDING=0 CELLSPACING=0><TR><TD>')

// create board (10 x 19)
for (var i = 0; i < 19; ++i) {
     for (var j = 0; j < 10; ++j) {
          write('<IMG SRC=' + off.src + ' HEIGHT=' + off.height +
                              ' WIDTH=' + off.width + '>')
     }
     write('<BR>')
}

// close table cell
write('</TD><TD VALIGN="top" ALIGN="center">')

// make small header ("Netris Deluxe")
write('<B><FONT SIZE=+2>N</FONT>ETRIS <FONT SIZE=+2>D</FONT>
                    ELUXE</B><BR>')

// create form for lines and level displays
write('<FORM NAME="lineslevel"><TABLE BORDER=0 CELLPADDING=5
                    CELLSPACING=0>')

// make "LINES" table cell and header
write('<TR><TD WIDTH=100 ALIGN="center"><FONT SIZE=2>LINES</FONT>
          <BR><INPUT TYPE="text" NAME="lines" VALUE="" SIZE=5></TD>')

// make "LEVEL" table cell and header
write('<TD WIDTH=100 ALIGN="center"><FONT SIZE=2>LEVEL</FONT><BR>
     <INPUT TYPE="text" NAME="level" VALUE="" SIZE=5></TD></TR>')

// create start button link
write('<TR><TD WIDTH=100 ALIGN="center"><A HREF="javascript:start()"
          onMouseOver="window.status=\'Start game\'; return true">')

// create start button image
write('<IMG SRC="start.gif" WIDTH=72 HEIGHT=24 BORDER=0></A></TD>')

// create pause button link
write('<TD WIDTH=100 ALIGN="center"><A HREF="javascript:pause()"
          onMouseOver="window.status=\'Pause / unpause game\';
          return true">')

// create pause button image
write('<IMG SRC="pause.gif" WIDTH=72 HEIGHT=24 BORDER=0></A>
               </TD></TR>')

// close start + pause table and form
write('</TABLE></FORM>')

// create table for shape statistics (two rows, seven columns)
write('<FORM NAME="stats"><TABLE BORDER=0 CELLPADDING=5
               CELLSPACING=0><TR>')
```

25 Chapter

```
// put one block of each type in each cell of upper row
for (var k = 0; k < 7; ++k) {
     write('<TD ALIGN="center"><IMG SRC="' + on[k].src + '" HEIGHT='
               + on[k].height + ' WIDTH=' + on[k].width + '></TD>')
}

// start new table row
write('</TR><TR>')

// create 7 text fields named "0", "1", "2", ..., "6"
for (var l = 0; l < 7; ++l) {
     write('<TD ALIGN="center"><INPUT TYPE="text" SIZE=2 VALUE="0"
                    NAME="' + l + '"></TD>')
}

// close statistics table and form
write('</TR></TABLE></FORM>')

// close table cell for header, start + pause buttons, and statistics,
                    and start new row in main table
write('</TD></TR><TR><TD>')

// center control panel (left, right, down, rotate)
write('<CENTER>')

// organize control panel in a table
write('<TABLE BORDER=0>')

// create left table cell and button
write('<TR><TD><A HREF="javascript:moveX(-1)" onMouseOver="window
          .status=\'Move left\'; return true" onMouseOut="window.
          status=\'\'; return true"><IMG SRC="left.gif" WIDTH=24
          HEIGHT=24 BORDER=0></A></TD>')

// create rotate table cell and button
write('<TD><A HREF="javascript:rotate()" onMouseOver="window
          .status=\'Rotate\'; return true" onMouseOut="window.
          status=\'\'; return true"><IMG SRC="rotate.gif" WIDTH=24
          HEIGHT=24 BORDER=0></A></TD>')

// create right table cell and button
write('<TD><A HREF="javascript:moveX(1)" onMouseOver="window
          .status=\'Move right\'; return true" onMouseOut="window.
          status=\'\'; return true"><IMG SRC="right.gif" WIDTH=24
          HEIGHT=24 BORDER=0></A></TD></TR>')

// create down table cell and button, preceded and proceeded by a
               black cell (placeholder)
write('<TR><TD></TD><TD><A HREF="javascript:moveY()" onMouseOver=
          "window.status=\'Move down\'; return true" onMouseOut=
```

```
                    "window.status=\'\'; return true"><IMG SRC="down.gif"
                    WIDTH=24 HEIGHT=24 BORDER=0></A></TD><TD></TD></TR>')

                // close table for control panel
                write('</TABLE>')

                // close center of control panel
                write('</CENTER>')

                // close control panel table cell (main table) and create another
                          main table cell with credits
                write('</TD><TD ALIGN="center">JavaScript code: Tomer Shiran<BR>
                    <FONT SIZE=2>Graphics: Dr. Clue</FONT><BR><FONT SIZE=2>
                    Music: Brian Kobashikawa</FONT></TD></TR></TABLE>')

                // close center of main table
                write('</CENTER>')
          }
     }

     // return index of image according to given x and y coordinates
     function computeIndex(x, y) {
               return (y * 10 + x) + firstImage
     }

     // returns state of square (true / false)
     function state(x, y) {
          // assign URL of image at given coordinates to local variable
          var source = document.images[computeIndex(x, y)].src

          // expression evaluates to 0 or 1
          return (source.charAt(source.lastIndexOf('/') + 1) == '0') ?
                              false : true
     }

     // set square to 1 / 0
     function setSquare(x, y, state) {
          if (state == 0)
               document.images[computeIndex(x, y)].src = off.src
          else
               document.images[computeIndex(x, y)].src = on[shape].src

          // if state is 1 square is active, so 1 is assigned to ar[x][y]
          // otherwise square is not active so 0 is assigned to ar[x][y]
          ar[x][y] = state
     }

     // clear array so no active squares exist
     function clearActive() {
          // scan entire array and assign 0 to all elements (no active squares)
          for (var i = 0; i < 10; ++i) {
               for (var j = 0; j < 19; ++j) {
```

25 Chapter

```
                ar[i][j] = 0
            }
        }

        // no shape is currently in screen
        shape = -1
    }

    // check if specified move (left or right) is valid
    function checkMoveX(step) {
        // scan screen (direction does not matter)
        for (var x = 0; x < 10; ++x) {
            for (var y = 0; y < 19; ++y) {
                // if current square is active
                if (ar[x][y] == 1) {
                    // check all conditions:
                    // not out of range and not colliding with existing not
                                    active block
                    if (x + step < 0 || x + step > 9 || (state(x + step, y) &&
                                    ar[x + step][y] == 0))
                        // return false if move (new situation) is not legal
                        return false
                }
            }
        }

        // return true if no invalid state has been encountered
        return true
    }

    // check if specified move (down) is valid
    function checkMoveY() {
        // only possible step is one to the bottom
        var step = 1

        // scan screen (direction does not matter)
        for (var x = 0; x < 10; ++x) {
            for (var y = 0; y < 19; ++y) {
                // if current square is active
                if (ar[x][y] == 1) {
                    // check all conditions:
                    // not out of range and not colliding with existing not
                                    active block
                    if (y + step > 18 || (state(x, y + step) && ar[x][y + step]
                                    == 0))
                        // return false if move (new situation) is not legal
                        return false
                }
            }
        }
```

```
        // return true if no invalid state has been encountered
        return true
    }

    // move all active squares step squares on the x axis
    function moveX(step) {
        // if specified move is not legal
        if (!checkMoveX(step))
            // terminate function (active blocks are not moved)
            return

        // if left movement then scan screen from left to right
        if (step < 0) {
            for (var x = 0; x < 10; ++x) {
                for (var y = 0; y < 19; ++y) {
                    // if current square is active
                    if (ar[x][y] == 1)
                        // call function to handle movement
                        smartX(x, y, step)
                }
            }
        } else

        // if right movement then scan screen from right to left
        if (step > 0) {
            for (var x = 9; x >= 0; --x) {
                for (var y = 0; y < 19; ++y) {
                    // if current square is active
                    if (ar[x][y] == 1)
                        // call function to handle movement
                        smartX(x, y, step)
                }
            }
        }
    }

    // responsible for the blocks' horizontal movement
    function smartX(x, y, step) {
        // if moving one step to the left
        if (step < 0)
            // if the destination square needs to be turned on explicitly
            if (ar[x + step][y] == 0)
                // if there is a block to the right of the current block
                if (x != 9 && ar[x - step][y] == 1)
                    // set square to the left on without clearing current
                                            block
                    setSquare(x + step, y, 1)
                else
                    // clear current block and turn square to the left on
                    warp(x, y, x + step, y)
            else
```

```
                // if there is no block to the right of the current block
                if (x == 9 || ar[x - step][y] == 0)
                      // clear current block
                      setSquare(x, y, 0)

    // if moving one step to the right
    if (step > 0)
          // if the destination square needs to be turned on explicitly
          if (ar[x + step][y] == 0)
                // if there is a block to the left of the current block
                if (x != 0 && ar[x - step][y] == 1)
                      // set square to the right on without clearing current
                                                 block
                      setSquare(x + step, y, 1)
                else
                      // clear current block and turn square to the right on
                      warp(x, y, x + step, y)
          else
                // if there is no block to the left of the current block
                if (x == 0 || ar[x - step][y] == 0)
                      // clear current block
                      setSquare(x, y, 0)
}

// move all active squares step squares on the x axis
function moveY() {
    // if specified move is not legal (shape is laid down on block or bottom
                                     panel)
    if (!checkMoveY()) {
          // active squares are not active anymore (should not be moved later)
          clearActive()

          // terminate function (active blocks are not moved)
          return
    }

    // scan screen from bottom to top
    for (var y = 18; y >= 0; --y) {
          for (var x = 0; x < 10; ++x) {
                // if current square is active
                if (ar[x][y] == 1)
                      // call function to handle movement
                      smartY(x, y)
          }
    }
}

// responsible for the blocks' vertical (downwards) movement
function smartY(x, y) {
    // if the destination square needs to be turned on explicitly
    if (ar[x][y + 1] == 0)
```

```
            // if there is a block above current block
            if (y != 0 && ar[x][y - 1] == 1)
                // set square below on without clearing current block
                setSquare(x, y + 1, 1)
            else
                // clear current block and turn square below on
                warp(x, y, x, y + 1)
        else
            // if there is no block above the current block
            if (y == 0 || ar[x][y - 1] == 0)
                // clear current block
                setSquare(x, y, 0)
}

// construct object containing shape
function shapeMap() {
    // set minimum and maximum coordinates to opposite (minimum and maximum
                            found thus far)
    var minX = 9
    var minY = 18
    var maxX = 0
    var maxY = 0

    // scan screen to find actual minimum and maximum coordinates of active
                            squares
    for (var y = 0; y < 19; ++y) {
        for (var x = 0; x < 10; ++x) {
            // if current coordinates reflect active square
            if (ar[x][y] == 1) {
                if (x < minX)
                    minX = x
                if (x > maxX)
                    maxX = x
                if (y < minY)
                    minY = y
                if (y > maxY)
                    maxY = y
            }
        }
    }

    // create a length property representing the x coordinate span
    this.length = maxX - minX + 1

    // create properties to hold minimum coordinates of both axes
    this.offsetX = minX
    this.offsetY = minY

    // construct minimum array containing all active squares respectively
    for (x = 0; x <= maxX - minX; ++x) {
        this[x] = new Array()
        for (y = 0; y <= maxY - minY; ++y) {
```

```
                this[x][y] = ar[x + minX][y + minY]
            }
        }
    }

    // random function to return an integer between 0 and 6
    function getRandom() {
        // use random number method to find integer between 0 and 8
        var randomNum = Math.round(Math.random() * 8)

        // call function again if random number is 0 or 8.
        if (randomNum == 0 || randomNum == 8)
            return getRandom()

        // 1 to 7 => 0 to 6
        randomNum--

        // update selected shape's statistics
        statistics[randomNum]++

        // update statistics display form (update *all* fields so user cannot
                                   enter any value in fields)
        for (var shape = 0; shape < 7; ++shape) {
            document.stats[shape].value = statistics[shape]
        }

        // return the random number
        return randomNum
    }

    // inserts a shape when there is no active shape
    function insertShape() {
        // initialize *global* variable
        shape = getRandom()

        // The following segment checks if the selected shape has room to enter.
        // If there is no room the game is over (function return false).
        // If there is room, the function inserts the shape by setting its initial
                                   coordinates.

        if (shape == 0) {
            if (state(3, 2) || state(3, 2) || state(3, 2) || state(3, 2))
                return false
            setSquare(3, 2, 1)
            setSquare(4, 2, 1)
            setSquare(5, 2, 1)
            setSquare(6, 2, 1)
        } else

        if (shape == 1) {
            if (state(4, 2) || state(5, 2) || state(4, 3) || state(5, 3))
                return false
```

```
        setSquare(4, 2, 1)
        setSquare(5, 2, 1)
        setSquare(4, 3, 1)
        setSquare(5, 3, 1)
    } else

    if (shape == 2) {
        if (state(3, 2) || state(4, 2) || state(5, 2) || state(3, 3))
            return false
        setSquare(3, 2, 1)
        setSquare(4, 2, 1)
        setSquare(5, 2, 1)
        setSquare(3, 3, 1)
    } else

    if (shape == 3) {
        if (state(3, 2) || state(4, 2) || state(4, 3) || state(5, 3))
            return false
        setSquare(3, 2, 1)
        setSquare(4, 2, 1)
        setSquare(4, 3, 1)
        setSquare(5, 3, 1)
    } else

    if (shape == 4) {
        if (state(4, 2) || state(5, 2) || state(3, 3) || state(4, 3))
            return false
        setSquare(4, 2, 1)
        setSquare(5, 2, 1)
        setSquare(3, 3, 1)
        setSquare(4, 3, 1)
    } else

    if (shape == 5) {
        if (state(3, 2) || state(4, 2) || state(5, 2) || state(4, 3))
            return false
        setSquare(3, 2, 1)
        setSquare(4, 2, 1)
        setSquare(5, 2, 1)
        setSquare(4, 3, 1)
    } else

    if (shape == 6) {
        if (state(3, 2) || state(4, 2) || state(5, 2) || state(5, 3))
            return false
        setSquare(3, 2, 1)
        setSquare(4, 2, 1)
        setSquare(5, 2, 1)
        setSquare(5, 3, 1)
    }

    // return true because shape was able to enter screen
```

```
        return true
    }

    // warp several squares if possible
    // initial x1, initial y1, destination x1, destination y1, initial x2, initial
                            y2, destination x2, destination y2, etc.
    function complexWarp() {
        // loop through arguments checking that each warp is valid
        for (var i = 0; i < arguments.length; i += 4) {
            // if warp is not valid
            if (!checkWarp(arguments[i], arguments[i + 1], arguments[i + 2],
                            arguments[i + 3]))
                // terminate the function -- no squares warped
                return
        }

        // loop through arguments again -- warp squares
        for (var i = 0; i < arguments.length; i += 4) {
            // call function to warp the current square corresponding to argument
                            coordinates
            warp(arguments[i], arguments[i + 1], arguments[i + 2], arguments[i
                            + 3])
        }
    }

    // check if warp is valid (used by complexWarp function)
    function checkWarp(startX, startY, endX, endY) {
        // if a destination coordinate is invalid or destination square is off
        // state(endX, endY) must be last due to short-circuit evaluation
        if (endX < 0 || endX > 9 || endY < 0 || endY > 18 || state(endX, endY))
            // return false because warp is invalid
            return false

        // return true because warp has not been proved to be invalid
                            (it is valid)
        return true
    }

    // rotate the current active shape
    function rotate() {
        // create instance of shapeMap object (similar to minimum 2D array
                            reflecting active shape)
        var curMap = new shapeMap()

        // note: all arguments handed to complexWarp are explained in that
                            function

        // if shape is 4 x 1 line
        if (shape == 0)
            // if line is in horizontal state
            if (curMap.length == 4)
```

```
                complexWarp(curMap.offsetX, curMap.offsetY, curMap.offsetX + 1,
curMap.offsetY + 1, curMap.offsetX + 2, curMap.offsetY, curMap.offsetX + 1,
curMap.offsetY - 1, curMap.offsetX + 3, curMap.offsetY, curMap.offsetX + 1,
curMap.offsetY - 2)
            // else line is in vertical state
            else
                complexWarp(curMap.offsetX, curMap.offsetY + 3, curMap.offsetX -
1, curMap.offsetY + 2, curMap.offsetX, curMap.offsetY + 1, curMap.offsetX + 1,
curMap.offsetY + 2, curMap.offsetX, curMap.offsetY, curMap.offsetX + 2,
curMap.offsetY + 2)

        // if shape is square
        if (shape == 1)
            // do not rotate shape because square does not change appearance
                              after rotation
            return

        // if shape is L
        if (shape == 2)
            // if shape is L tilted 90 degrees to the right
            if (state(curMap.offsetX, curMap.offsetY) && curMap.length == 3)
                complexWarp(curMap.offsetX, curMap.offsetY + 1, curMap.offsetX +
1, curMap.offsetY + 1, curMap.offsetX + 2, curMap.offsetY, curMap.offsetX + 1,
curMap.offsetY - 1, curMap.offsetX, curMap.offsetY, curMap.offsetX,
curMap.offsetY - 1)
            else
                // if shape is L titled 180 degrees
                if (state(curMap.offsetX + 1, curMap.offsetY) && curMap.length
                                      == 2)
                    complexWarp(curMap.offsetX + 1, curMap.offsetY + 2,
curMap.offsetX, curMap.offsetY + 1, curMap.offsetX + 1, curMap.offsetY,
curMap.offsetX + 2, curMap.offsetY, curMap.offsetX, curMap.offsetY,
curMap.offsetX + 2, curMap.offsetY + 1)
                else
                    // if L is tilted 90 degrees to the left
                    if (curMap.length == 3)
                        complexWarp(curMap.offsetX, curMap.offsetY + 1,
curMap.offsetX + 1, curMap.offsetY, curMap.offsetX + 2, curMap.offsetY,
curMap.offsetX + 2, curMap.offsetY + 2, curMap.offsetX + 2, curMap.offsetY + 1,
curMap.offsetX + 1, curMap.offsetY + 2)
                    // else L is not tilted
                    else
                        complexWarp(curMap.offsetX, curMap.offsetY,
curMap.offsetX + 1, curMap.offsetY + 1, curMap.offsetX, curMap.offsetY + 2,
curMap.offsetX - 1, curMap.offsetY + 2, curMap.offsetX + 1, curMap.offsetY + 2,
curMap.offsetX - 1, curMap.offsetY + 1)

        if (shape == 3)
            if (curMap.length == 3)
                complexWarp(curMap.offsetX + 1, curMap.offsetY + 1,
curMap.offsetX, curMap.offsetY + 1, curMap.offsetX + 2, curMap.offsetY + 1,
curMap.offsetX + 1, curMap.offsetY - 1)
```

```
            else
                complexWarp(curMap.offsetX, curMap.offsetY + 2, curMap.offsetX +
        1, curMap.offsetY + 2, curMap.offsetX + 1, curMap.offsetY, curMap.offsetX + 2,
        curMap.offsetY + 2)

        if (shape == 4)
            if (curMap.length == 3)
                complexWarp(curMap.offsetX, curMap.offsetY + 1, curMap.offsetX,
        curMap.offsetY, curMap.offsetX + 2, curMap.offsetY, curMap.offsetX,
        curMap.offsetY – 1)
            else
                complexWarp(curMap.offsetX, curMap.offsetY, curMap.offsetX + 2,
        curMap.offsetY + 1, curMap.offsetX, curMap.offsetY + 1, curMap.offsetX,
        curMap.offsetY + 2)

        if (shape == 5)
            if (curMap.length == 3 && state(curMap.offsetX, curMap.offsetY))
                complexWarp(curMap.offsetX + 2, curMap.offsetY, curMap.offsetX
                            + 1, curMap.offsetY – 1)
            else
                if (curMap.length == 2 && state(curMap.offsetX + 1,
                            curMap.offsetY))
                    complexWarp(curMap.offsetX + 1, curMap.offsetY + 2,
                                curMap.offsetX + 2, curMap.offsetY + 1)
                else
                    if (curMap.length == 3)
                        complexWarp(curMap.offsetX, curMap.offsetY + 1,
                                curMap.offsetX + 1, curMap.offsetY + 2)
                    else
                        complexWarp(curMap.offsetX, curMap.offsetY, curMap
                                .offsetX – 1, curMap.offsetY + 1)

        if (shape == 6)
            if (curMap.length == 3 && state(curMap.offsetX + 1, curMap.offsetY))
                complexWarp(curMap.offsetX, curMap.offsetY, curMap.offsetX,
        curMap.offsetY + 1, curMap.offsetX + 2, curMap.offsetY + 1, curMap.offsetX + 1,
        curMap.offsetY + 1, curMap.offsetX + 2, curMap.offsetY, curMap.offsetX + 1,
        curMap.offsetY – 1)
            else
                if (curMap.length == 2 && state(curMap.offsetX + 1,
        curMap.offsetY + 1))
                    complexWarp(curMap.offsetX, curMap.offsetY + 2,
        curMap.offsetX, curMap.offsetY, curMap.offsetX + 1, curMap.offsetY + 2,
        curMap.offsetX, curMap.offsetY + 1, curMap.offsetX + 1, curMap.offsetY,
        curMap.offsetX + 2, curMap.offsetY + 1)
            else
                if (curMap.length == 3)
                    complexWarp(curMap.offsetX + 1, curMap.offsetY + 1,
        curMap.offsetX + 1, curMap.offsetY, curMap.offsetX + 2, curMap.offsetY + 1,
        curMap.offsetX, curMap.offsetY + 2)
                else
```

```
                    complexWarp(curMap.offsetX, curMap.offsetY, curMap.offsetX
+ 1, curMap.offsetY + 1, curMap.offsetX + 1, curMap.offsetY, curMap.offsetX + 2,
curMap.offsetY + 1, curMap.offsetX, curMap.offsetY + 2, curMap.offsetX + 2,
curMap.offsetY + 2)
}

// flood entire screen with given state
function flood(state) {
     for (var x = 0; x < 10; ++x) {
          for (var y = 0; y < 19; ++y) {
               if (state == 0)
                    document.images[computeIndex(x, y)].src = off.src
               else
                    document.images[computeIndex(x, y)].src = on[3].src
          }
     }
}

// return true if no active squares are found and false otherwise
function noActive() {
     // scan board from top to bottom
     for (var y = 0; y < 19; ++y) {
          for (var x = 0; x < 10; ++ x) {
               if (ar[x][y] == 1)
                    return false
          }
     }

     // no active square found on the board
     return true
}

// return true if the line with the given coordinate is completed
function isLine(y) {
     // horizontal scan of current line
     for (var x = 0; x < 10; ++x) {
          // if a square is off the line is not completed
          if (!state(x, y))
               return false
     }

     // no square was found off
     return true
}

// move block from one position to another
function warp(startX, startY, endX, endY) {
     document.images[computeIndex(endX, endY)].src = document.images
                         [computeIndex(startX, startY)].src
     document.images[computeIndex(startX, startY)].src = off.src

     // block in new position is now active
```

25

Chapter

```
        ar[endX][endY] = 1

        // previous position is no longer active
        ar[startX][startY] = 0
    }

    // function that starts game (*works with global variables only*)
    function start() {
        // accept level from user (no validation to save space)
        tempLevel = prompt("Enter level to begin game (0 - 10):", "0")

        // if user cancelled prompt
        if (!tempLevel)
            // abort function
            return

        // tempLevel is the actual level
        level = tempLevel

        // clear states, blocks, and timer
        clearActive()
        flood(0)
        clearTimeout(timerID)

        // clear statistics
        for (var i = 0; i < 7; ++i) {
            statistics[i] = 0
        }

        // convert input from string to integer
        level = parseInt(level)

        // calculate speed
        speed = 800 - (level * 80)

        // game begins with no lines completed!
        lines = 0

        // game starts
        timerRunning = true

        // game is not paused for sure
        paused = false

        // start actual playing
        play()
    }

    // check if lines have been completed and drop accordingly
    function dropLines() {
        // on line has been found
        var aLine = -1
```

```
	// scan screen from top to bottom and stop when first complete line is
	                   found and assigned
	for (var y = 0; y < 19; ++y) {
		if (isLine(y)) {
			aLine = y
			break
		}
	}

	// if a complete line has been found
	if (aLine != -1) {
		// increment lines
		lines++

		// if enough lines have been made increment level
		if (lines > level * 10 + 9)
			level++

		if (level == 11)
			alert("You are a champion!")

		// scan screen from one line above the complete one to top
		                   of screen
		for (y = aLine - 1; y >= 0; --y) {
			for (var x = 0; x < 10; ++x) {
				// if current square is on
				if (state(x, y))
					// call function to warp it down
					warp(x, y, x, y + 1)
				else {
					// clear square below (similar to a warp because
					                   initial square is off)
					setSquare(x, y + 1, 0)
				}
			}
		}

		// recursive call (maybe more than one line was completed)
		dropLines()
	}

	// no square should be active
	clearActive()
}

// main function responsible for game action
function play() {
	// place values in form fields (display)
	document.lineslevel.lines.value = lines
	document.lineslevel.level.value = level
```

```
        // if no shape is falling
        if (noActive()) {
            // check for line completions and drop them
            dropLines()

            // insert a new shape (if shape is not able to enter)
            if (!insertShape()) {
                // flood screen to black
                flood(1)

                // flood screen to blank
                flood(0)

                // display final results
                alert('Game over!\r\rlevel = ' + level + '\rlines = '+
                                    lines)

                // clear timeout
                clearTimeout(timerID)

                // timer is not running
                timerRunning = false

                // terminate function (and game)
                return
            }
        } else
            // a shape is currently falling so move it one square downwards
            moveY()

        // call after speed milliseconds
        timerID = setTimeout('play()', speed)
    }

    // constructs an object representing a specific position
    function characteristics(x, y) {
        // create property to hold status (block or empty)
        this.state = state(x, y)

        // if block found in specified position
        if (state(x, y)) {
            // local variable to hold URL of image at specified location
            var src = document.images[computeIndex(x, y)].src

            // local variable to hold color (0, 1, 2, ..., 6)
            var color = src.charAt(src.lastIndexOf('/') + 2)

        } else
            // no color because no block found at specified position
            color = -1

        // convert color from string to integer and assign to property
```

```
        this.color = parseInt(color)

        // create property to hold square's current state (active or not,
                                    1 or 0)
        this.activity = ar[x][y]
    }

    // contructs a map of entire board and status
    function fullMap() {
        for (var x = 0; x < 10; ++x) {
            this[x] = new Array(10)
            for (var y = 0; y < 19; ++y) {
                this[x][y] = new characteristics(x, y)
            }
        }

        this.shape = shape
    }

    // pause and unpause game
    function pause() {
        // if game is not paused
        if (!paused) {
            // stop timer
            clearTimeout(timerID)

            // game is now paused
            paused = true

            // create global map of board
            map = new fullMap()

            // flood board so player cannot see current status
            flood(1)

            // no active blocks so user cannot move anything with buttons
            clearActive()

            alert('Oh no, not the boss...')
        } else {
            // return board to status before game was paused, according to the
                                    map object
            for (var x = 0; x < 10; ++x) {
                for (var y = 0; y < 19; ++y) {
                    if (!map[x][y].state)
                        document.images[computeIndex(x, y)].src = off.src
                    else
                        document.images[computeIndex(x, y)].src = on[map
                                            [x][y].color].src

                    ar[x][y] = map[x][y].activity
                }
```

```
            }
            shape = map.shape

            // game is no longer paused
            paused = false

            // play ball!
            play()
        }
    }


    // -->
    </SCRIPT>
    </HEAD>
    <BODY>
    <EMBED SRC="tetris1a.mid" AUTOSTART=TRUE LOOP=TRUE HIDDEN=TRUE>
    </BODY>
    </HTML>
```

***Example 25-8**. A 1,000-line script creates a Tetris game on a Web page.*

Global Statements

```
// array to hold number of shapes used from each type
var statistics = new Array(7)
for (var shapeNum = 0; shapeNum < 7; ++shapeNum) {
     statistics[shapeNum] = 0
}
```

Tetris is based on seven shapes, so an array of seven elements named `statistics` is created first, and its elements are 0-initialized. The first element, `statistics[0]`, is associated with the first shape, and so forth. The array holds the shape statistics from the beginning of the game, so the element `statistics[2]`, for example, holds the number of times shape #3 appeared.

```
// set pause to false
var paused = false

// game is currently running
var timerRunning = false

// no shape currently falling
var shape = -1

// timer is not running
var timerID = null
```

Since the game is paused only when the user clicks the Pause button, we set the paused variable to false. The second variable, timerRunning, is also set to false, as no time out has been set by the setTimeout() method. The shape variable normally holds the index of the shape that is currently falling down on the screen. It is initialized to –1, indicating that no shape is falling yet (the game has not started). Another global variable, timerID, is initialized to null.

```
// initialize image variables for seven shapes
var on = new Array()
on[0] = new Image(12, 12)
on[1] = new Image(12, 12)
on[2] = new Image(12, 12)
on[3] = new Image(12, 12)
on[4] = new Image(12, 12)
on[5] = new Image(12, 12)
on[6] = new Image(12, 12)

// create a transparent block
var off = new Image(12, 12)
```

Like the LED Sign, Netris Deluxe is based on image manipulations. In this script we create a seven-element global array named on and a variable named off, and assign an instance of the Image object to each element of the array and to the variable. Notice that all images are the same size, 12 pixels by 12 pixels. The off variable holds a transparent gif image for the background.


```
// set image URLs
on[0].src = "10.gif"
on[1].src = "11.gif"
on[2].src = "12.gif"
on[3].src = "13.gif"
on[4].src = "14.gif"
on[5].src = "15.gif"
on[6].src = "16.gif"
off.src = "0.gif"
```

After creating the Image instances, we set the src property of each instance to the URL of its image. The images for the seven color blocks (those used to construct shapes) are "10.gif", "11.gif", "12.gif", ..., "15.gif", and "16.gif". The URL of the transparent image is "0.gif". Notice that the first character of all block images is "1", whereas the first character of the "off image" (the transparent one) is "0".

```
// get number of images already laid out in the page
var firstImage = document.images.length

// create initial screen
drawScreen()

// array of screen (10 x 19)
var ar = new Array()
for (var i = 0; i < 10; ++i) {
     ar[i] = new Array(19)
     for (var j = 0; j < 19; ++j) {
          ar[i][j] = 0
     }
}
```

Once the essential instances of the `Image` object are ready, we compute the document index of the first image. Since the `document.images` array starts from index 0, the index of the last image in the document, before loading the game, is `document.images.length –1`. The value assigned to `firstImage`, then, is the index of the first image of the game and is equal to `document.images.length`. The function `drawScreen()` creates the initial screen of the game, as illustrated in Figure 25-3:

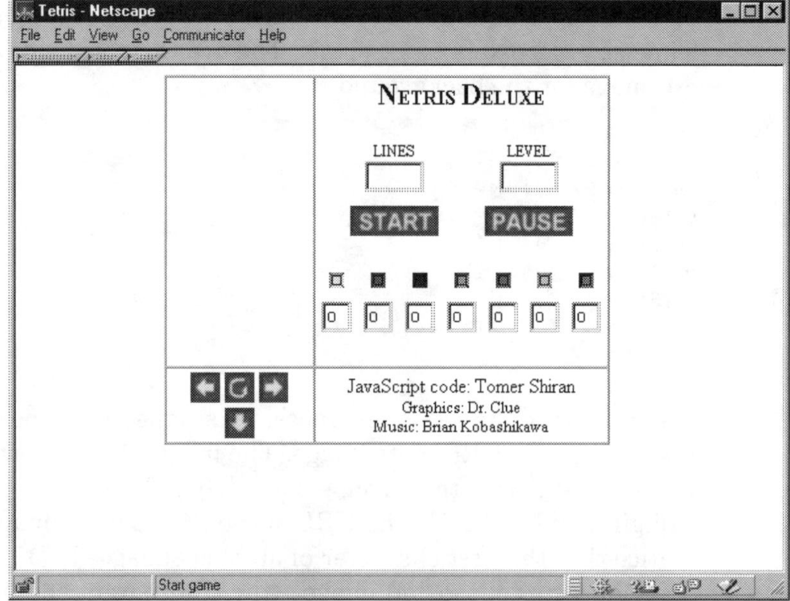

Figure 25-3*.* *The initial screen of Netris Deluxe, as printed by the* `drawScreen()` *function.*

The last portion of the global statements creates a simple 10 x 19 2D array. Since the actual height of a Tetris screen is 17 squares instead of 19, all shapes enter two lines above the top. This two-line margin enables the user to see the entire shape, even if he or she rotates it immediately upon entering the game (17th row). Figure 25-4 shows the position of a "line" shape when it enters a 17+2-row board, and its position after an in-place rotation (center of rotation is on the 17th row). It clearly demonstrates that the two extra rows at the top are essential.

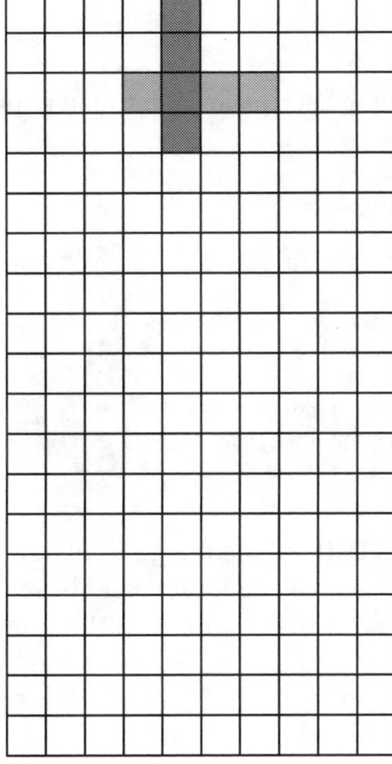

Figure 25-4. The light gray shape is the initial position when it enters the board, and the darker one is the shape's position after being rotated immediately afterwards.

drawScreen()

The `drawScreen()` function simply uses `document.write()` statements to generate the game, as presented in Figure 25-3. Notice that we use the `with(document)` construct so that we can use `write()` rather than `document.write()`. The function creates several forms and buttons:

- The first form includes the "LINES" and "LEVEL" text fields, referenced as `document.lineslevel.lines` and `document.lineslevel.level`, respectively.

- The Start and Pause buttons are images linked with the `start()` and `pause()` functions, respectively.
- The second form is named "`stats`". It includes seven two-character text fields, named "0", "1", …, "5" and "6".
- The control panel includes direction and rotation buttons as well. The left movement button calls `moveX()` with the argument –1, the right movement button invokes `moveX()` with the argument 1, the downward movement button calls the `moveY()` function with no argument, and the rotation button calls the `rotate()` function.

computeIndex(x, y)

See the listings for the previous script for a detailed explanation of this function.

state(x, y)

```
// returns state of square (true / false)
function state(x, y) {
     // assign URL of image at given coordinates to local variable
     var source = document.images[computeIndex(x, y)].src

     // expression evaluates to 0 or 1
     return (source.charAt(source.lastIndexOf('/') + 1) == '0') ?
                        false : true
}
```

This function first finds the URL of the image located at the given *x* and *y* coordinates and assigns it to the local variable `source`. You may recall from the beginning of our discussion that the filename of an image starts with either a "0" (for the off image) or a"1" (for a color block). Since `source.lastIndexOf('/') + 1` is the index of the first character of the image's filename, the following expression evaluates to either a "1" or a "0":

```
source.charAt(source.lastIndexOf('/') + 1)
```

This computation also applies to the case when the images are stored in the same directory in which the document resides (there is no slash in the URL expression). The `source.lastIndexOf('/')` evaluates to –1, and `source.lastIndexOf('/') + 1` yields a 0 value, the index of the first character.

The `state()` function returns `true` if the image at the given coordinates is a block (its filename starts with a "1"), and `false` if it is a transparent image (its filename starts with a "0").

setSquare(x, y, state)

```
// set square to 1 / 0
function setSquare(x, y, state) {
     if (state == 0)
          document.images[computeIndex(x, y)].src = off.src
     else
          document.images[computeIndex(x, y)].src = on[shape].src

     // if state is one square is active, so 1 is assigned to ar[x][y]
     // otherwise square is not active so 0 is assigned to ar[x][y]
     ar[x][y] = state
}
```

The `setSquare()` function accepts three arguments: the *x* coordinate of a square, its *y* coordinate, and a `state` (0 or 1) assignment. If the value of `state` is 0, the square at the given position is cleared by assigning `off.src` to its `src` property. On the other hand, if `state` is 1 (or any other value), the box at the given position is assigned the block image whose index is `shape`, where `shape` is a global integer between 0 and 6. The current state of the square, at the specified position, is stored in the global array, `ar`. See the inline comments for additional explanations regarding this statement.

clearActive()

```
// clear array so no active squares exist
function clearActive() {
     // scan entire array and assign 0 to all elements (no active squares)
     for (var i = 0; i < 10; ++i) {
          for (var j = 0; j < 19; ++j) {
               ar[i][j] = 0
          }
     }

     // no shape is currently in screen
     shape = -1
}
```

The `ar` array, which is 10 x 19, keeps track of all current "active" blocks, i.e., those that belong to a falling shape. Moving blocks around is done simply by visiting all active ones and assigning their next locations. Whenever a block hits the bottom of the board or lies on top of another block, the falling shape is inactivated by the `clearActive()` function, which clears the entire board. The last statement of the function sets `shape` to –1, signaling that there is no falling shape on the board.

checkMoveX(step)

```
// check if specified move (left or right) is valid
function checkMoveX(step) {
     // scan screen (direction does not matter)
     for (var x = 0; x < 10; ++x) {
          for (var y = 0; y < 19; ++y) {
               // if current square is active
               if (ar[x][y] == 1) {
                    // check all conditions:
                    // not out of range and not colliding with existing
                                   not active block
                    if (x + step < 0 || x + step > 9 || (state(x + step,
                                   y) && ar[x + step][y] == 0))
                         // return false if move (new situation) is not
                                   legal
                         return false
               }
          }
     }

     // return true if no invalid state has been encountered
     return true
}
```

This function accepts one argument, either 1 or –1, and checks if it is possible to move the active shape one square to the right (if the argument is 1) or to the left (if the argument is –1). The function looks for all active squares on the board and the following condition is evaluated for each active one:

```
x + step < 0 || x + step > 9 || (state(x + step, y) && ar[x + step]
[y] == 0)
```

This expression yields `true` if the active square, after moving it `step` positions to the right, finds itself out of the board's range, or in the territory of an inactive block (an active block obviously belongs to the same shape). If the specified movement is not valid, the function returns `false`. Otherwise, it returns `true`.

The efficiency of this function can be improved in two ways. First, to reduce the number of checks, the function can be spliced into `CheckMoveXright()` and `CheckMoveXleft()`. Second, instead of searching the whole board for active squares, a more localized algorithm, which takes advantage of the current shape and position information, can be devised.

checkMoveY()

```
// check if specified move (down) is valid
function checkMoveY() {
     // only possible step is one to the bottom
     var step = 1

     // scan screen (direction does not matter)
     for (var x = 0; x < 10; ++x) {
          for (var y = 0; y < 19; ++y) {
               // if current square is active
               if (ar[x][y] == 1) {
                    // check all conditions:
                    // not out of range and not colliding with existing
                                   not active block
                    if (y + step > 18 || (state(x, y + step) && ar[x]
                                   [y + step] == 0))
                         // return false if move (new situation) is not
                                   legal
                         return false
               }
          }
     }

     // return true if no invalid state has been encountered
     return true
}
```

This function is very similar to checkMoveX(), except that, since the movement is always downward, it does not accept any argument. The step variable appears in this function for historical reasons; it could have been replaced by 1.

moveX(step)

```
// move all active squares step squares on the x axis
function moveX(step) {
     // if specified move is not legal
     if (!checkMoveX(step))
          // terminate function (active blocks are not moved)
          return

     // if left movement then scan screen from left to right
     if (step < 0) {
          for (var x = 0; x < 10; ++x) {
               for (var y = 0; y < 19; ++y) {
                    // if current square is active
                    if (ar[x][y] == 1)
                         // call function to handle movement
                         smartX(x, y, step)
               }
```

```
                }
        } else

        // if right movement then scan screen from right to left
        if (step > 1) {
                for (var x = 9; x >= 0; --x) {
                        for (var y = 0; y < 19; ++y) {
                                // if current square is active
                                if (ar[x][y] == 1)
                                        // call function to handle movement
                                        smartX(x, y, step)
                        }
                }
        }
}
```

The moveX() function accepts one argument, specifying the number of positions that all active squares need to be moved. A positive value means that they should be moved to the right, while a negative value means that they should be moved to the left. The scanning algorithm is coordinated with the movement direction, so it does not visit the same square again (after it has been moved). The movement itself is accomplished by the smartX() function. Refer to inline comments for statement-specific notes.

smartX(x, y, step)

```
// responsible for the blocks' horizontal movement
function smartX(x, y, step) {
        // if moving one step to the left
        if (step < 0)
                // if the destination square needs to be turned on explicitly
                if (ar[x + step][y] == 0)
                        // if there is a block to the right of the current block
                        if (x != 9 && ar[x - step][y] == 1)
                                // set square to the left on without clearing current
                                           block
                                setSquare(x + step, y, 1)
                        else
                                // clear current block and turn square to the left on
                                warp(x, y, x + step, y)
                else
                        // if there is no block to the right of the current block
                        if (x == 9 || ar[x - step][y] == 0)
                                // clear current block
                                setSquare(x, y, 0)

        // if moving one step to the right
        if (step > 0)
                // if the destination square needs to be turned on explicitly
```

```
            if (ar[x + step][y] == 0)
                  // if there is a block to the left of the current block
                  if (x != 0 && ar[x - step][y] == 1)
                        // set square to the right on without clearing
                                    current block
                        setSquare(x + step, y, 1)
                  else
                        // clear current block and turn square to the
                                    right on
                        warp(x, y, x + step, y)
            else
                  // if there is no block to the left of the current block
                  if (x == 0 || ar[x - step][y] == 0)
                        // clear current block
                        setSquare(x, y, 0)
}
```

The `smartX()` function is responsible for the horizontal movement of the affected blocks. Notice that when you move a horizontal bar (four blocks) shape to the right, for example, you only need to move the far-right block to the right of the shape, and clear the premovement far-left block. Figure 25-5 illustrates this concept with an "L" shape. Moving a shape consisting of four blocks one step to the right requires the setting of two blocks and the clearing of two other blocks.

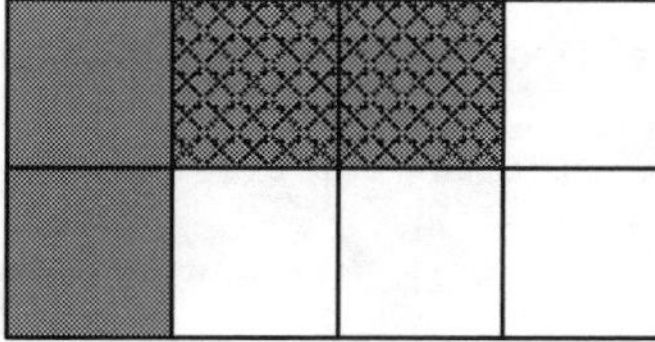

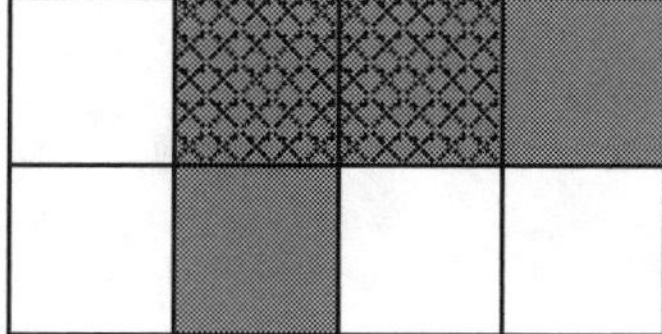

Block that did not move

Block that moved

Figure 25-5*. A shape can move without moving all the blocks in the shape.*

moveY()

```
// move all active squares step squares on the x axis
function moveY() {
      // if specified move is not legal (shape is laid down on block
                              or bottom panel)
      if (!checkMoveY()) {
            // active squares are not active anymore (should not be
                              moved later)
```

```
                clearActive()

                // terminate function (active blocks are not moved)
                return
        }

        // scan screen from bottom to top
        for (var y = 18; y >= 0; --y) {
                for (var x = 0; x < 10; ++x) {
                        // if current square is active
                        if (ar[x][y] == 1)
                                // call function to handle movement
                                smartY(x, y)
                }
        }
}
```

The moveY() function is identical to the moveX() function, except that, in the case the move is not possible, the clearActive() function is called, inactivating the whole board. Also, since the movement is always downward, no argument is needed.

smartY(x, y)

```
// responsible for the blocks' vertical (downward) movement
function smartY(x, y) {
        // if the destination square needs to be turned on explicitly
        if (ar[x][y + 1] == 0)
                // if there is a block above current block
                if (y != 0 && ar[x][y - 1] == 1)
                        // set square below on without clearing current block
                        setSquare(x, y + 1, 1)
                else
                        // clear current block and turn square below on
                        warp(x, y, x, y + 1)
        else
                // if there is no block above the current block
                if (y == 0 || ar[x][y - 1] == 0)
                        // clear current block
                        setSquare(x, y, 0)
}
```

This function is the Y-axis equivalent of the smartX() function presented earlier. See the listings for that function.

shapeMap()

```
// construct object containing shape
function shapeMap() {
        // set minimum and maximum coordinates to opposite (minimum and
                                        maximum found thus far)
```

```
        var minX = 9
        var minY = 18
        var maxX = 0
        var maxY = 0

        // scan screen to find actual minimum and maximum coordinates
                        of active squares
        for (var y = 0; y < 19; ++y) {
            for (var x = 0; x < 10; ++x) {
                // if current coordinates reflect active square
                if (ar[x][y] == 1) {
                    if (x < minX)
                        minX = x
                    if (x > maxX)
                        maxX = x
                    if (y < minY)
                        minY = y
                    if (y > maxY)
                        maxY = y
                }
            }
        }

        // create a length property representing the x coordinate span
        this.length = maxX - minX + 1

        // create properties to hold minimum coordinates of both axes
        this.offsetX = minX
        this.offsetY = minY

        // construct minimum array containing all active squares respectively
        for (x = 0; x <= maxX - minX; ++x) {
            this[x] = new Array()
            for (y = 0; y <= maxY - minY; ++y) {
                this[x][y] = ar[x + minX][y + minY]
            }
        }
}
```

25 Chapter

Before the script rotates a shape, it must know which shape is currently active and its exact position. The `shapeMap()` constructor builds the minimum 2D array which encloses the current shape, as illustrated in Figure 25-6:

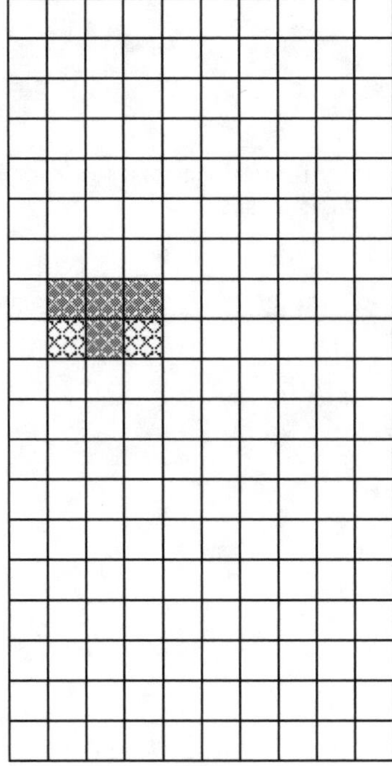

Block in shape

Blocks in shape map

Figure 25-6. A shape map reflects the minimum rectangle necessary to include the entire shape.

In addition to the array elements, an instance of `shapeMap` features the board's *x* and *y* coordinates (`offsetX` and `offsetY`) of the shape-enclosing rectangle's top left square (*`shapeMapInstance`*`[0][0]`). The 2D array and these two properties are enough to determine the current active shape and its location. For a complete discussion of each statement in the function refer to the comments.

getRandom()

```
// random function to return an integer between 0 and 6
function getRandom() {
     // use random number method to find integer between 0 and 8
     var randomNum = Math.round(Math.random() * 8)

     // call function again if random number is 0 or 8.
     if (randomNum == 0 || randomNum == 8)
          return getRandom()

     // 1 to 7 => 0 to 6
     randomNum--
```

```
        // update selected shape's statistics
        statistics[randomNum]++

        // update statistics display form (update *all* fields so user
                                 cannot enter any value in fields)
        for (var shape = 0; shape < 7; ++shape) {
             document.stats[shape].value = statistics[shape]
        }

        // return the random number
        return randomNum
}
```

The getRandom() function returns a random integer between 0 and 6. First, it uses the Math object's random() method to generate a random number. Peculiarly enough, we found out that the random generator prefers the inner integers (1, 2, 3, 4, and 5) over the boundary ones (0 and 6). To remedy the situation, we decided to generate random integers between 0 and 8, and then do some juggling to fit the result into the 0-to-6 range. If the integer is 0 or 8, the function invokes itself recursively, until an integer between 1 and 7 is randomly generated. The number then decrements by 1 to fit the 0-to-6 range, and is returned by the function. After updating the statistics array, the text fields, representing the number of appearances of each shape, are updated as well.

insertShape()

This function inserts a new shape whose index is a random integer stored in the global variable shape. Take a look at the following code segment:

```
if (shape == 4) {
        if (state(4, 2) || state(5, 2) || state(3, 3) || state(4, 3))
             return false
        setSquare(4, 2, 1)
        setSquare(5, 2, 1)
        setSquare(3, 3, 1)
        setSquare(4, 3, 1)
}
```

The insertShape() function includes such a script segment for each of the seven supported shapes. The coordinates used in this script are illustrated in Figure 25-7.

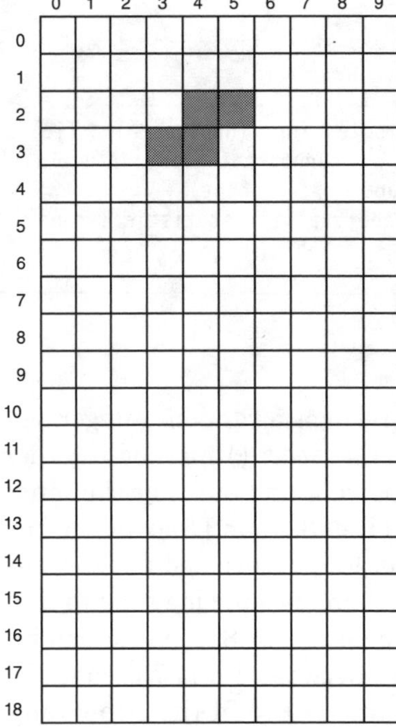

***Figure 25-7**. Shape #4 in its initial position.*

The conditional statement uses the function `state()` to check whether all four squares are empty. If one of the four is blocked, the `insertShape()` function returns `false` and terminates. Otherwise, the function proceeds by invoking the `setSquare()` function four times, one for each block of the new shape.

complexWarp()

```
// warp several squares if possible
// initial x1, initial y1, destination x1, destination y1, initial x2,
initial y2, destination x2, destination y2, etc.
function complexWarp() {
    // loop through arguments checking that each warp is valid
    for (var i = 0; i < arguments.length; i += 4) {
        // if warp is not valid
        if (!checkWarp(arguments[i], arguments[i + 1], arguments[i + 2],
                                arguments[i + 3]))
            // terminate the function -- no squares warped
            return
    }

    // loop through arguments again -- warp squares
    for (var i = 0; i < arguments.length; i += 4) {
```

```
            // call function to warp the current square corresponding to
                                    argument coordinates
            warp(arguments[i], arguments[i + 1], arguments[i + 2],
                                    arguments[i + 3])
        }
}
```

This function moves a shape's blocks from their current positions to their new ones. The argument list includes sets of four coordinates: *x* and *y* values of these positions. Since the number of sets depends on the shape type, the arguments are accessed via the `arguments` array, rather than as parameters.

First, the function calls `checkWarp()` to check if the destination squares are populated or not. The `complexWarp()` function terminates immediately whenever one of the squares is occupied. The warping itself is accomplished by calling the `warp()` function, once for each set of four arguments.

checkWarp(startX, startY, endX, endY)

```
// check if warp is valid (used by complexWarp function)
function checkWarp(startX, startY, endX, endY) {
    // if a destination coordinate is invalid or destination square
                                    is off
    // state(endX, endY) must be last due to short-circuit evaluation
    if (endX < 0 || endX > 9 || endY < 0 || endY > 18 || state(endX,
                                    endY))
        // return false because warp is invalid
        return false

    // return true because warp has not been proved to be invalid (it
                                    is valid)
    return true
}
```

Out of the four arguments this function accepts, it uses the last two (`endX`, `endY`) to check if the given position is occupied.

rotate()

First, the function assigns an instance of the `shapeMap` object to a local variable, `curMap`. Refer back to Figure 25-6 for an explanation about the enclosing rectangle concept of `shapeMap`. The `shapeMap` object is used to find out the current angle of the shape. The "L" shape, for example, has four different angles, whereas a "square" (2 x 2) shape has only one. It then calls the `complexWarp()` function with the coordinates of the blocks that need to be "warped" during rotation.

flood(state)

```
// flood entire screen with given state
function flood(state) {
     for (var x = 0; x < 10; ++x) {
          for (var y = 0; y < 19; ++y) {
               if (state == 0)
                    document.images[computeIndex(x, y)].src = off.src
               else
                    document.images[computeIndex(x, y)].src = on[3].src
          }
     }
}
```

When its argument is 0, the `flood()` function clears the entire board by setting the URL of all images to `off.src`. If the argument is not 0, all board images are replaced with `on[3].src`. Note that, instead of the doubly-nested loop, you can use a single loop to fill the `document.images` 1-D array. Since you would not have to invoke the `computeIndex()` function for each position, the flooding would have been more efficient.

noActive()

```
// return true if no active squares are found and false otherwise
function noActive() {
     // scan board from top to bottom
     for (var y = 0; y < 19; ++y) {
          for (var x = 0; x < 10; ++ x) {
               if (ar[x][y] == 1)
                    return false
          }
     }

     // no active square found on the board
     return true
}
```

This function is self-explanatory.

isLine(y)

```
// return true if the line with the given coordinate is completed
function isLine(y) {
     // horizontal scan of current line
     for (var x = 0; x < 10; ++x) {
          // if a square is off the line is not completed
          if (!state(x, y))
               return false
     }
```

```
        // no square was found off
        return true
}
```

This function looks for complete lines, i.e., lines with all squares checked.

warp(startX, startY, endX, endY)

```
// move block from one position to another
function warp(startX, startY, endX, endY) {
        document.images[computeIndex(endX, endY)].src = document.images
                                    [computeIndex(startX, startY)].src
        document.images[computeIndex(startX, startY)].src = off.src

        // block in new position is now active
        ar[endX][endY] = 1

        // previous position is no longer active
        ar[startX][startY] = 0
}
```

The `warp()` function "warps" a block from one position to another, by setting the URL of the destination image to that of the source one, and then setting the URL of the source image to that of the transparent one, `off.src`. The `ar` array is also being updated with the recent changes in square assignments.

start()

```
// function that starts game (*works with global variables only*)
function start() {
        // accept level from user (no validation to save space)
        tempLevel = prompt("Enter level to begin game (0 – 10):", "0")

        // if user cancelled prompt
        if (!tempLevel)
                // abort function
                return

        // tempLevel is the actual level
        level = tempLevel

        // clear states, blocks, and timer
        clearActive()
        flood(0)
        clearTimeout(timerID)

        // clear statistics
```

```
        for (var i = 0; i < 7; ++i) {
            statistics[i] = 0
        }

        // convert input from string to integer
        level = parseInt(level)

        // calculate speed
        speed = 800 - (level * 80)

        // game begins with no lines completed!
        lines = 0

        // game starts
        timerRunning = true

        // game is not paused for sure
        paused = false

        // start actual playing
        play()
}
```

This function is very well documented and explained. Use it as an example for how to comment a script.

dropLines()

```
// check if lines have been completed and drop accordingly
function dropLines() {
        // on line has been found
        var aLine = -1

        // scan screen from top to bottom and stop when first complete
                                line is found and assigned
        for (var y = 0; y < 19; ++y) {
                if (isLine(y)) {
                        aLine = y
                        break
                }
        }

        // if a complete line has been found
        if (aLine != -1) {
                // increment lines
                lines++

                // if enough lines have been made increment level
                if (lines > level * 10 + 9)
                        level++
```

```
            if (level == 11)
                alert("You are a champion!")

            // scan screen from one line above the complete one to top
                                    of screen
            for (y = aLine - 1; y >= 0; --y) {
                for (var x = 0; x < 10; ++x) {
                    // if current square is on
                    if (state(x, y))
                        // call function to warp it down
                        warp(x, y, x, y + 1)
                    else {
                        // clear square below (similar to a warp because
                                    initial square is off)
                        setSquare(x, y + 1, 0)
                    }
                }
            }

            // recursive call (maybe more than one line was completed)
            dropLines()
        }

        // no square should be active
        clearActive()
}
```


The dropLines() function loops over the board rows, from top to bottom, searching for fully blocked rows to clear. After finding a line, all blocks above the line are warped one position downward, and the dropLines() function is called recursively to search and clear other rows. Since there are no active shapes after clearing, the clearActive() function is invoked to clear all board squares. The script also checks if the user has completed enough lines to up the current level of play.

play()

```
// main function responsible for game action
function play() {
    // place values in form fields (display)
    document.lineslevel.lines.value = lines
    document.lineslevel.level.value = level

    // if no shape is falling
    if (noActive()) {
        // check for line completions and drop them
        dropLines()

        // insert a new shape (if shape is not able to enter)
```

```
               if (!insertShape()) {
                    // flood screen to black
                    flood(1)

                    // flood screen to blank
                    flood(0)

                    // display final results
                    alert('Game over!\r\rlevel = ' + level + '\rlines = '+
                                                lines)

                    // clear timeout
                    clearTimeout(timerID)

                    // timer is not running
                    timerRunning = false

                    // terminate function (and game)
                    return
               }
          } else
               // a shape is currently falling so move it one square downward
               moveY()

          // call after speed milliseconds
          timerID = setTimeout('play()', speed)
     }
```

characteristics(x, y)

```
     // constructs an object representing a specific position
     function characteristics(x, y) {
          // create property to hold status (block or empty)
          this.state = state(x, y)

          // if block found in specified position
          if (state(x, y)) {
               // local variable to hold URL of image at specified location
               var src = document.images[computeIndex(x, y)].src

               // local variable to hold color (0, 1, 2, ..., 6)
               var color = src.charAt(src.lastIndexOf('/') + 2)

          } else
               // no color because no block found at specified position
               color = -1

          // convert color from string to integer and assign to property
          this.color = parseInt(color)
```

```
        // create property to hold square's current state (active or not,
                                  1 or 0)
        this.activity = ar[x][y]
    }
```

fullMap()

```
    // contructs a map of entire board and status
    function fullMap() {
        for (var x = 0; x < 10; ++x) {
            this[x] = new Array(10)
            for (var y = 0; y < 19; ++y) {
                this[x][y] = new characteristics(x, y)
            }
        }

        this.shape = shape
    }
```

pause()


```
    // pause and unpause game
    function pause() {
        // if game is not paused
        if (!paused) {
            // stop timer
            clearTimeout(timerID)

            // game is now paused
            paused = true

            // create global map of board
            map = new fullMap()

            // flood board so player cannot see current status
            flood(1)

            // no active blocks so user cannot move anything with buttons
            clearActive()

            alert('Oh no, not the boss...')
        } else {
            // return board to status before game was paused, according
                                  to the map object
            for (var x = 0; x < 10; ++x) {
                for (var y = 0; y < 19; ++y) {
                    if (!map[x][y].state)
                        document.images[computeIndex(x, y)].src =
                                                        off.src
                    else
```

```
                              document.images[computeIndex(x, y)].src=
                                           on[map[x][y].color].src

                         ar[x][y] = map[x][y].activity
                    }
               }
               shape = map.shape

               // game is no longer paused
               paused = false

               // play ball!
               play()
          }
     }
```

The `pause()` function is responsible for pausing and unpausing the game, depending on its current state.

MUSIC

The background music featured by Netris Deluxe is embedded via a Netscape Navigator 3.0 HTML statement:

```
<EMBED SRC="tetris1a.mid" AUTOSTART=TRUE LOOP=TRUE HIDDEN=TRUE>
```

Summary

In this chapter we discussed the `Image` object, and how it is implemented in client-side JavaScript. Bear in mind that Navigator 2.0x and MSIE 3.0 do not support this object, so test carefully the version you are going to use. Mastering the usage of the `Image` object and the `document.images` array is not trivial, but will become easier with experience. This is the reason why we included three image-based comprehensive demonstrations, including a 1,000-line script (Netris Deluxe). JavaScript is very useful when you want to interact with the user (as in games), or when the animation is customized (as in the updating clock and in the LED sign). Plain animation is better created with gif89, rather than with JavaScript.

Chapter 26

Frames

What are Frames?

Frames provide the ability to divide the browser's window into several sections, each containing a distinct HTML document. There are many different ways to use frames. You can display, for instance, the table of contents on one side of the window, and the content itself on the other side. You can then direct all links in the table of contents to load documents in the other frame, thus ensuring that the table of contents is present at all times. While surfing the Web, you can occasionally recognize a frame-separated window by the frames' borders. Borderless frames, though, have recently become much more popular.

Creating Frames

Frames are basically plain HTML which are loaded by a parent document. In order to specify the frames in the top-level document, you must use the <FRAMESET> definition. This tag specifies how to divide the window. A single <FRAMESET> tag can divide a document into a set of rows or columns, depending on the desired design. For example, the following definition divides a document into two frames:

```
<FRAMESET COLS="50, *">
```

These two frames are organized in columns. The left frame is 50 pixels wide, whereas the other frame fills the rest of the document. An asterisk (*) represents the remaining space in a document, after allocating space for the other frames.

You can also specify the percentage width of a column frame out of the window's width, or the percentage height of a row frame out of the window's height. The following definition, for instance, divides a document into two frames (laid out as rows), where the upper one takes up one quarter of the document, and the bottom one takes up three quarters of it:

```
<FRAMESET ROWS="25%, *">
```

The following tags are equivalent to the preceding one:

```
<FRAMESET ROWS="*, 75%">
```

```
<FRAMESET ROWS="25%, 75%">
```

The <FRAMESET> tag must always be specified along with its closing counterpart, </FRAMESET>. The basic attributes of the <FRAMESET> tag are cols and rows (they cannot be present simultaneously). Netscape Navigator 3.0 introduced two more attributes:

- FRAMEBORDER
- BORDERCOLOR

The FRAMEBORDER attribute accepts either a no or a yes. Alternatively, you can replace the "no" with a 0 digit, and the "yes" with a 1 digit. This attribute enables you to create a document that consists of frames with invisible borders. The BORDERCOLOR attribute accepts a color, either in the form of a hexadecimal triplet or a recognized color name. Since there is a plain gray transition line between two borderless frames, you should specify a white border even when setting FRAMEBORDER to no. Setting FRAMEBORDER to no is not sufficient to completely hide the transition from one frame to another under IE 3.0x. To work around this problem, you should set the FRAMESPACING attribute to 0 under IE 3.0x.

The <FRAMESET> tag specifies a set of frames, each defined by a <FRAME> tag and usually a URL which reflects the initial document in the frame. The following construct creates a document consisting of two frames:

```
<FRAMESET COLS="100, *">
     <FRAME SRC="frame1.html">
     <FRAME SRC="frame2.html">
</FRAMESET>
```

The SRC attribute specifies the URL of the document in the frame. You can always load a different document in that frame by clicking a link, submitting a form, and so forth. The preceding source requires three documents: the parent HTML document that includes the

<FRAMESET> definition, `frame1.html`, and `frame2.html` (note that you can use either a relative or absolute URL). Take a look at the following documents:

```
<HTML>
<HEAD>
<TITLE>Frames</TITLE>
</HEAD>
<FRAMESET COLS="150, *">
     <FRAME SRC="ex26-1a.htm">
     <FRAME SRC="ex26-1b.htm">
</FRAMESET>
<NOFRAMES>
You must download a frame-capable browser in order to view this document.
</NOFRAMES>
</HTML>
```

Example 26-1 (ex26-1.htm). *The top-level FRAMESET document.*

```
<HTML>
<HEAD>
<TITLE>First frame</TITLE>
</HEAD>
<BODY BGCOLOR="white">
Frame #1
<HR>
</BODY>
</HTML>
```

Example 26-1a—first frame (ex26-1a.htm). *The initial document for the left frame.*

```
<HTML>
<HEAD>
<TITLE>Second frame</TITLE>
</HEAD>
<BODY BGCOLOR="white">
Frame #2
<HR>
</BODY>
</HTML>
```

Example 26-1b—second frame (ex26-1b.htm). *The initial document for the right frame.*

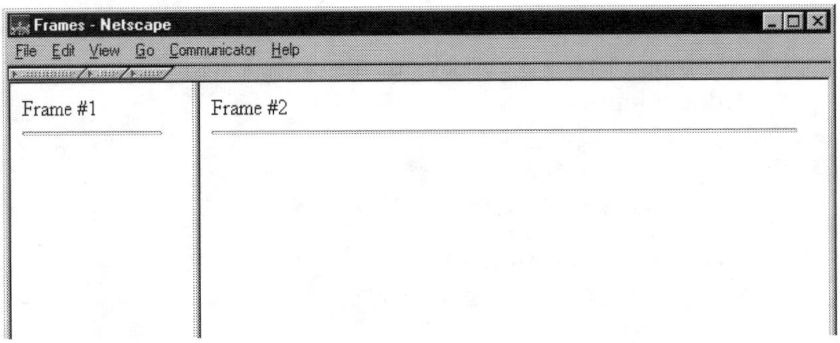

***Figure 26-1**. A simple frames document.*

You can delete the borders by replacing the <FRAMESET> tag in Example 26-1 by the following definition:

```
<FRAMESET COLS="150, *" FRAMEBORDER="no" FRAMESPACING=0 BORDER="0"
BORDERCOLOR="#ffffff">
```

The result is illustrated in Figure 26-2:

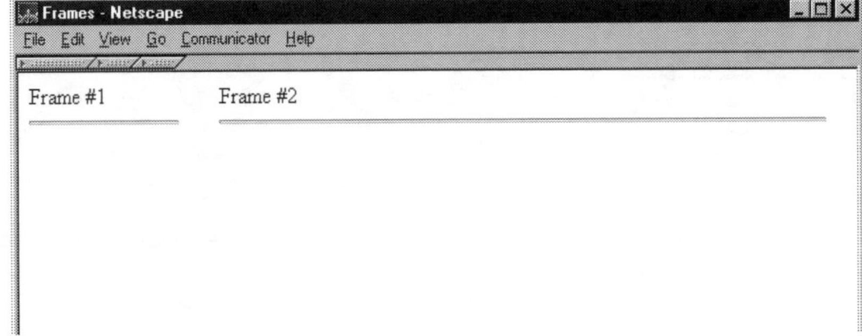

***Figure 26-2**. A frames document without a border.*

Now take another look at Example 26-1, and notice the <NOFRAMES>...</NOFRAMES> portion. These tags enclose alternative content for browsers which do not support frames. They are similar to the <NOSCRIPT>...</NOSCRIPT> tags which specify alternative content for browsers that do not support JavaScript or have their JavaScript disabled by the user.

Besides the SRC attribute, the <FRAME> tag features several other attributes, the NAME attribute being the most important one. You can target a link or a form submission return by a frame's name. Names must start with an alphanumeric character.

There are two attributes that deal with a frame's margin:

- MARGINHEIGHT
- MARGINWIDTH

The "margin" is the spacing between the frame's content and its borders. The minimum value for a margin's width or height is 1, and its maximum value is the frame's thickness. Both `MARGINHEIGHT` and `MARGINWIDTH` specify the margin value (height or width, respectively) in pixels.

The `SCROLLING` attribute is another important one. It accepts one of three values:

- `"yes"`
- `"no"`
- `"auto"`

The default value `"auto"` instructs the browser to make a scrolling frame (with a scrollbar) whenever needed. The browser's algorithm is very simple—if the length or width of the frame's content exceeds the frame's physical size, a scrollbar is provided. The other options, `"yes"` and `"no"`, force a decision on the browser.

A powerful feature of frames is that the user can resize them by dragging. You can disable this option by specifying the `NORESIZE` option.

Targeting Frames

Frames are powerful because they enable the content provider to direct various documents to specific frames. Directing a document to a frame is referred to as *targeting*. Targeting is supported in HTML via the `TARGET` attribute, which you can add to a variety of tags in the following fashion:

```
TARGET="windowName"
```

Since frames act as independent browser windows, they are often called as such. The classic usage of the `TARGET` attribute is with hypertext links, according to the following syntax:

```
<A HREF="URL" TARGET="windowName">text or image</A>
```

You should place such a link in a document that resides within a frame. *windowName* is the name of the frame in which the *URL* document should load.

You can use the `<BASE>` tag's `TARGET` attribute for targeting most of a document's links to a single common frame. The `TARGET` attribute establishes a default *windowName* that all links in a document will be targeted to. This default can be overridden by specific instances of the

TARGET attribute in individual anchor tags. The general syntax of the <BASE> tag's TARGET attribute is as follows:

```
<BASE TARGET="windowName">
```

Note that this definition should be placed at the beginning of the HTML document.

As you can see, it is possible to target a document to a named frame. There are reserved names that define specific locations:

- TARGET="_blank" loads a new, empty window.
- TARGET="_self" loads the same window the anchor was clicked in.
- TARGET="_parent" loads the FRAMESET (parent) document.
- TARGET="_top" loads the full body of the browser window.

Nested Frames

There are basically two ways to nest frames.

The easiest way is to use a simple <FRAMESET> tag in the top-level document to define several rows or columns of frames, and then use another <FRAMESET> tag in one or more of the frame documents to further divide it. Suppose you want to divide a window into two columns, where the second column is divided into two rows. You can define a two-frame <FRAMESET COLS="..."> construct in the parent document as follows:

```
<FRAMESET COLS="50%, *">
     <FRAME SRC="left.html" NAME="left">
     <FRAME SRC="right.html" NAME="right">
</FRAMESET>
```

The document right.html would then need to be subdivided into frames by including the following definition:

```
<FRAMESET ROWS="50%,50%">
     <FRAME SRC="topRight.html" NAME="topRight">
     <FRAME SRC="bottomRight.html" NAME="bottomRight">
</FRAMESET>
```

Figure 26-3 demonstrates the deeply nested frame hierarchy:

parent
left
right
topRight
bottomRight

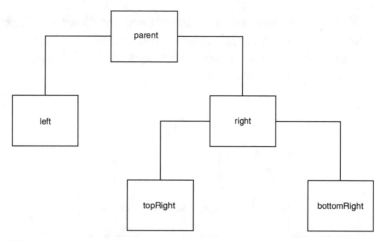

***Figure 26-3**. <FRAMESET> definitions are present in different documents so the hierarchy is deeply nested.*

A more convenient way to nest frames is as follows:

```
<FRAMESET COLS="50%, *">
     <FRAME SRC="left.html" NAME="left">
     <FRAMESET ROWS="50%,50%">
          <FRAME SRC="topRight.html" NAME="topRight">
          <FRAME SRC="bottomRight.html" NAME="bottomRight">
     </FRAMESET>
</FRAMESET>
```

In this code, we define a set of two frames, where the second one is not specified via a <FRAME> but rather as another inner <FRAMESET> definition.

Notice that this technique differs from the previous one, because all frames are directly defined in the top-level document. Figure 26-4 illustrates the structure of such a document.

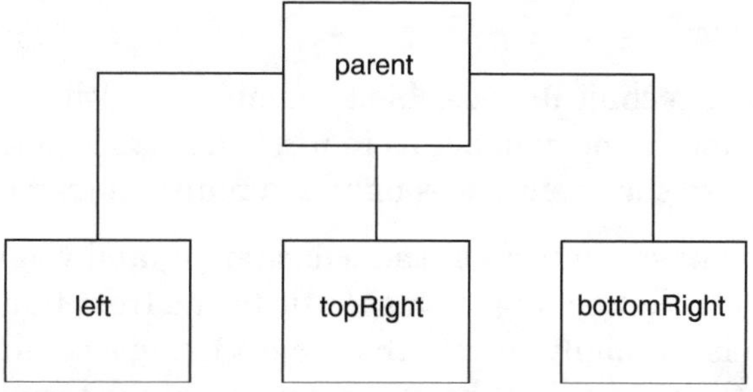

***Figure 26-4**. Frames are not actually nested when all definitions are in the top-level document.*

Notice that frames in a document are not directly connected to each other. However, HTML enables you to reference one frame directly from another one. Figure 26-5 shows the HTML connections between frames in such a structure:

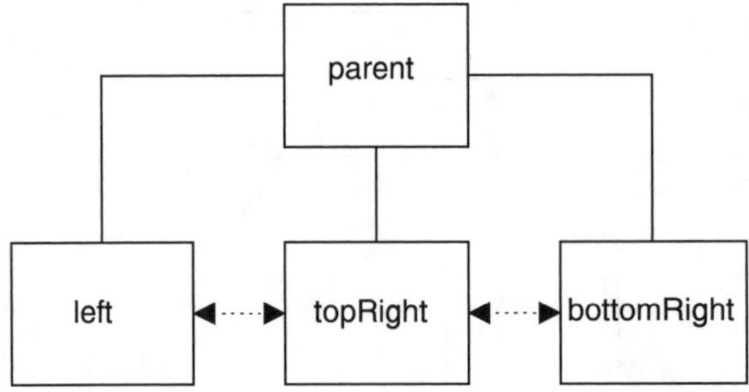

***Figure 26-5**. HTML enables direct connection between frames.*

JavaScript and Frames

In JavaScript, each frame acts as a full-fledged `window` object. A frame consists of a complete set of browser objects, including its own `document` object, `status` object (which is a bit tricky), and so forth.

self

The `self` object is equivalent to the `window` one. The background color of a document in a single-frame window can be referenced in one of the following fashions:

```
window.document.bgcolor
```

```
self.document.bgcolor
```

```
document.bgcolor
```

Although it is technically possible to combine multiple references within a single-frame window, as in `window.self.document.bgcolor`, you should use such references only in a multiple-frame window.

Suppose you have a multiple-frame document, and you want to reference an object that belongs to a specific frame from that same frame. One option is to simply specify that object using a common syntax. Specifying the `self` object, however, can make the script crystal clear and its debugging much easier. You can use the following code, for instance, to display the title of that frame:

```
alert(self.document.title)
```

In summary, when the HTML document appears in one frame of a multiple-frame document, it is recommended to precede all `window` object references with the `self` object.

Note that you can also precede all function calls with the `self` object specification:

```
self.functionName()
```

parent

A script running in a frame of a multiframe document can reference objects or properties of its parent document (the one that sets the frames) via the `parent` property.

Figure 26-6 shows the exact relations between a frame-setting document and its frames.

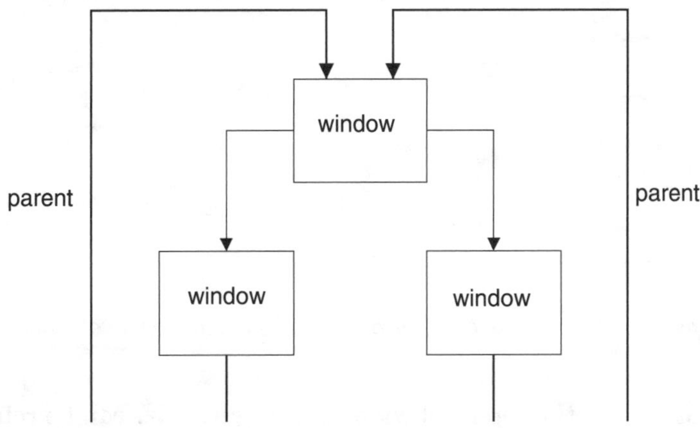

***Figure 26-6**. The structure of a multiple-frame window.*

Notice that the `window` object of the frame-setting document is equivalent to the `window.parent` (or `self.parent` or `parent`) of a document in one of the frames. In a way, since it points to a higher level of hierarchy, the `parent` property may seem to violate the object hierarchy rules.

A child window can also call a function of the parent window. The reference would be as follows:

```
parent.functionName([arguments])
```

The `parent` property of a frame's `window` object does not always point to the top-level window. If one of the children of the top-level window is also a frame-setting window, then you wind up with three levels of hierarchies. The `parent` property of the bottom level of hierarchy points to the second one. Figure 26-7 demonstrates this concept.

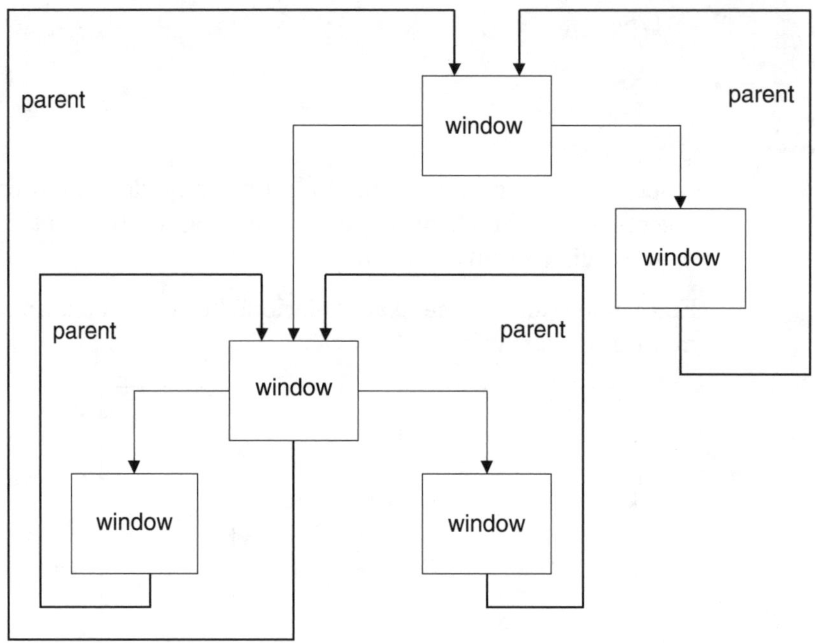

Figure 26-7*. The "youngest" child's parent is not the top-level window.*

Notice that the top-level window in Figure 26-7 can be referenced from the "youngest" child as `window.parent.parent`. We recommend that you draw such flowcharts when you design a site with deeply nested frames. (See the section "Nested Frames," earlier in this chapter, for a discussion of the different types of nesting.)

top

The window object's top property refers to the topmost window in a JavaScript hierarchy. For a single-frame window, top is equivalent to window, which in turn is equivalent to self and parent. In a multiple-frame window, the top object always reflects the topmost window that defines the first frameset. In a window that contains several frames, where at least one of the frames also contains a frameset, the top property of all window objects (including all generations in the hierarchy) refers to the window with the first frameset. In terms of flowcharts, the top property always refers to the highest rectangle.

Take another look at Figure 26-7. The top-level window can be referenced from the "youngest" child as parent.parent, top, window.top, or self.top.

frames

In a multiple-frame window, all frames act like full-fledged window objects. The frames property plays an important role when a statement in one frame must access an object or property located in a different frame.

The frames property is an array that reflects all direct children of a given window object. The property window.frames.length reflects the number of direct children from the point of view of that window object.

The browser stores information about all visible frames in an indexed array, where the first frame is stored in index 0:

```
window.frames[0]
```

Since you should never deeply nest frames using several frame-setting documents, the frames array should usually be referenced as parent.frames or top.frames. Suppose you have a window divided into three frames. You can access the title of the second frame from a script in the first frame as parent.frames[1].document.title.

You can also access frames by their names. You can use the following syntax to retrieve (from any frame) the background color of a document in a frame named myFrame:

```
parent.myFrame.document.bgcolor
```

You can also refer to the frames array as an associative array, in the following fashion:

```
parent.frames["myFrame"].document.bgcolor
```

Consider a window divided into three frames, all defined in a single frameset. The hierarchy is illustrated in Figure 26-8.

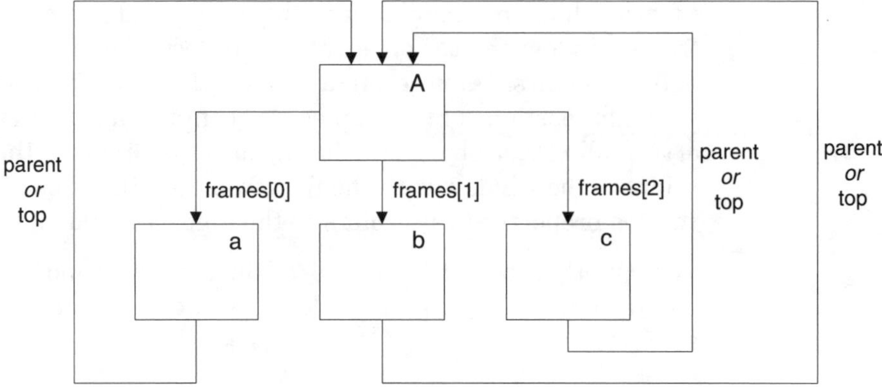

Figure 26-8*. The complete object hierarchy of a frameset window that defines three frames.*

You can use Figure 26-8 to trace the following references in this structure:

```
parent // references A from a, A from b, or A from c
parent.frames[0] // references a from b, a from c
parent.frames[1] // references b from a, b from c
parent.frames[2] // references c from a, c from b
frames[0] // references a from A
frames[1] // references b from A
frames[2] // references c from A
```

An Example—the Color Center

The Color Center is a JavaScript application that enables the user to test a variety of colors in order to find the best configurations for his or her Web site. There are five distinct attributes that play a role in this tool:

- `bgcolor`—the background color
- `link`—the color of standard links
- `alink`—the color of active links

- `vlink`—the color of visited links
- `text`—the color of plain text

The Color Center is compatible with both IE and Navigator. It is divided into three frames, as shown in Figure 26-9. The upper frame includes the red, green, and blue text fields which display the RGB values of the current color. It also features a menu enabling the user to select the attribute (one of five) that he or she wants to customize. A Save button stores the settings in a cookie, and a Load button retrieves them from the cookie.

The left frame displays the Color Cube—a complete set of 216 non-dithering colors. It is almost identical to Example 21-1 (in Chapter 21, The document Object—Colors, Output, and Properties). The user can select a color from the Color Cube and assign it to the attribute selected in the upper frame.

The right frame is the most simple one. Its initial document does not contain any data besides the basic HTML tags. Its content is generated by `document.write()` statements, executed in the parent frame-setting document.

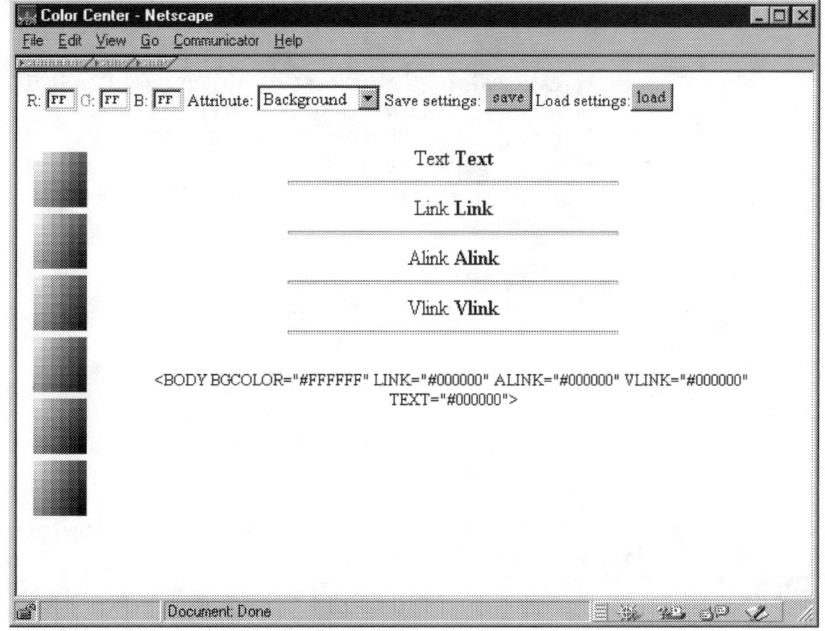

Figure 26-9. *The Color Center is divided into three frames with invisible borders.*

The Frame-setting window

Example 26-2 shows the frame-setting document.

```
<HTML>
<HEAD>
<TITLE>Color Center</TITLE>
<SCRIPT LANGUAGE="JavaScript">
<!--

// Boolean variable specified if alert should be displayed if
                    cookie exceeds 4KB
var caution = false
deleteCookie("slot")
// name - name of the cookie
// value - value of the cookie
// [expires] - expiration date of the cookie (defaults to end of
                         current session)
// [path] - path for which the cookie is valid (defaults to path of
                         calling document)
// [domain] - domain for which the cookie is valid (defaults to domain
                         of calling document)
// [secure] - Boolean value indicating if the cookie transmission
                         requires a secure transmission
// * an argument defaults when it is assigned null as a placeholder
// * a null placeholder is not required for trailing omitted arguments
function setCookie(name, value, expires, path, domain, secure) {
     var curCookie = name + "=" + escape(value) +
          ((expires) ? "; expires=" + expires.toGMTString() : "") +
          ((path) ? "; path=" + path : "") +
          ((domain) ? "; domain=" + domain : "") +
          ((secure) ? "; secure" : "")
     if (!caution || (name + "=" + escape(value)).length <= 4000)
          document.cookie = curCookie
     else
          if (confirm("Cookie exceeds 4KB and will be cut!"))
               document.cookie = curCookie
}

// name - name of the desired cookie
// * return string containing value of specified cookie or null if
                         cookie does not exist
function getCookie(name) {
     var prefix = name + "="
     var cookieStartIndex = document.cookie.indexOf(prefix)
     if (cookieStartIndex == -1)
          return null
     var cookieEndIndex = document.cookie.indexOf(";", cookieStartIndex
                         + prefix.length)
     if (cookieEndIndex == -1)
          cookieEndIndex = document.cookie.length
```

```
     return unescape(document.cookie.substring(cookieStartIndex
                         + prefix.length, cookieEndIndex))
}

// name - name of the cookie
// [path] - path of the cookie (must be same as path used to
                         create cookie)
// [domain] - domain of the cookie (must be same as domain used to
                         create cookie)
// * path and domain default if assigned null or omitted if no explicit
                         argument proceeds
function deleteCookie(name, path, domain) {
     if (getCookie(name)) {
          document.cookie = name + "=" +
          ((path) ? "; path=" + path : "") +
          ((domain) ? "; domain=" + domain : "") +
          "; expires=Thu, 01-Jan-70 00:00:01 GMT"
     }
}

// date - any instance of the Date object
// * you should hand all instances of the Date object to this function
                         for "repairs"
// * this function is taken from Chapter 14, Time and Date in JavaScript,
                         in "Learn Advanced JavaScript Programming"
function fixDate(date) {
     var base = new Date(0)
     var skew = base.getTime()
     if (skew > 0)
          date.setTime(date.getTime() - skew)
}

// updates the R, G, and B text fields (invoked as a method)
function display() {
     frames[0].document.forms[0].red.value = this.r
     frames[0].document.forms[0].green.value = this.g
     frames[0].document.forms[0].blue.value = this.b
}

// constructs an attribute
function makeAttribute(r, g, b) {
     this.r = r + ""
     this.g = g + ""
     this.b = b + ""
     this.display = display
}

// create instances for all attributes
var link = new makeAttribute("00", "00", "00") // black
var alink = new makeAttribute("00", "00", "00") // black
var vlink = new makeAttribute("00", "00", "00") // black
var text = new makeAttribute("00", "00", "00") // black
```

```
var bgcolor = new makeAttribute("FF", "FF", "FF") // white

// invoked when user selects a color from swatches
function select(r, g, b) {
     // assign string reflecting selected attribute ("text", "bgcolor",
etc.)
     var attribute = curAttribute()

     // assign new descriptors
     eval(attribute).r = r
     eval(attribute).g = g
     eval(attribute).b = b

     // display new descriptors in R, G, and B text fields
     eval(attribute).display()

     // update main frame
     update()
}

// return string reflecting selected attribute ("text", "bgcolor", etc.)
function curAttribute() {
     var list = frames[0].document.forms[0].attribute
     return list.options[list.selectedIndex].value
}

// returns <BODY> tag (excluding ">" and "<") reflecting all selections
function bodyDefinition() {
     var str = 'BODY '
     str += 'BGCOLOR="#' + bgcolor.r + bgcolor.g + bgcolor.b + '" '
     str += 'LINK="#' + link.r + link.g + link.b + '" '
     str += 'ALINK="#' + alink.r + alink.g + alink.b + '" '
     str += 'VLINK="#' + vlink.r + vlink.g + vlink.b + '" '
     str += 'TEXT="#' + text.r + text.g + text.b + '"'
     return str
}

// update main window
function update() {
     var bodyDef = bodyDefinition()
     var result = ""
     result += '<HTML><HEAD><TITLE>Main</TITLE></HEAD>'
     result += '<' + bodyDef + '>'
     result += '<CENTER>'
     result += 'Text <B>Text</B><HR WIDTH=50%>'
     result += '<FONT COLOR="#' + link.r + link.g + link.b + '">
                         Link <B>Link</B><HR WIDTH=50%></FONT>'
     result += '<FONT COLOR="#' + alink.r + alink.g + alink.b + '">
                         Alink <B>Alink</B><HR WIDTH=50%></FONT>'
     result += '<FONT COLOR="#' + vlink.r + vlink.g + vlink.b + '">
                         Vlink <B>Vlink</B><HR WIDTH=50%></FONT>'
     result += '<BR><FONT SIZE=2>&lt;' + bodyDef + '&gt;</FONT>'
```

```
		result += '</CENTER></BODY></HTML>'

		// assign document object of main frame to local variable
		var doc = frames[2].document

		// close data stream to document
		doc.close()

		// open new data stream to document (text/html)
		doc.open('text/html')

		// print HTML content
		doc.write(result)

		// close data stream to document
		doc.close()
	}

	// stores all selections as a cookie
	function save() {
		var slot = link.r + link.g + link.b +
				alink.r + alink.g + alink.b +
				vlink.r + vlink.g + vlink.b +
				text.r + text.g + text.b +
				bgcolor.r + bgcolor.g + bgcolor.b
		var now = new Date()
		fixDate(now)
		now.setTime(now.getTime() + 31 * 24 * 60 * 60 * 1000) // one month
		setCookie("slot", slot, now)
	}

	// load values from cookie (concatenation order in save() matters!)
	function load() {
		var slot = getCookie("slot")
		if (slot != null) {
			link.r = slot.substring(0, 2)
			link.g = slot.substring(2, 4)
			link.b = slot.substring(4, 6)
			alink.r = slot.substring(6, 8)
			alink.g = slot.substring(8, 10)
			alink.b = slot.substring(10, 12)
			vlink.r = slot.substring(12, 14)
			vlink.g = slot.substring(14, 16)
			vlink.b = slot.substring(16, 18)
			text.r = slot.substring(18, 20)
			text.g = slot.substring(20, 22)
			text.b = slot.substring(22, 24)
			bgcolor.r = slot.substring(24, 26)
			bgcolor.g = slot.substring(26, 28)
			bgcolor.b = slot.substring(28, 30)
			eval(curAttribute()).display()
			update()
```

```
    }
}

// -->
</SCRIPT>
</HEAD>
<FRAMESET
    ROWS="50, *"
    BORDER="0"
    FRAMEBORDER="no"
    FRAMESPACING="0"
    BORDERCOLOR="#ffffff">
    <FRAME
        NAME="control"
        SRC="ex26-2a.htm"
        NORESIZE
        SCROLLING="no">
    <FRAMESET
        COLS="80, *"
        BORDER="0"
        FRAMEBORDER="no"
        FRAMESPACING="0"
        BORDERCOLOR="#ffffff">
        <FRAME
            NAME="swatches"
            SRC="ex26-2b.htm"
            NORESIZE
            SCROLLING="no">
        <FRAME
            NAME="main"
            SRC="ex26-2c.htm"
            NORESIZE>
    </FRAMESET>
</FRAMESET>
<NOFRAMES>Please download a frames-capable browser!</NOFRAMES>
</HTML>
```

Example 26-2 (ex26-2.htm). *The frame-setting document serves as a "control center," because it contains most of the scripts that connect between the other frames.*

The first portion of the script in Example 26-2 consists of a complete set of cookie functions, which are not repeated here. This chapter focuses on functions which are specific to the Color Center application.

display(r, g, b)

```
// updates the R, G, and B text fields (invoked as a method)
function display() {
    frames[0].document.forms[0].red.value = this.r
```

```
        frames[0].document.forms[0].green.value = this.g
        frames[0].document.forms[0].blue.value = this.b
}
```

All attributes are defined as instances supporting the `display()` method. You can call this function, for example, to display the color of `bgcolor`:

```
bgcolor.display()
```

The `display()` method sets the values of the R, G, and B fields in the upper frame to the corresponding RGB values of the calling instance. Those values, named `r`, `g`, and `b`, are stored as properties of the calling instance.

The upper frame is the first frame to be defined, so we reference it as `frames[0]`. You can alternatively use `self.frames[0]`, `window.frames[0]`, `parent.frames[0]`, or `top.frames[0]`.

makeAttribute(r, g, b)

```
// constructs an attribute
function makeAttribute(r, g, b) {
        this.r = r + ""
        this.g = g + ""
        this.b = b + ""
        this.display = display
}
```

`makeAttribute()` is a constructor function. All attributes are created as instances of this object, so each attribute has three properties (`r`, `g`, and `b`) and one method (`display()`). The function accepts three arguments representing the red, green, and blue descriptors. Just to be on the safe side, the arguments are converted to strings.

Global Statements

```
// create instances for all attributes
var link = new makeAttribute("00", "00", "00") // black
var alink = new makeAttribute("00", "00", "00") // black
var vlink = new makeAttribute("00", "00", "00") // black
var text = new makeAttribute("00", "00", "00") // black
var bgcolor = new makeAttribute("FF", "FF", "FF") // white
```

We define five global variables in this script segment. All variables are defined as instances of the `makeAttribute` object. The arguments handed to the `makeAttribute()` function reflect the default colors for each attribute.

select(r, g, b)

```
// invoked when user selects a color from swatches
function select(r, g, b) {
     // assign string reflecting selected attribute ("text",
                         "bgcolor", etc.)
     var attribute = curAttribute()

     // assign new descriptors
     eval(attribute).r = r
     eval(attribute).g = g
     eval(attribute).b = b

     // display new descriptors in R, G, and B text fields
     eval(attribute).display()

     // update main frame
     update()
}
```

The `select()` function is invoked when the user selects a color from the swatches in the left frame, and it accepts the red, green, and blue descriptors of the selected color. The function first assigns the currently selected attribute to the local variable `attribute`. For example, if the current attribute (chosen from the menu in the upper frame) is "Visited link," the value of `attribute` is `"vlink"`. Therefore, `eval(attribute)` is an instance of the `makeAttribute` object, holding the red, green, and blue descriptors of the attribute.

curAttribute()

```
// return string reflecting selected attribute ("text", "bgcolor", etc.)
function curAttribute() {
     var list = frames[0].document.forms[0].attribute
     return list.options[list.selectedIndex].value
}
```

This function returns the currently selected attribute in the form of a string. First, the object representing the `select` element of the form in the upper frame is assigned to the local variable `list`. The text value of the selected option is then returned. As shown above, it is often convenient to assign an object reference to a local variable, especially when that reference is extremely lengthy. In this case, we specify the variable `list` twice, instead of specifying twice the entire object reference, `frames[0].document.forms[0].attribute`.

bodyDefinition()

```
// returns <BODY> tag (excluding ">" and "<") reflecting all selections
function bodyDefinition() {
     var str = 'BODY '
     str += 'BGCOLOR="#' + bgcolor.r + bgcolor.g + bgcolor.b + '" '
     str += 'LINK="#' + link.r + link.g + link.b + '" '
     str += 'ALINK="#' + alink.r + alink.g + alink.b + '" '
     str += 'VLINK="#' + vlink.r + vlink.g + vlink.b + '" '
     str += 'TEXT="#' + text.r + text.g + text.b + '"'
     return str
}
```

The bodyDefinition() function constructs and returns a complete <BODY> tag, based on the current values of the descriptors of each attribute. For instance, the function might return the following string:

```
BODY BGCOLOR="#FFFFCC" LINK="#FF00CC" ALINK="#00FF99" VLINK="#006633"
TEXT="#0000FF"
```

Notice that we do not include the less than ("<") and greater than (">") characters in the final string.

update()

```
// update main window
function update() {
     var bodyDef = bodyDefinition()
     var result = ""
     result += '<HTML><HEAD><TITLE>Main</TITLE></HEAD>'
     result += '<' + bodyDef + '>'
     result += '<CENTER>'
     result += 'Text <B>Text</B><HR WIDTH=50%>'
     result += '<FONT COLOR="#' + link.r + link.g + link.b + '">
                    Link <B>Link</B><HR WIDTH=50%></FONT>'
     result += '<FONT COLOR="#' + alink.r + alink.g + alink.b + '">
                    Alink <B>Alink</B><HR WIDTH=50%></FONT>'
     result += '<FONT COLOR="#' + vlink.r + vlink.g + vlink.b + '">
                    Vlink <B>Vlink</B><HR WIDTH=50%></FONT>'
     result += '<BR><FONT SIZE=2>&lt;' + bodyDef + '&gt;</FONT>'
     result += '</CENTER></BODY></HTML>'

     // assign document object of main frame to local variable
     var doc = frames[2].document

     // close data stream to document
     doc.close()

     // open new data stream to document (text/html)
     doc.open('text/html')
```

26 Chapter

```
        // print HTML content
        doc.write(result)

        // close data stream to document
        doc.close()
}
```

The update() function generates the HTML content of the main frame (the right one). The first portion of the function simply assigns the new HTML document to the local variable result. We then assign the document object of that frame window to the local variable doc. In order to replace the old HTML content with the newly generated one, we close the current data stream to the right frame document and reopen a new one to it. Since there is no apparent reason for the current data stream to be open, its closing is optional, and is done here just to be on the safe side. Forgetting to reopen the data stream, though, will crash the browser under certain situations. Since we are printing ASCII text with HTML formatting, we specify the MIME type as text/html, which is also the default MIME value. After printing the entire HTML content to the frame's document via the write() method, we close the data stream. Note that it is very important to open a stream before printing to a document, and to close the stream afterwards. The close() method displays text or images that were previously sent to layout.

save()

```
// stores all selections as a cookie
function save() {
        var slot = link.r + link.g + link.b +
                   alink.r + alink.g + alink.b +
                   vlink.r + vlink.g + vlink.b +
                   text.r + text.g + text.b +
                   bgcolor.r + bgcolor.g + bgcolor.b
        var now = new Date()
        fixDate(now)
        now.setTime(now.getTime() + 31 * 24 * 60 * 60 * 1000) // one month
        setCookie("slot", slot, now)
}
```

This function combines the descriptors of all attributes to one string and stores it as a cookie, set to expire one month later. Since the load() function relies on the order in which the descriptors are concatenated, the order cannot be altered.

load()

```
// load values from cookie (concatenation order in save() matters!)
function load() {
     var slot = getCookie("slot")
     if (slot != null) {
          link.r = slot.substring(0, 2)
          link.g = slot.substring(2, 4)
          link.b = slot.substring(4, 6)
          alink.r = slot.substring(6, 8)
          alink.g = slot.substring(8, 10)
          alink.b = slot.substring(10, 12)
          vlink.r = slot.substring(12, 14)
          vlink.g = slot.substring(14, 16)
          vlink.b = slot.substring(16, 18)
          text.r = slot.substring(18, 20)
          text.g = slot.substring(20, 22)
          text.b = slot.substring(22, 24)
          bgcolor.r = slot.substring(24, 26)
          bgcolor.g = slot.substring(26, 28)
          bgcolor.b = slot.substring(28, 30)
          eval(curAttribute()).display()
          update()
     }
}
```

The `load()` function retrieves the descriptors for each attribute stored in the cookie. If the cookie does not exist (the user did not press "Save" within the last month), the function is terminated. Otherwise the function extracts each descriptor from the string and assigns it to the corresponding property. The function then displays the new values in the upper frame and updates the main frame accordingly.

HTML

```
<FRAMESET
     ROWS="50, *"
     BORDER="0"
     FRAMEBORDER="no"
     FRAMESPACING="0"
     BORDERCOLOR="#ffffff">
     <FRAME
          NAME="control"
          SRC="ex26-3a.htm"
          NORESIZE
          SCROLLING="no">
     <FRAMESET
          COLS="80, *"
          BORDER="0"
          FRAMEBORDER="no"
```

```
            FRAMESPACING="0"
            BORDERCOLOR="#ffffff">
            <FRAME
                NAME="swatches"
                SRC="ex26-3b.htm"
                NORESIZE
                SCROLLING="no">
            <FRAME
                NAME="main"
                SRC="ex26-3c.htm"
                NORESIZE>
        </FRAMESET>
</FRAMESET>
<NOFRAMES>Please download a frames-capable browser!</NOFRAMES>
```

As you can see, all frames are defined in one frame-setting document. The upper frame is named "control," the bottom left frame is named "swatches," and the bottom right frame is named "main." Their URLs are `ex26-3a.htm`, `ex26-3b.htm`, and `ex26-3c.htm`, respectively. Notice the configurations used to create "borderless" frames.

The "control" Frame

Example 26-2a shows that the upper frame consists of very little JavaScript. The only JavaScript in this document is used to interact with the JavaScript objects in the frame-setting window (`self.top` or `self.parent`).

```
<HTML>
<HEAD>
<TITLE>Control Panel</TITLE>
<SCRIPT LANGUAGE="JavaScript">
<!--

function display() {
    top[top.curAttribute()].display()
}

// -->
</SCRIPT>
</HEAD>
<BODY BGCOLOR="#ffffff" onLoad="self.display()">
<FORM>
<FONT SIZE=2>
<FONT COLOR="#ff0000">R</FONT>:
<INPUT TYPE="text" SIZE=3 VALUE="" NAME="red" onFocus="this.blur()">
<FONT COLOR="#00ff00">G</FONT>:
<INPUT TYPE="text" SIZE=3 VALUE="" NAME="green" onFocus="this.blur()">
<FONT COLOR="#0000ff">B</FONT>:
<INPUT TYPE="text" SIZE=3 VALUE="" NAME="blue" onFocus="this.blur()">
Attribute:
```

```
<SELECT NAME="attribute" onChange="self.display()">
<OPTION VALUE="bgcolor">Background
<OPTION VALUE="text">Text
<OPTION VALUE="link">Link
<OPTION VALUE="alink">Active link
<OPTION VALUE="vlink">Visited link
</SELECT>
Save settings:
<INPUT TYPE="button" VALUE="save" onClick="top.save()">
Load settings:<INPUT TYPE="button" VALUE="load" onClick="top.load()">
</FONT>
</FORM>
</BODY>
</HTML>
```

Example 26-2a (ex26-2a.htm)*. The "control" frame consists of mostly plain HTML.*

display()

```
function display() {
	top[top.curAttribute()].display()
}
```

The script in the "control" frame's document consists of just one function, `display()`. There is a function named `display()` in the frame-setting document as well, but due to JavaScript's object hierarchy, each function is actually a method of a different object. The `display()` function in the "control" frame document invokes the `display()` function of the frame-setting document as a method of the selected attribute's instance. For example, if the selected attribute is "Background color," the function's statement is equivalent to:

```
top.bgcolor.display()
```


Event Handlers

The "control" frame's document features an `onLoad` event handler that invokes the local `display()` function. This is why the text fields in the upper frame are not empty when you first load the Color Center application. When the user selects a new option, the `onChange` event handler, associated with the select object, invokes the local `display()` function.

Notice that the text fields in this frame are read-only, thanks to the `onFocus` event handler which, whenever the user attempts to gain focus, immediately issues the `blur()` method to remove focus from the field. This "trick" does not work under IE 3.0x.

Both the Save and the Load buttons feature `onClick` event handlers which invoke the corresponding functions in the frame-setting document.

The "swatches" Frame

```
<HTML>
<HEAD>
<TITLE>Swatches</TITLE>
</HEAD>
<BODY BGCOLOR="#ffffff">
<SCRIPT LANGUAGE="JavaScript">
<!--

// create 6-element array
var hex = new Array(6)

// assign non-dithered descriptors
hex[0] = "FF"
hex[1] = "CC"
hex[2] = "99"
hex[3] = "66"
hex[4] = "33"
hex[5] = "00"

// accept triplet string and display as background color
function display(triplet) {
     // set color as background color
     self.document.bgColor = '#' + triplet

     // display the color hexadecimal triplet
     self.alert('Background color is now ' + triplet)
}

// draw a single table cell based on all descriptors
function drawCell(red, green, blue) {
     // open cell with specified hexadecimal triplet background color
     self.document.write('<TD BGCOLOR="#' + red + green + blue + '">')

     // open a hypertext link with javascript: scheme to call display
                         function
     self.document.write('<A HREF="javascript:top.select(\'' + (red + '\',
                         \'' + green + '\', \'' + blue) + '\')">')

     // print transparent image (use any height and width)
     self.document.write('<IMG SRC="place.gif" BORDER=0 HEIGHT=7
                         WIDTH=7>')

     // close link tag
     self.document.write('</A>')
```

```
          // close table cell
          self.document.write('</TD>')
     }

     // draw table row based on red and blue descriptors
     function drawRow(red, blue) {
          // open table row
          self.document.write('<TR>')

          // loop through all non-dithered color descripters as green hex
          for (var i = 0; i < 6; ++i) {
               drawCell(red, hex[i], blue)
          }

          // close current table row
          self.document.write('</TR>')
     }

     // draw table for one of six color cube panels
     function drawTable(blue) {
          // open table (one of six cube panels)
          self.document.write('<TABLE CELLPADDING=0 CELLSPACING=0 BORDER=0>')

          // loop through all non-dithered color descripters as red hex
          for (var i = 0; i < 6; ++i) {
               drawRow(hex[i], blue)
          }

          // close current table
          self.document.write('</TABLE>')
     }

     // draw all cube panels inside table cells
     function drawCube() {
          // open table
          self.document.write('<TABLE CELLPADDING=0 CELLSPACING=5 BORDER=0>')

          // loop through all non-dithered color descripters as blue hex
          for (var i = 0; i < 6; ++i) {
               // open table cell with white background color
               self.document.write('<TR><TD>')

               // call function to create cube panel with hex[i] blue hex
               drawTable(hex[i])

               // close current table cell
               self.document.write('</TD></TR>')
          }

          // close table row and table
          self.document.write('</TABLE>')
     }
```

```
// call function to begin execution
drawCube()

// -->
</SCRIPT>
</BODY>
</HTML>
```

***Example 26-2b (ex26-2b.htm)**. The "swatches" frame displays the Color Cube, consisting of all 216 non-dithering colors.*

The "swatches" frame's document is almost identical to Example 21-1 in Chapter 21. The major differences are as follows:

1. The `self` reference was added to precede all objects, methods, and properties of the frame window.
2. Each face of the Color Cube appears on a distinct table row, so the Color Cube is drawn vertically, in order to match the frame's physical dimensions.
3. Each color is a link to the frame-setting document's `select()` function. Instead of using one string of six characters as the argument, we invoke the function with three strings of two characters each, one for each descriptor (red, green, and blue).

The "main" Frame

Here is the complete source for the main frame:

```
<HTML>
<HEAD>
<TITLE>Main</TITLE>
</HEAD>
<BODY onLoad="top.update()">
</BODY>
</HTML>
```

***Example 26-2c (ex26-2c.htm)**. The "main" frame does not require any content because the frame-setting window dynamically generates its HTML content.*

Notice the `onLoad` event handler which invokes the `update()` function of the frame-setting document's script.

Frames, Events, and Event Handlers

Using Event Handlers Within a Frame

A child frame normally contains an HTML document. As opposed to a frame-setting document, an HTML document in a child frame is structured as a standard HTML document:

```
<HTML>
<HEAD>
<TITLE></TITLE>
</HEAD>
<BODY>
</BODY>
</HTML>
```

You can load any document in a frame, regardless of its content. If a frame does not contain another frame-setting document, you can use any event handler in its document. You can issue, for example, an onLoad event handler in the <BODY> tag, an onSubmit event handler in a <FORM> tag, and so forth.

HTML documents that users see in frames of a multiple-frame browser window are different from the frame-setting document, in that the latter remains in memory and is not otherwise visible to the user. It only instructs the browser to divide the window into sections, and assigns a visible document to each one of them. Since a child frame's document is visible, it can consist of forms, links, image maps, images, etc., which are rich in events and event handlers. As a document in a frame behaves exactly like a document in a single-frame browser window, the common event handler rules apply.

Using Event Handlers in a Frame-Setting Document

A frame-setting document differs from a regular HTML document in that it is not visible, and, therefore, does not include any output-generating HTML tags. Nevertheless, a frame-setting document can feature several event handlers which are very important for a frame set.

All event handlers that you normally issue within a <BODY> tag can be issued within a <FRAMESET> tag. An onLoad event handler within a <FRAMESET> tag, for example, specifies a JavaScript code to be executed when all frames defined in that frameset have finished loading. Therefore, the onLoad event handler in the <BODY> tag of a child frame triggers before the onLoad event handler in the <FRAMESET> tag. When all frames under its control have finished loading, the frameset that governs the frames receives a separate `load` event.

onFocus and onBlur

Netscape Navigator 3.0 introduced a new functionality to the `onFocus` and `onBlur` event handlers. You can use these event handlers to capture `focus` and `blur` events that are associated with a frame. A frame gains focus when the user clicks anywhere in that frame or issues a focus event in an element of that frame. A frame's `blur` event occurs when the frame loses focus.

There are two equivalent ways to specify an `onFocus` or an `onBlur` event handler for a single frame:

1. In the `<BODY>` tag of the frame's document.
2. In the `<FRAMESET>` tag of the frame-setting document. You can execute, for example, the statement `frames[0].onfocus = display` from a script within the frame-setting document. An event handler specified using this technique overrides an event handler issued in the child frame's `<BODY>` tag.

Never use an `alert()` method or any other dialog box within a frame's `onFocus` event handler. Doing so results in an endless loop: When you press OK to dismiss the alert, the underlying window gains focus again, and produces another `focus` event.

The following `<BODY>` definition of a frame's document demonstrates a common usage of the `onBlur` and `onFocus` event handlers:

```
<BODY BGCOLOR="lightgray" onBlur="document.bgColor='lightgray'"
onFocus="document.bgColor='antiquewhite'">
```

The frame's background color depends on whether or not the frame has focus.

Emulating Events

As with many other events, you can emulate the `blur` and `focus` events via their corresponding methods. You can use, for instance, the following statement to focus on the first frame from the point of view of another frame:

```
self.parent.frames[0].focus()
```

The same applies to the `blur()` method:

```
self.parent.frames[0].blur()
```

Since it is barely noticeable when a frame gains or loses focus, these methods are not that useful. They are not supported altogether by IE 3.0x.

Targeting Multiple Frames

Creating a link in one frame to load a document in a different frame requires a simple HTML attribute—TARGET. Consider the following frameset:

```
<FRAMESET ROWS="150, *">
     <FRAME NAME="one" SRC="docA.htm">
     <FRAMESET COLS="120, *">
          <FRAME NAME="two" SRC="docB.htm">
          <FRAME NAME="three" SRC="docC.htm">
     </FRAMESET>
</FRAMESET>
```

A link in docA.htm that loads Netscape's homepage in the right frame (three) would use the following syntax:

```
<A HREF="http://www.netscape.com/" TARGET="three">Netscape</A>
```

Now suppose you want a single link in docA.htm to load both Netscape's page in the frame named three and Microsoft's page in the frame named two. JavaScript's object hierarchy enables such operations:

```
<SCRIPT LANGUAGE="JavaScript">
<!--

function loadPages() {
     parent.two.location.href = 'http://www.microsoft.com/'
     parent.three.location.href = 'http://www.netscape.com/'
}

// -->
</SCRIPT>
<A HREF="javascript:loadPages()">Microsoft and Netscape</A>
```


Summary

Frames are widely used because they enable Web site designers to organize data in a pleasant, structured format. Frames are very easy to handle with JavaScript. An understanding of the JavaScript object model is required in order to take advantage of the language's powerful frame-handling features. Some frame operations can be accomplished only by JavaScript. The only way, for example, to load several documents in different frames when the user clicks a link is by scripting the link's event handler via JavaScript. Referencing objects in JavaScript can be done with the `self`, `window`, or no prefix at all. Mastering frames usually requires practice. After creating a few JavaScript applications with frames, you will have the knowledge to do virtually anything with frames. In the following chapter, we take a look at creating and handling browser windows with JavaScript. Windows are very similar to frames.

Chapter 27

Windows

What are Windows?

When you load your browser application (Netscape Navigator or Microsoft Internet Explorer), a window immediately appears. This window is known as a *browser window*, or a *window* for short. Figure 27-1 shows a single image.

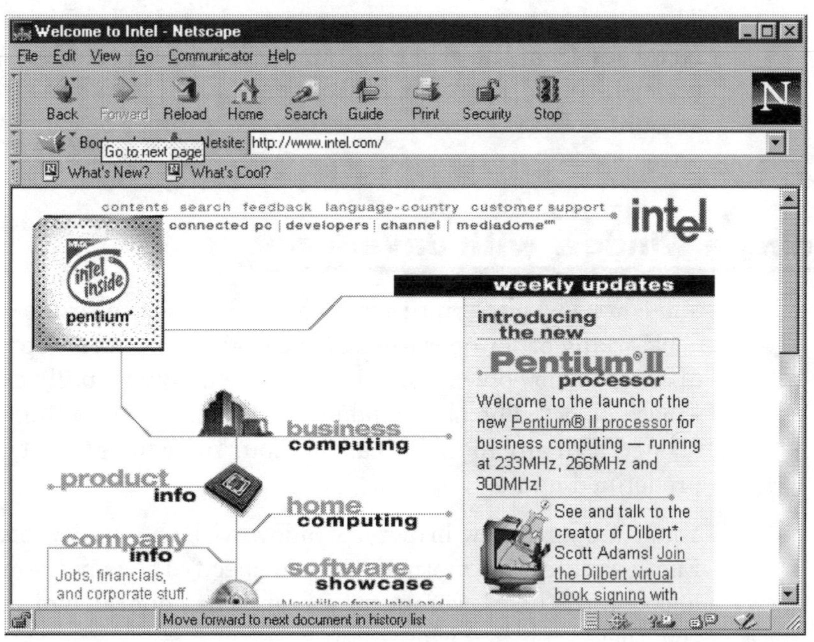

Figure 27-1. A standard browser window.

A browser window does not have to feature buttons, a location field, and so on. As a matter of fact, a browser window can consist of only the content zone and a title bar, as shown in Figure 27-2.

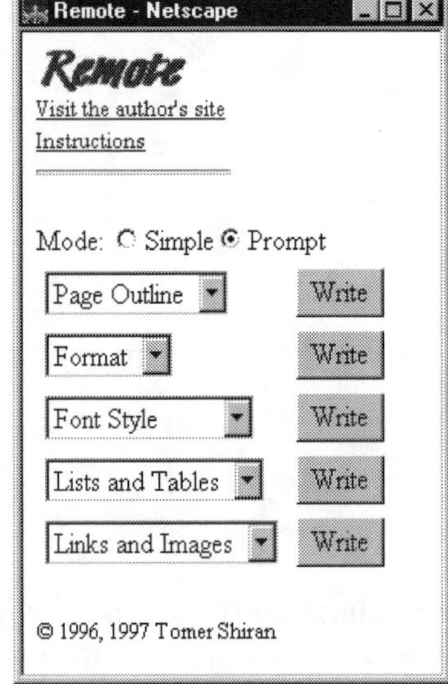

Figure 27-2*. A browser window does not have to contain a status bar, menus, and other navigation tools.*

It is possible to have several browser windows simultaneously open. The simplest way to open a window is by selecting **New Web Browser** from the File menu under Navigator, or **New Window** under Internet Explorer. Since each window requires a reasonable amount of RAM, there is a limit to the number of windows you can open.

Opening a Window with JavaScript

You can use JavaScript to open a window, as the result of a button click or any other operations. Since each window is represented as a distinct `window` object, opening a new window actually creates another `window` object. The new window is not connected to the window that opened it in any hierarchical relation. You can access it, though, by its predefined name.

You can open a new browser window with the `window.open()` method. Furthermore, this method lets you specify the way the new window looks on the user's computer screen. The general syntax of the `window.open()` method is as follows:

```
[windowVar = ][window].open("URL", "windowName", ["windowFeatures"])
```

"`windowVar =` " is required if you want to establish a connection between the current window and the new one. You can use this variable to reference the window object of the new window. Consider, for example, the following statement:

```
var homeWindow = open("http://www.geocities.com", "geo")
```

This statement creates a new window of the same dimensions and features as if it were opened through the browser's File menu. The initial document loaded into the new window is http://www.geocities.com, but a new one can be loaded via a script in the original window, using such a statement as:

```
homeWindow.location.href = "http://www.netscent.com/"
```

Since it is impossible to access a window's properties without assigning its object reference to a variable, it is a good practice to specify a variable for every window you create via JavaScript. Also, in order to ensure control over the window throughout the script, it is better to use a global variable rather than a local one. This is why some JavaScript programmers never use the var keyword with the window.open() method.

There are many reasons for a new window to fail during opening. Lack of resources and closing by the user are only two possibilities. Before addressing any property, method, or function of a window, you should test if that window exists by comparing the variable holding its object reference to null. Here is a simple example:

```
var homeWindow = open("http://www.geocities.com", "geo")
if (homeWindow != null)
      homeWindow.location.href = "http://www.netscent.com/"
```

The first argument accepted by the window.open() method is the URL of the initial document to be loaded in the new window. Use an empty string if you do not want any document to load in the new window. You might want, for example, to open a new window and generate its HTML content via a data stream from the originating window. You would then use the following syntax:

```
var win = open("", "myWindow")
if (win != null) {
      win.document.open("text/html")
      win.document.write("<H1>This is a new window!</H1><HR>")
      win.document.close()
}
```

There are two different open() methods in this script. While the first one is invoked as a method of the window object, the second open() is called as a method of the document object, and is used to open a data stream to the new window's document. Figure 27-3 illustrates these two `open()` methods.

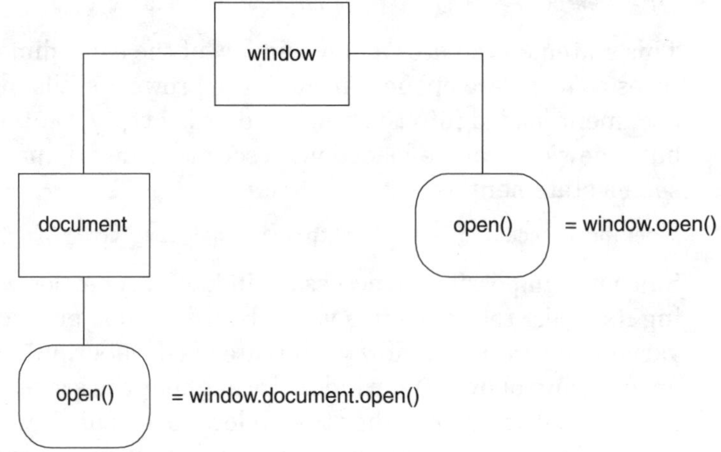

***Figure 27-3**. JavaScript features two different open() methods.*

The `window.open()` method's second argument, *`windowName`*, is the window name to use in the `TARGET` attribute of the `<FORM>` or `<A>` tag. This argument must be a string containing alphanumeric characters and underscores. Do not confuse this value with the variable that is assigned the returned value by the method. A window's name does not play any practical role in terms of JavaScript, but rather enables you to direct documents to that window in the same way you would target a document to a frame. The variable that we assigned `window.open()` method to, on the other hand, has a major role in JavaScript. It is the `window` object of the new window, through which the window's elements can be manipulated. Internet Explorer 3.0x does require a name (an empty one is OK) for every new window. You must use a distinct name for each new window, or else the new window won't open and the contents of the old window bearing the same name will be replaced by the new window's document.

The third argument of the `window.open()` method is a comma-separated list of window features, specified as a single string (enclosed in a single pair of quotes). (Be careful not to specify each feature as an independent argument of the `window.open()` method.) If you omit the `window.open()` method's third argument, the window features default to those of a new window manually opened from the browser's File menu. Any specification for the third argument value, including an empty string, turns off all unspecified attributes of the new window. Table 27-1 lists all window attributes you can control:

***Table 27-1**. The `window.open()` method attributes.*

Attribute	Value	Description (Navigator)	Description (Internet Explorer)
`toolbar`	Boolean	**Back**, **Forward**, and other buttons in that row	**Back**, **Forward**, other buttons in that row, and Address field, displaying the current URL
`location`	Boolean	Field displaying the current URL	N/A (always defaults to the value of `toolbar`)
`directories`	Boolean	**What's new?**, **What's cool?**, and other buttons in that row	N/A (always defaults to the value of `toolbar`)
`status`	Boolean	Status bar at the bottom of the window	Status bar at the bottom of the window
`menubar`	Boolean	Menu bar at the top of the window (File, Edit, View, Go, etc.)	Menu bar at the top of the window (File, Edit, View, Go, etc.)
`scrollbars`	Boolean	Scrollbars if the document is larger than the window (no scrollbars if the document is smaller than the window)	N/A (always defaults to "yes")
`resizable`	Boolean	Elements allowing resizing of window by dragging	N/A (always defaults to "yes")
`width`	Pixels	Window's width in pixels	Window's width in pixels
`height`	Pixels	Window's height in pixels	Window's height in pixels

As is obvious from these major differences, Microsoft Internet Explorer and Netscape Navigator are designed differently. Here are a few minor distinctions:

- Netscape Navigator requires that you either specify both the height and width of the new window, or do not specify them at all. Microsoft Internet Explorer works fine even if you specify only one of the dimensions.
- IE's toolbar includes the section beneath it, which you can alternate between a field displaying the location and fields displaying various directories. Navigator, on the other hand, has a separate attribute for each of these fields.

As menu bars are foreign to the Macintosh OS, the `menubar` option is not supported by browser windows on the Mac.

The attribute copyhistory is omitted from Table 27-1 because it is buggy and tends not to work on some browser-platform combinations. This attribute specifies if the originating window's history list should be copied to the new window. If not specified, the history list of the new window starts from scratch.

As emphasized above, the third argument of the window.open() method is a single string. A call to this function can look like this:

```
var remote = open("http://www.yahoo.com", "win1",
"height=300,width=400,toolbar")
```

First, notice that there are no spaces between the attributes. Then, be aware that there are basically three ways to specify a value for a Boolean attribute (all attributes except for the window's height and width):

1. Literally specifying an attribute's name implicitly assigns it a true value. All nonspecified attributes default to false.
2. Explicitly assigning a Boolean literal to an attribute (e.g., toolbar=false, toolbar=true).
3. Explicitly assigning a binary digit to an attribute, resembling C++'s Boolean values (e.g., toolbar=0, toolbar=1).

You can use the window.open() method to create a customized alert box, for example. Example 27-1 shows a general function for this purpose.

```
<HTML>
<HEAD>
<TITLE>A custom "alert"</TITLE>
<SCRIPT LANGUAGE="JavaScript">
<!--

function pop(height, width, content) {
     win = window.open("", "", "height=" + height + ",width=" + width)
     if (win != null) {
          win.document.open('text/html')
          win.document.write("<HTML><HEAD><TITLE>JavaScript Alert
                         </TITLE></HEAD><BODY>")
          win.document.write(content)
          win.document.write("</BODY></HTML>")
          win.document.close()
     }
}

// -->
```

```
</SCRIPT>
</HEAD>
<BODY>
<FORM>
<INPUT TYPE="button" VALUE="custom alert" onClick="pop(75, 250, 'You
               can use such windows instead of alert dialog boxes!')">
</FORM>
</BODY>
</HTML>
```

***Example 27-1**. A small window can replace the classic alert dialog box.*

This alternative to the built-in `window.alert()` method gives you a way to get rid of the annoying "JavaScript Alert:" message under Netscape Navigator, to size the window as you like, and to display images in the window. Later in this chapter, we show how to keep the window in front of other ones and how to implement an OK button for closing the window.

Figures 27-4 and 27-5 show the windows generated by Example 27-1 under Navigator and IE, respectively.

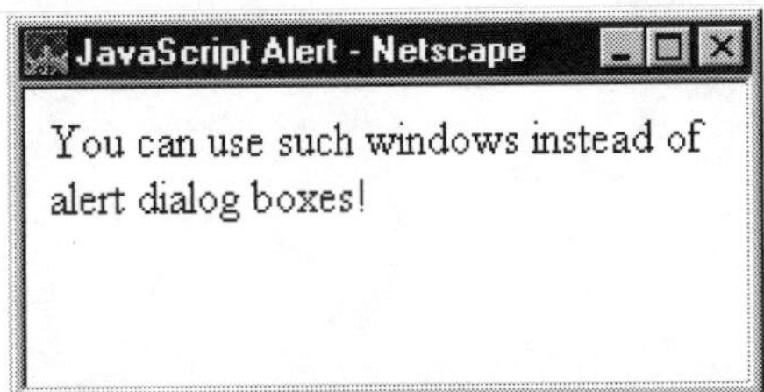

***Figure 27-4**. A small window under Netscape Navigator for Windows 95.*

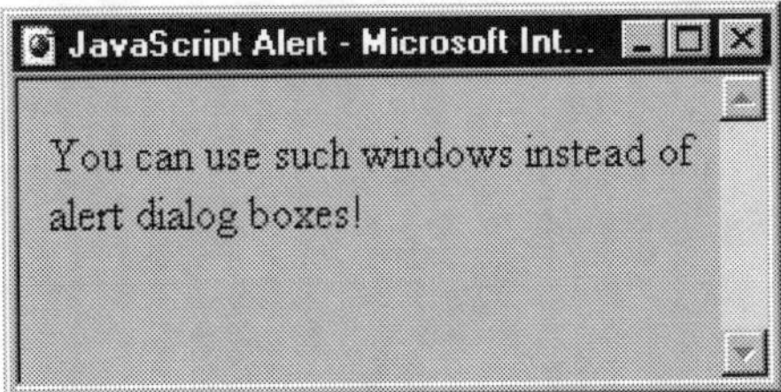

***Figure 27-5**. A small window under Microsoft Internet Explorer for Windows 95.*

An IE 3.0x Bug Workaround

A very bizarre bug in Internet Explorer 3.0x is that it does not like assigning the `document` object to a variable before invoking its methods. The following script, for example, should be equivalent to Example 27-1, but fails to work properly (the window opens but nothing is written to it):

```
<HTML>
<HEAD>
<TITLE>A custom "alert"</TITLE>
<SCRIPT LANGUAGE="JavaScript">
<!--

function pop(height, width, content) {
     win = window.open("", "", "height=" + height + ",width=" +
                      width)
     if (win != null) {
          doc = win.document
          doc.open('text/html')
          doc.write("<HTML><HEAD><TITLE>JavaScript Alert
                      </TITLE></HEAD><BODY>")
          doc.write(content)
          doc.write("</BODY></HTML>")
          doc.close()
     }
}

// -->
</SCRIPT>
</HEAD>
<BODY>
<FORM>
<INPUT TYPE="button" VALUE="custom alert" onClick="pop(75, 250,
                'You can use such windows instead of alert
                dialog boxes!')">
</FORM>
</BODY>
</HTML>
```

The workaround to this problem is not to assign the `document` object to a local variable before invoking its methods.

Referencing Windows

When assigning the returned value of the `window.open()` method to a variable, that variable represents the `window` object of the new window in the originating window's document.

When a document opens a new window by invoking the `window.open()` method, the `opener` property of the new window's `window` object is the `window` object of the originating document's window. The only way to change the `opener` property is by explicitly assigning it a new value. (Even unloading the document from the new window does not change it.) Figure 27-6 illustrates the relationship between an originating window and a new one.

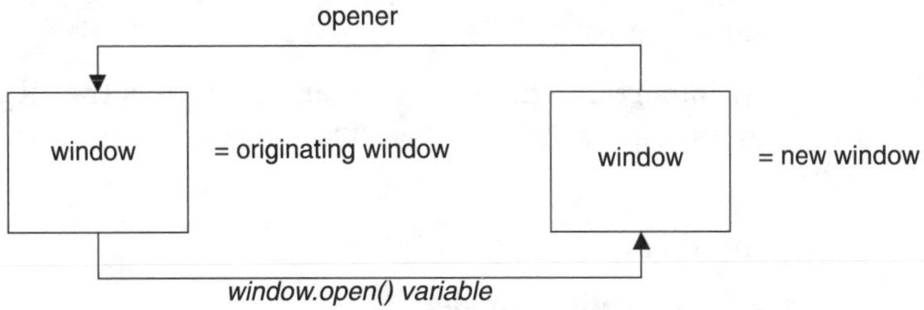

***Figure 27-6**. A two-way connection is established between the originating window and the new one.*

Later in this chapter we take a look at a popular application of windows—remotes.

Window Names

A window's name is used for its targeting by the `TARGET` attribute of the `<A>`, `<FORM>`, or any other tags that support this attribute. A new window's name can be passed to the `window.open()` method on its second argument. You cannot specify the window's name, however, when you open a new window from the File menu, or when you launch the browser. In both cases, you can apply a name to a window by assigning it to the window's `window.name` property.

It is a good practice to define names for all windows of a multiple-window site. Since a new window references its originating one, be sure to name the originating window as follows:

```
window.name = "name of window"
```

All objects feature a name property which differentiates each. The name property is extensively used in scripts which involve remotes, introduced in the following section.

Remotes

You have probably seen the button "Yahoo! Remote" while searching Yahoo!. When you click the button, a little window pops up and services your searching requests. When you use this window to search Yahoo!, the search engine's results are loaded into the originating window instead of the new popped-up one. As with any other window, you can either minimize the new window, send it behind the main browser window, leave it alone, or call it back. This little device is called a *remote*, just like your TV's.

The most important characteristic of a remote is that it must have access to its originating window. There are basically two ways to do that:

1. With plain HTML
2. Via JavaScript's object model

HTML-Based Remotes (Recommended)

An HTML-based remote relies on the name property of its originating window's window object. The remote can use the TARGET attribute of various HTML tags to target documents to the originating window. Take a look at the originating window's document and the remote window's HTML in Example 27-2.

```
<HTML>
<HEAD>
<TITLE>Remote Launcher</TITLE>
<SCRIPT LANGUAGE="JavaScript">
<!--

window.name = "main"
function launchRemote() {
    remote = window.open("ex27-2a.htm", "remote", "height=120,width=490")
}

// -->
</SCRIPT>
</HEAD>
<BODY>
<FORM>
```

```
<INPUT TYPE="button" VALUE="launch remote" onClick="launchRemote()">
</FORM>
</BODY>
</HTML>
```

Example 27-2 (ex27-2.htm)*. An HTML-based remote "launcher."*

The first statement of the script is an immediate one, and it sets the name of the originating window to `main`. When the user clicks the button, the function `launchRemote()` is invoked to open the remote window. Notice that the returned value of the `open()` method is assigned to a global variable. The document loaded into the new window is Example 27-2a:

```
<HTML>
<HEAD>
<TITLE>Remote</TITLE>
</HEAD>
<BODY BGCOLOR="#ffffff">
<A HREF="http://www.altavista.digital.com/" TARGET="main">
                            Altavista</A><BR>
<FORM METHOD="get" ACTION="http://www.altavista.digital.com/cgi-bin
                            /query" TARGET="main">
<INPUT TYPE="hidden" NAME="pg" VALUE="q">
<B>Search
<SELECT NAME="what">
<OPTION VALUE="web" SELECTED>the Web
<OPTION VALUE="news">Usenet
</SELECT>
and Display the Results
<SELECT NAME="fmt">
<OPTION VALUE="." SELECTED>in Standard Form
<OPTION VALUE="c">in Compact Form
<OPTION VALUE="d">in Detailed Form
</SELECT>
</B>
<BR>
<INPUT NAME="q" size=55 maxlength=200 VALUE="">
<INPUT TYPE=submit VALUE="Submit">
</FORM>
</BODY>
</HTML>
```

Example 27-2a—remote document (ex27-2a.htm)*. The remote document does not include any JavaScript statements!*

The remote document consists of two important elements:

1. A link (to `http://www.altavista.digital.com`)
2. A form (submitted to `http://www.altavista.digital.com/cgi-bin/query`)

Figure 27-7 shows the remote alongside the originating window.

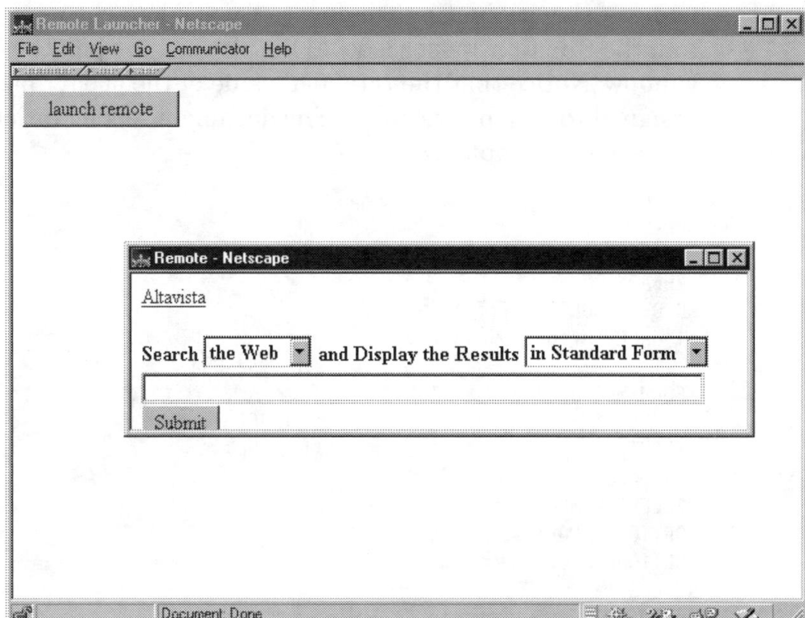

Figure 27-7. The originating window and the remote window.

Since the form is targeted to `main`, the AltaVista server will display its search results in the originating window.

Instead of specifying the originating window's name in its own source document, you might want to name it from the remote document, using the following statement:

```
window.opener.name = "main"
```

This statement must be an immediate one because it must execute before the user has a chance to click a link or send a document to the originating window.

JavaScript-Based Remote

A JavaScript-based remote relies only on JavaScript to connect between the originating window and the remote one. Example 27-3 shows how to use a JavaScript-based remote with links (it is more difficult to apply this technique to forms).

```
<HTML>
<HEAD>
<TITLE>Remote Launcher</TITLE>
<SCRIPT LANGUAGE="JavaScript">
<!--

function launchRemote() {
    remote = window.open("ex27-3a.htm", "remote", "height=75,width=200")
}

// -->
</SCRIPT>
</HEAD>
<BODY>
<FORM>
<INPUT TYPE="button" VALUE="launch remote" onClick="launchRemote()">
</FORM>
</BODY>
</HTML>
```

Example 27-3 (ex27-3.htm). *A JavaScript-based remote "launcher."*

Notice that you launch a JavaScript-based remote in the same way you launch an HTML-based remote. The only difference between the two is that we do not assign a string to the `name` property in JavaScript-based remotes (because it is not needed). Now, take a look at the following HTML document for the remote.

```
<HTML>
<HEAD>
<TITLE>Remote</TITLE>
<SCRIPT LANGUAGE="JavaScript">
<!--

function fetch(url) {
    window.opener.location.href = url
}

// -->
</SCRIPT>
</HEAD>
<BODY BGCOLOR="#ffffff">
```

```
<A HREF="javascript:fetch('http://www.altavista.digital.com/')">
                    Altavista</A><BR>
<A HREF="javascript:fetch('http://www.yahoo.com/')">Yahoo</A><BR>
<A HREF="javascript:fetch('http://www.lycos.com/')">Lycos</A>
</BODY>
</HTML>
```

Example 27-3a—remote document (ex27-3a.htm)*. Links are loaded in the source window via JavaScript.*

Three hypertext links invoke the `fetch()` function, with the desired URL as an argument. By assigning it to the `location.href` property of the originating window's `window` object, the function loads the new URL's document in the originating window. After opening the remote window, the originating window's `window` object is addressed as `window.opener`. Figure 27-8 shows both the originating window and the remote one, on the same desktop.

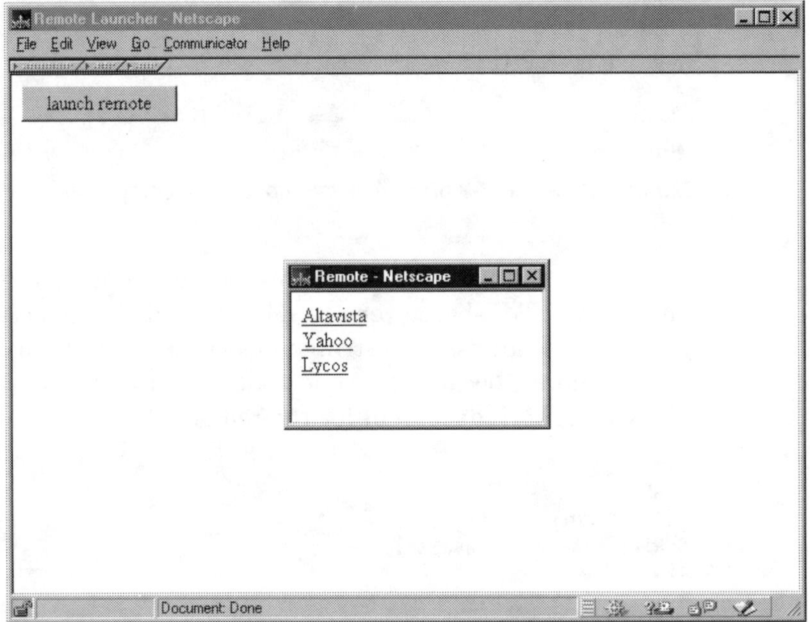

Figure 27-8*. The originating and remote windows.*

Another Algorithm to Open Windows

Yahoo! was the first to feature a remote for its site. Other sites followed suit, using exactly the same code (with different variable names, of course). Eventually, a standard algorithm for opening windows has emerged. Here is the source for the function that opens the window:

```
function launch() {
     var remote = null
     remote =
window.open('','remote','width=100,height=250,resizable')
     if (remote != null) {
          if (remote.opener == null)
               remote.opener = self
          remote.location.href = 'http://www.lycos.com/remote.html'
     }
}
```

First, the new window opens without an initial document in it. If the value of `remote` remains `null`, it is an indication that the remote failed to load for some reason and the function terminates. If the new window's `opener` property is `null`, the function explicitly assigns it the originating window. The desired URL is then loaded into the remote by assigning its `location.href` property.

Closing a Window

You can use JavaScript's `close()` method to close a window that has been opened via JavaScript's `open()` method. Attempting to close any other window results in a confirmation dialog box which asks the user whether to close the window or not. This security feature is designed to prevent "mail bombs" containing `self.close()` (yes, people did do that!). However, if the window has only one document (the current one) in its session history, closing is allowed without any confirmation. The general syntax of the `close()` method is as follows:

```
windowReference.close()
```

You can use this method to create a customized alert dialog box with an OK dismissing button, as demonstrated in Example 27-4.

```
<HTML>
<HEAD>
<TITLE>Custom Alert</TITLE>
<SCRIPT LANGUAGE="JavaScript">
<!--

function makeAlert(height, width, message) {
     var win = window.open("", "", "height=" + height + ",width=" + width)
     win.document.open()
     var text = ""
     text += "<HTML><HEAD><TITLE>Alert</TITLE></HEAD><BODY BGCOLOR=
                              '#ffffff'>"
     text += message + "<FORM><CENTER>"
     text += "<INPUT TYPE='button' VALUE='    OK    ' onClick=
                              'self.close()'>"
     text += "</CENTER></FORM></BODY></HTML>"
     win.document.write(text)
     win.document.close()
}

// -->
</SCRIPT>
</HEAD>
<BODY>
<FORM>
<INPUT
     TYPE="button"
     VALUE="make an alert"
     onClick="makeAlert(85, 200, '<CENTER>This is a custom alert!
                              </CENTER>')">
</FORM>
</BODY>
</HTML>
```

***Example 27-4 (ex 27-4.htm)**. A customized alert dialog box with an OK button.*

Load Example 27-4 in your browser, and click the button. A small window, consisting of a short message and an OK button (see Figure 27-9), should pop up. Click **OK** to close the window.

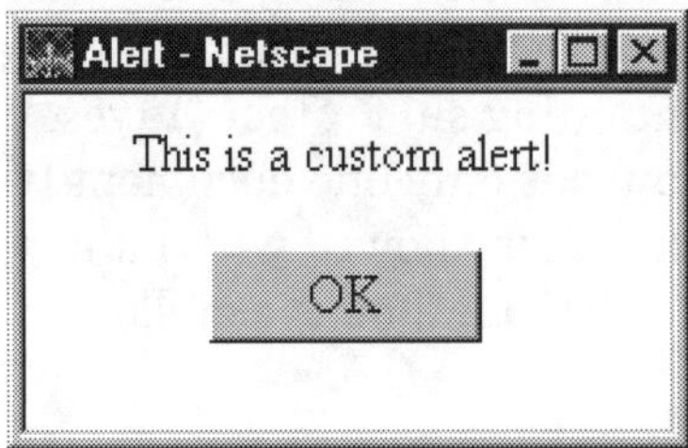

***Figure 27-9**. A regular window resembling an alert dialog box.*

Scrolling a Window

The `scroll()` method enables you to scroll a window to specified coordinates. This method is not implemented in Netscape Navigator 2.0x and Microsoft Internet Explorer 3.0x. The general syntax is:

```
windowReference.scroll(x-coordinate, y-coordinate)
```

Both arguments (the *x* and *y* coordinates) are specified in pixels. A document's upper left coordinates are 0, 0. Navigator 3.0x does not provide an event handler for a user-initiated scrolling (no `onScroll` event handler), so you cannot create an application where a user's scrolling of one window triggers an automatic scrolling of another window.

Windows, Events, and Event Handlers

Windows support the focus event by the `onFocus` event handler and the `focus()` method. Similarly, they support the blur event by the `onBlur` event handler and the `blur()` method. For more details, see the listings for these event handlers and methods in the previous chapter about frames.

Netscape Navigator 3.0x introduced the capability to focus on a window, by bringing it in front of all other windows. You can use the following statement from within a script to put focus on a window:

```
windowReference.focus()
```

windowReference is the name of the window's `window` object. You can use the `blur()` method to send a browser window behind the main window:

```
windowReference.blur()
```


A classic application of these methods to remotes and other floating toolbar-type windows is a window that always stays in front of other windows. When using such a window, you should provide a way to stop the "always-on-top" script, and you should also ensure that only one "always-on-top" window exists at any given period. Example 27-5 shows how to create an "always-on-top" window with these special restrictions.

```
<HTML>
<HEAD>
<TITLE>Remote Launcher</TITLE>
<SCRIPT LANGUAGE="JavaScript">
```

```
<!--

window.name = "main"
var onTop = false
function launchRemote() {
     remote = window.open("ex27-5a.htm", "remote", "height=200,width=490")
}

// -->
</SCRIPT>
</HEAD>
<BODY>
<FORM>
<INPUT TYPE="button" VALUE="launch remote" onClick="launchRemote()">
</FORM>
</BODY>
</HTML>
```

***Example 27-5 (ex27-5.htm)**. The source document that opens the new window.*

Example 27-5 is almost identical to Example 27-2. The only differences are:

1. The `onTop` variable indicates if there is currently a window which is being kept "on top." This variable only refers to the status of windows that were opened by the originating one.
2. The initial URL of the new window is `ex27-5a.htm`.

Here is the document for the new window:

```
<HTML>
<HEAD>
<TITLE>Remote</TITLE>
<SCRIPT LANGUAGE="JavaScript">
<!--

var onTop = false

function toggle() {
     if (opener.onTop && !onTop) return
     if (!onTop)
          self.focus()
     onTop = !onTop
     opener.onTop = onTop
     document.controls.status.value = (onTop) ? 'focus forced' :
                                   'focus not forced'
}

function focusRemote() {
     if (onTop)
          setTimeout('self.focus()', 200)
}
```

```
// -->
</SCRIPT>
</HEAD>
<BODY BGCOLOR="#ffffff" onBlur="focusRemote()" onLoad="toggle()">
<FORM NAME="controls">
<TABLE BORDER=2>
<TR><TD>
<INPUT TYPE="button" VALUE="TOGGLE" onClick="toggle()">
<INPUT TYPE="text" VALUE="focus not forced" SIZE=15 NAME="status">
</TD></TR>
</TABLE>
</FORM>

<A HREF="http://www.altavista.digital.com/" TARGET="main">
                              Altavista</A><BR>
<FORM METHOD="get" ACTION="http://www.altavista.digital.com/cgi-bin/
                              query" TARGET="main">
<INPUT TYPE="hidden" NAME="pg" VALUE="q">
<B>Search
<SELECT NAME="what">
<OPTION VALUE="web" SELECTED>the Web
<OPTION VALUE="news">Usenet
</SELECT>
and Display the Results
<SELECT NAME="fmt">
<OPTION VALUE="." SELECTED>in Standard Form
<OPTION VALUE="c">in Compact Form
<OPTION VALUE="d">in Detailed Form
</SELECT>
</B>
<BR>
<INPUT NAME="q" size=55 maxlength=200 VALUE="">
<INPUT TYPE=submit VALUE="Submit">
</FORM>
</BODY>
</HTML>
```

Example 27-5a—remote document (ex27-5a.htm). *The document for the new window.*

The first statement sets the variable onTop to false. Since it belongs to a different window object, the variable onTop in Example 27-5a is different than the variable onTop in Example 27-5. You can access, though, the onTop variable in Example 27-5 through opener.onTop. When the document in the new window is loaded, the onLoad event handler invokes the toggle() function, which turns on and off the "always-on-top" mode. After the toggle() function verifies that there is currently no other window which is in "always-on-top" mode (opener.onTop is true), it puts the remote window in focus. The Boolean value of onTop is then negated, and the text field displaying the current mode is updated. Note that each click on the TOGGLE button initiates the toggle() function.

Whenever the user removes focus from the window, the onBlur event handler calls the focusRemote() function, which repeatedly gives the window focus, provided that it is in "always-on-top" mode.

Accessing a Window's Objects—An Example

In order to manipulate a window's objects via JavaScript, you need to have a reference to the window's window object. This is why, when referencing a new window from its originating one, you should assign the returned value of the window.open() method to a variable. On the other hand, you should use the opener property when referencing an originating window from a new one. In the following example, we show how a script in one window can handle forms in two different windows. The originating window in Example 27-6 features a large text area with a few buttons, and a new remote one that includes some form elements, mimicking command buttons of an HTML editor. The editing zone is the text area in the originating window, whereas the buttons and HTML shortcuts are in the remote. Figure 27-10 shows both windows.

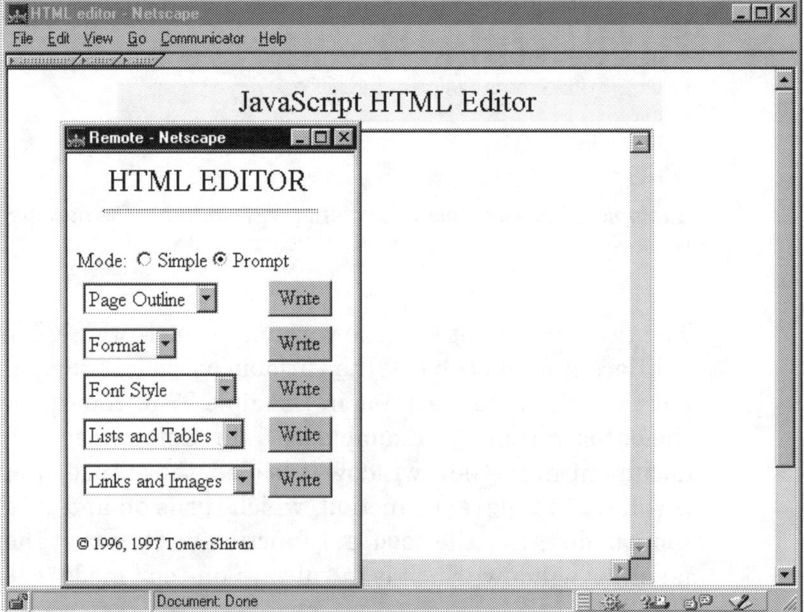

Figure 27-10. A two-piece JavaScript HTML editor.

Here is the source document:

```
<HTML>
<HEAD>
<TITLE>HTML editor</TITLE>
<SCRIPT LANGUAGE="JavaScript">
<!--

window.name = "source"
function launchEditor() {
     editor = window.open("ex27-6a.htm", "editor", "height=330,width=230")
}

function viewPage() {
     view = window.open("", "view")
     view.document.open()
     view.document.write(document.forms[0].elements[0].value) // value
                         of text area
     view.document.write("<BR>") // solves a bug
     view.document.close()
}

// -->
</SCRIPT>
</HEAD>
<BODY onLoad="launchEditor()" BGCOLOR="#ffffff">
<FORM ACTION="mailto:any@email.address" METHOD="post">
<CENTER>
<TABLE BORDER=0 CELLPADDING=2>
<TR><TD BGCOLOR="#ffffcc">
<CENTER>
<FONT SIZE=+2>JavaScript HTML Editor</FONT>
</CENTER>
</TD></TR>
<TR><TD>
<TEXTAREA COLS=50 ROWS=20 NAME="body"></TEXTAREA>
</TD></TR>
<TR><TD BGCOLOR="#ffffcc">
<CENTER>
<INPUT TYPE="button" VALUE="launch editor" onClick="launchEditor()">
<INPUT TYPE="button" VALUE="view page" onClick="viewPage()">
<INPUT TYPE="submit" VALUE="submit document">
</CENTER>
</TD></TR>
</TABLE>
</CENTER>
</FORM>
</BODY>
</HTML>
```

***Example 27-6 (ex27-6.htm)**. The source document consists of a large text area and some buttons.*

The source document (ex27-6.htm) creates a text area and some buttons below it. When the document loads, the `onLoad` event handler invokes the `launchEditor()` function, which generates a new window containing the HTML editing tools. That function consists of one statement that opens the new window and loads ex27-6a.htm into it.

Notice that the text area is named `body`, because the new remote window (`editor`) references it by that name. If the window fails to open automatically when the document loads, or is accidentally closed by the user, the user can open the new window explicitly via a button. The "view page" button calls the `viewPage()` function to create a new window and to write the HTML output in the text area of that window. Take another look at the function:

```
function viewPage() {
     view = window.open("", "view")
     view.document.open()
     view.document.write(document.forms[0].elements[0].value) // value
                         of text area
     view.document.write("<BR>") // solves a bug
     view.document.close()
}
```

First, the function opens the new window with no URL and no particular features (so the window opens with the same features as the originating window). The function opens a data stream to the new window, and then writes to it the text area's content, followed by a line break. Example 27-6a shows the document loaded into the new window.

```
<HTML>
<HEAD>
<TITLE>Remote</TITLE>
<SCRIPT LANGUAGE="JavaScript">
<!--

// variable to hold string to create new line in text field
var nl = getNewLine()

function getNewLine() {
     var agent = navigator.userAgent

     // if platform is Windows
     if (agent.indexOf("Win") >= 0)
          return "\r\n"
     else
          // if platform is Macintosh
          if (agent.indexOf("Mac") >= 0)
               return "\r"
```

```
        // if platform is not Windows or Macintosh
        return "\n"
}

function getInput(func, form) {
        // current value of text area in source window
        var text = form.body.value

        // determine current mode
        if (document.forms[0].mode[0].checked)
                var mode = 0 // simple
        else
                var mode = 1 // prompt

        if (func == 1)
                text += outline(mode)
        if (func == 2)
                text += vertical(mode)
        if (func == 3)
                text += font(mode)
        if (func == 4)
                text += list(mode)
        if (func == 5)
                text += link(mode)

        // update text area in source document
        form.body.value = text
}

function vertical(mode) {
        var ind = document.forms[0].select2.selectedIndex
        if (ind == 0)
                return ""
        if (ind == 1)
                return "<BR>" + nl
        if (ind == 2)
                if (mode == 0)
                                return "<HR>" + nl
                else {
                                var prompt1 = prompt("Enter width:", "100%")
                                prompt1 = (prompt1) ? " WIDTH=" + prompt1 : ""
                                var prompt2 = prompt("Enter size:", "2")
                                prompt2 = (prompt2) ? " SIZE=" + prompt2 : ""
                                return "<HR" + prompt1 + prompt2 + ">" + nl
                }
        if (ind == 3)
                return "<P>" + nl
}

function outline(mode) {
        var ind = document.forms[0].select1.selectedIndex
```

```
        if (ind == 0)
            return ""
        if (ind == 1)
            return "<HTML>" + nl
        if (ind == 2)
            return "</HTML>" + nl
        if (ind == 3)
            return "<HEAD>" + nl
        if (ind == 4)
            return "</HEAD>" + nl
        if (ind == 5)
            if (mode == 0)
                        return "<BODY>" + nl
            else {
                var prompt1 = prompt("Enter background color:",
                                     "white")
                prompt1 = (prompt1) ? " BGCOLOR=\"" + prompt1 + "\"" : ""
                var prompt2 = prompt("Enter background image:", "")
                prompt2 = (prompt2) ? " BACKGROUND=\"" + prompt2 + "\""
                                     : ""
                return "<BODY" + prompt1 + prompt2 + ">" + nl
            }
        if (ind == 6)
            return "</BODY>" + nl
        if (ind == 7)
            if (mode == 0)
                return "<TITLE></TITLE>" + nl
            else {
                var prompt1 = prompt("Enter title:", "My Document")
                prompt1 = (prompt1) ? prompt1 : ""
                return "<TITLE>" + prompt1 + "</TITLE>" + nl
            }
    }

    function font(mode) {
        var ind = document.forms[0].select3.selectedIndex
        if (ind == 0)
            return ""
        if (ind == 1)
            if (mode == 0)
                return "<H></H>" + nl
            else {
                var prompt1 = prompt("Enter header level:", "1")
                prompt1 = (prompt1) ? prompt1 : ""
                var prompt2 = prompt("Enter header text:", "")
                prompt2 = (prompt2) ? prompt2 : ""
                return "<H" + prompt1 + ">" + prompt2 + "</H" + prompt1
                            + ">" + nl
            }
        if (ind == 2)
            if (mode == 0)
                return "<FONT></FONT>" + nl
```

```
            else {
                var prompt1 = prompt("Enter font size:", "")
                prompt1 = (prompt1) ? " SIZE=" + prompt1 : ""
                var prompt2 = prompt("Enter font color:", "")
                prompt2 = (prompt2) ? " COLOR=\"" + prompt2 + "\"" : ""
                var prompt3 = prompt("Enter font text:", "")
                prompt3 = (prompt3) ? prompt3 : ""
                return "<FONT" + prompt1 + prompt2 + ">" + prompt3
                            + "</FONT>" + nl
            }
        if (ind == 3)
            if (mode == 0)
                return "<B></B>" + nl
            else {
                var prompt1 = prompt("Enter bold text:", "")
                prompt1 = (prompt1) ? prompt1 : ""
                return "<B>" + prompt1 + "</B>" + nl
            }
        if (ind == 4)
            if (mode == 0)
                return "<BLINK></BLINK>" + nl
            else {
                var prompt1 = prompt("Enter blinking text:", "")
                prompt1 = (prompt1) ? prompt1 : ""
                return "<BLINK>" + prompt1 + "</BLINK>" + nl
            }
        if (ind == 5)
            if (mode == 0)
                return "<U></U>" + nl
            else {
                var prompt1 = prompt("Enter underlined text:", "")
                prompt1 = (prompt1) ? prompt1 : ""
                return "<U>" + prompt1 + "</U>" + nl
            }
        if (ind == 6)
            if (mode == 0)
                return "<PRE></PRE>" + nl
            else {
                var prompt1 = prompt("Enter PRE text:", "")
                prompt1 = (prompt1) ? prompt1 : ""
                return "<PRE>" + prompt1 + "</PRE>" + nl
            }
        if (ind == 7)
            if (mode == 0)
                return "<I></I>" + nl
            else {
                var prompt1 = prompt("Enter italic text:", "")
                prompt1 = (prompt1) ? prompt1 : ""
                return "<I>" + prompt1 + "</I>" + nl
            }
        if (ind == 8)
            if (mode == 0)
```

```
                return "<EM></EM>" + nl
            else {
                var prompt1 = prompt("Enter text:", "")
                prompt1 = (prompt1) ? prompt1 : ""
                return "<EM>" + prompt1 + "</EM>" + nl
            }
        if (ind == 9)
            if (mode == 0)
                return "<CENTER></CENTER>" + nl
            else {
                var prompt1 = prompt("Enter centered text:", "")
                prompt1 = (prompt1) ? prompt1 : ""
                return "<CENTER>" + prompt1 + "</CENTER>" + nl
            }
    }

    function list(mode) {
        var ind = document.forms[0].select4.selectedIndex
        if (ind == 0)
            return ""
        if (ind == 1)
            return "<OL>" + nl
        if (ind == 2)
            return "</OL>" + nl
        if (ind == 3)
            return "<UL>" + nl
        if (ind == 4)
            return "</UL>" + nl
        if (ind == 5)
            if (mode == 0)
                return "<LI></LI>" + nl
            else {
                var prompt1 = prompt("Enter text of list item:", "")
                prompt1 = (prompt1) ? prompt1 : ""
                return "<LI>" + prompt1 + "</LI>" + nl
            }
        if (ind == 6)
            if (mode == 0)
                return "<TABLE>" + nl
            else {
                var prompt1 = prompt("Enter border:", "")
                prompt1 = (prompt1) ? " BORDER=" + prompt1 : ""
                var prompt2 = prompt("Enter cell padding:", "")
                prompt2 = (prompt2) ? " CELLPADDING=" + prompt2 : ""
                var prompt3 = prompt("Enter cell spacing:", "")
                prompt3 = (prompt3) ? " CELLSPACING=" + prompt3 : ""
                var prompt4 = prompt("Enter table width:", "100%")
                prompt4 = (prompt4) ? " WIDTH=" + prompt4 : ""
                var prompt5 = prompt("Enter table alignment:", "")
                prompt5 = (prompt5) ? " ALIGN=\"" + prompt5 + "\"" : ""
                return "<TABLE" + prompt1 + prompt2 + prompt3 + prompt4
                              + prompt5 + ">" + nl
```

```
        }
    if (ind == 7)
        if (mode == 0)
            return "<TH>" + nl
        else {
            var prompt1 = prompt("Enter horizontal alignment:", "")
            prompt1 = (prompt1) ? " ALIGN=\"" + prompt1 + "\"" : ""
            var prompt2 = prompt("Enter vertical alignment:", "")
            prompt2 = (prompt2) ? " VALIGN=\"" + prompt2 + "\"" : ""
            var prompt3 = prompt("Enter cell background color:", "")
            prompt3 = (prompt3) ? " BGCOLOR=\"" + prompt3 + "\"" : ""
            var prompt4 = prompt("Enter column span:", "100%")
            prompt4 = (prompt4) ? " COLSPAN=" + prompt4 : ""
            var prompt5 = prompt("Enter row span:", "left")
            prompt5 = (prompt5) ? " ROWSPAN=\"" + prompt5 + "\"" : ""
            return "<TH" + prompt1 + prompt2 + prompt3 + prompt4
                            + prompt5 + ">" + nl
        }
    if (ind == 8)
        return "</TH>" + nl
    if (ind == 9)
        if (mode == 0)
            return "<CAPTION></CAPTION>" + nl
        else {
            var prompt1 = prompt("Enter text alignment:", "")
            prompt1 = (prompt1) ? " ALIGN=\"" + prompt1 + "\"" : ""
            var prompt2 = prompt("Enter text:", "")
            prompt2 = (prompt2) ? prompt2 : ""
            return "<CAPTION" + prompt1 + ">" + prompt2 +
                                "</CAPTION>" + nl
        }
    if (ind == 10)
        if (mode == 0)
            return "<TR>" + nl
        else {
            var prompt1 = prompt("Enter horizontal alignment:", "")
            prompt1 = (prompt1) ? " ALIGN=" + prompt1 : ""
            var prompt2 = prompt("Enter vertical alignment:", "")
            prompt2 = (prompt2) ? " VALIGN=\"" + prompt2 + "\"" : ""
            var prompt3 = (confirm("Enable wrap-around?")) ? ""
                                : " NOWRAP"
            return "<TR" + prompt1 + prompt2 + prompt3 + ">" + nl
        }
    if (ind == 11)
        return "</TR>" + nl
    if (ind == 12)
        if (mode == 0)
            return "<TD>" + nl
        else {
            var prompt1 = prompt("Enter horizontal alignment:", "")
            prompt1 = (prompt1) ? " ALIGN=\"" + prompt1 + "\"" : ""
            var prompt2 = prompt("Enter vertical alignment:", "")
```

```
                prompt2 = (prompt2) ? " VALIGN=\"" + prompt2 + "\"" : ""
                var prompt3 = prompt("Enter cell background color:", "")
                prompt3 = (prompt3) ? " BGCOLOR=\"" + prompt3 + "\"" : ""
                var prompt4 = prompt("Enter column span:", "100%")
                prompt4 = (prompt4) ? " COLSPAN=" + prompt4 : ""
                var prompt5 = prompt("Enter row span:", "")
                prompt5 = (prompt5) ? " ROWSPAN=\"" + prompt5 + "\"" : ""
                return "<TD" + prompt1 + prompt2 + prompt3 + prompt4
                                        + prompt5 + ">" + nl
            }
        if (ind == 13)
            return "</TD>" + nl
        if (ind == 14)
            return "</TABLE>" + nl
    }

    function link(mode) {
        var ind = document.forms[0].select5.selectedIndex
        if (ind == 0)
            return ""
        if (ind == 1)
            if (mode == 0)
                return "<A>" + nl
            else {
                var prompt1 = prompt("Enter URL or anchor name:", "")
                prompt1 = (prompt1) ? " HREF=\"" + prompt1 + "\"" : ""
                return "<A" + prompt1 + ">" + nl
            }
        if (ind == 2)
            if (mode == 0)
                return "<A>" + nl
            else {
                var prompt1 = prompt("Enter anchor name:", "")
                prompt1 = (prompt1) ? " NAME=\"" + prompt1 + "\"" : ""
                return "<A" + prompt1 + ">" + nl
            }
        if (ind == 3)
            return "</A>" + nl
        if (ind == 4)
            if (mode == 0)
                return "<IMG>" + nl
            else {
                var prompt1 = prompt("Enter image URL:", "")
                prompt1 = (prompt1) ? " SRC=\"" + prompt1 + "\"" : ""
                var prompt2 = prompt("Enter image height:", "")
                prompt2 = (prompt2) ? " HEIGHT=" + prompt2 : ""
                var prompt3 = prompt("Enter image width:", "")
                prompt3 = (prompt3) ? " WIDTH=" + prompt3 : ""
                var prompt4 = prompt("Enter image border:", "")
                prompt4 = (prompt4) ? " BORDER=" + prompt4 : ""
                var prompt5 = prompt("Enter image alignment:", "")
                prompt5 = (prompt5) ? " ALIGN=\"" + prompt5 + "\"" : ""
```

```
                return "<IMG" + prompt1 + prompt2 + prompt3 + prompt4
                                     + prompt5 + ">" + nl
           }
}

// -->
</SCRIPT>
</HEAD>
<BODY BGCOLOR="white">
<CENTER>
<FONT SIZE=+2>HTML EDITOR</FONT>
</CENTER>
<HR WIDTH=80%>
<FORM>
  Mode: <INPUT NAME="mode" TYPE="radio">Simple<INPUT NAME="mode"
                                  TYPE="radio" CHECKED>Prompt
  <BR>
  <TABLE>
    <TR>
      <TD>
        <SELECT NAME="select1">
           <OPTION>Page Outline
           <OPTION>HTML
           <OPTION>/HTML
           <OPTION>HEAD
           <OPTION>/HEAD
           <OPTION>BODY
           <OPTION>/BODY
           <OPTION>TITLE
        </SELECT>
      </TD>
      <TD>
        <INPUT TYPE="button" VALUE="Write" onClick="getInput(1, opener.
                                    document.forms[0])">
      </TD>
    </TR>
    <TR>
      <TD>
        <SELECT NAME="select2">
          <OPTION>Format
          <OPTION>BR
          <OPTION>HR
          <OPTION>P
        </SELECT>
      </TD>
      <TD>
        <INPUT TYPE="button" VALUE="Write" onClick="getInput(2, opener.
                                    document.forms[0])"><BR>
      </TD>
    </TR>
    <TR>
      <TD>
```

```
          <SELECT NAME="select3">
            <OPTION>Font Style
            <OPTION>H (H1, H2)
            <OPTION>FONT
            <OPTION>B (bold)
            <OPTION>BLINK
            <OPTION>U (underline)
            <OPTION>PRE
            <OPTION>I (italics)
            <OPTION>EM (emphasis)
            <OPTION>CENTER
          </SELECT>
        </TD>
        <TD>
          <INPUT TYPE="button" VALUE="Write" onClick="getInput(3, opener.
                                          document.forms[0])"><BR>
        </TD>
      </TR>
      <TR>
        <TD>
          <SELECT NAME="select4">
            <OPTION>Lists and Tables
            <OPTION>OL
            <OPTION>/OL
            <OPTION>UL
            <OPTION>/UL
            <OPTION>LI
            <OPTION>TABLE
            <OPTION>TH
            <OPTION>/TH
            <OPTION>CAPTION
            <OPTION>TR
            <OPTION>/TR
            <OPTION>TD
            <OPTION>/TD
            <OPTION>/TABLE
          </SELECT>
        </TD>
        <TD>
          <INPUT TYPE="button" VALUE="Write" onClick="getInput(4, opener.
                                          document.forms[0])"><BR>
        </TD>
      </TR>
      <TR>
        <TD>
          <SELECT NAME="select5">
            <OPTION>Links and Images
            <OPTION>A HREF
            <OPTION>A NAME
            <OPTION>/A
            <OPTION>IMG
          </SELECT>
```

```
        </TD>
        <TD>
          <INPUT TYPE="button" VALUE="Write" onClick="getInput(5, opener.
                                                  document.forms[0])">
        </TD>
      </TR>
    </TABLE>
</FORM>
<FONT SIZE=2>&#169; 1996, 1997 Tomer Shiran</FONT>
</BODY>
</HTML>
```

***Example 27-6a—new document (ex27-6a.htm)**. The new document includes most of the JavaScript code.*

This script is extremely long, because some parts are repeated for every HTML tag supported by the editor. Let's take a look at the functions used in the script.

getNewLine()

```
function getNewLine() {
     var agent = navigator.userAgent

     // if platform is Windows
     if (agent.indexOf("Win") >= 0)
          return "\r\n"
     else
          // if platform is Macintosh
          if (agent.indexOf("Mac") >= 0)
               return "\r"

     // if platform is not Windows or Macintosh
     return "\n"
}
```

This function returns the characters required to create a new line in a fixed text (such as text in a field or a text area). Since we haven't discussed the `navigator` object yet, you can ignore the content of this function for a while. To use this function, assign its returned value to a variable and then use the variable to print a new line in the originating window's text area:

```
// variable to hold string to create new line in text field
var nl = getNewLine()
```

getInput(func, form)

```
function getInput(func, form) {
     // current value of text area in source window
     var text = form.body.value

     // determine current mode
     if (document.forms[0].mode[0].checked)
          var mode = 0 // simple
     else
          var mode = 1 // prompt

     if (func == 1)
          text += outline(mode)
     if (func == 2)
          text += vertical(mode)
     if (func == 3)
          text += font(mode)
     if (func == 4)
          text += list(mode)
     if (func == 5)
          text += link(mode)

     // update text area in source document
     form.body.value = text
}
```

The first parameter, `func`, receives the index of the Write button that the user clicked, whereas the second parameter receives a reference to the form in the originating document. The function first copied the value of the text area to a local variable and, at the end of the function, copied the value of the variable (which changed throughout the function) back to the text area.

Two values determine the function's actions:

- the editing mode (prompt or simple)
- the Write button clicked by the user

The local variable mode is set to 0 if the editing mode is "simple," and to 1 if the mode is "prompt."

The script in this document consists of a function for each select object (Write button). The first select object, for example, is associated with the `outline()` function, the second one with the `vertical()` function, and so on. The value returned by the function is concatenated to the value of the `text` variable. Since all five functions associated with the document's select objects have the same structure, we analyze only one of them.

vertical()

```
function vertical(mode) {
     var ind = document.forms[0].select2.selectedIndex
     if (ind == 0)
          return ""
     if (ind == 1)
          return "<BR>" + nl
     if (ind == 2)
          if (mode == 0)
                    return "<HR>" + nl
          else {
                    var prompt1 = prompt("Enter width:", "100%")
                    prompt1 = (prompt1) ? " WIDTH=" + prompt1 : ""
                    var prompt2 = prompt("Enter size:", "2")
                    prompt2 = (prompt2) ? " SIZE=" + prompt2 : ""
                    return "<HR" + prompt1 + prompt2 + ">" + nl
          }
     if (ind == 3)
          return "<P>" + nl
}
```

This function is called by the `getInput()` function, when the user clicks the second Write button. For each selected index, we create a set of statements that constitute the definition of the corresponding HTML tag. Selecting a category, such as "Page Outline" or "Format," yields a 0 index for which no HTML tag is generated (an empty string is returned).

Since the `<BR>` tag does not receive any attributes, the function returns `"<BR>"` plus a new line (see Figure 27-11). The second option, `<HR>`, accepts two attributes, `WIDTH` and `SIZE`. If the current mode is "simple," the function returns `"<HR>"` and a new line, just like the `<BR>` tag (first option). If the editing mode is "prompt," the function prompts the user for the values of these attributes. The following script segment prompts the user for the attributes of the `<HR>` tag when the mode is "prompt":

```
var prompt1 = prompt("Enter width:", "100%")
prompt1 = (prompt1) ? " WIDTH=" + prompt1 : ""
var prompt2 = prompt("Enter size:", "2")
prompt2 = (prompt2) ? " SIZE=" + prompt2 : ""
return "<HR" + prompt1 + prompt2 + ">" + nl
```

The value returned by the first prompt dialog box is assigned to `prompt1`, the value of the second prompt box is assigned to `prompt2`, and so on (if there are more than two). If the user clicks the Cancel button, the value of that variable (`prompt1`, `prompt2`, etc.) evaluates to `false` (because `null` automatically becomes `false` in a Boolean condition), and an empty string is returned. Otherwise, a string in the form of `ATTRIBUTE="value"` is returned. The same structures and algorithms are used for the other HTML tags supported by our editor.

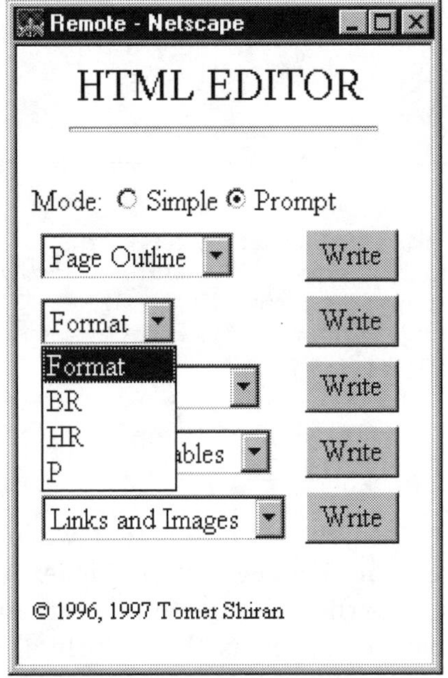

***Figure 27-11**. The HTML editor with the second select object pulled down.*

Take your time to play around with the HTML editor. The script will become much more understandable then.

Summary

A good understanding of JavaScript's object model is required in order to script windows properly and easily. This chapter serves as a complete reference for writing a JavaScript code related to windows. We have attempted to list as many window-handling applications as possible, for two reasons:

- A better understanding of the concepts presented in this chapter
- So you don't have to work hard when you need one of these scripts

In the following chapters we will focus on built-in objects and new features in Netscape Navigator 3.0x and 4.0.

Chapter 28

Evaluation and Compilation

Evaluating a String

The eval() function is the easiest way to evaluate a string expression. There are, however, several other ways:

```
var abc = "def"
document.write(abc)                     // 1
document.write("<BR>")
document.write(eval("abc"))             // 2
document.write("<BR>")
document.write(window.abc)              // 3
document.write("<BR>")
document.write(window["abc"])           // 4
document.write("<BR>")
document.write(window.eval("abc")) // 5
```

In the preceding script segment, all five lines (1, 2, 3, 4, 5) print the same output: def (except for the fifth one, due to a bug).

Line 1 The document.write() method automatically evaluates its argument, whether it is stored in a variable or handed to the function in the form of a literal. In this particular case, we hand the function a data structure (a variable), which evaluates to def. This method always evaluates the argument, so you must surround a string literal with quotes (of any type).

Line 2 The eval() function evaluates its argument and returns it as is. Unlike the document.write() function, except for returning it, eval() does not do anything with the value. In this case, the function returns abc (not "abc"), and document.write(eval("abc")) is then equivalent to document.write(abc), which outputs def, as explained above.

Line 3 Since all variables in a document are actual properties of the window object, the variable abc can be specified with a complete object reference, as shown on this line.

Line 4 You can use the array notation instead of the "dot" syntax (window["abc"] is equivalent to window.abc). Since the square brackets evaluate their content, you should place a quoted string in between.

Line 5 Based on the preceding discussion, window.eval("abc") is equivalent to window.abc which outputs def on Navigator. On Microsoft Internet Explorer 3.0, however, this line prints abc.

Here is another set of slightly more complicated statements:

```
var abc = "def"
var def = "abc"
document.write(eval('eval("abc")'))          // 1
document.write("<BR>")
document.write(eval(eval("abc")))            // 2
document.write("<BR>")
document.write(eval('window.eval("def")')) // 3
document.write("<BR>")
document.write(eval(window.eval("def")))     // 4
document.write("<BR>")
document.write(window[eval("def")])          // 5
document.write("<BR>")
document.write(eval(window[eval("def")]))  // 6
```

These statements output different strings, as explained below.

Line 1 eval('eval("abc")') evaluates to eval("abc") because the top-level eval() "removes" the quotes. The expression eval("abc") evaluates to abc, so the output of this statement is "def".

Line 2 eval("abc") is evaluated first, because the innermost function call is always evaluated before any other function call in the same expression. (In the previous statement, as the "inner" function call is actually a string, there is only one function call besides the document.write() statement.) Therefore, eval("abc") evaluates to abc, and eval(eval("abc")) evaluates to eval("def"), which, in turn, evaluates to def. The statement's output is then "def".

Line 3 You should have guessed that the output of this statement differs from browser to browser (IE and Navigator). On both browsers, eval('window.eval("def")') evaluates to window.eval("def"). This statement evaluates to "def" on MSIE, and "abc" on Netscape Navigator. (See the explanation for the last statement in the previous script segment.)

Line 4 We already know that `window.eval("def")` evaluates to "def" on MSIE, and "abc" on Netscape Navigator. Therefore, `eval(window.eval("def"))` evaluates to the exact opposite: "abc" on MSIE, and "def" on Netscape Navigator.

Line 5 `eval("def")` evaluates to `def`, so `window[eval("def")]` evaluates to `window[def]`, which evaluates to `window["abc"]`. Therefore, this statement prints "def".

Line 6 `eval(window[eval("def")])` is actually the value handed to the `document.write()` method in the previous statement, evaluated by another `eval()` function call. Therefore, it evaluates to `eval("def")`, which evaluates to `def`, so this statement prints "abc".

You should now know exactly how Netscape Navigator handles string evaluation. When it comes to MSIE 3.0x, you cannot always know what is going to happen, so the best solution is to simply try it. Sometimes, you'll have to work around a bug by using an alternative expression, as is demonstrated by the Color Center application in Chapter 26.

Function References and Calls

Take a look at the following function definition:

```
function multiply(op1, op2) {
     var result = op1 * op2
     return result
}
```

A function call is an expression that invokes a function. The following statement, for example, consists of a function call:

```
var num = multiply(5, 8)
```

Function calls are very convenient, because you can specify arguments for the function and accept the returned value. JavaScript, however, does not always permit function calls. You cannot use, for example, a function call as a constructor function's method. Instead, you should use a function reference:

```
function makeOperator() {
     this.multiply = multiply // not multiply()
}
```

All functions in JavaScript are objects, so a function reference is actually an object reference. Suppose you want to use a function in one window as a method in a constructor function located in a different window. You should specify the full function reference, using the following format:

```
this.methodName = windowReference.functionName
```

A function reference, as opposed to a function call, is not a command—the JavaScript interpreter cannot execute it. You should treat a function like any other object in JavaScript: Assign it to a variable, hand it to a function, and so forth. Here's an example:

```
function myAlert(msg) {
    alert("*** " + msg + " ***")
}

function test(func) {
    func("Hello!")
}

test(myAlert)
```

In this script segment we invoke the `test()` function with the function `myAlert` (a reference) as an argument. We then refer to the function `myAlert` as `func`, because the parameter is named `func`. Since `func` is equivalent to `myAlert`, we can call it in the same fashion we would call the `myAlert()` function.

Compiling Code as a Function

The `Function` object specifies a string of JavaScript code to be compiled as a function. The general syntax is:

```
var functionTarget = new Function ([arg1, arg2, …, argn], functionBody)
```

`functionTarget` is the name of a variable or a property of an existing object. It can also be a browser object followed by an event handler such as `window.onerror`.

`arg1, arg2, …, argn` are string arguments to be used by the function as formal parameter names.

`functionBody` is a string specifying the JavaScript code to be compiled as the function body.

The `Function` object is not implemented in Netscape Navigator 2.0x and Microsoft Internet Explorer 3.0x. An instance of the `Function` object is evaluated each time it is used. This is much less efficient than declaring a function and invoking it within your code, because declared functions are compiled. Declared functions are evaluated as the page loads, and are stored in memory as machine code. Instances of the `Function` object are stored in memory as objects (consisting of strings), and are converted to machine code for each execution.

Specifying the Function's Body

The function body, *functionBody*, is a string consisting of JavaScript statements. You could use, for example, the following string:

```
"document.bgColor='antiquewhite'"
```

Things become more complicated when you want to create an instance with a body of several statements. The string should then include all statements separated by semicolons. Although you will rarely use this feature, we show you how to write the function according to your personal preferences and have a distinct script convert it to valid, one-line JavaScript code.

Take a look at the following function:

```
function getCookie(name) {
     var prefix = name + "="
     var cookieStartIndex = document.cookie.indexOf(prefix)
     if (cookieStartIndex == -1)
          return null
     var cookieEndIndex = document.cookie.indexOf(";", cookieStartIndex
                              + prefix.length)
     if (cookieEndIndex == -1)
          cookieEndIndex = document.cookie.length
     return unescape(document.cookie.substring(cookieStartIndex +
                              prefix.length, cookieEndIndex))
}
```

Example 28-1 prints the body of this function on one line, including semicolons where needed.

```
<HTML>
<HEAD>
<TITLE>Function body string</TITLE>
</HEAD>
<BODY>
<SCRIPT LANGUAGE="JavaScript">
<!--

function getCookie(name) {
     var prefix = name + "="
     var cookieStartIndex = document.cookie.indexOf(prefix)
     if (cookieStartIndex == -1)
          return null
```

```
        var cookieEndIndex = document.cookie.indexOf(";", cookieStartIndex
                                + prefix.length)
        if (cookieEndIndex == -1)
            cookieEndIndex = document.cookie.length
        return unescape(document.cookie.substring(cookieStartIndex +
                                prefix.length, cookieEndIndex))
}

// print function body
document.write(getCookie)

// -->
</SCRIPT>
</BODY>
</HTML>
```

***Example 28-1 (ex28-1.htm)**. You can print a function reference to see its one-line equivalent.*

The technique demonstrated in Example 28-1 works only under Netscape Navigator. Its output is as follows:

```
function getCookie(name) { var prefix = name + "="; var cookieStartIndex =
document.cookie.indexOf(prefix); if (cookieStartIndex == -1) { return null;
} var cookieEndIndex = document.cookie.indexOf(";", cookieStartIndex +
prefix.length); if (cookieEndIndex == -1) { cookieEndIndex =
document.cookie.length; } return unescape(document.cookie.substring
(cookieStartIndex + prefix.length, cookieEndIndex)); }
```

You should extract the function's body from this long string. This script does not work properly under MSIE 3.0x, because it does not display the entire function body. Instead, the script's output is:

```
function getCookie() { [native code] }
```

Using the Function Object with a Variable

The following statement assigns a function to a variable:

```
var setBGColorBeige = new Function("document.bgColor = 'beige'")
```

Since it serves as a function, it is a good practice to include a verb form in the variable's name. You can call the variable as if it were a regular function:

```
setBGColorBeige()
```

Assigning a function to a variable is similar to declaring a function, with some differences, as expressed in Table 28-1.

Table 28-1. The differences between declaring a function and assigning a function to a variable.

Assigning a function to a variable *functionName* = new Function("...")	Declaring a function function *functionName*() {...}
functionName is a variable for which the current value is a reference to the function created with new Function().	*functionName* is the name of a function, not a variable.
The function's body is evaluated each time you call the function.	The function's body is evaluated only once—when the browser parses the script.
The function's parameters and body are specified as strings.	The function's parameters and body are plain code, not an explicit data type.

Specifying Arguments

As you already know, you can create an instance of the Function object that takes arguments. Take a look at the following statement:

```
var multiply = new Function("x", "y", "return x * y")
```

The last argument handed to the Function() constructor is the function's body (in the form of a string). Preceding string arguments are formal parameter names that are used in the function's body. Although they do not act as strings in the function, the arguments must be specified as strings. If you do not specify them as string literals, JavaScript attempts to evaluate them. If you use the following statement, for example, JavaScript will look for two variables, named x and y:

```
var multiply = new Function(x, y, "return x * y")
```

You can invoke a function reference created with the Function() constructor as if it were a declared function.

Using the Function Object with an Event Handler

You have already seen how to assign a function reference to an event handler. Here is a simple example:

```
<SCRIPT LANGUAGE="JavaScript">
<!--

function bye() {
     alert("Bye!")
}

window.onunload = bye
```

```
// -->
</SCRIPT>
```

We assign the window's `onunload` event handler a function reference, not a function call. Note that you cannot use arguments with an event handler. When you want to assign a statement to an event handler with this technique, you must use a function reference, even if you want to specify only a single statement as demonstrated in the preceding script. It may seem very annoying to create a function for each event handler. Therefore, you can assign a function reference to an event handler via the `Function()` constructor. The preceding script would then be much more simple and organized:

```
<SCRIPT LANGUAGE="JavaScript">
<!--

window.onunload = new Function('alert("Bye!")')

// -->
</SCRIPT>
```

When the user unloads a document containing such a script, an alert dialog box pops up. When you assign a function reference to an event handler in this fashion, the event handler becomes a reference to a function object. When you use it as a function, the event handler method will be converted from an object to a function:

```
window.onunload()
```

Properties of the Function Object

Instances of the `Function` object do not feature any properties. But, like all other dynamic objects in JavaScript (not in Navigator 2.0x or MSIE 3.0x), you can use its `prototype` property to extend the object by adding properties to it. Here is an interesting example:

```
function execute(x, y) {
     var now = new Date()
     if (now.getDay() == 5 && now.getDate() == 13) // Friday 13
          alert("This function does not execute on Friday the 13th")
     else
          this(x, y)
}

Function.prototype.exec = execute
var add = new Function("x", "y", "alert(x + y)")
add.exec(3, 4)
```

We use a function reference, `execute`, as a property (method) of `Function.prototype`, so the function `execute()` becomes a method of all instances of the `Function` object. Note that we could have used the `Function()` directly, instead of declaring a function and assigning its reference. Now, let's take a look at the `execute()` function. It first creates an instance of the `Date` object reflecting the current time and date. We check if the current date happens to be Friday the 13th, and if so, a corresponding message is displayed via the `window.alert()` method. If it is not Friday the 13th, the statement `this(x, y)` executes. We shall refer to our specific instance, `add`, in order to make this clear. When we assign an instance of the `Function` object to the variable `add`, it becomes an object. You can invoke that object as a function:

```
add(3, 4)
```

You can also invoke its method, `exec()`, in the following fashion:

```
add.exec(3, 4)
```

When you call `exec()` as a method of the `add` object, its calling object is obviously `add`. Therefore, the keyword `this` refers to `add`, and `this(x, y)` is equivalent to `add(x, y)`.

The `Function` object is quite extraordinary, because it is also a function. Figure 28-1 should make this object hierarchy very clear:

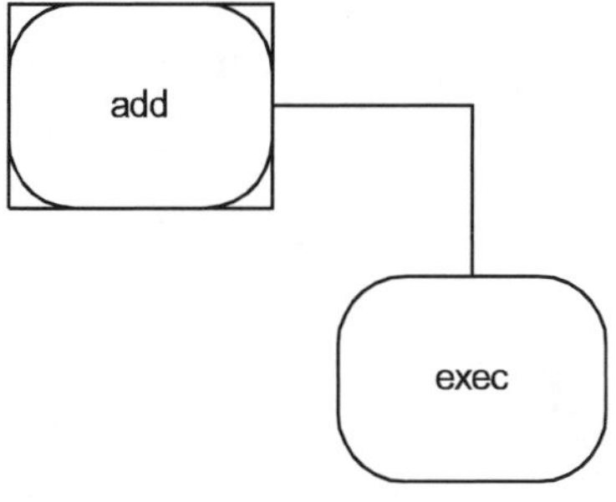

Figure 28-1*. A rounded rectangle represents a function or method, and a rectangle represents an object.*

Summary

In this chapter, we dealt mostly with function references. We also discussed various evaluation methods and their behavior under specific conditions, including the MSIE 3.0x. We have discussed many advanced applications of the `Function` object, so you should have no problems using it. Bear in mind that all functions are objects, and parentheses are used only to invoke a function. As you will find out with practice, there are many things you can do with functions besides calling them.

Chapter 29
General Software Detection

Browser Detection

A major problem with JavaScript is that it is not a compiled language but rather an interpreted one. Furthermore, unlike a server-side Perl script, it is interpreted by a different interpreter each time. For example, if you put some JavaScript code on a Web page, it is interpreted by Netscape Navigator 2.0x, 3.0x, Microsoft Internet Explorer 3.0x, and so forth. Each of these browsers is available on various platforms, so there are hundreds of possibilities (yes, hundreds!).

Some JavaScript features or elements are compatible only with some of the JavaScript-enabled browsers. For example, the `Image` object is not supported by Netscape Navigator 2.0x or MSIE 3.0x but is supported by Navigator 3.0x. In the heart of a Web content provider, you usually want to make sure that your Web pages are compatible with all browsers, or at least the most recent ones. For instance, if the most recent browser is Navigator 3.0x, you would want your Web pages to be suitable for Navigator 2.0x and MSIE 3.0x users. Microsoft, being aware of the differences between its implementation of JavaScript and Netscape's implementation, hurried to rename its JavaScript "JScript." There are basically two possibilities to provide Web pages that are compatible with most, if not all, JavaScript browsers:

- You can choose to stick with the most scaled-down version of JavaScript. That is, make sure that the page works with Netscape Navigator 2.0 and MSIE 3.0. This technique is possible because newer browsers always support the features of those that precede them. For example, JavaScript for Netscape Navigator 4.0 supports all features in JavaScript for Netscape Navigator 3.0x. This remedy's disadvantage is obvious—you cannot take advantage of the powerful features supported only by the most recent JavaScript-enabled browsers.

- You can use JavaScript to find out what browser the user is running, and provide scripts of HTML content accordingly. You can invoke, for example, one function if the user is running Netscape Navigator, and a different one if the user is running Microsoft Internet Explorer. You can also use two different statements depending on the user's platform (e.g., Windows 95, Macintosh PPC).

What is the navigator Object?

The `navigator` object does not belong to JavaScript's bulk of browser objects. It is an independent object, just like the `Math` object. This object combines various methods and properties providing information related to the user's software. For example, you can use this object to detect the user's browser, platform, plug-ins, and many other essential pieces of information.

You do not create instances of the `navigator` object in order to use it. You simply use the values of its properties and the values returned by its methods. Since the main topic of this chapter is software detection, we will deal with this object throughout the entire chapter.

Using the navigator Object to Detect the User's Browser and Platform

The `navigator` object features four properties on all versions of JavaScript:

- `appName`
- `appVersion`
- `appCodeName`
- `userAgent`

Figure 29-1 lists the value of each of these properties on Netscape Navigator 4.0 Preview Release 3 (Windows 95), and Figure 29-2 lists them on MSIE 3.0x (Windows 95).

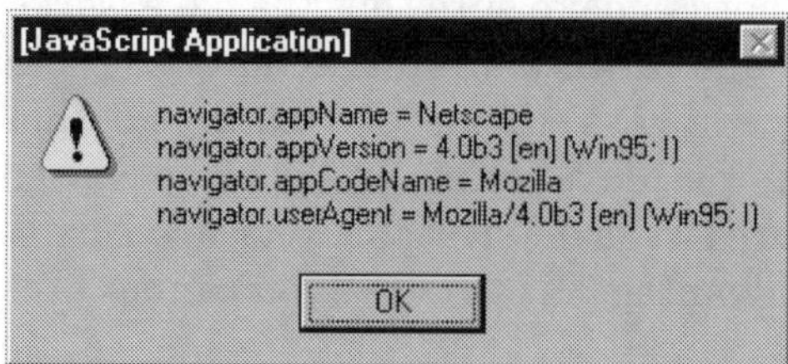

***Figure 29-1**. Property dumps for the `navigator` object under Netscape Navigator 4.0b3 (Windows 95).*

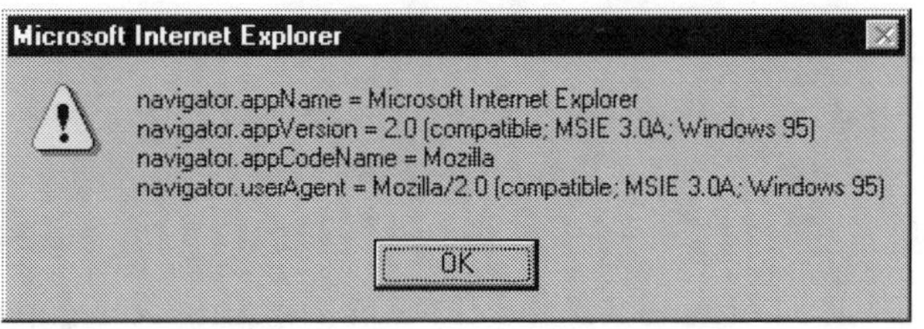

Figure 29-2. *Property dumps for the `navigator` object under MSIE 3.0x (Windows 95).*

Here is the script that we used to create these dialog boxes:

```
var text = ""
text += "navigator.appName = " + navigator.appName + "\n"
text += "navigator.appVersion = " + navigator.appVersion + "\n"
text += "navigator.appCodeName = " + navigator.appCodeName + "\n"
text += "navigator.userAgent = " + navigator.userAgent
alert(text)
```

The User Agent

Among all properties, the most useful one is `navigator.userAgent`. The roots of this property are held tightly in CGI programming. In the initial communication between the client and the server during an HTTP request, the browser sends the server bits of information, such as all the valid cookies stored on the client. Among this information, the browser sends the user-agent string to the server. This string is available to a CGI application through the HTTP_USER_AGENT variable. The exact definition of this variable is the browser that the client is using to send the HTTP request. Its general format is as follows:

```
software/version library/version
```

The `navigator.userAgent` variable is similar to the HTTP_USER_AGENT environment variable. This property is a combination of the `navigator.appCodeName` and `navigator.appVersion` properties. As a matter of fact, it is simply these two values separated by a slash. Therefore the following expression evaluates to `true`:

```
navigator.userAgent == navigator.appCodeName + "/" + navigator.appVersion
```

Determining the User's Browser

There are many ways to determine what browser the client is using, with the minimum number of `if` statements. For example, you can use the following function:

```
function getBrowser() {
     if (navigator.userAgent.indexOf("Mozilla/3.0") != -1)
          return 3
```

```
    if (navigator.userAgent.indexOf("MSIE 3.0") != -1)
        return 1
    if (navigator.userAgent.indexOf("Mozilla/2.0") != -1)
        return 2
    return 0
}
```

This function returns 3 if the client is running Netscape Navigator 3.0x, 2 if the client is running Netscape Navigator 2.0x, 1 if the client is running Microsoft Internet Explorer 3.0x, and 0 otherwise (any other JavaScript-enabled browser). We prefer to write a customized function for each script. For example, a function to check if the client is using Netscape Navigator would be the following:

```
function isNetscape() {
    return navigator.appName == "Netscape"
}
```

Figures 29-1 and 29-2 are a good reference for the properties you can use to accomplish your particular task.

Redirecting the User to a Browser-Specific Page

The easiest way to provide a distinct page for users with different browsers is to redirect some or all of them to another page. Here is a simple example, which loads a distinct Web page if the client is running Navigator 3.0x:

```
function getBrowser() {
    if (navigator.userAgent.indexOf("Mozilla/3.0") != -1)
        return 3
    if (navigator.userAgent.indexOf("MSIE 3.0") != -1)
        return 1
    if (navigator.userAgent.indexOf("Mozilla/2.0") != -1)
        return 2
    return 0
}

if (getBrowser() == 3)
    location.href = "URL of Navigator 3.0x-specific page"
```

The problem with this technique is that the user must wait for the new page to load (if he or she is using Netscape Navigator 3.0x). The first waiting period consists of the time until the document containing this script begins to load and the script is interpreted. If the client is using Navigator 3.0x, the condition `getBrowser() == 3` evaluates to `true`, and the user must wait until another page loads. In the following section, you will find out how to use an interesting technique involving frames to avoid the long waiting period.

Using Frames to Display Different Pages for Each Browser

You can use a hidden frame to display a different HTML document for each browser or version. This enables you to provide a page for Netscape Navigator 3.0 and up browsers, and another one just for Netscape Navigator 2.0 and MSIE 3.0. The main document is simply a frame-setting document that defines one frame. This technique even handles users with browsers that do not support JavaScript (or have it turned off) or frames. We'll use the following function to detect the user's browser:

```
function getBrowser() {
     var browserName = navigator.appName
     var browserVer = parseInt(navigator.appVersion)
     if (browserName == "Netscape" && browserVer >= 3)
          return "n3"
     if (browserName == "Netscape" && browserVer == 2)
          return "n2"
     // if (browserName == "Microsoft Internet Explorer" &&
                                   browserVer >= 2)
          return "e3"
}
```

Notice the use of the >= operator. We use it to check if the version of the user's browser is equal to or greater than the specified browser. The usage of the `browserName` variable is very simple, because it holds a plain JavaScript string for which we test equality. The usage of the `browserVer` variable, though, is somewhat more complicated. You may recall that `navigator.appVersion` is a string that begins with the browser version (e.g., 3.01). The `parseInt()` function evaluates a string from left to right, until it reaches a nondigit character. In the case of `navigator.appVersion`, it evaluates the string up to the space that separates the version number from the opening bracket, and returns the number in the form of an integer. If the user is running Netscape Navigator 3.01, for instance, the value of `browserVer` is 3. Since the value of `browserVer` is always a number, it is correct to compare it to a literal integer via a Boolean comparison operator. Note that the last `if` statement in the function can be commented out, because the `return` statement terminates the function, and there is only one possibility left.

In summary, this `getBrowser()` function returns one of three values (be prepared to modify it as new browsers are released):

- `"n3"` for Netscape Navigator 3.0x and above (Netscape Navigator 4.0 and so forth).

- "n2" for Netscape Navigator 2.0x.
- "e3" for Microsoft Internet Explorer 3.0x and above.

The next step is to display a different Web page for each browser, or browsers. Example 29-1 shows how to display a different one for each scenario:

```
<HTML>
<HEAD>
<TITLE>Actual title of page</TITLE>
<SCRIPT LANGUAGE="JavaScript">
<!--

function getBrowser() {
      var browserName = navigator.appName
      var browserVer = parseInt(browserVer = navigator.appVersion)

      if (browserName == "Netscape" && browserVer >= 3)
            return "n3"
      if (browserName == "Netscape" && browserVer == 2)
            return "n2"
      if (browserName == "Microsoft Internet Explorer" && browserVer >= 2)
            return "e3"
}

// retrieve user's browser
var browser = getBrowser()

// if client is using Navigator 3.0 or above
if (browser == "n3")
      document.write('<FRAMESET ROWS="100%, *" FRAMEBORDER=NO BORDER=0>' +
                  '<FRAME NAME="main" SRC="ns3_page.html" ' +
                  'SCROLLING=AUTO MARGINHEIGHT=2 MARGINWIDTH=2>' +
                  '</FRAMESET>')
else if (browser == "n2")
      document.write('<FRAMESET ROWS="100%, *" FRAMEBORDER=NO BORDER=0>' +
                 '<FRAME NAME="main" SRC="ns2_page.html" ' +
                 'SCROLLING=AUTO MARGINHEIGHT=2 MARGINWIDTH=2>' +
                 '</FRAMESET>')
else if (browser == "e3")
      document.write('<FRAMESET ROWS="100%, *" FRAMEBORDER=NO BORDER=0>' +
                  '<FRAME NAME="main" SRC="ie3_page.html" ' +
                  'SCROLLING=AUTO MARGINHEIGHT=2 MARGINWIDTH=2>' +
                  '</FRAMESET>')

// -->
</SCRIPT>
</HEAD>
</HTML>
```

***Example 29-1**. A frames document with only one frame.*

Example 29-1 displays a frameset containing one frame. A frameset avoids redirecting the browser to a distinct page, while still keeping the advantages of displaying a different page for each browser. Since the `<BODY>` tag disables frames, be careful not to place this script within `<BODY>` tags. The filenames `ns3_page.html`, `ns2_page.html`, and `ie3_page.html` are the URLs of the documents that you want to load for each browser. The file `ns3_page.html`, for example, loads if the user is running Netscape Navigator 3.0 or above.

Checking if Java is Enabled

We have already discussed the four basic properties of the `navigator` object, which also happen to be the only properties of this object under Netscape Navigator 2.0x and MSIE 3.0x. Under Navigator 3.0x, though, the `navigator` object features other important properties.

Select **Network Preferences...** from the Options menu, and click on the **Languages** tab. You should see two check boxes:

- Enable Java
- Enable JavaScript

The Enable JavaScript box should always be checked, unless you want to disable JavaScript. Provided it is checked, you can use the `navigator` object to detect the Enable Java box's state. The method that returns a Boolean value according to the box's state is `navigator.javaEnabled()`. This method returns `true` if Java is enabled, and `false` otherwise. The `navigator.javaEnabled()` is used mostly in concert with LiveConnect, because LiveConnect requires both Java and JavaScript to be enabled.

Summary

In this chapter, we discussed one of the most important features of JavaScript—browser detection. The ability to detect the user's browser is extremely useful, because it enables you to provide distinct Web pages to users with different browsers. Thus, your pages can be compatible with all browsers, and at the same time take advantage of features that are available only on the newest versions of Netscape Navigator and Microsoft Internet Explorer. We have also discussed the `navigator.javaEnabled()` method. The following chapter will suggest some applications of this method.

Chapter 30

Plug-ins

This chapter deals with JavaScript features that are not compatible with Netscape Navigator 2.0x and Microsoft Internet Explorer 3.0x.

In this chapter we do not discuss the connection between Java, JavaScript, and plug-ins, known as LiveConnect. LiveConnect is presented in the following chapter.

Embedding a Plug-in Object in HTML

A *plug-in* is a piece of software that the browser calls to process data referenced in an HTML document. In order to reference such data in an HTML tag, you must use the <EMBED> tag. This tag's general syntax is as follows:

```
<EMBED
      SRC=source
      NAME=appletName
      HEIGHT=height
      WIDTH=width>
      [<PARAM NAME=parameterName VALUE=parameterValue>]
      [...<PARAM>]
</EMBED>
```

SRC=*source* specifies the URL containing the source content to be interpreted by the plug-in.

NAME=*appletName* specifies the name of the embedded object in the document.

HEIGHT=*height* specifies the height of the applet in pixels within the browser window.

WIDTH=*width* specifies the width of the applet in pixels within the browser window.

`<PARAM>` defines a parameter for the embedded object.

`NAME=`*`parameterName`* specifies the name of the parameter.

`VALUE=`*`parameterValue`* specifies a value for the parameter (an argument).

We will refer to such `<EMBED>` definitions as plug-ins, although that is not entirely correct.

Referencing Plug-ins in JavaScript

You can reference the plug-ins in your code by using the `embeds` array, a property of the `document` object. This array contains an entry for each `Plugin` object (`<EMBED>` tag) in a document, in source order. That is, the first `Plugin` object in the document is reflected by the first element of the array, `document.embeds[0]`, and so on. The `length` property of this array, `document.embeds.length`, holds the number of `Plugin` objects in the document. Elements in the `embeds` array are read-only, so a statement such as the following has no effect:

```
document.embeds[0]="myVideo.avi"
```

It is important to understand that each element of the `embeds` array is a `Plugin` object. As you will see later in this chapter, referencing a `Plugin` object is very useful, because some plug-ins feature JavaScript methods.

You can also reference a `Plugin` object by its name. Take a look at the following HTML definition:

```
<EMBED SRC="rabin.avi" AUTOSTART=FALSE LOOP=FALSE HEIGHT=120 WIDTH=159
NAME="rabin">
```

Assuming this is the first plug-in in the HTML document, you can reference it via JavaScript in two ways:

1. `document.embeds[0]`
2. `document.rabin`

We recommend that you use the second fashion, because it is more convenient. It does not rely on the order in which the plug-ins are defined, so you do not have to modify your scripts if you choose to change the order of the plug-ins in the document. Secondly, you can choose meaningful names for your plug-ins so your code becomes much easier to understand.

Determining Installed Plug-ins with JavaScript

You can use JavaScript to determine if a user has installed a plug-in (the software). You can then display embedded plug-in data if the plug-in is installed, or alternative content if it is not. You can also determine whether a client is capable of handling a particular MIME (Multipart Internet Mail Extension) type. The `navigator` object has two properties for checking installed plug-ins:

- The `mimeTypes` object is an array of all the MIME types supported by the client. A MIME type can be supported either internally, via a helper application, or by plug-ins. Each element of this array is an object that has properties for its type, description, file extensions, and enabled plug-ins. The array is named `mimeTypes`, and each element is a `mimeTypes` object.
- The `plugins` object is an array of all the plug-ins installed on the client. Each element of this array has properties for its name and description as well as an array of `mimeTypes` objects for the MIME types supported by that plug-in. Each element of the `plugins` array is a `plugins` object.

In order to check if a plug-in is supported, you must know that plug-in's name. The general syntax used to check if a specific plug-in is installed is as follows:

```
if (navigator.plugins["name of the plug-in"]) …
```

The name often consists of space characters or other non-alphanumeric characters, so it is a common practice to use the array notation, even if the "dot" syntax is possible. The following script segment checks if the Shockwave plug-in is installed, and provides data for that plug-in if it is:

```
if (navigator.plugins["Shockwave"])
    document.writeln("<EMBED SRC='myMovie.dir' HEIGHT=100 WIDTH=100>")
else
    document.writeln("You don't have Shockwave installed!")
```

Once you have installed a plug-in on your computer, it is very easy to find its name.

Some JavaScript programmers prefer to write a simple Boolean function to assist in determining whether a given plug-in is installed. Here is the function:

```
function isInstalled(plugName) {
          if (navigator.plugins[plugName])
        return true
```

```
        else
            return false
}
```

The following script checks whether the client is capable of displaying QuickTime movies.

```
if (navigator.mimeTypes["video/quicktime"])
    document.writeln("Click <A HREF='movie.qt'>here</A> to see
                                a QuickTime movie")
else
    document.writeln("Sorry, can't show you any movies.")
```

You should use such plug-in detection routines with care, because they often conflict with LiveConnect routines located in the same document.

Properties of the mimeTypes Object

A `mimeTypes` object, as found in the `mimeTypes` array (as an element), features the following properties:

- `type`—the name of the MIME type, such as `"video/mpeg"` or `"audio/x-wav"`. This property is obviously a string.
- `description`—a description of the MIME type, such as `"JPEG Image"`.
- `enabledPlugin`—a reference to the `plugins` object that handles the MIME type.
- `suffixes`—a string listing possible filename extensions (suffixes) for the MIME type. This property is a string consisting of any valid suffix, typically three letters long, separated by commas.
- `length`—the number of elements in the array.

Example 30-1 shows a list of the MIME types supported by the browser, including all three string properties of each `mimeTypes` object.

```
<HTML>
<HEAD>
<TITLE>Supported MIME types</TITLE>
</HEAD>
<BODY>
<SCRIPT LANGUAGE="JavaScript">
<!--

// notice that you do not have to issue </TH> and </TD> tags!

document.write("<TABLE BORDER=1><TR VALIGN=TOP>" +
```

```
                  "<TH ALIGN=left><I>i</I>" +
                  "<TH ALIGN=left><I>type</I>" +
                  "<TH ALIGN=left><I>description</I>" +
                  "<TH ALIGN=left><I>suffixes</I></TR>")

for (var I = 0; i < navigator.mimeTypes.length; ++i) {
      document.writeln("<TR VALIGN=TOP><TD>" +
          i +
          "<TD>" +
          navigator.mimeTypes[i].type +
          "<TD>" +
          navigator.mimeTypes[i].description +
          "<TD>" +
          navigator.mimeTypes[i].suffixes +
          "</TR>")
}

document.writeln("</TABLE>")

// -->
</SCRIPT>
</BODY>
</HTML>
```

***Example 30-1**. We use tables to organize the list of supported MIME types.*

Try loading Example 30-1 in your browser. You should see a fairly long list of MIME types. Figure 30-1 shows the beginning of the list as it appeared on our computer.

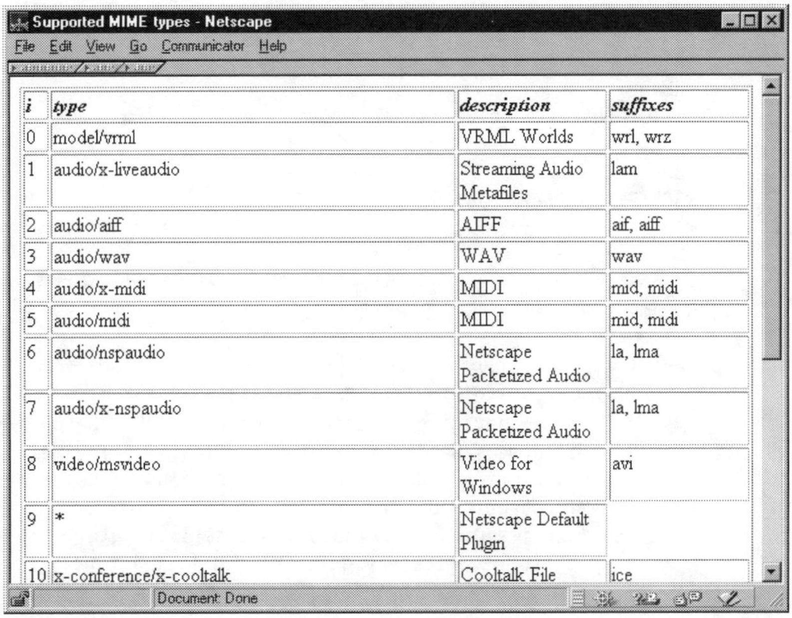

Supported MIME types - Netscape

File Edit View Go Communicator Help

i	*type*	*description*	*suffixes*
0	model/vrml	VRML Worlds	wrl, wrz
1	audio/x-liveaudio	Streaming Audio Metafiles	lam
2	audio/aiff	AIFF	aif, aiff
3	audio/wav	WAV	wav
4	audio/x-midi	MIDI	mid, midi
5	audio/midi	MIDI	mid, midi
6	audio/nspaudio	Netscape Packetized Audio	la, lma
7	audio/x-nspaudio	Netscape Packetized Audio	la, lma
8	video/msvideo	Video for Windows	avi
9	*	Netscape Default Plugin	
10	x-conference/x-cooltalk	Cooltalk File	ice

Document: Done

***Figure 30-1.** The scrollbar's position indicates that the number of MIME types supported by our browser is much more than 10.*

Notice that in Example 30-1 we referred to elements of the `mimeTypes` array by indexes. You can also use the MIME type's name as shown earlier in this chapter. Here are a few examples:

```
navigator.mimeTypes["image/jpeg"].type
navigator.mimeTypes["image/jpeg"].description
navigator.mimeTypes["image/jpeg"].suffixes
```

Properties of the plugins Object

The `plugins` object features the following properties:

- `name`—the name of the plug-in
- `filename`—the name of the plug-in file on disk.
- `description`—a description supplied by the plug-in itself.
- `length`—the number of elements in the array.
- [...]—array of `mimeTypes` objects, indexed by number or type, that the plug-in can handle.

The following statement, for example, assigns shorthand variables for the predefined Shockwave properties:

```
var myPlugin = navigator.plugins["Shockwave"].name
var myPluginFile = navigator.plugins["Shockwave"].filename
var myPluginDesc = navigator.plugins["Shockwave"].description
```

Example 30-2 lists the installed plug-ins, including each plug-in's name, filename, description, and MIME types that it handles.

```
<HTML>
<HEAD>
<TITLE>Installed plug-ins</TITLE>
</HEAD>
<BODY>
<SCRIPT LANGUAGE="JavaScript">
<!--

// notice that you do not have to issue </TH> and </TD> tags!
document.write("<TABLE BORDER=1>")

for (i = 0; i < navigator.plugins.length; ++i) {
     document.writeln("<TR><TD><FONT SIZE=2>" +
     "<U><B>" + navigator.plugins[i].name + "</B></U><BR>" +
     "<U>Filename:</U> " + navigator.plugins[i].filename + "<BR>" +
     "<U>Description:</U> " + navigator.plugins[i].description + "<BR>" +
     "<U>MIME types:</U> ")
     for (var j = 0; j < navigator.plugins[i].length; ++j) {
          document.write(navigator.plugins[i][j].type + "; ")
     }
```

```
        document.write("</FONT></TD></TR>")
}

document.write("</TABLE>")

// -->
</SCRIPT>
</BODY>
</HTML>
```


Example 30-2. *We use the navigator.plugins to list the installed plug-ins and their properties.*

Figure 30-2 shows the exact output of Example 30-2 on our PC.

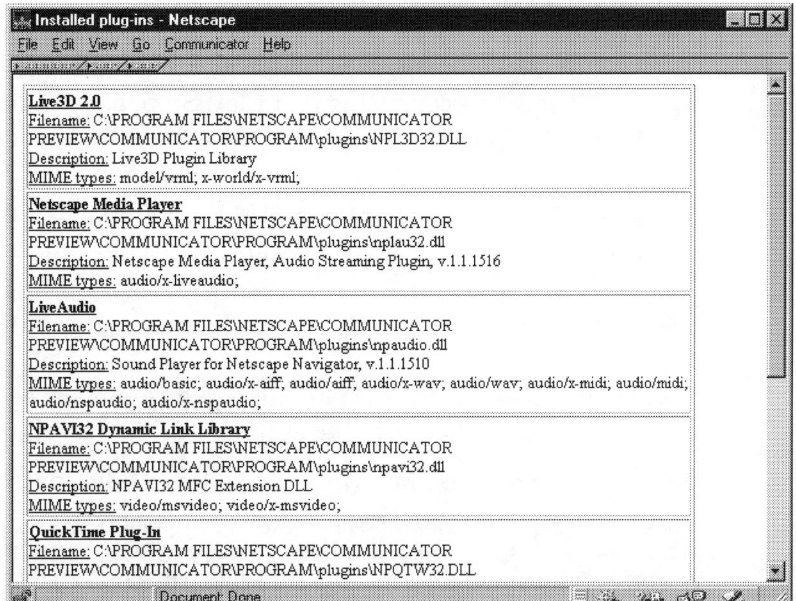

Figure 30-2. *The plug-ins installed on our computer.*

The following statement assigns the string `"LiveAudio"` to a variable:

```
var audioPlugin = navigator.mimeTypes["audio/basic"].enabledPlugin.name
```

The `name` property belongs to a `plugins` object, because `navigator.mimeTypes["audio/basic"].enabledPlugin` is equivalent to `navigator.plugins["LiveAudio"]`.

LiveAudio and LiveVideo

LiveAudio and LiveVideo are plug-ins that come built into Netscape Navigator 3.0x and above. LiveAudio enables you to embed audio in a Web page, whereas LiveVideo supports various video formats. Since both LiveAudio and LiveVideo are plug-ins, you include them in an HTML document via the standard `<EMBED>` tag.

LiveAudio

LiveAudio plays audio files in WAV, AIFF, AU, and MIDI formats. Audio controls appear according to the size specified in the `WIDTH` and `HEIGHT` parameters in the `<EMBED>` tag. You can create an audio console with any of the following views:

- `console`—consisting of a Play, Pause, Stop, and volume control lever. This is the most complete suite of controls.
- `smallConsole`—consisting of a Play, Stop, and volume control lever. The buttons in this view are somewhat smaller than those in a `console`.
- `playButton`—a button that starts the sound playing.
- `pauseButton`—a button that pauses (without unloading) the sound while it is playing.
- `stopButton`—a button that ends the playing of sound and unloads it.
- `volumeLever`—a lever that adjusts the volume level for playback of the sound (and adjusts the system's volume level).

Here is the general HTML syntax for a LiveAudio control:

```
<EMBED SRC=[URL] AUTOSTART=[TRUE|FALSE] LOOP=[TRUE|FALSE|INTEGER]
STARTTIME=[MINUTES:SECONDS] ENDTIME=[MINUTES:SECONDS] VOLUME=[0-100]
WIDTH=[#PIXELS] HEIGHT=[#PIXELS] ALIGN=[TOP|BOTTOM|CENTER|BASELINE
|LEFT|RIGHT|TEXTTOP|MIDDLE|ABSMIDDLE|ABSBOTTOM] CONTROLS=[CONSOLE
|SMALLCONSOLE|PLAYBUTTON|PAUSEBUTTON|STOPBUTTON|VOLUMELEVER] HIDDEN=[TRUE]
MASTERSOUND NAME=[UNIQUE NAME TO GROUP CONTROLS TOGETHER SO THAT THEY
CONTROL ONE SOUND]...>
```

The syntax may seem very complicated, but a close look shows that it does not consist of many attributes. The misleading fact is that there are many different values that can be given to each attribute. Here is a short description of each attribute and the values it accepts:

`SRC=[URL]`—The URL of the source sound file. It can be either a relative URL or a full one, including the server's identification.

AUTOSTART=[TRUE|FALSE]—When set to TRUE, the sound will begin playing automatically upon loading the Web. The default is FALSE.

LOOP=[TRUE|FALSE|*INTEGER*]—When set to TRUE, the sound will play continuously until the stop button is clicked on the console, or the user goes to another page. If an *INTEGER* value is used, the sound repeats the number of times indicated.

STARTTIME=[*MINUTES:SECONDS*]—Use STARTTIME to specify where the playback should begin. If you want to begin the sound at 30 seconds, you would set the value to 00:30 (implemented only on Windows 95, NT, and Macintosh).

ENDTIME=[*MINUTES:SECONDS*]—Use ENDTIME to specify where in the sound file you would like playback to end. If you want to stop the sound at 1.5 minutes, you would set the value to 01:30 (implemented only on Windows 95, NT, and Macintosh).

VOLUME=[0-100]—This value must be a number between 0 and 100 to represent 0 to 100 percent. This attribute sets the volume for the sound that is playing or for the entire system if MASTERVOLUME (see NAME attribute below) is used. The default volume level is the current system volume.

WIDTH=[*#PIXELS*]—Use WIDTH to change the width of the console or console element. For the CONSOLE and SMALLCONSOLE, the default is WIDTH=144. For the VOLUMELEVER, the default is WIDTH=74. For a button, the default is WIDTH=37 (WIDTH=34 looks much better). We suggest that you specify this attribute regardless of whether it is the default value.

HEIGHT=[*#PIXELS*]—Use HEIGHT to change the height of the console. For the CONSOLE, the default is HEIGHT=60. For the SMALLCONSOLE, the default is HEIGHT=15. For the VOLUMELEVER, the default is HEIGHT=20. For a button, the default is HEIGHT=22. We strongly recommend specifying this attribute even if it is the default.

ALIGN=[TOP|BOTTOM|CENTER|BASELINE|LEFT|RIGHT|TEXTTOP|MIDDLE|ABSMIDDLE|ABSBOTTOM]—While RIGHT and LEFT specify the position of the console with respect to the page, the other options tell Netscape Navigator how you want to align text as it flows around the consoles. It acts similarly to the ALIGN attribute of the IMG tag. The default value is BOTTOM.

CONTROLS=[CONSOLE|SMALLCONSOLE|PLAYBUTTON|PAUSEBUTTON|STOPBUTTON|VOLUMELEVER]—Use this attribute to select the control you want to place on your page. The default for this field is CONSOLE.

HIDDEN=[TRUE]—The value for this attribute should be TRUE, or it should not be included in the EMBED tag. If it is specified as TRUE, no controls will load and the sound will act as a background one.

MASTERSOUND—This value must be used when grouping sounds together in a NAME group. It takes no value (it must merely be present in the EMBED tag), but tells LiveAudio which file is a genuine sound file and allows it to ignore any stub files. In order to associate several EMBEDs with one sound file, all EMBEDs should have the same name (see the NAME attribute). The SRC attribute of one of those EMBEDs should be the URL of the actual sound file, whereas the other SRC attributes should specify the URL of a stub file. A stub file is a text file containing a single space (that's the recommended content). Its name should consist of a sound extension (e.g., .mid, .wav, .aif). To create a page with four LiveAudio elements (Play, Pause, Stop, and Volume) all controlling the same file, you need to create three sound stubs and of course have one legitimate sound file (for a total of four EMBEDs). Anytime you use the NAME attribute in a LiveAudio <EMBED>, you must also use a MASTERSOUND attribute. LiveAudio will play no sound when a NAME attribute exists without a corresponding MASTERSOUND attribute, even if that is the only EMBED with that name on the page. Since you do not want LiveAudio to attempt to play a stub file (it contains no sound data), you should specify a NAME attribute with no MASTERSOUND attribute. The <EMBED> reflecting the legitimate sound file, on the other hand, should feature MASTERSOUND in order to play.

NAME=[*UNIQUE NAME*]—This attribute sets a unique ID for a group of EMBEDs (each with a distinct CONTROLS attribute), so they all act on the same sound as it plays. The deficiency of EMBED's syntax is that it takes only one value for CONTROLS. For example, if a content creator wishes to have one sound controlled by two embedded objects (a PLAYBUTTON and a STOPBUTTON), he or she must use two separate EMBEDs and group them by the NAME attribute. In this case, the MASTERSOUND tag is necessary to flag LiveAudio and let it know which of the two EMBED tags actually has the sound file you wish to control. LiveAudio ignores any EMBED(s) with no MASTERSOUND tag.

If you want one VOLUMELEVER to control multiple NAMEs (or the system volume), create an EMBED using VOLUMELEVER as the CONTROL. Then set NAME to "_MASTERVOLUME".

Example 30-3 is a nice summary of the LiveAudio features.

```
<HTML>
<HEAD>
```

```
<TITLE>LiveAudio</TITLE>
</HEAD>
<BODY>
<TABLE BORDER=1><TR>
<TD BGCOLOR="black" ALIGN="center">
<FONT COLOR="white" SIZE=2>Beverly Hills</FONT><BR>
<EMBED SRC="bh190210.mid"
       AUTOSTART=FALSE
       LOOP=FALSE
       CONTROLS=PLAYBUTTON
       WIDTH=34
       HEIGHT=22
       MASTERSOUND
       NAME="90210">
<EMBED SRC="stub1.aif"
       AUTOSTART=FALSE
       LOOP=FALSE
       CONTROLS=STOPBUTTON
       WIDTH=34
       HEIGHT=22
       NAME="90210">
<EMBED SRC="stub2.aif"
       AUTOSTART=FALSE
       LOOP=FALSE
       CONTROLS=PAUSEBUTTON
       WIDTH=34
       HEIGHT=22
       NAME="90210">
</TD>
<TD BGCOLOR="black" ALIGN="center">
<FONT COLOR="white" SIZE=2>Melrose</FONT><BR>
<EMBED SRC="melrose.mid"
       AUTOSTART=FALSE
       LOOP=FALSE
       CONTROLS=PLAYBUTTON
       WIDTH=34
       HEIGHT=22
       MASTERSOUND
       NAME="melrose">
<EMBED SRC="stub1.aif"
       AUTOSTART=FALSE
       LOOP=FALSE
       CONTROLS=STOPBUTTON
       WIDTH=34
       HEIGHT=22
       NAME="melrose">
<EMBED SRC="stub2.aif"
       AUTOSTART=FALSE
       LOOP=FALSE
       CONTROLS=PAUSEBUTTON
       WIDTH=34
       HEIGHT=22
```

```
        NAME="melrose">
</TD>
</TR><TR>
<TD COLSPAN=2 BGCOLOR="black" ALIGN="center">
<FONT COLOR="white" SIZE=2>Master Volume</FONT><BR>
<EMBED SRC="stub1.aif"
        CONTROLS=VOLUMELEVER
        WIDTH=74
        HEIGHT=20
        NAME="_MASTERVOLUME">
</TD>
</TR></TABLE>
</BODY>
</HTML>
```

Example 30-3 (ex30-3.htm)*. Two sound files, with three `EMBED`s for each and an EMBED to control the system volume.*

Figure 30-3 shows the exact output of Example 30-3 by Netscape Navigator.

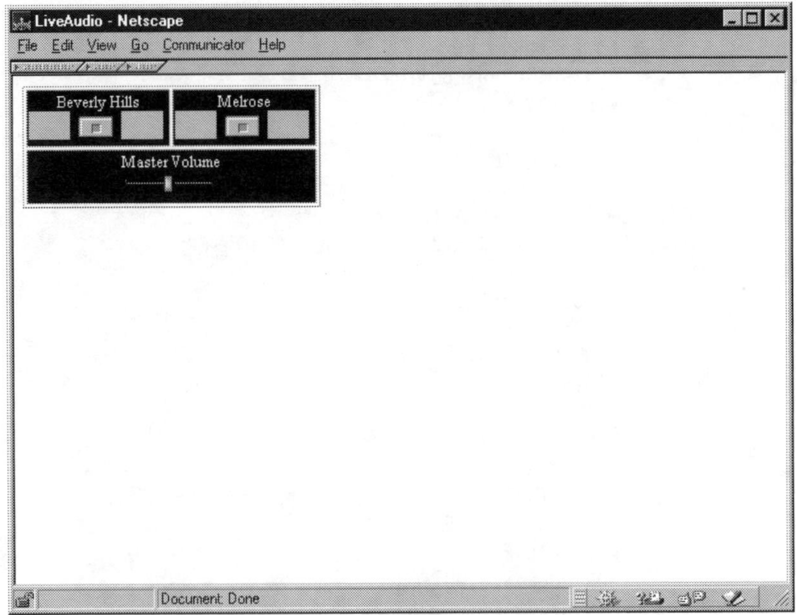

Figure 30-3*. You can create custom consoles using several elements (`EMBED`s).*

Since each `EMBED` statement can specify one control object, we need three of them to place the `PLAYBUTTON`, `STOPBUTTON`, and `PAUSEBUTTON`. Here's the syntax for the Master Volume control:

```
<EMBED SRC="stub1.aif"
        CONTROLS=VOLUMELEVER
```

```
        WIDTH=74
        HEIGHT=20
        NAME="_MASTERVOLUME">
```

Notice the underscore which is the first character in the object's name.

LiveVideo

LiveVideo plays video files in AVI format. It is currently supported for Windows 95 and NT only. Use the <EMBED> tag to place AVI movies in your Web page. The general syntax for this tag is as follows:

```
<EMBED SRC=[URL] AUTOSTART=[TRUE|FALSE] LOOP=[TRUE|FALSE] WIDTH=
                                     [#PIXELS] HEIGHT=[#PIXELS]
ALIGN=[TOP|BOTTOM|CENTER|BASELINE|LEFT|RIGHT|TEXTTOP|MIDDLE|ABSMIDDLE|
                                     ABSBOTTOM]...>
```

The attributes should be obvious, because we have already discussed them in the LiveAudio section.

Once the AVI video loads, you can start it with a click (only if you didn't set AUTOSTART to TRUE). Click the right mouse button over the video panel for a list of operations.

Other Plug-ins

There are currently hundreds of plug-ins besides LiveAudio and Live-Video. We decided to focus on these for several reasons:

- They come bundled with Netscape Navigator 3.0, so anyone running this browser can view audio and video files without downloading any external software.
- Both LiveAudio and LiveVideo enable LiveConnect, so you can control them with JavaScript (and Java).

Live3D lets you access distributed 3D spaces rendered at maximum speed with adaptive rendering, background processing, hardware acceleration, and GZIP data compression. This plug-in also matches the preceding features, but it is beyond the scope of this book because it requires VRML.

Summary

In this chapter we focused on embedding plug-ins in HTML, and referencing them with JavaScript. We also introduced LiveAudio and LiveVideo, mostly for the sake of the following chapter. Before you move on to the following chapter, be sure you know how to reference plug-ins with JavaScript, both with the `embeds` array and by name. In the following chapter we discuss LiveConnect, one of the strongest features implemented by Netscape in Navigator 3.0 and above.

Chapter 31

LiveConnect—Connecting JavaScript, Java, and Plug-ins

What is LiveConnect?

LiveConnect enables communication between JavaScript and Java applets in a page, and between JavaScript and plug-ins loaded on a page. Originally named JavaScript Wiring at the March 1996 Netscape Developer Conference, this technology has been recently renamed LiveConnect. With LiveConnect you can:

- Use JavaScript to access Java variables, methods, classes, and packages directly.
- Control Java applets or plug-ins with JavaScript.
- Use Java code to access JavaScript methods and properties.

Enabling LiveConnect

LiveConnect is enabled by default in Netscape Navigator 3.0x and 4.0. Because LiveConnect enables communication between JavaScript and Java, both these languages should be enabled. To confirm that LiveConnect is enabled, choose **Network Preferences** from the Options menu, then choose the **Languages** tab. Make sure that both check boxes are checked. Note that even if you plan to use LiveConnect to control plug-ins with JavaScript, the Enable Java box must be checked.

LiveConnect doesn't work on Netscape Navigator 3.0x for Mac 68K or Windows 3.1x operating systems.

The Java Console

The Java Console is a Navigator window that displays Java messages. When you use the class variables `out` or `err` in `java.lang.System` to output a message, the message appears in the Java Console. For example, the following `init()` method of a Java class displays the message "`Class loaded!`" in the Java Console:

```
public void init() {
   System.out.println("Class loaded!");
}
```

Figure 31-1 shows the Java Console after loading an applet consisting of the preceding `init()` method.

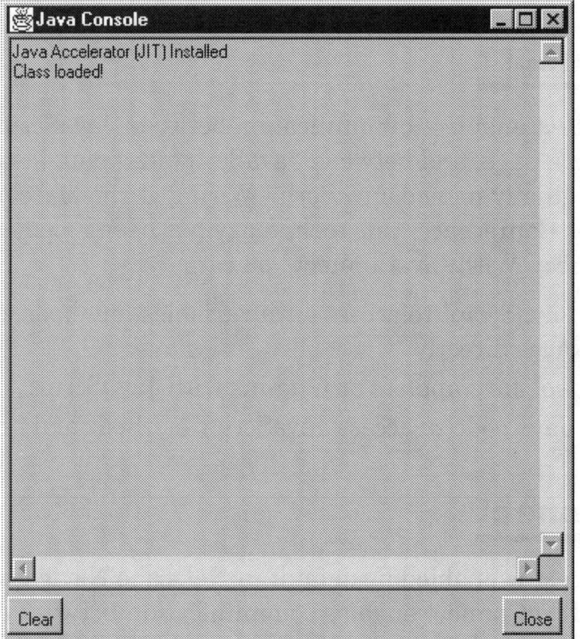

Figure 31-1. *The Java Console after printing a short message in it.*

You can use the Java Console to present messages to the user or to trace the values of variables at different stages of an applet's execution. However, do not rely on it for presenting messages to the user because the Java Console is rarely open.

Load the Java Console in Netscape Navigator 3.0x from the Options menu. In Netscape Navigator 4.0, this feature is available in the Window menu.

Netscape Packages

LiveConnect-enabled versions of Netscape Navigator come with a file that includes the following Java packages:

- `netscape` packages to enable JavaScript and Java communication.
- `java` and `sun` packages to provide security enhancements for LiveConnect.

In Netscape Navigator 3.0x this file is named java_30 (or java_301 for Navigator 3.01), whereas in Navigator 4.0 it is named java_40.

If you have some Java programming experience, you probably know that the `java` and `sun` packages already exist in the Sun 1.0.2 Java Development Kit (JDK). These packages replace packages in the JDK src.zip archive.

The file java_*x*0 contains the following packages:

- `netscape.javascript` implements the `JSObject` class to let your Java applet access JavaScript methods and properties. It also implements `JSException` to throw an exception when JavaScript code returns an error.
- `netscape.plugin` implements the `Plugin` class to enable JavaScript and plug-in communication. Compile your plug-in with this class to allow applets and JavaScript code to manipulate the plug-in.

In addition, java_*x*0 contains some other `netscape` packages: `netscape.applet` is a replacement for the Sun JDK package `sun.applet`, and `netscape.net` is a replacement for the Sun JDK package `sun.net`.

Compiling Java Code with Netscape Packages

The java_*x*0 file is delivered in the Program\java\classes directory beneath the Navigator directory. To access the packages in java_*x*0, place the file in the `classpath` of the JDK compiler in either of the following ways:

- Create a `CLASSPATH` environment variable to specify the paths and names of java_*x*0 and classes.zip.
- When you compile the Java code, specify the location of java_*x*0 and classes.zip by using the `-classpath` command line parameter.

If you are using an application such as Visual J++, you should specify the path in that application. For example, choose the **Settings...**

option from the Build menu in Visual J++ 1.0 to specify the directories containing the classes.

For some reasons, the internal structure of java_30 is not as expected by the Java compiler. Therefore, you cannot use the following statement:

```
import netscape.javascript.*
```

Instead, you must specify the actual names (e.g., `netscape.javascript.JSObject`). One workaround is to rename the java_30 file to java_30.zip (by adding a .zip extension). Then, create a new directory, and unzip the archive to that directory. Specify the directory in the `CLASSPATH` environment variable, the `-classpath` parameter, or the corresponding field in Visual J++. Note that all applets in this chapter were built with Visual J++ (it shouldn't matter much).

Java to JavaScript Communication

To access JavaScript methods, properties, and data structures from your Java applet, import the Netscape `javascript` package in the following form:

```
import netscape.javascript.*
```

If this technique does not work properly, try the following format:

```
import netscape.javascript.JSObject
import netscape.javascript.JSException
```

The package `netscape.javascript` defines the `JSObject` class and the `JSException` exception object.

Not all applets have permission to access JavaScript. You may permit such access by specifying the `MAYSCRIPT` attribute of the `APPLET` tag. Accessing JavaScript when `MAYSCRIPT` is not present results in an exception. The following HTML code shows how to grant a Java applet permission to access JavaScript:

```
<APPLET CODE="className" NAME="appletName" HEIGHT=height WIDTH=width
MAYSCRIPT>
```

Passing Values Between Java and JavaScript

JSObject allows Java to manipulate objects that are defined in JavaScript. Values passed from Java to JavaScript are converted as follows:

- `JSObject` is converted to the original JavaScript object.
- Any other Java object is converted to a JavaScript wrapper, which can be used to access methods and fields of the `java` object. Converting this wrapper to a string will call the `toString()` method on the original object; converting it to a number will call the `floatValue()` method if possible, and will fail otherwise. Converting it to a Boolean value will try to call the `booleanValue()` method in the same way.
- Java arrays are wrapped with a JavaScript object that understands *array*`.length` and *array*`[`*index*`]`—the `Array` object. Therefore, a Java array in JavaScript is actually an instance of the `Array` object, thus featuring the same properties and methods of any other instance of this object.
- A Java `boolean` is converted to a JavaScript Boolean value.
- Java `byte`, `char`, `short`, `int`, `long`, `float`, and `double` are converted to JavaScript numbers. Since JavaScript is loosely typed, these data types are not distinguished in JavaScript as they are in Java.

Values passed from JavaScript to Java are converted as follows:

- Objects which are wrappers around `java` objects are unwrapped. This conversion is the opposite of the second one in the Java-to-JavaScript conversion listing.
- Other objects, which were not originally Java objects, are wrapped with a `JSObject`.
- Strings, numbers, and Boolean values are converted to `String`, `Float`, and `Boolean` objects, respectively.

All JavaScript values show up as some kind of `java.lang.Object` in Java. In order to make use of them, you will have to cast them to subclasses of `java.lang.Object`, using the regular casting technique.

Getting a Handle for the Browser Window

Before you can access JavaScript, you must get a handle for the browser window. Use the `getWindow()` method of the `JSObject` class to do so.

The following Java class gets a handle for the browser window containing the applet:

```
import netscape.javascript.JSObject;
import java.applet.Applet;

public class js extends Applet {
     JSObject win;
```

```
        public void init() {
              win = JSObject.getWindow(this);
        }
}
```

Accessing JavaScript Objects and Properties

The getMember() method in the class netscape.javascript.JSObject enables you to access JavaScript objects and properties. You should invoke this function as a method of a JavaScript object reflected in Java (the JavaScript object is wrapped with a JSObject). The getMember() method retrieved a named property of a JavaScript object, thus returning a value equivalent to this.*name* in JavaScript. This method receives the name of the desired property in the form of a string. The following Java method provides you the value of a check box in an HTML document (provided that the applet is loaded from the same HTML document):

```
public void init() {
      win = JSObject.getWindow(this);
      JSObject doc = (JSObject) win.getMember("document");
      JSObject myForm = (JSObject) doc.getMember("myForm");
      JSObject check = (JSObject) myForm.getMember("myBox");
      Boolean isChecked = (Boolean) check.getMember("checked");
}
```

Since data type casting is often very confusing, take special precautions when using such routines.

Don't worry if you don't completely understand this topic. As you will see later, you will probably never need to use it, because it is much easier to hand values from JavaScript to Java rather than the opposite way.

Calling JavaScript Methods

The eval() method in the class netscape.javascript.JSObject enables you to execute any valid JavaScript statement within a Java code. Use getWindow() to get a handle for the JavaScript window (the window containing the desired JavaScript functions or methods), then use eval() to execute a JavaScript statement. The eval() method is mostly used to invoke JavaScript methods, using the following syntax:

```
JSObject.getWindow().eval("expression")
```

Be aware that if you want to hand an argument to a JavaScript method in the form of a Java data structure (e.g., a String or an int), the argument should first be evaluated to its literal value in the Java applet. For example, you can use the following Java method to invoke the JavaScript's `alert()` method:

```
public void JSalert(String str) {
     win.eval("alert(\"" + str + "\")");
}
```

Example 31-1 shows how to invoke a JavaScript method and a JavaScript function using Java.

```
<HTML>
<HEAD>
<TITLE>Invoking a JavaScript method from a Java Applet</TITLE>
<SCRIPT LANGUAGE="JavaScript">
<!--

function myAlert(str) {
     window.alert(str)
}

// -->
</SCRIPT>
</HEAD>
<BODY>
<APPLET CODE="callMe" NAME="callMe" MAYSCRIPT>
</APPLET>
</BODY>
</HTML>
```

Example 31-1 (ex31-1.htm)*. A simple HTML document with a Java applet and a deferred JavaScript function.*

Here's the source code for the `callMe` class in Example 31-1:

```
import netscape.javascript.JSObject;
import java.applet.Applet;

public class callMe extends Applet {
     JSObject win;

     public void init() {
          win = JSObject.getWindow(this);
          makeAlert1();
          makeAlert2();
     }

     private void makeAlert1() {
          win.eval("alert(\"LiveConnect is cool.\")");
     }

     private void makeAlert2() {
          win.eval("myAlert(\"LiveConnect is cool.\")");
```

```
    }
}
```

***Example 31-1a (callMe.java)**. The source code for the callMe class.*

First, we declare a variable (which is an object) of type JSObject. The init() method associates this variable with the browser window using the getWindow() method in netscape.javascript.JSObject. It then invokes the other methods in order. The method makeAlert1() generates a JavaScript alert dialog box by calling the window object's alert() method with a literal argument. The second method, makeAlert2(), does exactly the same by calling a user-defined JavaScript function in the HTML document. Both methods use the eval() method in netscape.javascript.JSObject.

Other methods in the JSObject class

Here is a complete listing of all the methods in the netscape.javascript.JSObject class, as explained in Netscape's documentation.

- public Object getMember(String *name*)—Retrieves a named member of a JavaScript object. Equivalent to "this.name" in JavaScript.
- public Object getSlot(int *index*)—Retrieves an indexed member of a JavaScript object. Equivalent to "this[*index*]" in JavaScript.
- public void setMember(String *name*, Object *value*)—Sets a named member of a JavaScript object. Equivalent to "this.*name* = *value*" in JavaScript.
- public void setSlot(int *index*, Object *value*)—Sets an indexed member of a JavaScript object. Equivalent to "this[*index*] = *value*" in JavaScript.
- public void removeMember(String *name*)—Removes a named member of a JavaScript object.
- public Object call(String *methodName*, *args[]*)—Calls a JavaScript method. Equivalent to "this.*methodName*(*args*[0], *args*[1], ...)" in JavaScript.
- public Object eval(String *s*)—Evaluates a JavaScript expression. The expression is a string of JavaScript source code which will be evaluated in the context given by "this".
- public String toString()—Converts a JSObject to a String. This method overrides toString() in class Object.

- `public static JSObject getWindow(Applet applet)`—Gets a `JSObject` for the window containing the given applet.
- `protected void finalize()`—Finalizing decrements the reference count on the corresponding JavaScript object. This method overrides `finalize()` in class `Object`.

JavaScript Exception

The `netscape.javascript.JSException` class enables you to catch JavaScript exceptions. A JavaScript exception occurs as a result of a JavaScript error caused by a Java applet. In order to execute Java code when a JavaScript exception occurs, you must catch the exception using the following syntax:

```
try {
    Java code involving JSObject methods
}
catch (JSException e) {
    Java code to execute when a JavaScript exception occurs
}
```

Bear in mind that you should either import `netscape.javascript.JSException` or use this complete specification instead of `JSException`. For more information regarding the `netscape.javascript.JSException` class, take a look at `<http://home.netscape.com/eng/mozilla/3.0/handbook/javascript/packages/netscape.javascript.JSException.html>`.

JavaScript to Java Communication

LiveConnect provides three ways for JavaScript to communicate with Java:

1. JavaScript can call Java methods directly.
2. JavaScript can control Java applets.
3. JavaScript can control Java plug-ins.

You may have noticed that we did not introduce many examples and detailed explanations in the previous section. As a JavaScript scripter, you do not need to know how to write a Java applet (though it would be very useful). However, in the way Java programmers need to know how to access JavaScript from Java, you should know how to access existing applets from JavaScript. In this section we discuss each of the three techniques in depth, including some useful examples.

Accessing Java Directly

When LiveConnect is enabled, JavaScript can make direct calls to Java methods. For example, you can call `System.out.println()` to display a message on the Java Console.

In JavaScript, Java packages and classes are properties of the `Packages` object. So the general syntax for invoking a Java method in a JavaScript script is as follows:

```
[Packages.]packageName.className.methodName
```

The name of the `Packages` object is optional for `java`, `sun`, and `netscape` packages. For example, the `System` class can be referenced in one of the following ways:

```
Packages.java.lang.System

java.lang.System
```

Access properties and methods in a class in the same way you would access them in Java. The following script segment, for instance, displays a message in the Java Console:

```
var System = java.lang.System
System.err.println("This is JavaScript invoking a Java method!")
```

Because `println()` expects a `String (java.lang.String)` argument, the JavaScript interpreter automatically converts the JavaScript string to a Java `String` data type.

Example 31-2 shows how to extract the dimensions and resolution of the user's screen and assign them to JavaScript variables.

```
<HTML>
<HEAD>
<TITLE>Accessing Java directly</TITLE>
<SCRIPT LANGUAGE="JavaScript">
<!--

var toolkit = java.awt.Toolkit.getDefaultToolkit()
var screenSize = toolkit.getScreenSize()
var width = screenSize.width
var height = screenSize.height
var dpi = toolkit.getScreenResolution()
alert("Your screen resolution is " + width + " x " + height + " at "
                                + dpi + " dpi!")

// -->
</SCRIPT>
</HEAD>
```

```
<BODY>
</BODY>
</HTML>
```

Example 31-2 (ex31-2.htm). *Using LiveConnect, you can find the exact dimensions of the user's screen, and even its resolution (dots per inch).*

Controlling Java Applets

The idea of enabling JavaScript scripts to control Java applets is to allow scripters to control the behavior of an applet without having to know much Java. However, in order to understand how to create an applet suitable for JavaScript access, or to control an existing Java applet with no documentation, you must know some Java basics.

Java applets employ many of the same programming concepts as JavaScript. Applet writers can determine which variables and methods are accessible to calls from outside the applet. All public items can be accessed from JavaScript. For example, instead of defining an instance variable like this:

```
int speed;
```

a Java programmer would make the variable accessible by JavaScript with the following variable declaration:

```
public int speed;
```

The same applies to methods in a class, so a method such as the following could be invoked by a JavaScript script:

```
public void start() {
     if(thread == null) {
          thread = new Thread(this);
          thread.start();
     }
}
```

Variables and methods which are not declared with the `public` keyword are not accessible by JavaScript, and thus play no role in LiveConnect. In this section, we'll base our discussion on the nervous class. Here is the source code for that class:

```
import java.awt.Graphics;
import java.awt.Font;
import java.applet.Applet;

public class nervous extends Applet implements Runnable {
     // array declarations
     char separated[];
```

```
// thread declarations
Thread killme = null;

// font declarations
Font displayFont;

// integer declarations
int i;
int xCoordinate = 0, yCoordinate = 0;
int speed;
int counter = 0;
int fontSize;
int fontStyle;

// string declarations
String num;
String fontName;
String text = null;

// Boolean declarations
boolean threadSuspended = false;

public void init() {
     getAttributes();
     separated = new char[text.length()];
     text.getChars(0, text.length(), separated, 0);
     resize(460, 60);
     displayFont = new Font(fontName, fontStyle, fontSize);
}

public void start() {
     if (killme == null) {
          killme = new Thread(this);
          killme.start();
     }
}

public void stop() {
     killme.stop();
     killme = null;
}

public void run() {
     while (killme != null) {
          try {
               Thread.sleep(speed);
          } catch (InterruptedException e) {}
          repaint();
     }
     killme = null;
}
```

```
public void paint(Graphics g) {
     g.setFont(displayFont); // set current font
     for (i = 0; i < text.length(); ++i) {
          xCoordinate = (int) (Math.random() * 10 + 15 * i);
          yCoordinate = (int) (Math.random() * 10 + 36);
          g.drawChars(separated, i, 1, xCoordinate, yCoordinate);
     }
}

/*************************************
     private methods for internal use
*************************************/

private void getAttributes() {
     // get text parameter
     text = getParameter("text");
     if (text == null)
          text = "JavaScript"; // default value

     // get speed parameter
     String speedString = getParameter("speed");
     if (speedString == null)
          speedString = "100"; // default value
     speed = Integer.parseInt(speedString);

     // get font parameter
     fontName = getParameter("font");
     if (fontName == null)
          fontName = "TimesRoman"; // default value

     // get size parameter
     String temp = getParameter("size");
     setFontSize(temp); // invoke function to set size

     // get style parameter
     temp = getParameter("style");
     setFontStyle(temp); // invoke function to set style
}

private void setFontSize(String size) {
     try {
          fontSize = Integer.parseInt(size);
     }
     catch (Exception e) {
          fontSize = 36;
     }
}

private void setFontStyle(String style) {
     try {
          if (style.equalsIgnoreCase("Plain"))
               fontStyle = Font.PLAIN;
```

```
                else if (style.equalsIgnoreCase("Italic"))
                    fontStyle = Font.ITALIC;
                else
                    fontStyle = Font.BOLD;
            }
            catch(Exception e) {
                fontStyle = Font.BOLD;
            }
        }
    }
```

Example 31-3a (nervous.java). *The source code for a simple "nervous text" applet.*

If you are a Java programmer, you'll immediately notice that the preceding Java code is not perfect, but it's good enough to demonstrate LiveConnect features.

The public method `start()` launches the thread that allows the applet to run. The public method `stop()` halts the applet from running, by terminating the current thread.

Since both of these methods are public, we can invoke them from JavaScript. Figure 31-2 shows a very simple way of implementing LiveConnect: Invoking Java statements from JavaScript when the user triggers an event.

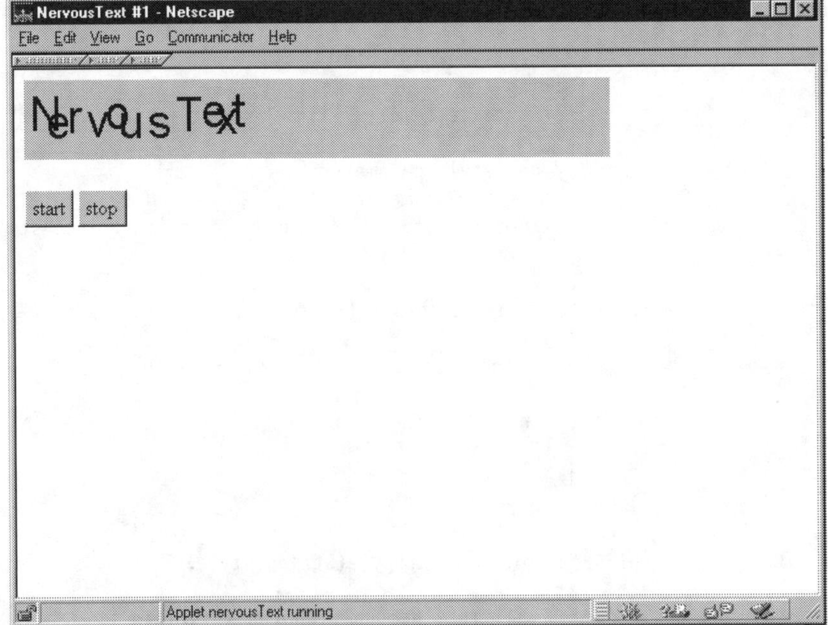

Figure 31-2. *The start and stop buttons call the applet's* `start()` *and* `stop()` *public methods, respectively.*

Take a look at the HTML document that lays out the Web page as seen in Figure 31-2:

```
<HTML>
<HEAD>
<TITLE>NervousText #1</TITLE>
</HEAD>
<BODY>
<APPLET CODE="nervous" WIDTH=460 HEIGHT=60 NAME="nervousText">
<PARAM NAME="text" VALUE="Nervous Text">
<PARAM NAME="speed" VALUE="100">
<PARAM NAME="font" VALUE="Arial">
<PARAM NAME="size" VALUE="36">
<PARAM NAME="style" VALUE="plain">
</APPLET>
<FORM NAME="attributes">
<INPUT TYPE="button" VALUE="start" onClick="document.nervousText.start()">
<INPUT TYPE="button" VALUE="stop" onClick="document.nervousText.stop()">
</FORM>
</BODY>
</HTML>
```

Example 31-3 (ex31-3.htm)*. Two HTML buttons controlling a Java applet.*

Now we'll see how those buttons can invoke the applet's methods.

The applet Object

You are probably familiar with the object concept of JavaScript. Frames, documents, forms, and form elements are all different types of JavaScript objects. Any applet loaded in your document becomes an object, contained by a `document` object.

The HTML definition for the applet in Example 31-3 is as follows:

```
<APPLET CODE="nervous" WIDTH=460 HEIGHT=60 NAME="nervousText">
<PARAM NAME="text" VALUE="Nervous Text">
<PARAM NAME="speed" VALUE="100">
<PARAM NAME="font" VALUE="Arial">
<PARAM NAME="size" VALUE="36">
<PARAM NAME="style" VALUE="plain">
</APPLET>
```

The `CODE` attribute points to the compiled applet, saved with the filename extension .class. Notice that the extension specification can be omitted in this case. Some applets let the HTML author set some initial values by the `<PARAM>` tags. Each parameter's name is defined in the Java applet code, while its value is set as the applet initializes itself by the `<APPLET>` statement. Another feature of LiveConnect is the ability to modify the applet's parameters while the applet is running.

Once the applet is running, these parameters are accessible from JavaScript or HTML but only with LiveConnect.

You can access the applet using one of several procedures. References begin with the container object, `document`, followed by the applet name (by name or position in the `document.applets[i]` array), and then either the applet's variable or method name. Last, there are arguments (enclosed in parentheses) to be passed to the applet. Here are the four possible references:

```
document.appletName.varName
document.appletName.methodName(arguments)
document.applets[i].varName
document.applets[i].methodName(arguments)
```

Bear in mind that *varName* and *methodName* should be defined as `public` in their class. Now, take another look at the HTML code in Example 31-3. The applet is named `nervousText` via the `NAME` attribute. The Stop and Start buttons are defined as follows (pay special attention to their event handlers):

```
<INPUT TYPE="button" VALUE="start" onClick="document.nervousText.start()">
<INPUT TYPE="button" VALUE="stop" onClick="document.nervousText.stop()">
```

The first button invokes the applet's `start()` method. It is easy to see that this method belongs to the applet, because it is preceded by the applet's standard reference—`document.nervousText`. The second button's `onClick` event handler calls the `nervousText` applet's `stop()` method. Notice that the name of the applet's class (which is also the name of the .class file) is irrelevant when invoking an applet's method or handling a public variable from JavaScript.

What Else is Scriptable in an Applet?

The best way to find out what methods are available for scripting is to investigate the source code on your own. Most applets currently in circulation on the Web were not designed for external access, so there are probably only a few public methods defined that will let scripters control the applet. Since the documentation for most applets does not deal with minor details such as variable declarations and method definitions, you will have to study the source code for the desired Java class.

As you study the code, focus on searching the `public` keyword. Also, pay attention to the data type that a method returns. The following declaration, for instance, belongs to a method that returns a string via a `return` statement:

```
public String methodName(parameters)
```

A method that does not return a value is defined with the keyword `void`.

Modifying an Applet

Modifying simple applets to be scriptable is usually not a difficult task. Going through some basic Java tutorials is a good idea to start with. If you are an experienced Java programmer, go ahead and write your own applets. If you are not a native Java developer, however, try playing around with an existing applet's source code. First, look for variables that have an important role in the applet. In an applet that involves text, for example, look for a variable that holds the name of the current font. If you cannot find such a variable, search for a font name expressed as a literal in the code, and try replacing that literal with your own variable (define it as a `String`, of course).

Once you've spotted variables that you would like to control via JavaScript, write public methods to control the value of these variables. Although it is also possible to access public instances (variables) from JavaScript, we recommend that you modify the applet entirely by methods. Looking back at the source code for nervous.class (Example 31-3a), there are no methods designed for JavaScript access. Nevertheless, there are quite a few instances that we would like to control by JavaScript, such as `fontName`, `fontSize`, `fontStyle`, and `text`. Here is a modified version of that example, explicitly designed for JavaScript access:

```
import java.awt.Graphics;
import java.awt.Font;
import java.applet.Applet;

public class nervous extends Applet implements Runnable {
     // array declarations
     char separated[];

     // thread declarations
     Thread killme = null;

     // font declarations
     Font displayFont;

     // integer declarations
     int i;
     int xCoordinate = 0, yCoordinate = 0;
     int speed;
     int counter = 0;
```

```
    int fontSize;
    int fontStyle;

    // string declarations
    String num;
    String fontName;
    String text = null;

    // Boolean declarations
    boolean threadSuspended = false;

    public void init() {
        getAttributes();
        separated = new char[text.length()];
        text.getChars(0, text.length(), separated, 0);
        resize(460, 60);
        displayFont = new Font(fontName, fontStyle, fontSize);
    }

    public void start() {
        if (killme == null) {
            killme = new Thread(this);
            killme.start();
        }
    }

    public void stop() {
        killme.stop();
        killme = null;
    }

    public void run() {
        while (killme != null) {
            try {
                Thread.sleep(speed);
            } catch (InterruptedException e) {}
            repaint();
        }
        killme = null;
    }

    public void paint(Graphics g) {
        g.setFont(displayFont); // set current font
        for (i = 0; i < text.length(); ++i) {
            xCoordinate = (int) (Math.random() * 10 + 15 * i);
            yCoordinate = (int) (Math.random() * 10 + 36);
            g.drawChars(separated, i, 1, xCoordinate, yCoordinate);
        }

    }

    /**************************************
```

```
          private methods for internal use
     *************************************/

     private void getAttributes() {
          // get text parameter
          text = getParameter("text");
          if (text == null)
               text = "JavaScript"; // default value

          // get speed parameter
          String speedString = getParameter("speed");
          if (speedString == null)
               speedString = "100"; // default value
          speed = Integer.parseInt(speedString);

          // get font parameter
          fontName = getParameter("font");
          if (fontName == null)
               fontName = "TimesRoman"; // default value

          // get size parameter
          String temp = getParameter("size");
          setFontSize(temp); // invoke function to set size

          // get style parameter
          temp = getParameter("style");
          setFontStyle(temp); // invoke function to set style
     }

     private void setFontSize(String size) {
          try {
               fontSize = Integer.parseInt(size);
          }
          catch (Exception e) {
               fontSize = 36;
          }
     }

     private void setFontStyle(String style) {
          try {
               if (style.equalsIgnoreCase("Plain"))
                    fontStyle = Font.PLAIN;
               else if (style.equalsIgnoreCase("Italic"))
                    fontStyle = Font.ITALIC;
               else
                    fontStyle = Font.BOLD;
          }
          catch(Exception e) {
               fontStyle = Font.BOLD;
          }
     }
```

```
        /*********************************************
             public methods for LiveConnect access
         *********************************************/

        public String getInfo() {
             String result = "nervous.class\r\n";
             result += "Version/Date: 1.0 January 1997\r\n";
             result += "Author: Tomer Shiran\r\n";
             result += "Public Variables:\r\n";
             result += "   (none)\r\n";
             result += "Public Methods:\r\n";
             result += "   setFont(fontName, \"Plain\" | \"Bold\"
                                 | \"Italic\", fontSize)\r\n";
             result += "   setText(newText)\r\n";
             return result;
        }

        public void setFont(String newFont, String newStyle, String
                                 newSize) {
             stop(); // stop applet before setting font
             if (newFont != null && newFont != "")
                  fontName = newFont;
             if (newStyle != null && newStyle != "")
                  setFontStyle(newStyle);
             if (newSize != null && newSize != "")
                  setFontSize(newSize);
             displayFont = new Font(fontName, fontStyle, fontSize);
             start(); // restart applet
        }

        public void setText(String newText) {
             stop();
             text = newText;
             separated =  new char[text.length()];
             text.getChars(0, text.length(), separated, 0);
             start();
        }
   }
```

***Example 31-4 (nervous.java)**. The source code for a "nervous text" applet with public methods designed for JavaScript access.*

First we added the `getInfo()` method, which returns a string containing general information regarding the applet, such as the author, the version, and, most importantly, the public items. This method actually provides documentation for the applet in the applet itself, so you do not have to provide any external documentation. We suggest that you use the name `getInfo()` for such methods, so a scripter will immediately know how to get information, even when the source code for the class is not available. When you assign the returned value of the method to a variable, or a property of an existing object in JavaScript, the value is automatically converted from a Java `String` to a JavaScript string. Thus, if you embedded this applet in an HTML document under the name `nervousText`, you would retrieve the information using the following statement:

```
var info = document.nervousText.getInfo()
```

The `getInfo()` method does not control the applet in any way. The second method we designed for JavaScript access is `setFont()`, which is invoked to change the current font of the text in the applet. This method receives three `String` arguments, specifying the name of the font, its style, and its new size. The `setFont()` method changes the current font by assigning those strings to the corresponding variables. Note that we could have defined `setFontStyle()` and `setFontSize()` as public methods, and added another public method `setFontName()`, instead of writing a general function to change all of the font attributes at once.

Last, but not least, the public method `setText()` receives one string and sets the applet's text to that value. When invoking this method from JavaScript, you should hand it a JavaScript string (an instance of JavaScript's `String` object). Since this method is defined to receive an instance of Java's `String` object, the value is automatically converted.

Once you write some public methods for JavaScript access, you can try them out by creating an HTML document with the corresponding elements. The following is an HTML document, designed to take advantage of the modifications we made to the `nervous` class:

```
<HTML>
<HEAD>
<TITLE>NervousText #2</TITLE>
</HEAD>
<BODY onLoad="document.attributes.info.value =
document.nervousText.getInfo()">
<APPLET CODE="nervous" WIDTH=460 HEIGHT=60 NAME="nervousText">
<PARAM NAME="text" VALUE="Nervous Text">
<PARAM NAME="speed" VALUE="100">
<PARAM NAME="font" VALUE="Arial">
<PARAM NAME="size" VALUE="36">
<PARAM NAME="style" VALUE="plain">
</APPLET>
<SCRIPT LANGUAGE="JavaScript">

<!--
```

```
function getInfo() {
        document.attributes.info.value = document.nervousText.getInfo()
}

function setFont() {
        var fontSelect = document.attributes.fontName
        var fontName = fontSelect[fontSelect.selectedIndex].value
        var styleSelect = document.attributes.fontStyle
        var fontStyle = styleSelect[styleSelect.selectedIndex].value
        var sizeSelect = document.attributes.fontSize
        var fontSize = sizeSelect[sizeSelect.selectedIndex].value
        document.nervousText.setFont(fontName, fontStyle, fontSize)
}

function changeText() {
        document.nervousText.setText(document.attributes.message.value)
}

// -->

</SCRIPT>

<FORM NAME="attributes">
<INPUT TYPE="button" VALUE="start" onClick="document.nervousText.start()">
<INPUT TYPE="button" VALUE="stop" onClick="document.nervousText.stop()">
<BR>
Font name:
<SELECT NAME="fontName" onChange="setFont()">
<OPTION VALUE="Arial" SELECTED>Arial
<OPTION VALUE="Courier">Courier
<OPTION VALUE="Helvetica">Helvetica
<OPTION VALUE="TimesRoman">Times Roman
</SELECT>
Font style:
<SELECT NAME="fontStyle" onChange="setFont()">
<OPTION VALUE="Bold">Bold
<OPTION VALUE="Italic">Italic
<OPTION VALUE="Plain" SELECTED>Plain
</SELECT>
Font size:
<SELECT NAME="fontSize" onChange="setFont()">
<OPTION VALUE="18">18
<OPTION VALUE="24">24
<OPTION VALUE="36" SELECTED>36
</SELECT>
<BR>
<INPUT TYPE="text" VALUE="Nervous Text" NAME="message" SIZE=20>
<INPUT TYPE="button" VALUE="change text" onClick="changeText()">
<BR>
<TEXTAREA COLS=62 ROWS=15 NAME="info">
</TEXTAREA>
```

```
</FORM>
</BODY>
</HTML>
```

***Example 31-4a (ex31-4.htm)**. An HTML document with many form elements to control the applet.*

The `getInfo()` function invokes the `getInfo()` method of the `nervous` class, and displays the returned value in the text area (named `info`).

The `setFont()` function retrieves the value of the selected option in each `select` object on the page. In total, there are three `select` objects, each standing for one font attribute:

- The font's name
- The font's style
- The font's size

This function is invoked by the `select` object's `onChange` event handler, so it executes whenever the user changes one of the font attributes. After gathering the essential data, `setFont()` calls the applet's `setFont()` method, which is referenced in Java as `document.nervousText.setFont()`.

The `changeText()` function is invoked by the "change text" button's `onClick` event handler. It invokes the applet's `setText()` method, handing it the string located in the text field named `message`.

Why Make an Applet Scriptable?

The prospect of scriptability should open up a new avenue for applet developers. Java programmers are no longer limited to building the entire user interface in the applet window. Applet developers can now let HTML and JavaScript authors create their own interface to an applet, matching their personal needs. With just a few HTML elements, such as tables and layers, one can redesign an applet's interface.

LiveConnect enables JavaScript-Java integration. Java's strength can contribute to various JavaScript applications. You can use JavaScript, for instance, to call a Java method to spell-check the content of an HTML form element. Java's ability to read and write files on the server can add power to a simple JavaScript device. As you can see, LiveConnect has opened a whole new world for HTML, JavaScript, and Java programmers.

Controlling Plug-ins

As explained in the previous chapter, each plug-in in a document is reflected in JavaScript as an element in the `document.embeds` array. If the plug-in is associated with the Java class `netscape.plugin.Plugin`, you can access its static variables and methods in the same way you access an applet's variables and methods. Plug-in development is beyond this book's scope. Take a look at *The LiveConnect/Plug-in Developer's Guide* at <http://home.netscape.com/eng/mozilla/3.0/handbook/plugins/index.html>. In this section we'll show you how JavaScript can control plug-ins that were developed with LiveConnect in mind. We'll focus on LiveAudio and LiveVideo, because these plug-ins come bundled with Netscape Navigator.

Accessing a Plug-in's Elements

Plug-ins can be controlled by JavaScript (and Java) if they were developed with support for LiveConnect. Although it is possible to provide public variables in a plug-in, most plug-ins provide methods that you can use in JavaScript. The general JavaScript syntax for invoking a plug-in's methods is:

```
document.embedName.methodName(arguments)
document.embeds[index].methodName(arguments)
```

JavaScript and LiveAudio

LiveAudio is LiveConnect-enabled. Generally speaking, LiveAudio provides two sets of JavaScript methods that enable you to interact with a LiveAudio instance via JavaScript:

- Methods to control a loaded LiveAudio plug-in instance. These functions return Boolean values, but the returned value is rarely ever referred to.
- Methods that indicate the current state of a loaded LiveAudio plug-in instance.

Let's take a look at the JavaScript methods that control a LiveAudio plug-in instance.

```
play(loop, 'URL_of_sound')
```

`loop` is a Boolean value or an integer. If set to `true`, the specified sound file is played repeatedly in an infinite loop. If set to `false`, the sound plays once and stops at the end of the track. If you specify an integer as the first argument for this method, LiveAudio plays the sound the specified number of times.

URL_of_sound is the URL of the desired sound file.

This method plays a specified number of times.

`stop()`

Stops the current sound playing.

`pause()`

Pauses and unpauses the current sound playing. Invoking this method when the sound is paused causes it to continue playing from where it was paused.

`start_time(seconds)`

seconds is an integer specifying the number of seconds from the beginning where the sound should start playing. Use this method if you do not want the sound to start playing from the beginning. `start_time()` does not actually start playing a sound but rather specifies where it should start when it starts.

`end_time(seconds)`

seconds is an integer specifying the number of seconds from the end where the sound should stop playing. Use this method if you do not want the sound to stop playing at the natural end of the sound track.

`setvol(percent)`

percent is an integer from 0 to 100, specifying the desired volume (0 is silent, 100 is the loudest).

This method sets the current volume of a LiveAudio instance, whether or not it is currently playing.

`fade_to(to_percent)`

to_percent is an integer specifying the final volume to which the sound fades. Use this method to fade from the current volume to the specified one.

`fade_from_to(from_percent, to_percent)`

from_percent is an integer specifying the initial volume where the fade starts. *to_percent* is an integer specifying the final volume to which the sound fades. Use this method to fade from a specified volume to another specified volume (both provided as arguments).

`start_at_beginning()`

Use this method to override a `start_time()`. That is, if you used the `start_time()` to specify where the sound should start playing, this method cancels that. It is equivalent to `start_time(0)`.

```
stop_at_end()
```

Similarly, this method overrides an `end_time()`, and is equivalent to `end_time(0)`.

There are also JavaScript methods that indicate the current state of a LiveAudio plug-in instance. Except for `GetVolume()`, which returns an integer, these methods return Boolean values.

```
IsReady()
```

This method returns `true` if the plug-in instance has completed loading, and `false` otherwise.

```
IsPlaying()
```

This method returns `true` if the sound is currently playing, and `false` otherwise.

```
IsPaused()
```

This method returns `true` if the sound is currently paused, and `false` otherwise.

```
GetVolume()
```

This method returns the current volume as a percentage. The returned value is an integer.

Note that all values are Java-equivalent data types. That is, a method that returns an integer actually returns an `int`. These data types are wrapped to JavaScript types, as explained earlier in the chapter.

Since you already know how to use the preceding methods, check out Example 31-5 to see how you can use them to create a useful JavaScript application.

```
<HTML>
<HEAD>
<TITLE>Juke Box</TITLE>
</HEAD>
<BODY onLoad="setVolume(50)">
<SCRIPT LANGUAGE="JavaScript">
<!--

function changeVolume(step) {
     var vol = document.jukebox.GetVolume()
     vol += step
```

```
          if (vol > 100)
               vol = 100
          else
               if (vol < 0)
                    vol = 0
          setVolume(vol)
     }

     function makeVolume() {
          for (var i = 0; i < 10; ++i) {
               document.write("<IMG SRC='" + off.src + "' HEIGHT="
                              + off.width + " WIDTH=" + off.width + "
                              NAME='vol" + (9 - i) + "'><BR>")
          }
     }

     function display(text) {
          window.status = text
          return true
     }

     function pause() {
          document.jukebox.pause()
     }

     function stop() {
          document.jukebox.stop()
     }

     function play() {
          var sel = document.jukeboxform.elements[0]
          var songURL = sel.options[sel.selectedIndex].value
          if (document.jukebox.IsPaused())
               pause()
          else
               document.jukebox.play(false, songURL)
     }

     function makeControlButtons() {
          with (document) {
               write("<FONT SIZE=2 COLOR='#ffffff'>Control</FONT><BR>")
               write("<A HREF='javascript:play()' onMouseOver='return display
                    (\"Play\")' onMouseOut='return display(\"\")'>")
               write("<IMG SRC='play.gif' WIDTH=12 HEIGHT=9 HSPACE=2 VSPACE=3
                    BORDER=0></A>")
               write("<A HREF='javascript:pause()' onMouseOver='return display
                    (\"Pause\")' onMouseOut='return display(\"\")'>")
               write("<IMG SRC='pause.gif' WIDTH=12 HEIGHT=9 HSPACE=2 VSPACE=3
                    BORDER=0></A>")
               write("<A HREF='javascript:stop()' onMouseOver='return display
                    (\"Stop\")' onMouseOut='return display(\"\")'>")
```

```
            write("<IMG SRC='stop.gif' WIDTH=12 HEIGHT=9 HSPACE=2 VSPACE=3
                                BORDER=0></A>")
        }
    }

    function makeVolumeButtons() {
        with (document) {
            write("<FONT SIZE=2 COLOR='#ffffff'>Volume</FONT><BR>")
            write("<A HREF='javascript:changeVolume(10)' onMouseOver=
                    'return display(\"Increase volume\")' onMouseOut=
                    'return display(\"\")'>")
            write("<IMG SRC='volup.gif' WIDTH=9 HEIGHT=10 HSPACE=2 VSPACE=3
                    BORDER=0></A>")
            write("<A HREF='javascript:changeVolume(-10)' onMouseOver=
                    'return display(\"Decrease volume\")' onMouseOut=
                    'return display(\"\")'>")
            write("<IMG SRC='voldown.gif' WIDTH=9 HEIGHT=10 HSPACE=2
                    VSPACE=3 BORDER=0></A>")
        }
    }

    function setVolume(vol) {
        document.jukebox.setvol(vol)
        var lights = Math.round(vol / 10)
        for (var i = 0; i < lights; ++i) {
            document.images["vol" + i].src = on.src
        }
        while (i < 10) {
            document.images["vol" + i].src = off.src
            i++
        }
    }

    function makeSong(url, name) {
        this.url = url // url of sound file
        this.name = name // name of sound file
    }

    // array of songs
    var songs = new Array()
    songs[0] = new makeSong("baywatch.mid", "Baywatch")
    songs[1] = new makeSong("bh190210.mid", "Beverly Hills 90210")
    songs[2] = new makeSong("melrose.mid", "Melrose Place")
    songs[3] = new makeSong("simpsons.mid", "The Simpsons")
    document.write("<EMBED NAME='jukebox' SRC='" + songs[0].url + "' HIDDEN=
                    TRUE AUTOSTART=FALSE MASTERSOUND>")

    var off = new Image(4, 4)
    off.src = "off.gif"
    var on = new Image(4, 4)
    on.src = "on.gif"
```

```
// create custom console
with (document) {
     write("<FORM NAME='jukeboxform'>")
     write("<TABLE BORDER=3><TR><TD>")
     write("<TABLE BORDER=0 CELLSPACING=0 CELLPADDING=4><TR><TD COLSPAN=3
                BGCOLOR='#000000'>")
     write("<SELECT onChange='play()'>")
     for (var i = 0; i < songs.length; ++i) {
          write("<OPTION VALUE='" + songs[i].url + "'>" + songs[i].name)
     }
     write("</SELECT>")
     write("</TD></TR>")
     write("<TR><TD BGCOLOR='#000000' WIDTH=15>")
     makeVolume()
     write("</TD><TD BGCOLOR='#000000'><CENTER>")
     makeVolumeButtons()
     write("</CENTER></TD><TD BGCOLOR='#000000'><CENTER>")
     makeControlButtons()
     write("</CENTER></TD></TR>")
     write("</TABLE></TABLE>")
     write("</FORM>")
}

// -->
</SCRIPT>
</BODY>
</HTML>
```

Example 31-5 (ex31-5.htm). *A juke box involving JavaScript, LiveAudio, and LiveConnect.*

Figure 31-3 illustrates the juke box application generated by Example 31-5. The difference between this "juke box" and the regular console is that it enables multiple sound files and features a different interface.

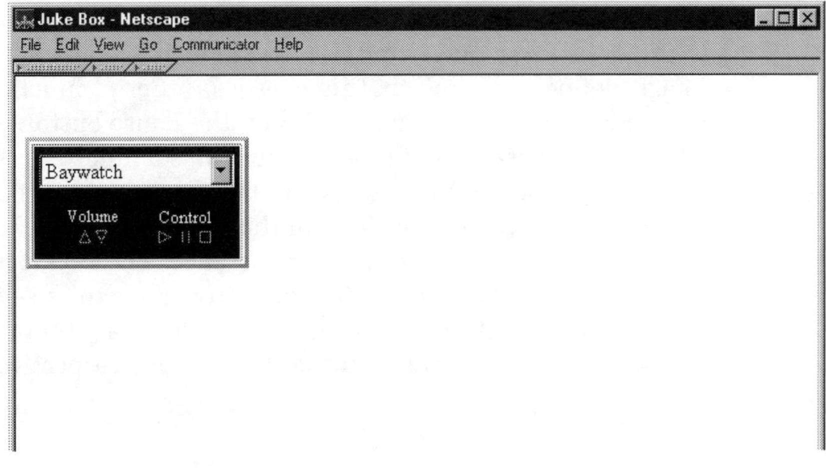

Figure 31-3. *A juke box as an alternative to the standard LiveAudio console.*

The onLoad event handler invokes the setVolume() function, handing it the integer 50.

The changeVolume() function accepts one integer value, specifying the desired volume increment or decrement. If the current volume is 50%, for instance, and you call the function with the argument 10, the new volume is 60%. Use negative integers to decrease the current volume. Note that a volume exists whether or not the sound is playing. The changeVolume() function simply calculates the new volume, making sure it is within the 0-100 range, and invokes the setVolume() to set the volume to that figure.

The makeVolume() function is called only once—while the page is loading. It prints ten images in a column, serving as a volume gauge.

The display() function accepts a string argument and displays it in the browser's status bar. It returns a true Boolean value.

The pause() function invokes the LiveAudio instance's pause() method, which is referenced in JavaScript as document.jukebox.pause().

The stop() function calls the LiveAudio instance's stop() method, which is referenced in JavaScript as document.jukebox.stop().

The play() function first finds the value of the selected option in the select object. This value is the URL of the selected sound. If the LiveAudio instance is currently paused, the function invokes the instance's pause() method to unpause it. If the LiveAudio instance is stopped or is currently playing, the function calls its play() method. The first argument is false, so there is no looping, and the second argument is simply the URL of the selected sound file.

The makeControlButtons() function is called while the page is loading, to print the Play, Pause, and Stop buttons. Each button is a small image, defined as a link that invokes a JavaScript function. The Play button is a link to javascript:play(), the Pause button is a link to javascript:pause(), and the Stop button is a link to javascript:stop(). They do not call the LiveAudio instance's methods directly but rather invoke functions located in the local script, which in turn call the desired methods of the plug-in instance. The makeVolumeButtons() function prints two volume control buttons: one to raise the current volume and the other to lower it. They link to javascript:changeVolume(10) and javascript:changeVolume(-10) respectively.

The `setVolume()` function accepts an integer representing the desired volume. After calling the LiveAudio instance's `setvol()` method to set the volume, it updates the volume gauge. First, the new volume is divided by 10, and its rounded value is assigned to the local variable `lights`. The `Math.round()` method is not required, but it makes the algorithm crystal clear. Bear in mind that there are 10 images that combine to create the volume gauge, so `lights` images should be "lit," whereas the others should be "turned off." The images are referenced by their names rather than by their index in the document, where the bottom image is named `vol1`, the one above it is named `vol2`, and so forth, up to `vol9`.

The `makeSong()` constructor function accepts two arguments representing the URL and the name of a sound file. Instances of the `makeSong` object feature two properties:

- *`instanceName`*`.url`
- *`instanceName`*`.name`

Adding or modifying the sound file entries in the juke box is as simple as creating instances of this object. The section following the `makeSong()` function creates an array named `songs`, and assigns an instance of the `makeSong` object (representing a song) to each element. The number of songs in the juke box is reflected by the array's `length` property—`songs.length`.

After creating the required instances of the `makeSong` object, two instances of the built-in `Image` object are defined. The first reflects the "off" image, which is a small black image, and the second one reflects the "on" image, which is a small green image.

The final section of global statements is a command block, in which `document` is a default object. It simply prints the entire juke box interface via `write()` (`document.write()`) statements.

JavaScript and LiveVideo

LiveVideo is LiveConnect-enabled, providing several JavaScript (and Java) functions. The supported functions are as follows:

`play()`

This method starts playing the source file at the current location.

`stop()`

This method stops the currently playing video.

```
rewind()
```

This method rewinds the currently loaded video.

```
seek(frame_number)
```

This method sets the current frame of the video to the given frame. It is broken on some platforms.

Example 31-6 shows how to use the first three methods to provide buttons controlling a LiveVideo plug-in instance.

```
<HTML>
<HEAD>
<TITLE>Rabin Movie</TITLE>
<SCRIPT LANGUAGE="JavaScript">
<!--

function play() {
     document.rabin.play()
}

function stop() {
     document.rabin.stop()
}

function rewind() {
     document.rabin.rewind()
}

function exec(func) {
     func()
}

// -->
</SCRIPT>
</HEAD>
<BODY>
<SCRIPT LANGUAGE="JavaScript">
<!--

with (document) {
     write('<TABLE BORDER=2 CELLPADDING=7><TR><TD ALIGN="center">')
     write('<EMBED SRC="rabin.avi" AUTOSTART=FALSE LOOP=FALSE HEIGHT=120
                                  WIDTH=159 NAME="rabin">')
     write('</TD></TR><TR><TD ALIGN="center"><FORM>')
     write('<INPUT TYPE="button" VALUE="play" onClick="exec(play)">')
     write('<INPUT TYPE="button" VALUE="stop" onClick="exec(stop)">')
     write('<INPUT TYPE="button" VALUE="rewind" onClick="exec(rewind)">')
     write('</TD></TR></TABLE></FORM>')
}

// -->
```

```
</SCRIPT>
</BODY>
</HTML>
```

Example 31-6 (ex31-6.htm). *A LiveVideo plug-in controlled by JavaScript statements.*

First of all, take a look at Figure 31-4 so you have a general idea of the page's appearance.

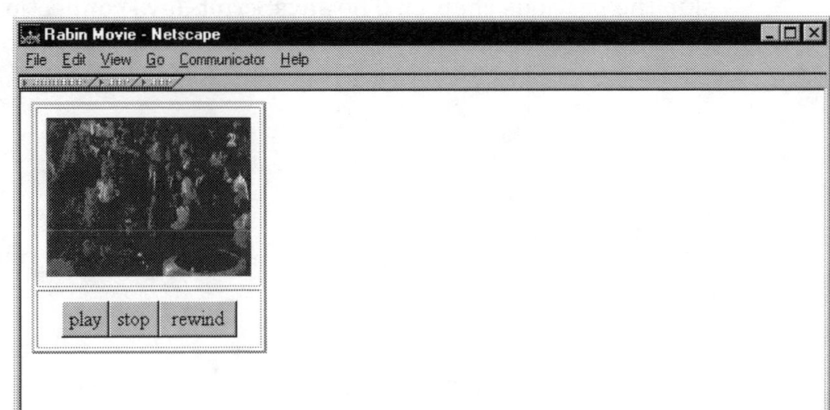

Figure 31-4. *The small view along with some HTML buttons to control it.*

First of all, notice that all buttons invoke the same function, `exec()`. They specify which function the `exec()` function should invoke by handing an object reference of the desired function to the `exec()` function. We do not call the corresponding functions directly, in order to demonstrate this important technique, which is highly useful when you want to check that the user has the required plug-in and browser. Also note that the value handed to the `exec()` function is an object reference, not a string, so you do not need the `eval()` function to evaluate it. You merely invoke the function by enclosing the parameter within parentheses.

Summary

This chapter deals with LiveConnect, the powerful feature that enables communication between JavaScript, Java, and plug-ins. We did not fully cover LiveConnect, because it is a very complex topic. Instead, we focused on those JavaScript aspects which are relevant to you as a JavaScript scripter and as a Java programmer. The JavaScript-plug-in connection should be clear, provided you did not skip the previous chapter. The JavaScript-Java connection isn't difficult either, and relies mostly on basic JavaScript knowledge.

Chapter 32

JavaScript Extensions for Layers

Introduction to Layers

Netscape Navigator 4.0 introduces functionality that allows you to define precisely positioned, overlapping layers of transparent or opaque content on a Web page. A single Web page can consist of several layers, stacked like papers. Think of a layer as an overhead transparency (those transparent sheets used with overhead projectors).

Layers can be controlled by JavaScript. You can use JavaScript, for example, to move layers, hide them, and change the order in which they overlap. Layers enable you to create various elements on a Web page that would otherwise be very difficult or even impossible.

The `<LAYER>` tag starts a layer definition, and the `</LAYER>` tag ends it. The content between the opening tag and the closing one can be treated as a single item that can be moved and altered in many ways. In a document consisting of multiple layers, each layer is a distinct tag.

Using JavaScript, you can dynamically control whether a layer is visible or not, so you can hide a layer and make it reappear again if you want. You can also use JavaScript to move a layer, and, in concert with other methods such as `setTimeout()`, you can create dynamic animation.

Layers have a stacking order (z-order), which determines the order of layers overlapping each other. You can specify the stacking order of layers as relative to each other (e.g., Layer A is immediately beneath Layer B), or you can specify numerical z-orders (e.g., the z value of

Layer A is 1). The z-order is important because the content of underlying layers shows through a transparent layer. A layer defined with a background image or a background color (as you do for the body of an HTML document) is not transparent, so it obscures any layers that lie below it. When using a transparent layer, although the actual content on the layer is opaque, you can see through it.

Layers can be nested inside layers, so you can have a layer containing a layer containing a layer and so forth.

You can define layers that have explicit positions, and you can define layers whose position follows the natural flow of the page. A layer that is explicitly positioned is known as a positioned, or out-of-flow, layer, while a layer that follows the natural flow of the page is known as an inflow layer. For inflow layers the `<ILAYER>` and `</ILAYER>` tags are used rather than the `<LAYER>` and `</LAYER>` tags.

Defining a Layer

The `<LAYER>` and `<ILAYER>` tags start a new layer (different types of layers), and the `</LAYER>` and `</ILAYER>` tags end the layer. Layers defined with the `<LAYER>` tag and its counterpart can be explicitly positioned by setting the `LEFT` and `TOP` attributes. Layers defined with the `<ILAYER>` tag (inflow layers) appear wherever they naturally fall in the flow of the document. Such layers are:

- inflow—they occupy space in the document flow.
- inline—they share line space with other HTML elements, such as text, images, tables, form elements, and so on.

An inflow layer resembles any other HTML element. The browser determines its position like it determines the position of an image embedded with the `<IMG>` tag. It also takes up space in the document like a standard HTML element. On the contrary, positioned layers differ from standard HTML elements, and they introduce an entirely new aspect in HTML design (remember how frames were revolutionary when Navigator 2.0 was introduced). In this section, we discuss the various attributes that you can specify with the `<LAYER>` and `<ILAYER>` tags.

NAME

```
NAME="layerName"
```

The NAME attribute is an ID tag for the layer. It accepts a string beginning with an alphabetic character. This attribute is optional, so layers are unnamed by default. You can use the layer's name for referencing from within HTML and external scripting languages such as JavaScript.

LEFT and TOP

```
LEFT=num1 TOP=num2
```

The LEFT and TOP attributes specify the horizontal and vertical positions of the top left corner of the layer. Both attributes are optional. The default values are the horizontal and vertical position of the tag's contents, as if they were not enclosed in a <LAYER> tag. That is, if you do not specify one of these attributes, it defaults to 0.

For positioned layers, the origin is the upper left-hand corner of the document or containing layer (for nested layers), with coordinates increasing downward and to the right. Take a look at the following layer definition:

```
<LAYER LEFT=100 TOP=200>
This layer appears 100 pixels in from the left and 200 pixels down from the
top.
</LAYER>
```

We suggest that you do not rely on these attributes to default properly when they are not specified, due to some bugs in the software. Thus, if you want the layer on the top, use TOP=0, and if you want it on the left, specify LEFT=0.

Since inflow layers occupy space in the document flow, the origin is the layer's natural position in the flow, rather than the upper left corner of the containing page or layer. You can specify the <LAYER> tag with an INFLOW=TRUE attribute, or simply use the <ILAYER> tag. The following layer definitions, for example, nudge one word in a sentence down 3 pixels.

```
<P>This <ILAYER TOP=3>word</ILAYER> is nudged down 3 pixels.</P>
```

```
<P>This <LAYER INFLOW=TRUE TOP=3>word</LAYER> is nudged down 3 pixels.</P>
```

Suppose you want to create two layers at the same position. Specifying the same numerical literals for both layers is not recommended because you will have to change the values for both layers if you choose to change the layers' position. Although we haven't introduced JavaScript properties for layers, you should be able to understand the following multiple-layer definition.

```
<LAYER NAME="myLayer1" TOP=20 LEFT=20>
<P>This layer appears on top of myLayer2.</P>
</LAYER>
<LAYER NAME="myLayer2" VISIBILITY=HIDE
    LEFT=&{document.layers['myLayer1'].left};
    TOP=&{document.layers['myLayer1'].top};>
<P>This layer appears beneath myLayer1.</P>
</LAYER>
```

We use JavaScript entities to set the value of the HTML attributes. Don't worry about the VISIBILITY attribute and the JavaScript property references, because they are discussed later in this chapter.

Note that like many other layer-related features, the ability to use inline Javascript code to define the values of <LAYER> attributes is not implemented in the Beta 1 release of Netscape Navigator 4.0 (as a component of Communicator).

WIDTH

```
WIDTH=num
```

The WIDTH attribute determines how the HTML contents of the <LAYER> tag are wrapped.

If elements that cannot be wrapped, such as images, extend beyond the width specified, the actual width of the contents of the layer will be larger than the specified value. This behavior is analogous to the way in which the width of a window sets the default wrapping for any HTML it contains, and elements that cannot be wrapped (because they are wider than the window's total width) simply extend the window to the right by adding a scrollbar. Since layers do not include scrollbars, though, a layer whose right boundary exceeds the right boundary of the window or the containing layer causes the containing element to stretch to the right.

The WIDTH attribute is optional; by default, the layer contents wrap at the right boundary of the enclosing block.

Example 32-1 shows how to use this attribute.

```
<HTML>
<HEAD>
<TITLE>Using the WIDTH attribute</TITLE>
</HEAD>
<BODY>
<LAYER TOP=0 LEFT=0 WIDTH=150>
<P>
The width of this layer is 150.
```

```
The width of this layer is 150.
The width of this layer is 150.
The width of this layer is 150.
</P>
</LAYER>
<LAYER TOP=150 LEFT=0 WIDTH=300>
<P>
The width of this layer is 300.
The width of this layer is 300.
The width of this layer is 300.
The width of this layer is 300.
</P>
</LAYER>
<LAYER TOP=300 LEFT=0 WIDTH=450>
<P>
The width of this layer is 450.
The width of this layer is 450.
The width of this layer is 450.
The width of this layer is 450.
</P>
</LAYER>
</BODY>
</HTML>
```

***Example 32-1 (ex32-1.htm)**. The `WIDTH` attribute sets the layer's horizontal span.*

In this case a picture is worth a thousand words, so take a look at Figure 32-1.

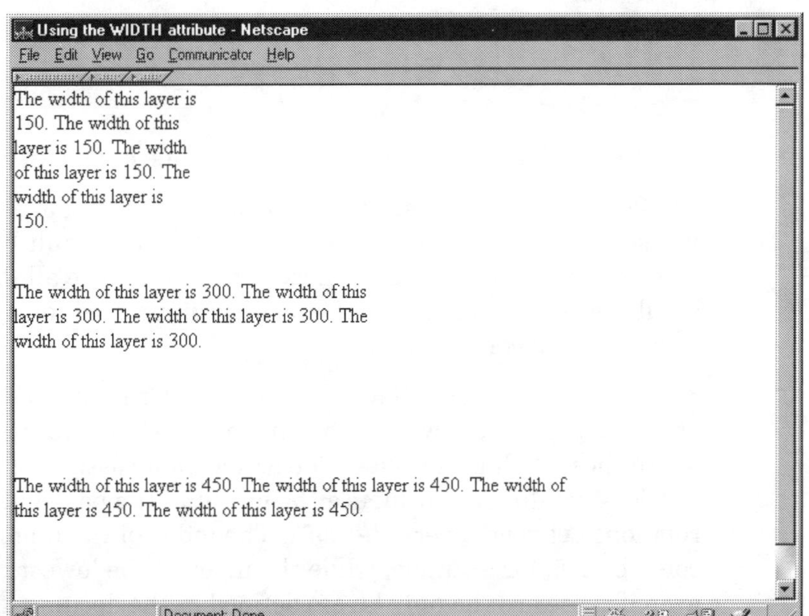

***Figure 32-1**. A layer's width affects the vertical span of its HTML content.*

CLIP

```
CLIP=leftVal,topVal,rightVal,bottomVal
```

The `CLIP` arguments determine the clipping rectangle of the layer; that is, they define the boundaries of the visible area of the layer. These values do not affect the dimensions of a layer, just the size of the layer's visible area. Since these four values are considered a single value (an HTML attribute can only accept one value), delimiting spaces are not permitted.

The value is a set of four numbers indicating, in order, the left value, the top value, the right value, and the bottom value. The left and right values are specified as pixels from the left, while the top and bottom values are specified as pixels down from the origin of the layer (see the listings for the `LEFT` and `TOP` attributes).

You can also specify the value as a set of two integers, in which case the left and top values default to `0`.

Note that the `CLIP` attribute is optional. If it is omitted, the clipping rectangle of a layer is the same size as the HTML content of the layer. By default, a layer expands to contain all of its content.

Z-INDEX, ABOVE, and BELOW

```
Z-INDEX=num

ABOVE=layerName

BELOW=layerName
```

`num` is any integer, and *`layerName`* is the name of an existing layer.

These three attributes specify the z-order (stacking order) of layers. If you set one of these attributes, it overrides the default behavior of placing new layers on top of all existing ones. Since all three of these attributes specify the z-order, only one can be used for a given layer (in order to avoid conflicts).

The `Z-INDEX` attribute allows a layer's z-order to be specified in terms of an integer. Layers with high-numbered `Z-INDEX` values are stacked above those with lower ones. The actual value assigned to this attribute does not directly influence the layout of the page but rather the relations between layers' `Z-INDEX`. The index of the topmost layer could be `100`, for example, while the index of the lowest layer is `75`, even if those are the only layers defined in the document. Positive `Z-`

INDEX values cause the layer to be stacked above its parent, while negative values cause the layer to be stacked below its parent.

The ABOVE attribute specifies the layer immediately above the layer whose <LAYER> tag contains the ABOVE=*layerName* attribute. That is, the new layer is created just below the layer specified by the ABOVE attribute.

The BELOW attribute specifies the layer immediately beneath the layer whose <LAYER> tag contains the BELOW=*layerName* attribute. That is, the new layer is created just above the layer specified by the BELOW attribute. Note that the layer specified by either the ABOVE or the BELOW tag must exist when the browser evaluates the corresponding <LAYER> tag (the one containing the attribute).

For simple layer constructions, you should avoid using these attributes. It is much easier to understand the code if you define the layers in the HTML document according to the desired stacking order. If you prefer to use these attributes, we suggest that you provide comments in the code.

Currently, all nested layers exist above their parent layer in the stacking order. The Z-INDEX, ABOVE, and BELOW values are relative to sibling layers; that is, other layers that have the same parent layer. This rule is very easy to remember, because it states that a high-level layer in the hierarchy exists beneath a low-level layer. Picture a hierarchy road map (or a family tree) to see how obvious this is.

VISIBILITY

```
VISIBILITY=SHOW|HIDE|INHERIT
```

The VISIBILITY attribute determines whether the layer is visible or not. A value of HIDE hides the layer, SHOW shows the layer, and INHERIT causes the layer to have the same visibility as its parent layer. This attribute is optional, as it defaults to INHERIT.

Remember that even if the visibility of a layer is set to SHOW, you will only be able to see the layer if there are no other visible, solid layers stacked on top of it.

BGCOLOR and BACKGROUND

```
BGCOLOR=color
```

```
BACKGROUND=color
```

These attributes control the solid background color or tiled image backdrop of a layer. They are similar to the BGCOLOR and BACKGROUND attributes of the <BODY> tag. BGCOLOR is either the name of a standard color or an RGB value. BACKGROUND is the URL of a backdrop image. Backdrop images may contain transparent pixels. Both of these attributes are optional.

By default, a layer is transparent, so layers below one with neither of these attributes show through in the areas in which a background color or pattern would have been visible.

The Layer Object

For each layer in a document there is a corresponding Layer object. A Layer object has various properties reflecting the layer's properties. Among these properties are some that can be set such as visibility.

A Layer object also features some useful methods that enable you to control the corresponding layer in various ways. A Layer object's properties and methods are referenced as follows:

```
layerObject.propertyName
layerObject.methodName(arguments)
```

Layer Object Properties

The properties featured by a Layer object reflect the <LAYER> tag's HTML attributes. See the listings for each attribute for detailed explanations.

name

```
layerObject.name
```

The name property reflects the name assigned to the layer through the NAME attribute in the <LAYER> tag. You will not find this property very useful because you already know the names of layers defined in your HTML document. Note that this property is read-only, so you cannot change a layer's name by assignment (or in any other way).

width and height

```
layerObject.width
layerObject.height
```

The `width` and `height` properties reflect a layer's width and height in pixels, respectively.

left and top

```
layerObject.left
```

```
layerObject.top
```

These properties represent the horizontal and vertical position of the layer, respectively, relative to the origin of its parent layer. Note that both are specified as integers and measured in pixels.

Setting the value of any of these properties should normally cause the layer to move.

zIndex

```
layerObject.zIndex
```

This property reflects the relative z-order of this layer (the one represented by the specified `Layer` object) with respect to its siblings and parent. Sibling layers with lower numbered z-indexes are stacked underneath this layer. A layer with a negative z-index value is always stacked below its parent layer and a layer with a non-negative z-index always appears above its parent layer.

Adjusting the value of this property immediately influences the stacking of the layers in the document.

visibility

```
layerObject.visibility
```

The `visibility` property determines whether or not the layer is visible. It initially reflects the value of the `<LAYER>` tag's `VISIBILITY` attribute. Therefore, this property evaluates to one of three string values:

- `"hide"`
- `"show"`
- `"inherit"`

It is very convenient to set the `visibility` property, especially when creating a Web page design involving several alternating layers.

clip.top, clip.left, clip.right, clip.bottom, clip.width, and clip.height

```
layerObject.clip.top
layerObject.clip.left
layerObject.clip.right
layerObject.clip.bottom
layerObject.clip.width
layerObject.clip.height
```

These modifiable properties define the clipping rectangle, which specifies the part of the layer that is visible. Any part of the layer outside of the clipping rectangle is transparent. The `clip.x` properties are measured in integral number of pixels.

background

```
layerObject.background
```

The `background` property contains the URL of the layer's tiled backdrop image, or `null` if the layer has no backdrop. This property can be set via JavaScript to change the current backdrop image.

bgColor

```
layerObject.bgColor
```

This property holds the encoded RGB value of the layer's solid background color, or `null` if the layer is transparent.

siblingAbove and siblingBelow

```
layerObject.siblingAbove
layerObject.siblingBelow
```

The `siblingAbove` and `siblingBelow` properties evaluate to the `Layer` object above or below, respectively, the current one. The terms "above" and "below" in this case refer to the z-order among all layers that share the same parent layer. `siblingAbove` is `null` if the layer is topmost in the stack, whereas `siblingBelow` is `null` if the layer is bottommost. Like all other properties that evaluate to an object, these two properties are read-only.

above and below

```
layerObject.above
layerObject.below
```

The `above` and `below` properties evaluate to the `Layer` object above or below, respectively, this one in z-order, among all layers in the document, or `null`, if layer is topmost or bottommost, respectively. Notice the difference between these properties and the `siblingAbove` and `siblingBelow` properties—these refer to all the layers in the document, not only those sharing the same parent. As with `siblingAbove` and `siblingBelow`, `above` and `below` are read-only properties.

parentLayer

```
layerObject.parentLayer
```

This property reflects the `Layer` object that contains this layer, or `null` if this layer is not nested in another one.

layers

```
layerObject.layers
```

This property is an associative array, enumerating all child layer objects by both name and index, or `null` if no child layers exist. For example, the first sibling of a given layer is referenced as:

```
layerObject.layers[0]
```

or

```
layerObject.layers["nameOfFirstSibling"]
```


Layer Object Methods

Methods of a `Layer` object handle the current position of the layer. They affect the layout of the page when they are called.

offset()

```
layerObject.offset(deltaX, deltaY)
```

This method changes the layer's position by applying the specified deltas, measured in pixels. Table 32-1 shows how the sign of the argument affects the movement.

Table 32-1. *Various arguments for the offset() method.*

	deltaX	***deltaY***
Positive integer	Layer moves to the right.	Layer moves downward.
Negative integer	Layer moves to the left.	Layer moves upward.

moveTo()

```
layerObject.moveTo(x, y)
```

This method sets the layer's position to the specified pixel coordinates. The coordinates refer to the position of the layer's top left corner.

resize()

```
layerObject.resize(width, height)
```

This method resizes the layer according to the specified height and width values (in pixels). It does not relayout any HTML content in the layer. Instead, the layer contents may be clipped by the new boundaries of the layer. When you resize a layer you should be certain that necessary HTML content is not excluded.

moveAbove() and moveBelow()

```
layerObject.moveAbove(layer)
```

```
layerObject.moveBelow(layer)
```

These methods stack the layer (represented by the specified `Layer` object) above or below the layer specified in the argument, respectively. The horizontal and vertical positions of the layer do not change when you invoke one of these methods. After restacking, both layers will share the same parent layer.

Demonstration: A Pictorial Album of U.S. Presidents

We demonstrate the usage of layers in a script that implements a pictorial album of U.S. presidents. Figure 32-2 shows the first page of the album. The user can choose a president from a list of names, displayed by the pull-down menu (Clinton, Kennedy, and Theodore Roosevelt in this case).

Example 32-2 shows the script.

```
<HTML>
<TITLE>U.S. presidents</TITLE>
<HEAD>
</HEAD>
<BODY BGCOLOR="white">
<CENTER><FONT SIZE=+3 FACE="arial">U.S. Presidents</FONT></CENTER>
                         <HR WIDTH=95%>
<LAYER TOP=70 LEFT=10 WIDTH=350 NAME="clinton">
<FONT SIZE=2>
<TABLE BORDER=0>
<TR>
```

```
<TD WIDTH=200>
<CENTER>
<IMG SRC="clinton.gif" HEIGHT=268 WIDTH=164>
</CENTER>
</TD>
<TD WIDTH=200>
<CENTER>
<I>
<B>William J. Clinton</B><BR>
Forty-second president
</I>
</CENTER>
</TD>
</TR>
</TABLE>
</FONT>
</LAYER>

<LAYER TOP=70 LEFT=10 WIDTH=350 VISIBILITY=HIDE NAME="kennedy">
<FONT SIZE=2>
<TABLE BORDER=0>
<TR>
<TD WIDTH=200>
<CENTER>
<IMG SRC="kennedy.gif" HEIGHT=268 WIDTH=164>
</CENTER>
</TD>
<TD WIDTH=200>
<CENTER>
<I>
<B>John F. Kennedy</B><BR>
Thirty-fifth president
</I>
</CENTER>
</TD>
</TR>
</TABLE>
</FONT>
</LAYER>

<LAYER TOP=70 LEFT=10 WIDTH=350 VISIBILITY=HIDE NAME="roosevelt">
<FONT SIZE=2>
<TABLE BORDER=0>
<TR>
<TD WIDTH=200>
<CENTER>
<IMG SRC="roosevelt.gif" HEIGHT=268 WIDTH=164>
</CENTER>
</TD>
<TD WIDTH=200>
<CENTER>
<I>
```

```
<B>Theodore Roosevelt</B><BR>
Twenty-sixth president
</I>
</CENTER>
</TD>
</TR>
</TABLE>
</FONT>
</LAYER>

<LAYER TOP=280 LEFT=64 NAME="selection">
<FORM>
<SELECT NAME="list" onChange="changePresident(this.selectedIndex); return
false">
<OPTION SELECTED VALUE="clinton">Clinton
<OPTION VALUE="kennedy">Kennedy
<OPTION VALUE="roosevelt">Roosevelt
</SELECT>
</FORM>
</LAYER>

<SCRIPT LANGUAGE="JavaScript">
<!--

function hidePresidents() {
     var args = hidePresidents.arguments
     for (var i = 0; i < args.length; ++i) {
          document.layers[args[i]].visibility = "hide"
     }
}

function changePresident(president) {
     hidePresidents('clinton', 'kennedy', 'roosevelt')
     document.layers[president].visibility = "show"
}

// -->
</SCRIPT>
</BODY>
</HTML>
```

Example 32-2 (ex32-2.htm)*. This script for a pictorial album of U.S. presidents demonstrates an application of layers.*

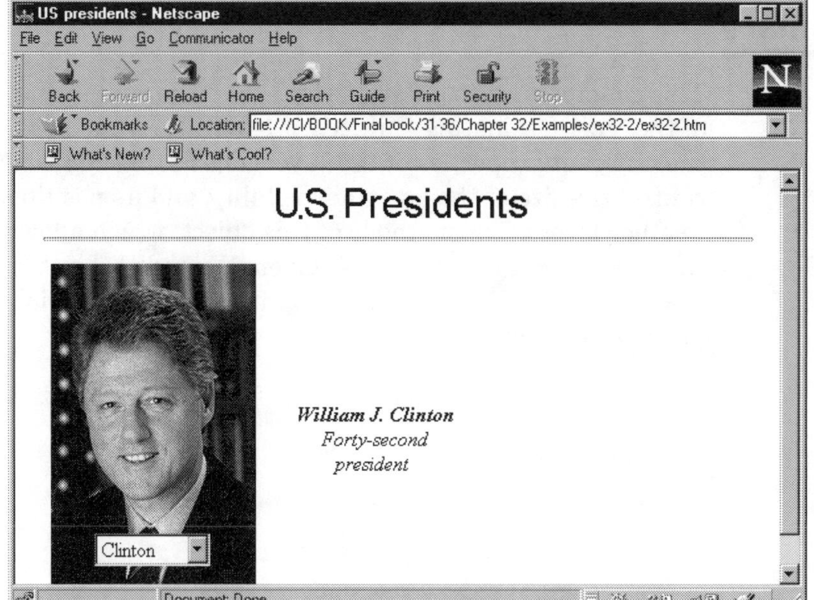

Figure 32-2. Pictorial album of U.S. presidents demonstrates the use of layers.

The script consists of four layers, one for each of the three presidents and an additional one for the pull-down selection menu. The three president layers are identical in size and span the entire browser's window. The Kennedy and Roosevelt layers are defined with `VISIBILITY=HIDE`, leaving the front page for Clinton's layer which, by default, has `VISIBILITY=SHOW`. The pull-down menu is a layer by itself and has, by default, `VISIBILITY=SHOW` as well. Since both the pull-down layer and the Clinton layer are shown, part of the Clinton image is obstructed by the pull-down menu.

Selecting an entry from the pull-down menu invokes the `changePresident()` function. Upon invocation, `changePresident()` hides all three president layers via the `hidePresident()` function and converts the selected president's layer to a `VISIBILITY=SHOW` status. In order to make the script general enough, the `hidePresident()` function reads its arguments (president names) from the standard `args` array, rather than a fixed-size argument list. Notice the different ways to index the `layers` array. The `changePresident()` function accesses it via a president's layer index in the page, in source order. The `hidePresident()` function, on the other hand, indexes the `layers` array by name.

Summary

This chapter describes JavaScript's extension for layers, which is one of the most fascinating features of Navigator Version 4.0. We detailed the different properties of the `layer` object, through which you can control the size of the layer, its visibility, and its positional relationship to other layers. The methods of this object, which allow you to change the layers' positions, were also given. We ended the chapter with an example script that shows how to implement a pictorial album of U.S. presidents by way of layers.

Chapter 33

Style Sheets

Introduction

Prior to Netscape Navigator Version 4, Web page authors have had limited control over the page style. They could not, for example, specify the left margin for their pages. The World Wide Web Consortium (W3C) has solved this problem by introducing standards for defining stylistic attributes for Web pages.

Using style sheets, you can specify many such attributes, ranging from text color, margins, and element alignments to font styles, sizes, and weights.

Netscape Communicator supports two types of style sheets: cascading style sheets (CSS) and JavaScript-accessible style sheets. The W3C has defined a set of properties and syntax for CSS and its proposal is posted at `http://www.w3.org/pub/WWW/TR/PR-CSS1`. Each style item is defined by a relevant attribute. The left margin, for example, is set by `margin-left`, and the interword spacing by `word-spacing`.

In this book, the JavaScript-accessible style sheet syntax will be used to manipulate style sheets. For each stylistic property, there is a JavaScript equivalent. Generally, property names are the same for both types, with some minor differences due to JavaScript naming restrictions.

Using JavaScript, you can specify styles for all elements of a particular kind (all paragraphs should be displayed in green, for example) or you can declare classes of styles to which you can assign any element you want. You can define, for instance, a class called BAR whose style is green, bold, large text. Any document element (paragraph, block quote, heading) can be a member of the class BAR, and it will be displayed in green, bold, large text. You can also specify local styles for individual instances of document elements. You can specify, for example, that the color for a single, particular paragraph is blue.

Content Layout

Using style sheets, you can determine margins for individual elements on a page, or for all elements on a page. The following code, for instance, specifies that all paragraphs will have a right margin of 20 pixels:

```
<STYLE>
tags.P.rightmargin=20;
</STYLE>
```

Font Properties

You can create styles that determine font size and font style (such as bold). The following code, for example, specifies that all block quote elements will appear in bold:

```
<STYLE>
document.blockquote.fontStyle="bold";
</STYLE>
```

Text Properties

The modifiable attributes of text properties include line height, text decoration (such as underlined), horizontal and vertical alignment of text, and text indent (which allows indented and outdented paragraphs). For example:

```
<STYLE>
// the line height for block quotes is increased by 150 percent
tags.blockquote.lineHeight* = 1.5
// level four headings are underlined
tags.H4.textDecoration = "underline"
// bold elements are vertically aligned with the top of their parent
tags.B.verticalAlign = "top"
// level five headings are displayed in uppercase
tags.H5.textTransform = "uppercase"
// the text in all paragraphs is centered
tags.P.align = "center"
// the first line of each paragraph is indented 20 pixels
tag.P.indent = 20
</STYLE>
```

Inheritance of Styles

JavaScript-based style sheets use the notion of parent and child elements. For example, in the following HTML source, the <H1> element is the parent one, while the <EM> element is a child of the <H1> element.

```
<H1>The headline <EM>is</EM> important!</H1>
```

In general, child elements acquire or inherit the styles of their parent elements. Look at the following example:

```
<H1 CLASS="boldBlue">The headline <EM>is</EM> important!</H1>
```

The child element (the <EM> element) inherits the style of its parent, so the word "is" will appear emphasized in the boldBlue style. However, if you had previously set up a style that specified that the <EM> element should be displayed in red, then the word "is" would be displayed in red, since properties set on the child override properties inherited from the parent. Inheritance starts at the oldest ancestor, at the top-level element. In HTML, this is the <HTML> element which is followed by <BODY>.

To set default style properties, just define the style before the <BODY> element. For example, the following code sets the default text color to green:

```
<STYLE>document.tags.BODY.color="green";</STYLE>
```

If you want to change the color in a specific place, you can set styles for different kinds of elements, or you can set up classes of styles. Some style properties cannot be inherited from the parent, background color being one of those.

Creating Style Sheets and Assigning Styles

There are three ways to specify styles using Javascript-based style sheets: (1) create external style sheets and link them into your document, (2) create style sheets within a document, or (3) specify specific styles for certain elements within a document.

The simplest way to assign styles is to apply them to all elements of a certain type. For example, the following code indicates that all level one headings will be displayed in green:

```
<STYLE>document.tags.H1.color = "green"</STYLE>
```

Setting up classes of styles within a document (bold, blue style, for example) will allow you to apply styles to some elements but not others. Then, whenever you want an element to be displayed in that style, you simply tell the browser what class of style to use. For example:

```
<style type="text/javascript">
     classes.boldBlue.all.color = "blue";
     classes.boldBlue.all.fontWeight = "bold";
</style>
<P CLASS="boldBlue">This paragraph appears in bold, blue style</P>
<P>This should be in the normal document color<P>
```

The rest of this chapter describes the different ways to assign styles.

Defining Styles with the <STYLE> Tag in the Header

You can use the <STYLE> tag within the header of a document to define styles for specified elements used in the document. You can specify, for instance, that all level one headings are blue, all block quotes are red, all paragraphs are emphasized, and so on. For example:

```
<HTML>
   <HEAD>
      <TITLE>A Grand Title</TITLE>
      <STYLE TYPE="text/javascript">
            tags.H1.color = "blue"
      </STYLE>
   </HEAD>
<BODY>
   <H1>This heading is in blue</H1>
```

Specifying Styles for Individual Elements

You can use the `STYLE` attribute to specify a style for a particular instance of an element. You can specify, for example, that a particular paragraph is green or a particular block quote is bold. This approach mixes style with content, as opposed to style sheets where they are separated. For example:

```
<BODY>
  <P STYLE="color = 'green'">This paragraph is green.</P>
  <P>This paragraph is in the usual color </P>
</BODY>
```

Defining Classes of Styles

You can declare classes of styles by using the `CLASSES` attribute inside the <STYLE> tag. You can define, for example, a green, bold class. Whenever you want an element to be displayed in green bold, you can specify that the element is a member of the green bold class. For example:

```
<HTML>
<HEAD>
    <TITLE>Title</TITLE>
    <STYLE TYPE="text/javascript">
        classes.greenbold.all.color = "#00FF00"
         classes.greenbold.all.fontWeight = "bold"
    </STYLE>
</HEAD>
<BODY>
    <H1 CLASS=greenbold>This heading is way too green</H1>
```

You can use the keyword `all` to specify that all tags within the class are affected by the style property or you can selectively identify which elements belong to the class. The following code, for instance, creates a class called `red1`. Only paragraphs and block quotes can be displayed in this style:

```
<HTML>
  <HEAD>
     <TITLE>Title</TITLE>
     <STYLE TYPE="text/javascript">
         classes.red1.P.color = "red"
         classes.red1.blockquote.color = "red"
     </STYLE>
  </HEAD>
<BODY>
  <H1 CLASS=red1>This paragraph is in red</H1>
  <P>This paragraph is in the default color, since it is not a member
     of class red1.</P>
  <BLOCKQUOTE CLASS="red1">Oh what a beautifully red quote this is.
  </BLOCKQUOTE>
```


Format Properties

Javascript-accessible style sheets treat each block level element as if it is surrounded by a box. (Block level elements start on a new line, for example, <H1> and <P> are block level elements, but <EM> is not.) Each box can have padding, border, and margins. You can set values for top, bottom, left, and right paddings and margins. The padding area uses the same background as the element itself (which is set with the background property). The margins are always transparent, so the parent element shines through. The width of the box is the sum of the element width (that is, the width of the formatted text or image), the padding, and the border. Padding and margin properties are not inherited, but, since the placement of an element is relative to its ancestors and siblings, the parent's padding and margin properties affect its children.

Box Math

Seven length units influence the horizontal dimension of a box: left margin, left border, left padding, width, right padding, right border, right margin. The width of the element has to be equal to the sum of these units. Therefore, you cannot specify values for all seven properties and expect them to be honored. The relative strengths between them are as follows:

1. left border
2. right border
3. left padding
4. right padding
5. width
6. left margin
7. right margin

By default, the value of the `width` property is automatically calculated based on the other properties' values (`auto`). If `width`, however, is assigned another value, or the dimensions do not add up for other reasons, the property with the lowest rank (closest to 7) will automatically be calculated (`auto`).

Replaced Elements

A replaced element is an element which is replaced by a content pointed to from the element. For example, in HTML, the <IMG> element is replaced by the image pointed to by the `SRC` attribute.

Replaced elements often come with their own intrinsic width and height. If the value for `width` is `auto`, the intrinsic width is used as the width of the element. If a value other than `auto` is specified in the style sheet, this value is used and the replaced element should be resized accordingly (the resize method will depend on the media type). The height of the element is determined in a similar way.

Setting Margins

You can set the size of the margins for a block level element by specifying the `marginLeft`, `marginRight`, `marginTop`, and `marginBottom` properties. You can also use the predefined `margins()` method to set all four properties simultaneously. For example:

```
// manual assignment
with(tags.P) {
      marginTop = 30;
      marginBottom = 40;
      marginRight = 50;
      marginLeft = 60;
}
```

The above manual assignment has the same result as the call to the `margins()` method shown below:

```
// assignment using a method
// margins(top, right, bottom, left)
tags.P.margins(30, 50, 40, 60);
```

To set the default margins for everything in a document, specify the margin properties for the <BODY> tag. The following code, for example, sets the left and right margins to 20:

```
tags.BODY.margins(0, 20, 0, 20);
```

The actual distances between boxes is equal to the sum of two adjoining margins. A box with no border, padding, or content is a legal element and may be used to increase the margin between two real boxes. If there are negative margins, the absolute maximum of the negative adjoining margins is deducted from the maximum of the positive adjoining margins.

Settting Border Width

You can set the width of the border surrounding a block level element by specifying the `borderTopWidth`, `borderRightWidth`, `borderBottomWidth`, and `borderLeftWidth` properties. You can also use the predefined `borderWidths()` method to set all four properties simultaneously. The style of the border can be specified using the `borderStyle` property.

Settting the Padding Size

You can set the size of the padding surrounding a block level element by specifying the `paddingTop`, `paddingRight`, `paddingBottom`, and `paddingLeft` properties. You can also use the predefined `paddings()` method to set all four properties simultaneously.

Summary

In this chapter, we have introduced new ways to specify a page's style via JavaScript. You can specify specific styles for certain element types or instances. Style sheets can be specified outside the page and linked into it, or created within a document. The concepts of style class and style inheritance are explained. We described how to specify a page's paddings and margins, and what the mathematical rules are for governing a page's settings.

Chapter 34

Security Issues

Security issues are every surfer's and homestead's top concerns when surfing the net or posting homepages to it. There are several flavors of security issues. This chapter deals with those related to protecting your private information such as e-mail address, directory structures, user session history, or objects and properties of a loaded page.

History

Netscape Navigator 2.0 was the first browser to include support for JavaScript. The language provided Intranet managers with some very powerful methods to access user information for beneficial purposes. But JavaScript also allowed hackers to use these methods for not-so-beneficial purposes. They intercepted client computer information such as file directories, user history, and even passwords you may have entered to access secure sites. The trade and even popular press were all over Netscape for compromising users' privacy and security.

Netscape fixed the problems in two versions. Navigator 2.02 took care of the security problems by taking some capabilities off the release. One could no longer capture visitors' browser history, local file directory listings, or silent e-mail. Navigator 3.0 is better than Navigator 2.02 in error reporting, and is also more verbose in warning you when a loaded document is about to reveal normally secured information.

e-mail Address Security

Navigator 3.0 warns you when a loaded document is about to reveal normally hidden information, even if the trigger for this action is your own action. A classic example is clicking on a Submit button, which, unless you won't approve it, will reveal your e-mail address to the site's author. Figure 34-1 shows the e-mail warning you get in this case:

Figure 34-1. E-mail warning window pops up when you submit a form.

URL to URL Access Security

When you challenge the security of a URL which resides on a different server, an error message pops up, specifying your script's URL and the URL of the document you are trying to access without permission. Note that you can still load the document from another domain into any of your windows or frames, but you won't be able to read any information from this document, including its location properties or form element values. Let's demonstrate this situation, trying to get the title of Yahoo!'s index page, as shown in Example 34-1.

```
<HTML>
<HEAD>
<TITLE>Security</TITLE>
<SCRIPT LANGUAGE="JavaScript">
<!--
var URL = "http://www.yahoo.com/index.html"
function openYahoo() {
    win = window.open(URL, "win")
}

function alertTitle() {
    alert(win.document.title)
}

// -->
</SCRIPT>
</HEAD>
```

```
<BODY>
<FORM>
<INPUT TYPE="button" VALUE="open Yahoo!" onClick="openYahoo()">

<INPUT TYPE="button" VALUE="display title" onClick="alertTitle()">
</FORM>
</BODY>
</HTML>
```

Example 34-1 (ex34-1.htm). *A script that attempts to access properties of a document on a different server.*

The `alert()` function tries to access the `title` property of Yahoo!'s window `document`. Figure 34-2 shows the alert box that pops up with an error message, specifying the URLs of both the script and the document for which its security is being challenged.

Figure 34-2. *When challenging document security, an error message shows the URLs of both the offending script and the document.*

The Concept of Tainting

Obviously, the security measures make scripters' lives difficult, especially if a site consists of multiple servers, and documents from different servers need to interact with each other. Security upon demand is Netscape's answer to scripters' needs, and is being achieved by the concept of *data tainting*. This feature allows the page's publisher to mark the specific properties he or she wants to secure. *Data tainting* is turned off by default and you can turn it on from within your script, as will be shown later. When data tainting is enabled, JavaScript in one window can see properties of another window, no matter what server the other window's document was loaded from. However, the author of the other window taints (marks) property values or other data that should be secure or private, and JavaScript cannot pass these tainted values on to any server without the user's permission. When data tainting is disabled, a script cannot access any properties. Again, notice that the page's reader has no control on data tainting; it's the publisher's exclusive right. Obviously, data tainting is supported only by tainting-enabled browsers.

Tainting terminology applies to both the page author and the browser. The publisher has tainting control over his or her document. The browser must be manually enabled by the individual browser user before it can recognize that data has been tainted. If the browser does not have data tainting enabled, it just ignores the tainting attributes of the document and the access to the document properties is not allowed.

Values derived from tainted data elements are also tainted. If a tainted value is passed to a function, the return value of the function is tainted. If a string is tainted, any of its substrings is tainted. If a script examines a tainted value in an `if`, `for`, or `while` statement, the script itself accumulates taint in what will be explained later under "taint accumulator."

Enabling Data Tainting

To enable data tainting, the end user sets the NS_ENABLE_TAINT environment variable as follows:

- On Unix, use the setenv command in csh, `setenv NS_ENABLE_TAINT`.
- On Windows, use set in autoexec.bat or NT user settings, `SET NS_ENABLE_TAINT=1`. Be sure not to include any spaces around the equal sign. The variable applies to all copies of Navigator 3.0 (for different languages).
- On Macintosh, edit the resource with type "Envi" and number 128 in the Netscape application, by removing the two ASCII slashes "//" before the `NS_ENABLE_TAINT` text, at the end of the resource.

`NS_ENABLE_TAINT` can have any value; "1" will do. If the end user does not enable tainting and a script attempts to access properties of a window on another URL, a message is displayed, indicating that access is not allowed. To determine whether tainting is enabled, use the `taintEnabled()` method. The following code executes `function1()` if data tainting is enabled; otherwise it executes `function2()`:

```
if (navigator.taintEnabled()) {
   function1()
}
else function2()
```

You can also enable tainting interactively in your browser. Navigate to `javascript:` URL and enter `navigator.taintEnabled()`.

Specific Tainting

Navigator marks a specific set of objects, their properties, and their methods as tainted. The user should not care about the taint value Navigator assigned to them. These items are identified as a source for a potential security risk if abused. Table 34-1 shows items which are automatically tainted when in a document.

window.status	document.length
window.defaultStatus	document.element
	document.forms[]
location.href	document.links[]
location.protocol	document.title
location.host	document.location
location.hostname	document.referrer
location.port	document.lastModified
location.pathname	document.cookie
location.hash	document.domain
location.search	
location.toString()	form.action
history.previous	inputObject.name
history.current	inputObject.value
history.next	inputObject.defaultValue
history.toString()	iputObject.status
	inputObject.defaultStatus
option.text	inputObject.toString()
option.value	
option.defaultSelected	
option.selected	

***Table 34-1.** Default tainted elements in a document.*

Taint-enabled browsers can view tainted items, but they cannot send the information to any location on the Internet that is not on the same domain and server. If, on the other hand, you want some snoopy scripts to propagate your homepage information (form entries for example) to wherever they want, you can use the `untaint()` method to make an untainted reference of the object:

```
var prevHistoryFree = untaint(history.previous)
```

By making an untainted reference to your previous link, you have given the world explicit permission to take the data and propagate it wherever it wants. Of course, the author of such a snoopy script would have to study your HTML source to figure out how you have named the untainted data.

There are times when you want to secure more than what is tainted by default. You may have some custom functions or global variables that you do not want to share or allow some snoopy scripts to invoke. Sometimes, sensitive information about the document is hidden in one of your document's functions. Navigator 3.0 helps you protect this function or other entities by tainting them via the `taint()` method. For example, if you define a function named `mySecretAlgorithm()`, you can taint it as follows:

```
        function mySecretAlgorithm () {
    statements
}
taint(mySecretAlgorithm)
```

Foreign scripts may use `mySecretAlgorithm` but the result will be tainted, i.e., the function or any result computed by the function must stay in the foreign script scope and cannot be communicated to other domains or servers.

Window Taint Accumulator

The browser keeps track of tainted data exchanges between windows by updating each window's taint accumulator. The taint accumulator is the mechanism to watch your window's tainting status, as your scripts interact with items in other windows. When a document is loaded into a window, its taint accumulator is initialized to identity, which is the null value. Every time there is a tainted data exchange with another server, the accumulator mixes different taint codes to create new codes that identify the sources of data origins (server1, server2, server3, ...). Notice that all of the server's data elements share the same tainted code of the server.

The taint codes in the accumulator are checked whenever there is an attempt to pass data over the network. Three taint codes are checked: script's accumulated taint, taint code of targeted server, and taint code of data. For the transfer operation to succeed, either two taint codes are equal, or at least one is identity (null). If an incompatibility is identified, a dialog box pops up, asking for a confirmation or cancellation of the URL load or form post.

The taint accumulator changes dynamically upon interaction with another server, but it can also be manipulated by the page author. In general, taint accumulates until the document is unloaded and is reset to identity only if it contains the current document's original code. Also, all windows loading documents from the same server share the same taint accumulator. To manipulate the taint accumulator, call `taint()` or `untaint()` with no arguments. When calling `taint()`, JavaScript adds the current document's taint code to the accumulator. Calling `untaint()` removes taint from the accumulator only if it holds taint from the current window. If the current window has been tainted by other servers, `untaint()` will have no effect. Removing taint from the accumulator will reset the taint code to identity.

Summary

This chapter describes the security issues of the Internet and Netscape's tainting mechanism which answers some of them. Tainting can be applied to specific elements, to the whole document, or to a window. The concept of a taint accumulator is described. Users of Navigator 3.0 and up find themselves answering many more dialog boxes than with Navigator 2.0. There is no way to circumvent this situation but to untaint specific elements. Security on the Web is critical for its growth and commercial usage. Netscape does not have the last word on it, so you can expect some changes in this direction. Changes may vary in range from revolutionary (adopting the digital signature algorithm) to evolutionary (improving on the current methods of tainting and taint accumulator).

Chapter 35

JavaScript Authoring Tools

Introduction

Several authoring tools have shown up recently. These tools aim at helping you ramp up faster on HTML and JavaScript. We have chosen to introduce you to Infuse by Acadia, but other competitive tools are also available. Notice that Infuse sometimes refers to LiveWire. That subject is outside the scope of this book and therefore is not covered.

Top 10 Tips

The next 10 paragraphs show the top 10 tips given by Infuse.

Tip #1. Navigate Your Code with the Script Navigator

Infuse includes the Script Navigator window from which you can navigate your HTML or JavaScript code. The window displays all functions and objects in the current page (see Figure 35-1). Double-click on any function or object to jump to its location.

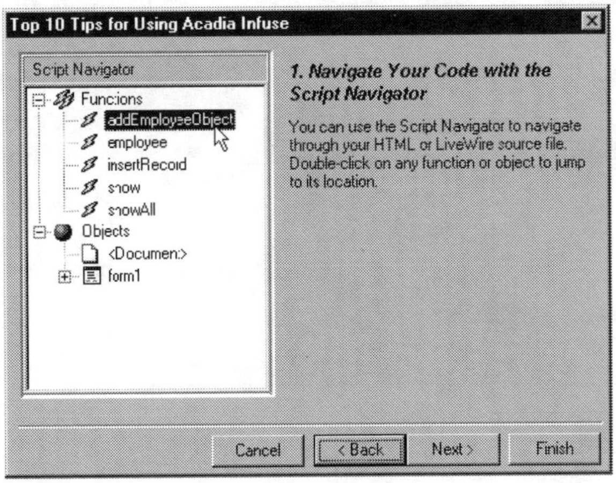

Figure 35-1. *Tip #1. Navigate your code with the Script Navigator.*

Tip #2. Integrated JavaScript Reference

Netscape's official JavaScript reference is built into Infuse. Right-click anywhere in either the Object or the Language Tree to convert the cursor to a Help cursor (question mark), and then click on the language element item you wish to get help on. Help will then be displayed in a pop-up window, as shown on the left-hand side of Figure 35-2 (for `appName` property).

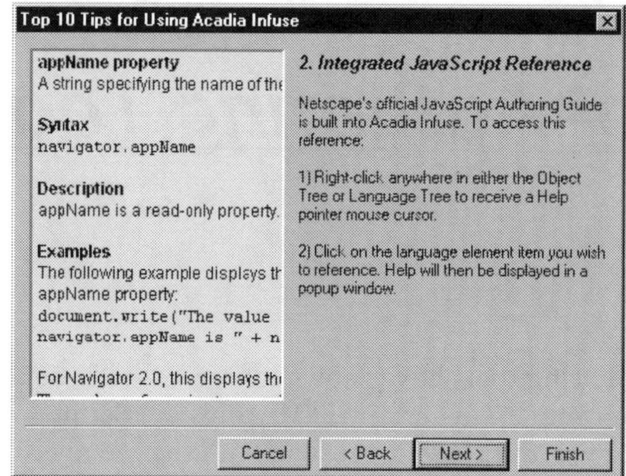

Figure 35-2. Tip #2. You can invoke Netscape's JavaScript Authoring Guide from Infuse.

Tip #3. Drag-&-Drop Into Your Source File

There are three index tabs at the top left corner of the Acadia Infuse window: Objects, Language, and HTML. You can use these trees to drag-&-drop objects, properties, methods, and other language elements into your code. This feature is handy, for example, when you forget the exact syntax of an HTML tag, or the parameter order of a method. If you don't like to drag-&-drop, you can simply double-click any time to place it at the current cursor position in the editor. Figure 35-3 shows that portion of the Acadia Infuse window.

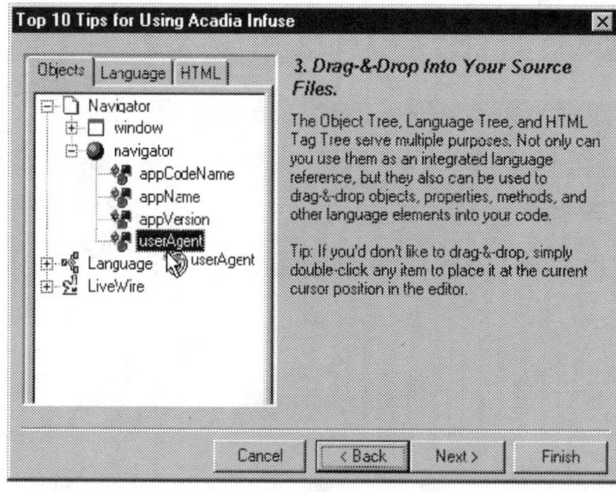

Figure 35-3. Tip #3. Drag-&-Drop into your source file.

Tip #4. Instantiate JavaScript Objects

The JavaScript Object Tree serves two purposes. First, you can visualize the object hierarchy (see Figure 35-4). Then, you can instantiate JavaScripts objects by holding down **Ctrl** while you drag-&-drop an object into the editor. Dragging-&-dropping JavaScript objects (without holding the Ctrl key) will have no effect. Since not all JavaScript objects can be explicitly instantiated, holding down the Ctrl key when dragging-&-dropping these objects will have no effect as well.

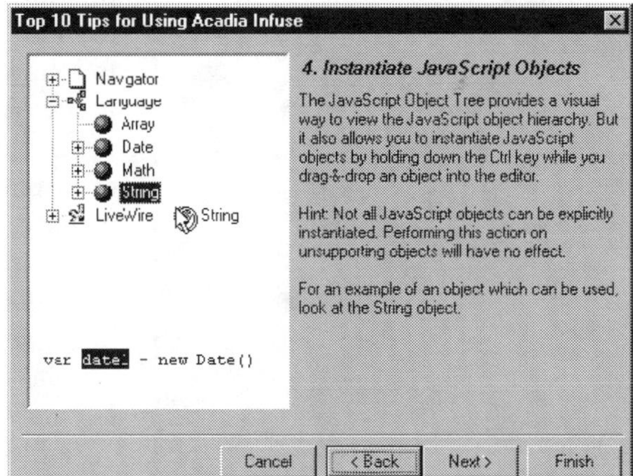

Figure 35-4. Tip #4. Instantiate JavaScript objects.

Tip #5. Using Special Inline Characters

As with any other language, JavaScript has a special treatment for certain characters, such as carriage returns or tabs. The Inline Character subtree of the Language Tree eliminates the need to remember the specific syntax of these characters (see Fig 35-5). Again, drag-&-drop or double-click the characters to place them in your code as global variables. Keep using the global names in the rest of the code.

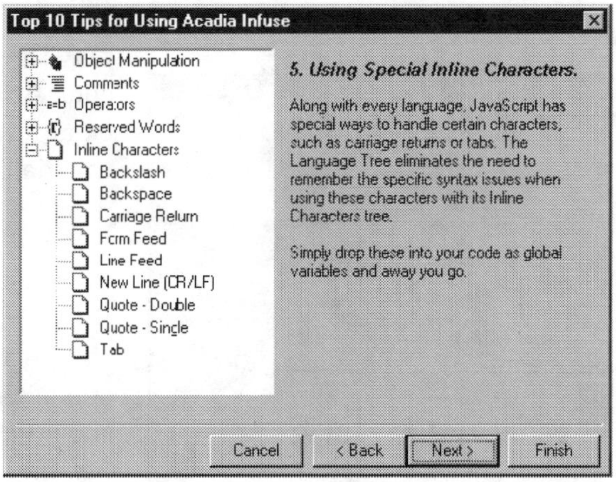

Figure 35-5. Tip #5. Using special inline characters.

Tip #6. Speed Up Your Typing with Natural Cursor Positioning

When you place an object by dragging-&-dropping (or by double-clicking) it to your editor, the cursor is automatically positioned at the most natural location for that particular object. You can begin typing instantly instead of manually searching for the insertion point followed by a positioning of the cursor. The example in Figure 35-6 shows how a `for` loop is placed in your document when the loop generic limit (`value`) is selected. Upon typing the real variable name, the generic one will be instantly erased.

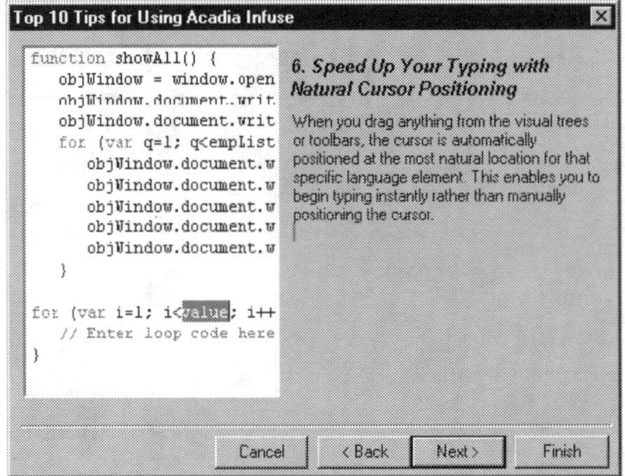

Figure 35-6. Tip #6. Speed up your typing with natural cursor positioning.

Tip #7. Reuse Your JavaScript Code

Acadia Infuse supports the concept of Frequent Scripts. You can store your favorite JavaScript routines and retrieve them for later use. In order to save your code, select it using your mouse, right-click to display the pop-up menu, click **Add Frequent Script**, and fill out the dialog box. To insert a favorite script, select **Favorite Scripts** from the Insert menu and then choose a script from one of the categories, shown in Figure 35-7. Acadia Infuse comes with over 30 commonly used routines.

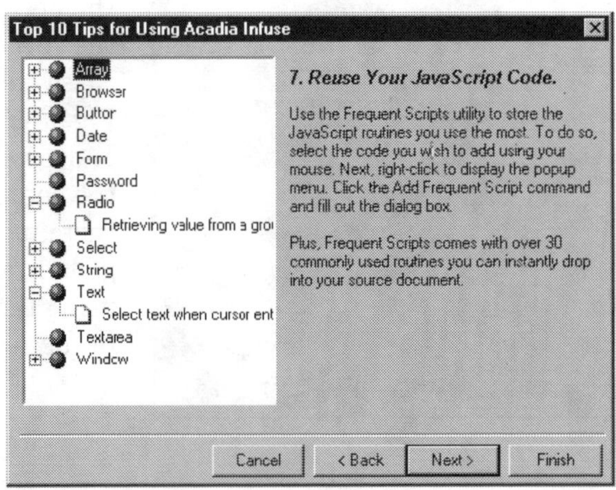

Figure 35-7. Tip #7. Reuse your JavaScript code.

Tip #8. Customize Your Editor

As with other editors, Acadia Infuse lets you customize the look and feel of its windows. Just invoke the Preferences menu from Tools main menu and try the different options. For example, you can change the color of HTML tags, strings, comments, etc. The window portion shown in Figure 35-8 displays the foreground and background colors of text and its selection.

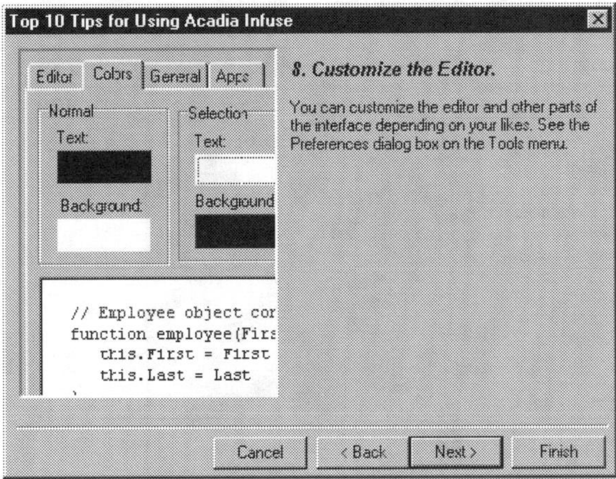

Figure 35-8. *Tip #8. Customize the editor.*

Tip #9. Create Custom Objects

Upon mastering JavaScript, you will want to create your own custom objects. Acadia Infuse helps you accomplish that by providing you with a dialog box that guides you during the process. From Insert main menu, click **Custom Object** and use the dialog box interface to fill in the details such as the object name, its properties, methods, etc. Figure 35-9 shows an object called "customer" having the properties "name," "address," "city," and "state."

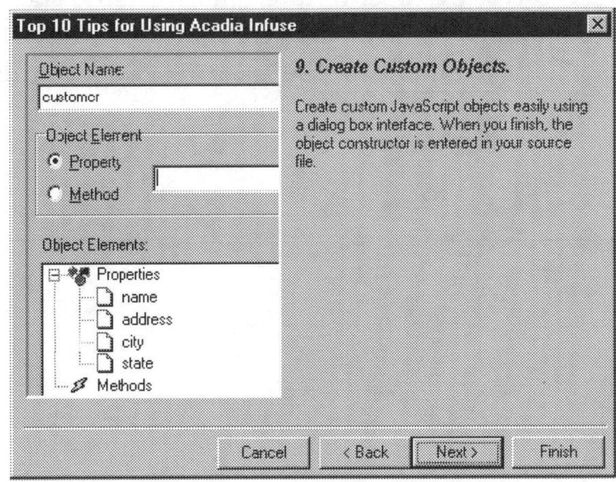

Figure 35-9. *Tip #9. Create custom objects.*

Tip #10. Finding That Matching Brace

This feature helps you keep track of those unpaired braces. Select the open brace (see Figure 35-10) and then from Search main menu, click **Find Matching Brace**. The cursor will select the matching brace.

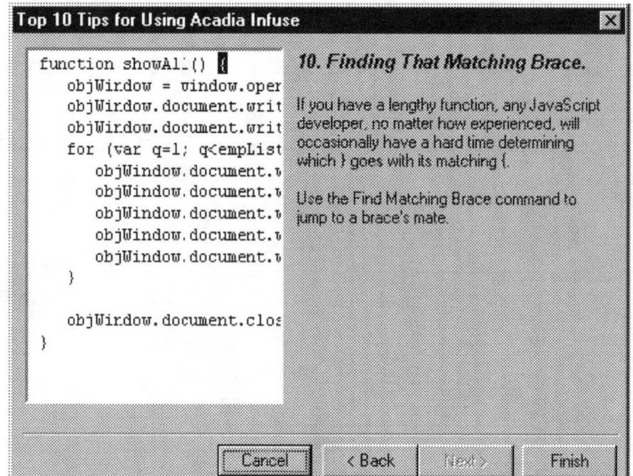

Figure 35-10. *Tip #10. Finding that matching brace.*

Summary

In this chapter, we introduced a JavaScript editor called Infuse. This application may help you create scripts faster. You can navigate your code with Infuse, drag-&-drop items into your code, create your own objects, save and retrieve useful functions, and find the matching brace you are looking for. Over the years, more JavaScript editing applications will be available on the Internet. Choose the one that suits you best.

Chapter 36

Debugging Scripts

Development environments usually include at least one powerful debugger, and sometimes a multitude of them. In fact, experienced programmers, when introduced to a new language, are concerned first and foremost about the power and the productivity factor of the debugger. The debugger is the most powerful tool an advanced computer scientist uses to find his or her bugs, and we have yet to meet a programmer who does not have bugs in his or her code. Sources for bugs range from simple ones like typos to logic problems in very complex applications like the Tetris game.

JavaScript is not in the same league as other development environments in providing a debugger for its developers. The smartest JavaScript editor to date is Infuse by Acadia (see `www.acadians.com`). This environment provides you with all language features online, and thus can help you write a better code with less bugs. But, at the end, you still end up with a script that can have bugs and there is no debugger to find it with. You have to revert to the old way people used to debug their programs: printing messages and progressive commenting of lines.

Types of Errors

In a traditional language, such as C, there are two main types of errors: compiletime errors (syntax) and runtime errors. Since JavaScript is not a compiled language, the boundaries between these two types of errors are blurred. As the page loads, the first type of errors the browser is looking for are *syntax* ones. These are relatively easy to detect and fix. Misspelling *else* in the *if-else* construct is one example of a syntax error. Runtime errors involve mismatching between function definitions and function calls, undeclared variables located on the right-hand side of assignment operators, mismatches between object types, etc. If the script lines execute immediately as the page loads, undeclared variables will be flagged immediately. Other errors will be detected when culprit functions execute, which may occur upon loading or while responding to user actions. In fact, some errors, if not invoked as a response to user actions, may never be detected. This kind of issue belongs to a wider field of Coverage Analysis. There are methodologies and tools for mainstream languages that measure the percentage of code covered by a specific testing suite, where the coverage can be measured by the percentage of lines or functions executed by the suite. Such a tool is yet to be developed for JavaScript.

Error Messages

Navigator and Explorer behave very similarly when detecting a problem. They produce a large alert box (Figure 36-1a and Figure 36-1b) specifying:

- The URL or filename of the document causing the problem
- The line number
- A description of the problem in a very condensed and terse statement
- An extract of the code that JavaScript could not handle
- An arrow marker pointing to the offending word

The line number shown in the alert box is exactly the line count of the code extract shown in the alert box, where the first line of the file is at count one. Some authors mistakenly write that the line number is counted from the opening `<script>` tag of the group that contains the code extract.

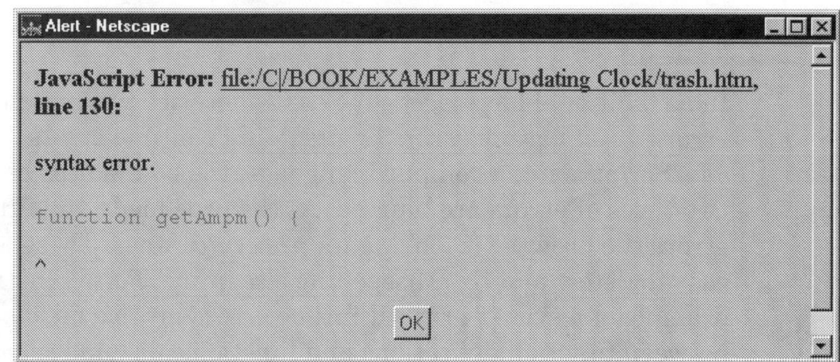

Figure 36-1a: A typical Navigator error message window.

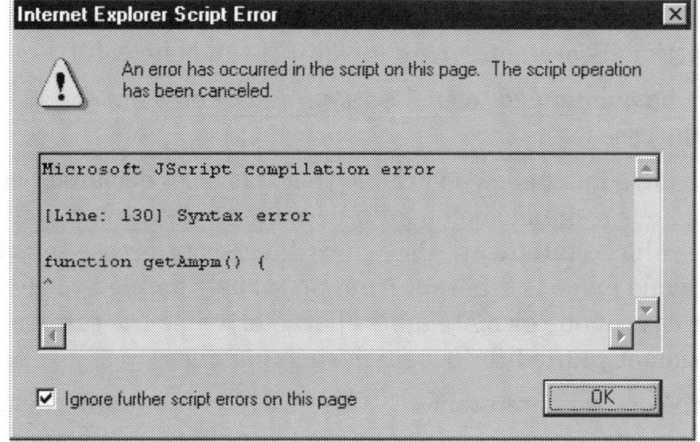

Figure 36-1b: A typical Internet Explorer error message window.

Debugging JavaScript may be tricky at times. You have to infer from the shown code extract what might be the real problem. In Figures 36-1a and 1b, for example, the problem is a missing closing brace for the function defined before the shown `getAmpm()` function. Some error messages, as Figure 36-2 shows, do not provide the code extract but rather the offending element (a property name for example) instead.

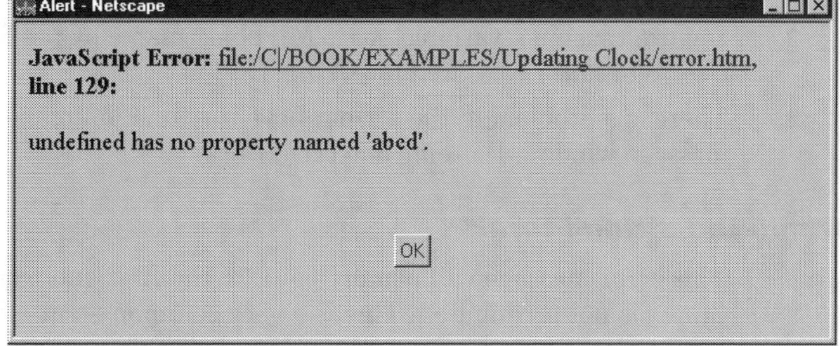

Figure 36-2: The property "abcd" is provided instead of the code extract.

The number of error message types is large and we do not list all of them here. The rest of this chapter provides the most important ones with some explanations on proper remedies to the problems.

"string is not defined"

This error usually points to an uninitialized variable being referenced to another variable (two-operands statement) or to itself (unary-operand statement). Obviously, this variable has not been declared or assigned a value prior to the line provided in the error message window. There may be several reasons for this bug:

1. The variable *string* has been initialized as a local variable in another function. Search for *string* in your file and check if this is the case.
2. You have intended to enclose *string* in quotes but forgot. Check if this is the case.
3. You have misspelled a variable that has been declared before. Check if you have a similar name for a variable that has been initialized before the culprit statement. Also, since JavaScript is case sensitive, see if the variable name is different from previously defined variable names by the case of one or more of its characters. Use the case-insensitive option of your editor to search such matches.
4. If the erroneous statement starts with a function, you either have a bug in the script above the flagged line (failed to balance braces for example) or are calling a function that is defined in another window or frame, but you forgot to include the reference to that window or frame.

"string is not a function"

The following problems are the most common sources for such a bug:

1. There is a mismatched case of letters between the calling statement and function definition.
2. You are reusing a variable or HTML object name by the function name. Use your editor to search for *string*.
3. There is a problem in the script above the function named in the error message window. Do some detective work.

"unterminated string literal"

This error message will usually point to the first quote of a string it thinks is not terminated. This is a very common error when trying to concatenate strings or nest them. You can avoid nesting strings by using a pair of \" in-line quote symbols or using a variable to indirectly reference a string.

"missing } after function body"

A brace is missing somewhere in the function, not necessarily where the error message says. When a function includes several nested items such as `if..else` or `for` loop constructs, it is not so obvious where the brace is missing. An intelligent editor can be of help here to match braces, pair by pair.

"string is not a number"

The erroneous line has an operator that requires a number, but a different type of variable has been found instead. You either have declared the variable (with `var` statement) but have not initialized it, or have not initialized it. It is always preferred to use `parseInt()` or `parseFloat()` to convert strings to numbers.

"string has no property named property"

JavaScript did not find the property provided for the object referenced on the specified line number. There may be few explanations for this bug. You are either trying to reference a property that does not exist for the relevant object, or failing to reference the right object. The latter often occurs when you forget to specify the index of an arrayed object. Look closely at the error message to see if it includes a reference to an entire array rather than just one of its elements. Common arrays are `forms`, `links`, and `buttons`.

"string has no property indexed by [i]"

This error is the opposite of the previous one. Look at the last item and prove to yourself that it is not an element of an array. This is a very common mistake when references become very long and cumbersome, especially when creating radio buttons and select options. Just scan the reference elements one by one, and determine which are simple object names and which are arrays.

"string cannot be set by assignment"

You are either trying to assign a value to a read-only property, or assigning a value to an object reference which must be created via a constructor function, rather than by simple assignment.

"test for equality (==) mistyped as assignment (=)? Assuming equality test"

JavaScript is usually right here. You meant to use the equality comparison test (==) but had typed a single equal sign only.

"function does not always return a value"

JavaScript checks the organization of every function and verifies that a value is always returned. It is very common to focus on a single logic path while designing deeply nested `if..else` loops, and to overlook other cases in which the decision process "falls through" all the way to the bottom, without returning any value.

"access disallowed from scripts at Url_1 to documents at URL_2"

Cross-domain security, which is covered in Chapter 34, is being violated.

"Lengthy JavaScript still running. Continue?"

JavaScript provides a safeguard against the infamous bug of infinite loop. After processing a large number of cycles, JavaScript asks the user whether the script should continue. This safety net is for developers and users both. Developers use it for debugging infinite loops and freeing up the browser which would have been locked up forever otherwise. The safety net also protects users against JavaScript's harmful hackers.

"syntax error"

This is every compiler's classic error message. The alert box provides you with the code extract and the pointer to the exact location of the error.

Manual Debugging Techniques

Sometimes, the error messages are of no help in giving directions towards finding the bug and you have to resort to manual and other techniques for debugging.

Match Those Tag Pairs

Before checking the code itself, go over the document carefully and check that all tags have matching pairs. Be sure to check that each tag is closed by a closing angle bracket.

View the Intermediate HTML Source

Just click in a frame to select it and choose **Frame Source** from the View menu. The displayed results include the HTML code that the script generates. Debugging often involves examining intermediate results. The HTML source code is an excellent means for verifying that the computer does what you intend it to. You can also print and save this JavaScript-written HTML.

Reopen the File

Sometimes reloading a URL does not free the browser memory from a bug you are trying to debug. Try reopening the file via the File menu. It may clear the browser's memory completely and reload the fixed version of your source file. If this does not help, try quitting the browser and restart it again. Rebooting the computer may also help if you are still frustrated with not being able to load your fixed source code.

Good Old Print Messages

Senior programmers may identify with this method, very popular in the days when we did not have debuggers. Just put alert dialog boxes in your script with a brief message that you will recognize (such as `alert("Just before calling function xyz")`). These dialog boxes will tell exactly which parts are working and which parts are disconnected and cannot be reached. You can either work your way from top to bottom or use the binary search mechanism. This method is very popular in classic searching and sorting algorithm. Insert an alert dialog box in the middle of the script. If the flow reaches this point of the script, then focus your effort on the second half, since the problem is somewhere there. If the flow does not reach the script's midpoint, insert an alert box in the middle of the first half, and keep going until you quarantine the bug.

Comment Out Statements

Sometimes, the line number provided by the error message is not exactly the culprit one. To find out the exact one, start commenting the lines, one by one, starting from the given line number. Reload the source file after every additional commented line and observe when the error message goes away (and usually substituted with the next in order). At this stage, you know exactly which is the offending source line.

Watching and Tracing Variables

Watching and *tracing* variables, as well as *single-stepping*, are among the most powerful features of any programming environment. Most serious bugs occur when a variable holds an unexpected value, and the only way to find it is to single-step through the code and examine every variable upon its assignment. Unfortunately, JavaScript does not support these basic features, and you need to mimic them via alert boxes. Every time you change a variable by an assignment or invocation of string, math, or date method, insert an `alert()` method on the following line, and show the content of the variable in it. Repeat this sequence of edit, save, switch, and reload until you find a variable content which is not what you have expected.

This technique may seem to you very tedious and time-consuming and it is indeed. In some cases, you won't have any other way to find the bug. These cases usually involve a value coming back as `<undefined>` or `null`. Check for incomplete object reference (missing the top-level parent), misspelling an object name, or accessing an undefined property.

Sometimes you are not aware that an object property has been changed. To look for such cases, use the following function to list all object properties in your alert box:

```
function listProperties(object, objectName) {
     var message = ""
     for (var i in object) {
          message += objectName  +  "." + i + " = " + object[i] + "\n"
     }
alert(message)
}
```

You invoke this function with the object type (unquoted) and the name of the instance (quoted string).

Getting it Right the First Time

Some bug-preventing programming techniques are as valid for JavaScript as they are for any other languages, and they should always be used in order to prevent bugs in the first place. The lack of sophisticated debuggers in JavaScript only emphasizes the leverage you can get by using these techniques.

Build the Script's Skeleton First

Build your script in a top-down fashion. Start laying down your HTML parts first, including all form definitions. After you have designed the page layout, you can start filling in the JavaScript portions. When beginning a `function`, `repeat` loop, or `if` statement, fill out the entire structure before entering any details. For example, suppose you want to define a function `showProperties()`. Enter first the following structure:

```
function showProperties(){

}
```

and then add the parameters and the for structure

```
function showProperties(object, objectName){
   var message = ""
   for ( ) {
   }



}
```

and so on. This technique has two advantages. It assures you have the closing character always attached at the end of the structure, as well as aligning the indentations. If you want, you can prepare a file with all JavaScript structure templates to copy from and paste in your document. You can also use JavaScript editor applications as explained in Chapter 35.

Keep Testing While Developing

This technique cannot be overemphasized. Always test your code after an incremental development. Don't write pages of code and only then test it. Test the script whenever you have a new feature, function, algorithm, or any other complete chunk that can be tested by itself. The edit-save-switch-reload sequence is relatively fast and not as painful as compiling the code all over again, although this technique is very useful in a compiled language development environment as well.

Evaluate Expressions Outside Your Source

Instead of printing variable contents via an alert box, it is much faster to evaluate certain expressions in an independent, isolated environment such as a separate document you write with a few `text` or `textarea` objects in it. You can also use the internal `javascript:` URL for testing out expressions. This technique is especially recommended for beginners who need to gain confidence in their knowledge of what different methods (such as `string`, `math`, and `date`) yield.

Test Your Functions Outside Your Source

The same arguments presented above for expressions are applicable to functions as well. It is much easier to debug a function in an independent, isolated environment than inside a complex scripted document. Develop your function in a separate document that includes the minimum number of user interface elements you need for the testing. Of course, you will find it more and more difficult to develop your functions in isolation, because they are usually tied to numerous objects in the original document. It will encourage you, though, to develop much more generalized functions that have fewer ties to the environment.

Testing Your Script

Writing JavaScript is development and should be treated as such when you come to test your piece of art. Management bodies of development projects often allocate 50% of the resources for testing. You should anticipate similar proportions in your own work plans.

Making a script robust for the World Wide Web audience is not an easy task and should not be taken lightly. You have to anticipate what the user can do at any point and make sure your code handles it correctly. You should not make any assumptions on either the sequence of operations the user is going to follow or the type of data the user is going to enter into forms. You should assume, on the contrary, that the user is not going to follow your instructions (accidentally or intentionally). The user will enter characters in numeric fields, and will fill the form bottom up. Your script should handle all weird and incorrect data, giving the proper feedback to the user. If a form field accepts character values only, give the user an error message. Make sure your script does not crash the system if the input is not valid. Specifically check for the following items:

- Unexpected reloading. Check how it affects the relationship between frames.
- Suspending a document loading. Does it affect your script?
- Bad data. Does the script crash when the data is not valid?

Test your pages extensively and on as many browsers as you can. Users expect the same robustness from your script as from the most professional software published on earth.

Summary

In this chapter, we gave some tips for debugging JavaScript scripts. We first listed common error messages, and explained what they mean and how you can use them to find bugs. We also provided some manual debugging techniques, which are very important in JavaScript, because, in contrast to other languages, it does not come with a debugger.

Appendix A

HTML-Generated Object Map

This appendix shows a comprehensive map of all objects generated by an HTML document. As you can see from a quick glance, the object map is quite complex: Objects are linked to each other in many different ways and directions. Although the object map is transparent to an HTML author, it is very useful to a JavaScript programmer. The shown objects are created automatically from the HTML document; take the time to educate yourself about which HTML construct generates a specific object.

The book references many of these objects. When studying a specific example or explanation, you can go to the map and look for the objects dealt with in the example, as well as the objects which are linked to them in any way. It is always good to understand which other objects a particular object is related to, as this will extend your understanding and increase the number of options you have to accomplish a specific task.

The map in this appendix also shows the properties, methods, and event handlers of every object, in a very succinct way. If you forget the name of an attribute, method, or event handler of an object, it is always good to consult this map first.

The essence of JavaScript is the ability to manipulate the objects in this map (as well as your own). Use this map to achieve more from your script.

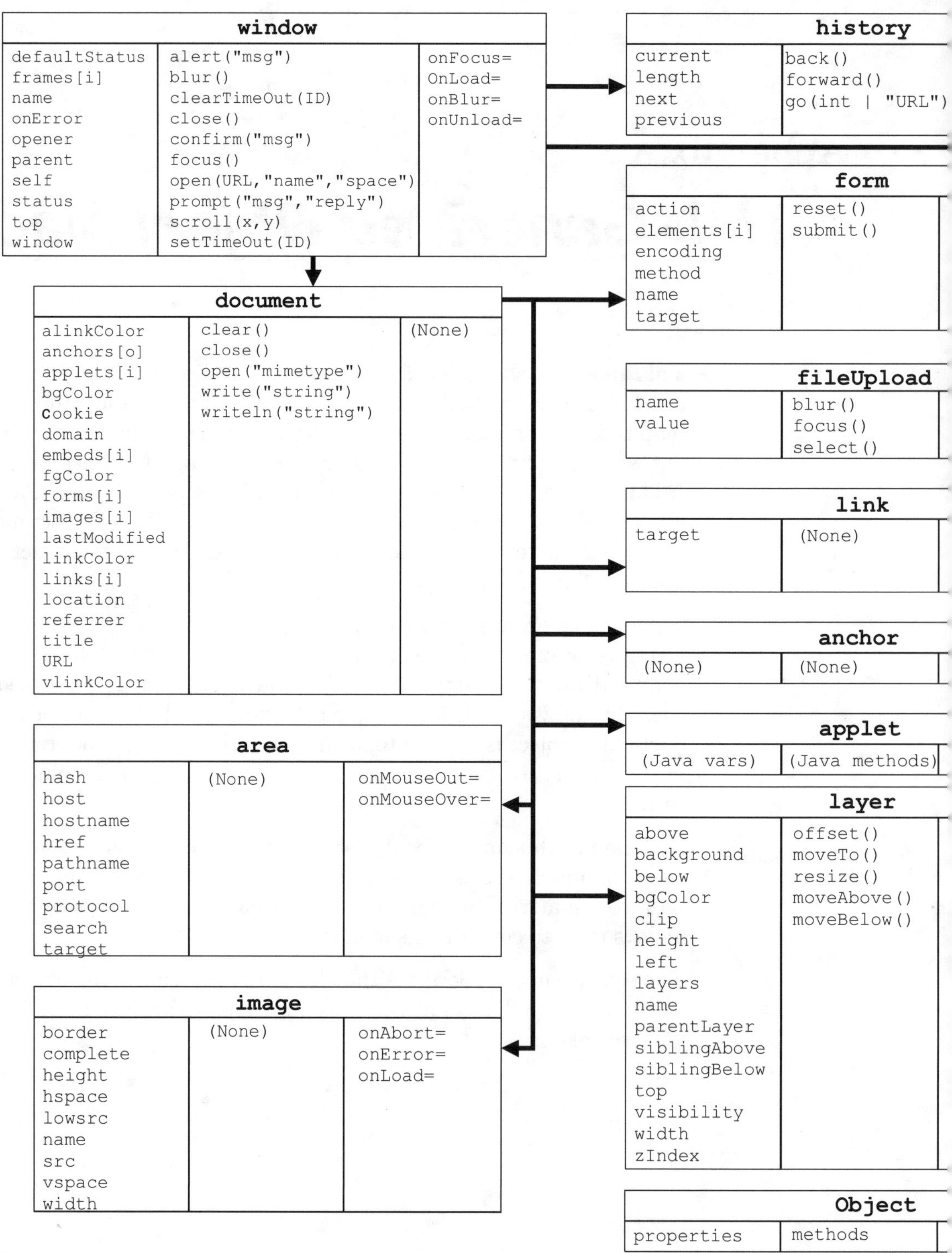
window
defaultStatus
frames[i]
name
onError
opener
parent
self
status
top
window
alert("msg")
blur()
clearTimeOut(ID)
close()
confirm("msg")
focus()
open(URL,"name","space")
prompt("msg","reply")
scroll(x,y)
setTimeOut(ID)
onFocus=
OnLoad=
onBlur=
onUnload=
history
current
length
next
previous
back()
forward()
go(int | "URL")
form
action
elements[i]
encoding
method
name
target
reset()
submit()
document
alinkColor
anchors[o]
applets[i]
bgColor
Cookie
domain
embeds[i]
fgColor
forms[i]
images[i]
lastModified
linkColor
links[i]
location
referrer
title
URL
vlinkColor
clear()
close()
open("mimetype")
write("string")
writeln("string")
(None)
fileUpload
name
value
blur()
focus()
select()
link
target
(None)
anchor
(None)
(None)
applet
(Java vars)
(Java methods)
area
hash
host
hostname
href
pathname
port
protocol
search
target
(None)
onMouseOut=
onMouseOver=
layer
above
background
below
bgColor
clip
height
left
layers
name
parentLayer
siblingAbove
siblingBelow
top
visibility
width
zIndex
offset()
moveTo()
resize()
moveAbove()
moveBelow()
image
border
complete
height
hspace
lowsrc
name
src
vspace
width
(None)
onAbort=
onError=
onLoad=
Object
properties
methods

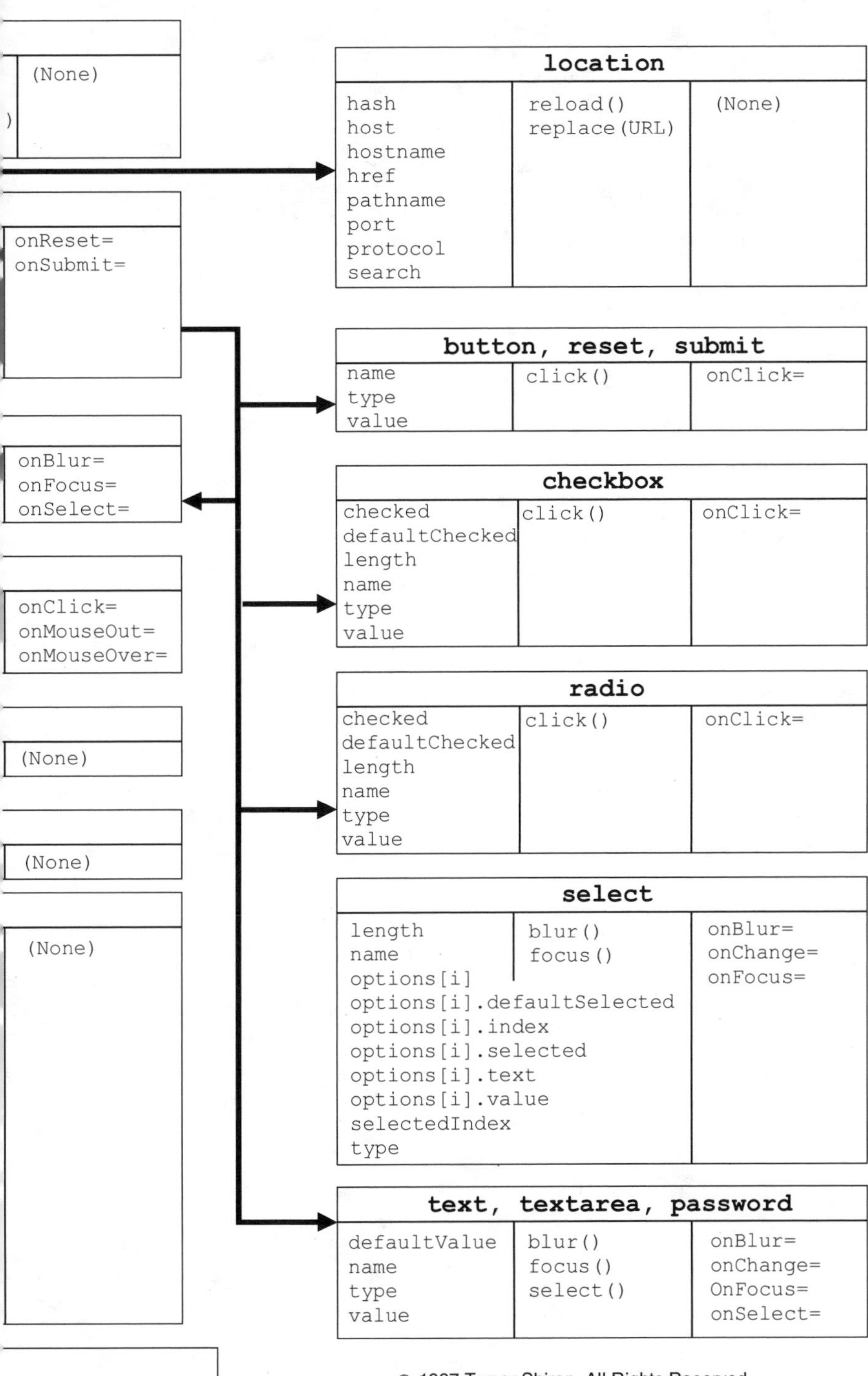
(None)
onReset=
onSubmit=
onBlur=
onFocus=
onSelect=
onClick=
onMouseOut=
onMouseOver=
(None)
(None)
(None)
Event Handlers
location
hash
host
hostname
href
pathname
port
protocol
search
reload()
replace(URL)
(None)
button, reset, submit
name
type
value
click()
onClick=
checkbox
checked
defaultChecked
length
name
type
value
click()
onClick=
radio
checked
defaultChecked
length
name
type
value
click()
onClick=
select
length
name
options[i]
options[i].defaultSelected
options[i].index
options[i].selected
options[i].text
options[i].value
selectedIndex
type
blur()
focus()
onBlur=
onChange=
onFocus=
text, textarea, password
defaultValue
name
type
value
blur()
focus()
select()
onBlur=
onChange=
OnFocus=
onSelect=

Appendix B

JavaScript Object Specification Syntax

Anchor Object

Creating

```
<A NAME="anchorName">
    textOrImageAnchor
</A>
```

Applet Object

Creating

```
<APPLET
    CODE="AppletURL"
    HEIGHT="PixelCount"
    NAME="AppletName"
    WIDTH="PixelCount"
    [ALIGN="AlignmentLocation"]
    [ALT="AlternateTextDisplay"]
    [CODEBASE="ClassFileDirectory"]
    [HSPACE="MarginPixelCount"]
    [VSPACE="MarginPixelCount"]>
        <PARAM NAME="AppletParameterName" VALUE="ParameterValue">
        ...
        <PARAM NAME="AppletParameterName" VALUE="ParameterValue">
</APPLET>
```

Properties

```
name                (string)
```

(Java variables)

Event Handlers

```
onMouseOut=
onMouseOver=
```

Methods

(Java methods)

Area Object

Creating

```
<MAP NAME="areaMapName">
  <AREA
     COORDS="x1,y1,x2,y2...." | "x-center,y-center,radius"
     HREF="URLorLocation"
     [NOHREF]
     [SHAPE="rect" | "poly" | "circle" | "default" ]
     [TARGET="windowName"]
     [onFocus="EventHandlerTextOrFunction"]
     [onMouseOut="EventHandlerTextOrFunction"]
     [onMouseOver="EventHandlerTextOrFunction"]>
</MAP>
```

Properties

```
links[index].target          (window name)
[location object properties]
```

Event Handlers

```
onMouseOut=
onMouseOver=
```

Array Object

Creating

```
var myArray = new Array([integer] | [val1 [ , val2 ... [ , valn]]])
```

Properties

```
length                    (integer)
prototype                 (expression)
```

Methods

```
join("delimiterChar")
reverse()
sort(compareFunc)
```

Button, Submit, and Reset Objects

Creating

```
<FORM>
  <INPUT
     TYPE="button" | "submit" |"reset"
     [NAME="buttonName]
     [VALUE="labelText"]
     [onClick="EventHandlerTextOrFunction"]
     [onFocus="EventHandlerTextOrFunction"]
     [onLoad="EventHandlerTextOrFunction"]
     [onUnLoad="EventHandlerTextOrFunction"]>
</FORM>
```

Properties

```
name          (string)
type          (string)
value         (string)
```

Methods

```
click()
```

Event Handlers

```
onClick=
```

Checkbox Object

Creating

```
<FORM>
  <INPUT
     TYPE="checkbox"
     [CHECKED]
     [NAME="boxName]
     [VALUE="buttonValue"]
     [onClick="EventHandlerTextOrFunction"]>
```

```
    buttonText
</FORM>
```

Properties

```
checked              (Boolean)
defaultChecked       (Boolean)
name                 (string)
type                 (string)
value                (string)
```

Methods

```
click()
```

Event Handlers

```
onClick=
```

Date Object

Creating

```
var myDate = new Date("Month dd, yyyy, hh:mm:ss")
var myDate = new Date("Month dd, yyyy")
var myDate = new Date("yy,mm,dd,hh,mm,ss")
var myDate = new Date("yy, mm, dd")
var myDate = new Date(millisecondsInteger)
```

Properties

```
prototype                 (expression)
```

Methods

```
myDate.getDate()            (1-31)
myDate.getDay()             (0-6)
myDate.getHours()           (0-23)
myDate.getMinutes()         (0-59)
myDate.getMonth()           (0-11)
myDate.getSeconds()         (0-59)
myDate.getTime()            (0-...)
myDate.getTimezoneOffset()  (0-...)
myDate.getYear()            (70-...)
myDate.setDate()            (1-31)
myDate.setDay()             (0-6)
```

```
myDate.setHours()          (0-23)
myDate.setMinutes()        (0-59)
myDate.setMonth()          (0-11)
myDate.setSeconds()        (0-59)
myDate.setTime()           (0-...)
myDate.setYear()           (70-...)
myDate.toGMTString()       (String)
myDate.toLocaleString()    (String)
Date.parse("dateString")
Date.UTC("date values")
```

Document Object

Creating

```
<BODY
     [ALINK="#activatedLinkColor"]
     [BACKGROUND="backgroundImageURL"]
     [BGCOLOR="#backgroundColor"]
     [LINK="#unfollowedLinkColor"]
     [TEXT="#foregroundColor"]
     [VLINK="#followedLinkColor"]
     [onLoad="#handlerTextOrFunction"]
     [onUnload="#handlerTextOrFunction"]
</BODY>
```

Properties

```
alinkColor    (hexadecimal triplet or constant)
anchors       (array)
applets       (array)
bgColor       (hexadecimal triplet or constant)
cookie        (string)
domain        (string)
embeds        (array)
fgColor       (hexadecimal triplet or constant)
forms         (array)
images        (array)
lastModified  (date string)
linkColor     (hexadecimal triplet or constant)
links         (array)
location      (string)
referrer      (string)
```

```
title          (string)
URL            (string)
vlinkColor     (hexadecimal triplet or constant)
```

Methods

```
write("string1" [,"string2",…, "stringn"])
write("string1" [,"string2",…, "stringn"])
write("string1" [,"string2",…, "stringn"])
open("mimeType")
close()
clear()
```

FileUpload Object

Creating

```
<FORM>
<input
     TYPE="file"
     [NAME="fieldName"]
     [SIZE="numberOfCharacters"]>
</FORM>
```

Properties

```
name           (string)
value          (string)
type           (string)
```

Methods

```
blur()
focus()
select()
```

Event Handlers

```
onBlur=
onChange=
onFocus=
onSelect=
```

Form Object

Creating

```
<FORM
    [ACTION="serverURL"]
    [ENCTYPE="MIMEType"]
    [METHOD=GET | POST]
    [NAME="formName"]
    [onSubmit="eventHandlerTextOrFunction"]
    [onReset="eventHandlerTextOrFunction"]
</FORM>
```

Properties

```
action          (URL)
elements        (array)
encoding        (MIME type)
method          (GET or POST)
name            (string)
target          (window name)
```

Methods

```
reset()
submit()
```

Event Handlers

```
onReset=
onSubmit=
```

Function Object

Creating

```
function functionName( [parameter1]…[, parameterN] ) {
        statements
    }

var myFunction = new function([parameter1]…[, parameterN], statements)
```

Properties

```
arguments       (array)
caller          (function)
```

```
prototype       (expression)
```

Methods

```
reset()
submit()
```

Event Handlers

```
onReset=
onSubmit=
```

Hidden Objects

Creating

```
<FORM>
  <INPUT
     NAME="fieldName"
     TYPE="hidden"
     [VALUE="contents"]>
</FORM>
```

Properties

```
defaultValue    (string)
name            (string)
type            (string)
value           (string)
```

History Object

Properties

```
length          (integer)
```

Methods

```
back()
forward()
go(relativeNumber |"URLorTitleSubstring")
```

Image Object

Creating

```
<IMG
    NAME="imageName"
    SRC="imageURL"
    [ALIGN="left" | "right" | "top" | "absmiddle" | "absbottom" |
        "texttop" | "middle" | "baseline" | "bottom" ]
    [BORDER="pixelCount"]
    [HEIGHT="pixelCount" | "percentageValue%"]
    [HSPACE="pixelCount"]
    [ISMAP]
    [LOWSRC="lowResImageURL"]
    [USEMAP="areaMapName"]
    [VSPACE="pixelCount"]
    [WIDTH="pixelCount" | "percentageValue%"]
    [onAbort="EventHandlerTextOrFunction"]
    [onError="EventHandlerTextOrFunction"]
    [onLoad="EventHandlerTextOrFunction"]>
```

Properties

```
border      (integer)
complete    (Boolean)
height      (integer)
hspace      (integer)
lowsrc      (string)
src         (string)
vspace      (integer)
```

Event Handlers

```
onAbort=
onError=
onLoad=
```

Layer Object

Properties

```
above
background      (colorValue)
below           (layerObject)
```

```
bgColor            (colorValue)
clip.top           (pixelCount)
clip.left          (pixelCount)
clip.right         (pixelCount)
clip.bottom        (pixelCount)
clip.width         (pixelCount)
clip.height        (pixelCount)
height             (pixelCount)
left               (pixelCount)
layers             (array)
name               (string)
parentLayer        (layerObject)
siblingAbove       (layerObject)
siblingBelow       (layerObject)
top                (pixelCount)
visibility         (hide|show|inherit)
width              (pixelCount)
zIndex             (integer)
```

Methods

```
offset()
moveTo()
resize()
moveAbove()
moveBelow()
```

Link Object

Creating

```
<A HREF="URLorLocation"
     [NAME="anchorName"]
     [TARGET="windowName"]
     [onClick="EventHandlerTextOrFunction"]
     [onMouseOut="EventHandlerTextOrFunction"]
     [onMouseOver="EventHandlerTextOrFunction"]>
     TextOrImageLink
</FORM>
```

Properties

```
links[index].target          (window name)
[location object properties]
```

Event Handlers

```
onClick=
onMouseOut=
onMouseOver=
```

Math Object

Properties

```
Math.E
Math.LN2
Math.LN10
Math.LOG2E
Math.LOG10E
Math.PI
Math.SQRT1_2
Math.SQRT2
```

Methods

```
Math.abs()
Math.acos()
Math.asin()
Math.atan()
Math.atan2()
Math.ceil()
Math.cos()
Math.exp()
Math.floor()
Math.log()
Math.max()
Math.min()
Math.pow()
Math.random()
Math.round()
Math.sin()
Math.sqrt()
Math.tan()
```

MimeType Object

Properties

```
description      (string)
enabledPlugin    (string)
type             (string)
suffixes         (string)
```

Navigator Object

Properties

```
appName          (string)
appVersion       (string)
appCodeName      (string)
mimeTypes        (string)
plugins          (string)
userAgent        (string)
```

Methods

```
javaEnabled()
taintEnabled()
```

Plugin Object

Properties

```
description      (string)
enabledPlugin    (string)
type             (string)
suffixes         (string)
```

Methods

```
javaEnabled()
taintEnabled()
```

Radio Object

Creating

```
<FORM
   <INPUT
```

```
    NAME="buttonGroupName"
    TYPE="radio"
    [CHECKED]
    [VALUE="buttonValue"]
    [onClick="EventHandlerTextOrFunction"]
    buttonText
</FORM>
```

Properties

```
checked             (Boolean)
defaultChecked      (Boolean)
name                (string)
value               (string)
type                (string)
```

Methods

```
click()
```

Event Handlers

```
onClick=
```

Select Object

Creating

```
<FORM
   <SELECT
    NAME="listName"
    [MULTIPLE]
    [SIZE="NumberOfCharacters"]
    [onBlur="EventHandlerTextOrFunction"]
    [onChange="EventHandlerTextOrFunction"]
    [onFocus="EventHandlerTextOrFunction"]>
    <OPTION [SELECTED] [VALUE="string"]>listItem
    [...<OPTION [VALUE="string"]>listItem
   </SELECT>
</FORM> >
```

Properties

```
length                        (integer)
name                          (string)
options[index]                (array)
```

```
options[index].defaultSelected    (Boolean)
options[index].index              (integer)
options[index].value              (string)
options[index].selected           (Boolean)
options[index].text               (string)
selectedIndex                     (integer)
type                              (string)
```

Methods

```
blur()
focus()
```

Event Handlers

```
onBlur=
onChange=
onFocus=
```

String Object

Creating

```
var myString = new String(["stringExpression"])
```

Properties

```
length                   (integer)
prototype                (expression)
```

Methods

```
myString.anchor("anchorName")
myString.big()
myString.blink()
myString.bold()
myString.charAt(index)
myString.fixed()
myString.fontcolor(colorValue)
myString.fontsize(integer1to7)
myString.indexOf(searchString [ , startIndex])
myString.italics()
myString.lastIndexOf(searchString [ , startIndex])
myString.link(locationOrURL)
myString.small()
myString.split("delimitingChar")
```

```
myString.strike()
myString.sub()
myString.substring(beginIndex, endIndex)
myString.sup()
myString.toLowerCase()
myString.toUpperCase()
```

Text, Textarea, and Password Objects

Creating

```
<FORM
   <INPUT
     NAME="fieldName"
     TYPE="text"
     [MAXLENGTH="MaxLengthAllowed"]
     [SIZE="NumberOfCharacters"]
     [VALUE="contents"]
     [onBlur="EventHandlerTextOrFunction"]
     [onChange="EventHandlerTextOrFunction"]
     [onFocus="EventHandlerTextOrFunction"]
     [onSelect="EventHandlerTextOrFunction"]>
</FORM>

<FORM
   <TEXTAREA
     COLS="NumberOfColumns"
     NAME="fieldName"
     ROWS="NumberOfRows"
     [WRAP="off" | "virtual" | "physical"]
     [onBlur="EventHandlerTextOrFunction"]
     [onChange="EventHandlerTextOrFunction"]
     [onFocus="EventHandlerTextOrFunction"]
     [onSelect="EventHandlerTextOrFunction"]
     defaultText
   </TEXTAREA
</FORM>

<FORM
   <INPUT
     NAME="fieldName"
     TYPE="password"
```

```
    [MAXLENGTH="MaxLengthAllowed"]
    [SIZE="CharacterLength"]
    [VALUE="contents"]>
</FORM>
```

Properties

```
defaultValue        (string)
name                (string)
value               (string)
type                (string)
```

Methods

```
blur()
focus()
select()
```

Event Handlers

```
onBlur=
onChange=
onFocus=
onSelect=
```

Window and Frame Objects

Creating

```
windowObject = window.open([parameters])

<BODY
    ...
    [onBlur="EventHandlerTextOrFunction"]
    [onFocus="EventHandlerTextOrFunction"]
    [onLoad="EventHandlerTextOrFunction"]
    [onUnLoad="EventHandlerTextOrFunction"]
</BODY>

<FRAMESET
    COLS="valueList"
    ROWS="valueList"
    [BORDER=pixelSize]
    [BORDERCOLOR=colorSpecs]
    [FRAMEBORDER=YES | NO]
```

```
    [onBlur="EventHandlerTextOrFunction"]
    [onFocus="EventHandlerTextOrFunction"]
    [onLoad="EventHandlerTextOrFunction"]
    [onUnLoad="EventHandlerTextOrFunction]
        <FRAME
            SRC="locationOrURL"
            NAME="firstFrameName"
            [BORDER=pixelsize]
            [BORDERCOLOR=colorSpecs]
            ....
</FRAMESET>
```

Properties

```
defaultStatus  (string)
frames         (array)
name           (string)
onerror        (function)
opener         (window object)
parent         (window object)
self           (window object)
status         (window object)
top            (window object)
window         (window object)
```

Methods

```
alert(message)
blur()
clearTimeout(timeoutIDnumber)
close()
confirm(message)
focus()
open("URL", "windowName"[,,"windowSpecification"])
prompt(message,defaultReply)
scroll(horizontalPixel, verticalPixel)
setTimeout("expression", millisecondsDelay)
```

Event Handlers

```
onBlur=
onFocus=
onLoad=
onUnload=
```

Control Structures

```
if (condition)= {
     statements
}

if (condition)= {
     statements
}
else {
     statements
}

variable = (condition) ? val1 : val2

for ( [ initial expression]; [condition]; [update expression]){
     statements
}

while (condition) {
     statements
}

for (var in object) {
     statements
}

with (object) {
     statements
}
```

Operators

Comparison

==	Equals
!=	Does not equal
>	Is greater than
>=	Is greater than or equal to
<	Is less than
<=	Is less than or equal to

Binary & Unary

```
+       Plus
-       Minus
*       Multiply
/       Divide
%       Modulo
++      Increment
--      Decrement
-val    Negation
```

Assignment

```
=       Equals
+=      Add the RHS (Right Hand Side)
-=      Subtract the RHS
*=      Multiply by the RHS
/=      Divide by the RHS
%=      Modulo by the RHS
<<=     Left shift by the RHS
>>=     Right shift by the RHS
>>>=    Right shift by the RHS, zero fill
&=      Bitwise AND by the RHS
|=      Bitwise OR by the RHS
^=      Bitwise XOR by the RHS
```

Boolean

```
&&      And
||      Or
!       Not
```

Bitwise

```
&       Bitwise And
|       Bitwise Or
^       Bitwise XOR
~       Bitwise Not
<<      Left Shift
>>      Right Shift
>>>     Zero Fill Right Shift
```

Miscellaneous

```
new
typeOf
void
```

JavaScript Functions and Methods

```
eval("string")
isNan(expression)
object.toString()
parseFloat("string")
parseInt("string")
taint([object])
untaint([object])
```

Appendix C
ASCII Character Set

Char	Oct	Dec	Hex	Ctrl-key	Control Action
NUL	0	0	0	^@	Null character
SOH	1	1	1	^A	Start of heading, = console interrupt
STX	2	2	2	^B	Start of text, maintenance mode on HP console
ETX	3	3	3	^C	End of text
EOT	4	4	4	^D	End of transmission, not the same as ETB
ENQ	5	5	5	^E	Enquiry, goes with ACK; old HP flow control
ACK	6	6	6	^F	Acknowledge, clears ENQ logon hang
BEL	7	7	7	^G	Bell, rings the bell
BS	10	8	8	^H	Backspace, works on HP terminals/computers
HT	11	9	9	^I	Horizontal tab, move to next tab stop
LF	12	10	a	^J	Line Feed
VT	13	11	b	^K	Vertical tab
FF	14	12	c	^L	Form Feed, page eject
CR	15	13	d	^M	Carriage Return
SO	16	14	e	^N	Shift Out, alternate character set
SI	17	15	f	^O	Shift In, resume default character set
DLE	20	16	10	^P	Data link escape
DC1	21	17	11	^Q	XON, with XOFF to pause listings; "okay to send"
DC2	22	18	12	^R	Device control 2, block-mode flow control
DC3	23	19	13	^S	XOFF, with XON is TERM=18 flow control
DC4	24	20	14	^T	Device control 4
NAK	25	21	15	^U	Negative acknowledge
SYN	26	22	16	^V	Synchronous idle

Char	Oct	Dec	Hex	Ctrl-key	Control Action
ETB	27	23	17	^W	End transmission block, not the same as EOT
CAN	30	24	18	^X	Cancel line, MPE echoes !!!
EM	31	25	19	^Y	End of medium, Control-Y interrupt
SUB	32	26	1a	^Z	Substitute
ESC	33	27	1b	^[	Escape, next character is not echoed
FS	34	28	1c	^\	File separator
GS	35	29	1d	^]	Group separator
RS	36	30	1e	^^	Record separator, block-mode terminator
US	37	31	1f	^_	Unit separator
SP	40	32	20		Space
!	41	33	21		Exclamation mark
"	42	34	22		Quotation mark (" in HTML)
#	43	35	23		Cross hatch (number sign)
$	44	36	24		Dollar sign
%	45	37	25		Percent sign
&	46	38	26		Ampersand
'	47	39	27		Closing single quote (apostrophe)
(	50	40	28		Opening parentheses
)	51	41	29		Closing parentheses
*	52	42	2a		Asterisk (star, multiply)
+	53	43	2b		Plus
,	54	44	2c		Comma
-	55	45	2d		Hypen, dash, minus
.	56	46	2e		Period
/	57	47	2f		Slant (forward slash, divide)
0	60	48	30		Zero
1	61	49	31		One
2	62	50	32		Two
3	63	51	33		Three
4	64	52	34		Four
5	65	53	35		Five
6	66	54	36		Six
7	67	55	37		Seven
8	70	56	38		Eight
9	71	57	39		Nine
:	72	58	3a		Colon
;	73	59	3b		Semicolon
<	74	60	3c		Less than sign (< in HTML)
=	75	61	3d		Equals sign
>	76	62	3e		Greater than sign (> in HTML)
?	77	63	3f		Question mark

Char	Oct	Dec	Hex	Ctrl-key	Control Action
@	100	64	40		At sign
A	101	65	41		Uppercase A
B	102	66	42		Uppercase B
C	103	67	43		Uppercase C
D	104	68	44		Uppercase D
E	105	69	45		Uppercase E
F	106	70	46		Uppercase F
G	107	71	47		Uppercase G
H	110	72	48		Uppercase H
I	111	73	49		Uppercase I
J	112	74	4a		Uppercase J
K	113	75	4b		Uppercase K
L	114	76	4c		Uppercase L
M	115	77	4d		Uppercase M
N	116	78	4e		Uppercase N
O	117	79	4f		Uppercase O
P	120	80	50		Uppercase P
Q	121	81	51		Uppercase Q
R	122	82	52		Uppercase R
S	123	83	53		Uppercase S
T	124	84	54		Uppercase T
U	125	85	55		Uppercase U
V	126	86	56		Uppercase V
W	127	87	57		Uppercase W
X	130	88	58		Uppercase X
Y	131	89	59		Uppercase Y
Z	132	90	5a		Uppercase Z
[	133	91	5b		Opening square bracket
\	134	92	5c		Reverse slant (Backslash)
]	135	93	5d		Closing square bracket
^	136	94	5e		Caret (Circumflex)
_	137	95	5f		Underscore
`	140	96	60		Opening single quote
a	141	97	61		Lowercase a
b	142	98	62		Lowercase b
c	143	99	63		Lowercase c
d	144	100	64		Lowercase d
e	145	101	65		Lowercase e
f	146	102	66		Lowercase f
g	147	103	67		Lowercase g
h	150	104	68		Lowercase h
i	151	105	69		Lowercase i

Char	Oct	Dec	Hex	Ctrl-key	Control Action
j	152	106	6a		Lowercase j
k	153	107	6b		Lowercase k
l	154	108	6c		Lowercase l
m	155	109	6d		Lowercase m
n	156	110	6e		Lowercase n
o	157	111	6f		Lowercase o
p	160	112	70		Lowercase p
q	161	113	71		Lowercase q
r	162	114	72		Lowercase r
s	163	115	73		Lowercase s
t	164	116	74		Lowercase t
u	165	117	75		Lowercase u
v	166	118	76		Lowercase v
w	167	119	77		Lowercase w
x	170	120	78		Lowercase x
y	171	121	79		Lowercase y
z	172	122	7a		Lowercase z
{	173	123	7b		Opening curly brace
|	174	124	7c		Vertical line
}	175	125	7d		Closing curly brace
~	176	126	7e		Tilde (approximate)
DEL	177	127	7f		Delete (rubout), cross-hatch box

Index

P

Q

R

S

T

U

Other Books from Wordware Publishing, Inc.

Popular Applications Series

Build Your Own Computer (2nd Ed.)
Creating Help for Windows Applications
Developing Utilities in Assembly Language
Developing Utilities in Visual Basic 4.0
Getting the Most From Your HP LaserJet
HP LaserJet Handbook
Learn AutoCAD in a Day
Learn AutoCAD 12 in a Day
Leran AutoCAD LT for Windows in a Day
Learn AutoCAD LT Rel. 2 for Win in a Day
Learn C in Three Days
Learn CompuServe for Windows in a Day
Learn Computers in a Day
Learn DOS 6.2 in a Day
Learn Generic CADD 6.0 in a Day
Learn Lotus 1-2-3 Rel. 4 for DOS in a Day
Learn Lotus 1-2-3 Rel. 4 for Win in a Day
Learn Lotus 1-2-3 Rel. 5 for Win in a Day
Learn MS Access 2.0 for Win 95 in a Day
Learn MS Access 7.0 for Win in a Day
Learn MS Assembler in a Day
Learn MS Excel 7.0 for Win 95 in a Day
Learn MS PowerPoint 7.0 for Win 95 in a Day
Learn MS Publisher 2.0 for Win in a Day
Learn MS Word 6.0 for Win in a Day
Learn MS Word 7.0 for Win 95 in a Day
Learn MS Works 3.0 for Win in a Day
Learn Novell NetWare Software in a Day
Learn PageMaker 5.0 in a Day
Learn PAL 4.5 in a Day
Learn PROCOMM PLUS 2.0 for Win in a Day
Learn to Use Your Modem in a Day
Learn Turbo Assembler in a Day
Learn Visual Basic 4.0 in Three Days
Learn Visual dBASE 5.5 for Windows in a Day
Learn Windows in a Day
Learn Windows 95 in a Day
Learn WordPerfect 5.2 for Windows in a Day
Learn WordPerfect 6.0 for Windows in a Day
Learn WordPerfect Presentations in a Day
Moving from WP for DOS to WP for Windows
Networks for Small Businesses
Write TSRs Now
Write Your Own Programming Language Using C++ (2nd Ed.)

At A Glance Series

ACT! 2.0 for Windows at a Glance
CorelDRAW 5.0 for Windows at a Glance
Lotus 1-2-3 Rel. 4 for Windows at a Glance
Microsoft Word 6.0 for Windows at a Glance
Paradox 5.0 for Windows at a Glance
Quattro Pro 5.0 for Windows at a Glance
WordPerfect 6.0 for Windows at a Glance

Games and Entertainment

Alliances Revealed: A Review of the Magic: The Gathering Alliances Edition
The Art of Limited Formats for Magic: The Gathering
Baxter on Magic: A Guide to Proper Playing Techniques
Deep Magic: Advanced Strategies for Experienced Players of Magic: The Gathering
Dolan's Almanac of Magic
Dominating Dominia: A Type II Tournament Player's Guide for Magic: The Gathering
HeroZero: The Uncollectable Card Collection Game
Magic Cards Simplified: For Player Parents and Beginners of Magic: The Gathering
Mastering Middle-earth: Strategies for Middle-earth: The Wizards
Mastering Netrunner
Mastering Portal
Mirage Revealed: A Review of the Mirage Edition of Magic: The Gathering
Pro Magic: The Art of Professional Deck Construction
Single Card Strategies for Magic: The Gathering
The Tables of Magic: The Ultimate Reference Guide to Magic: The Gathering
Tournament Reports for Magic: The Gathering
Visions Revealed: A Review of the Visions Edition of Magic: The Gathering
Weatherlight Revealed: A Review of the Weatherlight Edition of Magic: The Gathering

Other Books from Wordware Publishing, Inc.

General and Advanced Topics

Advanced CGI Techniques for Information Processing
The Complete Communications Handbook (2nd Ed.)
Demystifying ISDN
Demystifying SNA
Demystifying TCP/IP
Demystifying TCP/IP (2nd Ed.)
Developer's Guide to HP Printers
Developing Internet Information Services
Developing Enterprise Applications with PowerBuilder
Digital Imaging in C and the World Wide Web
Illustrated UNIX System V
Innovation, Inc.
Integrating TCP/IP into SNA
Internet Publishing with Microsoft Word 7.0
Learn ActiveX Development Using Visual Basic 5.0
Learn ActiveX Development Using Visual C++ 5.0
Learn ACT! 3.0 for Windows 95
Learn Advanced JavaScript Programming
Learn Advanced Internet Relay Chat
Learn AutoCAD LT for Windows 95
Learn Internet Publishing with Microsoft Publisher 97
Learn Internet Relay Chat
Learn Lotus Domino
Learn Microsoft Exchange Server 5.0 Core Technologies
Learn Microsoft FrontPage 97
Learn Microsoft Office 95
Learn Microsoft Office 97
Learn the MFC C++ Classes
Learn Multimedia Programming with Visual Basic
Learn Visio 5.0
Learn Oracle 7.3 and PowerObjects 2.0
Learn Pascal in Three Days (2nd Ed.)
Learn P-CAD Master Designer
Learn Visual Basic 5.0 in Three Days
Lotus Notes Developer's Guide
Networking with Windows NT
Object-Oriented Software Management
Practical Guide to Intranet Client-Server Applications Using the Web
Practical Guide to SGML Filters
The Ultimate Computer Buyer's Guide
Visio 4 for Everyone
World Wide Web Site Development with PowerBuilder

Delphi Series

Collaborative Computing with Delphi 3
The Delphi 3 Example Book
Learn Graphics File Programming with Delphi 3
Software and Interface Design Guide for Delphi 3
The Tomes of Delphi 3: Win 32 Core API
The Tomes of Delphi 3: Win 32 Graphical API

Programmer's Example Series

The HTML Example Book
The Microsoft WordBasic Example Book
The Visual Basic 4.0 Example Book

Hands-on Windows Programming Series

1 Introduction to Window Programming
2 Child Windows
3 Painting the Screen
4 Transferring Data To and From Windows
5 Mouse, Timer, and Keyboard Inputs
6 Text and Special Fonts, Menus, and Printing
7 AppStudio Graphics Editor
8 C to C++ Conversion
9 Special Topics, Master Index for Books 1-9
Nine Book Set

What's on the CD?

The CD included with this book contains the html source for all examples referred to throughout the book. GIF files with graphics for these examples are also included. The goal in adding these examples is to let you cut and paste applicable examples so you can quickly reuse them during your JavaScript learning experience, and long after that.

The CD contains several subdirectories located off the root directory. The directories are organized by examples, a separate directory for each example. A directory's name is identical to that of the appropriate example in the book. Directory ex25-2, for example, includes all relevant material for example ex25-2, which is the second example in Chapter 25. Inside each directory are the html sources and, if applicable, gif files. Directory ex25-2, for example, includes the source code ex25-2.htm and the gif files 10.gif, 11.gif, 12.gif, 13.gif, 14.gif, 15.gif, and 16.gif.

These examples can be used in various ways. The easiest way is to just copy them to your hard disk and load them with your favorite browser. Your learning will much improve if you get hands-on experience running the book's examples. Once you master these examples, you can start to change them. Copy source codes to different files and play around with the JavaScript code. Be sure to test your creations from time to time, so you will be able to easily return to your last working version.

Acadia Infuse software package is also included for your convenience. It allows you to visually create JavaScript code, prepare and store reusable JavaScript code, etc. This package is described in the book.